U1069937

东南大学建筑学院2007—2008年鉴
SEU-ARCH Yearbook 2007—2008
东南大学出版社
南京

东南大学出版社出版发行
（南京四牌楼2号　邮编210096）
南京工大印务有限公司印刷
开本：889㎜×1194㎜　1/16
印张：16.25
字数：600千字
2008年11月第1版
2009年4月第2次印刷
ISBN 978-7-900714-26-8
定价：80.00元

若有印装质量问题，请同读者服务部联系。电话：025-83792328

院长按语

王建国
Wang Jianguo

2007-2008年，我们着重针对国家重大社会需求对学科布局和发展进行了深入考虑，并确定构建建筑学数字技术科技创新和冬冷夏热地区资源节约型和环境友好型规划设计两大科技创新平台。

在具体的事业发展方面，也有一些是值得提及的：

学院建筑设计及其理论和建筑历史与理论两个国家重点学科点顺利通过评估验收，并被批准为建筑学一级学科国家重点学科；

继“中国建筑史”课程，学院本科生“建筑设计”课程再次荣获国家精品课程称号；

配合教育部理工科工程教学改革项目的实施，招收了第一届“杨廷宝班”学生，并在建筑学与土木工程的交叉等方面做出了初步的教改创新；

南京近代史遗址博物馆文化服务中心等一批建筑设计作品获得国家优秀建筑工程银奖、铜奖和省部级奖；

配合学院院庆80周年，学院编辑出版建筑设计教学研究丛书一套、国际联合教学成果一本，系统总结了东大近十多年来建筑设计核心课程建设持续改革的成果，同时，学院实施了硕士研究生论文统一开题和答辩时间制度；

学院成功组织主办了亚洲计算机辅助建筑设计研究协会（CAADRIA）2007年年会，来自国内外114名代表参加了会议，其中国外代表105名。同时，学院与瑞士苏黎世高等工业大学（ETHZ）续签2008－2010年交流合作协议，与法国拉维莱特建筑学院签订2008－2010年交流合作协议。国际联合教学开展的也有声有色，先后与美国加州大学伯克利分校（UC Berkeley）和伍德博瑞大学（Woodbury）、瑞士联邦苏黎世高等工业大学（ETHZ）、澳大利亚新南威尔士大学（UNSW）、TU Delft等开展国际联合教学取得成功。2007－2008年，学院还连续两年开展了与国内兄弟院校之间的联合毕业设计，并出版了相关成果。

2007年是一个特殊的年份，10月20日，建筑学院（系）迎来了八十周年华诞。吴良镛、齐康、钟训正、关肇邺、戴复东、程泰宁6位院士和近千名校友参加了庆典活动。庆典同期举行了鲍鼎先生铜像揭幕仪式和刘敦桢先生诞辰110周年纪念会。院庆前夕，前工院北楼教室装修改造工作完成，本科生全部迁至新的学习环境，教学条件得到显著改善。

2008年同样是一个特殊的年份，因为它是改革开放实施的第三十个年头。伴随着思想解放的洪流，全国建筑教育事业空前繁荣。群峰竞秀、百舸争流构成了近三十年中国各大高校建筑教育发展的基本走向，今天，快速城市化进程和经济持续高速增长再一次使新世纪的中国建筑教育遭遇新机遇和新挑战。但不管怎样，我认为，建筑教育终究要体现博雅和通识的平衡，继承和展拓的并举。东大建筑发展历史上所一以贯之的严谨求实的治学精神，以及历史上创立的“严、实、活、透、硬”的建筑教学思想，体现了现代大学教育中崇尚知识诚笃（intellectual integrity）、崇尚学术尊严、崇尚理性的精神。正是这种办学理念、教学思想和学术精神引领和培育，并将继续造就一代又一代的东大建筑人才。

Dean's Message

In the year 2007 and 2008, we pored deeply on the layouts and developments of our academic subject, which was influenced by the important social needs of the country. Then we decided to build two platforms of scientific and technological innovation. They are digital technique innovation of architecture, as well as the conservation-minded and eco-friendly planning of the area where is cold in winter hot in summer.

There is something deserved to be mentioned at the aspect of concrete developments of our work:

The two national key subjects, architectural design and theory as well as architectural history and theory passed through the evaluation successfully. Meanwhile they were approved to be the national key subjects for the first level subject of architecture.

After the course of Chinese architectural history had won the title of "National Level Excellent Course", the course of architectural design for undergraduate students also won the title.

In conjunction with the educational reform of science and engineering by the Ministry of Education, we recruited the first batch of students for the "Class of Yang Tingbao" .Besides that we also did some preliminary work to achieve educational reform innovation, which was about intersection between architecture and civil engineering.

The design of the cultural services centre for the Museum of Nanjing Modern History and some other architectural works won the silver medal and bronze medal of the national best architectural project, as well as ministerial and provincial awards.

Match with the 80th anniversary of the founding of Architecture Institute (Department), we published a series about educatory research on architecture design, as well as a book about achievement of international consociation for teaching. Therefore we systematically summarized the achievements of our continuous reform, which was about the establishment of core curricular for architectural design, for the recent 10 years. At the same time, we carried out the new system, that the graduate students should decide the subjects of their master's thesis in an unified time, and also reply them in an unified time.

We succeeded in holding the annual academic conference of Computer Aided Architectural Design Research in Asia(CAADRIA), which 114 representatives from home and abroad took part in, moreover 105 of them were from abroad. Meanwhile, we continued to sign on an exchange and cooperation agreement with ETHZ in Swiss for 2008 to 2010, and signed with La Villette School of Architecture in France for the same period.

The international consociation for teaching has also developed vividly and dramatically. We did successful cooperation with UC Berkeley, Woodbury, ETHZ, UNSW and TU Delft successively . We also did our diploma-winning designs in cooperation with universities in brotherhood during the year 2007 and 2008 , some related achievements were being published.

The year 2007 was an unusual year, we welcomed the 80th anniversary of the founding of Architecture Institute(Department) on Oct.20th. The six academicians Wu Liangyong, Qi Kang, Zhong Xunzheng, Guan Zhaoye, Dai Fudong, Cheng Taining and nearly a thousand former students of our school took part in the celebration. Meanwhile, we held ceremonies respectively for the unveiling of Mr. Bao Ding's bronze statue and the 110th anniversary of Mr. Liu Dunzhen. The conversion work of the north part of Qiangongyuan Building into classrooms was completed before the celebration of the 80th anniversary, so that the undergraduate students moved into the totally new learning environment, where the teaching conditions had been improved a great lot.

The year 2008 was also an unusual year, since it was the 30th year to carry out the reform and opening-up. With the onrush of emancipating the mind, the educational business of architecture in our country is flourishing as never before. Nobody is willing to lag behind, which is the basic trend of the development of architectural education for the recent 30 in China. In the new century, the Chinese architectural education is being confronted with new opportunities and challenges for one more time, because of the fast urbanization together with the sustained and rapid development of economy. Anyhow, I think the architectural education should reflect the Liberal Arts Education as well as the simultaneous development of inheriting and expansion. The school of architecture in SEU always holds the preciseness and matter-of-fact attitude for teaching .With the teaching thought "strict, concrete, active, clear, well-knit", which was established during the history of its development, the school of architecture shows the spirit of modern university education. That is the advocation for intellectual integrity, academic dignity and rationality. Because of all these, we will lead and cultivate generations of architectural talents.

学院概况与组织结构
Introduction & Organization

东南大学建筑学院简介
School Introduction

东南大学（国立中央大学、南京工学院）建筑系创立于1927年，是中国现代建筑教育的发源地。

我国著名建筑教育先驱刘福泰、鲍鼎、卢树森等先生先后执掌建筑系，著名建筑家杨廷宝和刘敦桢学部委员、童寯教授等曾长期在该系任教和主持工作，其中杨廷宝还是中国建筑学会理事长，国际建筑师协会副主席。

本学科由建筑学院、建筑研究所、建筑历史遗产保护研究院、CAAD国家专业实验室、SEU-UNESCO GIS中心等构成，并与校城市规划设计研究院、建筑设计研究院形成产学研一体的体制。80年来，建筑学院已为国家培养了近3000名高级建设人才，其中院士6名，建筑工程设计大师10名。

1. 学科建设

东南大学建筑学科为一级学科博士学位授权点；2001年，“建筑设计及其理论”和“建筑历史与理论”双双被评为国家重点学科（均为所在二级学科排名第一），2007年评为一级学科国家重点学科。学科构建了“地域性建筑创作和城市设计”、“冬冷夏热地区建筑技术集成”和“数字技术应用”三大科技创新平台，基本形成科学合理的学科布局和优势互补、共同发展的学科态势。

本学科所在学院是全国高等院校建筑学学科专业指导委员会历届主任挂靠单位，一直是国家“985工程”和“211工程”重点建设的学科。

2. 学术队伍

本学科拥有3名院士、16名博士生导师、2名教育部“长江学者”特聘教授（全国同类学科中仅有）、1名“国家杰出青年基金”获得者，3人入选教育部“新世纪优秀人才支持计划”，5人入选省人才培养计划。

目前已形成一支以院士、长江学者等中青年学术带头人为骨干，年龄结构合理，年富力强、视野开阔、勇于开拓的学科队伍，并培养出在国内具有较大学术影响力的新一代学科带头人多人。师资队伍的博士比例明显提高，在建筑、规划、历史、技术等主要二级学科方向，博士学位教师已达到55%，其中超过70%的教师有国外攻读学位、学习进修和科研合作的经历。

The School of Architecture of Southeast University (which was renamed National Central University in 1920-1950, Nanjing Institute of Technology in 1950-1988) was founded in 1927, it is the cradle of modern architecture education in China.

Famous Chinese architectural education pioneers, including Professor Liu Futai, Bao Ding, Lu Shusen, etc , have been as director here successively. Famous Chinese architects, such as Professor Yang Tingbao, Liu Dunzhen and Tong Jun had been teaching here for a long time. Among them, Yang Tingbao was ever the chairman of Architectural Society of China, vice-chairman of International Union of Architects.

SEU-ARCH is constituted by School of Architecture, Research Institute of Architecture, Research Institute of Architectural Heritage Protection, the State Specialized Laboratory of CAAD, SEU-UNESCO Geography Information System (GIS) Center , with the Research Institute of Urban Planning and Design, and the Research Institute of Architecture Design to form a system of studying and researching. In 80 years, the School of Architecture has taught and trained nearly 3000 senior architects, including 6 academicians, and 10 Famous Designers of Architecture and Construction.

1. Subject Development

SEU-ARCH is the national first-class discipline and specialties for doctor degree. In 2001, “Architectural Design and Theory”, “Architectural History and Theory” were both commented as national key subjects. In 2007, SEU-ARCH was commented as a national key subject of the first-class disciplines. SEU-ARCH established “Regional Architecture and Urban Design”, “Construction Technology Integration in the Area Where the Summer is Hot and the Winter is Cold” and “Application of Digital Technology”, the three major scientific and technological innovation platforms, forming a scientific and rational arrangement in the subjects and a subject situation which complemented each other’s advantages and jointly developed.

2. Faculties

SEU-ARCH has 3 academicians,16 doctoral students' supervisors, 2 Distinguished Professors of “CHANGJIANG Scholars” of the Ministry of Education, 1 winner of “The National Fund for Distinguished Young Scholars”, 3 scholars in the “Program for New Century Excellent Talents in University” of the Ministry of Education, 5 scholars in the “Human Resource Development Project” in the province.

Now there is a young and energetic faculties team with the reasonable age structure , broad vision, and the courage to open up, in which the academicians, CHANGJIANG Scholars, and other middle-aged and young academic leaders and scholars have been the mainstay. And the school has cultivated a lot of new scholars who have a great influence on the academic fields.

3. 科学研究

学科主要研究方向包括：地域建筑学和城镇建筑规划设计，现代城市设计理论与方法，高速城镇化背景下的城镇空间形态转型理论及相关技术，数字技术在城镇建筑学中的应用，中外建筑理论和遗产保护，小城镇人居环境规划建设理论及相关技术等。

2005年以来，学科梯队主持完成和承担国家自然科学基金重点项目1项，国家杰出青年科学基金1项，国家自然科学基金和青年基金10项。主持科技部“十一五”国家科技支撑计划重大（点）项目1项，参加4项。建筑设计获得国家优秀设计银奖2项、铜奖1项，部省优秀规划和建筑设计一等奖8项、二等奖8项；两人获中国建筑教育奖、两人获中国建筑教育奖特别奖；此外学院教师还获得中国建筑创作奖、青年建筑师奖、优秀图书奖、国内外规划设计竞赛奖。在国家和省部级项目的主持数量上在国内同类学科中处于领先地位。

2005-2007年间，出版专著、教材及译著54部，在本学科最高级学术期刊发表论文34篇，在其他核心期刊发表学术论文82篇。

4. 人才培养

学科拥有两门国家精品课程（建筑设计、中国建筑史）、一门江苏省精品课程（城市规划），承担教育部理工类教学改革课题1项（获准年度全国仅11项），获江苏省教学成果奖一等奖1项、二等奖2项。

新增“景观建筑学”和“遗产保护与管理”博士点两个（2004年）；培养博士生92人、硕士生333人、博士后6人，获全国优秀博士论文提名奖3篇，省级优秀博士和硕士论文多篇。

在历届全国大学生建筑学设计竞赛和作业评比中，本学科均名列前茅（包括中国首届建筑艺术双年展国际青年学生展唯一特等奖）。

5. 国际学术交流

主办有重要学术影响的国际学术会议6次，与美、英、法、日、瑞士、瑞典、荷、德、奥、韩、澳、新加坡等国建立了院际学术交流关系，与UNESCO等国际组织一直保持着经常性的联系，同多所国际知名大学展开了系列国际联合教学并互认学分，开展多项重要的国际和国内科研合作项目。

3. Research Achievements

The main research subjects include: regional architecture, urban planning and design, modern urban design theory and methods, theory and related technology of urban spatial patterns transition in the context of high-speed urbanization, application digital technology in urban architecture, Chinese and foreign architectural theory and heritage conservation, theory and related technology of town environment plan, etc.

Since 2005, SEU-ARCH has assumed and completed various projects of the Natural Science Foundation of China(NSFC),5 projects of the National Science and Technology Support Program from “11th Five-Year Plan” supported by the Ministry of Science and Technology, won 2 Silver Awards and 1 Bronze Medal of the National Award for Excellent Design, 8 first prizes and 8 second prizes of the Award of Ministry of Construction and Jiangsu Province for Excellent Planning and Architect Design. Two scholars won the Chinese Architectural Education Award, two scholars won the special prizes of the Chinese Architectural Education Award. Furthermore, the teachers in the school have won the Chinese Architecture Design Award, the Young Architects Award, the Outstanding Book Award, the awards for domestic and overseas planning and design competition. The amount of projects, at the national and provincial and ministerial level, is in a leading position in similar subjects in the country.

In 2005-2007, 54 monographs, textbooks and translated works have been published, 34 dissertations have been published on highest level academic journals of the same specialities, and 82 on other core journals.

4. Education

SEU-ARCH has 2 National Level Excellent Courses: “Architecture Design” and “History of Chinese Architecture” , 1 excellent course in the province, “Urban Planning”.

Two specialties for doctors were newly added, including “Landscape Architecture” and “Heritage Conservation and Management” in 2004.

In the national architecture design competitions, the School is always among the best, including the only grand prize of International Exhibition of Architectural works of Students and Young Architects in the first Chinese Architecture Biennale in Beijing.

5. Academic Exchanges

6 international academic conferences with wide academic influence have been held here. The School has established academic relationship with architecture schools from the United States, UK, France, Japan, Switzerland, Sweden, the Netherlands, Germany, Austria, South Korea, Australia, Singapore and other countries, and has maintained regular contacts with UNESCO and other international organizations. Also, the School has established united teaching system with architecture schools of internationally renowned universities, and carried out a number of important international and domestic scientific research and cooperation projects.

学院组织结构
School Organization

东南大学建筑学院实行党委和行政共同负责的运行机制及党政联席会议办公制度。学院管理设院务办公室、学生办公室和院长办公室，教学与科研分为4个系和5个研究中心（所），另有城市规划设计研究院、实验中心、图书资料中心和期刊编辑室等单位。学院设有学术委员会、学位委员会、教学委员会、职称评审委员会。学院党总支委员会下设各党支部、院共青团分团委及院工会委员会（教代会）。

东南大学建筑学院机构设置示意如下：

The School sets up the school affairs' office, the students' office and deans' office, four departments, five research centers (institutes), Research Institute of Urban Planning & Design, Experiment Center, Library and Archive Center and Journal Editing Section, etc. Under the departments and the institutes, there are teaching research sections established. The School also sets up Academic Committee, Degree Committee, Teaching Committee and Professional Title Evaluation Committee.

The organizing diagram of SEU-ARCH is shown below:

东南大学建筑学院机构示意图
The organizing diagram of SEU-ARCH

- 东南大学建筑学院 SEU-ARCH
  - 学术委员会 Academic Committee
  - 学位委员会 Degree Committee
  - 教学委员会 Teaching Committee
  - 职称评审委员会 Professional Title Evaluation Committee
  - 城市规划设计研究院 Research Institute of Urban Planning & Design
  - 期刊编辑室 Journal Editing Section
  - 院务办公室 School Affairs' Office —— 人事室、行政室、财务室、教务室
  - 学生办公室 Students' Office —— 本科生工作室、研究生工作室
  - 建筑系 Department of Architecture —— 第一建筑设计教研室、第二建筑设计教研室、第三建筑设计教研室、第四建筑设计教研室
  - 城市规划系 Department of Urban Planning —— 第一城市规划教研室、第二城市规划教研室、第三城市规划教研室
  - 环境设计系 Department of Environmental Design —— 美术教研室、环境艺术设计室
  - 景观学系 Department of Landscape Architecture —— 景园设计教研室
  - 建筑与环境艺术研究中心 Research Center of Architecture and Environmental Art
  - 建筑历史与理论研究所 Research Institute of Architectural History & Theory —— 中国建筑史教研室、外国建筑史教研室
  - 建筑构造与技术研究所 Research Institute of Building Construction & Technology —— 构造与技术教研室
  - 建筑物理与设备研究所 Research Institute of Building Physics & Facilities —— 建筑物理与设备教研室
  - CAAD国家专业实验室 CAAD Lab
  - 东南大学-联合国教科文组织GIS中心 SEU-UNESCO GIS Center
  - 图书资料中心 Library and Archive Center —— 中文图书室、外文图书室、古籍图书室、文档资料室
  - 实验中心 Experiment Center —— 建筑物理实验室、造型艺术实验室、CAD学生机房、艺术设计实验室

院长:王建国教授，主持学院全面工作并主管学科建设、人事、财务等工作
Dean: Professor Wang Jianguo

总支书记:安宁高工，主持学院全面工作，主管学院党建、党群教育工作
General Secretary of Party Committee: Senior Engineer An Ning

副院长:董卫教授，主管纵向科研、外事等工作
Vice Dean: Professor Dong Wei

副院长:钱强教授，主管教学工作
Vice Dean: Professor Qian Qiang

副院长:段进教授，主管规划设计研究院工作
Vice Dean: Professor Duan Jin

副院长:刘博敏教授，主管研究生教学工作
Vice Dean: Professor Liu Bomin

副院长:冷嘉伟教授，主管院行政、横向科研、设备管理等工作
Vice Dean: Professor Leng Jiawei

副院长:郑炘教授，主管学院发展工作
Vice Dean: Professor Zheng Xin

副院长:高嵩讲师，主管本科生管理、学生党建工作
Vice Dean: Lecturer Gao Song

教学管理组织结构
Teaching Management Organization

建筑系系主任：龚恺教授
副系主任：单踊教授 张彤教授 鲍莉副教授
城市规划系系主任：阳建强教授
副系主任：吴晓副教授 王承慧副教授
环境设计系系主任：赵思毅副教授
副系主任：曾琼副教授
景观学系副系主任：唐军副教授
建筑历史与理论研究所所长：周琦教授
建筑构造与技术研究所所长：杨维菊教授
建筑物理与设备研究所所长：傅秀章副教授
CAAD实验室室主任：董卫教授
副主任：胡明星副教授

Director of Department of Architecture: Professor Gong Kai
Deputy Director: Professor Shan Yong, Professor Zhang Tong, Associate Professor Bao Li
Director of Department of Urban Planning: Professor Yang Jianqiang
Deputy Director: Associate Professor Wu Xiao, Associate Professor Wang Chenghui
Director of Department of Environmental Design: Associate Professor: Zhao Siyi
Deputy Director: Associate Professor Zeng Qiong
Deputy Director of Department of Landscape Architecture: Associate Professor Tang Jun
Director of Research Institute of Architectural History & Theory: Professor Zhou Qi
Director of Research Institute of Building Construction & Technology: Professor Yang Weiju
Director of Research Institute of Building Physics and Facilities: Associate Professor Fu Xiuzhang
Director of CAAD Lab: Professor Dong Wei
Deputy Director: Associate Professor Hu Mingxing

院学位评定分委会

负责对博士、硕士、学士学位的评定，讨论与审查重点学科、博士点、硕士点的工作，增补博士生导师及硕士生导师申报工作，讨论授予成人高等教育学位事宜。

主　席：齐　康
副主席：王建国
委员：朱光亚 仲德崑 刘博敏 安　宁
杜顺宝 郑　炘 钟训正 段　进 龚　恺
董　卫 韩冬青
秘书：王海华

Degree Evaluation Branch of School

To be in charge of the evaluation on the degrees for doctor, master and bachelor; to discuss the matters on granting degrees for adult higher education.

Chairman: Professor Qi Kang
Vice chairman: Professor Wang Jianguo
Committeemen: Zhu Guangya, Zhong Dekun, Liu Bomin, An Ning, Du Shunbao, Zheng Xin, Zhong Xunzheng, Duan Jin, Gong Kai, Dong Wei, Han Dongqing
Secretary: Wang Haihua

建筑学科评审委员会

负责初、中、高级职称的评定。

主任委员：　王建国
副主任委员：　安　宁
委员：王建国 仲德崑 安　宁 朱光亚
阳建强 齐　康 杜顺宝 张　宏
郑　炘 赵　军 钟训正 段　进
韩冬青
秘书：李芳芳　林　挺

Professional Title Evaluation Committee of School

To be in charge of the evaluation on junior, intermediate and senior professional titles.

Executive committeeman: Professor Wang Jianguo
Vice executive committeeman: Senior Engineer An Ning
Committeemen: Wang Jianguo, Zhong Dekun, An Ning, Zhu Guangya, Yang Jianqiang, Qi Kang, Du Shunbao, Zhang Hong, Zheng Xin, Zhao Jun, Zhong Xunzheng, Duan Jin, Han Dongqing
Secretaries: Li Fangfang, Lin Ting

院教学委员会

负责制订院所属专业的培养方案及教学计划，研讨并整体协调专业教学工作，成员由各专业教研室主任担任。

主任委员：钱强
委员：龚　恺　孔令龙　朱光亚　杨维菊
傅秀章　赵思毅
秘书：俞传飞

Teaching Committee of School

To be in charge of the cultivation plans and teaching plans of the specialties, to discuss and entirely assort with the professional teaching work; members comprise executives of all professional sections.

Executive committeeman: Professor Qian Qiang
Committeemen: Gong Kai, Kong Linglong, Zhu Guangya, Yang Weiju, Fu Xiuzhang, Zhao Siyi
Secretary: Yu Chuanfei

师资情况及结构
Teaching Staff

建筑学院现有专任教师117名，其中院士3名，博士生导师18名，教授29名，副教授34名，讲师52名，助教2名，平均年龄39.6岁。

The School has 117 teachers now, which comprises of 3 academicians, 18 supervisors of doctoral students, 29 professors, 34 associate professors, 52 lecturers and 2 assistants. The average age is 39.6.

1. 基本情况及年龄结构
1. Basic Information and Structure of Age

专任教师基本情况
Information of teachers

职 称 Professional Titles	人数 Number of Staff	男 Male	女 Female	备 注 Remarks
教 授 Professor	29	27	2	
副教授 Associate Professor	34	26	8	
讲 师 Lecturer	52	31	21	
助 教 Assistant	2	2		
合 计 In Total	117	86	31	

年龄结构情况表
Structure of age

教师年龄 Age of Teacher	人数 Number of Staff	比例 Proportion	教授 Professor	（博士生导师） (Supervisor of Doctoral Student)	副教授 Associate Professor	（硕士生导师） (Supervisor of Masteral Student)	讲师 Lecturer	助教 Assistant
Over 56	11	9.4%	9	（7）		（3）	2	
51-55	4	3.4%	4	(2)		（4）		
41-50	27	23.1%	14	(7)	9	（23）	4	
31-40	75	64.1%	2	（2）	25	（15）	46	2
合 计 In Total	117	100%	29	（18）	34	（45）	52	2

2. 职称结构
2. Structure of Professional Titles

本院教师中高级职称人数占全体教师人数的47.1%，具体如下：

The teachers with senior professional titles in our school occupy 47.1% of the total number of teachers. The details are as follows:

教师/职称 Teacher/Professional Title	教授 Professor	副教授 Associate Professor	讲师 Lecturer	助教 Assistant	合计 In Total
人数 Number of Staff	29	34	52	2	117
比例% Proportion %	24.8%	29.1%	44.4%	1.7%	100%

3. 教师学科分布
3. Distribution of Staff in Different Specialities

学科名称 Name of Subject	（博士生导师 Supervisor of Doctoral Student）	教授 Professor	副教授 Associate Professor	讲师 Lecturer	助教 Assistant	合计 In Total
建筑设计 Architectural Design	（9）	14	14	22		50
城市规划 Urban Planning	（4）	6	6	9	1	22
历史与理论 History & Theory	（2）	3	2	3		8
景观学 Landscape Architecture	（1）	2	1	6		9
建筑物理与设备 Building Physics & Facilities			3	1		4
建筑构造与技术 Building Construction & Technology	（1）	2	3			5
美术学 Fine Art	（1）	2	3	7		12
CAAD			2	4	1	7
合 计 In Total	（18）	29	34	52	2	117

建筑系
Department of Architecture

系主任：龚 恺
Director: Gong Kai

副系主任：单 踊
Deputy Director: Shan Yong

副系主任：张 彤
Deputy Director: Zhang Tong

副系主任：鲍 莉
Deputy Director: Bao Li

钟训正
Zhong Xunzheng

王建国
Wang Jianguo

仲德崑
Zhong Dekun

黎志涛
Li Zhitao

钱 强
Qian Qiang

韩冬青
Han Dongqing

冷嘉伟
Leng Jiawei

陈 烨
Chen Ye

王 静
Wang Jing

张玫英
Zhang Meiying

郑炘
Zheng Xin

孙茹雁
Sun Ruyan

薛 力
Xue Li

李 飚
Li Biao

周 颖
Zhou Ying

王 正
Wang Zheng

朱 雷
Zhu Lei

夏 兵
Xia Bing

屠苏南
Tu Sunan

刘 捷
Liu Jie

吴锦绣
Wu Jinxiu

陈秋光
Chen Qiuguang

张 嵩
Zhang Song

俞传飞
Yu Chuanfei

贺镇东
He Zhendong

王海宁
Wang Haining

王湘君
Wang Xiangjun

张 彧
Zhang Yu

郭 菂
Guo Di

张慧
Zhang Hui

顾震弘
Gu Zhenhong

陈 宇
Chen Yu

徐晓东
Xu Xiaodong

邓浩
Deng Hao

史永高
Shi Yonggao

城市规划系
Department of Urban Planning

系主任：阳建强
Director: Yang Jianqiang

副系主任：吴 晓
Deputy Director: Wu Xiao

副系主任：王承慧
Deputy Director: Wang Chenghui

吴明伟
Wu Mingwei

段 进
Duan Jin

董 卫
Dong Wei

刘博敏
Liu Bomin

孔令龙
Kong Linglong

杨俊宴
Yang Junyan

孙世界
Sun Shijie

巢耀明
Chao Yaoming

王兴平
Wang Xingping

徐春宁
Xu Chunning

张 倩
Zhang Qian

权亚玲
Quan Yaling

雒建利
Luo Jianli

王海卉
Wang Haihui

高 源
Gao Yuan

熊国平
Xiong Guoping

环境设计系
Department of Environment Design

系主任：赵思毅
Director: Zhao Siyi

副系主任：曾 琼
Deputy Director: Zeng Qiong

高祥生
Gao Xiangsheng

赵 军
Zhao Jun

李 哲
Li Zhe

张 蕾
Zhang Lei

朱 丹
Zhu Dan

沈 颖
Shen Ying

陈晓扬
Chen Xiaoyang

李向锋
Li Xiangfeng

戴 斐
Dai Fei

景观学系
Department of Landscape Architecture

副系主任：唐 军
Deputy Director: Tang Jun

杜顺宝
Du Shunbao

成玉宁
Cheng Yuning

王晓俊
Wang Xiaojun

杨冬辉
Yang Donghui

姚 准
Yao Zhun

谭 瑛
Tan Ying

陈洁萍
Chen Jieping

建筑历史与理论研究所
Research Institute of Architectural History & Theory

所长：朱光亚（1995-2007年先后任副所长、所长）
Director: Zhu Guangya

所长：周 琦（2007年至今任所长）
Director: Zhou Qi

潘谷西
Pan Guxi

刘先觉
Liu Xianjue

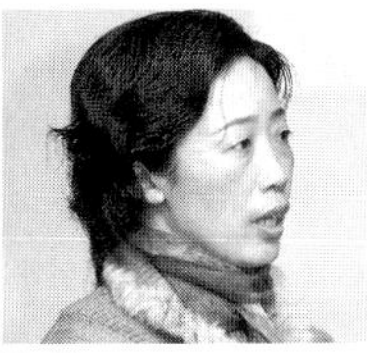
陈 薇
Chen Wei

葛 明
Ge Ming

汪晓茜
Wang Xiaoqian

诸葛净
Zhuge Jing

胡 石
Hu Shi

李新建
Li Xinjian

白 颖
Bai Ying

建筑构造与技术研究所
Institute of Building Construction & Technology
建筑物理与设备研究所
Institute of Building Physics & Facilities

所长：杨维菊
Director: Yang Weiju

张 宏
Zhang Hong

李海清
Li Haiqing

方立新
Fang Lixin

王伟成
Wang Weicheng

所长：傅秀章
Director: Fu Xiuzhang

柳孝图
Liu Xiaotu

吴 雁
Wu Yan

彭昌海
Peng Changhai

石 邢
Shi Xing

CAAD国家专业实验室 东南大学-联合国教科文组织GIS中心
The State Specialized Laboratory of CAAD, SEU-UNESCO GIS Center

主任：董 卫
Director: Dong Wei

副主任：胡明星
Deputy Director: Hu Mingxing

钱敬平
Qian Jingping

史 新
Shi Xin

彭 冀
Peng Ji

虞 刚
Yu Gang

杜 嵘
Du Rong

教学科研平台
Teaching and Scientific Research Platform

学院教学科研平台主要包括CAAD国家专业实验室、UNESCO与东南大学合作的GIS亚洲培训中心、VR工作站、建筑学院图书馆、物理环境与节能评价检测中心等，基本具备供重大研究项目使用的实验室条件和培养高层次科研教学人才的能力。

已经建成东大建筑(WWW.ARCH.SEU.EDU.CN)网站，通过网站实施了建筑设计和中国建筑史课程的网络教学，受到广泛好评，二者均已被遴选为国家精品课程，扩大了东南大学建筑学科的影响。

CAAD国家专业实验室

CAAD实验室在承担本科及研究生的计算机辅助建筑设计课程的基础上，全面参与专业基础课及建筑设计和规划设计教学，开设了GIS教学、VR教学、观众厅视线分析设计等相关课程，并参加AutoCAD的开发和应用。

主要设备有：SGI Octane R12000型图形工作站一套，Intergraph工作站一套，并有与此相配套的输入输出设备。微机方面现有PC-奔腾Ⅳ型以上113余台及其它微机多台，所有微机和工作站已全部联网工作并配备有关教学用正版软件。2005年以来，CAAD国家专业实验室增加IBM工作站二套，电脑终端一批。

东南大学-联合国教科文组织GIS中心

东南大学-联合国教科文组织地理信息系统亚洲培训中心（简称GIS亚洲培训中心）成立于2000年，是东南大学建筑学院与联合国教科文组织在城市空间研究及历史遗产保护等方面进行合作的一项重要成果。该中心在组织和技术方面基于CAAD国家专业实验室，在体系和操作方面是为联合国教科文组织亚太地区技术网络服务的中国中心，同时，该中心面向国内及亚太地区，开展与城市空间研究及历史遗产保护有关的专项或综合性培训。

建筑视觉艺术实验室

本实验室含建筑造型、摄影、视听、图文四个工作室，主要承担一年级的设计基础工作模型辅导，二年级至四年级建筑设计教学模型及毕业设计模型指导。主要设备有：Universal激光雕刻机、威克雕刻机等。

艺术设计（美术）实验室

本实验室有专门美术教室5间，主要承担环境设计系本科生基础教学及毕业设计，研究生专业学习及课程设计使用。现有画架126个，石膏模型98件，美术灯8个，静物台5个。

The platform for teaching and scientific research of the School mainly comprises CAAD Lab, SEU-UNESCO GIS Center, VR Station, Library of ARCH, Evaluation and Testing Center of Physics Environment and Energy Saving, etc.

The website for the School (www.arch.seu.edu.cn) has been built, which has expanded the influence of the architecture specialty of SEU, and exerted the architectural talents and information advantages of the university. Through the website, online teaching of Architectural Design and Chinese Architectural History have been implemented, which are widely praised and both awarded the National Level Excellent Courses.

State Specialized Laboratory of Computer Aided Architectural Design

SEU-UNESCO GIS Center

建筑物理实验室

建筑物理实验室有混响室、隔声室、消声室、光学实验室等，承担的主要实验有混响时间测量、墙体和楼板的隔声测量、噪声和震动测量、建筑采光模型实验、日照实验、建筑构件的总热阻及房间的热环境测量。

近年来，建筑物理实验室在“985”和“211”工程学科建设经费的持续支持下，在实验条件、实验水平上有了大幅提高。目前正在建设一个高水平的大型动态建筑环境舱实验平台，瞄准国际建筑物理界最新研究动态，争取达到国内领先、国际可比的水平。该环境舱计划在2009年中期建设完成并投入使用。

主要测量设备：声学有丹麦B&K公司生产的4418型建筑声学分析仪，2010型外差式频率分析仪，2230型精密声级计，2317型电平记录仪等台式与便携式测试设备20余种；光学有天体半球模型，光学积分球，各种光度、照度计量仪器10余件；热工有温度自动巡回测试仪，红外线测温仪、辐射仪、风速仪等数十件；日照方面有建筑模型日照仪。

建筑学院图书馆

建筑学院共有三个图书阅览室：中文图书室、外文图书室、古籍图书室。管理人员5人（其中2人外聘）。2000年我院投入近80万元对图书资料室的阅览环境进行了全面的装修改造，更换了所有的书架，阅览桌、椅，安装了空调、除湿机。同时对图书室的管理进行了根本性的改革，购买了图书馆管理软件，添置了12台计算机、1台服务器。改变了原来的手工借阅与检索，实现了计算机网络化管理，图书资料费比以往有加倍的投入，改善了藏书和阅览环境。目前图书规模与硬件设施在全国建筑院校中名列前茅。

中文图书室使用面积为240平方米，现有馆员2名，阅览座位20个，图书56400册，期刊现刊110种，过刊装订本260种（约5300册），素描图片2800张，建筑画彩色照片1185张，渲染图1050张。外文图书室使用面积为240平方米，现有馆员和管理人员各1名，阅览座位20个，目前藏有外文图书21400册，外文期刊现刊50余种，外文期刊装订本12000册。另有国内建筑院系中唯一的古籍图书室，使用面积80平方米，现有管理人员1名，阅览座位10余个，藏古籍20000余册。

建筑学院新教学楼

2007年，建筑学院改造了原前工院，增加了建筑面积4400平方米，作为建筑学院新的教学楼。

Architectural Physics Laboratory

School Library

中文阅览室

中文藏书库

外文阅览室

外文藏书库

古籍藏书库

New School Building

城市规划设计研究院
Research Institute of Urban Planning & Design

东南大学城市规划设计研究院行政隶属于东南大学建筑学院。1993年经国家建设部批准成立城市规划设计研究院（甲级资质）。由中国科学院院士齐康教授担任名誉院长，中国城市规划学会常务理事、著名城市规划专家吴明伟教授担任总规划师，中国风景园林学会理事杜顺宝教授任总建筑师，建筑学院院长、中国城市规划学会常务理事王建国教授兼任院长，常务副院长是中国城市规划学会理事段进教授。

东大规划院既有经验丰富、年富力强的博士生导师，也有一批崭露头角，在国内具有重要学术影响的青年学者和规划师，还有一批朝气蓬勃的博士、硕士生。规划院已经出版《现代城市设计理论与方法》等几十本学术专著，其中城市设计理论方法和实践在国内具有公认的学术领先地位，在国内外享有盛誉。

近年来，在桂林中心城环城水系规划、苏州火车站地区综合改造城市设计、南京红花机场地区概念性城市设计等多次国际规划竞赛中中标。承担了一批在国内外有影响的规划设计任务，其中曲阜五马祠地区规划、苏州古城控制性详细规划先后获得国家优秀规划设计银奖，苏州市环古城风貌保护工程西段详细规划获国家优秀规划设计一等奖。

The Research Institute of Urban Planning & Design of SEU belongs to SEU-ARCH. Upon the approval of the State Ministry of Construction in 1993, the Research Institute of Urban Planning & Design was established (with Grade A qualification). Professor Qi Kang, academician of Chinese Academy of Sciences acts as the honorary director; Professor Wu Mingwei, standing member of Urban Planning Society of China and famous expert of urban planning acts as the chief planner; Professor Du Shunbao, director of Chinese Society of Landscape Architecture acts as chief architect; Professor Wang Jianguo, dean of SEU-ARCH and director of Urban Planning Society of China acts as director. Standing vice director is Professor Duan Jin, director of Urban Planning Society of China .

南京红花机场地区概念性城市设计

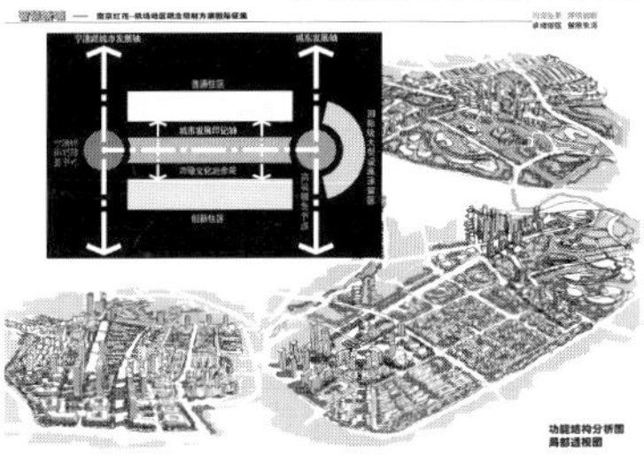

苏州火车站地区综合改造城市设计

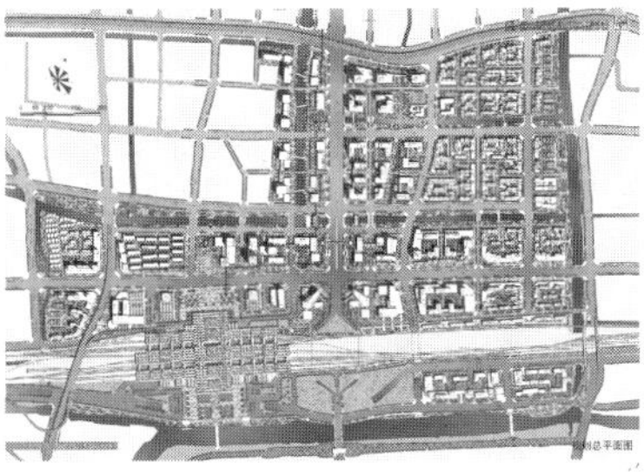

新闻
News

东南大学建筑学院八十周年院庆
the 80th Anniversary of the Founding of Architecture School

2007年10月20日，东南大学建筑学院在四牌楼校区（原中央大学校园）举行隆重的建院八十周年纪念活动，建筑学院全体师生员工和来自全国各地及世界多个国家的校友、嘉宾欢聚一堂。

上午8：30在中大院门前举行了《刘敦桢全集》首发式及《童寯文集》发行仪式，接着是鲍鼎先生铜像揭幕仪式，并由吴良镛院士和钟训正院士剪彩。鲍鼎先生在抗日战争时期，为建筑系的发展毅然负重，力挽困局，是建筑学院发展史册里的重要功臣。随后是学生集体艺术表演，他们身着统一的橘红色服装围绕着大礼堂前的水池，用鼓声和整齐的掌声和腾空而起的彩色气球为院庆活动增添了节日气氛。

上午10：00院庆大会隆重开幕，会议由建筑学院董卫副院长主持。出席会议的有江苏省副省长仇和，建设部规划司司长唐凯，吴良镛、齐康、关肇邺、戴复东、钟训正、程泰宁六位院士，东南大学校长易红，校党委常务副书记杨树林，清华大学、天津大学等兄弟建筑学院的院长，国外建筑院系代表及众多知名校友及各届校友和嘉宾。会上仇和副省长，唐凯司长、易红校长等发表了热情洋溢的讲话，大会还播放了建设部黄卫副部长的祝贺录像。王建国院长在会上发表主旨发言：建筑学院作为一个在全国创立最早，在国内外具有重要学术影响的建筑院系，未来的发展道路还很长。筚路蓝缕，继往开来，开拓耕耘乃是我们今天肩负的历史重任。吴良镛、齐康院士相继发言，畅谈80年艰辛与辉煌，更感谢杨廷宝、刘敦桢、童寯等多位恩师教育。另有教师代表和学生代表发言，大会在欢庆祥和的气氛中结束。

晚上7：30，以“建筑东南 筑梦中大”为主题，以建筑学院师生共同联欢的晚会开始了，多才多艺的学生和老师演绎了一个又一个精彩的节目，晚会在以师生同唱“明天会更好”的乐曲声中把院庆活动带入了高潮，使人们对未来充满了希望和信心。

开幕式

仇和副省长视察

庆典文艺晚会

On Oct. 20th 2007, the School of architecture of Southeast University held a ceremonious activity, which was for the 80th anniversary of the founding of Architecture Institute, in the Sipailou campus (the former campus of Central University). All the teachers and students of the SEU-ARCH, as well as the schoolfellows and guests from home and abroad enjoyed a happy get-together.

At 8:30 am, we held the release ceremony for the books Collected Edition of Liu Dunzhen and Collected Works of Tong Jun. After that the two academicians Wu Liangyong and Zhong Xunzheng cut the ribbon at the opening ceremony for the unveiling of Mr. Bao Ding's bronze statue. Mr. Bao Ding, who is one of the most important personages for the development of the SEU-ARCH, made every effort to save a desperate situation of the Architecture Department during the War of Resistance against Japan. Later was the collective artistic performance acted by students, those who stood around the pool which was in front of the auditorium wearing the orange color clothes. The regular drum and applause given by the students, as well as the flying color balloons added festival mood to the celebration.

At 10:00 am the celebration, which was hosted by the subdecanal of SEU-ARCH Dong Wei, opened ceremoniously. The conventioneers included the vice-governor of Jiangsu Province Qiu He, chief of the Planning Department in the Ministry of Construction Tang Kai and the six academicians Wu Liangyong, Qi Kang, Zhong Xunzheng, Guan Zhaoye, Dai Fudong, Cheng Taining, as well as the principal of SEU Yi Hong, the administrative vice secretary of the SEU party committee Yang Shulin. Deans from the Architecture Institute of Tsinghua University, Tianjin University and other brotherhood universities, as well as the representatives from oversea architecture institute and former students, guests also took part in the celebration. The vice-governor of Jiangsu Province Qiu He, the department chief Tang Kai and the principal Yi Hong, and so on, all gave ebullient speeches in the celebration. Meanwhile the video of Huang Wei, who is the undersecretary in the Ministry of Construction, was also broadcasted. Dean of SEU-ARCH Wang Jianguo also gave a speech in the celebration, he said the SEU-ARCH was a pioneer in our country, which had important influences on academic both home and abroad, and it will have a lot of progress in the future. Enduring great hardships in pioneer work, carrying forward the tradition into the future, bringing forth and cultivating were still our important task nowadays. Then academician Wu Liangyong and Qi Kang gave speeches in succession, they collogued about the hardship and refulgence of the past 80 years, and thanked Yang Tingbao, Liu Dunzhen, Tong Jun for their educations. After that the representatives of teachers and students gave speeches, and the celebration ended in the joyful and festival mood.

At 7:30 pm, with the theme "make your dream come true in SEU", all the teachers and students of SEU-ARCH had an evening party. The accomplished students and teachers acted many wonderful programs. With the song "Better Tomorrow", the celebration approached a climax, letting everyone feel full of hope and confidence for the future.

学术活动

鲍鼎铜像揭幕

刘敦桢、童寯文集发行

中国建筑史学研讨会

院庆期间学院还组织了多场高水平的学术讲座及学术交流和展览，其中包括：“海峡两岸大学的校园”学术研讨会、“中德国际联合教学展览”、“刘敦桢先生诞辰110周年纪念会暨中国建筑史学研讨会”、“中德联合学术研讨会”、“建筑教育的新内涵座谈会”。著名学者程泰宁院士、戴复东院士、钱方总建筑师、德国建筑师Aibert Speer、日本中央大学妹尾达彦教授、德国装置艺术家Markus Heinsdorff、斯图加特建筑与城市规划学院T. Jocher教授、法国拉维莱特建筑学院Michel Verne教授、德国建筑师Stefan Meyer-Miethker分别给同学做了精彩的学术报告。

During the anniversary, we organized many high level academic lectures, exchanges and exhibitions, including the seminar of The University Campuses Across The Taiwan Straits, the exhibition of The International Consociation for Teaching Between China and Germany, the commemoration of Liu Dunzhen's 110th anniversary and seminar of Chinese architectural history, the academic seminar between China and Germany, colloquium of the new meaning of architectural education. The following scholars gave wonderful lectures to our students respectively, they were the academician Chen Taining, Dai Fudong, chief architect Qian Fang, German architect Aibert Speer, professor SEO Tatsuhiko from Central University in Japan, German installation artist Markus Heinsdorff, professor T. Jocher from the College of Architecture and Urban Planning in Stuttgart, professor Michel Verne from La Villette School of Architecture in France, German architect Stefan Meyer-Miethker.

抗震救灾
Post-disaster Aid Projects for the Quake Area, Sichuan Province

四川汶川"5. 12"地震后，东南大学建筑学院王建国院长、安宁书记积极组织、召集院系骨干力量，投身抗震救灾工作，先后完成了绵竹县广济镇总体规划、广济镇村庄规划、广济镇灾后援建项目建筑设计、丽春镇灾后重建规划等，并结合工程实践，参与中国科学技术协会课题"地震建筑预案"研究。

Under the leadership and support of Jiangsu Province, Wang Jianguo and An Ning quickly organized groups which are the backbone of the School to enlist the post-disaster aid projects for the quake area in Sichuan Province.

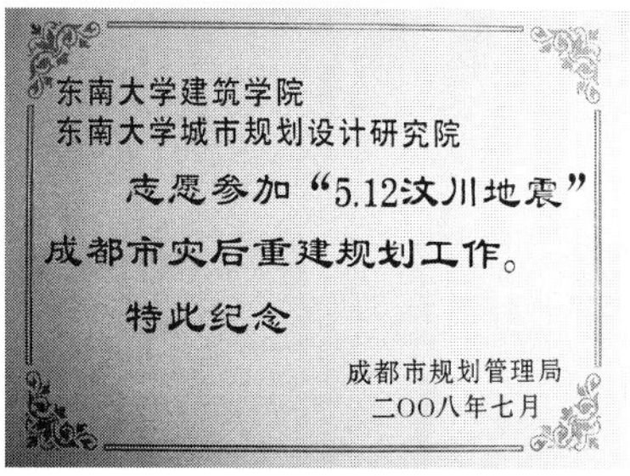

绵竹市广济镇总体规划
Guangji Town Master Plan, Mianzhu City

主要设计人：段进 孔令龙 徐春宁 熊国平 王志东 邵润清 杨俊宴 王敏等

规划将广济镇城镇性质定位为生态型工贸城镇、镇域综合服务中心。规模预测：2010年广济镇区人口为0.20万人，建设用地33.83公顷，人均建设用地169.15平方米。2020年城镇人口为0.40万人，建设用地47.89公顷。

镇域规划：结合灾损程度、未来发展的交通、区位条件等要素，沿山发展生态旅游，沿路发展工业贸易，构建一镇六村沿山沿路有序发展的空间格局。镇村体系遵从区位优势、联系合理、规模经济的原则，采取镇区、中心村、基层村三级设置，并配置相应的公共设施，构建宜居的居住环境。

镇区规划：镇区规划经多方案比较，最终从广济的发展趋势和当地政府的意愿出发，经过比选对"一心、一带、二轴、二区"的空间结构进行了深化。

防震规划：按规范紧急避震疏散场所服务半径500米，固定避震疏散场所服务半径1.5-3千米，规划利用学校操场、街头绿地和滨河绿地等作为避震疏散场地。规划以城镇主、次干道为避震疏散通道。

近期建设规划：充分利用现有设施和建设条件，具有可操作性，符合"恢复生产、和谐生活"的重建原则和目标，使城镇在近期形成比较合理的空间布局态势，为远期目标的实现提供坚实基础。根据开发规模和当地的实际需要，本规划确定广济镇灾后近期江苏援建项目10项。

镇域规划图

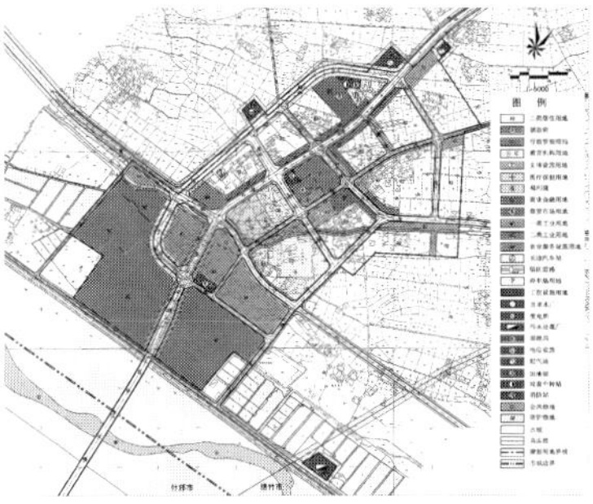
镇区总体规划图

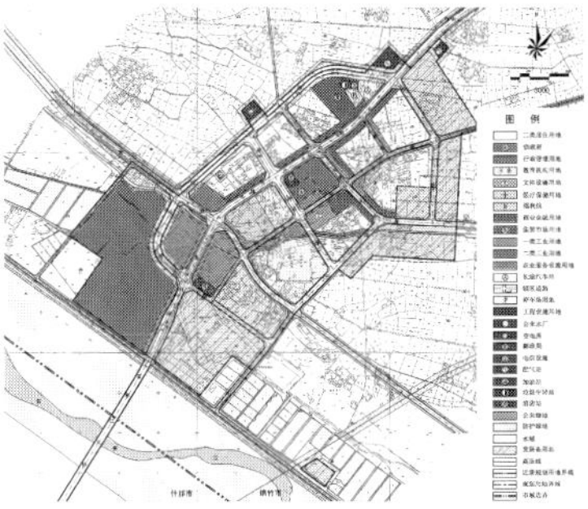
镇区近期建设规划图

Guangji is planned to be an eco-town of industry and trade.

Recent construction plan: to make full use of existing facilities and construction, with the principles and objectives of the reconstruction "the resumption of production, harmonious life", form a more reasonable spatial layout to provide a solid foundation for achieving long-term goals.

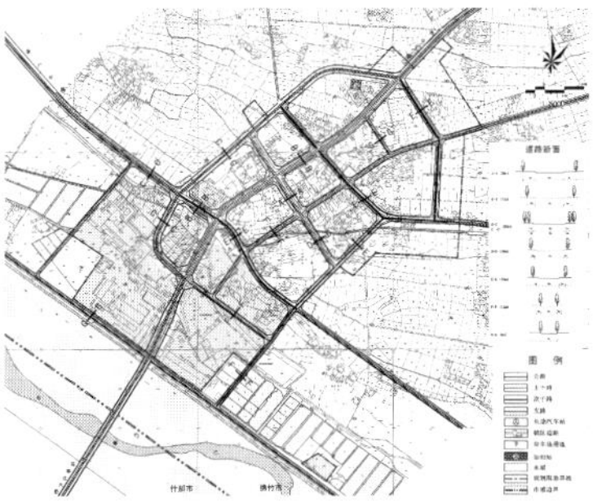
镇区道路交通规划图

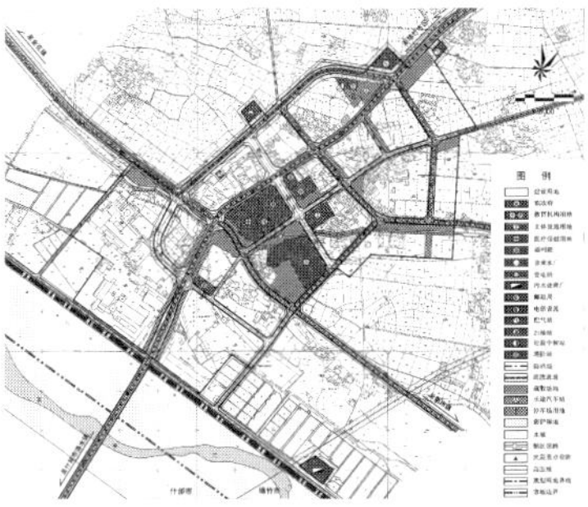
镇区防灾减灾规划图

绵竹市广济镇村庄规划
Guangji Village Plan, Mianzhu City

主要设计人：段进 孔令龙 张彤 徐春宁 王志东 吴锦绣 张玫英 杨静 王敏等

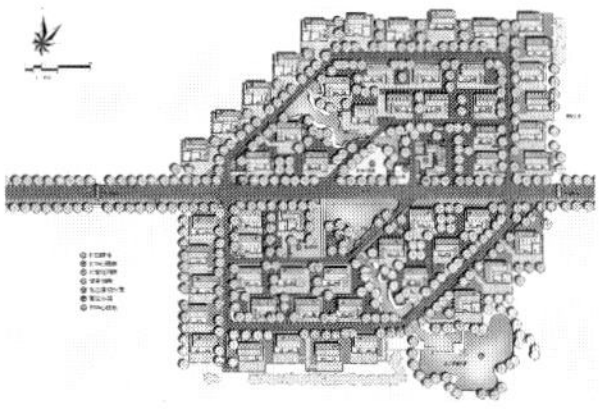

村庄建设规划总平面图

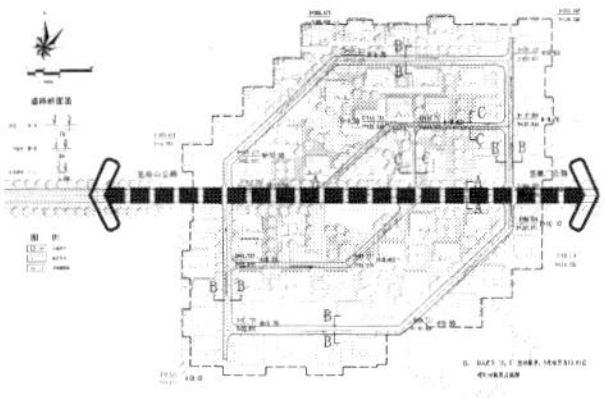

村庄道路及竖向规划图

村庄总体效果图

卧云村位于绵竹市西南边缘、广济镇域西北部，沿山公路南北向穿过。结合现有村庄产业特色和良好的自然景观，利用村级道路、配套公共设施、生产设施、农业基础设施，规划卧云村规划设置1个中心村、21个基层村。

卧云村五组地处规划卧云行政村东北约600米，规划尽量集中布局，考虑土地资源、公共资源有效利用，强调自然空间在村庄中的渗透，重塑传统乡村生活。形成“一轴两片，一心双环” 的结构，村庄形态具有可生长性。村庄建设用地0. 85公顷，人均建设用地42. 33平方米。规划居住建筑用地坚持以人为本的原则，选择环境宜人的地段安排，并在居民住宅布局和设计上承载当地传统农村的生活习惯和环境。居住点以规划道路进行分割，相互之间相对独立，又相互沟通，建筑布置以均质形态为主。建筑采用了白墙灰瓦的风格，既体现了当地居民质朴的性格，又与周边的田园景色浑然一体，使农村田园风貌得到更好的展现。

Woyun Village with a north-south road along the hillside, is lying southwest of Mianzhu City, northwest of Guangji town. By the combination of existing distinctive industries and good natural landscape, using the village road, public facilities, production facilities and agricultural infrastructure, planning a system of a village centre and 21 basic level villages.

Group five locates about 600 meters northeast of Woyun Village. To centralize land, make full use of land resources and public resources, emphasize infiltration of the natural space, and remodel traditional village life, planning a structure of "one axis-two area, one centre- double loop", with the form of growth. The amount of construction land can reach to 0.85 hm^2, and Per Capita construction land can be 42.33 m^2. Following the principle “putting people first”, residential land is planned in a pleasant place and the residential design embodies local rural environment and living habits. Residential districts divided by the road, are both dependent and intercommunicate, to form a homogeneous mainly building layout. Building design uses the style of white walls and grey roofing tiles, to reflect the local residents' earthiness character and the surrounding rural landscape as well.

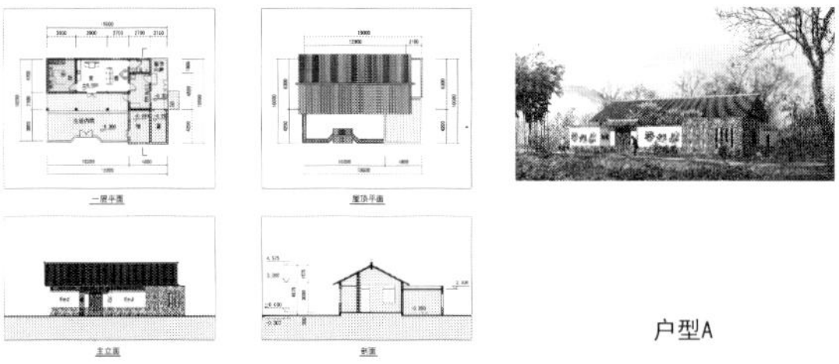

户型A

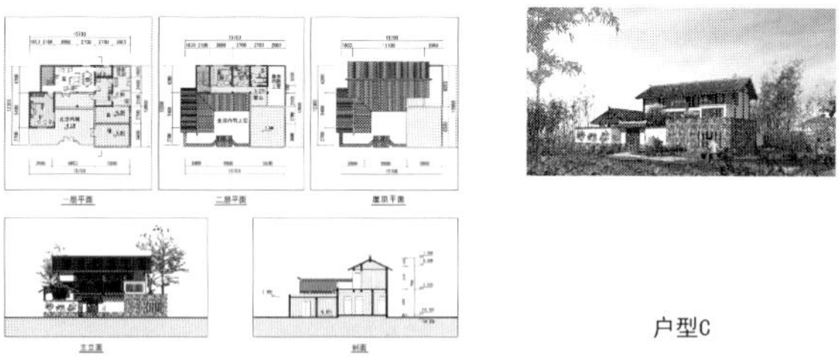

户型C

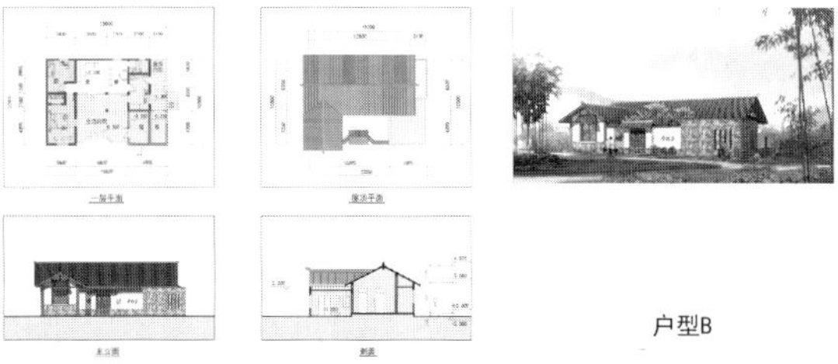

户型B

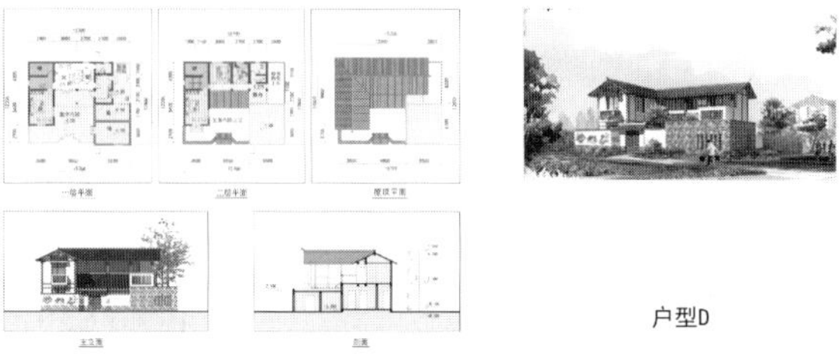

户型D

绵竹市广济镇灾后援建项目
Post-disaster Aid Projects of Guangji Town, Mianzhu City

主要设计人：张彤 韩冬青 邓浩 鲍莉 周颖 王建国 徐小东 顾震弘等

江苏省昆山市援建的广济镇灾后援建项目包括镇卫生院、镇幼儿园、镇福利院、镇小学校及202户廉租房（该项目后取消）。项目位于镇中心区，与镇政府行政服务地块共同形成未来镇区的核心地块与中心空间。

街区设计

街区设计根据各项目的功能性质与规模大小，对中心区四个地块进行了用地划分，并对各地块的机动车出入口作出规定。在地块划分中保留水渠，规划公共绿地，并在镇政府西南侧留出公共广场用地。作为震后新建镇区，本次设计力图通过对街墙的控制，形成明确的城市街道界面，以创造鲜明的城市空间特征。每个街区沿城镇道路规定统一的后退界面，在街区内部则形成活泼丰富的空间环境。

在四块用地交叉的十字路口，遵照总体规划，保留水渠，设置公共绿地，在镇政府前规划一个公共广场，该广场与绿地互为对角，共同形成镇区主要公共活动空间。保留水渠经改造成为景观水面。在十字路口的西南角，结合小学入口，水面适当扩大，形成一个湖面，设置市民休闲活动广场，并设立镇中心主题雕塑。

建筑设计

镇中心区各个援建项目遵循适用、安全、经济、美观的原则，以简洁明快的现代风格为主题基调，结合竹、木、卵石等地方材料和传统做法，体现地域风格。单体建筑设计遵照当地的气候特点，迎合主导风向，合理组织和利用自然通风和天然采光。所有建筑均采用植草屋面，提高完善围护结构的保温性能，结合建筑立面精心设计外遮阳系统。

援建各项目均采用现浇钢筋混凝土结构，结构设计达到八度抗震标准，结构布置均匀合理，提高受力的整体性，能满足“小震不坏、中震可修、大震不倒”的抗震要求。

卫生院

福利院

廉租房

小学校

幼儿园

鸟瞰图

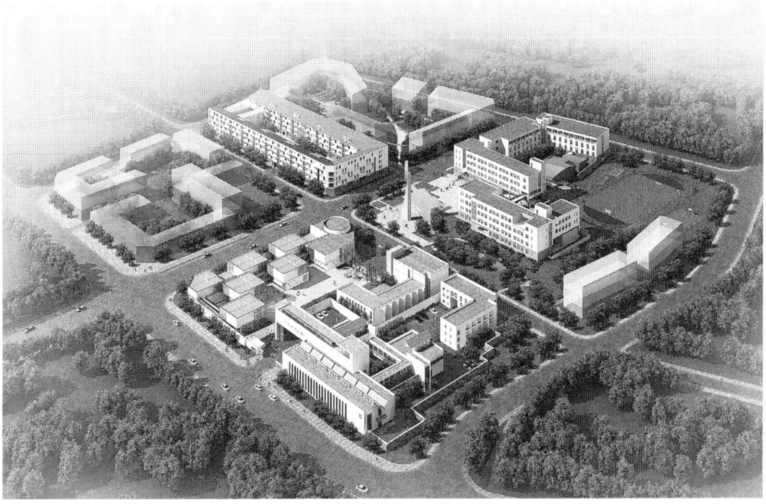

The post-disaster aid projects for Guangji Town are invested by Kunshan City, including a health center, a kindergarten, a welfare house, a primary school, and low-cost flats. The projects are located in the center of the town, which is the core of the new town, together with the new town government and civil service buildings.

彭州市丽春镇灾后重建规划

The Post-quake Reconstruction Plan of Lichun Town, Pengzhou City

主要设计人：王兴平 赵虎 袁新国 胡畔 李媚 席震 符彩云 吴珏

规划将丽春镇城镇性质定位为彭州市灾后经济重建的重要阵地，是彭州、郫县和都江堰市交界处的工贸型中心镇，是彭州市南部城镇密集区的副中心，远期是彭州市中心城区重要的城镇组团。规模预测：2010年丽春城镇人口3万人，建设用地269.48公顷，人均建设用地90平方米。2020年城镇人口为4万人，建设用地337公顷。

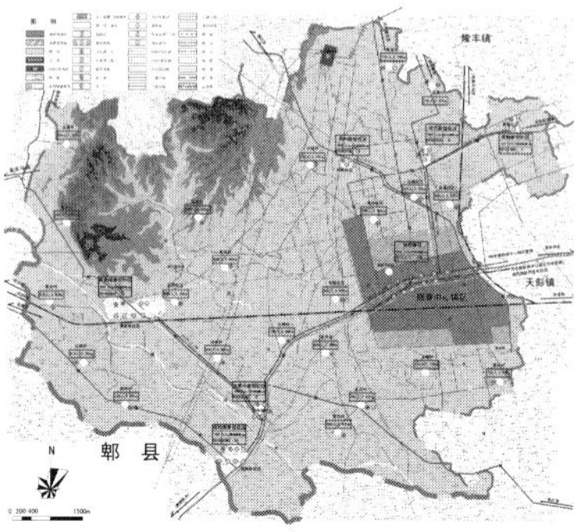

镇域规划：结合灾损程度、未来发展的交通、区位条件等，将镇域整体规划为“三心三轴三片区”的空间结构。“三心”分别为丽春城镇，作为全镇的经济发展核心；谭家场新型社区，作为西部发展的中心；草鞋街新型社区，作为南部发展的中心。“三轴”一为彭温公路的发展轴线；二为北桂路发展轴线，三为北部的旅游发展轴线。“三片区”指以人民渠和行政界线为界划分的东部片区、南部片区和西部片区。镇村体系遵从安置灾民、适当聚集的原则，采取镇区、农村新型社区、农村小型聚居点三级设置，并配置相应的公共设施，构建宜居的居住环境。

镇区规划：镇区规划采取多方案，从丽春的发展趋势和当地政府的意愿出发分别完成了两套方案，供灾区人民选择。最终经过比选对“一带三轴七小区”的空间结构进行了深化。

防震规划：根据成都市防震减灾局的《汶川8.0级地震成都市灾后重建地震评价规划用图》，按规范避震疏散场地疏散半径在1公里以内，规划利用公园、绿地、广场、运动操场等空旷地区作为避震疏散场地。规划以城镇主要道路作为人员疏散和物质运输的主要救援通道，救援通道要求保证灾后有7米以上的宽度。

近期建设规划：以灾后重建规划为依据，以现状情况为基础，适应市场经济的发展要求，规划提出了紧凑布局、滚动开发的思路，使城镇在近期形成比较合理的空间布局态势，为远期目标的实现提供坚实基础。在农村新社区要注意增加相应的公共设施，吸引人口向新型社区集中。根据开发规模和当地的实际需要，本规划确定丽春城镇灾后近期建设项目27项，6个农村新型社区近期建设项目61项，镇域基础设施建设项目6项。

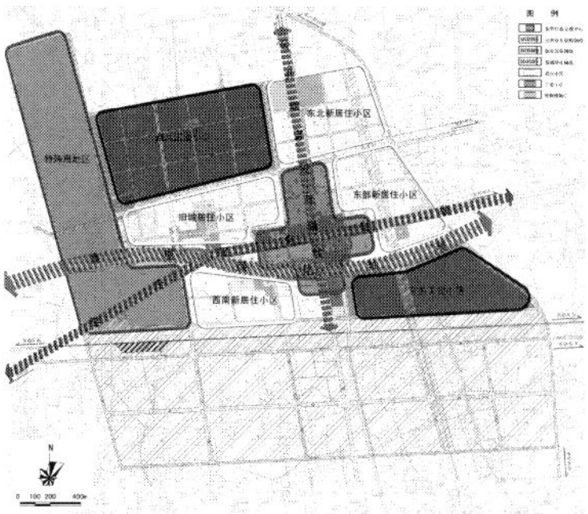

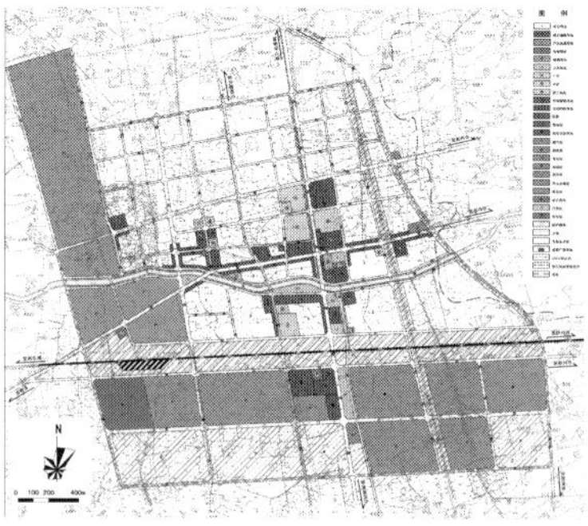

Lichun town is planned to be an important part of Pengzhou city's post-quake economy reconstruction, the industrial and commercial center town on the border of Pengzhou city, Pi town and Dujiangyan city and the auxiliary city center of south town concentrated areas in Pengzhou city.

Recent construction plan: The plan brings up a thinking of compact layout and rolling development which based on post-disaster reconstruction plan and the status quo situation to accommodate the development requirements of market economy. So that towns can form more reasonable spatial layout situation in the near future to provide a solid foundation for achieving long-term goals. We should pay attention to increase corresponding public facilities in the new rural community to attract population gather up to the new community.

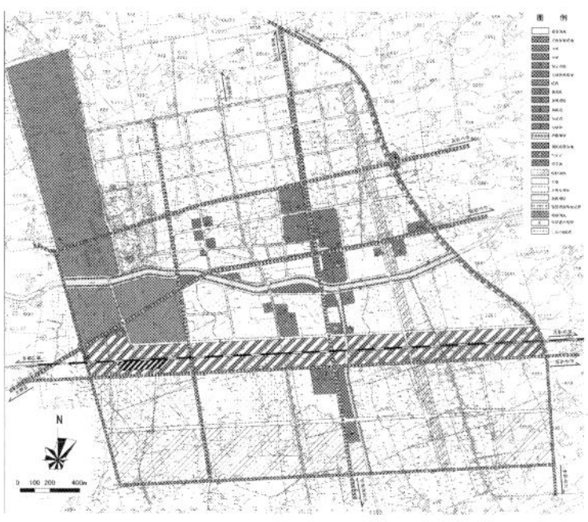

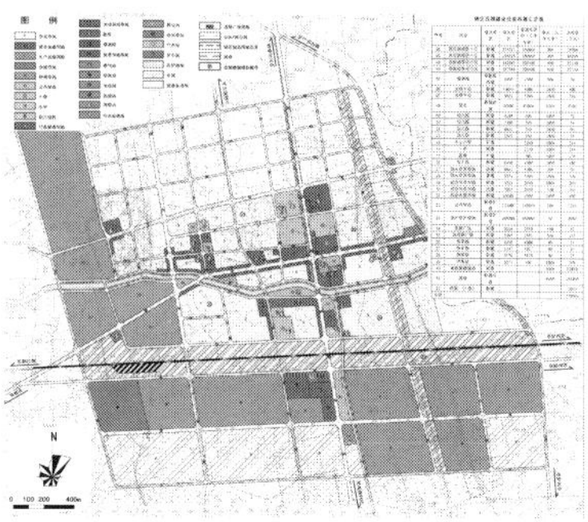

松潘县城北片区控制性详细规划和重点地段城市设计
Regulatory Plan and Urban Design of Strategic Section of North Town, Songpan County

主要设计人：徐春宁 应珺 吴增鑫 谢薇佳 陈黎娟 吴珏

松潘县位于四川省西北部，是黄龙-九寨沟风景旅游区的重要组成部分和旅游服务基地。“5.12”地震后，对口援建的安徽省和松潘县共同确定了未来城市发展的总体规划，即古城-川主寺一体化、组团式格局。而城北片区处于岷江河谷向北发展的主导方向，将建设成为新城政务中心及文教科研集中区，适宜建设用地75.45公顷，预计人口规模0.4万人。

作为灾后重建规划的重要环节，本次详细规划将与总体规划保持程序上的同步，应急救灾与恢复重建保持整体上的协调，有效落实三年近期建设和长远科学发展的双和谐。并加强防灾抗灾规划，初步建立地震监测预报、地震灾害防御、地震应急与救援三大体系。

空间规划注重对自然资源和历史要素的整合，突出两山夹一水的空间形态和因地就势的城市格局；探寻松潘故事情节，彰显藏、羌、回、汉多元民族，唐、明、现代多元文化，聚居、建设、旅游多元生活的水乳交融。

鸟瞰图

岷江两岸

行政广场鸟瞰

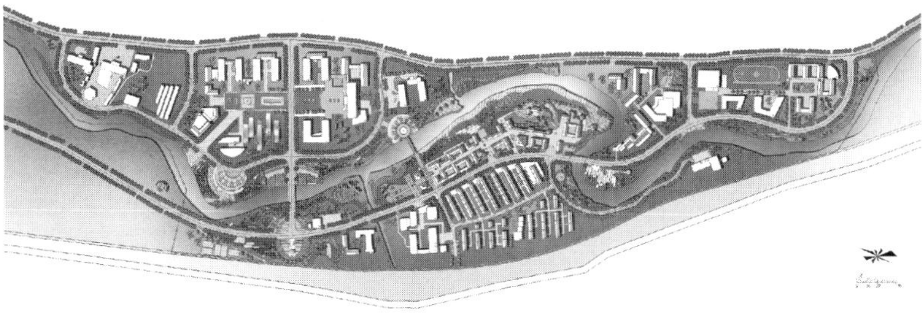
总平面图

松潘中学

行政广场

默默——2008威尼斯建筑双年展中国馆之一
MURMUR: Chinese Pavilion, La Bienale di Venezia, 2008

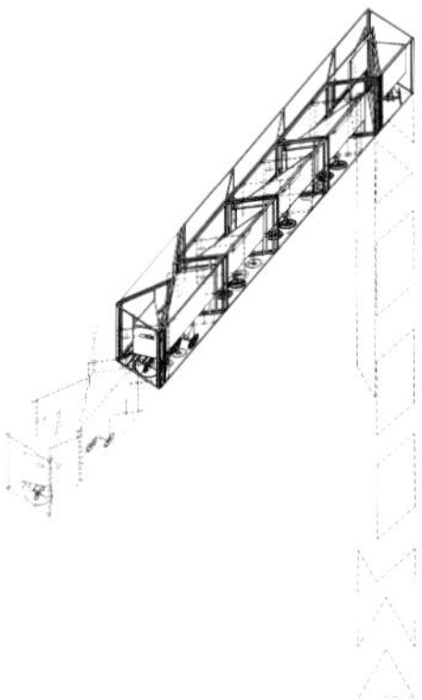

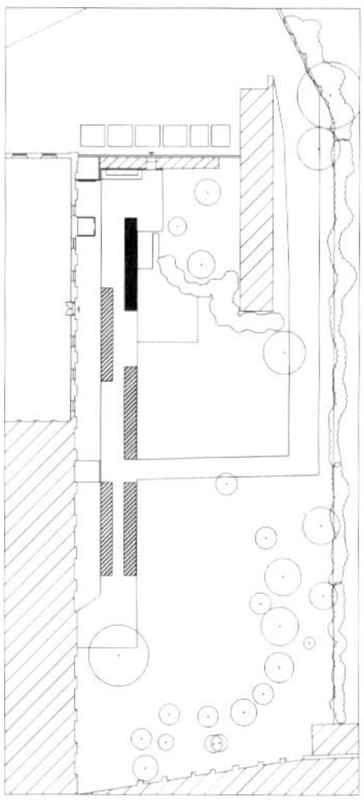

我们的作品名为Murmur，与中国馆的主题“Negotiation”呼应，意为威尼斯处女园中一群集身体-装置-建筑于一身的特殊物体，彼此低声细语，以微弱的声音构筑起一个公共领域。

它以钢为主材，由若干空房子构成，集体对环境作出默默反应。房子移动，互相低语，形成另一状态，又一次归于集体。作品以动为静，并以此纪念五月中的国难。

它也与双年展主题“Out There－Architecture Beyond Building”呼应，它是东方式的集合，不同于西方狂欢节中的假面舞会；它是身体劳动的表现，不同于当代图像社会的种种姿态。

它试图讨论建筑如何成为公共领域的边界条件，建筑如何在公共空间和私密空间中自然地呈现。因此Murmur是对公共语言和私人语言的一次讨论。

它还试图讨论建筑如何在极值条件下体现自己的猜想价值，建筑如何通过多种学科的过滤表现去芜存菁的能力。因此Murmur是一种对各种情形的应对策略。

Murmur表达了这样一种语言：重重叠叠，轻微难辨，似是而非。

状态：Uncanny，一面特殊的墙，在另四堵墙前突然整体轻轻移动，再分化为七个姿态不同的物体，三三两两游弋园中；或反之。其重点在于齐步走时的Murmur，而非简单拆分。各个体块互相位移，像中国古代的阵法——但速度缓慢，以动示静；它的竖框所勾画的背景在不断变化——但横向的金属体块却始终交叠不分，是一个还是七个？

建筑师：葛明
助手：王志强 蒋梦麟 韩曼 高勤 刘畅 王英哲

Architect: Ge Ming
Project assistants: Wang Zhiqiang, Jiang Menglin, Han Man, Gao Qin, Liu Chang, Wang Yingzhe

身体：整体为墙时逐个进入不同物体，分解时显露，并通过各种反射呈现多重迹象——但不是舞台，是为了实现身体在内外的角色转换——私人世界与生活世界的连接，而各个身体自身也因此似乎形成了机械的一个部分。真幻人像处于不同标高来回移动，四周看到投影时，以为人悬在不同高度，似乎在不断测量环境。

材料：以铁为框，勾勒出天空与各个物体的界限。竖向的线条包含着形态各异的几何体块，它们采用反光金属表面，使它可以放在南京、威尼斯、墨西哥、纽约各个地方，隐隐反射环境，反射其余四墙——但不是玻璃，灰灰的，沉沉的，反射景物时像里希特的照片画。是不均匀的图像衬托着真实材料，还是真实材料在衬托着虚幻图像？

结构：不动声色，诸多形体各有其难度和复杂度，重心、轴心、运动类型、运动轨迹、内外连接各不相同——但材料使它们似是而非，难以分辨，只有进入的身体才能区别；各个物体之中，各个构件可以彼此分开，各有其用——但它们又无法分离，外框是独立的，但又是结构校正的最后一道工序，底座是独立的，但当架上重物时，各个轮子才能共同作用成为车子。

其实Murmur是一种日常的语言，是常被忽略的语言，对我们来说却意义重大，它是一种发声的练习——是我们视建筑为一种技艺所需要的练习，是当代中国建筑一片喧闹之中的默默之语。

Murmur is our response to "negotiation", the theme of the Chinese Pavilion 2008. It's suggestive of the whispering of various body-installation-architecture objects in the Virgin Garden of Venice, where a new type of public sphere is formed through the aggregation of tiny voices.

Using steel as the main material, Murmur consists of several empty houses that respond to the environment collectively. They move around, whispering to each other, gathering in new form before resolving once again in the collective. It's a stationary presence consisting of movement, serving as a memorial to the national tragedy in May, 2008.

It also speaks to the biennale's theme "Out There--Architecture Beyond Building". Unlike the Masquerade in the western carnival, it's a collective in the style of the East; unlike the poses in the contemporary visual societies, it's an embodiment of craft and labor.

It tries to discuss how architecture becomes the boundary condition of the public sphere, how it's represented in a spontaneous way in public and private space. Therefore, Murmur is an alternative way to discuss the issues of public and private language.

It also asks the question of how architecture can realize its hypothetical value under extreme condition, how its filtering mechanism works by sifting through parallel disciplines. Therefore, Murmur is a kind of strategy which is able to respond to different situations.

Murmur is such a language: multi-layered, ambiguous,paradoxical.

State: Uncanny. A special wall suddenly moves silently in front of other four walls before splitting into seven objects of different shapes, lingering in the garden in pairs. (The process can also be reversed.) Here the emphasis is not on the deconstructing process, but rather on the tranquil silence when the objects are "walking" together. The position shifting of them is not unlike the movement of the army array in ancient China slowed down—a way to express the idea of silence through movement. The background views outlined by the vertical frame of the objects are constantly changing, while the horizontal metal blocks are always mingled together: are they seven objects, or just one?

Body: The body enters each objects when the collective manifests itself as a wall, when they part, the body will be revealed as multiple images through various reflection mechanism. This is not a stage though, but a way for the body to shift between internal and external characters—an intersection of one's private world and the real world out there. Here, the bodies become part of the mechanism, real and fake portraits are moving at different heights, creating the illusion of people being suspended and thus "measuring" the whole environment.

Material: The iron frame is used to sketch out the boundaries between the objects and the sky. Different shapes of geometric blocks are made visible by the vertical lines, their reflective metallic surface projecting the environment as well as the other four walls—whether they are placed in Nanjing, Venice, Mexico City or New York. The effect, however, doesn't resemble that of glass, it's rather grayish and dim, like the photograph-like paintings of Gerhard Richter. Is the uneven image simply a backdrop of the real materials, or the other way around?

Structure: Deadpan. Each of the different shapes and forms has its own complexity: centre of gravity, axis, type of movement, trajectory, connection type...But the materials used add ambiguity to the objects, making them indistinguishable unless the "body" enters their sphere. Each component of the objects can be disintegrated and utilized differently, but they are not to be separated from each other. The frame is independent, while also serving as the last step in the structural calibration work flow; the base is independent, but it's only when heavy object is placed on top that the wheels will be able to work together as parts of a cart.

In fact, Murmur is a kind of daily language. Although often neglected, it is significant for us. It's a kind of "vocal practice" for us who regard architecture as craft, the murmur among the brouhaha of the contemporary Chinese architecture scene.

专业设置与学科建设

Specialities Setup & Discipline Development

专业设置
Specialities Setup

一、建筑系

1. 办学思想

面向全球，面向社会，面向未来，建设整合、开放的建筑学专业教育新体系。

（1）建筑教育应当是职业教育与素质教育的统一，其教育过程是阶段性与持续性的统一，其目标是未来建筑师知识结构与综合能力的统一。因此，建筑教育应当以职业能力的培养为基础，进一步促进学生基本素质和综合创造能力的全面提高。通过整合与开放的专业教学体系，造就高素质、多层次、多类型的专业人才。

（2）以系统的观念重新审视已有教学体系，整合和加强课程之间的有机联系，提高教学效率，建立与此配套的教案、教材和师资组织构架。

（3）树立开放的教育理念，谋求多层面、多方位的合作途径，使学生具有宽阔的学术视野，灵活的实践能力和合作能力，以便进入社会后能尽快适应不断变化的社会需求。

2. 办学目标

本专业培养建筑学领域素质高、能力强、基础扎实、知识面宽、德智体美全面发展的，具有创造能力的复合型优秀建筑设计人才。围绕建筑学专业评估标准和国家一级注册建筑师的职业要求，学生应具有自然科学、人文科学的基本知识和扎实的专业基础理论，系统掌握专业知识和实践技能，具有在建筑学领域从事设计、研究、教学和管理的能力。

3. 办学特色

（1）继承和发展东南大学建筑教育“严谨求实、学以致用、中西兼蓄、锐意创新”的优良传统和基础扎实、要求严格、注重实践、综合发展的特点。

（2）突出“建筑设计”核心课程的地位，注重思维训练和技能训练的统一。

（3）注重科研成果与教学环节的整合。

（4）强调实践环节的重要性。集中实践教学环节包括认识实习、专业技能实习、工程实践和毕业设计等类型，共50个周时。各个实践环节均有明确的教学大纲及相应的考核标准。毕业设计的课题多数结合实际工程展开。

（5）关注本土问题。

（6）强调教学研究的日常化和教学改革的系统性和连续性，近几年来的教学改革主要包括如下内容：“建筑设计”核心课程的系统整合研究；“美术”课程教学中的“视觉设计”问题研究；相关专业课程群的建设；网络课程及多媒体课件研究；江苏省“建筑学”品牌专业建设研究；建筑学专业本科培养方案及教学计划修订工作。

Ⅰ. Department of Architecture

1. Philosophy

Facing the world, the society and the future, to construct new education system of the architecture specialty with national characteristics.

(1)Education on architecture shall be the unification of professional education and qualification education, the process of its education shall unite period and continuity, with the goal of unifying the knowledge structure and comprehensive ability of the future architects.

(2)The current teaching system will be inspected again with systematic views so as to conform and strengthen the organic connection among courses, enhance teaching efficiency, and establish mated teaching plans, text books and faculty structure.

(3)To establish open education concepts and seek for multi-level and multi-aspect cooperation ways so as to make the students possess wide academic view, flexible practice ability and cooperative ability.

2. Target

The target of education is to cultivate excellent comprehensive architectural designers with high qualifications in the architectural field, strong abilities, solid foundations, wide knowledge range, and all-round development in morality, intelligence, physique and art as well as creativities.

3. Characteristics

(1)To inherit and develop the excellent tradition of SEU-ARCH, “be prudent and down-to-earth, study in order to apply, combine Chinese and foreign cultures, and be creative and innovative”, and focusing on practice and comprehensive development.

(2)To highlight the position of “architectural design” as a core course.

(3)To focus on the conformation of scientific research achievements and teaching results.

(4)To strengthen the importance of the practice. The integrated practice teaching part will comprise such types as recognition practice, professional skills practice, engineering practice and graduation design, etc., in total 50 week hours. Each practice part has clarified teaching outline and corresponding inspection standard.

(5)To focus on local problems.

(6)To strengthen the daily teaching research, as well as systematization and continuation of teaching reform.

4.Course Setup for Undergraduates

4. 本科生课程设置

指导性教学计划
Instructive teaching plan

课程类别	课程名称	学分	课内学时			课外学时	各学期周学时分配														
			授课	实验	上机		一			二			三			四			五		
							1	2	3	1	2	3	1	2	3	1	2	3	1	2	3
通识教育基础课程	毛泽东思想概论	2	24			8					2										
	邓小平理论与三个代表的重要思想	2	32			16						2									
	马克思主义哲学	2	32			16								2							
	政治经济学	2	24			8												2			
	思想道德修养	1	12			4		1													

续表

课程类别	课程名称	学分	课内学时			课外学时	各学期周学时分配														
			授课	实验	上机		一			二			三			四			五		
							1	2	3	1	2	3	1	2	3	1	2	3	1	2	3
通识教育基础课程	形势与政策	1	10			6								1							
	就业导论	1	10			6											1				
	法律基础	2	32									2									
	文史类 哲学社科类 经典导读类 军事理论类	7	112																		
	大学英语	14	224					4	4		4	2									
	体育	4	128					2	2		1	1		1	1						
	高等数学E（建筑）	4	64					4													
大类学科基础课程	建筑设计基础	8	256					8	8												
	视觉设计基础	9	288					6	6		3	3									
	建筑制图	2	32					2													
	建筑学概论	1	16					1													
	建筑设计基础理论	1	16						1												
	计算机辅助设计	2	32						2												
	城市规划原理（双语）	2	32															2			
	居住环境与住宅设计原理	1	16															1			
	专业外语	4	64																	4	
	建筑力学	3	48						1		2										
专业主干课	建筑设计	24	768								8	8		8	8			8		8	
	中国建筑史	4	64											4							
	外国建筑史（双语）	4	64												4						
	建筑结构	3	48									2		1							
	建筑构造	6	96								2	1		1	2						
	建筑物理	4	64											2	2						
	建筑设备	3	48												3						
	建筑设计理论（双语）	4	64								1	1		1	1						
跨专业学科选课	中国近现代建筑解析	1.5	24																	15	
	西方当代建筑思潮（双语）	1	16															1			
	计算机建筑表现	1	16															1			
	古典亭榭与小品设计	3	48																	3	
	建筑经济与业务管理	2	32																	2	
	城市设计概论（双语）	2	32															2			
	建筑行为心理学	1	16												1						
	城市中心（区）发展与规划	1	16																	1	
	城市环境与城市生态	2	32																	2	
	城市道路与交通	2	32															2			
	城市地理学	2	32															2			
	城市规划管理与法规	2	32															2			

续表

课程类别	课程名称	学分	课内学时			课外学时	各学期周学时分配														
			授课	实验	上机		一			二			三			四			五		
							1	2	3	1	2	3	1	2	3	1	2	3	1	2	3
跨专业学科选课	摄影	1	16											1							
	建筑画技法	1	16											1							
	艺术概论	2	32															2			
	现代绘画	2	32															2			
	陶艺	1	16																	1	
	公共艺术	1	16															1			
	室内设计原理	2	32																		2
	景园植物学	2	32																	2	
	人体工程学	1	16															1			
	中外园林史	2	32																	2	
	中大跨建筑结构	1	16												1						
	建筑节能	1	16																	1	
	虚拟设计	2	32												1						

集中实践教学环节指导表
Guidance on integrated practice teaching

课程要求	课程名称	学分	学时			各学期周学时分配														
			授课	周数	天/周	一			二			三			四			五		
						1	2	3	1	2	3	1	2	3	1	2	3	1	2	3
课内	军训	2		3	3															
	工地实习	1		1					1											
	认识实习（一）	1		1					1											
	CAD理论与实践（一）	1		1					1											
	素描实习	1		1					1											
	色彩实习	2		2								2								
	认识实习（二）	1		1								1								
	CAD理论与实践（二）	1		1								1								
	建筑测绘	4		4											4					
	快速设计强化训练	2		2														2		
	城市环境调研	2		2														2		
	毕业设计	16		16																16
课外	工程实践	10		16												10				
	文献阅读	2																		
	学科竞赛	2																		
	科研实践																			

二、城市规划系

1. 办学思想

根据市场经济条件下城市规划学科内涵持续深化和外延不断拓展的发展态势，不断跟踪城市规划学科发展前沿，“面向现代化、面向世界、面向未来”，建设具有东南大学特色的城市规划专业教育体系，培养德智体美全面发展的国内领先、具有国际竞争力的城市规划高级专门人才。

（1）城市规划专业教育应当是职业教育与素质教育的统一，其教育过程是阶段性与连续性的统一，其教育目标是未来规划师知识教育、综合能力培养和职业道德教育的统一。

（2）以系统的观念审视和优化已有教学体系，建立以通识教育为基础，强化规划综合素质教育的课程体系，不断加强、完善、整合城市规划与建筑学、风景园林、艺术设计等多元学科之间的有机联系；提高教学效率，建立与此配套的教案、教材和师资组织构架。

（3）树立开放的教育理念，谋求多层面、多方位的合作途径，使学生具有宽阔的学术视野，灵活的实践能力、组织合作能力和创新能力，以便进入社会后能尽快适应不断变化的社会需求。

2. 办学目标

根据城市规划专业教育的客观规律和国家的发展与建设实际需要，围绕城市规划专业评估标准和国家注册规划师的职业要求，培养城市规划领域具有科学发展观，素质高、能力强、基础扎实、知识面宽、德智体美全面发展的城市规划复合型优秀专业人才。

学生应具有扎实的自然科学、人文科学和城市规划专业技术基础理论、系统的专业知识和实践能力；在城市规划领域中，具有独立或合作进行规划设计、科学研究、管理和教学工作的能力；具有较为广泛的知识面与知识结构，能与不同专业人员合作进行有关城市发展的咨询、评估、策划与决策研究工作。

3. 办学特色

（1）继承和发展东南大学建筑学院“严谨求实、学以致用、中西兼蓄、锐意创新”的优良传统和基础扎实、要求严格、注重实践、综合发展的特点。

（2）“规划设计”课程和规划理论教学两轴并重，注重理论思维训练和技能训练的统一，尤其以城市的物质形态规划教学为特色。

（3）注重科研成果与教学环节的整合互动，与学院其他学科之间的教学交叉互动。

（4）强调实践环节的重要性。各个集中实践教学环节均有明确的教学大纲及相应的考核标准。毕业设计的课题多数结合实际工程展开。

（5）对长三角经济发达地区城市问题的关注：注重引发学生对我国城市化和现代化进程、长三角经济发达地区持续发展和城市环境问题的广泛思考，注重人文环境和物质环境的共生创造。

（6）强调开放互动的教学特色，注重教学研究的日常化和教学改革的系统性和连续性。主要内容包括：“规划设计”核心课程的系统整合研究；相关专业课程群的建设；网络课程及多媒体课件研究；江苏省“城市规划”品牌专业建设研究以及城市规划专业本科培养方案及教学计划修订工作等。

4. 本科生课程设置

Ⅱ. Department of Urban Planning

1. Philosophy

According to the development tendency of continuous deepening of connotation and expanding of the extension of urban planning under market economic conditions, to trace the frontier of the development of urban planning; “facing modernization, facing the world and facing the future”, to construct professional education system of urban planning with SEU characteristics, and cultivate senior professional talents who are domestically leading in the development of morality, intelligence, physique and art as well as with international competitiveness.

(1) Education on urban planning shall be the unification of professional education and qualification education, the process of its education shall unite period and continuity. Its education target is the unification of the future planners in knowledge education, comprehensive ability cultivation and professional morality education.

(2) To inspect and optimize the current teaching system with systematic concept, and establish a course system that bases on general recognition education and strengthens comprehensive qualification education of planning; to continuously strengthen, perfect and conform the organic connections among multiple subjects such as architecture, landscape architecture, and art design; to enhance teaching efficiency, and establish mated teaching plans, textbooks and faculty structure.

(3) To establish open education concepts and seek for multi-level and multi-aspect cooperation ways so as to make the students possess wide academic view, flexible practice ability, organization-cooperative ability, and creativity, which will help them adapt the continuously changing demand from the society in the future.

2. Target

According to objective rules of professional education on urban planning and actual requirements of the state on development and construction, embracing the professional evaluation standard for urban planning and the requirements on state licensed planners, to cultivate excellent comprehensive professionals of urban planning with scientific development view, high qualification, strong ability, solid foundation, wide knowledge range and all-round development in morality, intelligence, physique and art.

Students shall possess solid theories in natural sciences, humanity sciences and urban planning, systematic professional knowledge and practice ability; in the urban planning field, the students shall possess the abilities of independently or cooperatively carrying out planning and design, scientific research, management and teaching. Also the students are required to have wide knowledge range and structure, be able to carry out consultation, assessment, planning and decision studying concerning urban development with people from different majors.

3. Characteristics

(1) To inherit and develop the excellent tradition of SEU-ARCH, “be prudent and down-to-earth, study in order to apply, combine Chinese and foreign cultures, and be creative and innovative”, and such characteristics as solid foundation, strict requirements, focusing on practice and comprehensive development.

(2) The “planning and design” course and planning theory teaching shall be focused at the same time, meanwhile, the unification of theory thinking training and skill training shall be unified, especially the urban material planning teaching shall be characteristic.

(3) To focus on the conformation and interaction of scientific research achievements and teaching results, and crossing interaction with other subjects of the school.

(4) To emphasize the importance of practice. Each practice part has clarified teaching outline and corresponding inspection standard. Most of the topics of graduation design are made with combination of actual projects.

(5) To pay attention to the urban problems in the economically developed areas in the Yangtze Delta: to attract the students' wide thinking on the urbanization and modernization process of China, the continuous development and urban environmental problems in the economically developed areas in the Yangtze Delta, and focus on the joint generation and creation of humanity environment and material environment.

(6) To strengthen the open and interactive teaching characteristics, focus on daily teaching research as well as systematization and continuation of teaching reform. Main content comprises the following: system conformation research on “Planning and Design” core course, construction of relevant professional course cluster, studying on online course and multimedia courseware, studying on branded “Urban Planning” construction of Jiangsu Province, and modification on the cultivation plan for undergraduates and teaching plan concerning urban planning major.

4. Course Setup for Undergraduates

指导性教学计划
Instructive teaching plan

课程类别	课程名称	学分	课内学时			课外学时	各学期周学时分配														
							一			二			三			四			五		
			授课	实验	上机		1	2	3	1	2	3	1	2	3	1	2	3	1	2	3
通识教育基础课程	毛泽东思想概论	2	24			8					2										
	邓小平理论与三个代表的重要思想	2	32			16						2									
	马克思主义哲学	2	32			16								2							
	政治经济学	2	24			8												2			
	思想道德修养	1	12			4		1													
	形势与政策	1	10			6								1							
	就业导论	1	10			6											1				
	法律基础	2	32						2												
	文史类 哲学社科类 经典导读类 军事理论	7	112																		
	大学英语	14	224					4	4		4	2									
	体育	4	128					2	2		1	1		1	1						
	高等数学E	4	64					4													
大类学科基础课程	建筑设计基础	8	256			256		8	8												
	视觉设计基础	9	288					6	6		3	3									
	建筑学概论	1	16					1													
	建筑制图	2	32					2													
	建筑设计	12	384			384					8	8		8							
	计算机辅助设计(规划CAD)	2	32						2												
	专业外语	4	64											1	1		1	1			
专业主干课程	城市规划初步	4	64								2	2									
	城市规划原理(一)(二)(三)	6	96											4			2				
	中外城市建设史	4	64											2	2						
	城市道路与交通	2	32												2						
	城市工程系统规划	2	32												2						
	城市地理学	2	32															2			
	城市经济学	2	32														2				
	城市环境与城市生态	2	32															2			
	城市规划管理与法规	2	32															2			
	详细规划(住区与景园)	4	128	128											8						
	详细规划(控规与城市设计)	4	128	128													8				
	城镇总体规划	4	128	128														8			
	建筑物理	4	64											2	2						

续表

课程类别	课程名称	学分	课内学时			课外学时	各学期周学时分配														
			授课	实验	上机		一			二			三			四			五		
							1	2	3	1	2	3	1	2	3	1	2	3	1	2	3
专业及跨学科选修课程	居住环境与住宅设计原理	2	32												2						
	城市设计概论（双语）	2	32														2				
	城市中心（区）的发展与规划	1	16														1				
	城市社会学	2	32															2			
	房地产经济导论	2	32															2			
	城市研究专题(讲座)	1	16															1			
	建筑设计基础理论	1	16						1												
	建筑设计理论	4	64								1	1		1	1						
	建筑构造	6	96								2	1		1	2						
	中国建筑史	4	64											4							
	外国建筑史(双语)	4	64												4						
	中国近现代建筑解析	1.5	24														1.5				
	西方当代建筑思潮	1	16															1			
	古典亭榭与小品设计	3	48														3				
	计算机建筑表现	1	16									1									
	建筑行为心理学	1	16									1									
	室内设计原理	2	32														1	1			
	中外园林史	2	32											2							
	城市更新与历史文化保护	1	16														1				
	城市景观与环境理论	2	32												2						
	GIS及在城市规划中的应用	1	16														1				
	虚拟设计（VR）	1	16															1			
	摄影	1	16								1										
	建筑画技法	1	16								1										
	艺术概论	2	32						2												
	现代绘画	2	32									2									
	陶艺	1	16								1										

集中实践教学环节指导表
Guidance on integrated practice teaching

课程要求	课程名称	学分	学时			各学期周数分配														
			授课	周数	天/周	一			二			三			四			五		
						1	2	3	1	2	3	1	2	3	1	2	3	1	2	3
课内	军训	2		3		3														
	工地实习	1		1					1											
	认识实习（一）	1		1					1											
	CAD理论与实践（一）	1		1					1											
	素描实习	1		1					1											
	色彩实习	2		2									2							
	认识实习（二）	1		1								1								
	CAD理论与实践（二）	1		1								1								
	规划表现实习	2		2											2					
	城市认知实习	2		2											2					
	快速设计强化训练	2		2															2	
	毕业设计	16		16																16
	工程实践(规划院)	10		18														4	12	
课外	社会实践	1																		
	文化素质教育实践	1																		
	科研实践	2		2																
	文献阅读																			

三、环境设计系

1. 办学思想

根据市场经济条件下建筑学学科内涵持续深化和延不断拓展的发展态势，不断跟踪环境设计学科发展前沿，“面向现代化、面向世界、面向未来”建设具有东南大学特色的环境设计专业教育体系，培养德智体美全面发展的国内领先、具有国际竞争力的环境艺术设计专门人才。

（1）艺术设计专业教育应当是职业教育与素质教育的统一，其教育过程是阶段性与连续性的统一，其教育目标是未来知识型艺术设计人才，是针对环境设计师未来发展方向的知识教育、综合能力培养和职业道德教育的统一。

（2）在不断补充新的教学内容基础上，以系统的观念审视和优化已有教学体系，建立以艺术设计教育为基础，强化综合素质教育的课程体系，不断加强、完善、整合环境设计与建筑学、风景园林、城市规划等多元学科之间的有机联系；提高教学效率，建立与此配套的教案、教材和师资组织构架。

（3）树立开放的教育理念，谋求多层面、多方位的合作途径，使学生具有宽阔的学术视野，灵活的实践能力、组织合作能力和创新能力，以便进入社会后能尽快适应不断变化的社会需求。

2. 办学目标

根据艺术设计专业教育的客观规律和国家的发展与建设实际需要，围绕艺术设计专业评估标准和国家相关职业教育的要求，培养艺术设计领域具有科学发展观，素质高、能力强、基础扎实、知识面宽、德智体美全面发展的复合型优秀专业人才。

经过系统的艺术设计教育，本科毕业生应具有扎实的艺术学、自然科学、人文科学和相关建筑学基础理论、系统的艺术设计专业知识和实践能力；在城市、建筑不同尺度内的空间环境设计领域中，具有独立或合作进行环境艺术设计、科学研究、管理和教学工作的能力；具有较为广泛的知识面与知识结构，能与不同专业人员合作进行有关城市、建筑发展的咨询、评估、策划与决策研究工作。

3. 办学特色

（1）继承和发扬东南大学建筑学院“严谨求实、学以致用、中西兼蓄、锐意创新”的优良传统和基础扎实、要求严格、注重实践、综合发展的特点。

（2）艺术设计技能和环境设计理论两轴并重，注重理论思维训练和技能训练的统一。

（3）注重科研成果与教学环节的整合互动，与学院其他学科之间的教学交叉互动。

（4）强调实践环节的重要性。各个集中实践教学环节均有明确的教学大纲及相应的考核标准。毕业设计的课题尽量结合实际工程。

（5）强调开放互动的教学特色，注重教学研究的日常化和教学改革的系统性和连续性。主要内容包括：艺术设计与景观设计核心课程的系统整合研究；相关专业课程群的建设；网络课程及多媒体课件研究。

4. 本科生课程设置

III. Department of Environmental Design

1. Philosophy

According to the development tendency of continuous deepening of connotation and expanding of the extension of architecture under market economic conditions, to trace the frontier of the development of environmental design; “facing modernization, facing the world and facing the future”, to construct professional education system of environmental design with SEU characteristics, and cultivate senior professional talents who are domestically leading in the development of morality, intelligence, physique and art as well as with international competitiveness.

(1) Education on art design shall be the unification of professional education and qualification education, the process of its education shall unite period and continuity. Its education target is to cultivate future knowledge type art design talents, which is the unification of environmental designers in knowledge education, comprehensive ability cultivation and professional morality education in the future.

(2) On the basis of continuous supplementing new teaching content, to inspect and optimize the current teaching system with systematic concept, establish a course system that bases on art design education and strengthen comprehensive qualification education; to continuously strengthen, perfect and conform the organic connections among multiple subjects such as architecture, landscape architecture, and urban planning; to enhance teaching efficiency, and establish mated teaching plans, textbooks and faculty structure.

(3) To establish open education concepts and seek for multi-level and multi-aspect cooperation ways so as to make the students possess wide academic view, flexible practice ability, organization-cooperative ability, and creativity, which will help them adapt the continuously changing demand from the society in the future.

2. Target

According to objective rules of professional education on art design and actual requirements of the state on development and construction, embracing the professional evaluation standard for art design and the requirements on state licensed planners, to cultivate excellent comprehensive professionals in the art design field with scientific development view, high qualification, strong ability, solid foundation, wide knowledge range and all-round development in morality, intelligence, physique and art.

Through systematic art design education, the undergraduate students shall possess solid theories in art, natural sciences, humanity sciences and related architecture, systematic professional knowledge concerning art design and practice ability; in the space environmental design field with different dimensions of cities and architecture, the students shall possess the abilities of independently or cooperatively carrying out environmental art design, scientific research, management and teaching. Also the students are required to have wide knowledge range and structure, be able to carry out consultation, assessment, planning and decision studying concerning urban development and architectural development.

3. Characteristics

(1) To inherit and develop the excellent tradition of SEU-ARCH, “be prudent and down-to-earth, study in order to apply, combine Chinese and foreign cultures, and be creative and innovative”, and such characteristics as solid foundation, strict requirements, focusing on practice and comprehensive development.

(2) The art design skills and environmental design theory shall be focused at the same time, meanwhile, the unification of theory thinking training and skill training shall be unified.

(3) To focus on the conformation and interaction of scientific research achievements and teaching results, and crossing interaction with other subjects of the school.

(4) To emphasize the importance of practice. Each practice part has clarified teaching outline and corresponding inspection standard. Most of the topics of graduation design are made with combination of actual projects.

(5) To strengthen the open and interactive teaching characteristics, focus on daily teaching research as well as systematization and continuation of teaching reform. Main content comprises the following: system conformation research on core courses of art design and landscape design; construction of relevant professional course cluster, studying on online courses and multimedia courseware.

4. Course Setup for Undergraduates

指导性教学计划
Instructive teaching plan

课程类别	课程名称	学分	课内学时			课外学时	各学期周学时分配														
			授课	实验	上机		一			二			三			四			五		
							1	2	3	1	2	3	1	2	3	1	2	3	1	2	3
通识教育基础课程	毛泽东思想概论	2	24			8					2										
	邓小平理论与三个代表的重要思想	2	32			16						2									
	马克思主义哲学	2	32			16								2							
	政治经济学	2	24			8												2			
	思想道德修养	1	12			4		1													
	形势与政策	1	10			6								1							
	就业导论	1	10			6											1				
	法律基础	2	32						2												
	文史类 哲学社科类 经典导读类 军事理论	7	112																		
	大学英语	14	224					4	4		4	2									
	体育	4	128					2	2		1	1		1	1						
	高等数学E	4	64					4													
大类学科基础课程	建筑设计基础	8	256					8	8												
	视觉设计基础	9	288					6	6		3	3									
	建筑学概论	1	16					1													
	建筑制图	2	32					2													
	建筑设计基础理论	1	16						1												
	计算机辅助设计	2	32						2												
专业主干课程	建筑设计	8	256								8	8									
	室内设计	8	256											8				8			
	室内设计原理	2	32												2						
	景观规划设计	8	256												8		8				
	中外园林史	2	32														2				
	室内设计史	2	32											2							
	城市景观与环境理论	2	32														2				
专业及跨学科任选课程	建筑结构概论	1	16								1										
	建筑设备	3	48															3			
	建筑构造	3	48								2	1									
	建筑物理	4	64											2	2						
	装饰构造和材料	2	32												2						
	家具设计	2	64														4				
	公共艺术	2	32															2			
	景园植物学	2	32												2						
	居住环境与住宅设计原理	1	16													1					
	城市规划原理	2	32															2			

续表

课程类别	课程名称	学分	课内学时			课外学时	各学期周学时分配														
							一			二			三			四			五		
			授课	实验	上机		1	2	3	1	2	3	1	2	3	1	2	3	1	2	3
	城市设计概论	2	32															2			
	城市道路与交通	2	32											2							
	城市环境与城市生态	2	32															2			
	中国建筑史	4	64											4							
	外国建筑史	4	64												4						
	城市规划管理与法规	2	32														2				
	建筑设计理论	2	32								1	1									
	中国近现代建筑解析	1.5	24														2				
	城市中心发展与规划	1	16														1				
	西方当代建筑思潮	1	16															1			
	计算机建筑表现	1	16									1		1							
	古典亭榭与小品设计	3	48														3				
	虚拟设计	2	32												2						
	人体工程学	1	16												1						
	艺术照明设计	1	32														2				
	影像综合设计	2	32									2									
	现代绘画	2	32											2							
	建筑画技法	1	16											1							
	艺术概论	1	16									1									
	建筑摄影	2	32									2									
	数字化技术与建筑	2	32														2				
	绿色建筑设计概论	1	16															1			
	中国传统陈设与家具	2	40												3						

集中实践教学环节指导表
Guidance on integrated practice teaching

课程要求	课程名称	学分	学时			各学期周学时分配														
			授课	周数	天/周	一			二			三			四			五		
						1	2	3	1	2	3	1	2	3	1	2	3	1	2	3
课内	军训	2		3	⑶															
	认识实习（一）	1		1					1											
	认识实习（二）	1		1								1								
	素描实习	1		1					1											
	色彩实习	2		2								2								
	CAD理论与实践（一）	1		1					1											
	CAD理论与实践（二）	1		1								1								
	测绘实习	4		4											4					
	工地实习	1		1					1											
	快图训练	2		2														2		
	环境调研	2		2														2		
	工程实践	10		16															14	
	实践总结																		2	
	毕业设计	16		16																16
课外	社会实践	1																		
	文化素质教育实践	1																		
	文献阅读	2																		
	科研实践																			
	学术竞赛																			

四、景观学系

1. 办学思想

面对景观学（风景园林）国际与国内多元化的教育现状，根据景观学学科领域和知识体系不断拓展、实践理论与方法持续深化的态势，以“面向世界、面向未来、面向现代化”的眼光，不断追踪景观学学科发展前沿，紧密结合社会与专业实践的发展，建设具有东南大学特色的景观学专业教育体系。培养德智体美全面发展，具有突出实践能力和扎实理论素养的具有国际先进水平的景观学高级专门人才。

作为一门实践性学科，东南大学景观学教育坚持职业教育与素质教育的统一，教育过程阶段性与持续性的统一，教育目标是未来景观设计师知识结构与综合能力的统一。强调职业素质和实践动手能力的培养。

在根据学科发展不断完善景观学教学内容的基础上，系统化地审视和优化已有教学体系，建立以培养景观规划设计职业能力为主要目标，以通识教育为基础，以规划设计课程为主干，整合相关各知识模块、层层递进的课程体系。提高教学效率及针对性，建立与之配套的教案、教材和师资组织结构。

树立开放的教育理念，谋求多方位、多层面的合作教学模式，使学生具有宽阔的学术视野、扎实的实践能力、灵活的组织能力和持续的创新能力，满足不断发展的社会需求。

2. 办学目标

根据景观学教育的客观规律，结合社会发展和建设的实际需要，围绕培养职业景观规划设计师的要求，培养具有较强的创造、开拓和适应能力，高度的责任感和团队精神，完善的个性、高尚的修养和健康的体魄，理论素养和设计基础扎实，知识结构全面合理，熟练掌握本专业知识与实践技能，具有景观设计、组织与管理能力的复合型专门人才。

毕业生应具有从事景观规划、设计、管理和教学、研究工作，并具有国土与区域景观规划、城市景观规划与设计、场地规划与设计、自然遗产保护与管理、游憩与旅游规划与设计等工作的基本能力。就业的部门和承担的工作包括：政府有关部门、土地综合利用和市场服务机构，项目策划、决策与工程等部门咨询工作；建设、国土、环保、旅游等政府部门管理工作；以及景观规划设计的相关教育及研究工作。

3. 办学特色

继承和发扬东南大学建筑学院“严谨求实、学以致用、中西兼蓄、锐意创新”的优良传统和基础扎实、要求严格、注重实践、综合发展的特点。

突出景观规划与设计系列课程的核心地位，以景观规划设计和景观建筑设计实践能力的培养为主线，整合植物、生态、地理、社会、艺术等相关知识传授及其运用能力的培养，实践技能和理论素养两轴并重。

注重科研成果与教学环节的整合互动，以及与学院建筑学、城市规划、艺术设计等其他学科之间的教学交叉互动。同时强调实践环节的重要性，要求各个集中实践教学环节均明确自身的特点和目标，有明确的教学大纲及相应的考核标准。

因材施教，坚持开放互动的教学特色，坚持师生面对面的教学与讨论，注重教学研究的日常化和教学改革的系统性和连续性。强化“景观规划设计”核心系列课程与各相关课程群的整合研究，与时俱进，完善科学、人文等各专业课程群的建设。

Ⅳ. Department of Landscape Architecture

1. Philosophy

Based on the policies of “facing the world, facing the future and facing modernization”, to cultivate senior professional talents who adapt the demand of socialist modernization construction, achieve all-round development of morality, intelligence, physique, possess good landscape design theories and qualifications, grasp knowledge and skills of the major, and are familiar with relevant professional knowledge.

2.Target

Graduates are able to engage in such jobs as landscape planning, designing, management, teaching and research, and possess fundamental abilities in carrying out the following work, including state-owned land and regional landscape planning, urban landscape planning and design, field planning and design, natural heritage protection and management, resting and tourism planning and design, etc.

3.Characteristics

The main employment orientation for the graduates of this major as well as their business range are: business job of landscape planning and design as well as relevant planning and design organizations; governmental departments, land comprehensive use and market service organizations, and consultation work in departments of project planning, decision-making and engineering; management work in governmental departments such as construction, state-owned land, environmental protection and tourism; and relevant education and research work concerning landscape planning and design.

4.Course Setup for Undergraduates

4. 本科生课程设置

指导性教学计划
Instructive teaching plan

课程类别	课程名称	学分	课内学时			课外学时	各学期周学时分配														
							一			二			三			四			五		
			授课	实验	上机		1	2	3	1	2	3	1	2	3	1	2	3	1	2	3
通识教育基础课程	毛泽东思想概论	2	32								2										
	邓小平理论概论	3	32/32									2									
	马克思主义原理	3	48											3							
	政治经济学	2	32														2				
	成才导论	2	32					2													
	法律基础	2	32						2												
	形势与政策	1	10			6								1							
	体育	4	128					2	1		1	1		1	1		1				
	大学英语	15	240					4	4		4	3									
	大学语文	2	32									2									
	高等数学D	4	64					4													
	经济管理基础	3	48															3			
美术基础课	素描	6	192					6	6												
	水彩与水粉	6	192								6	6									
	构成设计	4	64						2		2										
学科基础课	建筑制图	2	32					2													
	建筑设计初步	8	256					8	8												
	建筑设计	8	256								8	8									
	景观学概论	2	32											2							
	近现代景观史	4	64											2	2						
	中外园林史	4	64											2	2						
	景观规划设计（系列）	16	512											8	8		8	8			
	建筑设计基础理论	1	16						1												
	景观设计初步													2							
	景观资源学														2						
	种植设计																2				
	景观生态学与生态基础	2	32															2			
	景观工程与技术	4	64											2	2						
	景观植物学	2	32												2						
	景观规划设计原理	4	64														2	2			
	城市规划原理	2	32												2						
	城市设计概论	2	32														2				
	居住环境	2	32														2				
	园林美学	1	16															1			
	专业外语	4	64											1	1		1	1			

续表

课程类别	课程名称	学分	课内学时			课外学时	各学期周学时分配														
							一			二			三			四			五		
			授课	实验	上机		1	2	3	1	2	3	1	2	3	1	2	3	1	2	3
学科基础课	城市社会学	2																			
	区域规划	2																			
	资源与环境保护	2																			
	环境行为学	2																			
	游憩学	1																			
	景观与文化	1																			
	3S技术应用	4																			
	政策法规	1																			
	建筑结构	2	32									2									
	建筑构造	4	64						2		2										
	建筑材料	2	32								2										
	建筑设计理论	4	64								1	1		1	1						
	建筑学概论	1	16					1													
	建筑技术概论	2	32								2										
	中国建筑史	2	32									2									
	外国建筑史	2	32												2						
专业选修课	工程概预算	1	16																	1	
	建设项目可行性研究	1	16																	1	
	城市道路与交通	1	16														1				
	城市管理与法规	1	16														1				
	古典亭榭及小品设计	3	48												3						
	灯光设计	2	32															2			
	城市发展史	2	32														2				
	自然与人文地理	2	32														2				
	环境伦理	2	32														2				
艺术修养课	摄　影	1	16												1						
	模型制作	1	16												1						
	建筑画技法	1	16												1						
	艺术品分析	1	16						1												
	古代艺术史	1	16																		
	现代艺术史	1	16																		
人文社科类	创造学	2	32															2			
	中西文化比较	2	32															2			
	军事理论类课	2	32														2				

集中实践教学环节指导表
Guidance on integrated practice teaching

课程要求	课程名称	学分	课内学时			各学期周学时分配														
			授课	周数	天/周	一			二			三			四			五		
						1	2	3	1	2	3	1	2	3	1	2	3	1	2	3
课内	军训	3		3		(3)														
	建筑设计	1		1					(1)											
	工地实习	1		1					(1)											
	素描实习	1		1					(1)											
	CAD理论与实践(一)	1		1					(2)											
	认识实习(一)	1		1								(1)								
	景园设计(一)	1		1								(1)								
	水彩水粉实习	2		2								(2)								
	CAD理论与实践(二)	1		1								(1)								
	景园设计(二)	1		1											(1)					
	测绘实习	4		4											(4)					
	设计院实习	16		16														(16)		
	设计院实习总结与考核	1		1															(1)	
	景园设计(三)	1		1															(1)	
	景园规划调查实习																		(1)	
	快速设计强化训练	3		3															(2)	
	毕业设计	16		16																(16)

学科建设
Discipline Development

一、建筑设计及其理论学科

1. 学科建设

东南大学建筑设计与理论学科拥有博士学位授予点和博士后流动站。东南大学建筑学科1988年被评为全国首批国家重点学科，2007年被评为全国首批一级学科国家重点学科，2008年建筑设计课程被评定为国家精品课程，并一直是全国高等院校建筑学学科专业指导委员会挂靠单位。总体看，本学科整体科研水平、教学质量和办学条件等方面均在国内同类学科中处于领先地位。通过学科建设，目前已经形成了一支以中青年学术带头人为骨干、学术层次高、年富力强、敢于打硬仗的学科队伍，学科团队获江苏省“青蓝工程”省级优秀学科梯队称号。在原先建筑设计和城市设计的优势领域基础上，学科建设又向国内外学术前沿领域的深度和广度两方面拓展深化。学科先后申报获准国家“211工程”二期和“985工程”的支持，并成为东南大学“重中之重”的建设学科，其中“211工程”二期已经通过国家专家组验收，获得优秀成绩。在此基础上，建构了“地域性建筑创作和城市设计”、“冬冷夏热地区建筑技术集成”和“数字技术应用”三大科技创新平台，组织了三次有影响的国际学术会议，开展了多项重要的国际科研合作项目，与国际著名（知名）建筑院系开展了系列国际联合教学并互认学分。结合国家和社会重大需求，完成一批国家自然科学基金项目（含重点项目）和部省级科研项目，其中包括数项具有较高显示度的重大研究成果，建筑学专业被评为江苏省“品牌专业”，获江苏省“青蓝工程”优秀学科梯队称号，已经初步形成一个国内领先、国际可比的教学科研基地，地区建筑学、绿色城市设计和遗产保护数字技术应用等部分学科分支已经具有国际先进的研究水平。

2. 人才培养

培养建筑设计方面宽口径学术、技术的骨干，使其掌握坚实宽广的建筑学一级学科的基础理论，系统全面的建筑设计及其理论的专业知识，具备在某一方向独立研究的能力。

研究方向：

（1）可持续发展和人类住区规划设计理论和方法

（2）城市与建筑形态研究

（3）城镇开放建筑设计研究

（4）城市规划理论和方法

（5）可持续发展与城市物理环境

（6）现代建筑、技术和艺术及其交叉研究

（7）地方建筑学研究

Ⅰ. Architectural Design & Theory

1. Introduction

The SEU architectural design and theory is a doctoral degree post, possessing postdoctoral circulating station. As early as in 1988, it was evaluated as one of the state key subjects most early in China. It has always been the united affiliated by the Guidance Committee of Architecture of National Higher Education, and, it was listed into the first batch of “state key first-grade discipline” in 2007. In general, the entire research level, teaching quality and school running conditions of this subject have achieved certain progress, which is a big step for building the architecture major of a world top-rank university. Architectural design and theory, on its research depth, is extending to the aspects such as architectural reality rules and design methodology, etc.; while on the research width, is expanding to digitalization of urban designing and architectural design, and modern architectural technology structure, etc. The subject is also strengthening international communication and exchange, trying to get closer to the world high level with planned period.

Through the construction of the subject, a professional teaching team has been built, with mid-aged and young academic leaders as backbone, being high academic level, energetic and enterprising. The team has won the title as excellent subject echelon of the Blue Project of Jiangsu Province.

2. Education

To cultivate academic and technological backbones with wide caliber in architectural design, who grasp solid and broad basic theories concerning the first grade architecture subject, systematic and complete professional knowledge of architectural design and theory, and possess the ability of independent research in one field.

Research directions:

(1) Theory and method for sustainable development and human residential planning and design

(2) Research on urban and architectural forms

(3) Research on the design of open urban architectures

(4) Urban planning theory and method

(5) Sustainable development and urban physics environment

(6) Modern architecture, technology and art as well as their intercrossing research

(7) Local architectural research

3. 硕士研究生课程　　3. Course for Master's Candidates

组别	课程名称	学时	学分	授课方式	考试方式
A公共基础课	自然辩证法、科学社会主义理论和实践	60	2.0	面授讲课	笔试
	学位英语	60	3.0	面授讲课	笔试
	专业外语	18	1.0	面授讲课	笔试
B专业基础课	现代建筑理论	54	3.0	面授讲课	笔试
	现代城市规划原理	54	3.0	面授讲课	考查
	数字技术与建筑学（1）	54	3.0	面授讲课	笔试
C专业必修课	学术专题	18	1.0	其它	考查
	建筑设计	36	2.0	面授讲课	考查
	建筑设计（建研所）	36	2.0	面授讲课	考查
	现代城市设计方法	36	2.0	面授讲课	考查
	建筑设计思维和方法	36	2.0	面授讲课	考查
	建筑设计专题研究	54	3.0	面授讲课	考查
	建筑设计专题研究（建研所）	54	3.0	面授讲课	考查

4. 博士研究生课程　　4. Course for Doctor's Candidates

组别	课程名称	学时	学分	授课方式	考试方式
A公共基础课	科技革命与马克思主义	36	2.0	面授讲课	笔试
	博士英语	36	2.0	面授讲课	笔试
B专业基础课	学术专题	18	1.0	其它	考查
	建筑哲学	54	3.0	面授讲课	考查
	建筑遗产保护学	36	2.0	面授讲课	考查
	建筑设计专题研究	36	2.0	面授讲课	考查
	城市与风景旅游环境设计问题研究（1）	36	2.0	面授讲课	考查
	城市规划与设计专题研究	36	2.0	面授讲课	考查
	建筑与哲学	36	2.0	面授讲课	考查
	建筑文献阅读	36	2.0	面授讲课	考查
	建筑设计	36	2.0	面授讲课	考查
	景观规划与设计	36	2.0	面授讲课	考查
	城市规划与设计	36	2.0	面授讲课	考查
	城市物理环境与可持续发展（1）	36	2.0	面授讲课	其他
	建筑设计（建研所）	36	2.0	面授讲课	考查
	城市建筑形态（哲学思辨）	36	2.0	面授讲课	考查

二、建筑历史与理论学科

1. 学科建设

东南大学建筑历史与理论学科是我国第一批博士学位授予点，也长期是全国唯一的建筑历史与理论国家重点学科。从20世纪50年代开始，本学科就在中国科学院学部委员刘敦桢教授的领导下成立了建筑历史与理论研究室，70年代后期在童寯教授的领导下，正式奠定了本博士点。80年代以后，本博士点又拓宽为三个主要研究领域：中国建筑史、东方建筑史、现代建筑理论，研究成果在国内均具有领先水平。现已成立建筑历史与理论研究所，拥有一支精干、训练有素的学术队伍，总的研究方向为建筑历史与理论，涵盖了中外古今的建筑历史、建筑理论以及园林艺术研究。

本学科点承担了多项国家自然科学基金、教育部博士点基金、江苏省自然科学基金、各部委委托项目、中外合作项目，以及有关单位横向委托研究项目等。已出版专著数十本，发表论文数百篇，曾先后获得过国家科学大会奖，国家教委科技进步二等奖，建设部科技成果一等奖，建设部科技成果二等奖，江苏省教学成果奖等奖项。

2. 人才培养

本专业的目标是培养从事建筑历史、建筑理论与古典园林艺术方面的研究和应用，能在建筑历史与理论某一领域具有独立研究能力，并能提出一定的理论联系实际的见解的人才。

研究方向：

（1）中国古代建筑史研究
（2）东方建筑史研究
（3）现代建筑理论研究
（4）中国近现代建筑史研究
（5）中国城市史研究
（6）外国建筑史研究
（7）风景园林史研究
（8）建筑遗产保护理论及技术研究

Ⅱ. Architectural History &Theory

1. Introduction

The SEU architectural history and theory is a doctoral degree post of the first batch in China, and is a "state key subject", the only one in this field of China. Since the 1950s, the research section of architectural history and theory was established under the leadership of Professor LIU Dunzhen, commissioner of Science Department of Chinese Academy of Sciences, and the doctoral post was founded formally under the leadership of Professor TONG Jun in the late 70s. Since the 80s, the doctoral post has been expanded to three main research fields, including Chinese architectural history, oriental architectural history and modern architectural theory. The research results possess leading level in China. The general research direction is architectural history and theory, covering the architectural history of China, foreign countries, ancient and modern, as well as researches on architectural theory and landscape art.

The subject has undertaken several projects from the National Science Foundation of China, Doctoral Fund from the Ministry of Education, Jiangsu Province Fund of Natural Sciences and other projects entrusted by departments and ministries, Sino-foreign cooperative projects as well as horizontally entrusted projects from other units, etc. Dozens of monographs have been published, and several hundreds pieces of dissertation issued. Moreover, the subject has successively won many awards such as the National Science Conference Award, the second prize of scientific improvement of the State Education Commission, the first prize and the second prize of Technological Achievements of the Ministry of Construction, and Jiangsu Province teaching results award, etc. Now the Research Institute of architectural history and theory has been founded, possessing a capable and well-trained academic team.

2. Education

The purpose of the major is to cultivate research and application talents engaged in the studying of architectural history, theory and classical garden art, possessing independent research ability in some certain field concerning architectural history and theory, and being able to put forward certain ideas that connect reality with theory.

Research directions:

(1) Research on Chinese ancient architectural history
(2) Research on oriental architectural history
(3) Research on modern architectural theory
(4) Research on Chinese modern architectural history
(5) Research on Chinese urban history
(6) Research on foreign architectural history
(7) Research on landscape history
(8) Research on theory and technology of architectural heritage protection

3. 硕士研究生课程　　3. Course for Master's Candidates

组别	课程名称	学时	学分	授课方式	考试方式
A公共基础课	自然辩证法、科学社会主义理论和实践	60	2.0	面授讲课	笔试
	学位英语	60	3.0	面授讲课	笔试
	专业外语	18	1.0	面授讲课	笔试
B专业基础课	现代建筑理论	54	3.0	面授讲课	笔试
	现代城市规划原理	54	3.0	面授讲课	考查
	数字技术与建筑学（1）	54	3.0	面授讲课	笔试
C专业必修课	学术专题	18	1.0	其它	考查
	宋清营造法式	54	3.0	面授讲课	考查
	西方现代建筑	36	2.0	面授讲课	考查
	西方古典建筑	36	2.0	面授讲课	考查
	建筑史理论与实践	54	3.0	面授讲课	考查

4. 博士研究生课程　　4. Course for Doctor's Candidates

组别	课程名称	学时	学分	授课方式	考试方式
A公共基础课	科技革命与马克思主义	36	2.0	面授讲课	笔试
	博士英语	36	2.0	面授讲课	笔试
B专业基础课	学术专题	18	1.0	其它	考查
	建筑哲学	54	3.0	面授讲课	考查
	建筑遗产保护学	36	2.0	面授讲课	考查
	建筑设计专题研究	36	2.0	面授讲课	考查
	城市与风景旅游环境设计问题研究（1）	36	2.0	面授讲课	考查
	城市规划与设计专题研究	36	2.0	面授讲课	考查
	建筑与哲学	36	2.0	面授讲课	考查
	建筑文献阅读	36	2.0	面授讲课	考查
	建筑设计	36	2.0	面授讲课	考查
	景观规划与设计	36	2.0	面授讲课	考查
	城市规划与设计	36	2.0	面授讲课	考查
	城市物理环境与可持续发展（1）	36	2.0	面授讲课	其他
	建筑设计（建研所）	36	2.0	面授讲课	考查
	城市建筑形态（哲学思辨）	36	2.0	面授讲课	考查

三、城市规划与设计学科

1. 学科建设

本学科专业点是我国第四批博士学位授予点，于1995年被江苏省教委评为省重点学科。本专业点学术带头人为吴明伟教授。总的研究方向为城市规划设计及城市环境设计，近年承担国家自然科学基金、教委博士点及各部委基金和委托项目十余项。年平均在国际、国内学术刊物和重要学术会议上发表论文数十篇，参与国际国内重大规划设计投标和规划设计工程项目数十项。近年来获部委、省级科技进步一等奖一项，二等奖一项，三等奖三项，获国家和省部级优秀工程设计奖数十项。

2. 人才培养

培养适应我国社会主义建设需要，德、智、体、美全面发展，具备扎实的城市规划理论知识，掌握城市规划与设计专业技能，了解自然科学和人文科学相关知识的高级专门人才，有高度社会责任感的职业规划师、城市规划管理者、研究人员和高等学校教师。

研究方向：

（1）城市规划理论与方法

（2）城市设计及其理论

（3）城市环境设计理论与方法

（4）风景旅游环境设计理论与方法

III. Urban Planning & Design

1. Introduction

The SEU urban planning and design is a doctoral degree post of the fourth batch in China, and was evaluated as key subject by Jiangsu Province in 1995. The academic leader of this specialty is Professor Wu Mingwei. The general research direction comprises urban planning and design, and urban environmental design. In recent years, the subject has undertaken nearly ten projects from National Science Foundation of China, the doctoral post of the Education Commission and the funds from each ministry and commission as well as entrusted projects. Averagely, more than 10 pieces of dissertation are published in international and domestic academic magazines and important conferences every year. Moreover, the section has participated in a few dozens of significant planning and designing bidding and projects internationally and domestically. In recent years, the section has won one first prize, one second prize and three third prizes of Scientific Improvement from Commissions, Departments and the province.

2. Education

To cultivate senior professionals that are suitable for the Chinese socialist construction demand, develop in morality, intelligence, physique and art, possess solid theoretical knowledge in urban planning, and grasp urban planning and design skills; and professional planners, urban planning management staff, researchers and college teachers with a high sense of social responsibilities.

Research directions:

(1) Urban planning theory and method

(2) Urban planning and theory

(3) Urban environmental design theory and method

(4) Tourism environmental design theory and method

3. 硕士研究生课程

3. Course for Master's Candidates

组别	课程名称	学时	学分	授课方式	考试方式
A公共基础课	自然辩证法、科学社会主义理论和实践	60	2.0	面授讲课	笔试
	学位英语	60	3.0	面授讲课	笔试
	专业外语	18	1.0	面授讲课	笔试
B专业基础课	现代建筑理论	54	3.0	面授讲课	笔试
	现代城市规划原理	54	3.0	面授讲课	考查
	数字技术与建筑学（1）	54	3.0	面授讲课	笔试
C专业必修课	学术专题	18	1.0	其它	考查
	城市规划与设计	36	2.0	面授讲课	考查
	当代区域规划导论	36	2.0	面授讲课	笔试
	城市规划研究方法论	36	2.0	面授讲课	考查
	城市规划与设计专题研究	54	3.0	面授讲课	考查

4. 博士研究生课程

4. Course for Doctor's Candidates

组别	课程名称	学时	学分	授课方式	考试方式
A公共基础课	科技革命与马克思主义	36	2.0	面授讲课	笔试
	博士英语	36	2.0	面授讲课	笔试
B专业基础课	学术专题	18	1.0	其它	考查
	建筑哲学	54	3.0	面授讲课	考查
	建筑遗产保护学	36	2.0	面授讲课	考查
	建筑设计专题研究	36	2.0	面授讲课	考查
	城市与风景旅游环境设计问题研究（1）	36	2.0	面授讲课	考查
	城市规划与设计专题研究	36	2.0	面授讲课	考查

续表

组别	课程名称	学时	学分	授课方式	考试方式
B专业基础课	建筑与哲学	36	2.0	面授讲课	考查
	建筑文献阅读	36	2.0	面授讲课	考查
	建筑设计	36	2.0	面授讲课	考查
	景观规划与设计	36	2.0	面授讲课	考查
	城市规划与设计	36	2.0	面授讲课	考查
	城市物理环境与可持续发展（1）	36	2.0	面授讲课	其他
	建筑设计（建研所）	36	2.0	面授讲课	考查
	城市建筑形态（哲学思辨）	36	2.0	面授讲课	考查

四、建筑技术科学学科

1. 学科建设

我校的建筑技术学科自20世纪30年代刘敦桢学部委员、张镛森教授研究我国古建筑和近现代建筑中的建筑技术以来，已经发展到现今包括城市与建筑物理环境、现代建筑（诸如被动式太阳能建筑、节能建筑设计与优化、智能建筑）等方面的技术问题研究。建筑技术科学，作为现代技术与传统学科的交叉与互动发展建设的学科，在城市和建筑物理环境评价、控制和建筑节能技术研究方面达到国内先进水平。近年来承担国家自然科学基金项目及部、省级项目的研究，研究成果多次获奖。

2. 人才培养

培养建筑技术方面的学术、技术骨干，使其掌握较为坚实宽广的建筑学一级学科的基础理论，系统的建筑技术二级学科的专业知识，初步具备在某一方向独立研究的能力。

研究方向：

（1）物理环境与可持续发展
（2）建筑节能与能源再利用技术
（3）建筑技术与设计
（4）建筑结构技术与选型
（5）住宅技术研究

Ⅳ. Architectural Technology

1. Introduction

Since academician Liu Dunzhen and Professor Zhang Yongsen started studying the architectural technology of ancient Chinese architecture and modern architecture in the 1930s, the architectural technology of our university has been developed to study the technological problems today, comprising urban and architectural physics, modern architecture (such as passive solar energy architecture, energy-saving architecture design and optimization, intelligent architecture). Architectural technology, as the subject intercross and interact between modern technology and traditional subject, has reached top level in China in the aspects including urban and architectural physics environmental evaluation, control and architectural energy-saving technology. In recent years, the section has undertaken several projects from National Science Foundation of China and projects of ministry or provincial level. Research achievements have won prizes many times.

2. Education

To cultivate academic and technical backbones in the aspect of architectural technology, who can grasp solid and broad foundational theories of first level subject of architecture, and professional knowledge of the second level subject of systematic architectural technology, and initially possess the ability of independent research in some certain direction.

Research directions:

(1) Physics environment and sustainable development
(2) Architectural energy-saving and energy recycling technology
(3) Architectural technology and design
(4) Architectural structure technology and lectotype
(5) Residence technology research

3. 硕士研究生课程　　3. Course for Master's Candidates

组别	课程名称	学时	学分	授课方式	考试方式
A公共基础课	自然辩证法、科学社会主义理论和实践	60	2.0	面授讲课	笔试
	学位英语	60	3.0	面授讲课	笔试
	专业外语	18	1.0	面授讲课	笔试
B专业基础课	现代建筑理论	54	3.0	面授讲课	笔试
	现代城市规划原理	54	3.0	面授讲课	考查
	数字技术与建筑学（1）	54	3.0	面授讲课	笔试
C专业必修课	学术专题	18	1.0	其它	考查
	建筑技术与环境设计	36	2.0	面授讲课	考查
	城市物理环境与可持续发展（2）	36	2.0	面授讲课	考查
	建筑节能技术	36	2.0	面授讲课	考查
	建筑技术与环境设计专题研究	54	3.0	面授讲课	考查

4. 博士研究生课程　　4. Course for Doctor's Candidates

组别	课程名称	学时	学分	授课方式	考试方式
A公共基础课	科技革命与马克思主义	36	2.0	面授讲课	笔试
	博士英语	36	2.0	面授讲课	笔试
B专业基础课	学术专题	18	1.0	其它	考查
	建筑哲学	54	3.0	面授讲课	考查
	建筑遗产保护学	36	2.0	面授讲课	考查
	建筑设计专题研究	36	2.0	面授讲课	考查
	城市与风景旅游环境设计问题研究（1）	36	2.0	面授讲课	考查
	城市规划与设计专题研究	36	2.0	面授讲课	考查
	建筑与哲学	36	2.0	面授讲课	考查
	建筑文献阅读	36	2.0	面授讲课	考查
	建筑设计	36	2.0	面授讲课	考查
	景观规划与设计	36	2.0	面授讲课	考查
	城市规划与设计	36	2.0	面授讲课	考查
	城市物理环境与可持续发展（1）	36	2.0	面授讲课	其他
	建筑设计（建研所）	36	2.0	面授讲课	考查
	城市建筑形态（哲学思辨）	36	2.0	面授讲课	考查

五、美术学学科

1. 人才培养

本专业培养景观设计、室内设计、公共艺术领域素质高、能力强、基础扎实、知识面宽、德智体美全面发展，具有创新能力的复合型优秀设计人才。

研究方向：

（1）环境艺术设计
（2）可持续发展的环境艺术设计研究
（3）建筑室内设计
（4）室内设计理论与方法研究
（5）室内设计技术与材料研究
（6）建筑室外环境设计
（7）建筑室外环境理论与方法研究
（8）城市公共艺术研究

Ⅴ. Fine Arts

1. Education

The major is to cultivate excellent comprehensive designers with high qualifications, strong abilities, solid foundations, wide knowledge range, and all-round development in morality, intelligence, physique as well as creativities in such fields as landscape design, indoor design and public art.

Research directions:

(1) Environmental art design
(2) Research on sustainable developing environmental art design
(3) Architectural indoor design
(4) Research on indoor design theory and method
(5) Research on indoor design technology and materials
(6) Architectural outdoor environmental design
(7) Research on architectural outdoor environmental theory and method
(8) Research on public urban art

2. 硕士研究生课程

2. Course for Master's Candidates

组别	课程名称	学时	学分	授课方式	考试方式
A公共基础课	自然辩证法、科学社会主义理论和实践	60	2.0	面授讲课	笔试
	学位英语	60	3.0	面授讲课	笔试
	专业外语	18	1.0	面授讲课	笔试
B专业基础课	现代建筑理论	54	3.0	面授讲课	笔试
	现代城市规划原理	54	3.0	面授讲课	考查
	数字技术与建筑学（1）	54	3.0	面授讲课	笔试
C专业必修课	艺术设计	36	2.0	面授讲课	考查
	学术专题	18	1.0	其它	考查
	室内设计理论研究	36	2.0	面授讲课	考查
	环境艺术设计及理论	36	2.0	面授讲课	考查
	概念设计	18	1.0	面授讲课	笔试
	艺术设计专题研究	54	3.0	面授讲课	考查

六、景观学学科

1. 学科建设

东南大学景观学（风景园林）研究始于刘敦桢教授、童寯教授20世纪30至50年代开创的江南古典园林研究，继而由潘谷西教授、杜顺宝教授推陈出新，完善学科结构、拓展学科范畴、健全学科体系。

从1986年开始，我校连续招收了三届风景园林本科学生，是全国率先进行风景园林（工学）本科专业教育的高等院校之一。1989年，受国务院专业设置的影响而停止招生，但一直保留着教研室一级的机构和人员设置，保持着研究生（包括硕士、博士）一级的专业教育（附设于城市规划与设计）。2004年，成立景观学系，独立招收景观建筑学硕士、博士研究生，2007年恢复招收景观学（工学）专业5年制本科生，以现代景观学的专业教育思想和教学构架开展教学和研究工作。本专业学术带头人为杜顺宝教授。十多年来，本专业教师承担国家自然科学基金项目、博士点基金和部委基金研究项目十余项，获部委科技进步二等奖一项，工程实践项目获国家优质工程银奖一项，部省级优秀规划设计一等奖四项、二等奖九项。出版相关专著十余部，学术论文百余篇。

2. 人才培养

培养对景观学、建筑学、城市规划、区域规划、自然地理学、生态环境保护等交叉学科领域有较广泛的了解，掌握景观规划设计的一般方法、内容及其成果要求，熟悉景观规划设计相关法规，具备运用多学科理论成果和研究方法进行专业理论研究和实践工作的能力，具备独立承担景观规划设计实际工程的能力，适应实际工作需要的专门人才。

研究方向：

（1）城市扩展与环境问题研究
（2）城市景观规划设计理论与方法
（3）风景旅游与游憩景观规划设计理论与方法
（4）景观建筑设计理论与方法
（5）景观发展史研究
（6）景观技术研究
（7）城市公共艺术设计研究

Ⅵ. Landscape Architecture

1. Introduction

The specialty of landscape architecture was started by Professor Liu Dunzhen and Professor Tong Jun since 1930s to 1950s, and began with their research on traditional gardens in south Yangzi River. It had been a branch of urban planning and design (doctoral degree awarding post in the fourth batch in China) called landscape and garden planning until 2004, when it formally became an independent specialty called landscape architecture. The academic leader of the specialty is Professor Du Shunbao. The general research direction is planning and design of urban and landscape tourism. The section has undertaken more than 10 projects from the doctoral post of the Education Commission, the foundation research projects of Ministry or Commissions as well as entrusted projects for more than ten years, and has won one second prize of scientific improvement of Ministry, one national silver prize of construction project, four first prizes and nine second prizes of Excellent Planning and Design of ministry and the province.

2. Education

Talents shall have wide understanding on intercrossing fields such as landscape architecture, architecture, urban planning, regional planning, natural geography and ecological environmental protection, etc.; grasp general methods, content and achievement requirements concerning landscape planning and design, be familiar with relevant provisions of landscape planning and design; possess the ability of independently undertaking actual projects of landscape planning and design, so as to adapt the demand of actual work.

Research directions:

(1) Research on urban expansion and environmental problems
(2) Theory and method of urban landscape planning and design
(3) Theory and method of scenery tourism and leisure landscape planning and design
(4) Theory and method of landscape architectural design
(5) Research on landscape development history
(6) Landscape technology research
(7) Research on urban public art design

3. 硕士研究生课程　　3. Course for Master's Candidates

组别	课程名称	学时	学分	授课方式	考试方式
A公共基础课	自然辩证法、科学社会主义理论和实践	60	2.0	面授讲课	笔试
	学位英语	60	3.0	面授讲课	笔试
	专业外语	18	1.0	面授讲课	笔试
B专业基础课	现代建筑理论	54	3.0	面授讲课	笔试
	现代城市规划原理	54	3.0	面授讲课	考查
	数字技术与建筑学（1）	54	3.0	面授讲课	笔试
C专业必修课	学术专题	18	1.0	其它	考查
	景园规划与设计	36	2.0	面授讲课	考查
	现代景观设计理论与方法	36	2.0	面授讲课	考查
	城市规划研究方法论	36	2.0	面授讲课	考查
	景园规划与设计专题研究	54	3.0	面授讲课	考查

4. 博士研究生课程　　4. Course for Doctor's Candidates

组别	课程名称	学时	学分	授课方式	考试方式
A公共基础课	科技革命与马克思主义	36	2.0	面授讲课	笔试
	博士英语	36	2.0	面授讲课	笔试
B专业基础课	学术专题	18	1.0	其它	考查
	建筑哲学	54	3.0	面授讲课	考查
	建筑遗产保护学	36	2.0	面授讲课	考查
	建筑设计专题研究	36	2.0	面授讲课	考查
	城市与风景旅游环境设计问题研究（1）	36	2.0	面授讲课	考查
	城市规划与设计专题研究	36	2.0	面授讲课	考查
	建筑与哲学	36	2.0	面授讲课	考查
	建筑文献阅读	36	2.0	面授讲课	考查
	建筑设计	36	2.0	面授讲课	考查
	景观规划与设计	36	2.0	面授讲课	考查
	城市规划与设计	36	2.0	面授讲课	考查
	城市物理环境与可持续发展（1）	36	2.0	面授讲课	其他
	建筑设计（建研所）	36	2.0	面授讲课	考查
	城市建筑形态（哲学思辨）	36	2.0	面授讲课	考查

七、建筑遗产保护与管理

1. 学科建设

东南大学利用已有优势，依托国内唯一的建筑历史与理论的重点学科，通过学科交叉，与经验及成果丰富的文学院旅游专业整合，在建筑学一级学科博士授权范围内自主设置建筑遗产保护与管理专业。其总的研究方向是建筑遗产保护理论与技术体系、管理与规划，包含旅游资源的可持续利用与管理、非物质文化的保护与管理等。

2. 人才培养

面向建设部门、文物局及其所属研究与管理机构，面向各涉及历史名城的有关机构，面向各高等学校，培养建筑文化资源保护与管理领域中的研究和应用人才，能在该领域具有独立研究能力，并能提出一定的理论联系实际的见解。

研究方向：

（1）建筑遗产保护理论和技术
（2）历史名城史迹及其保护研究
（3）旅游资源保护与管理
（4）城乡非物质文化遗产保护研究
（5）景园历史研究及其保护

Ⅶ. Conservation and Management on Architectural Heritage

1. Introduction

China is now experiencing swift urbanization. The threats on cultural heritage, specially on architectural heritage are very serious. Protection on cultural heritage has become common understanding of people. The rising movement on protecting cultural heritage from down to up in the world formed since the 20th century has influenced China, too. In order to change the relevant backward situation in cultivation of talents in this field, SEU has used its own advantages, depending on the domestic unique key subject of architectural history and theory, set up the specialty of protection and management on architectural heritage in the range which was authorized by the first level doctoral degree of architecture through the conformation of tourism from School of Humanities who enjoy rich experience and achievements. The general research direction comprises theory and technology system of architectural heritage protection, management and planning, including the continuous utilization and management of tourism resources, and protection and management of non-material culture, etc.

2. Education

Facing the construction departments, the cultural relics bureau and affiliated research and management organizations, relevant organizations for designing historical cities and all colleges, to cultivate research and application talents in the field of protection and management on architectural cultural resources, who possess independent research ability in this field, and can put forward certain ideas that connect theories with realities.

Research directions:

(1) Theory and technology of architectural heritage protection
(2) Research on historical cities relics and protection
(3) Protection and management of tourism resources
(4) Research on protection of urban and rural non-material cultural heritage
(5) Research and protection of garden history

3. 研究生课程　　3. Course for Post-graduate Students

组别	课程名称	学时	学分	授课方式	考试方式
A公共基础课	自然辩证法、科学社会主义理论和实践	60	2.0	面授讲课	笔试
	学位英语	60	3.0	面授讲课	笔试
	专业外语	18	1.0	面授讲课	笔试
B专业基础课	现代建筑理论	54	3.0	面授讲课	笔试
	建筑遗产保护设计基础	54	3.0	面授讲课	考查
	现代城市规划原理	54	3.0	面授讲课	考查
C专业必修课	建筑遗产保护设计	36	2.0	面授讲课	考查
	学术专题	18	1.0	其它	考查
	宋清营造法式	54	3.0	面授讲课	考查
	西方古典建筑	36	2.0	面授讲课	笔试
	建筑遗产保护设计专题研究	54	3.0	面授讲课	考查

教学体系与特色办学
Teaching System & Characteristics

一年级设计课程教学大纲
Compendium_1st Year

一、课程的性质与目的

本课程是建筑学专业必修的主要的专业基础课，是建筑设计的入门课程。

本课程的教学目的为：①通过本课程，使学生初步掌握以设计图纸、模型作为设计研究和表达的工具。②熟悉掌握基本的建筑设计的方法（对环境、功能的分析，对方案的综合深入等），并树立一些相对完整的建筑设计方法和观念，形成初步的建筑技术概念。③培养和引导学生的专业兴趣，激发学生的创作热情。

二、课程内容的教学要求

1. 建筑设计基础Ⅰ

（1）小制作：使用纸板为材料，手工完成坐具：体会设计与生活、设计与建造、形式与结构等要素之间的相互关系。

（2）建筑测绘：测绘学校传达室或其他小型建筑，学习建筑制图，初步了解建筑构造。

（3）外部空间认知：认知某一城市公共空间，学习外部空间的认知、分析和表达的方法。

（4）外部空间设计：对一具体的城市外部空间加以设计，训练学生的空间尺度感和空间处理的方法。

（5）建筑空间认知：体验和分析、比较多个建筑空间，并以图示语言加以表达。培养空间观念，学习空间分析的方法，训练图示语言的表达方法。

（6）建筑空间设计：对一个给定的建筑空间加以设计，学习面对空间进行划分的空间设计方法，学习室内空间的功能组织和尺度关系。

2、建筑设计基础Ⅱ

（1）先例分析：树立正确的设计观和建筑观，掌握分析这一重要的学习手段。

（2）小型休闲展示建筑设计：较为综合地进行建筑设计训练，学习以环境分析和空间构成为出发点的建筑设计方法。

（3）设计建造：设计和建造结合；依照材料特点选用合理的结构形式，创造同时具有结构逻辑和形式逻辑的构筑物。

三、上机实习要求

学习Autocad、Sketchup等软件的基本操作。初步掌握应用以上软件进行设计研究和设计表达。通过互联网收集与课程有关的资料和信息。

四、能力培养的要求

1. 分析能力的培养：要求学生通过本课程的学习，具备独立的分析环境、建筑使用方式、建筑结构构造及其他限制要素的能力。

2. 设计研究能力的培养：要求学生通过本课程的学习，具备操作图纸、手工模型、电脑模型等多种工具进行建筑设计研究的能力。

3. 设计表达能力的培养：要求学生通过本课程的学习，具备操作图纸、手工模型、电脑模型等多种工具进行建筑设计表达的能力。

4. 自学能力的培养：通过本课程的教学，培养和提高学生对所学知识进行整理、概括、消化吸收的能力，以及围绕课堂教学内容，阅读参考书籍和资料自我扩充知识领域的能力。

5. 创新能力的培养：培养学生独立思考、深入钻研问题的习惯，以及对问题提出多种解决方案，选择不同设计方法，对设计方案进行推敲和深化的能力。

五、建议学时分配

课 程 内 容	讲 课	实习课程设计	上 机
建筑设计基础Ⅰ	20	108	16
小制作	2	6	
建筑测绘	2	14	
外部空间认知	4	12	
外部空间设计	4	28	
建筑空间认知	4	12	8
建筑空间设计	4	36	8
建筑设计基础Ⅱ	20	108	16
先例分析	6	26	8
小型休闲展示建筑设计	10	54	
设计建造	4	28	8

六、考核方式

总评成绩＝平时各设计作品成绩按学时比例换算的总和

七、教材及参考书

1. [美]弗朗西斯·D·K·钦. 建筑：形式、空间、秩序. 邹德侬，方千里译. 北京：中国建筑工业出版社，1987
2. 彭一刚. 建筑空间组合论. 北京：中国建筑工业出版社，2004
3. [日]芦原义信. 外部空间设计. 尹培桐译. 北京：中国建筑工业出版社，1988
4. [美]爱德华·艾伦. 建筑初步. 刘晓光，王丽华，林冠兴等译. 北京：知识产权出版社，2005
5. [荷]赫曼·赫兹伯格. 建筑学教程：设计原理. 天津：天津大学出版社，2003
6. 建筑设计资料集编委会. 建筑设计资料集. 北京：中国建筑工业出版社，1994

先例分析与环境设计
Case Study & Environmental Design

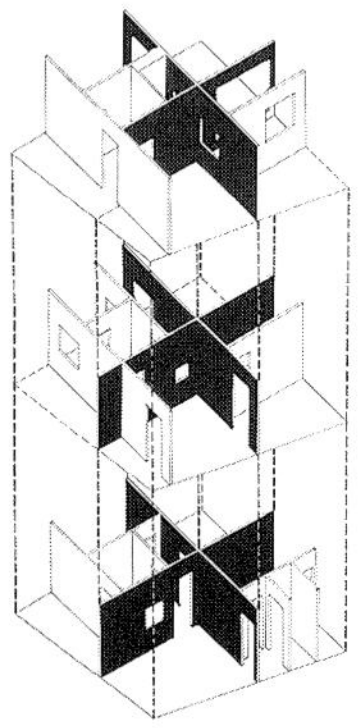

分层轴测

模型照片

作者：魏亚文 李文婷 刘一歌   指导老师：张彧

作者：申瑞雪   指导老师：李飚

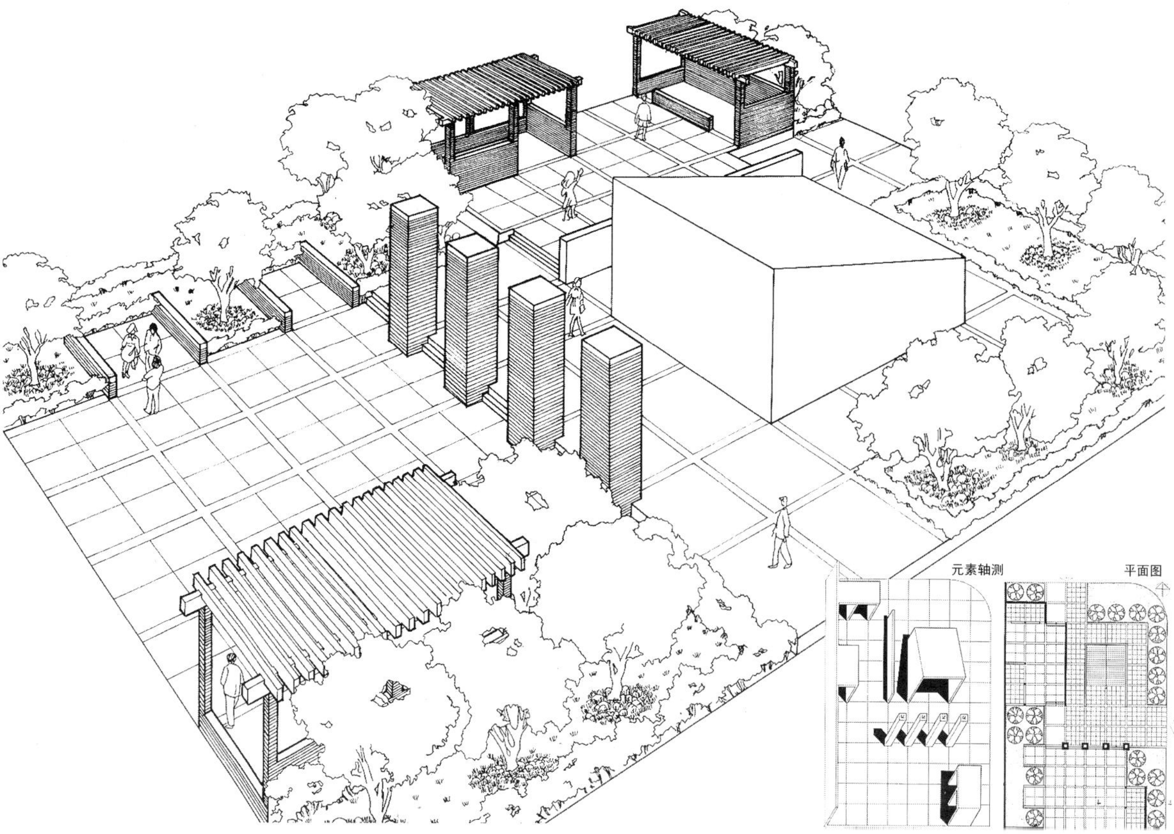

建筑师沙龙设计
Architects' Salon Design

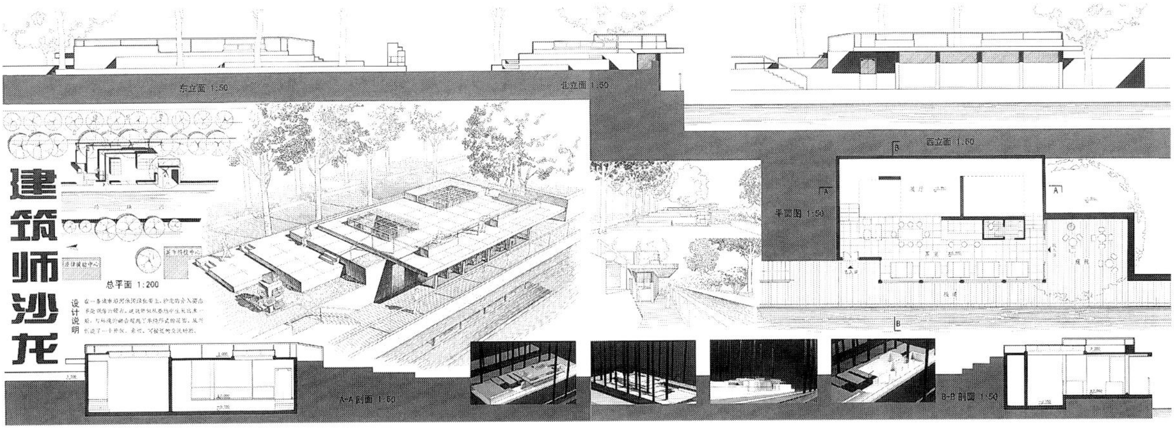

作者：吴程辉　指导老师：郭药
获2007年“Revit杯”全国大学生建筑设计作业优秀奖

作者：贾若　指导老师：杨靖

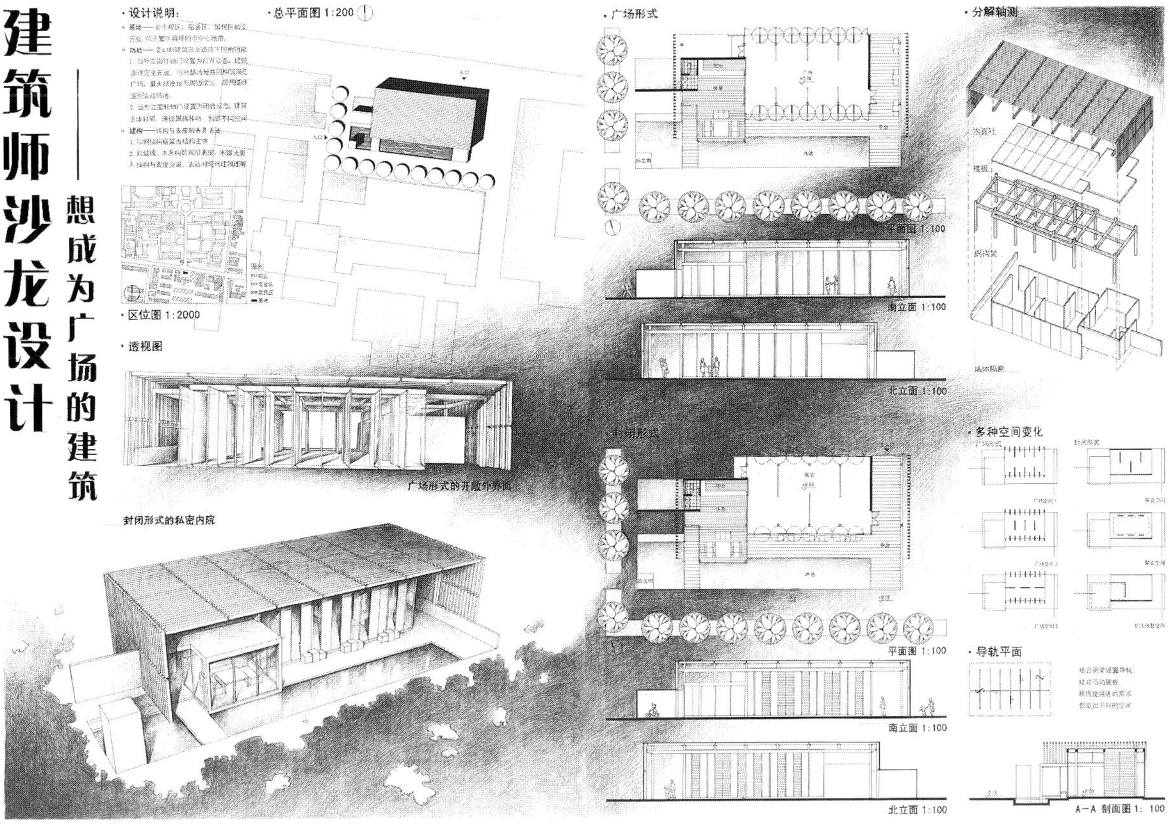

二年级设计课程教学大纲
Compendium_2nd Year

一、课程的性质与目的

本课程是建筑学、城市规划和环境艺术设计专业必修的一门专业主干课。课程的教学目的，是使学生建立基本的建筑观，掌握空间思维和相应的操作方法。

课程设置总体上仍旧采取原有的大框架，以建筑的三个基本问题——环境、空间、建构为主要线索，由浅入深地设置若干设计练习：包括单一形体与空间、连续空间、单元空间，最后发展到综合空间。对不同的课题，更加有针对性地匹配了不同类型的场地环境、使用功能、材料结构，以掌握建筑抽象的空间形式与具体的功能使用以及场地环境和材料结构之间互动的设计方法。

此外，在上述大框架下，近年来二年级的设计课程，重点强调了设计教学的过程和方法的训练，展开和推进设计构思和操作方法之间的互动性研究。

教学框图

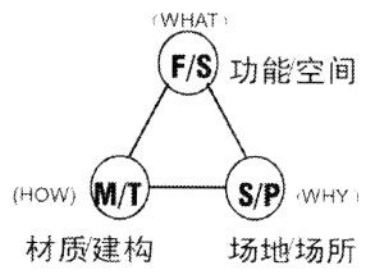

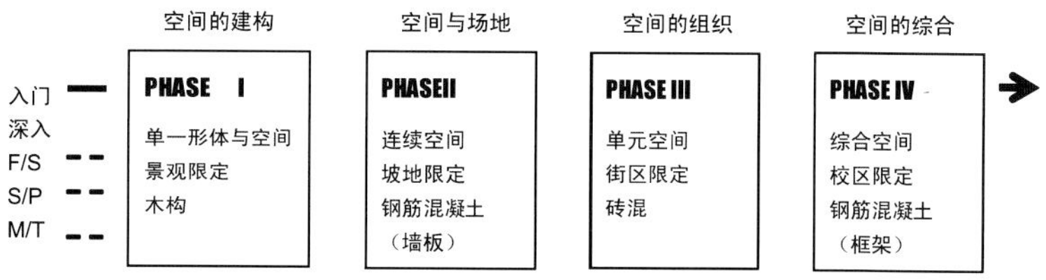

二、课程内容的教学要求

1. 空间的建构——临水小筑

（1）认识建筑材料及其相应的结构、构造与空间的互动，在设计中对其进行表现。

（2）考虑具体场地条件对建筑空间的影响。

（3）考虑建筑物的特定功能与空间和结构的互动。

（4）了解简单形体与空间设计的基本要素及其构成。

（5）掌握通过实物模型进行设计研究的工作方法。

2. 场地与空间——游客信息中心

（1）加强对现代建筑设计中“场地与空间”关系的理解，学习坡地建筑空间与地形及场地组织之间互动设计的方法，加深对场地环境分析及设计的认识。

（2）学习展示性连续空间的要素构成和系统组织特点，注重空间的路径组织与人的行为体验，了解类似公共建筑的一般设计原理及设计方法。

（3）基于坡地环境，探索不同比例的模型、不同的模型操作方法与连续空间设计的互动与表达。

3. 单元空间设计——青年旅社

（1）学习标准单元空间的设计与组合方式，在给定的用地范围内，按场地条件、环境特点、建筑功能及形式要求对空间进行围合、划分、引导及联系，并进行建筑形体的塑造。

（2）此设计练习着重训练由单一形体建筑向由若干个单一形体所组成的复合形体建筑的转化，以及复合形体的组合方式、手法和构成特点，即由单元空间所构成建筑的设计与组合。

（3）分析青年人对空间的基本需求，分析青年人在空间中的行为方式和感受，结合居住及出租特点分析此类建筑应有的形体特征、居住单元室内布置方式的各种可能性。

（4）理解结构形式对空间的限定及围合作用，掌握具体材料的建构方式和逻辑，注重其建筑构图的节奏及韵律。

（5）砖混结构是最基本的建筑结构形式，在这个设计练习中学习掌握这种结构形式的基本特点以及与之相关的物质技术手段，并着重研究其所形成的特有的结构形式逻辑。

（6）学习“空间”、“形”与“建构”之间互动的设计方法。理解环境条件对建筑生成的控制与限定作用，建筑与特定场地条件（城市街区）的互动、室内与室外空间的互动。

4. 综合空间设计——图书馆

（1）学习在一个简单形体内复杂空间关系的组织方法。

（2）建立在一个较紧凑的场地限定中，建筑的形体空间与周围建筑、道路及环境之间互动的设计态度。

（3）掌握以图书馆为代表的一般公共建筑的基本使用特征和要求，并理解功能使用的弹性及其与空间形式的互动。

（4）理解框架结构与空间形式的基本关系，着重结构要素（构件）与空间限定要素（构件）之间的基本关系研究。

（5）在设计的过程中加强不同比例的手工模型研究，同时利用手工模型和电脑模型，以及模型与图面作业的互动。

三、能力培养的要求

1. 抽象思维能力的培养：理解和建立抽象的空间概念，掌握一般空间设计的原理和基本形式分析及拓扑分析方法。
2. 具体感知力的培养：体验具体的物质空间，激发空间感知的觉醒。
3. 设计能力的培养：理解空间设计在抽象思维和具体感知之间的转换，熟习基本的空间设计模式及其操作要素、机制、工具（媒介）等。

四、建议学时分配

课 程 内 容	讲 课	实习课程设计	实　验	上 机
临水小筑设计	8	56		64
游客信息中心设计	8	56		64
青年旅社设计	8	56		64
图书馆设计	8	56		64

五、考核方式

总评成绩＝期中成绩+期末成绩
期中成绩50%
期末成绩50%

六、教材及参考书

1. 彭一刚. 建筑空间组合论. 北京：中国建筑工业出版社，1983
2. 鲍家声，杜顺宝. 公共建筑设计基础. 南京：南京工学院出版社，1986
3. [意]布鲁诺·塞维. 建筑空间论. 张似赞译. 北京：中国建筑工业出版社，1985
4. [荷]赫曼·赫兹伯格. 建筑学教程：空间与建筑师. 刘大馨，古红缨译. 天津：天津大学出版社，2003
5. [美]程大锦. 建筑：形式、空间和秩序. 刘丛红译. 天津：天津大学出版社，2005

临水小筑设计
Lakeside House Design

作者：黄灵卉　指导老师：雒建利

房子以格子墙为结构，人在房子里的活动与格子墙有着密切的关系：书桌、厨房电器，甚至床，都被安置在格子内。建筑立面也将由于使用者对格子的利用不同而产生不同的变化。

Structure of the house is made up of grid wooden walls to which activities are closely related. Desk, electrical apparatus and even bed, are set within the wall. Facade is varied with the use-change of these grid shelves.

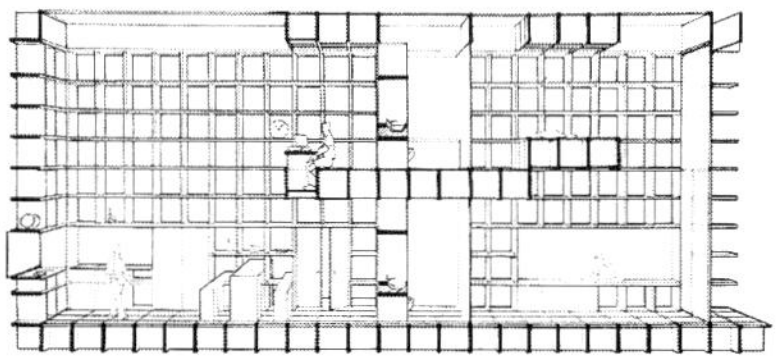

剖透视

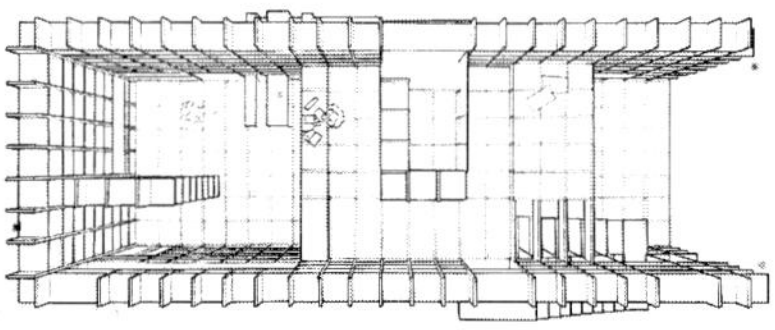

俯透视

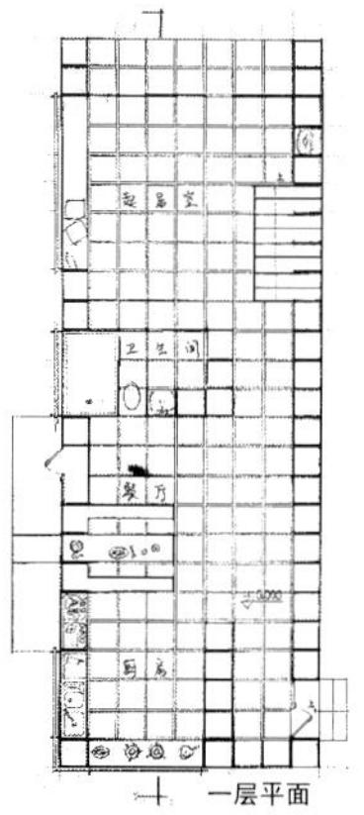

一层平面

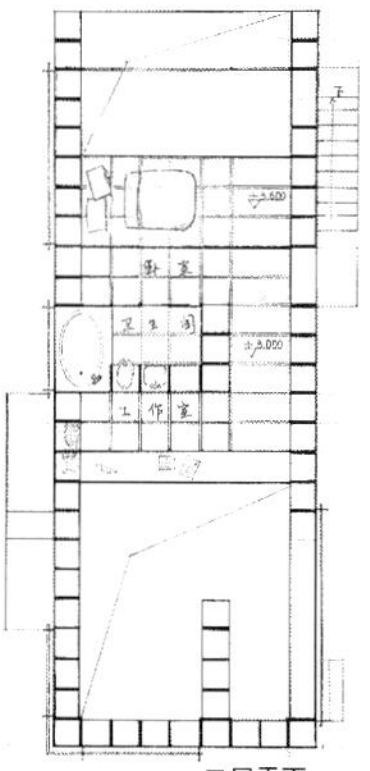

二层平面

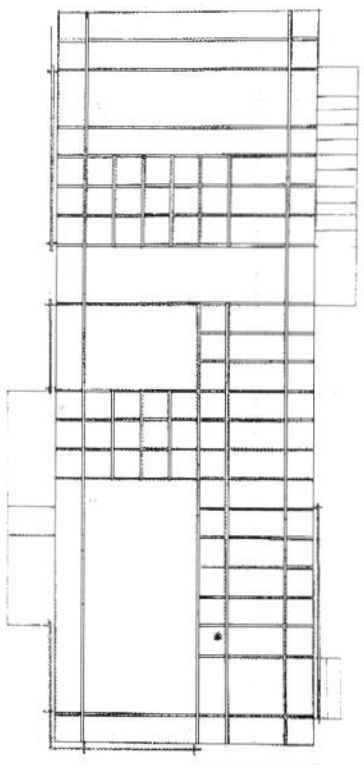

屋顶平面

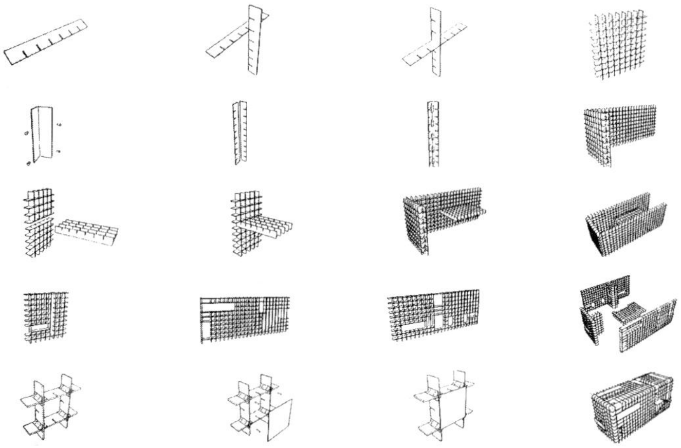

临水小筑设计
Lakeside House Design

作者：孔德钟　指导老师：史永高

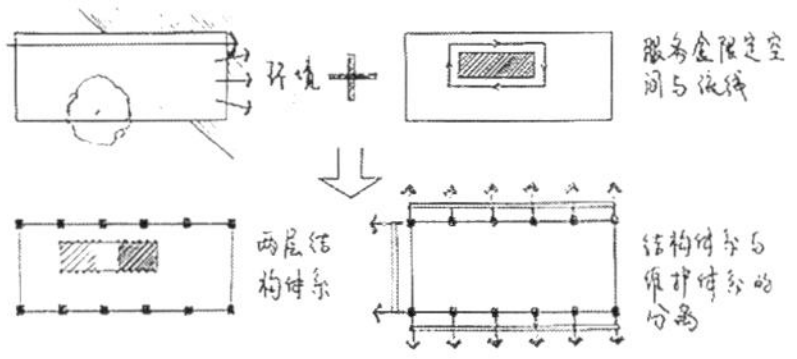

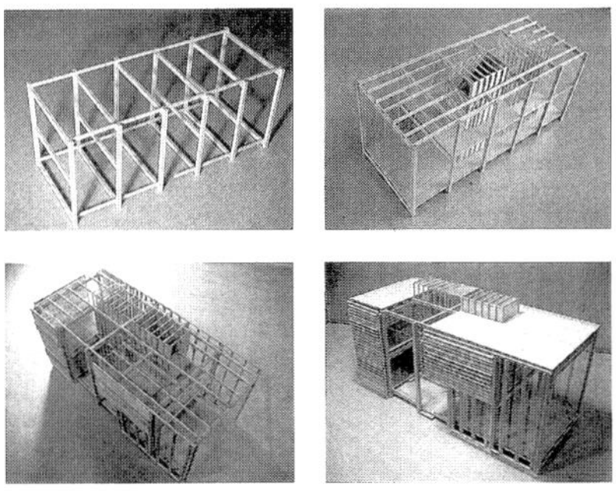

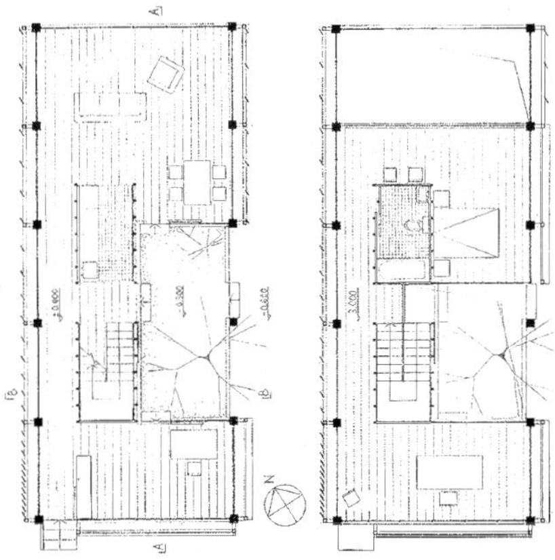

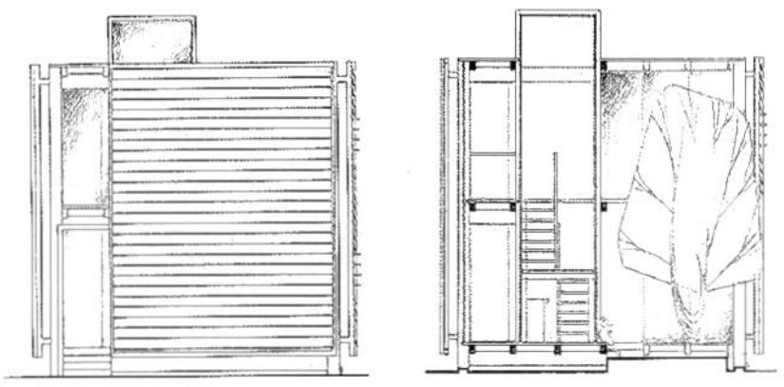

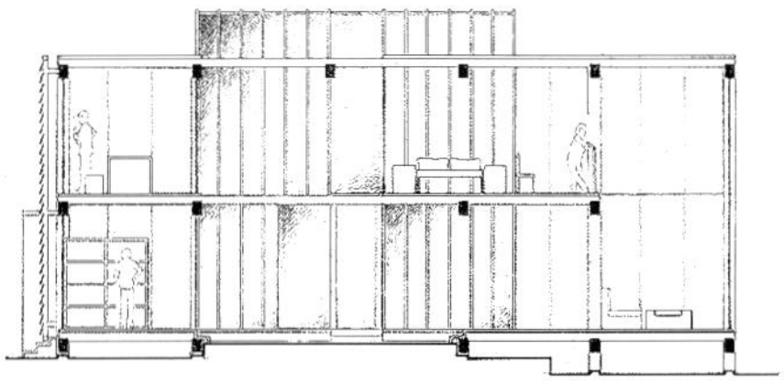

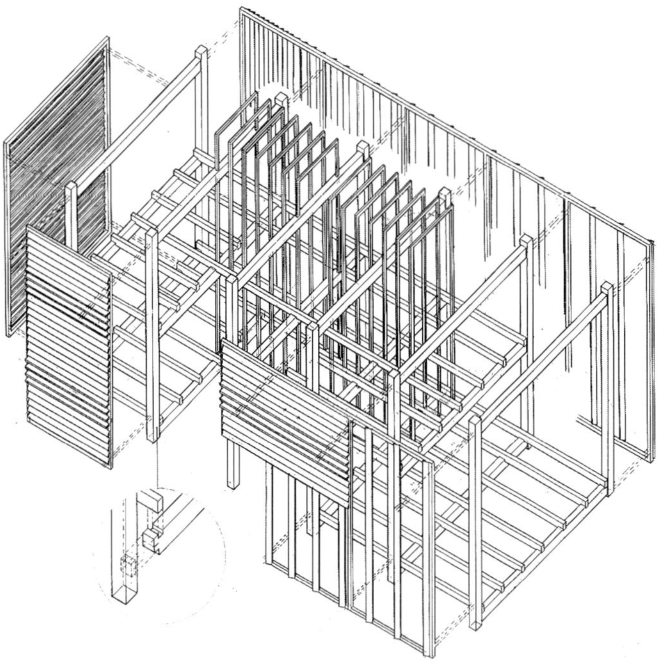

小筑位于玄武湖畔一块度假绿地之中，设计从环境因素启动。插入其中的服务盒和建筑主体对应了两层不同的结构体系，同时维护体系也从主体中脱离开来。

Located in a green land near the Xuanwu Lake, the design begins with positive response to environmental elements. Different structural systems are given to main body and the serving box inserted in while covering is detached from those two.

青年旅社设计
Youth Hotel Design

作者：张一楠　指导老师：鲍莉
获2007年“Revit杯”全国大学生建筑设计作业优秀奖

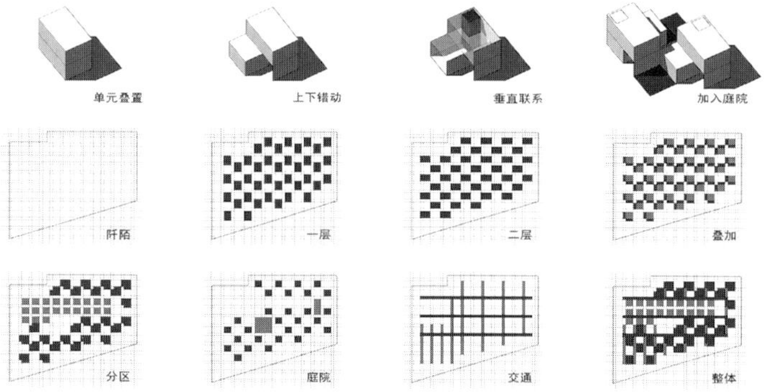

设计方案以一种阡陌纵横、交通相错的意象，试图恢复中国传统街巷生活的温馨。在保证公共与私密空间有机联系的同时，塑造了介于两者之间的模糊地带，从而给人与人之间的关系带来了无数可能性。设计方法上利用单元组合的生长性和适应性，创造了一种灵活有效的居住模式。框架以及砖混结构的交替、庭院与阳台的错动、光与风的筛入，带来了整体的舒适感。

The design creates some criss-cross paths which refer to traditional Chinese neighbourhood space which encourages more contacts between youth from different places. The repeated units bring much flexibility to users so that they may make the space more vivid and comfortable.

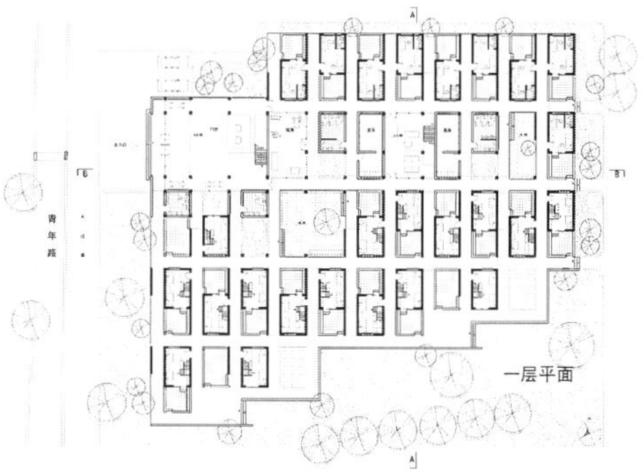
一层平面

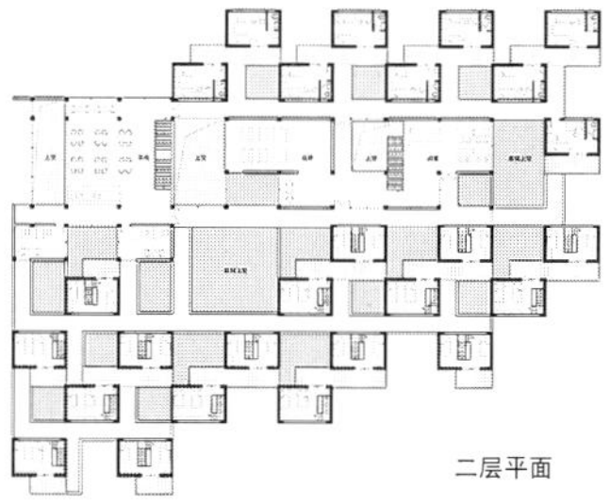
二层平面

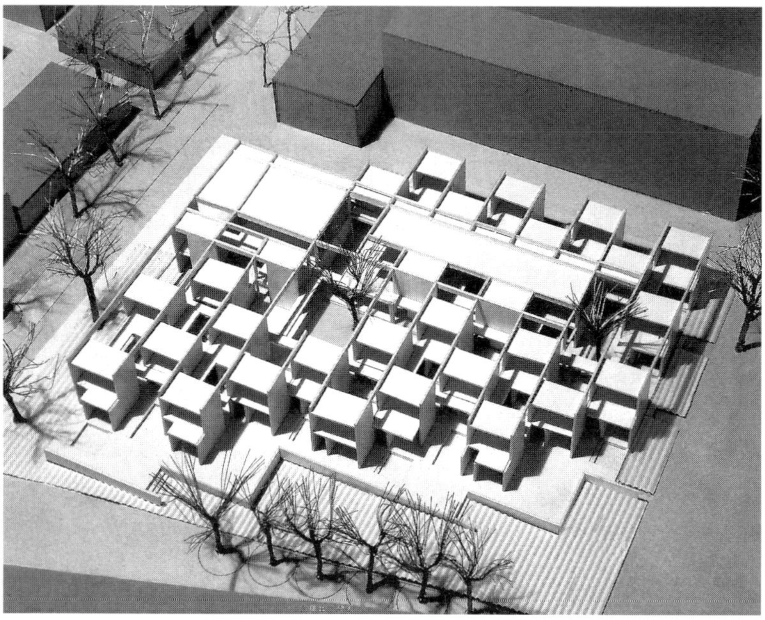

青年旅社设计
Youth Hotel Design

作者：李冠英　指导老师：杨东辉

针对青年旅社的特点，采用了将私密性强的居住单元沿轴线布置在外围以获得较好的采光和景观效果，并将其叠加区域作为公共空间的策略。结构上“十字”形墙的可扩展性在形成栏板、连廊、女儿墙等一系列构件的同时，创造出流动的空间。

Considering the characteristics of Youth Hotel, private accommodations aligned with axis are arranged outside to get better sunshine and views, while shared space serves as communication area. Moreover, structural cross wall is extended into a series of component parts such as balustrades and corridors, providing flow space at the same time.

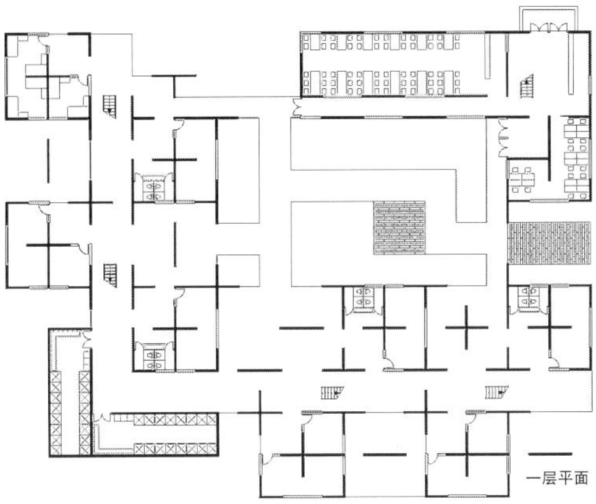

一层平面

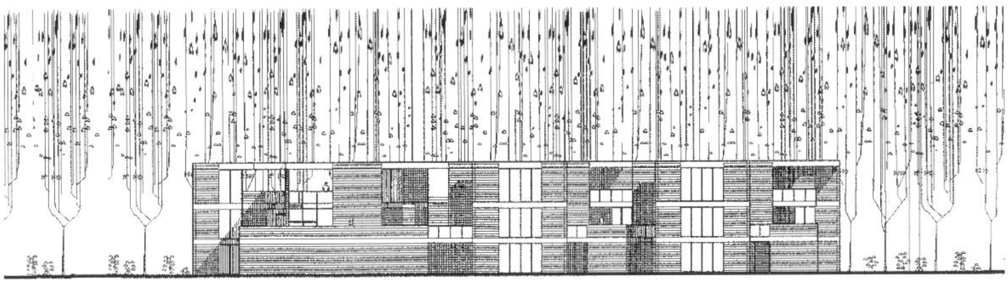

南立面

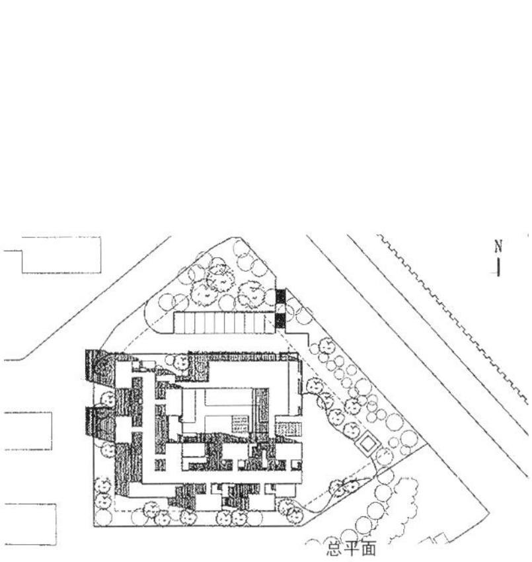

总平面

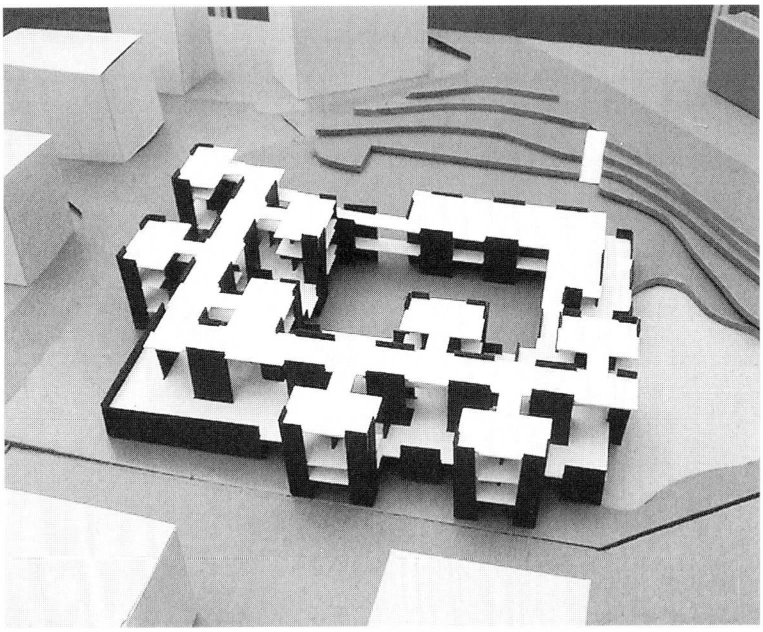

青年旅社设计
Youth Hotel Design

作者：申瑞雪　指导老师：史新

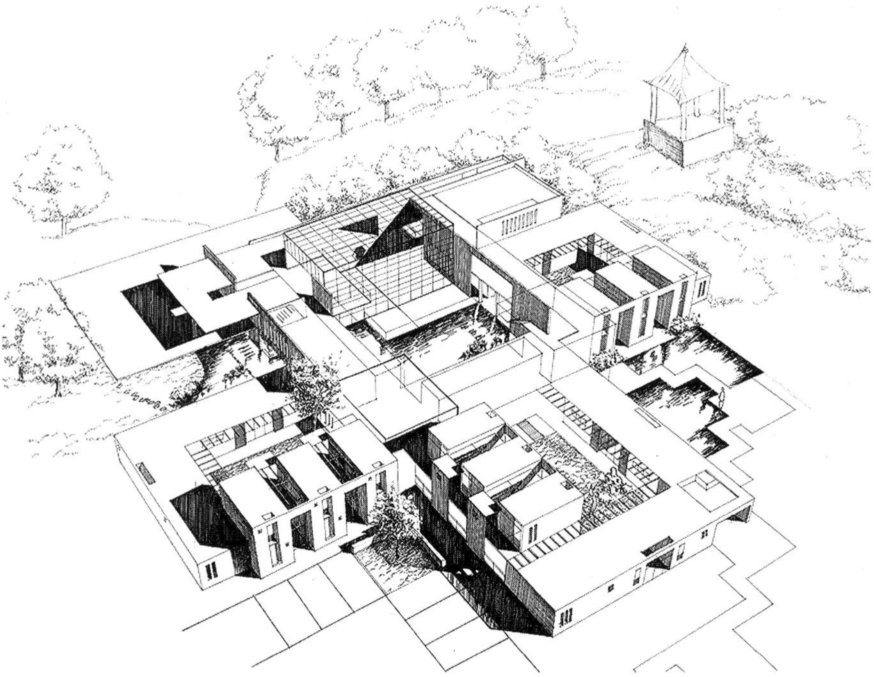

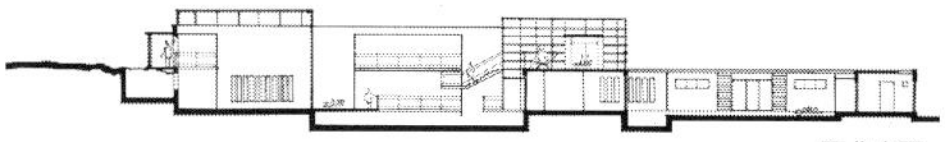

西北立面

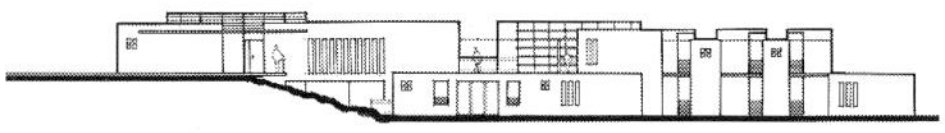

剖面B-B

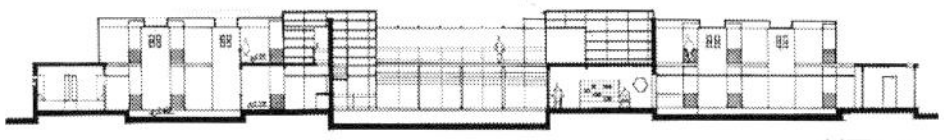

剖面A-A

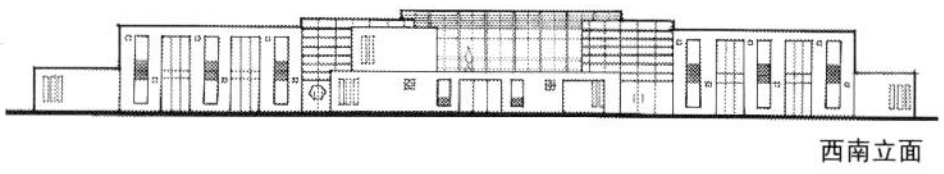

西南立面

一层平面

受城墙和玄武湖的影响，希望在这片区域创造一种整体景观，其外在传承着中国古典式的、并和邻近古建相呼应的形态。在动线的设计上充分考虑了步移景易的中国古典式园林空间带来的情节式体验，而在节点的设计上也尽量让人能感到整个大空间的存在性，以实现中国园林中的丰富性与细腻性。

An internal traditional Chinese garden plot is brought into the design for promoting a harmonious relationship between the ancient wall and the Xuanwu Lake. The trace of movement is elaborately set for a variation of views, while at the konts perception of the whole space would realize the complexity as in a Chinese garden.

游客信息中心设计
Tourists' Info. Center Design

作者：郭炜　指导老师：朱雷

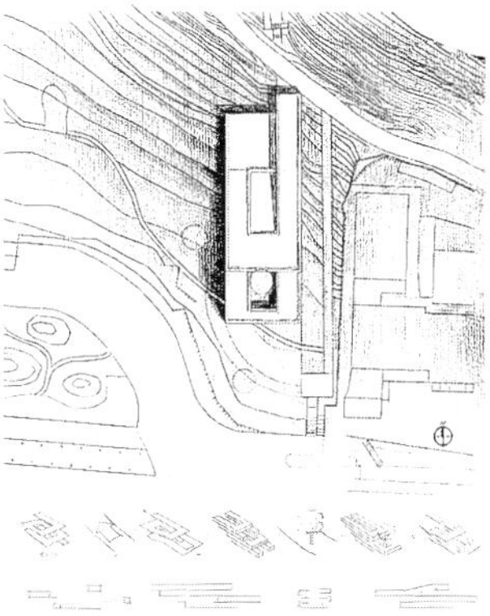

设计从基地和功能出发，结合坡地与参观功能形成了螺旋形的流线，同时对场地中的树作了回应，参观的过程也是上山的过程，视线在环境与建筑间转换，而位于中央的贯通空间起到了汇聚展览空间的作用。

The design starts from combination of site and function. What I did is to combine trace of visit with the slope, which leads to a spiral route covering all displays during climbing the hill.

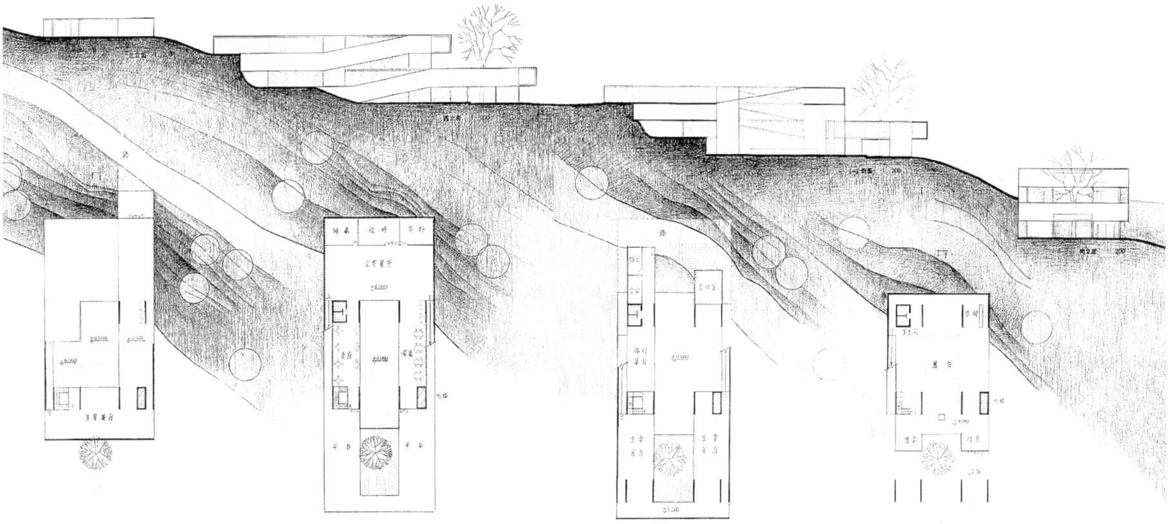

四层平面　三层平面　二层平面　一层平面

游客信息中心设计
Tourists' Info. Center Design

作者：蔡倩倩　指导老师：王湘君

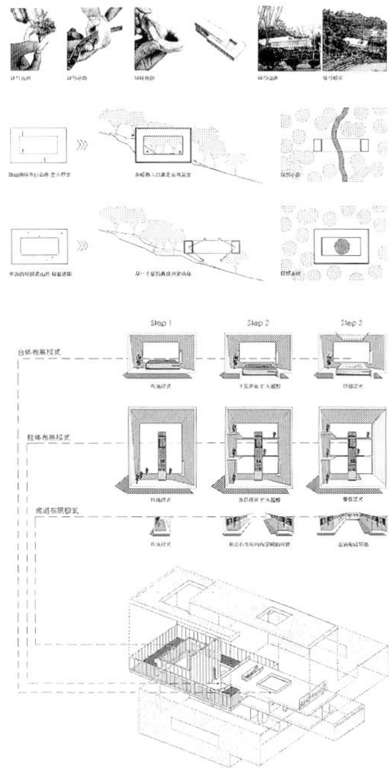

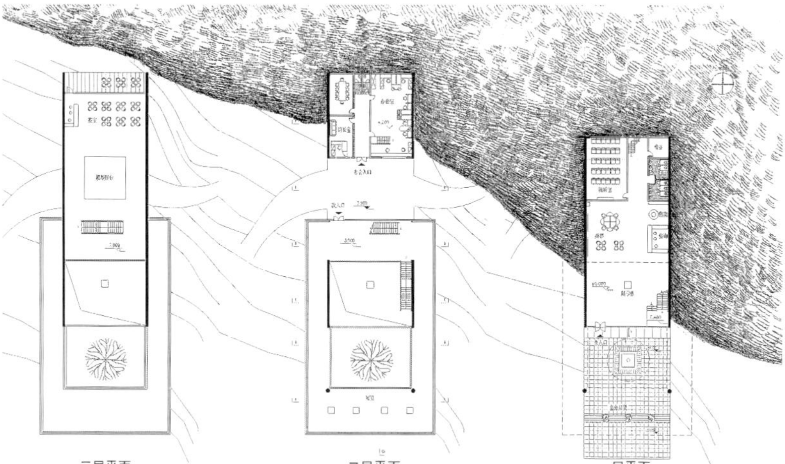

三层平面　　二层平面　　一层平面

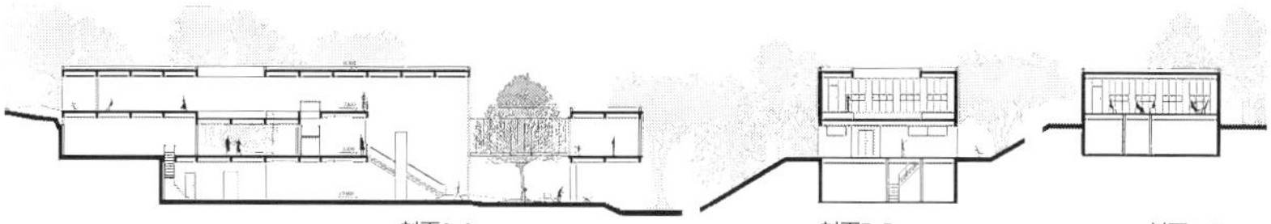

剖面C-C　　剖面E-E　　剖面F-F

基地位于城市中的一个山地上，面朝一条主干道，如何在此处创造出融入自然并适宜山地的游览空间成为设计的主要目标。设计保留了基地上的一棵古树、一条石阶路和一个广场，基本构思是两个套叠的“环”。使自然从多个方向渗透进建筑。一个剖面上的环和一个平面上的环的叠加使建筑完美地适应了山地，让人游历山体内外，产生奇特的空间体验。三种展示空间也被水平的环串了起来，垂直的环带来的不同标高上的两个入口又成功地实现了人员的分流。

Located on a small hill, the main aim of the design is to create a unique spatial experience with a harmonious relationship between architecture and nature. Reserving a tree, an alley and a plaza, two loops are concieved, horizontal and vertical, to fit the slope. Meanwhile, this operation classified three different kinds of exhibition spaces and made two entrances at both low and high levels.

游客信息中心设计
Tourists' Info. Center Design

作者：陈梦婕　指导老师：虞刚

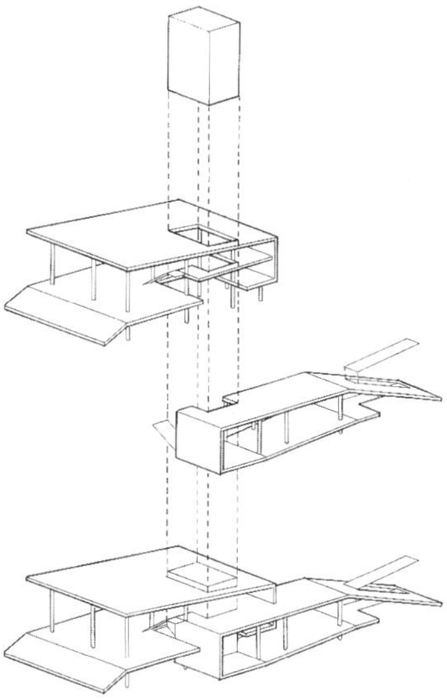

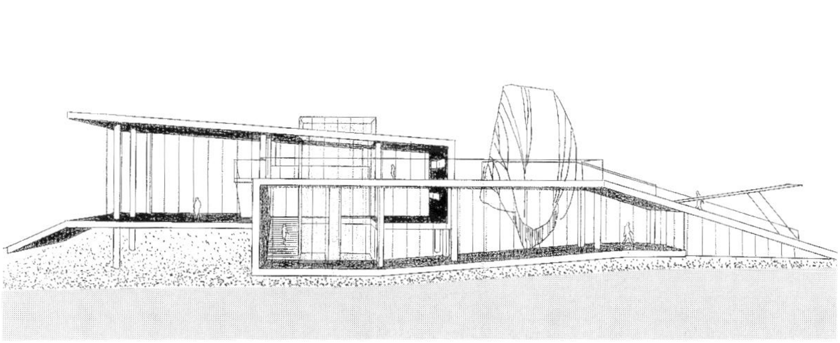

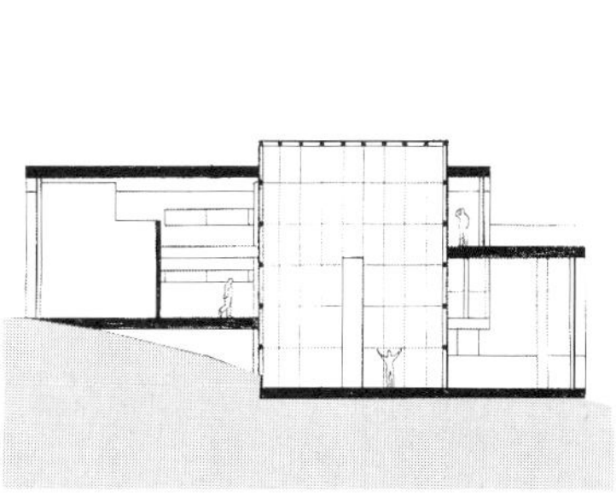

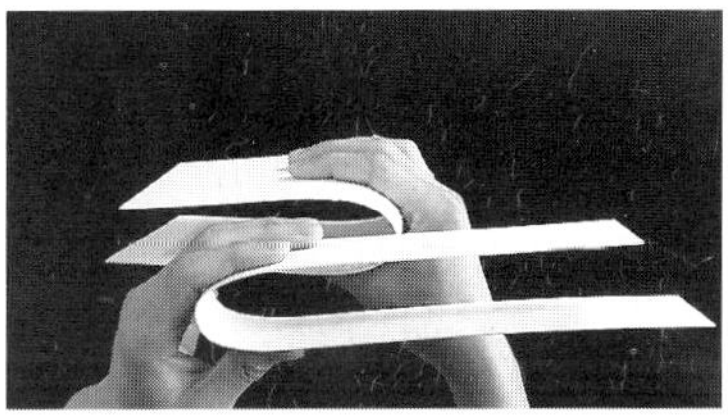

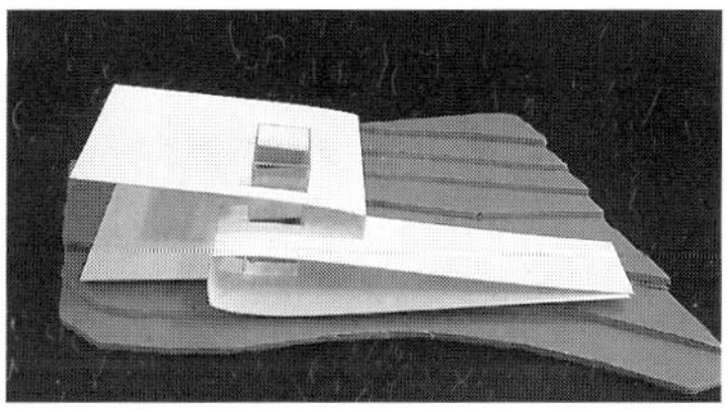

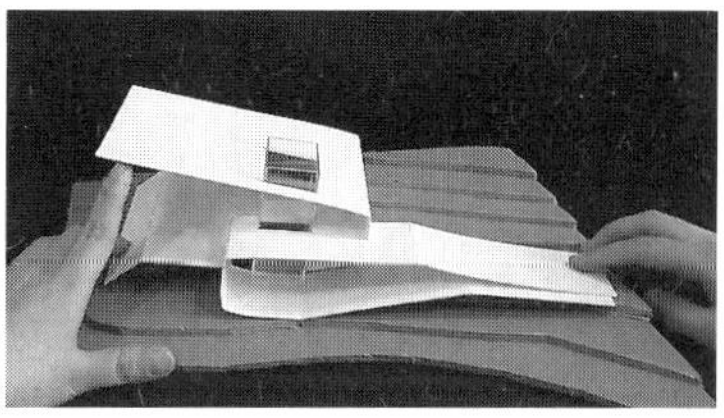

图书馆设计

Library Design

作者：汪澄波　指导老师：朱雷
获2007年“Revit杯”全国大学生建筑设计作业优秀奖

本建筑在两个方向上对建筑进行了分层：在竖直方向上，由下到上分为半地下的办公区、高敞外向的大厅及活动空间和上部内向的核心阅览书架区；在水平方向上分为中心由四个核心筒所支撑的书架区以及周围一圈阅览区，其中阅览区又分为强调阅览私密性的阅览单元和四角上对外开敞的休息讨论单元。设计中强调结构要素和空间限定要素区分明确、清晰易读。

The building is divided into several parts in two directions: office department, public area and reading department in the vertical direction; reading area and storing area in the horizontal direction. Thus the building is clearer to read.

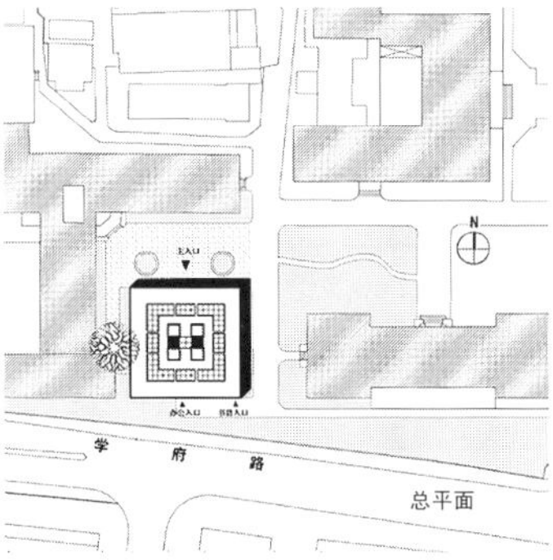

总平面

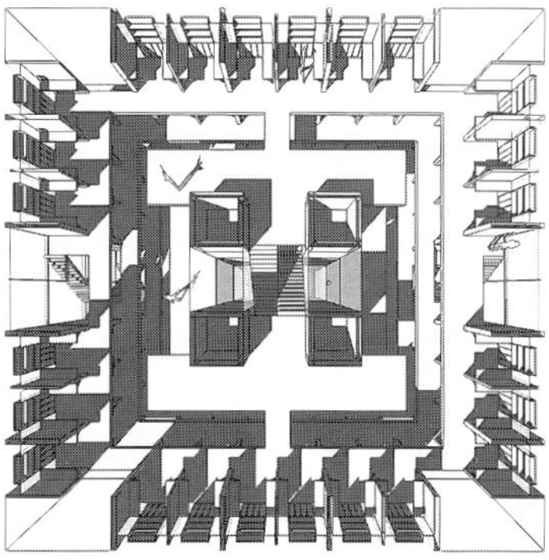

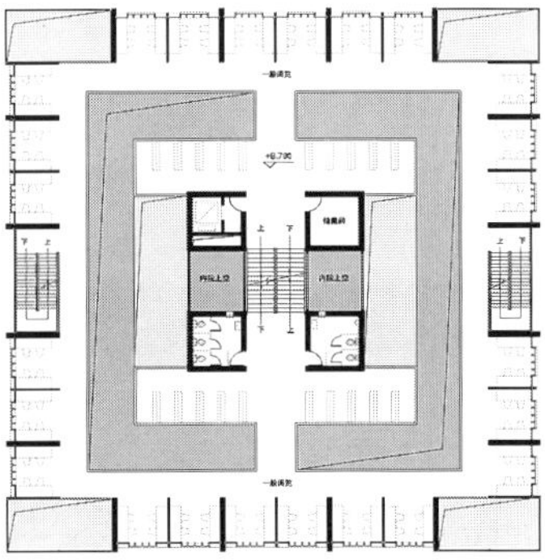
+8.700标高平面

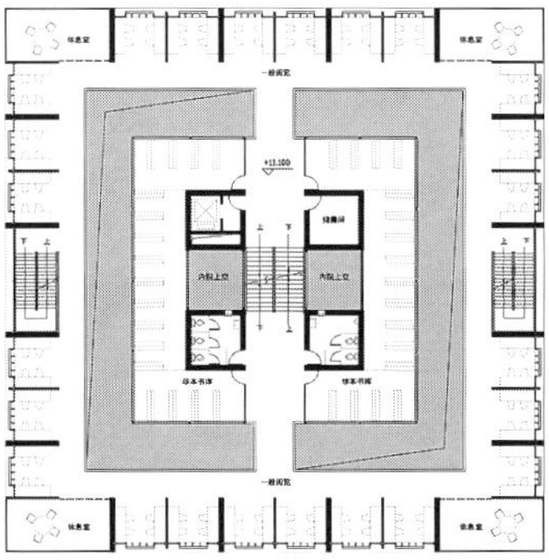
+10.000标高平面

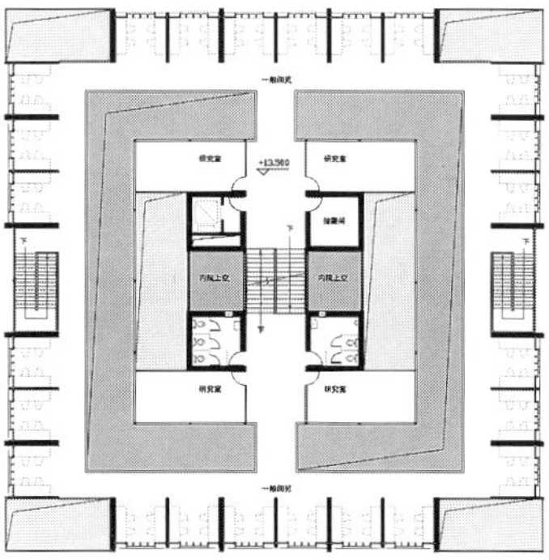
+13.300标高平面

图书馆设计
Library Design

作者：樊思嘉　指导老师：王正

基地位于校园一角，南望城市道路，东邻开敞绿地，西北向为“L”形建筑所围合。因此本设计试图创造一条“L”形绿色廊道，将东侧绿色空间延伸至室内，通过室内外绿色空间的整合使建筑锚固于环境中，同时缓解与西北侧建筑之间的紧张关系。建筑内部以不同的空间可达性和开敞度来满足图书馆不同使用功能以及对公共性与私密性的要求。阅览区采光充足，同时窗外的绿色更使借阅充满乐趣。

The design intends to connect outdoors and indoors by creating an L-shaped green corridor, which also acts as a buffer between the library and the already existed L-shaped teaching building, and therefore anchors the architecture into the environment around it.

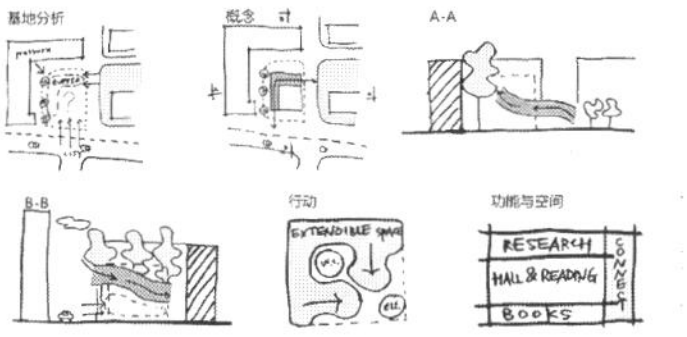

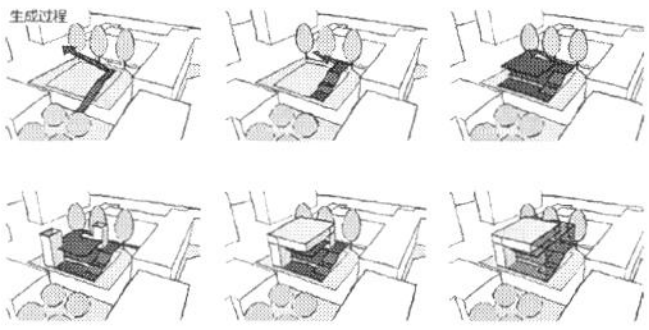

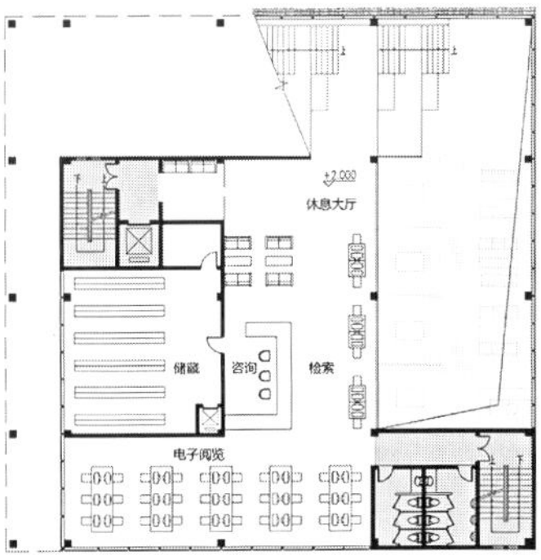

一层平面

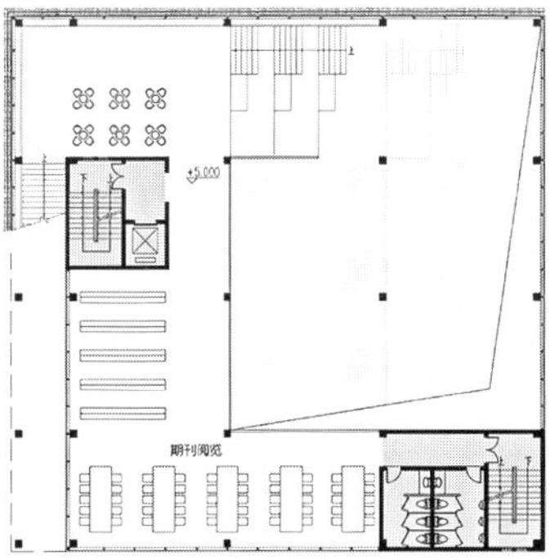

二层平面

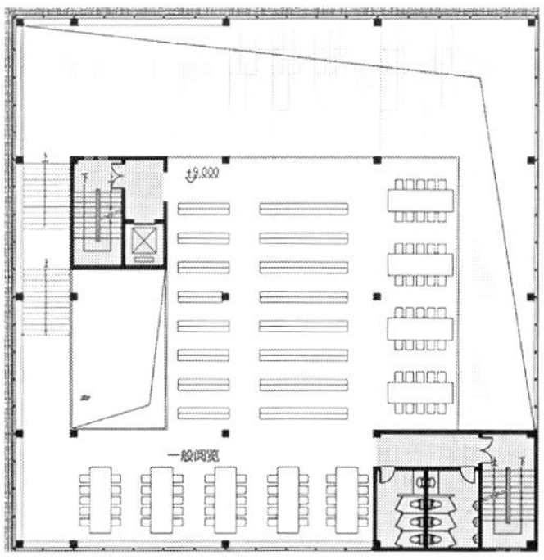

三层平面

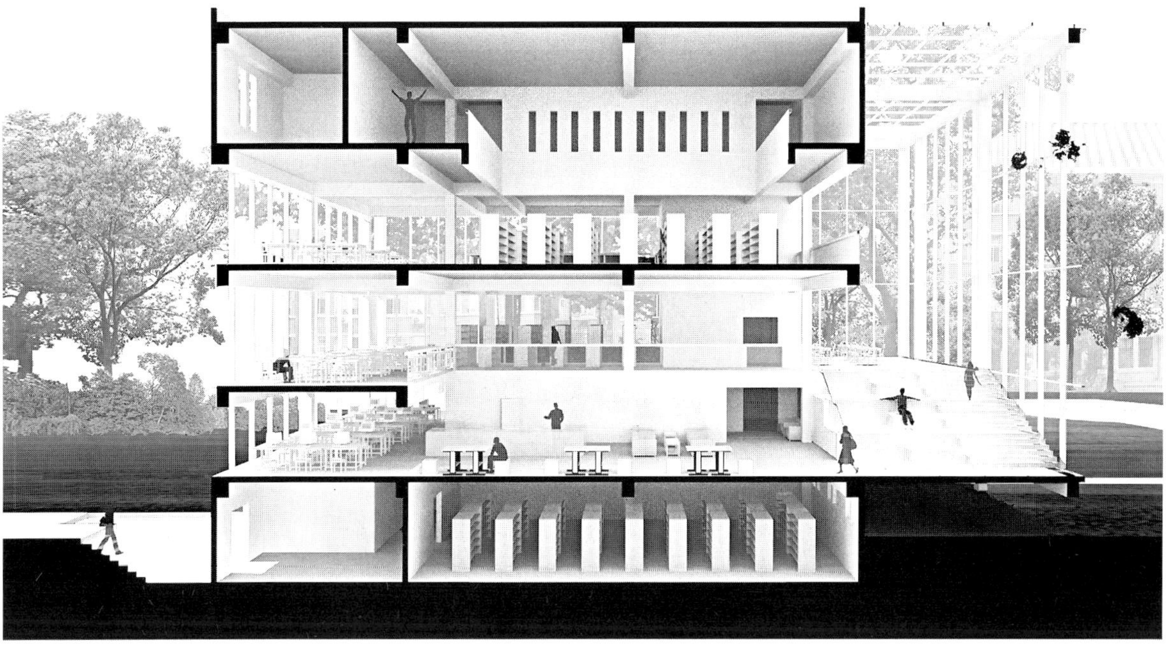

图书馆设计
Library Design

作者：唐超乐　指导老师：王湘君

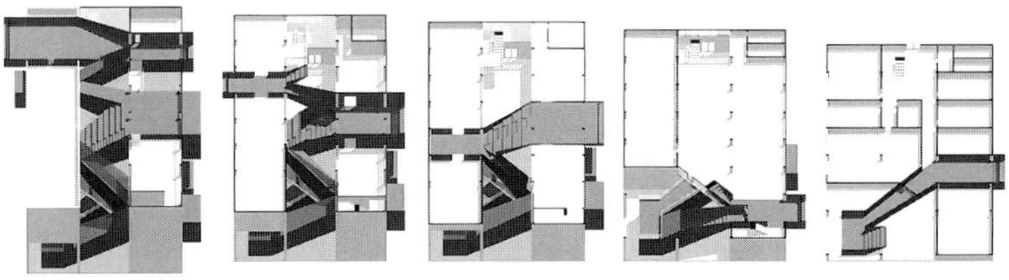

基地临街，处于校园环境向城市环境过渡的边界区域。方案试图将两种不同环境的转换在建筑中展开，一条“S”形的管道穿插在投射了两个环境属性的条状空间中，人在经历建筑的同时不断感受两种环境的转换，创造了一种有趣的体验。“S”形管道是承载了休息、阅览、展览、交通等多种功能的混合体。

The site next to the street is in a mediate zone between campus and city. The design trys to display the transition between two different atmospheres. An S-shaped tube which serves as mixture of different functions goes through the space definited by the two. Thus people feel the transition while walking in the building, which makes an interesting experience.

剖面

三年级设计课程教学大纲
Compendium_3rd Year

建筑设计

一、课程的性质与目的

本课程是建筑学专业必修的一门最重要的专业主干课。

本课程的教学目的，是使学生建立整体的建筑观，以建筑的三个基本问题——功能、环境、材料为线索，由浅入深地设置若干设计练习，从单一问题发展到综合问题，使学生初步掌握大中型建筑的设计原理。

二、课程内容的教学要求

1. 实验研究中心

（1）设计某研究所的化学实验研究中心，基地位于东南大学校园之内，两处地形可任选一处。要求初步掌握一般实验室建筑的设计原理并扩大公共建筑设计的基本知识。

（2）学习空间、功能、结构、场地互动的设计方法。学习分析类型载体的流程和分析场地内外关系的技巧，学习功能配置与结构配置结合的技巧，学习构建空间模式、组织空间秩序的技巧。

（3）培养利用手工模型进行快速推敲方案的能力。培养快速入手、多轮反复、逐轮深入的工作习惯。培养图纸、模型、设计对象之间想象的能力和把握秩序的能力。

2. 和平纪念中心

（1）设计南京国防园和平纪念中心，在指定的区域中选择一处自设纪念园区进行建筑设计及场地设计。要求初步掌握一般纪念建筑的设计原理，了解坡地建筑设计的基本方法。

（2）在第一个练习基础上深化学习空间、场地、结构和功能互动的设计方法，学习纪念建筑的仪式和流线特点，学习利用坡地塑造空间的技巧，学习构思空间原形，学习研究重点部分（如祭堂）特殊的光线设计与结构设计的技巧。

（3）培养利用手工模型与计算机辅助设计结合进行方案深化的能力。培养利用空间表现仪式的构思能力和对气氛、光线和结构的敏感性。

3. 铁路交通博物馆

（1）设计某铁路交通博物馆，基地位于南京市浦口区的南京北站（原浦口火车站）。要求初步掌握博览建筑的设计原理，并了解大型公共建筑设计的基本知识。

（2）学习场地、结构、空间、功能互动的设计方法，学习在旧城区复杂场地环境中开展调研工作以及分析新旧建筑关系的技巧，学习功能配置与结构选型相结合的技巧，了解旧建筑功能置换以及适应性再利用的策略、方法和技术细节，学习建筑细部处理和构造设计互动的技巧。

（3）培养利用手工模型进行快速推敲方案的能力。培养快速入手、多轮反复、逐层次深入的工作习惯。培养对于图纸、模型、设计对象三者之间在设计过程中同步推进的想象力和把握秩序的能力。

4. 文化艺术中心

（1）文化艺术中心设计，基地位于西安门或玄武门，两处地形可任选一处。要求初步掌握演艺类建筑的设计原理以及复合型公共建筑设计的基本方法。

（2）学习空间、功能、结构、场地互动的设计方法。学习分析类型载体的流程和分析场地内外关系的技巧，学习功能配置与结构配置结合的技巧，学习构想空间模式、建立空间秩序的技巧。

（3）培养利用手工模型进行快速推敲方案的能力。培养快速入手、多轮反复、逐轮深入的工作习惯。培养图纸、模型、设计对象之间想象的能力和把握空间秩序的能力。

三、上机实习要求

通过上机实习掌握电脑三维模型研究建筑空间的方法，并与实物模型和图纸互动。利用电脑模拟的方便性观察使用者在实际空间中的透视体验。

四、能力培养的要求

1. 设计分析能力的培养：主要是对功能、环境、材料等各因素进行分析的方法。
2. 设计综合能力的提高：要求学生通过本课程的学习，对上述各种因素具有一定的综合解决问题的能力。
3. 设计方法和表达能力的培养：学习模型、电脑和图纸等基本设计媒介对设计思维的推动和表达。
4. 参考资料和典例的学习能力：要求学生学会从阅读材料和典例中主动去吸收、整理和消化，转化为对自己有用的背景知识和参考范例。
5. 研究构思和研究能力的培养：初步培养学生独立思考、发现和研究设计问题的能力。
6. 培养对技术性规范的尊重与理解。

五、建议学时分配

课 程 内 容	讲 课	实习课程设计	实 验	上 机
实验研究中心设计	8	56		64
和平纪念中心设计	8	56		64
铁路交通博物馆设计	8	56		64
文化艺术中心设计	8	56		64

六、考核方式

总评成绩＝期中评图成绩＋期末评图成绩
期中评图成绩50％
期末评图成绩50％

七、教材及参考书

1. 鲍家声，杜顺宝. 公共建筑设计基础. 南京：南京工学院出版社，1986
2. 彭一刚. 建筑空间组合论. 北京：中国建筑工业出版社，1983
3. [荷]伯纳德·卢本等. 设计与分析. 林尹星译. 天津：天津大学出版社，2003
4. [荷]赫曼·赫兹伯格. 建筑学教程：设计原理. 仲德崑译. 天津：天津大学出版社，2003
5. [美]程大锦. 建筑：形式、空间和秩序. 刘丛红译. 天津：天津大学出版社，2005
6. 建筑设计资料集总编辑委员会. 建筑设计资料集（1-8）. 北京：中国建筑工业出版社，1994
7. 中国建筑工业出版社. 现行建筑设计规范大全. 北京：中国建筑工业出版社，2005

详细规划

一、课程的性质与目的

本校的城市规划专业是在建筑学专业基础上发展的，前两年学生是在建筑学背景下进行专业设计基础训练，从三年级起正式与规划设计衔接。三年级的教学目的是引导学生顺利渡过转型期，实现从建筑设计教学到规划设计教学的良性过渡，领会城市规划的设计思维模式和方法。

三年级规划教学组织，以景园—住区为线索，循序渐进、由简单到复杂地设置若干设计练习，从单一空间发展到多元空间，从对建筑本体的关注到对综合环境的兼顾，从小规模群体的营建到住区综合系统的建构，逐步增加基地规模、扩展设计要素的多样性。

二、课程内容的教学要求

1. 景园规划设计

（1）通过对城市公共空间的景观规划，学习并掌握景园规划的基本原理与设计方法。

（2）理解公共空间在城市中的作用，学习区位分析、视线分析等与城市规划调研的基本方式方法。

（3）认识城市景观的各类基本构成要素，将其有序组织，形成能与城市融合的、满足市民需求的景观空间。

2. 住区综合设计

（1）学习和理解住区规划的基本原理、设计过程与设计方法，培养建筑与环境、建筑与城市的整体观念与综合设计能力。体验和研究城市居民的生活状况、生活方式和生活需求，掌握满足这些需求的规划设计方法与技能。

（2）掌握综合系统建构的方法，使之具备合理的功能结构、完整的建筑布局、有序的交通组织、适宜的空间环境和优美的景观。

（3）对住区规划所涉及的多方社会力量及其社会角色（包括政府、开发商、城市居民、规划设计师）有所了解。掌握相关设计规范，了解相关住房制度、管理技术规定。

三、能力培养的要求

1. 调查研究的能力：强调不同层次、不同维度的物质空间环境的综合调查，以及社会调查在规划设计中的运用。
2. 综合分析的能力：要求学生在调研中善于发现问题，并理论联系实践加以深入思考，在设计中予以解决。
3. 自主学习和案例评析的能力：要求学生自主收集相关信息，并学会评析和鉴赏，转化为对自己有用的背景知识和参考范例。
4. 设计技能的培养：从微观的建筑设计逐渐过渡到综合系统的建构，继续强化通过手工模型、电脑模型和图纸等媒介辅助和推动设计的能力。
5. 表达能力的培养：包括最终设计成果的表达，以及平时学习过程中师生交流的表达，表达的方式除了图纸外，要求强化口头表达能力和多媒体表达能力。
6. 合作能力的培养：规划设计教学的前期调研要求多人合作进行，初步培养学生团队合作的意识和能力。

实验研究中心设计
Experiment Research Center Design

作者：唐静寅　指导老师：葛明

设计借助自然要素的介入，依据实验室建筑不同功能对采光、通风等的专业要求，着力营造出一屋一院、一行一停的修道院式宁谧舒适的校园科学研究环境。

Depending upon these specific demands for different parts in the experiment center, design was pushed forward on, following distribution of function and utility of nature.

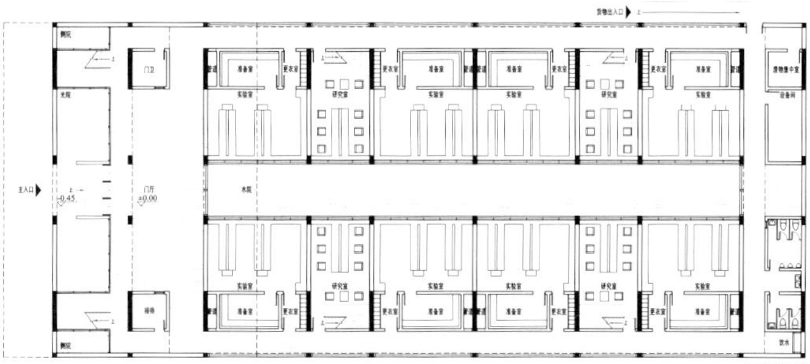

一层平面

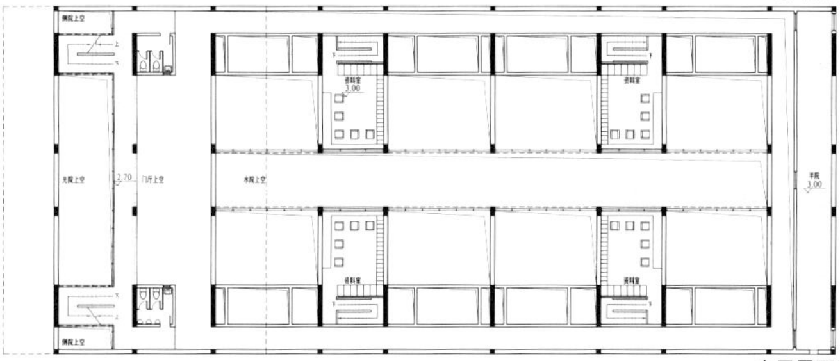

夹层平面

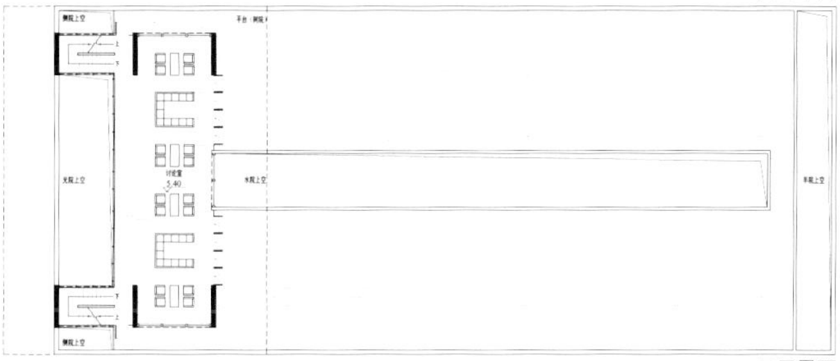

二层平面

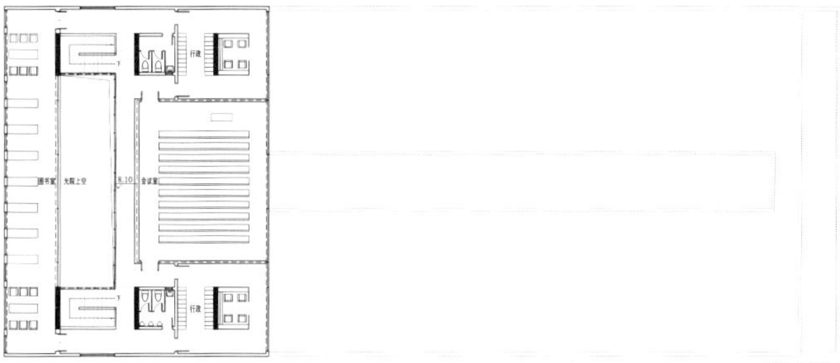

三层平面

剖面模型

实验研究中心设计

Experiment Research Center Design

作者：姜汶林　指导老师：薛力

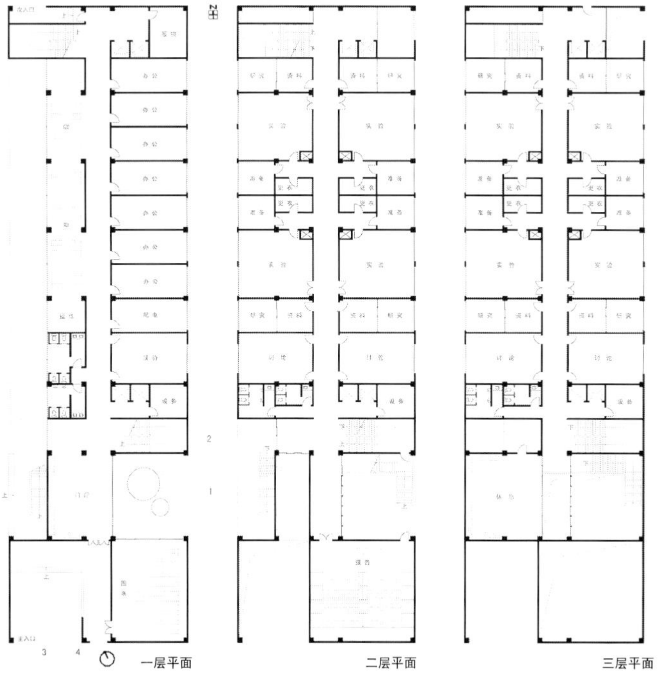

一层平面　　二层平面　　三层平面

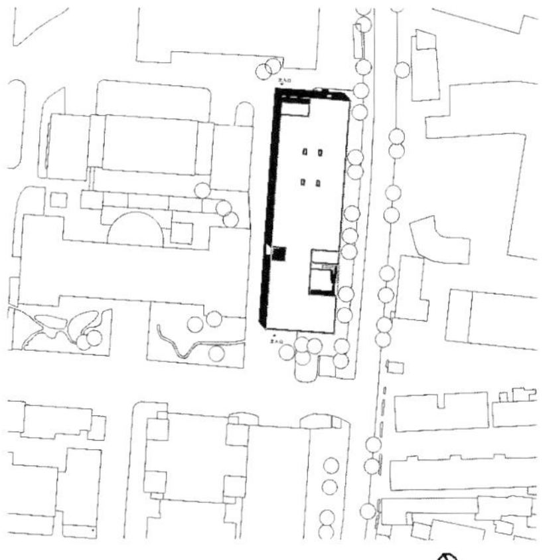

总平面

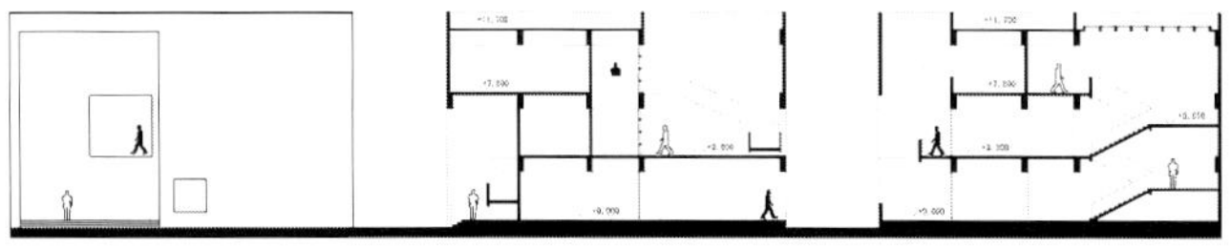

南立面　　剖面1-1　　剖面2-2

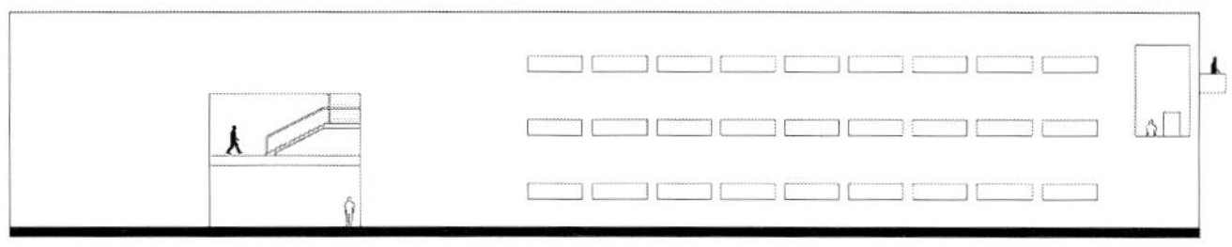

东立面

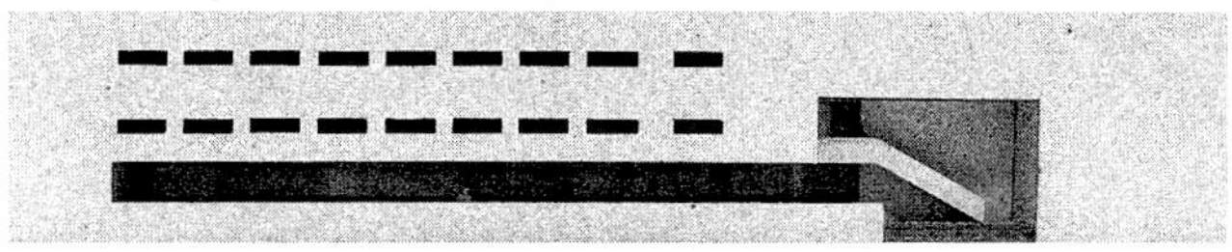

西立面

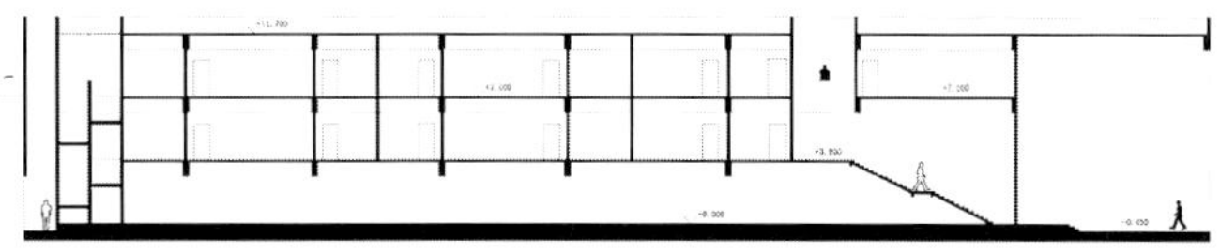

剖面3-3

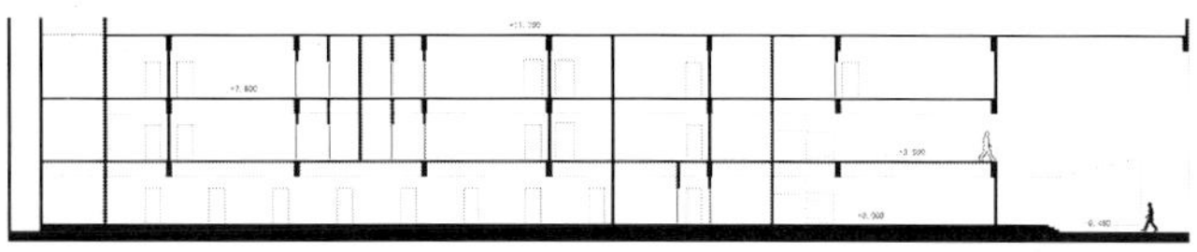

剖面4-4

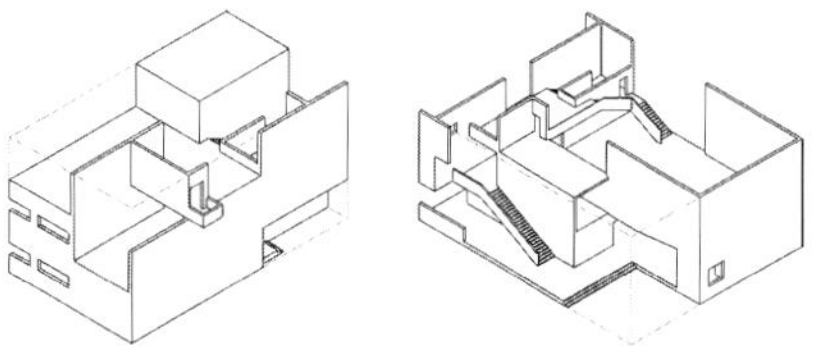

设计通过对公共空间、半公共空间以及单元空间的有序组织实现建筑内部的秩序和变化。在交通节点处设置院子，院子同时成了不同功能区间的过渡空间。

Through organization of public, semi-public and unit spaces, order and variation within the design of the architecture is fulfilled, with transition from courtyards as knots of transportation.

实验研究中心设计

Experiment Research Center Design

作者：周姝颖　指导老师：刘捷

建筑由单元组成，每个单元包括实验室、研究室和庭院。庭院有利于化学实验楼的通风以及与自然的交流。西侧的实验室部分与东侧的研究室部分错层形成设备夹层。

The chemistry lab is composed by units. Each unit contains a lab, a study room and a courtyard which help with ventilation and communication with the nature. The staggering floors form space for equipments of the lab.

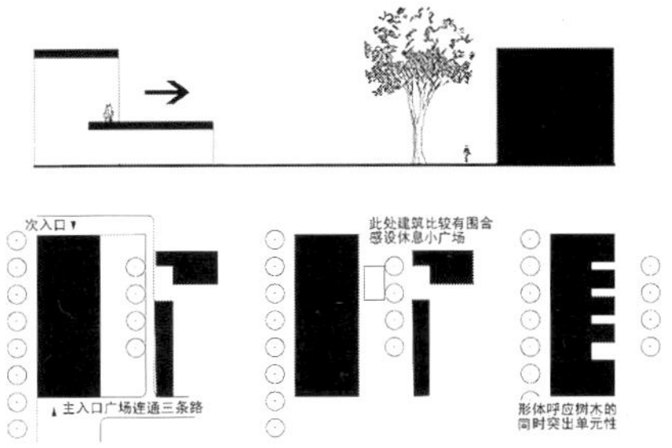

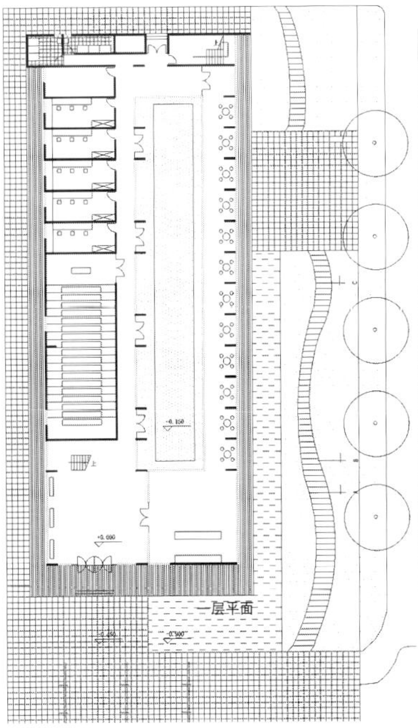

一层平面

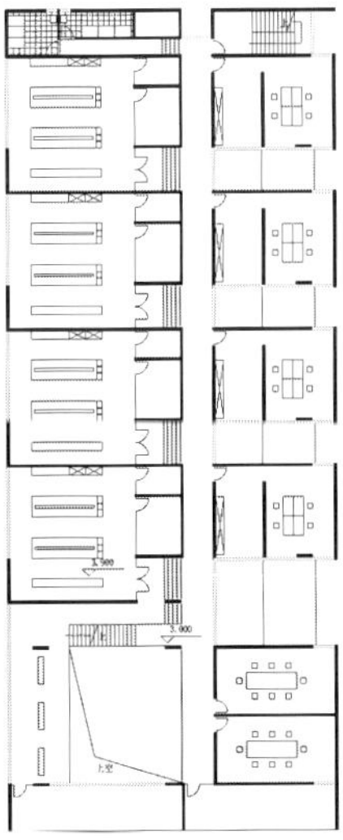

二层平面

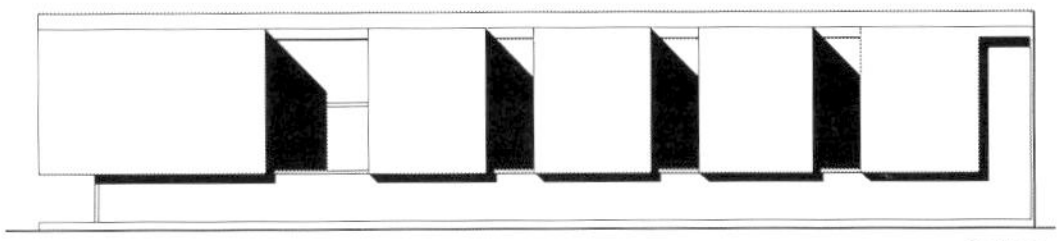

东立面

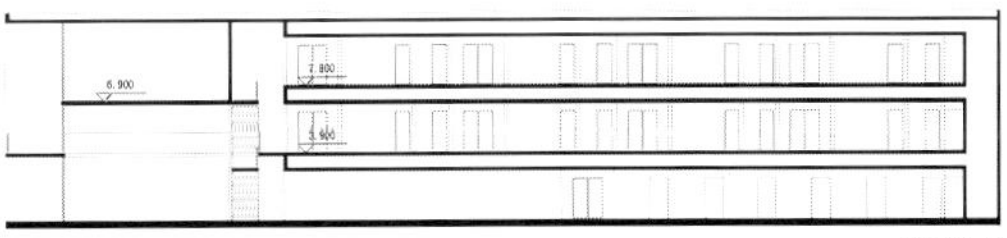

剖面C-C

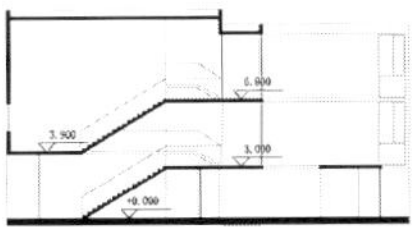

剖面A-A

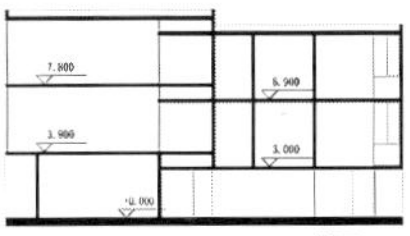

剖面B-B

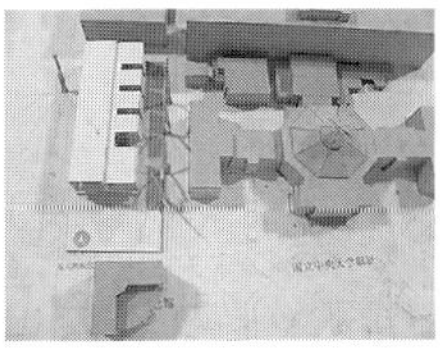

和平纪念中心设计
Peace Memorial Center Design

作者：吴静明　指导老师：夏兵

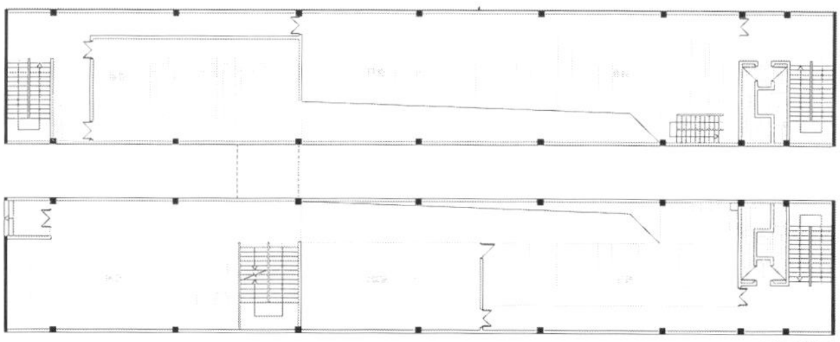
三层平面

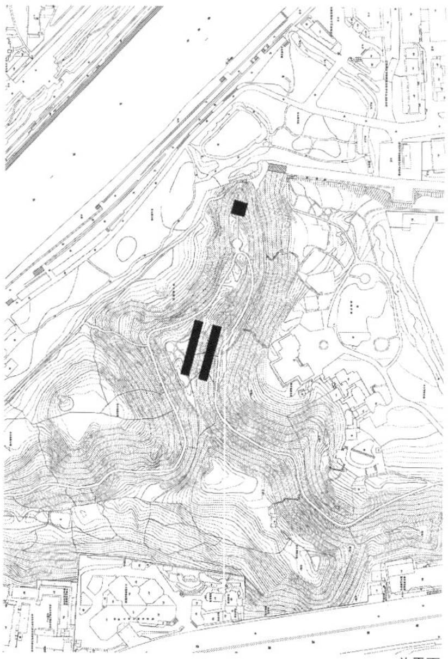
总平面

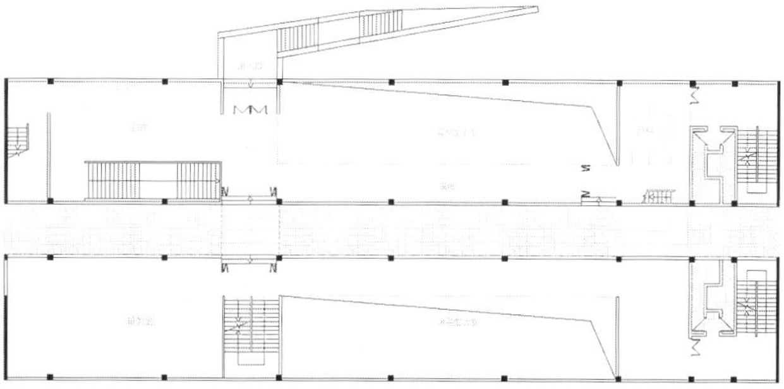
二层平面

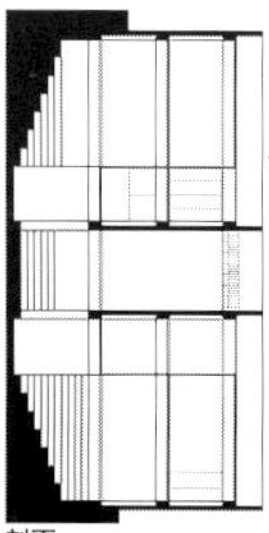
剖面

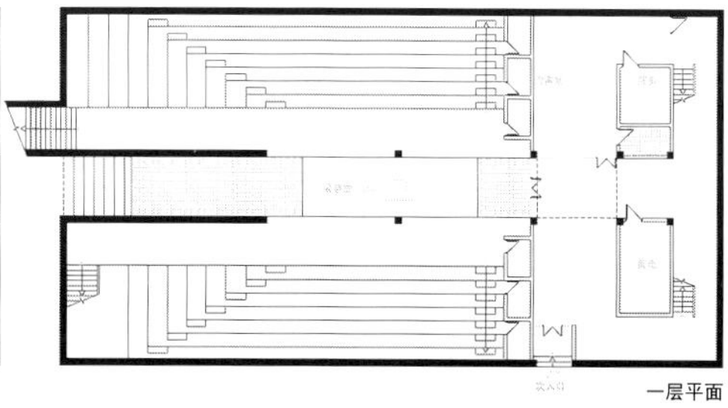
一层平面

基地位于山顶，面对一座碉堡。构思设计一条象征战争和死亡的“战壕”，直指碉堡，希望参观者在多次穿越它的体验中引发思考。

The site is on the top of the mountain facing a historic castle. The idea is to build a trench pointing to the castle, which stands for war and death. Thus the repeated action of walking through the trench may arise some kind of deep thinking.

和平纪念中心设计
Peace Memorial Center Design

作者：习超　指导老师：薛力

设计从纪念中心功能出发，分成世俗和神圣两个对峙而又联系的部分，中间的平台是冲突汇集的地方。利用山地组织交通，不同标高的入口将参观人流和工作人流区分开来。

Embarking from function, the memorial center is divided into two parts, the mundane and the sacred. As the two parts are both related and confronted, the platform between them becomes the place where confliction occurs. The organization of transportation depends on the mountainous terrain.

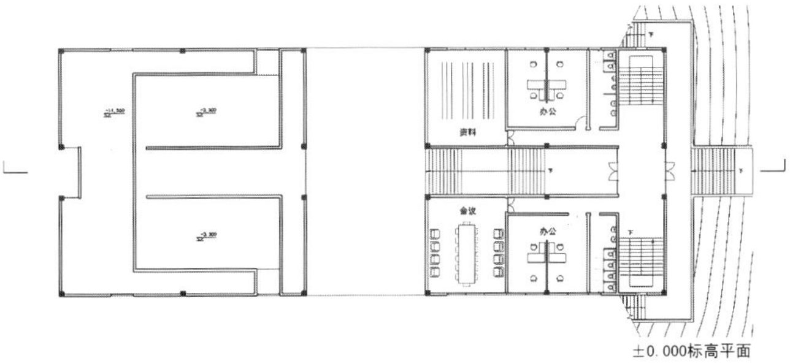

±0. 000标高平面

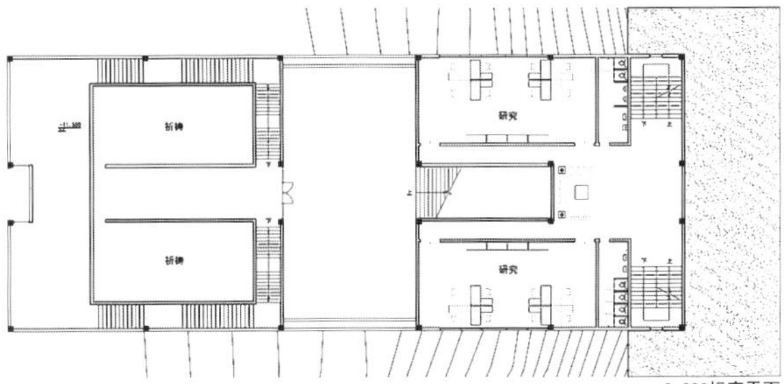

-3. 300标高平面

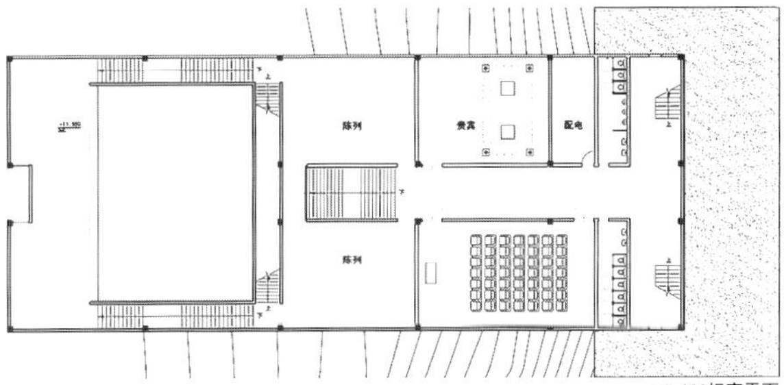

-6. 600标高平面

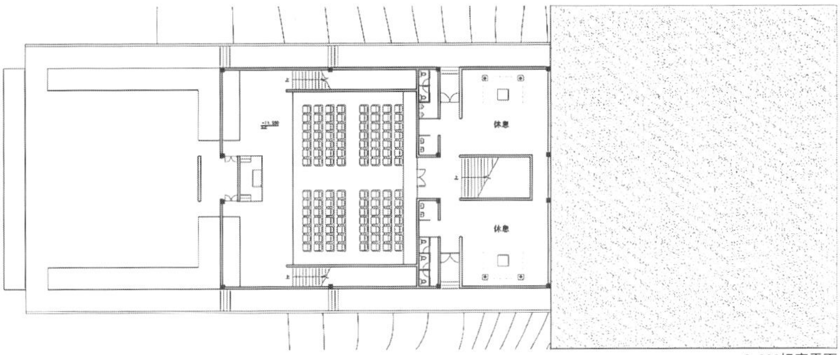

-9. 900标高平面

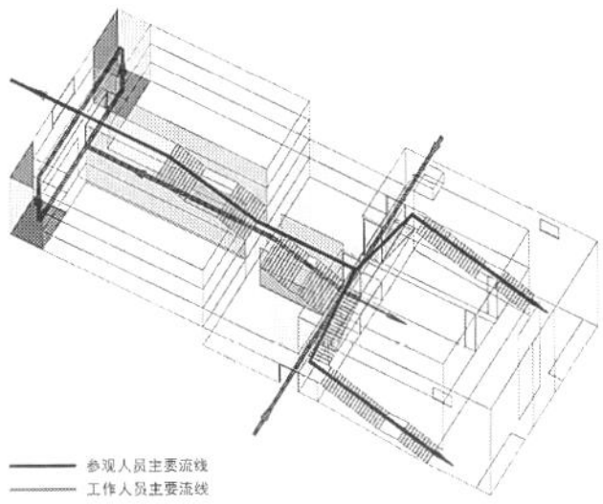

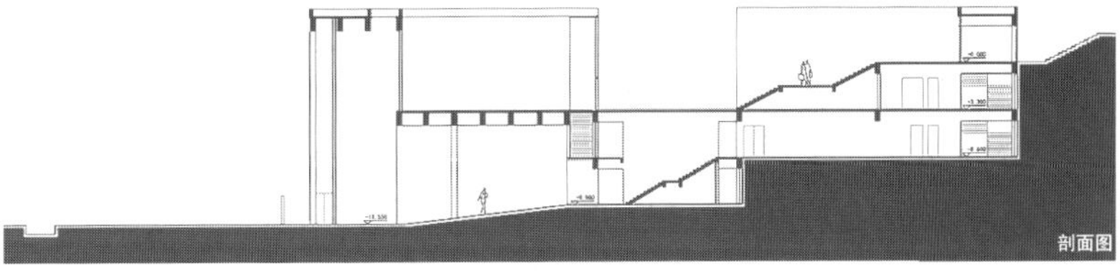

剖面图

和平纪念中心设计
Peace Memorial Center Design

作者：吴欢瑜　指导老师：薛力

它低低匍匐在山林中，白天将高度还给树木，夜晚用光为坡地勾勒边缘。这样的姿态暗合对和平的理解：世间光明时消隐，黑暗降临则刺破黑暗。

Never until the mankind
making Bird beast and flower
Fathering and all humbling darkness
Tells with silence the last light breaking
And the still hour
Is come of the sea tumbling in harness
——Dylan Thomas

"A Refusal To Mourn The Death, By Fire, Of A Child In London"

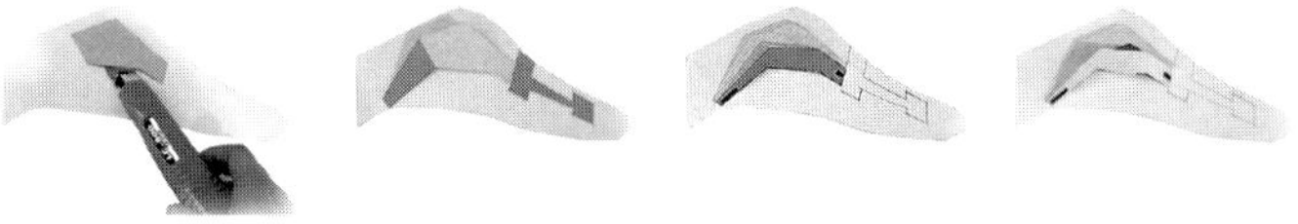

根据地形掀起主体区域　建筑贯通场地内外道路相连　切割出服务条与参观条以高度区分功能　根据建筑形体挖出光院，营造气氛

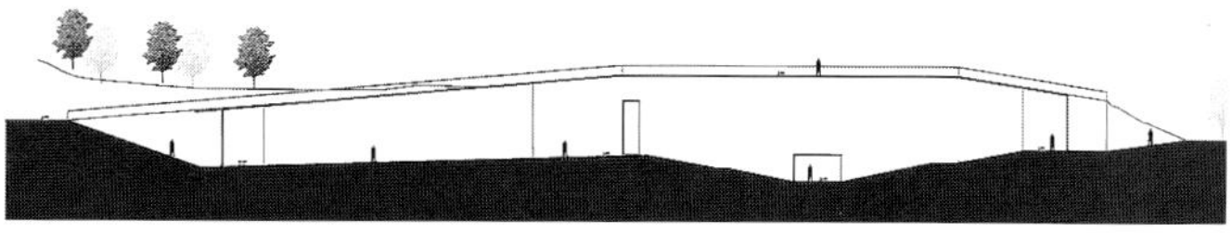

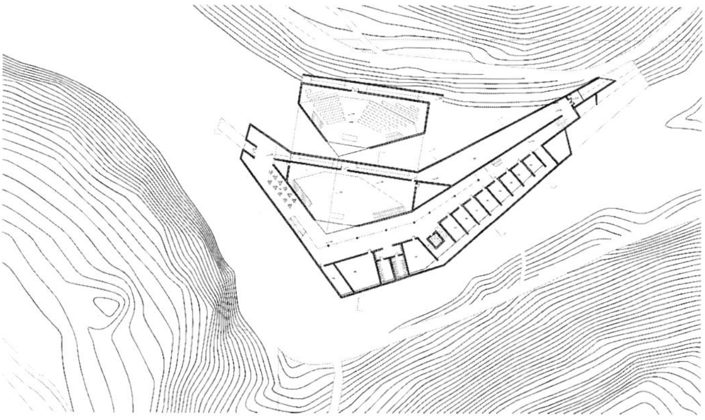

一层平面

铁路交通博物馆设计

Railway Transportation Museum Design

作者：姜汶林　指导老师：孙茹雁

获2007年“Revit杯”全国大学生建筑设计作业优秀奖

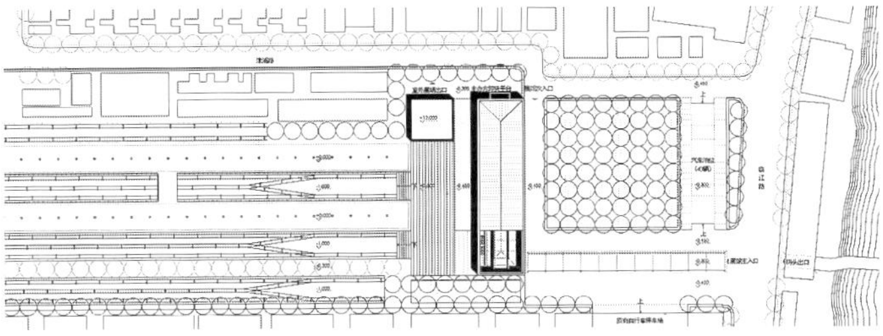

总平面

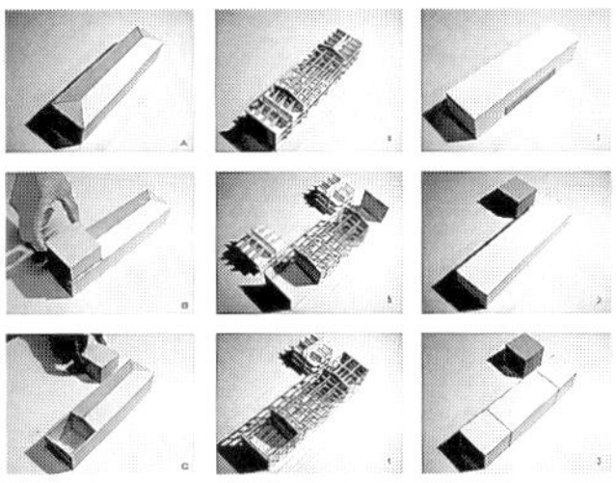

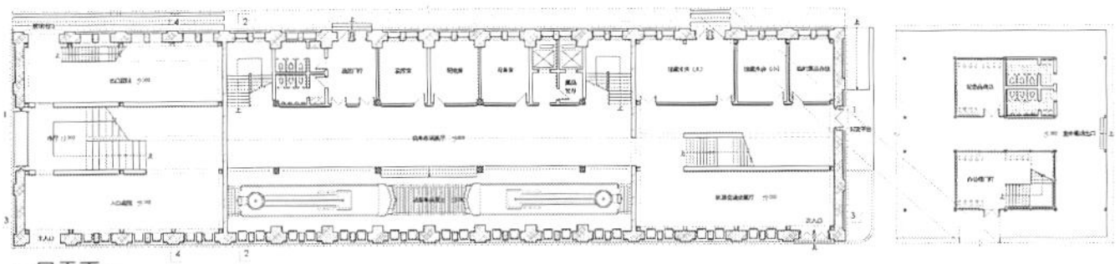

一层平面

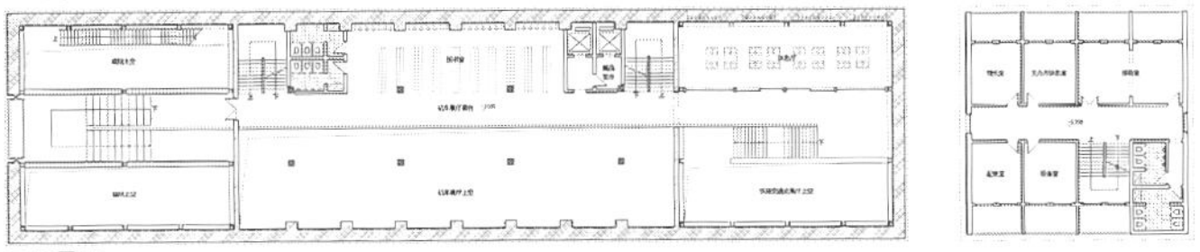

二层平面

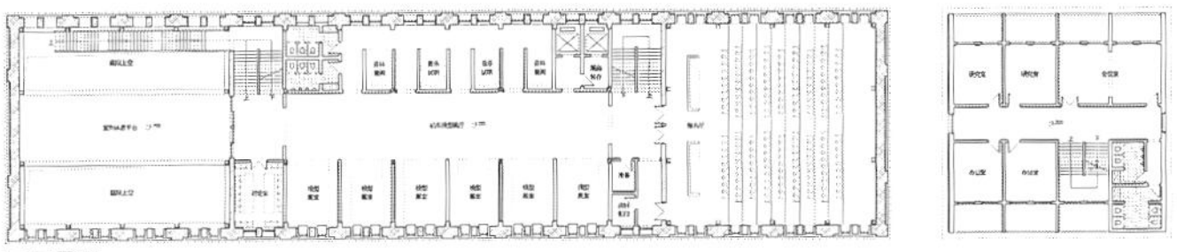

三层平面

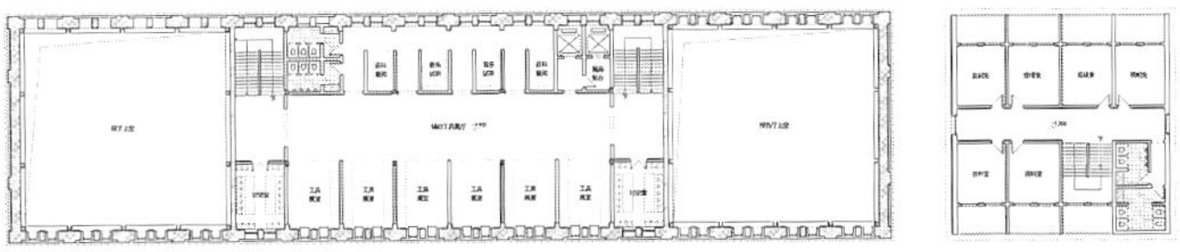

四层平面

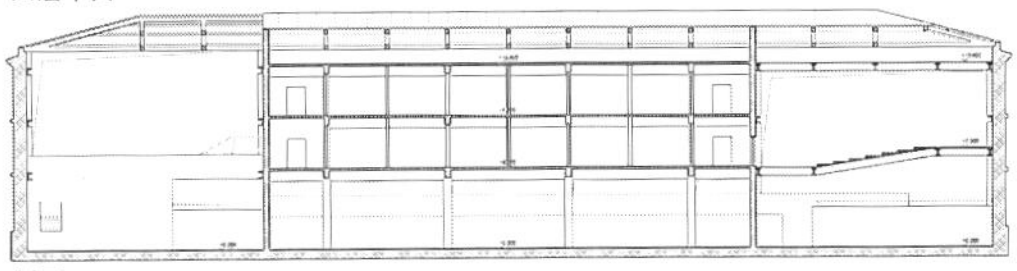

剖面3-3

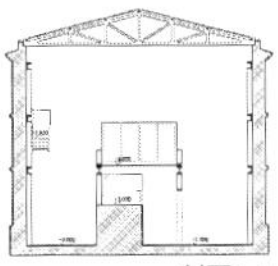

剖面1-1

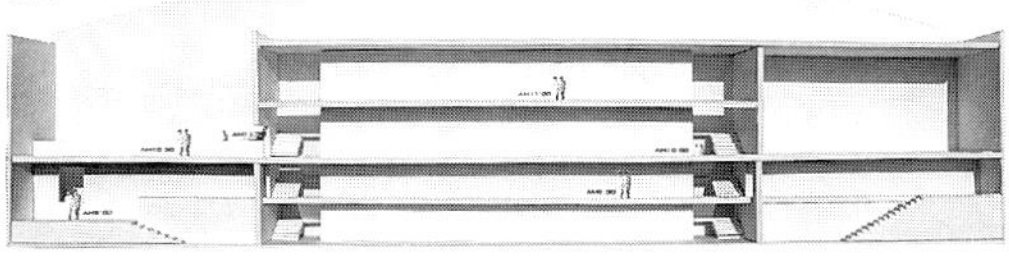

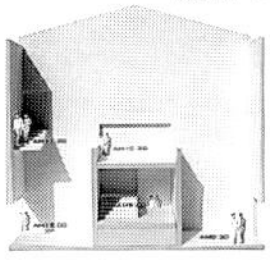

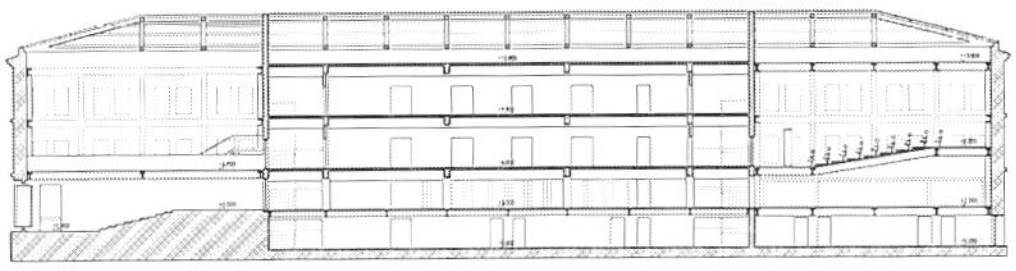

剖面4-4

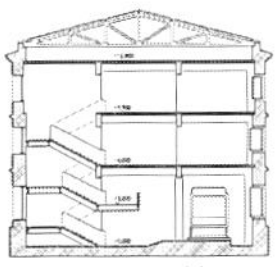

剖面2-2

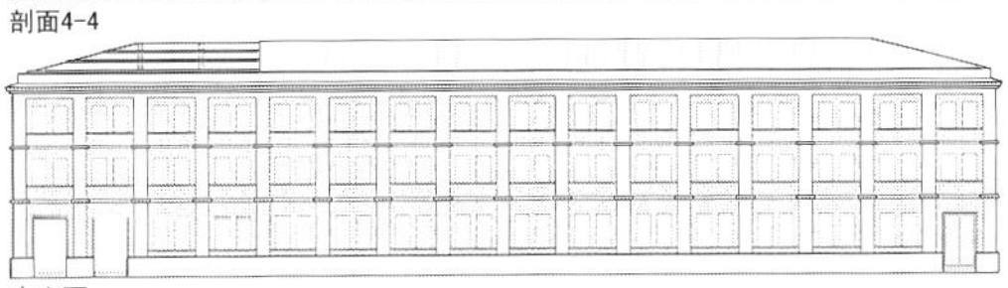

南立面

西立面

设计通过设置一个院子，将旧火车站由站前广场到月台广场的一条通畅流线打结，延长建筑的通行和体验时间。院子引导人流在横向的迂绕回弹中缓缓完成纵向的通行，从而完成由火车站到展览馆的功能置换。

Expressing the change of function in the way of change of circulation, a courtyard is set which would be experienced several times during the exhibition, leading people through visit.

铁路交通博物馆设计

Railway Transportation Museum Design

作者：李小溪　指导老师：刘捷

本方案尽可能保留老建筑，包括月台、站篷、拱廊、广场。同时把新建筑埋入地下，老建筑映射在新建筑之上，试图寻找新老建筑的一种关系。

This project is aimed to reserve the old railway transportation building as much as possible. As the new building is located underground reflecting the image of the old, a balance bewteen old and new is displayed and discussed.

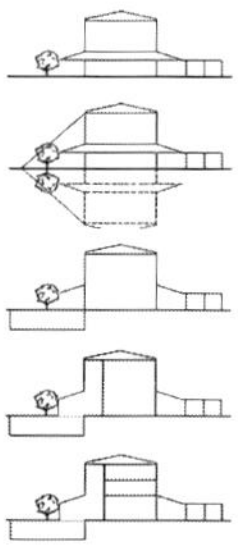

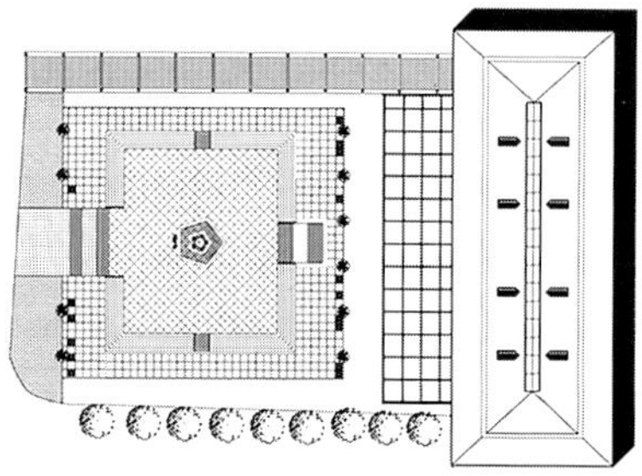

总平面

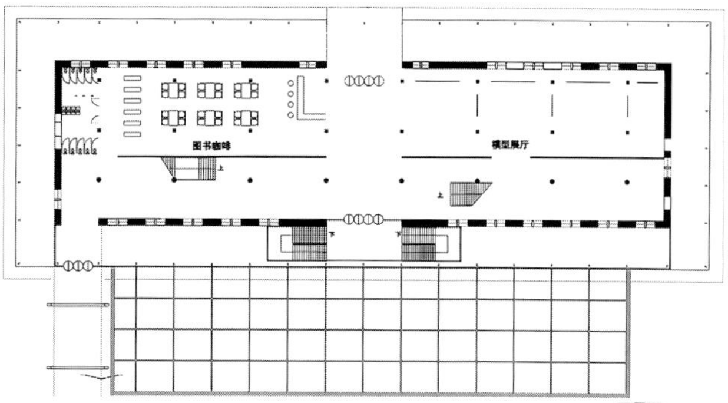

一层平面

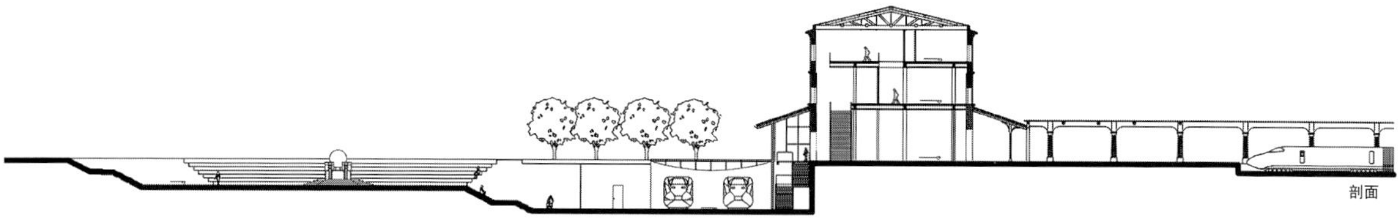

剖面

铁路交通博物馆设计
Railway Transportation Museum Design

作者：王伟实　指导老师：鲍莉
获2008年“Revit杯”全国大学生建筑设计作业优秀奖

老火车站位于一个具有历史感的城市语境中。方案通过对原有站墙肌理的变形与延续，组织建筑内外空间，在完成对旧站房功能置换的同时呼应了老城区的历史语境，整合了城市肌理。新建部分结构与老站房完全脱离，连续墙体既是主要结构构件也是空间展开的线索。

Located in a historical context, the project arranges indoors and outdoors by transforming the texture of the old wall of the station. The newly built structure is totally detached from the old. The continous wall is not only the structure but the way the space carries out as well.

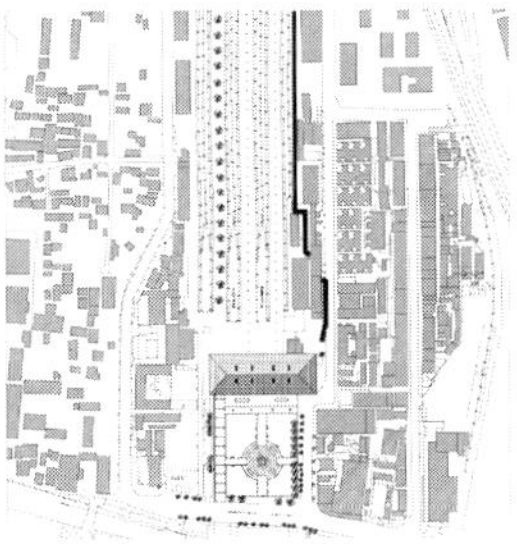

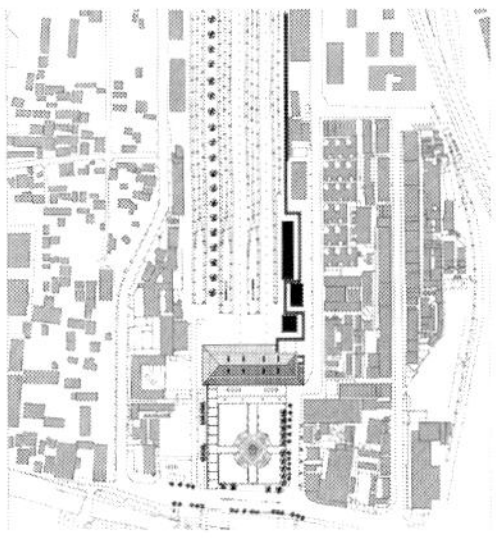

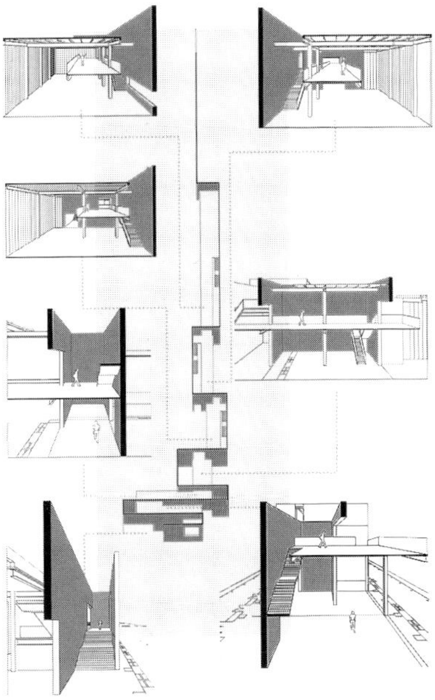

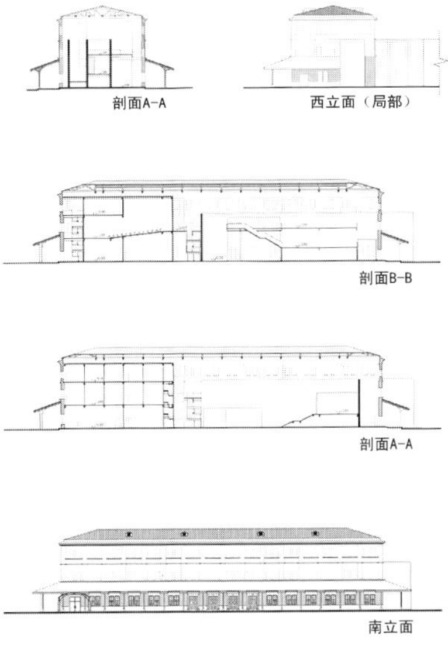

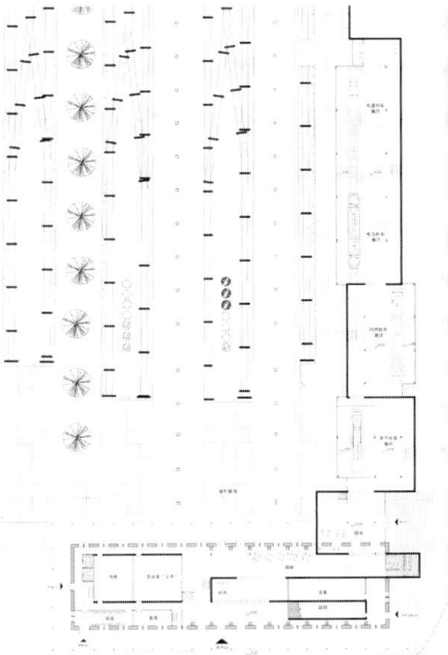
一层平面

文化艺术中心设计
Culture & Art Center Design

作者：何志鹏　指导老师：钱强
获2007年“Revit杯”全国大学生建筑设计作业优秀奖

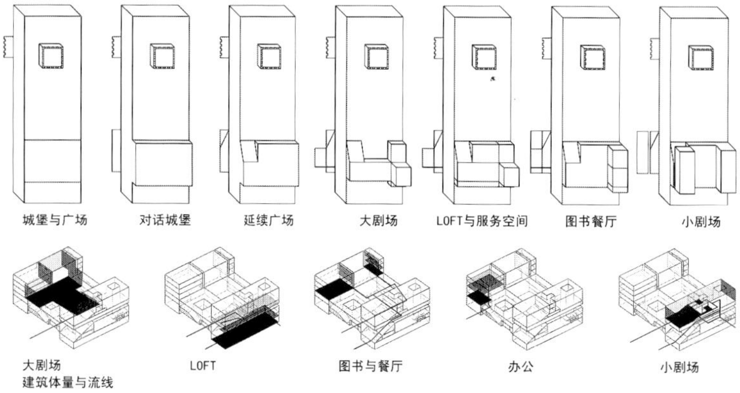

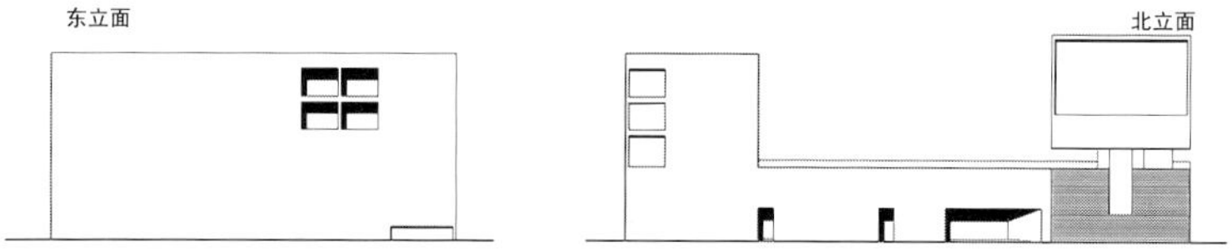

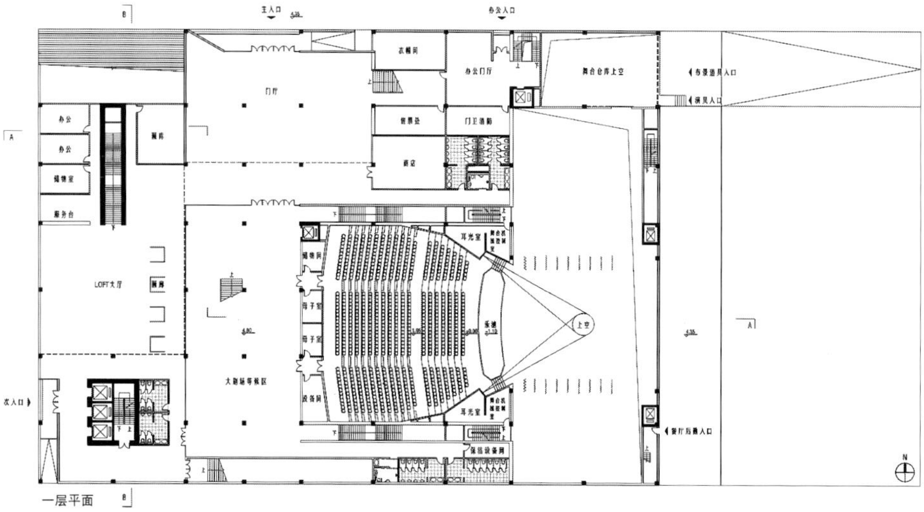
一层平面

关注建筑面对城市的姿态，以城市启动设计，通过平台对话城堡，以大台阶为连接，延续广场，组织建筑、城堡和广场三者为一整体，通过对功能体量的组织，建筑本身不只是剧场建筑，而是城市中的综合体。

Attention to the architecture's posture of facing the city, leads to the platform as a start of design, which expresses a dialogue to the castle and displays as an extension of the square at the same time. By the organization of functions and spaces, the architecture itself would be not only a theater building, but a urban compoundas well.

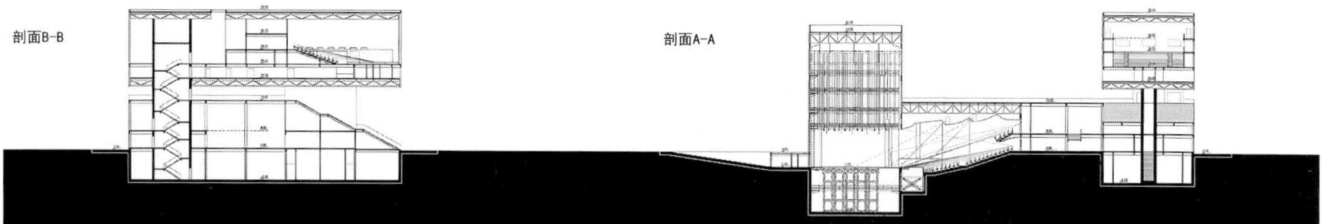

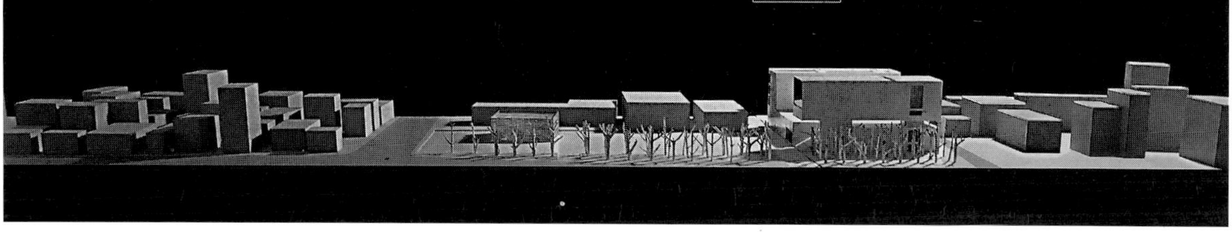

文化艺术中心设计
Culture & Art Center Design

作者：马晓君　指导老师：鲍莉

建筑，作为联系起喧嚣的商业街区和古老的历史文化氛围的载体，为周边环境添加新的观景点和兴奋点，功能流线也以此为基准展开，成为都市沙漠里的一片心灵绿洲。

Life can be expanded by music & art. The higher you go, the more your see. In this design, people slow their paces down, take a look around, and then realize that life is much more than just work. Definition of such a building is thus greenland among urban desert.

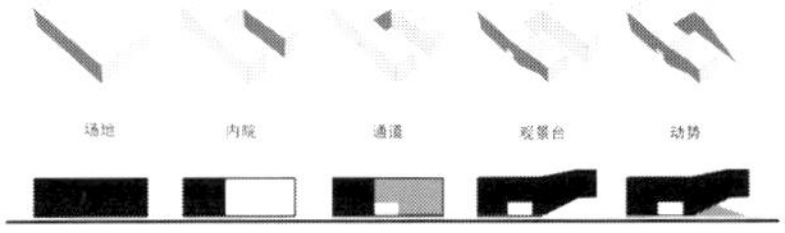

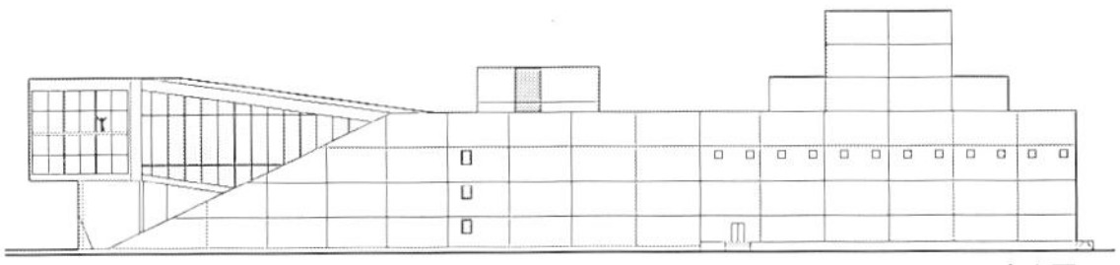
东立面

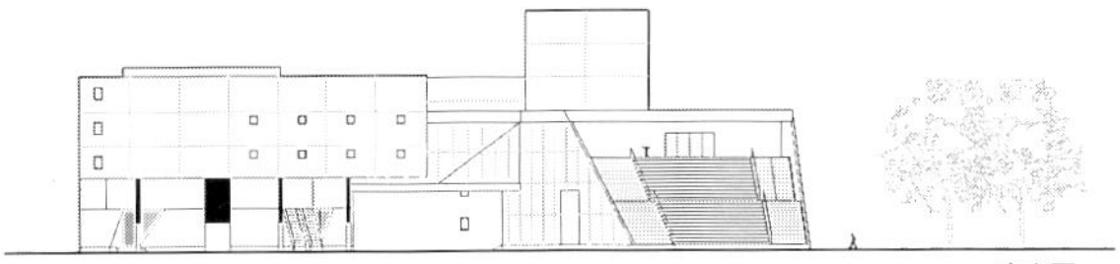
南立面

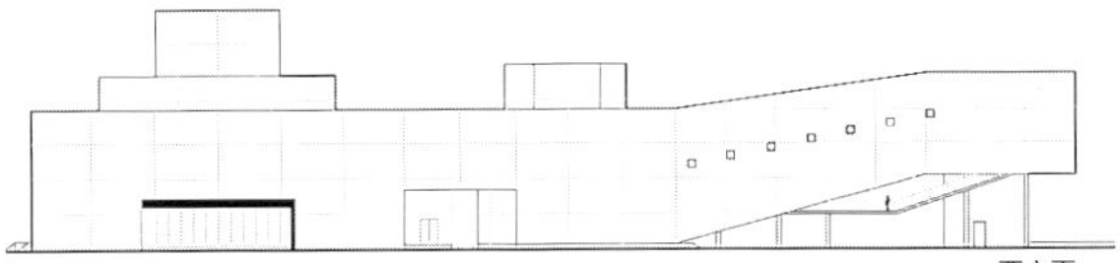
西立面

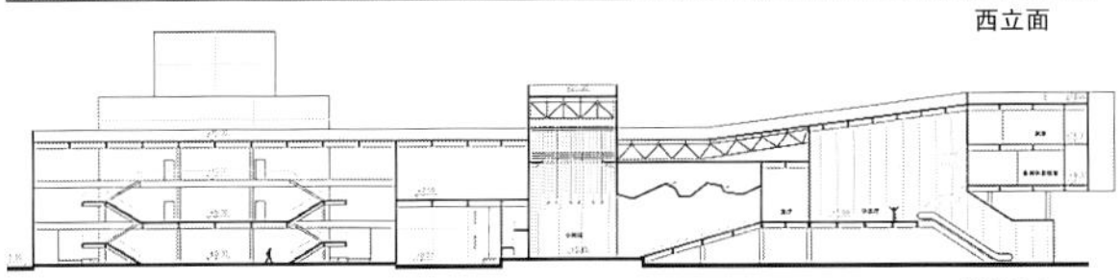
剖面B-B

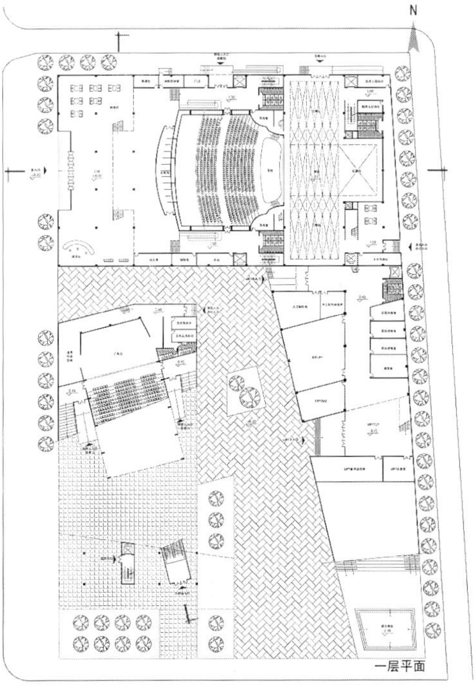

一层平面

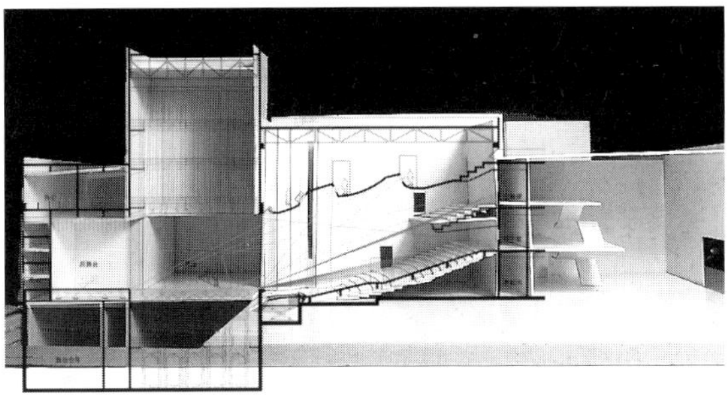

在餐厅远眺玄武门

小剧场入口透视

文化艺术中心设计
Culture & Art Center Design

作者：王欣　指导老师：夏兵
获2008年“Revit杯”全国大学生建筑设计作业优秀奖

设计构思从基地周边环境出发，目的在于将周围分别从广场、居民区、停车场三个主要来向的人流引入建筑内的街道，以提高该大型公建的亲和力。西华门城堡与剧场间的广场也纳入了设计范畴，力求创造出亲切活跃的氛围，形成城堡与广场、剧院三者之间的互动，吸引市民参与其间。

The design aims at attracting citizens around the site to ramble across the building, whose smooth skin creates a series of continuous space experience.A dialogue among square, castle and the center is set so that the new building will become part of the urban sequence within the site.

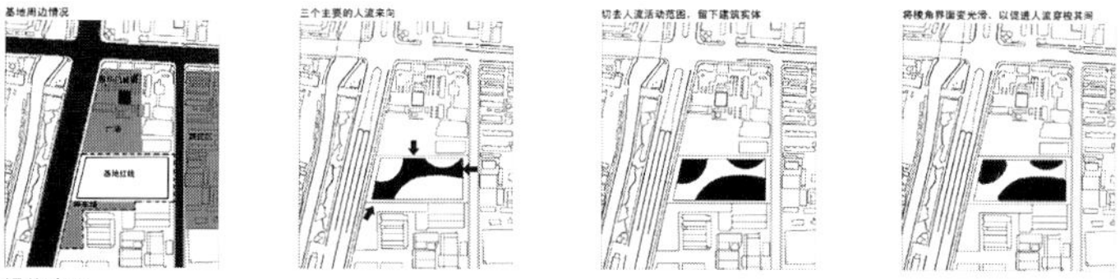

操作步骤

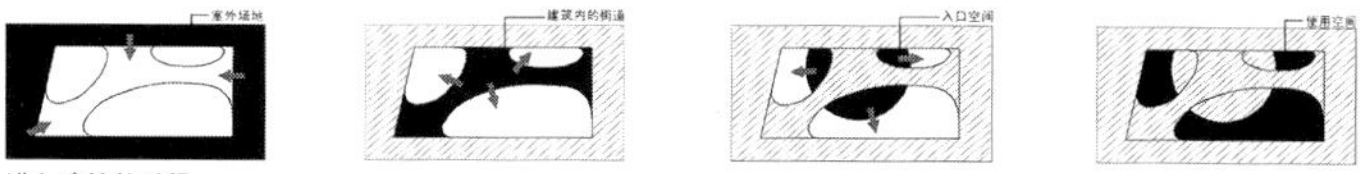
进入建筑的过程

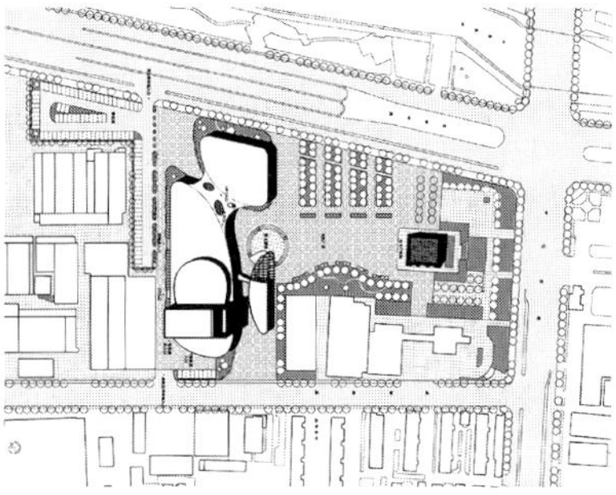
总平面

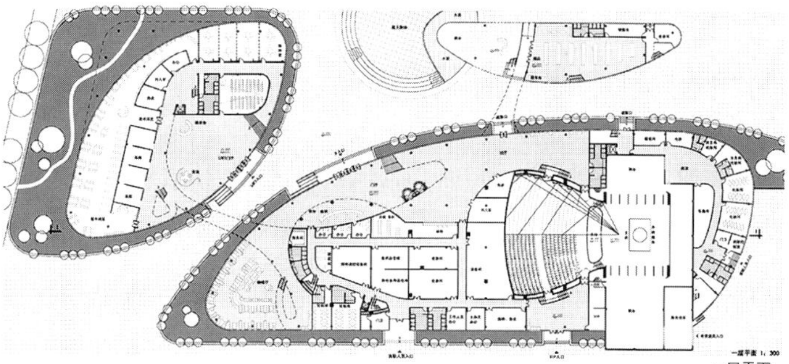
一层平面

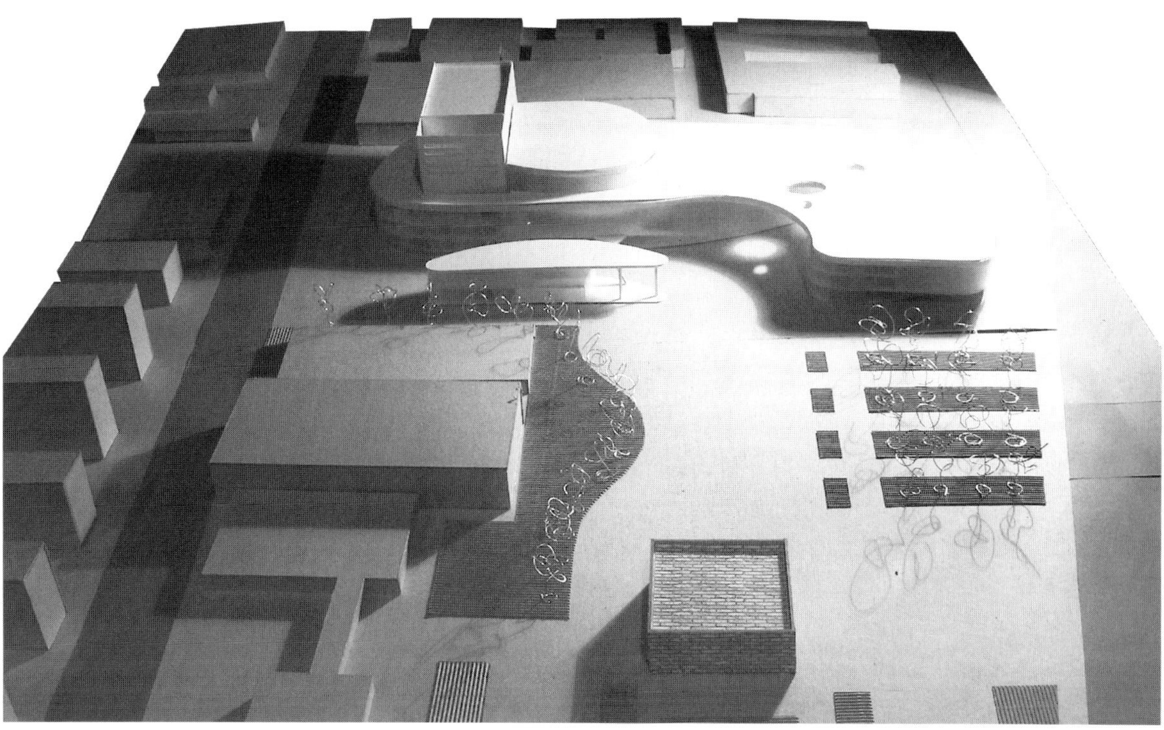

汉中门市民广场设计
Hanzhong Gate Square Design

作者：翟玉章　指导老师：王承慧

广场基地位于南京明城墙风光带西侧，现保留石城门、瓮城等重要文物。设计以凸显南京历史文化名城风貌特色的“山水城林”等元素为广场景观中心。分为西部（城市展示）、中部（静思纪念）和东部（市民生活）三部分。在强调传统轴线同时加入“信息轴线”，将景观串联。

The Hanzhong Gate Square locates in the west of scenery of Nanjing Ming dynasty wall. The design highlights history and culture of Nanjing with elements such as hill, water, wall and forest. The topic of the square is divided into three parts: west ,city show; center, meditation memorial; east, citizen life.

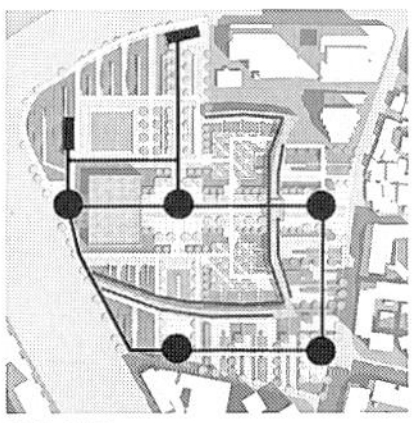
流线分析

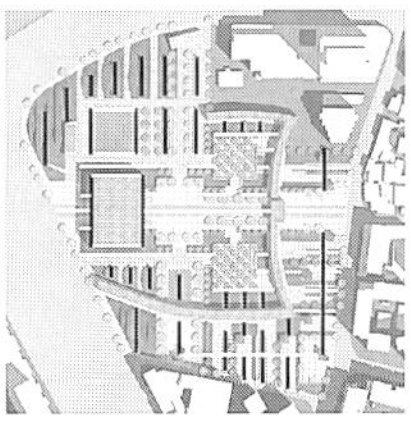
线性景观“阡陌”

活动场地

传统轴线 光带砖铺

信息轴转

荷塘叠水 历史追忆

城墙基址 重叠绿坡

广场总平面图

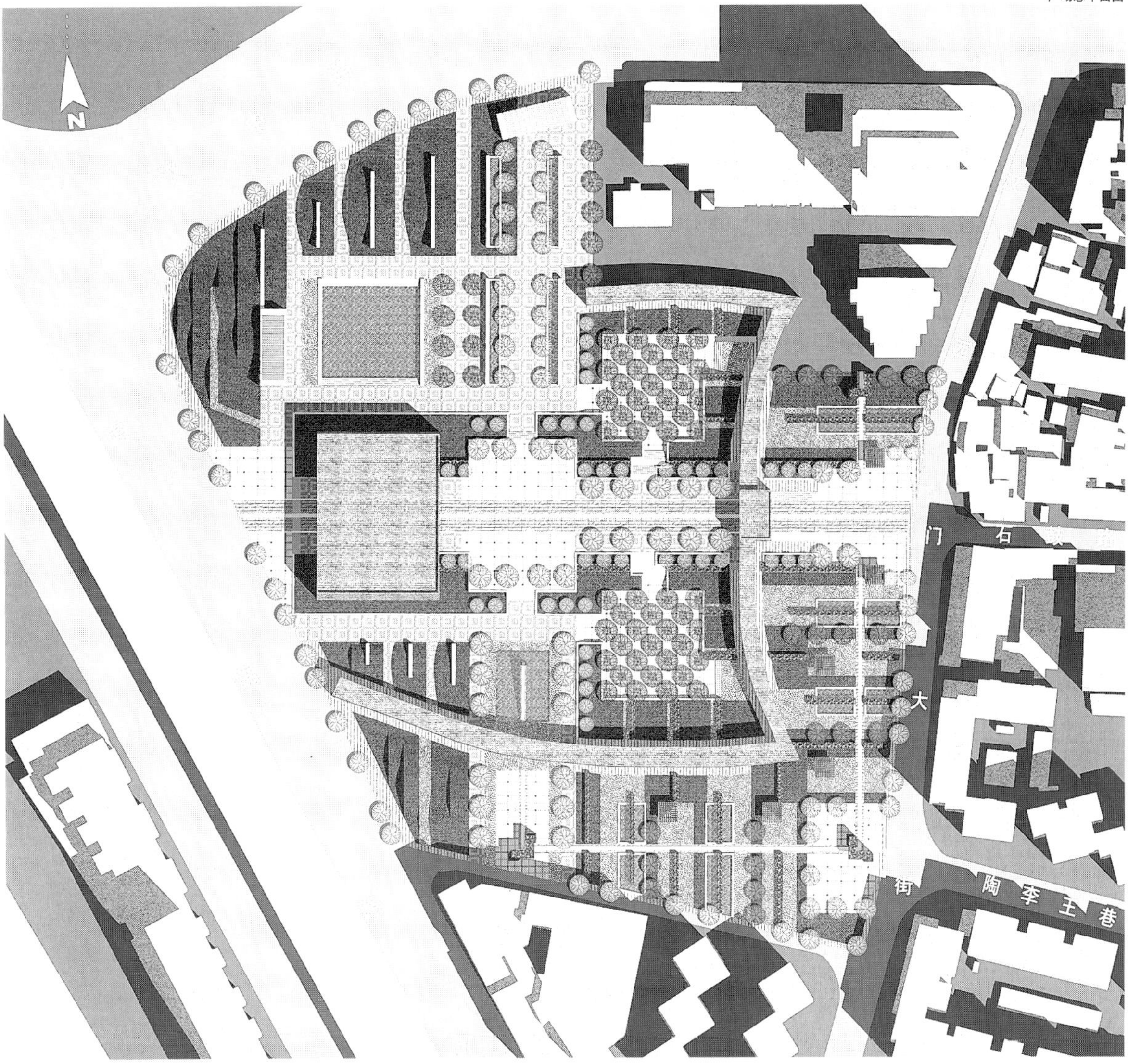

住区规划
Resident Area Plan

作者：周邹　指导老师：权亚玲

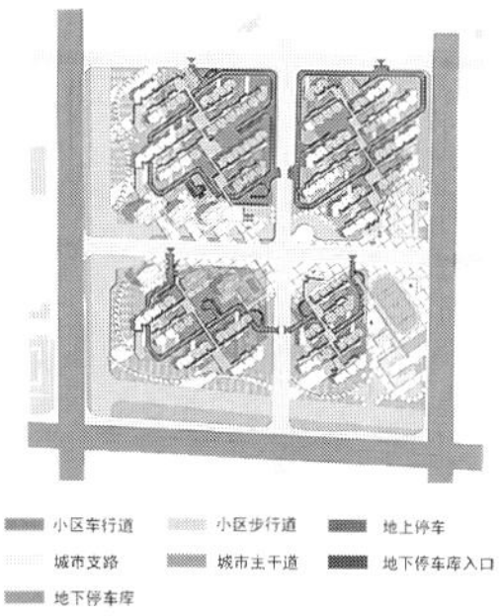

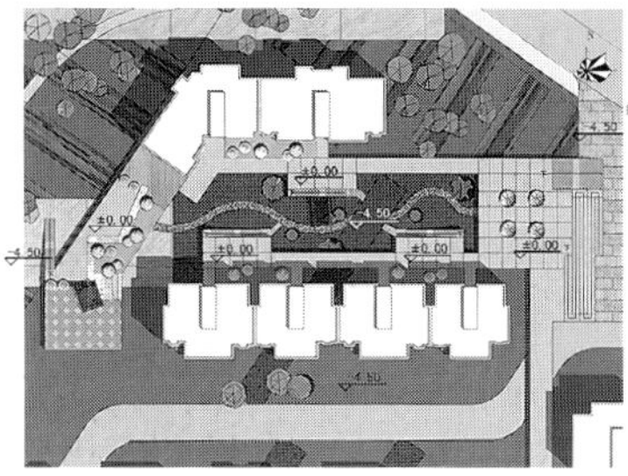

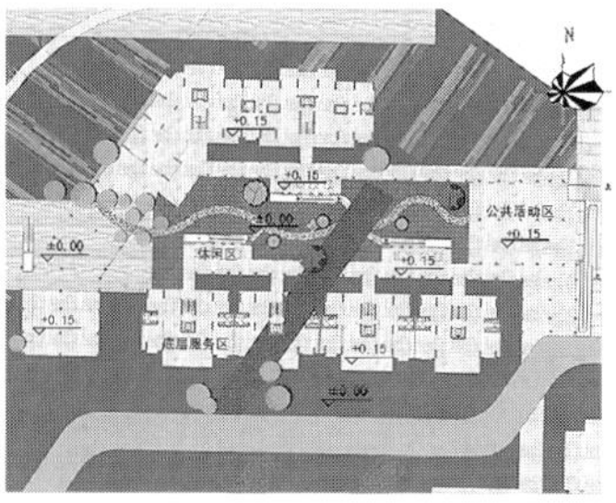

基地位于南京河西新城，靠近新城中心，毗邻河西中央商务区，特殊的区位决定了此住区应是面向城市的国际化住区，应具有很强的开放性。所以本设计力求打破“小家”概念，营造向城市开放的“大家”。

本设计采用了住房底层架空的方式，使住区土地的公共使用面积大幅增加。引入城市自然景观资源，借助底层架空，使城市与住区、住区内部的景观互相渗透，并形成一个水平向的开放空间网络，增加开放性。

住区主要步行道架空并与车行道分离（步行道为住区居民服务，车行道也作为外部人员活动的主要流线），减少干扰。其次在步行系统中设置不同等级的活动平台，与架空层活动场地构成了住区的垂直活动空间系统。

住区规划
Resident Area Plan

作者：秦静　指导老师：巢耀明

该基地位于紫金山脚下，所以借助地形，营造自己的山水小环境。该绿色空间不仅服务于本小区，且向城市开放，服务于城市公共空间。交通模式上侧重于对步行者的考虑，步行环线与水系景观交融。

This site lies at the foot of Purple Mountain,so the typology is used to create a green public space,which not only serves the residence but also the city doing huge good to urban public space. In addition, the pedestrian circle is being focused on which meets the water system on many junctions.

设计演变

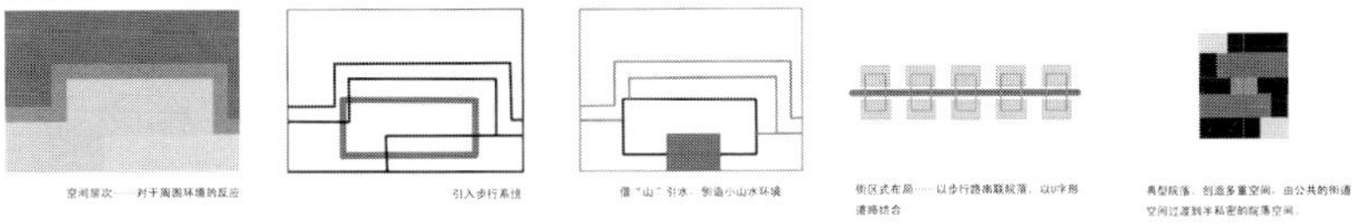

系统分析

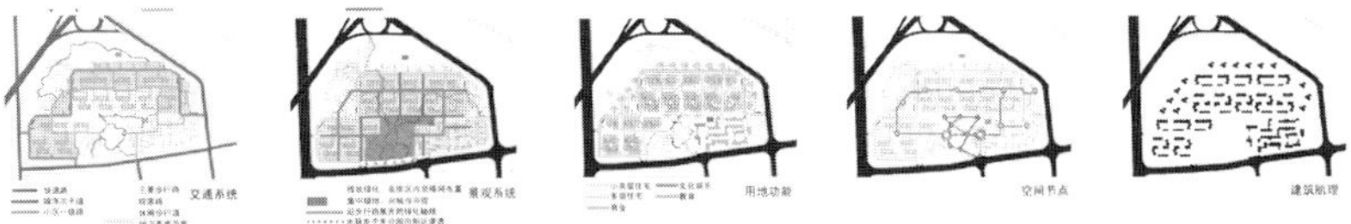

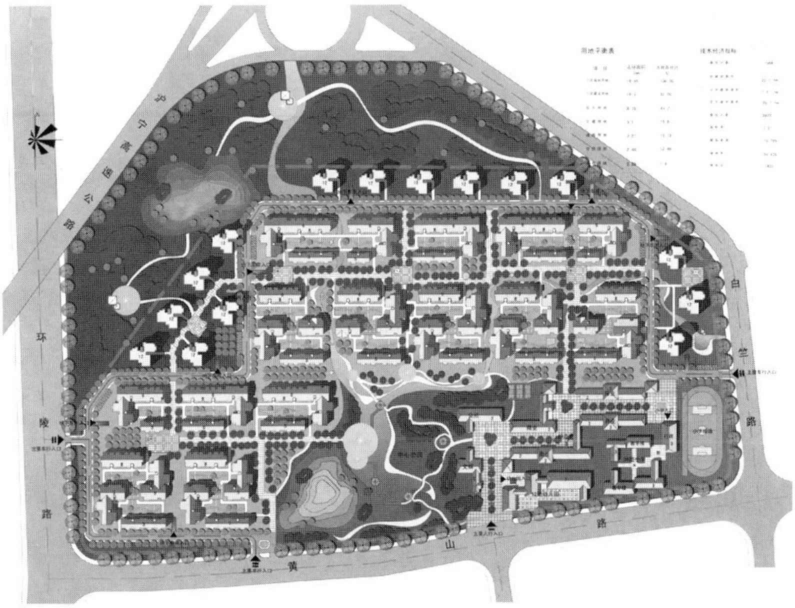

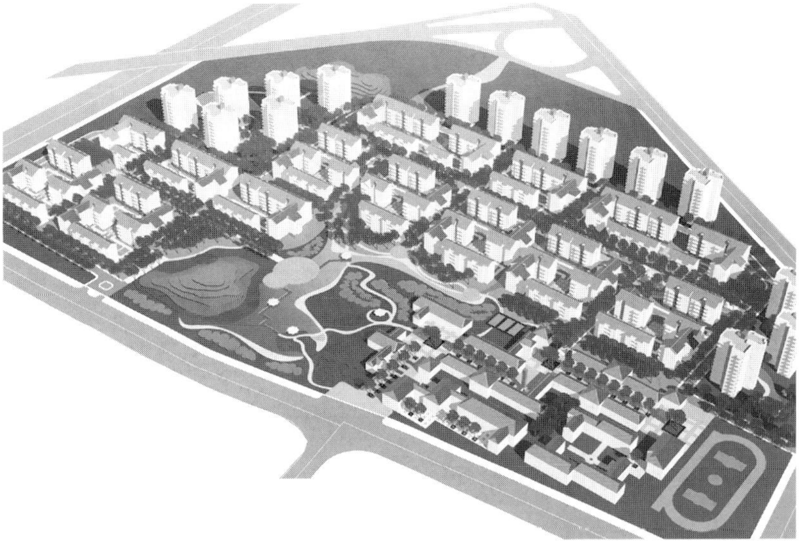

幕府30工园厂房改造设计
Mufu 30 Factory Renovation Design

作者：厉鸿凯　指导老师：李哲

幕府30工业区坐落在南京城幕府山脚下，旧为南京客车厂，现改为艺术创意园区。园区内废弃厂房的牛腿柱很漂亮，方案的着眼点也就在此。创造不同的高差，牛腿柱的各部分可以有不同的作用，如走廊、桌子、坐椅。通过对旧事物不同的体验，唤起一个年代或一段时期的记忆。透过厂房内高高的侧窗，光线打在牛腿柱上，穿过取景框入射到中庭。

Mufu30 industry area is located at the foot of the Mufu Mountain of Nanjing, which used to be the bus company of Nanjing. However, it currently has been reformed into an area for art. Columns of the room are significantly nice, which results in my concept as to create different levers to experience the columns, such as corridors, tables and seats. With these kinds of experiences, the memory of the old days is evoked. In addition, via the windows of the roof, light flushes onto the columns, then into the yard.

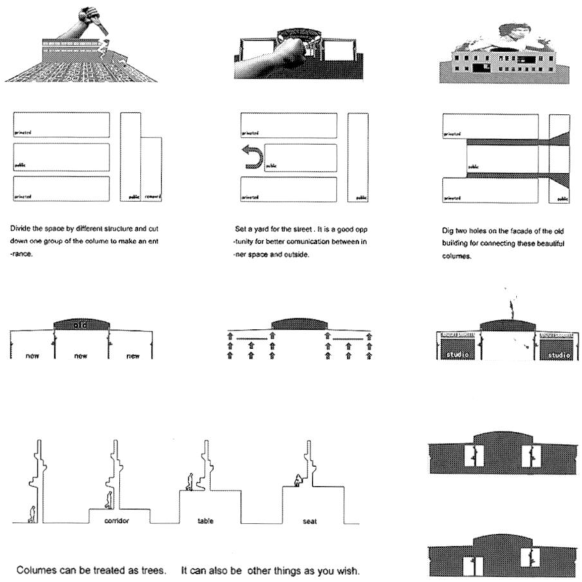

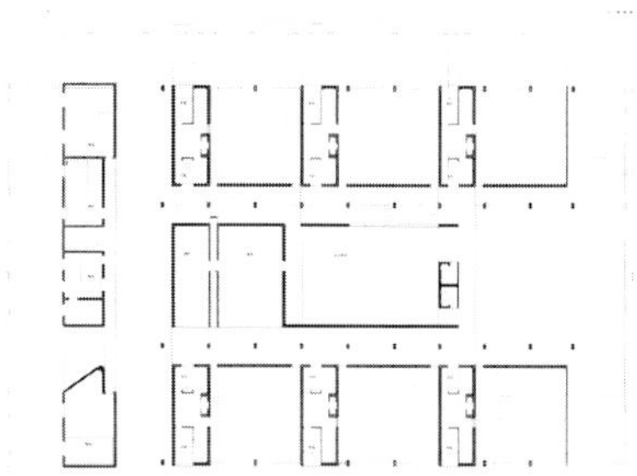

二层平面

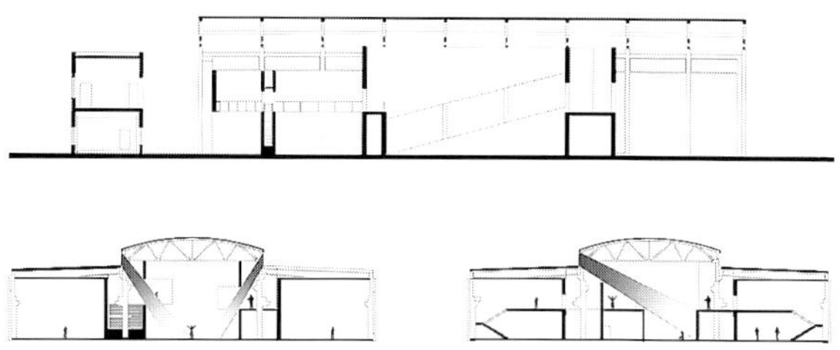

幕府30工园厂房改造设计
Mufu 30 Factory Renovation Design

作者：后文君　指导老师：陈晓扬

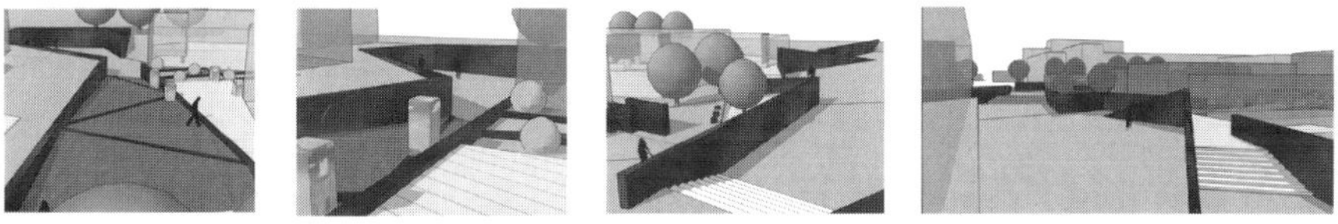

环境设计分成三个区域：左侧为安静的冥想空间，右侧为画廊、工作室等来客的活动空间，北部为公共交通区域

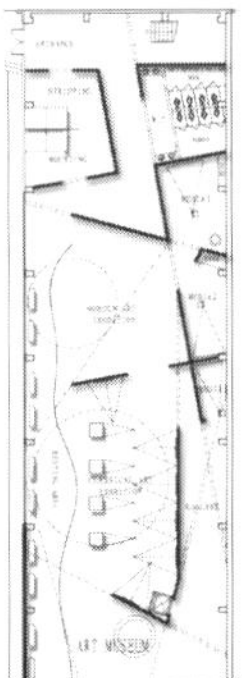

夹层可以作为小型平面作品展，也可以参与底层的行为艺术，换个角度欣赏装置等，为创作提供了更多的可能

夹层底部作为暗室，可以为现代的影像灯光装置等艺术形式提供空间，同时它本身也是一种很好的景观

入口的通高大厅为大型主题装置提供空间，旁边的纱帘隔断了空间，限定了休息区域，同时防止直射光

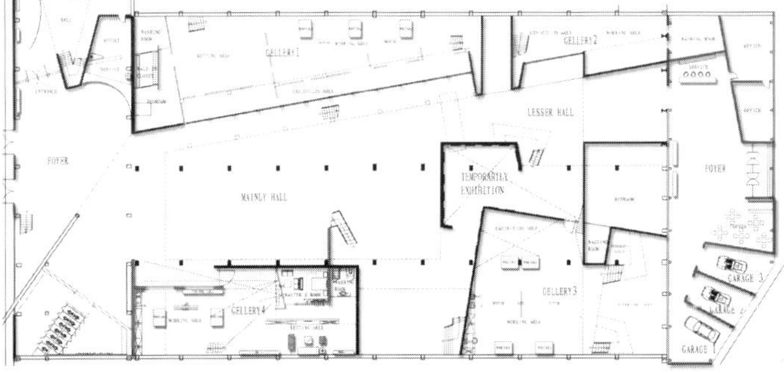

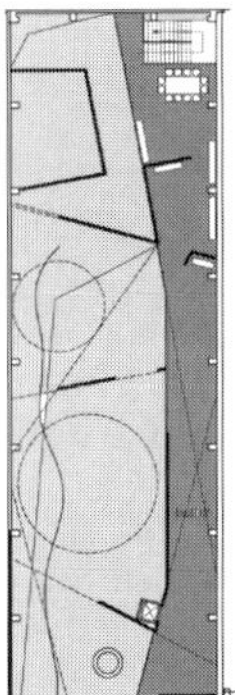

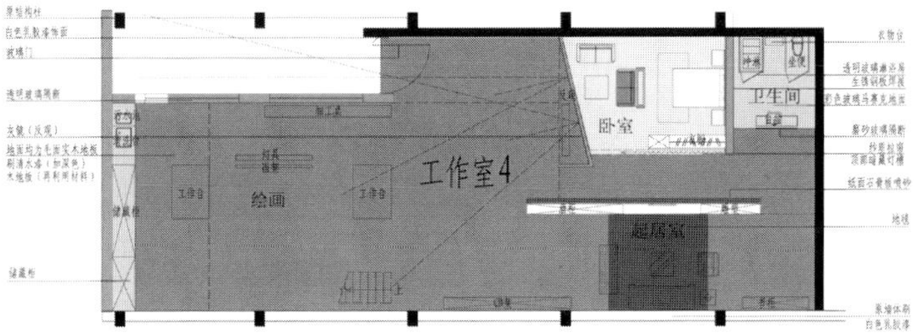

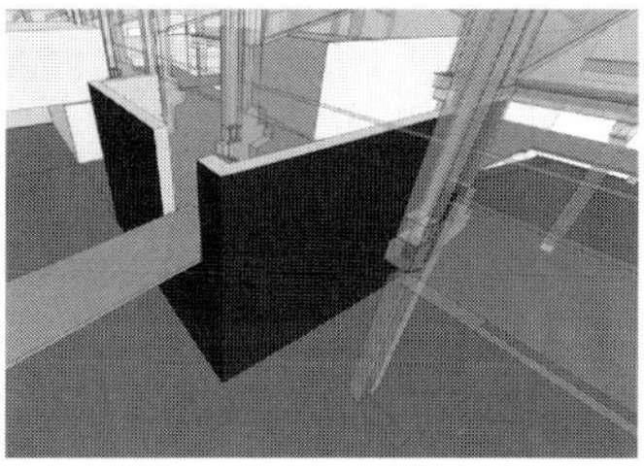

大厅中央厚重质感的体块与黑色挑出的连廊体量高大，构成视觉的焦点，能够迅速吸引观者的视线，同时视线也不能逾越。好奇感使人不自觉地绕过这一体块，体块的后面则是光照较强，且以暖光源为主的一个临时展示空间

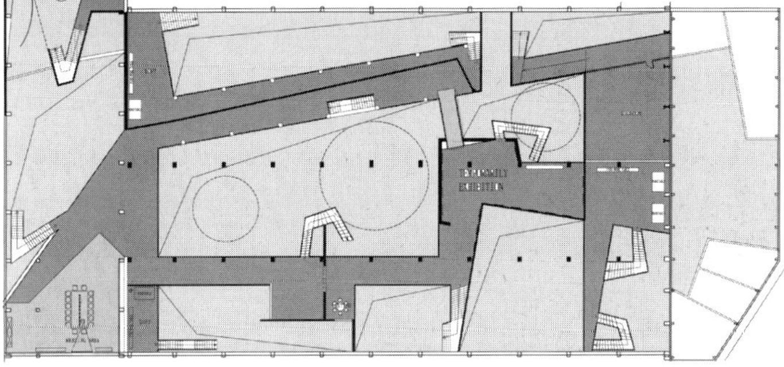

专卖店设计
Franchised Store Design

作者：后文君　指导老师：李哲

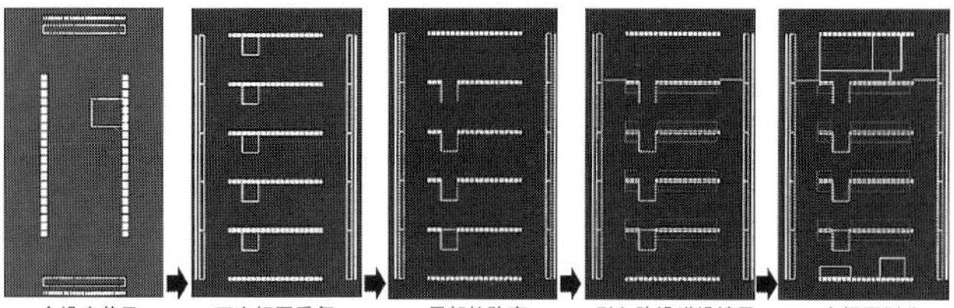

一个设定单元　五次相同重复　局部的改变　引入陈设增设镜子　空间再划分

结合功能，尝试将空间切片，以寻求独特的空间感受。室内以深色的产品形象墙纸为基调，辅以木本色家具

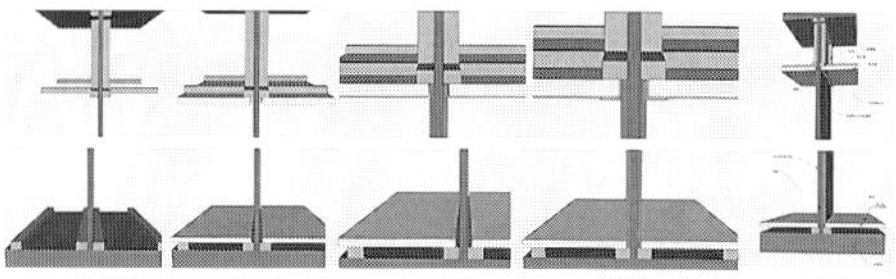

结构构建　基层　饰面　收边　成型

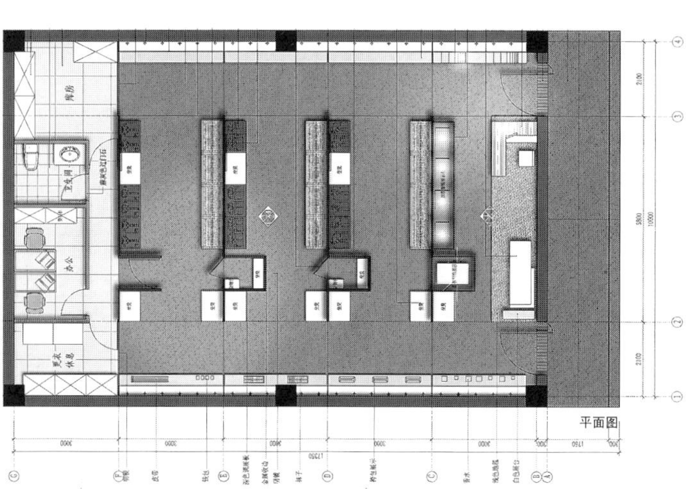

平面图

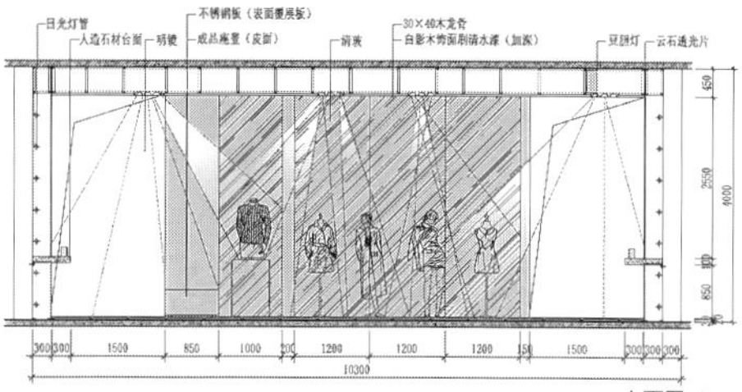

立面图 1

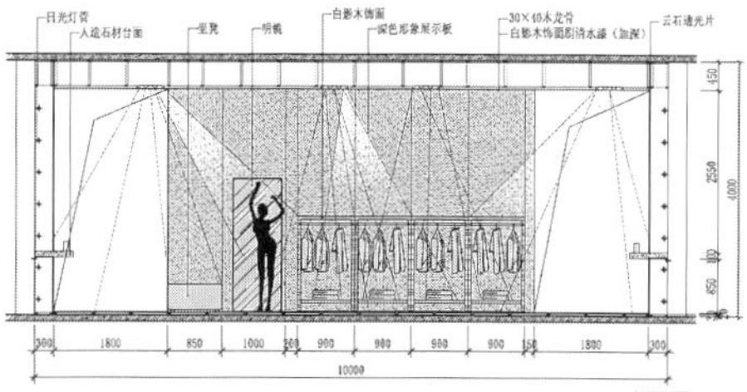

立面图 2

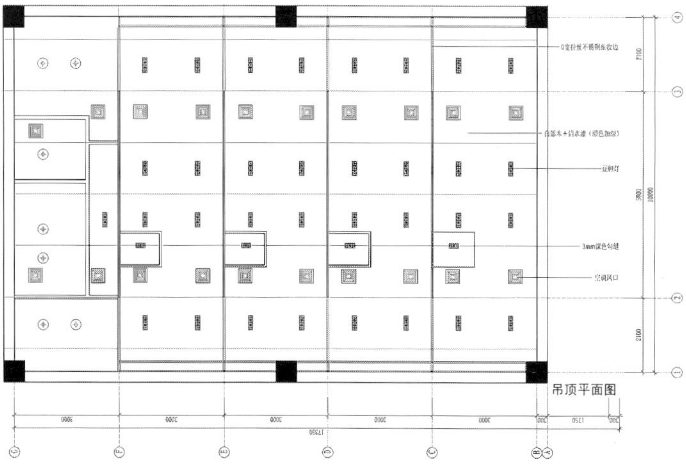

吊顶平面图

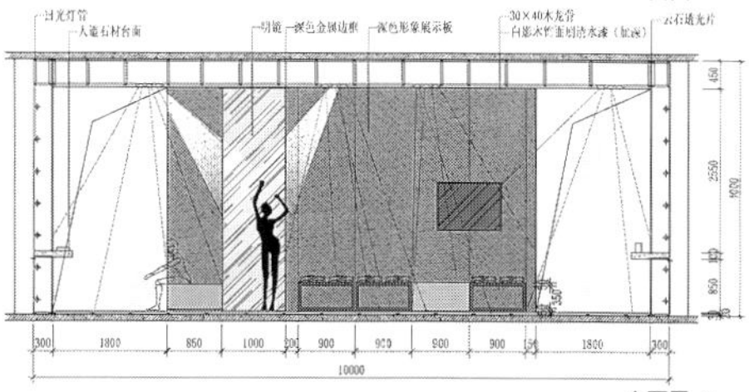

立面图 3

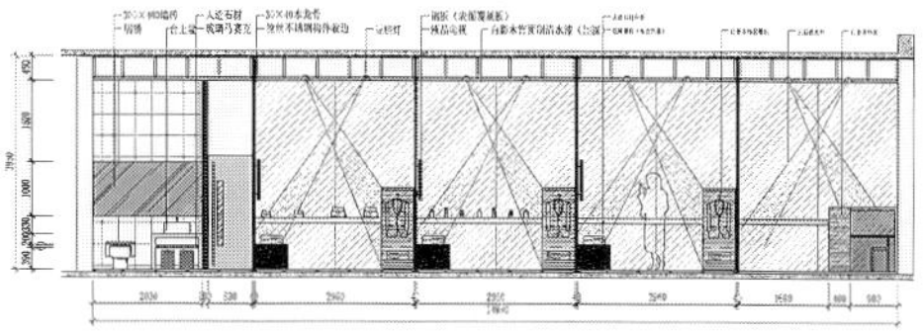

立面图 4

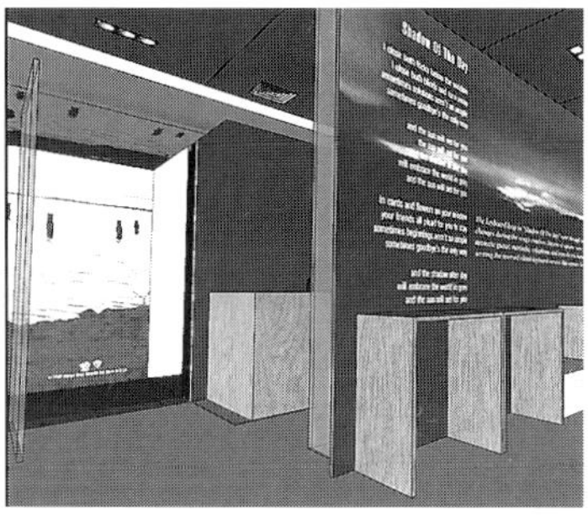

四年级设计课程教学大纲
Compendium_4th Year

建筑设计

一、课程的性质与目的

本课程是建筑学专业必修的一门最重要的专业主干课。

本课程的教学目的，是提高设计教学质量，形成具有研究性和个性化的特色教学，建构“开放性、多样化、个性化”的教学模式。鼓励学生在前三年设计课的基础上，在四年级多样化的综合教学结构中，学习和认识城市设计、住区设计、大型公建以及其他重要学科方向的基本理论和设计方法，重点培养综合设计能力，培育创新思维和设计研究能力的发展，形成东大建筑设计教学的特色。

四年级设计教学总的特色可以概括为：教授工作室制、教学课题多样化、评图开放化。

二、课程内容的教学要求

四年级设计教学的主题是“城市与建筑”，全学年设置四大类课题为基本知识模块，即：城市设计类、住区设计类、大型公建类和学科交叉类。该四大类课题同时开设，没有前后关系。学生在一个学年四个课题的选择中，城市设计类、住区设计类和大型公建类为必选，除此以外学生可选择学科交叉类课题或以上三类课题再选一次。学生不能选同一教授工作室三次或三次以上。各类课题的教学要求如下：

“城市设计类”：必须包含对设计地段的调查研究，应有城市或地段的总平面图、基本的城市结构分析图等，不能仅是一个形体设计。

“住区设计类”：研究人居环境的问题，必须包含对市场和开发的调查研究，包含住宅设计的基本要素，了解住宅和居住区设计规范，设计规模和深度相适配。

“大型公建类”：认识大型公建与城市环境及景观的关系，掌握大型公建的设计规律和造型处理，必须具有一定的技术含量（高层、大跨、钢结构等），掌握相应的技术规范（消防、设备、结构等），设计规模和深度相适配。

“多学科类”：这类课题一般邀请建筑系以外的教师承担，要求凸显一个方面的主题，如历史遗产保护、景观设计与规划、可持续性发展、构造技术等。

三、上机实习要求

四年级建筑设计教学要求在整个教学过程中学生的设计推进、完成和表达均采用电脑辅助设计手段和手工绘图及手工模型两种并行的手段，学生上机贯穿整个教学过程。

四、能力培养的要求

1. 设计分析能力的培养：主要培养对城市环境、居住空间、大型公共空间的分析方法和能力。
2. 设计综合能力的培养：在前三年设计基础教学的基础上，四年级设计教学着重培养学生对大型复杂项目的综合设计能力。
3. 技术设计能力的培养：除了综合设计能力以外，四年级设计教学的另一个重点是培养学生的技术设计能力，使学生初步掌握各项基本设计规范以及建筑设计中其他专业的技术要求，结合以上知识将设计深入到细部设计层次。
4. 设计表达能力的培养：进一步学习模型、电脑和图纸等基本设计媒介对设计思维的推动和表达，学习根据设计的内容和特点选择合适的表达方式，设计表达的形式。
5. 设计研究能力的培养：四年级的设计课题要求具有一定的研究性，旨在培养学生独立思考、发现和研究设计问题的能力，引导学生对与课题相关的内容进行一定的理论思考。

五、建议学时分配

课 程 内 容	讲 课	课程设计	上 机
城市设计类课题	32	224	256
住区设计类课题	32	224	256
大型公建类课题	32	224	256
学科交叉类课题或以上三类任一课题	32	224	256

注：各课程设计教学中的学时分配由任课教师根据教案自行决定。

六、考核方式

总评成绩＝每学期两次课程设计成绩的平均数

每次课程设计成绩的构成如下：

中期成绩（任课教师评定）占30%；

期末成绩（任课教师评定）占20%；

评图成绩（评图评委评定）占50%。

七、教材及参考书

教材：

1. 王建国. 现代城市设计理论和方法. 南京：东南大学出版社，1991
2. 王建国. 城市设计. 南京：东南大学出版社，1999
3. 齐康. 城市环境规划设计与方法. 北京：中国建筑工业出版社，1997
4. J Barnett. An Introduction to Urban Design. New York: Harper & Row，1982
5. Shirvani Hamid. The Urban Design Process. New York: Van Nostrand Reinhold Company, 1981
6. 彭一刚. 建筑空间组合论. 第2版. 北京：中国建筑工业出版社，2001
7. 鲍家声，杜顺宝. 公共建筑设计基础. 南京：南京工学院出版社，1986
8. 天津大学编. 公共建筑设计原理. 北京：中国建筑工业出版社，1981

参考书：

1. C. Alexander. A Pattern Language. Oxford: Oxford Unit. Press, 1977
2. J. Bacon. Design of Cities. London: Thomas and Hudson, 1974
3. J. Barnett. Urban Design as Public Policy. Architectural Record Book, 1974
4. L. Halprin. Cities.Cambridge, MA: MIT Press, 1980
5. Kevin Lynch. The Image of the City, Cambridge. MA: MIT Press, 1960
6. Sigfried Giedion. Space, Time and Architecture. 5th Edition. Harvard: Harvard University Press，1971
7. 黑川纪章. 都市デザンの思想と手法. 日本：彰国社，1996
8. [奥]卡米诺·西特. 城市建设艺术. 仲德崑译. 南京：东南大学出版社，1990
9. [英]吉伯德. 市镇设计. 程里尧译. 北京：中国建筑工业出版社，1983
10. [芬]沙里宁. 城市——它的发展、衰败与未来. 顾启源译. 北京：中国建筑工业出版社，1986
11. [美]罗杰·特兰西克. 找寻失落的空间. 谢庆达译. 台北：创兴出版社，1989
12. [美]麦克哈格. 设计结合自然. 芮经纬译. 北京：中国建筑工业出版社，1992
13. 韩冬青，冯金龙. 城市·建筑一体化设计. 南京：东南大学出版社，1999
14. 夏祖华，黄伟康. 城市空间设计. 南京：东南大学出版社，1992
15. [日]芦原义信. 外部空间设计. 尹培桐译. 北京：中国建筑工业出版社，1988
16. [英]埃比尼泽·霍华德. 明日的田园城市. 金经元译. 北京：商务印书馆，2000
17. 吴良镛. 广义建筑学. 北京：清华大学出版社，1991
18. 建筑设计资料集编委会. 建筑设计资料集（1-10）. 第2版. 北京：中国建筑工业出版社，1997
19. 现行建筑设计规范大全（修订缩印本）. 北京：中国建筑工业出版社，1994
20. [美]弗朗西斯·D·K·钦. 建筑：形式、空间和秩序. 第2版. 刘从红译. 邹德侬审校. 天津：天津大学出版社，2005
21. [荷]赫曼·赫兹伯格. 建筑学教程：设计原理. 仲德崑译. 刘先觉，薛皓东校订. 天津：天津大学出版社，2003
22. [美]诺伯格-舒尔茨. 存在·空间·建筑. 尹培桐译. 北京：中国建筑工业出版社，1984
23. [意]布鲁诺·赛维. 建筑空间论. 张似赞译. 北京：中国建筑工业出版社，1985
24. [意]布鲁诺·赛维. 现代建筑语言. 席云平译. 北京：中国建筑工业出版社，1986
25. [英]查尔斯·詹克斯. 后现代建筑语言. 李大厦译. 北京：中国建筑工业出版社，1986
26. 张伶伶，孟浩. 建筑设计指导丛书——场地设计. 北京：中国建筑工业出版社，1999
27. 徐卫国. 建筑设计指导丛书——快速建筑设计方法. 北京：中国建筑工业出版社，2001

城市设计

一、课程的性质与目的

本课程作为城市规划专业必修的一门重要专业课，注重的是从前期研究、实地调研、策划分析到概念构思、方案优化和深度表达，帮助学生建立一套集综合性、系统性和开放性于一身的研究策略和技术路线，同时培养职业性与创造性、思维能力与操作能力、分析能力与综合能力、自主能力与合作能力协调统一的多维能力，以突出人才培养的多元复合化目标。

围绕该核心课程，本专业经过多年的改革和完善，已逐步建构起相对成熟的“课程群”——以专业设计课“城市设计”和基础理论课“城市设计概论”、“城市规划原理”为主线，以专业设计课“控制性详细规划”和相关理论课“城市中心（区）的发展与规划”、“城市更新与历史文化保护”等为支撑。

二、课程内容的教学要求

1. 选择适宜的规划基地。
2. 规划基地现状、规划环境与背景调研。
3. 总平面规划与形体设计。
4. 专业系统规划。
5. 规划控制指标与相关概念的表述。
6. 规划方案的表现。
7. 规划成果汇编与规划说明的编写。

三、能力培养的要求

1. 分析能力的培养：主要培养对规划基地现状、规划环境与背景调研进行分析的能力。
2. 表达能力的培养：主要培养通过总平面规划与形体设计，清晰表达自己解决问题的思路和步骤的能力。
3. 创新能力的培养：培养学生独立思考、深入研究和针对问题提出解决方法以及在应用实践中的创新能力。

总体规划

一、课程的性质与目的

城市总体规划是法定城市规划中的核心层次，城市总体规划课程以其高度综合性，在整个城市规划专业教学环节中居于整体集成、综合检验的地位，是规划专业学生从非专业学生走向专业学生的重要的催化剂。城镇总体规划设计过程对学生各专门知识和综合能力进行检验，促使学生理论和实践融会贯通，提高解决现实问题的能力。

二、课程内容的教学要求

1. 总体规划案例研究

（1）了解总体规划解决的问题和包含的内容。

（2）熟悉总体规划的规范性表达。

2. 总体规划设计

（1）现场踏勘及规划基础资料收集。

（2）规划专题分析。

（3）市/县/镇域层面的空间规划。

（4）用地结构、交通系统、市政工程系统的综合规划。

（5）编制全套法定成果。

三、能力培养的要求

1. 规划能力的培养：包括城镇体系及城区空间布局结构规划能力的培养。
2. 分析能力的培养：包括对城市发展条件的分析能力，应用GIS对村、镇发展潜力进行分析的能力，以及对城市建设用地工程和经济分析的能力的培养。
3. 自学能力的培养：培养和提高学生对所学知识进行整理、概括、消化吸收的能力，以及围绕课堂教学内容，阅读参考书籍和资料，自我扩充知识领域的能力。
4. 表达能力的培养：主要是通过作业、课堂讨论和答辩等环节，培养学生清晰、完整地表达自己的观点，表达分析、解决问题的思路、步骤和结论的能力。
5. 分工合作能力的培养：结合城市总体规划工作的特点，采取以小组工作为主，个人、小组和班级相结合的教学方式，培养协调、合作工作的能力。

都市水岸城市设计
Waterfront Urban Design

作者：唐静寅 乔琦 指导老师：张彤

城墙和秦淮河在作为南京历史名城标志的同时，阻隔了新老两个城区的联系和发展，形成了一系列城市功能和行为的真空带。如何策动织补完整丰富的城市生活成为推进本地块设计的主要方向。

The strategy to connect two parts of city separated by substance and function is to fill the gap which lacks complexity of citizen life.

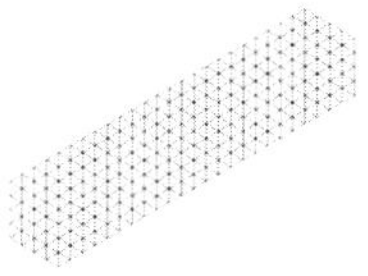

符合功能策划及发展

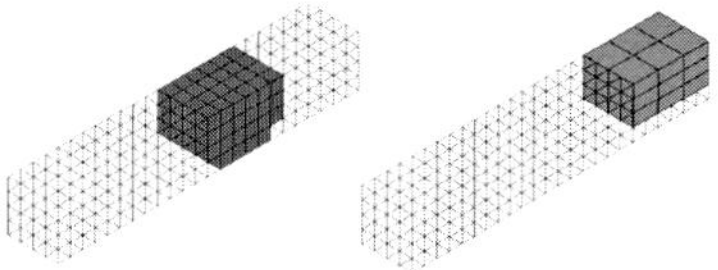

A 商业用途 8m×8m　　B 办公文化用途 16m×16m

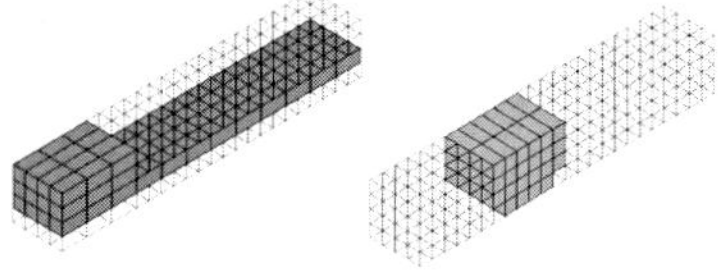

D 运动休闲用途 8m×16m　　E 休闲娱乐用途 16m×8m

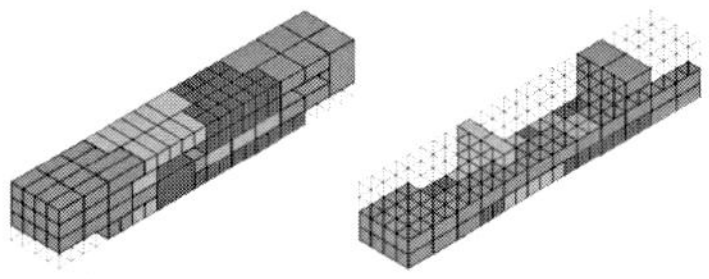

功能的叠错扩张

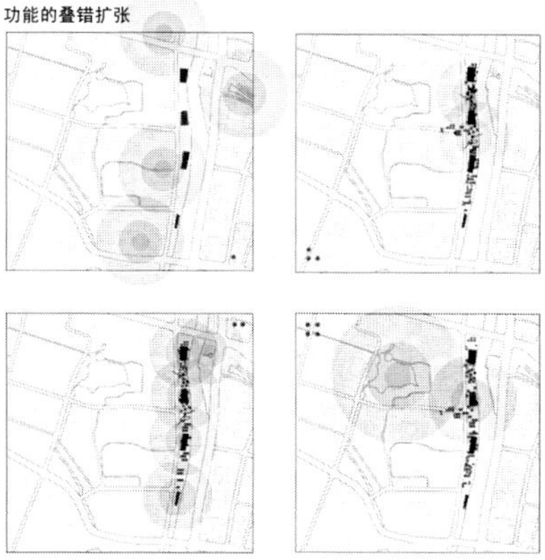

地块	面积(ha)	百分比(%)
A 商业金融业用地	2.408	10.96
B 文化娱乐用地	1.346	6.13
C 公共绿地	1.687	7.68
D 文化娱乐用地	0.578	2.63
E 文化娱乐用地	1.405	6.39
F 水域	12.925	58.82
G 代征用地	1.624	7.39
总用地面积	21.973	100

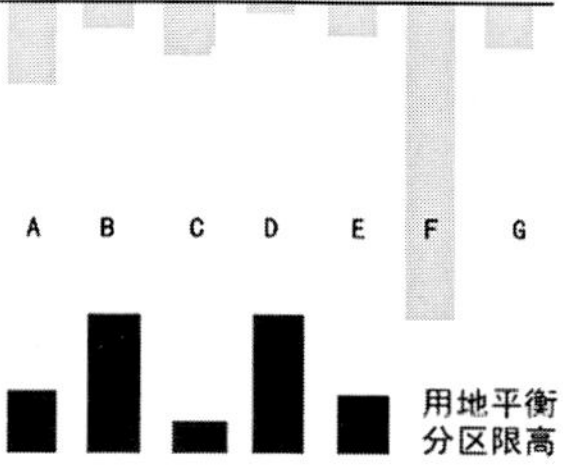

用地平衡
分区限高

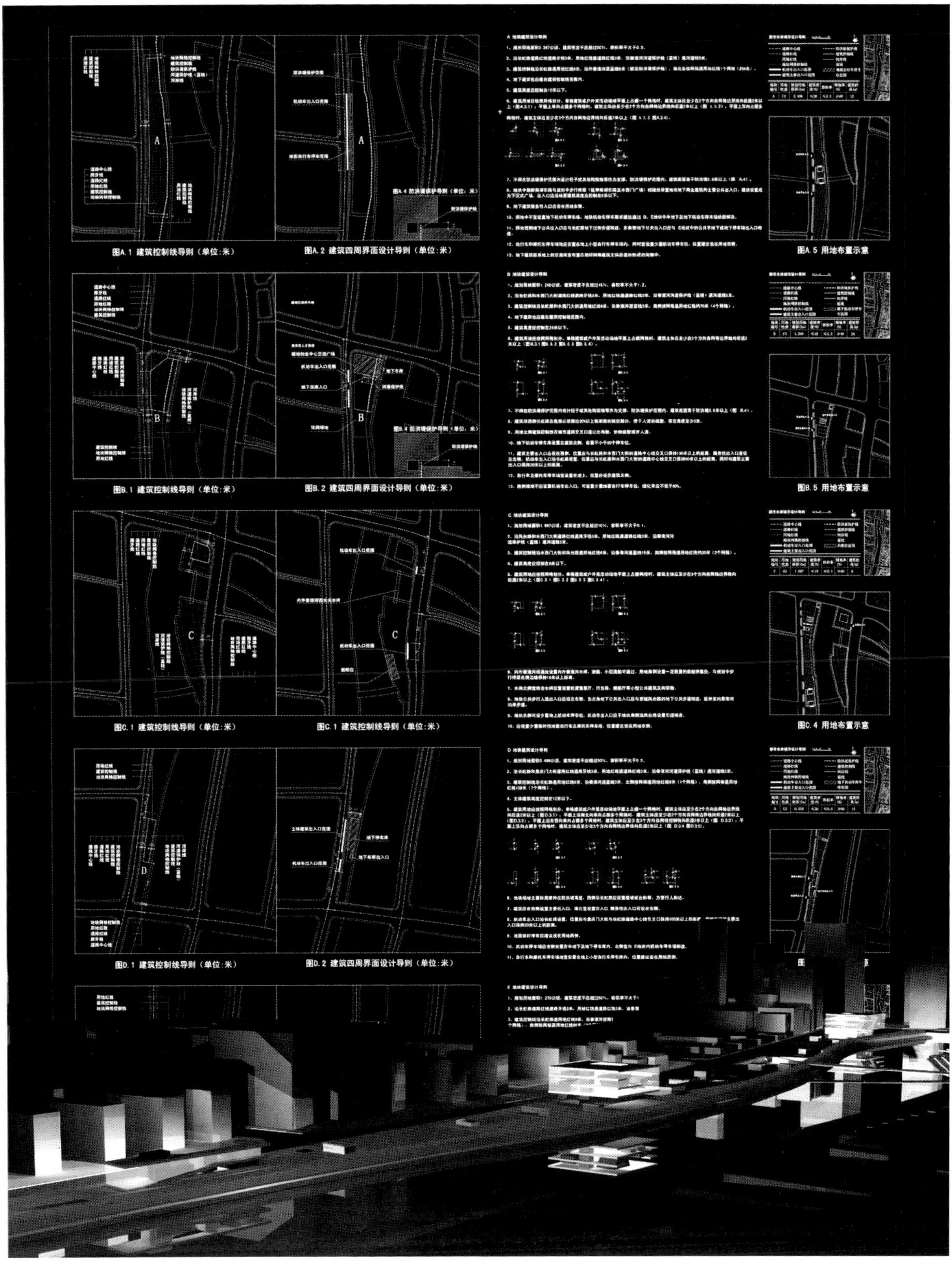
图A.1 建筑控制线导则（单位:米）
图A.2 建筑四周界面设计导则（单位:米）
图A.5 用地布置示意
图B.1 建筑控制线导则（单位:米）
图B.2 建筑四周界面设计导则（单位:米）
图B.5 用地布置示意
图C.1 建筑控制线导则（单位:米）
图C.1 建筑控制线导则（单位:米）
图C.4 用地布置示意
图D.1 建筑控制线导则（单位:米）
图D.2 建筑四周界面设计导则（单位:米）

城市设计
Urban Design

作者：杨晔 张弛 黄莘颖　指导老师：韩冬青

基地位于南京市中山东路与游府西街、太平南路与抄纸巷所限定的地块内，总用地面积约14.4公顷，包含公共建筑和不同时期的住宅及民国建筑遗存，多种肌理并存。在地段迅速发展的时期，该地段面临重要的发展机遇。

在区位认识的基础上，我们展开该区段城市路径、建筑功能及相关城市形态结构的调查研究，进而得出结论：新街口及大行宫两大城市中心不断发展，处在两大中心间的基地需要在功能业态、空间形态和活动方式上改变以适应城市发展。

通过对世界各大城市CBD模式的研究，我们提出了“连接双峰，塑造城市公共行为活动链”的设计目标。在空间形态上，表现为带状城市公共空间。通过对建筑类型、容积等方面的分析，我们提出了保留改造现有建筑，并适当加建新建筑的改造模式。进而，通过对人流活动特征，即“同时运动诸系统”的研究，以及对功能复合等多方面的分析，我们创造出了适合基地的城市公共连接体。这种连接是多种层面上的，包括视线关系、景观联系、业态互补、行为活动等各个方面，从而使新街口、大行宫成为南京市的整体中心区。

The site is located between Xinjiekou and Daxinggong, two business areas which are largely expanded during the rapid urbanization campaign in Chinese cities these years.

After research and analysis on common modes of central business districts around the world and the condition of the site, our proposal is made. By creating a chain-like urban space which connects the two expanding city centers in not only spatial aspects such as visual connections, but also function and behavior, etc. this area gets its chance for revitalization, while the original mixed context is reserved.

两大城市双峰在不断发展的过程中对中心区不断产生作用，现状闭塞的基地功能、业态、空间、形态和活动方式上都需要改变

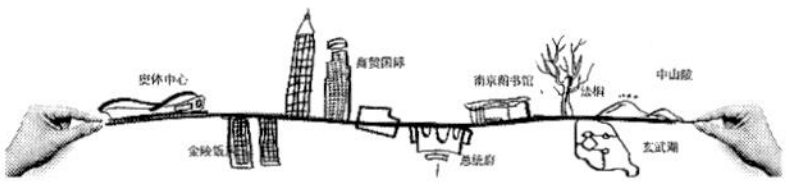

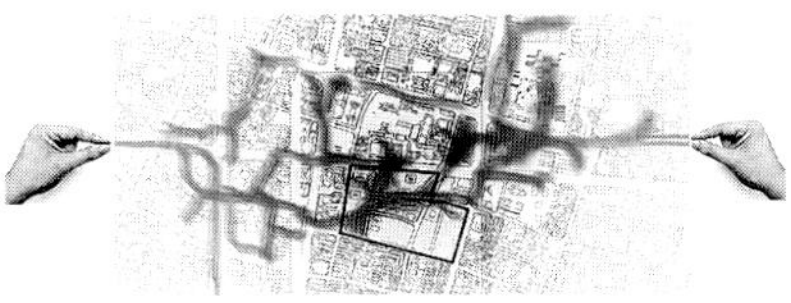

一个城市会有诸多著名的城市名片，我们希望会有一条连接体系串起它们以形成一个具有整个城市鲜明个性的形态

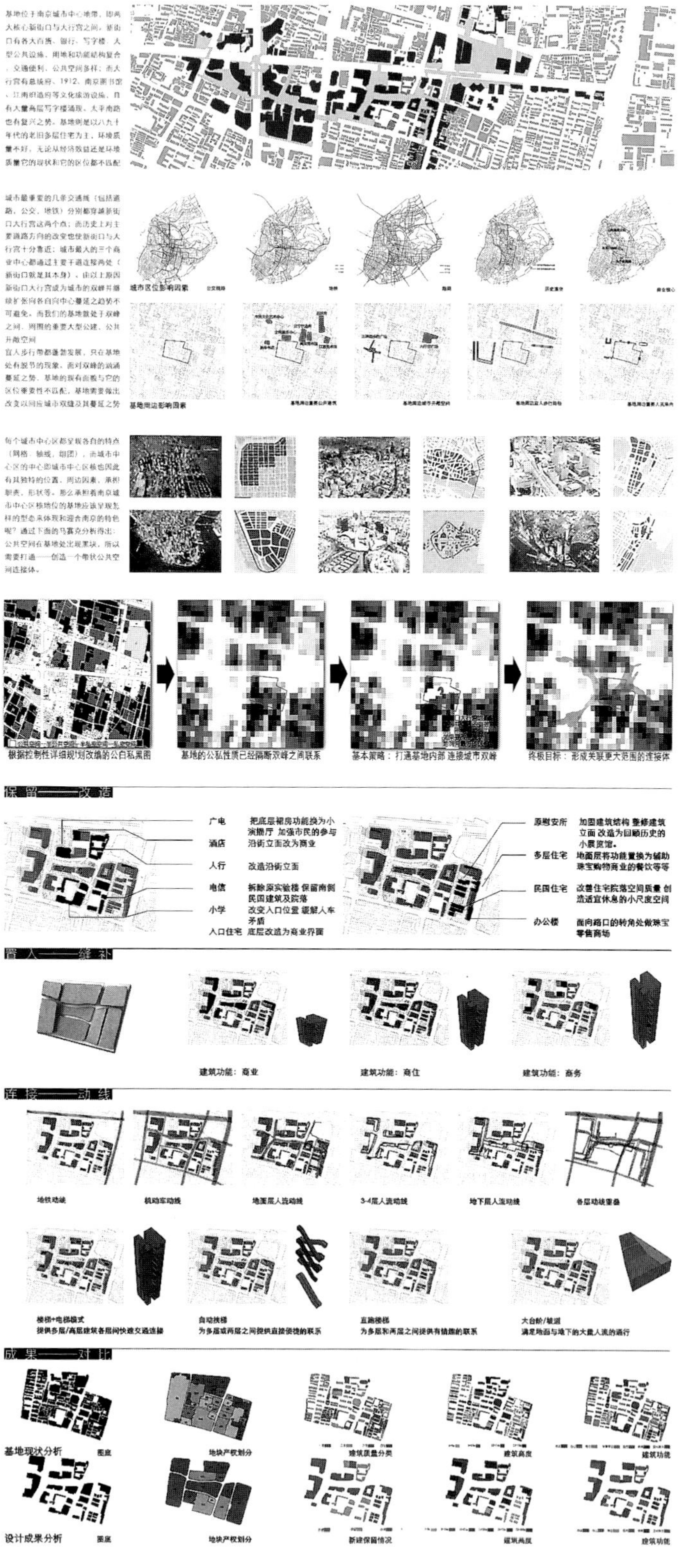

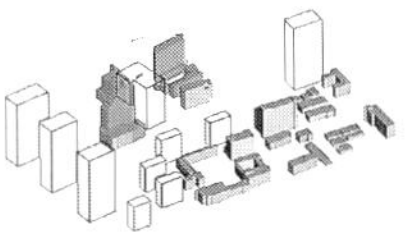

地块内保留建筑

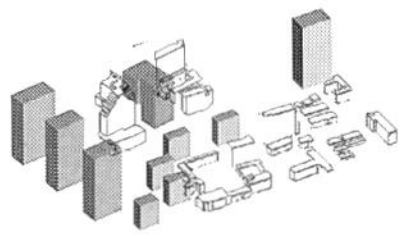

地块内新建建筑

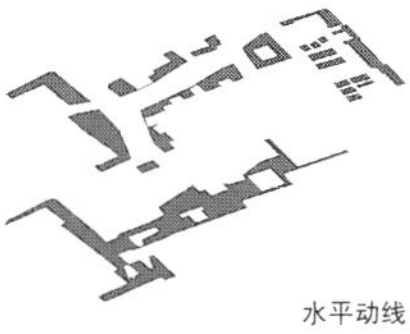

水平动线

地块垂直交通核心

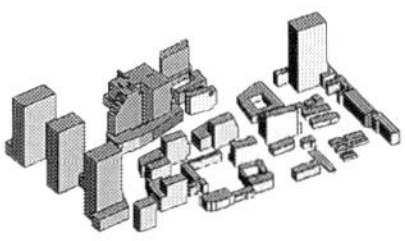

地块改造后体块模型

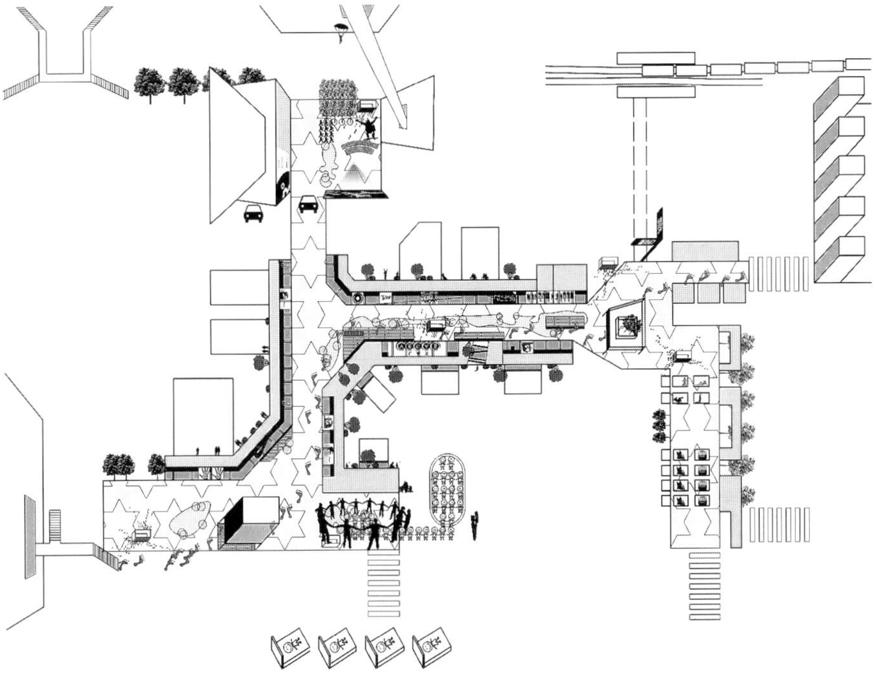

鼓励各种人流活动的带状城市公共连接空间意象

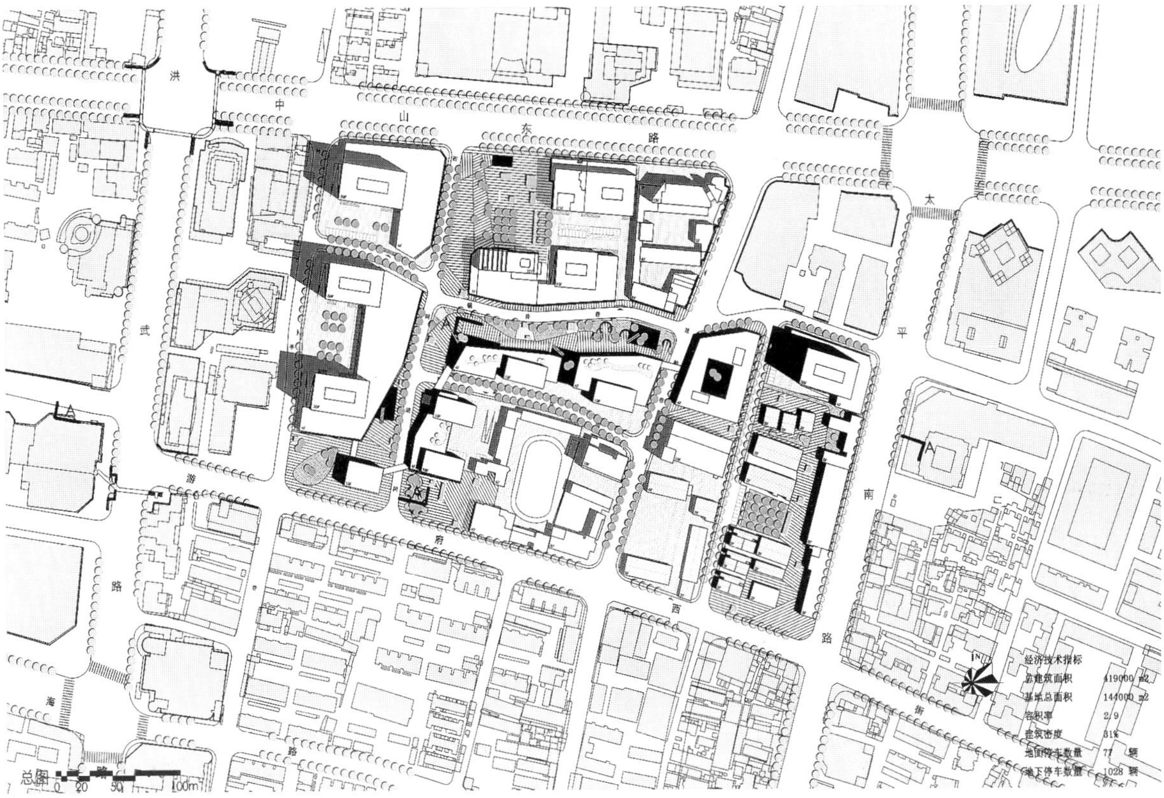

总图

古生物博物馆设计
Paleontology Museum Design

作者：李力 吴倩　指导老师：张彤
获2007年“Revit杯”全国大学生建筑设计作业优秀奖

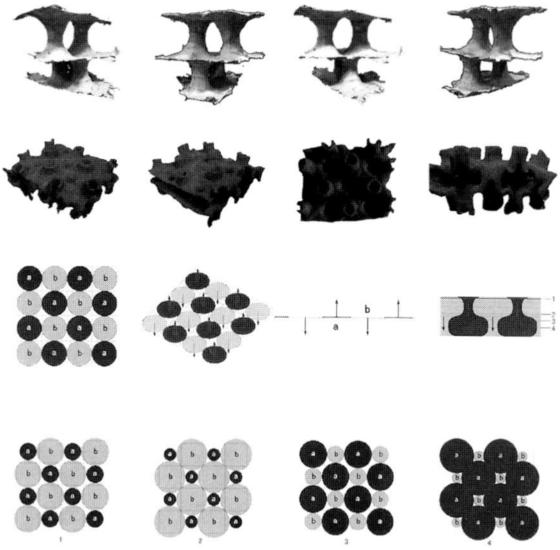

湖石的孔洞是年代的象征，设计中使用多孔贯通的空间原型模仿这种自然形态来获得古老的气质。细胞单元的排列组织是生物形体构成的根本，通过单元组织的手法使建筑更为整体有机。空间二等分体：其特点在于围合和被围合的空间的形体和体积是完全相同的，由此墙的概念被弱化了。空间围合的不明确性同时也导致了空间整体的连续性。内外表皮的翻转和相互置换、空间的贯通融合赋予了建筑神秘的特质。

The holes on lake stone show us the process of time, and the structures of tissues reveal the essence of life. By imitating these natural phenomena, we endow the museum with historical and organic structure. Furthermore, this structure enhances the continuity of the space and weakens the sensation of wall. Tourists will get different spatial feelings in this museum.

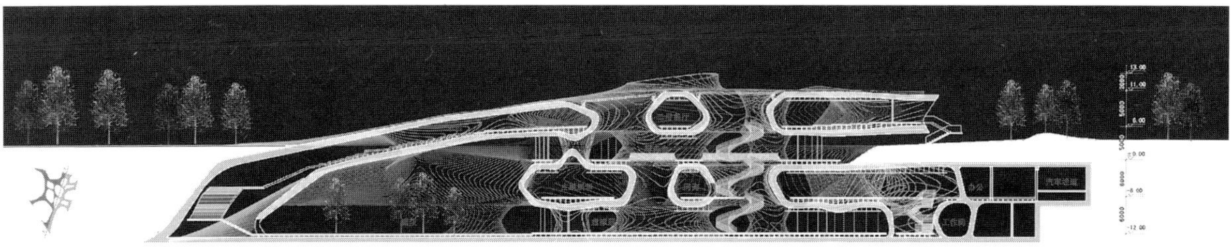

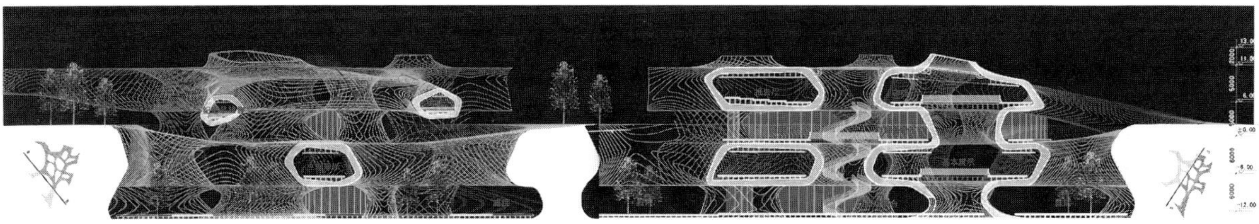

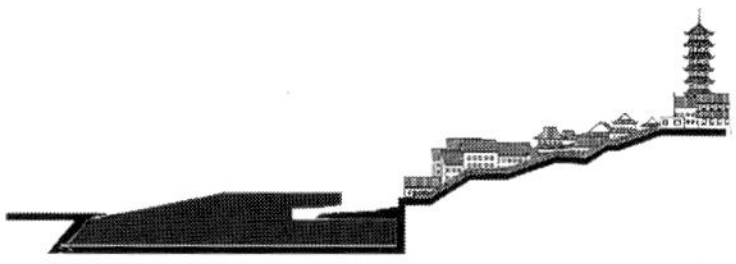

建筑形态与地形关系

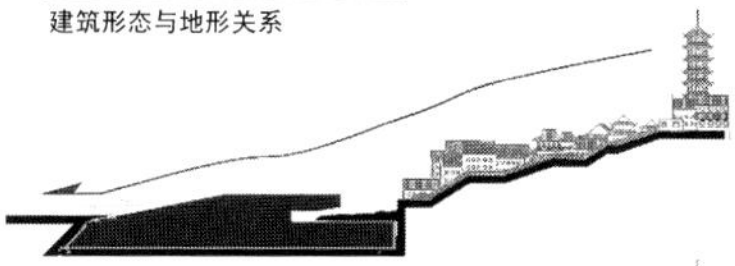

场地及建筑的走势

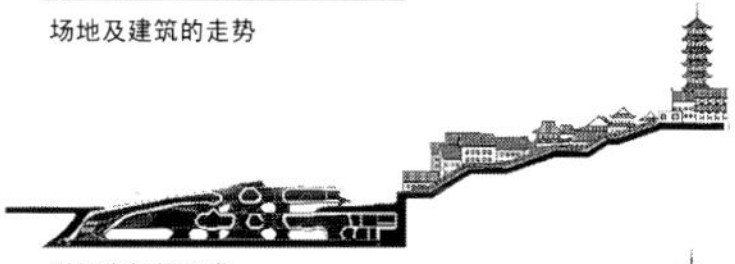

封闭空间的形成

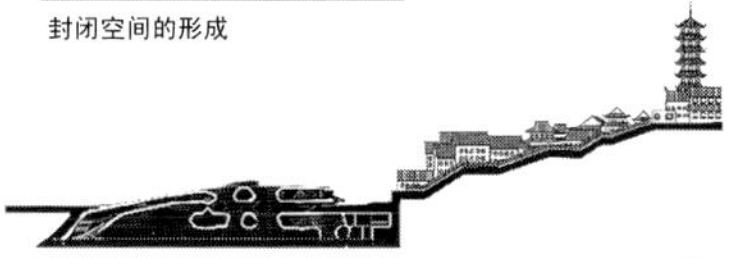

流通空间的形成

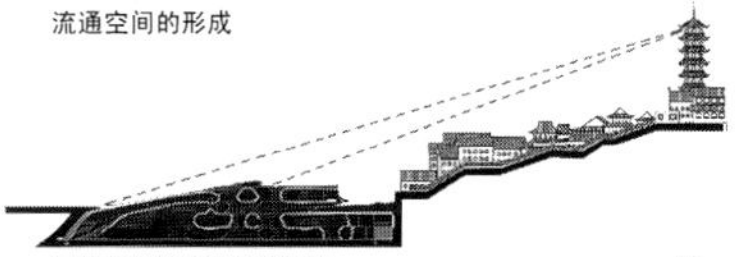

与场地的视线关系(被看)

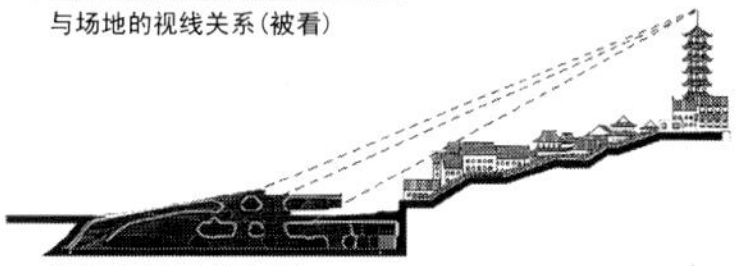

与场地的视线关系(看)

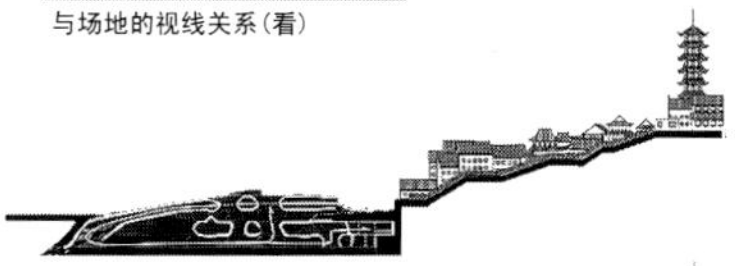

交通组织与场地关系

建筑的自然通风效果

复合式超高层设计
High-rise Building Design

作者：李晨星 郭东海　指导老师：钱强

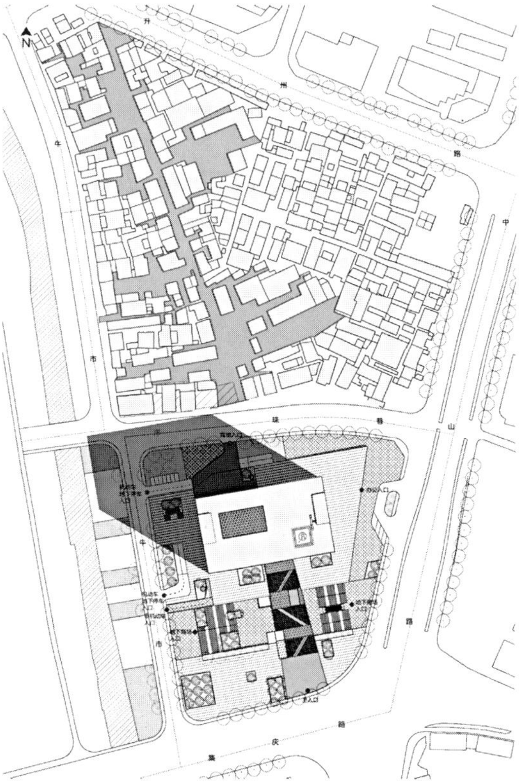

设计的最初概念源自对原始肌理的尊重和保留，意图将水平向的巷弄空间形式转之于竖向空间用之，在纪念的同时增加高层建筑内部新颖的空间体验。在处理手法上通过对原始肌理的格构化以及拆分组合形成独特中庭（共享空间）和立面效果。

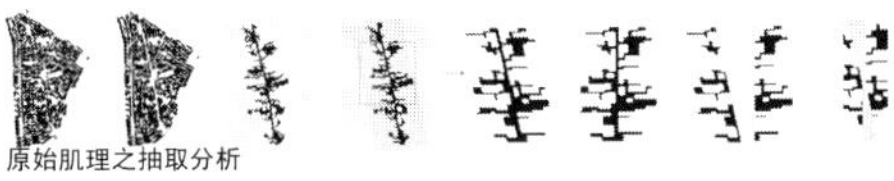

原始肌理之抽取分析

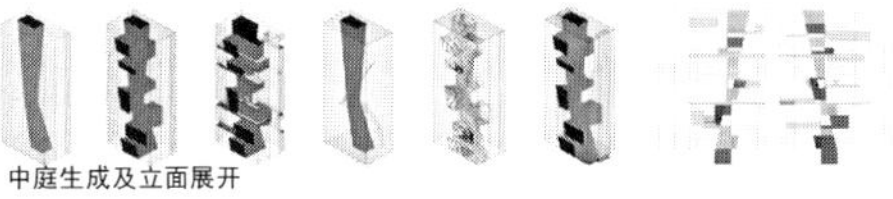

中庭生成及立面展开

剖面图

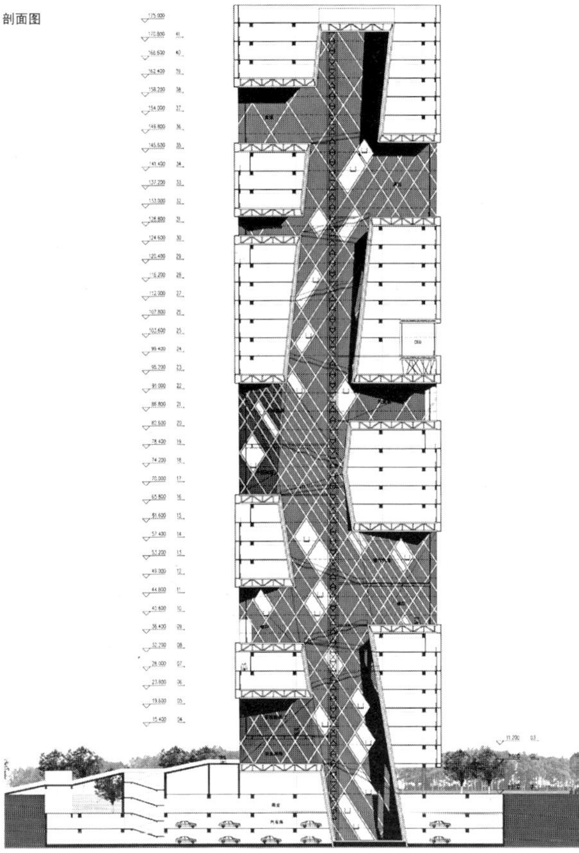

立面图

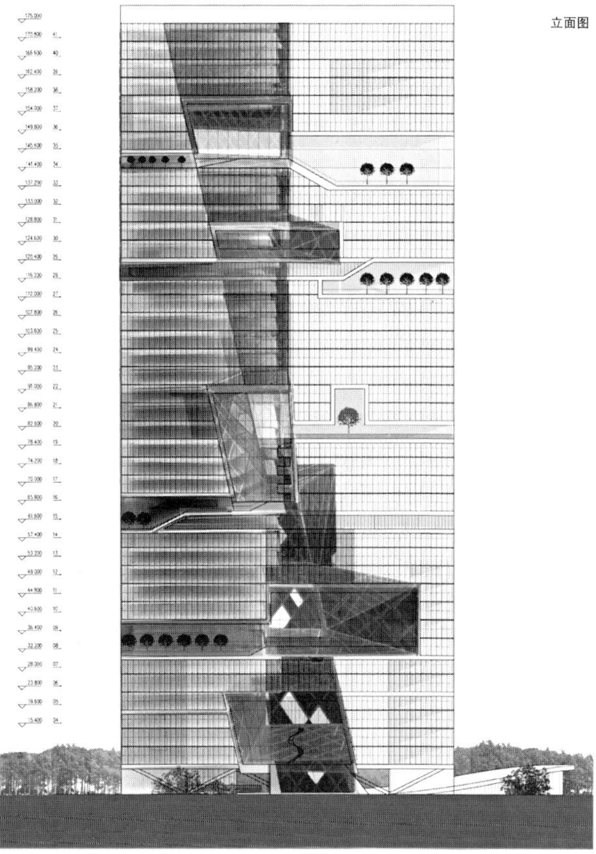

各层平面

经济技术指标
基地面积：21800m^2
建筑规模：138000m^2
容积率：5.7

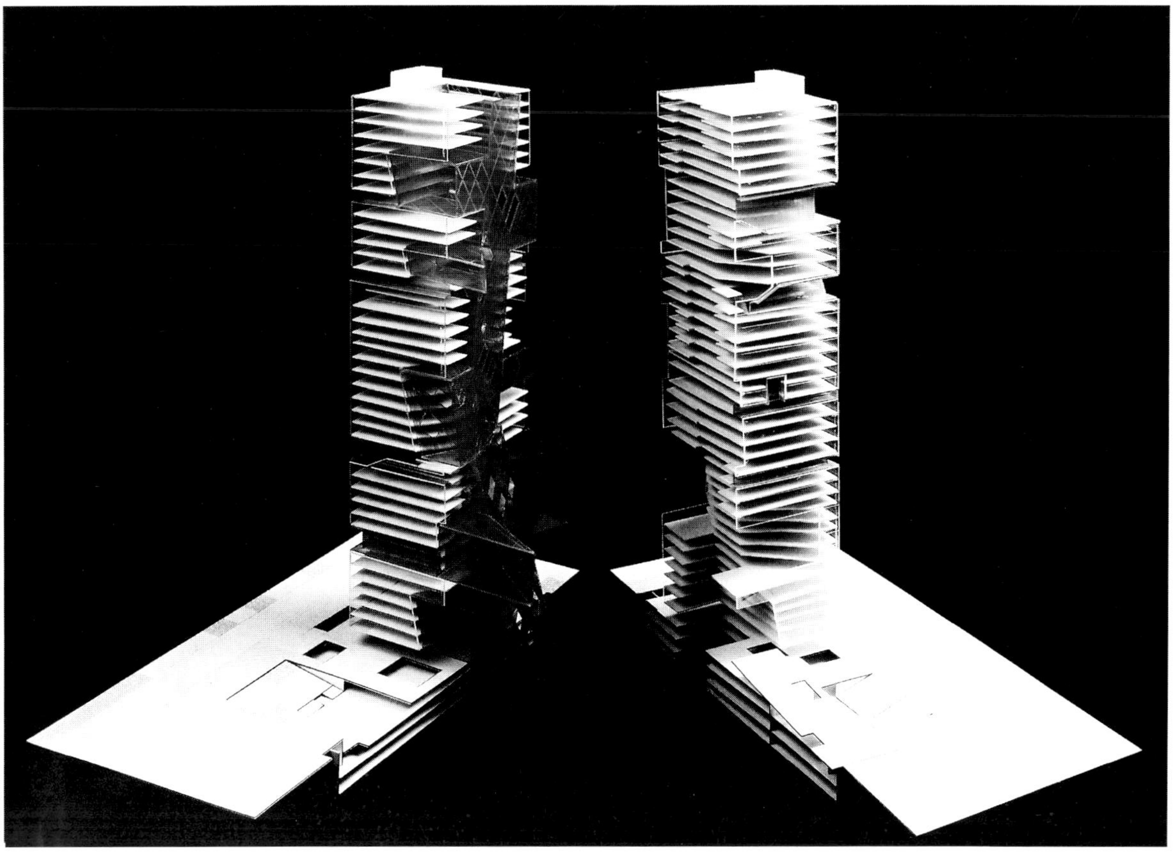

镇江市城市规划展览馆设计
Urban Planning Exhibition Hall, Zhenjiang, China

作者：栗茜 柴金戈 指导老师：龚恺

作为大型公共建筑，城市规划展览馆的设计关键在于人的行为，同时兼顾形式与文脉的契合。于是在行为方面，展区均匀分布并且尽量交融从而激活内部空间；在形式方面，通过对镇江地形和城市结构的研究，结合内部空间需要提炼出了岛的概念，以分散的流体和起伏的曲线来隐喻镇江地区的自然风光。

As an important architecture for public, the key to design Urban Planning Exhibition Hall is man's activity, considering context of the city at the same time. So firstly, we try to make the internal and external isotropically chiasma to vitalize the internal exhibition. While in consideration of context and form of architecture, by reseaching the topographical elements and cultural symbols, we abstracted "island" as our formal conception to reflect the regional characteristics.

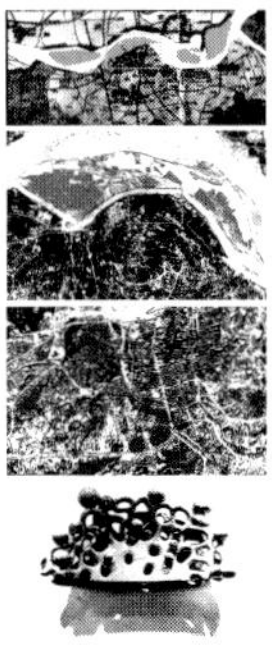

城市规划展览馆作为一个展示城市风采的窗口必须具有个性特点，于是从对镇江城市的总体印象开始，希望找到镇江独特的美。

脑海中最模糊的镇江是源于千古流传的诗句——京口瓜洲一水间，钟山只隔数重山。走近镇江，山水之城的感觉愈发清晰，作为长江中的一个节点，镇江的港口经济贸易发展迅猛，城市生活也是由一个个不同的功能岛屿组成的，绿岛、商业岛、居住岛，纵横交错的路网联系其中。

当我们继续深入，抽象城市各种功能的运作方式，一个作用于宏观和微观世界、独立而又相互联系中的结构体——岛的概念便产生了。

城市-生长
Development

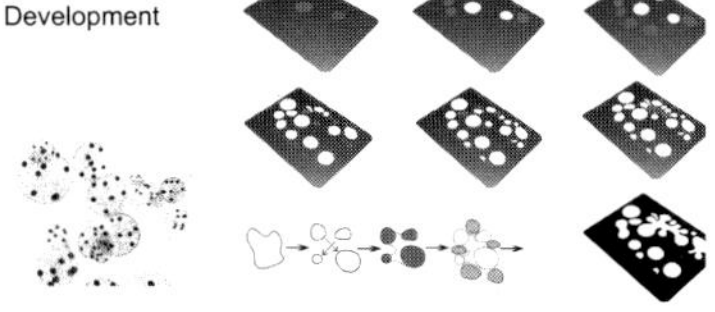

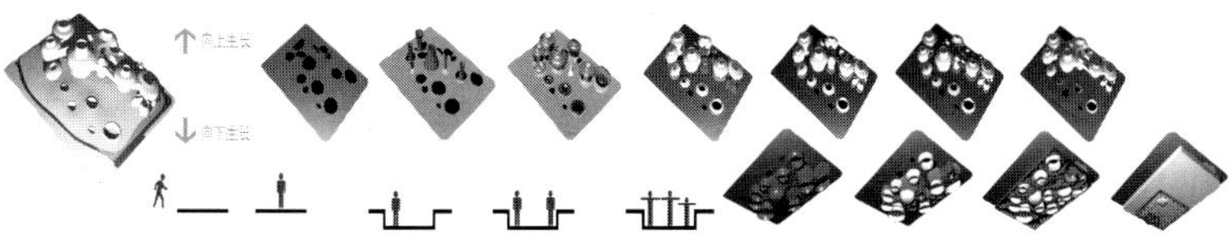

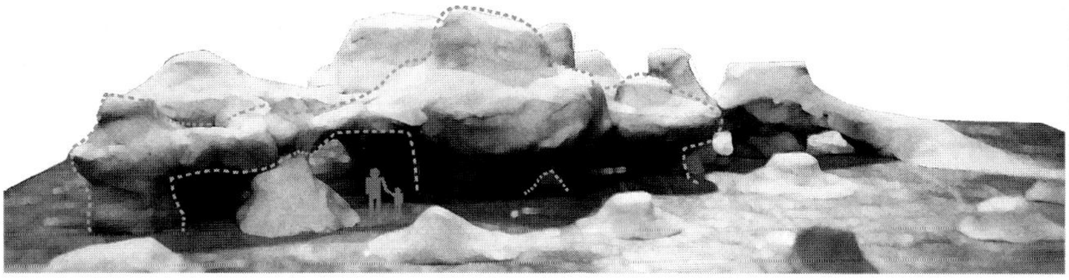

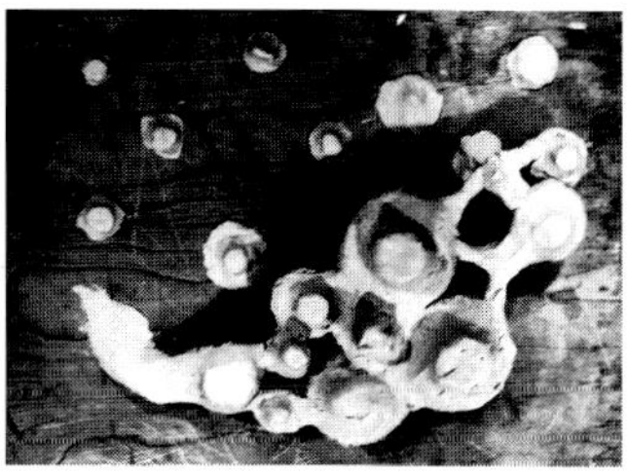

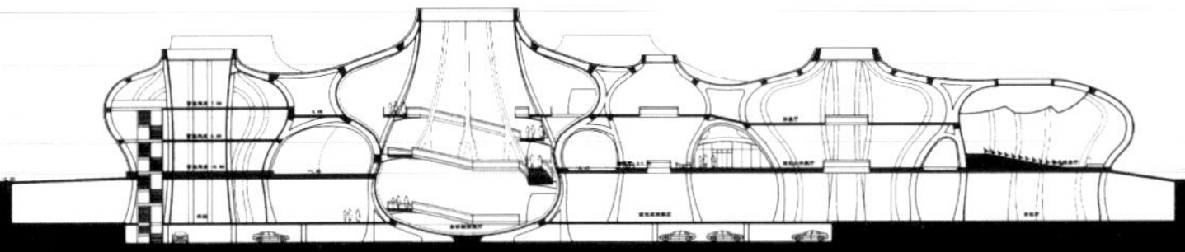

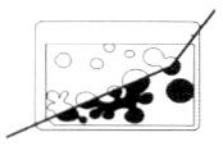

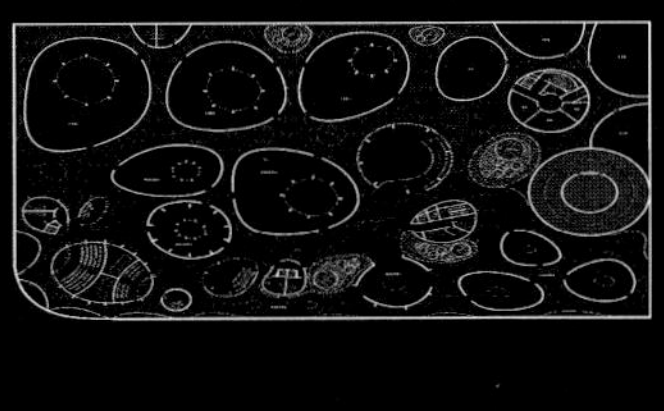

负一层平面 Underground Floor

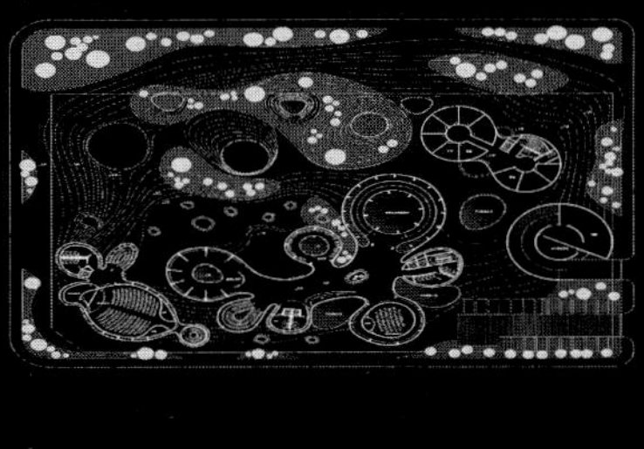

一层平面 First Floor

二层平面 Second Floor

高舒适度低能耗建筑设计
High Comfort Low Energy Architecture Design

作者：崔赟 徐旺　指导老师：李海清

我们的设计从生态角度出发，力图通过对建筑形态的设计在建筑物内部形成独特的微气候；对建筑表皮进行特殊处理以保证建筑的环保与节能，同时形成了独特的立面效果，Space-Condition建筑室内调节系统的引入能更好地保证建筑内部环境的质量。

We design in the ecological point of view and have sought in the form of construction in the design of the interior to form a unique micro-climate. We also do special treatment to the building's skin in order to ensure the construction of environmental protection and energy saving, from which we achieve a unique facade effect, too. Furthermore, Space-Condition indoor conditioning system is used to better ensure the construction quality of the internal environment.

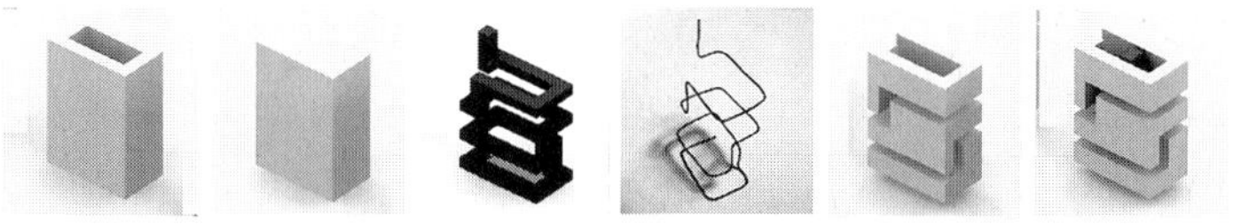

概念生成

平面形态

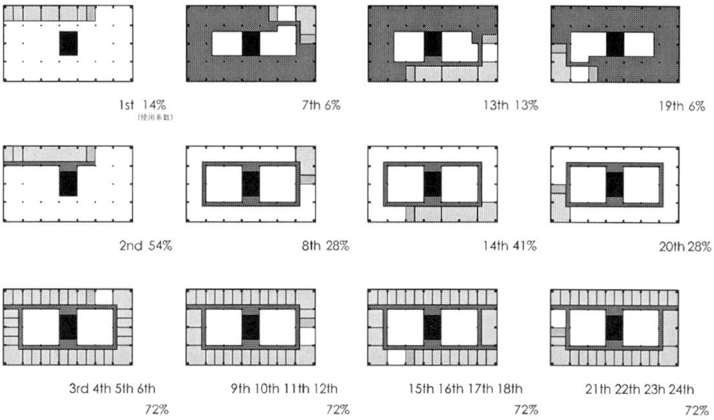

模型照片

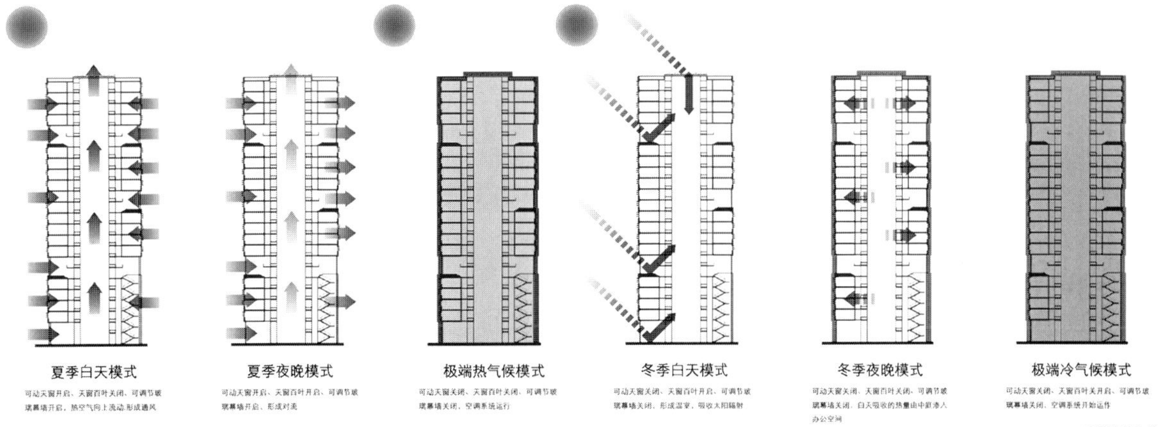

环境模式分析

剖面

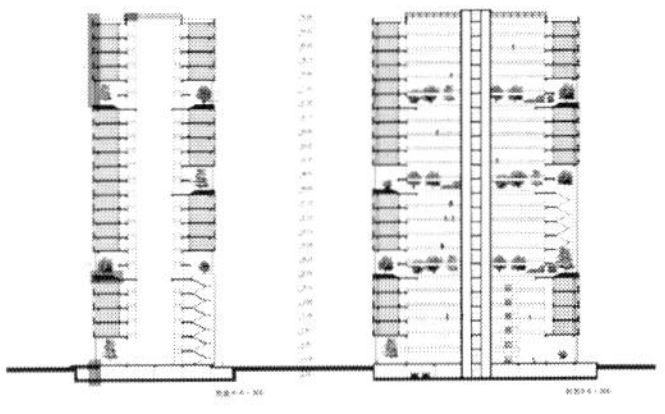

立面形态展开分析

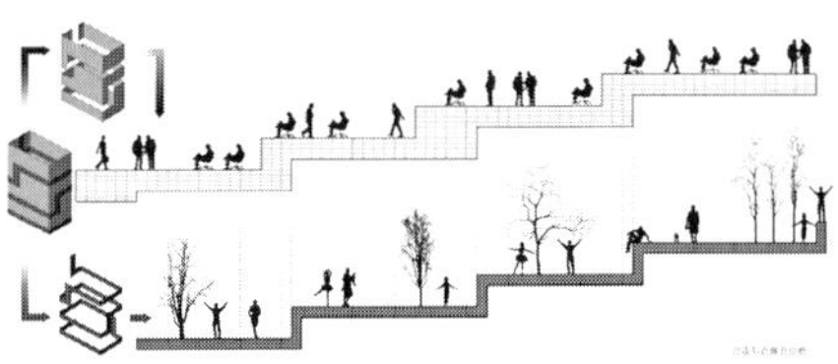

Delta Skin表皮构造

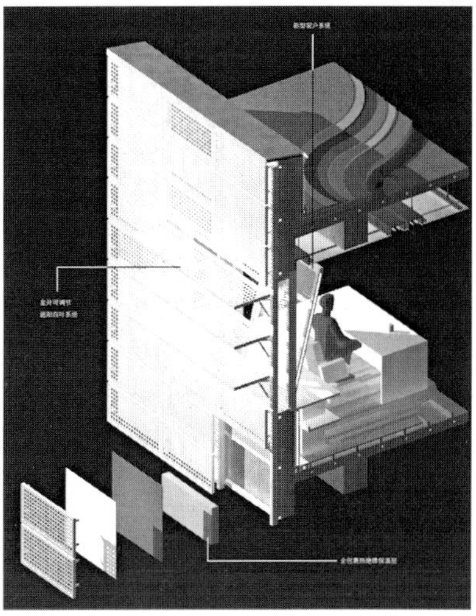

可开启玻璃幕墙构造

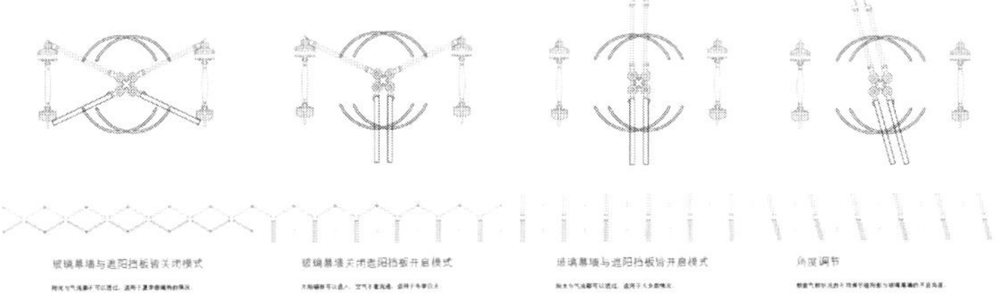

覆土建筑中大院前广场设计
Earth Sheltered Studios for SEU-ARCH Square Design

作者：郭东海　指导老师：周琦

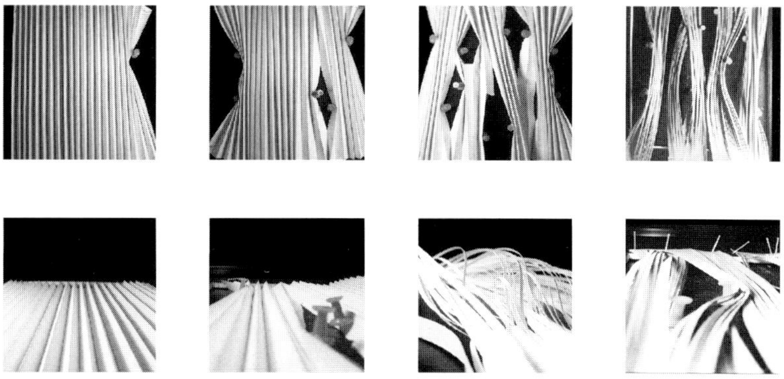

中大院前草坪位于校轴线东侧，被场地中的两条纵横交错的道路分成四块，植上了观赏性的草坪，现利用其地下空间扩展为建筑学院工作间。

纵观整个学校强有力的轴线关系控制了整个空间，休闲性活动场地缺乏，该草坪并没有达到它应有的活力值。

The site is located in front of Zhongda-yuan Building, at the east side of the campus axis, covered with grass. The underground space is to be used as the architects' studios. There is a strong order controlled by the axis in the university, resulting in lack of rest areas, I propose a fluid form to change stress from the axis and bring in new activities.

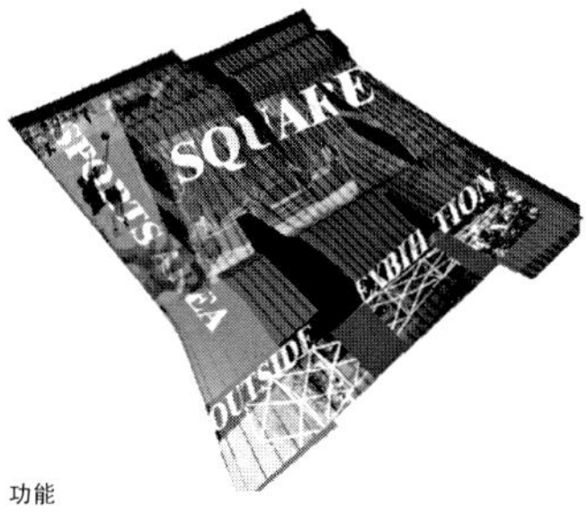

功能

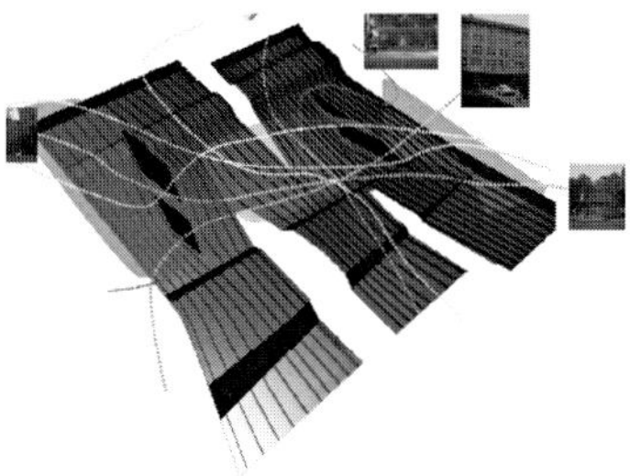

屋顶穿越路径

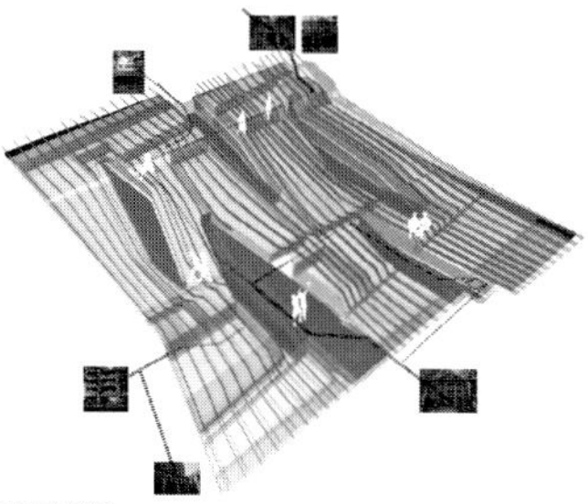

室内活动路径

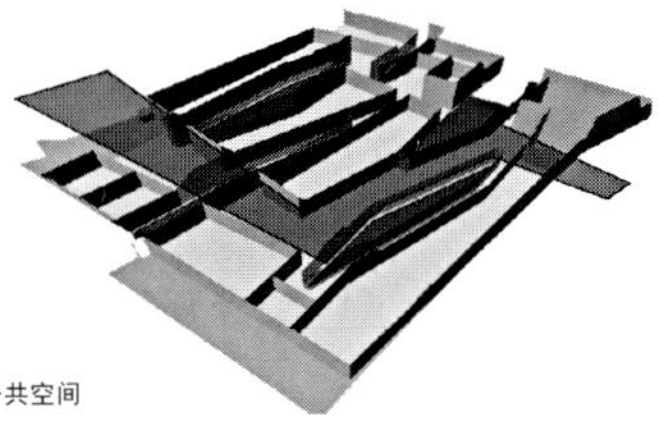

公共空间

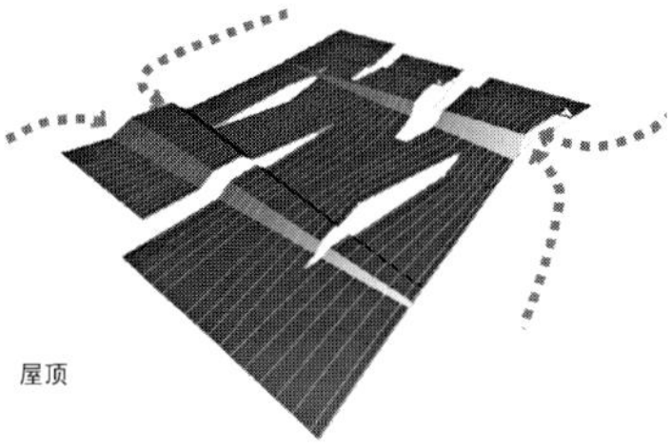

屋顶

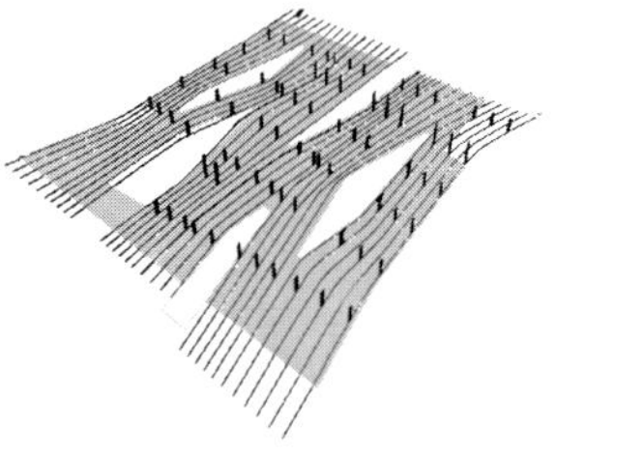

结构

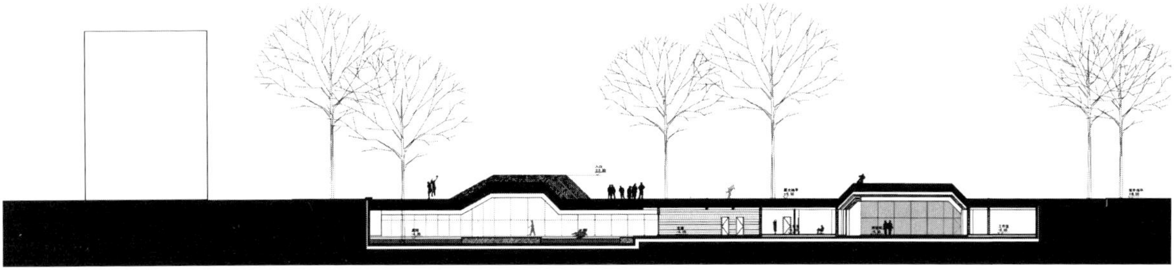

南北向剖面

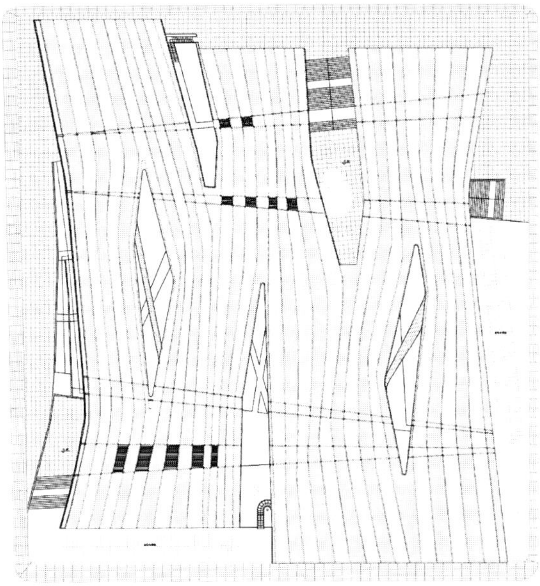

屋顶平面

地下层平面

玻璃幕墙办公建筑设计
Glass Curtain-wall Office Building Design

作者：吴倩　指导老师：王静

本设计针对普通玻璃幕墙办公建筑的光环境缺点，对办公建筑的内部空间和外部围护进行了独特的设计和改善。在设计的过程中，以ECOTECT软件作为辅助，检验并调整每一过程中的光环境质量，以获得一个光线均匀、空间积极的办公空间为最终目标。设计主张使建筑自身以积极自然的状态采光，因此将楼板的走势形态设为迎向自然光充足的一侧，最大程度地将光线导入建筑。其次，把楼板分成几个脱开的段落，空隙中布置交通，解决建筑楼板过长造成的受光不均，同时由于楼板的错动在室内形成丰富的空间和不同的分区使办公空间开阔而不单调，其尺度也更加人性化。在不同标高的平台工作，为使用者提供了更多的交流机会和活动场所。新型的空间给未来的办公生活带来全新的感受。

This program based on the light environment of popular glass curtain-wall office buildings, tries a particular design and promotion in inner space and outer skin. In the process, I pick the program with software ECOTECT as a tool, which helps me exam and adjust the light quality in every step. The aim is to create an active office space with plenty and average skylight. As the building itself should get light in a natural way, the tendency of its floors is to face the light source, leading the skylight in the building extremely. Divide the floors into several separate sections, put the stairs in the gaps, so that avoid various light caused by long floors. With separation of floors, complicated space and different divisions appear, coming with spacious but no monotonous inner space. Working on the various layers, users get more communicating chances. This new-fashion office space brings brand-new experience for future life.

普通办公空间形态

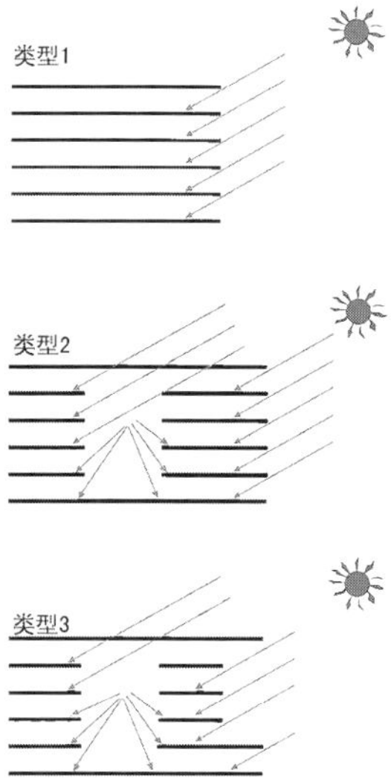

SECTION

类型1
特征：空间单一，各层楼板呈相同状态平铺
缺点：靠窗地带光照大，平面中部缺乏光照，内部空间缺乏变化，单调不宜交流

类型2
特征：空间有中心，共享空间增加了交流的机会，平面中部的光照问题得到解决
缺点：适宜规模较大的平面，平面尺寸超出一定数值时连续楼板的中部光照仍较弱，中庭无法适应多样的交流类型

类型3
特征：空间较丰富，共享空间增加了交流的机会，平面中部的光照问题得到解决，边庭解决中庭没有解决的采光问题
缺点：适宜规模较大的平面，用贯通空间来解决进深带来的采光问题在空间的利用上过于浪费

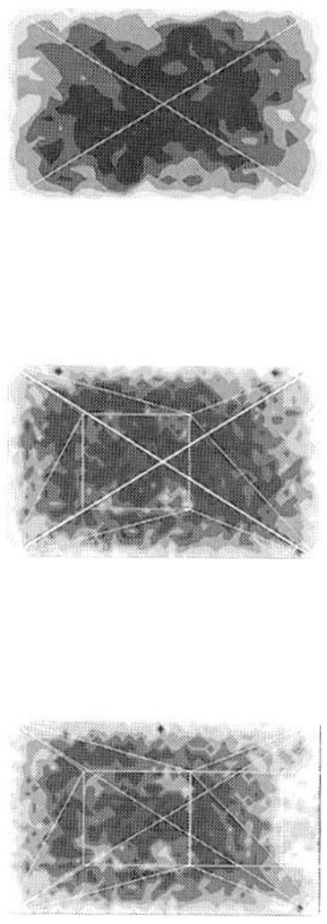

PLAN(BY ECOTECT)

设计后---办公空间形态

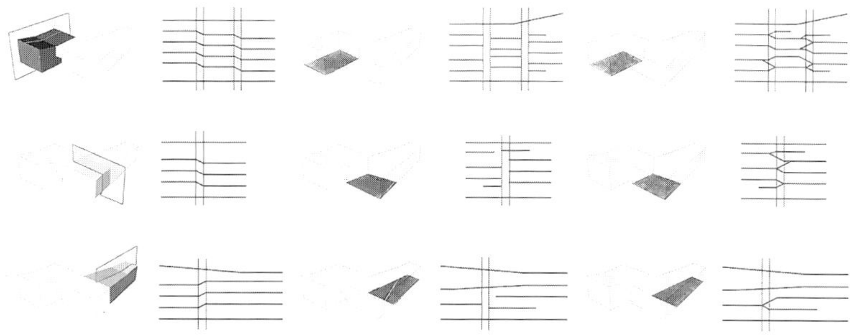

PROGRESS 1 标高错动　PROGRESS 2 原始采光状况　PROGRESS 3 调整高度关系　PROGRESS 4 调整后采光状况　PROGRESS 5 创造连贯空间

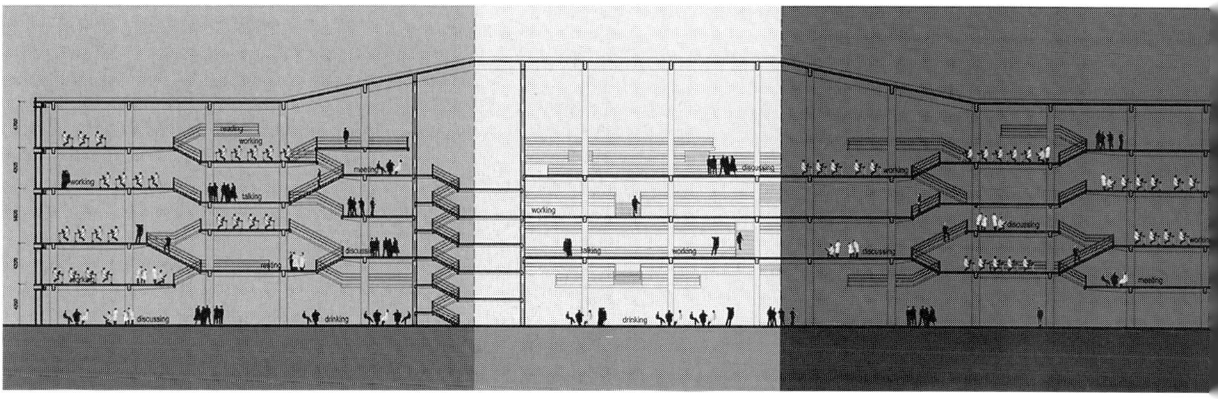

标准层平面采光系数示意

标准层平面

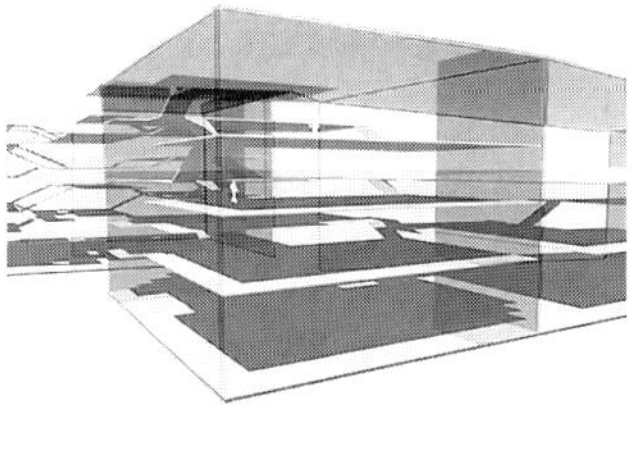

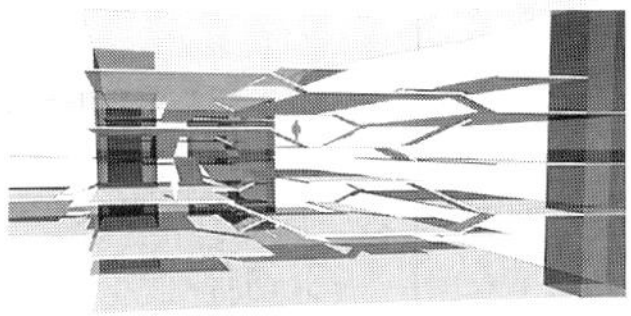

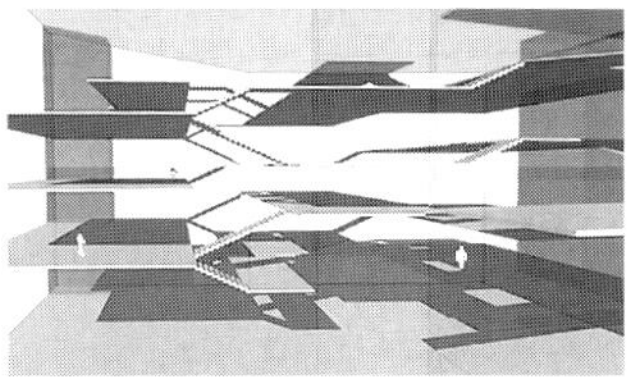

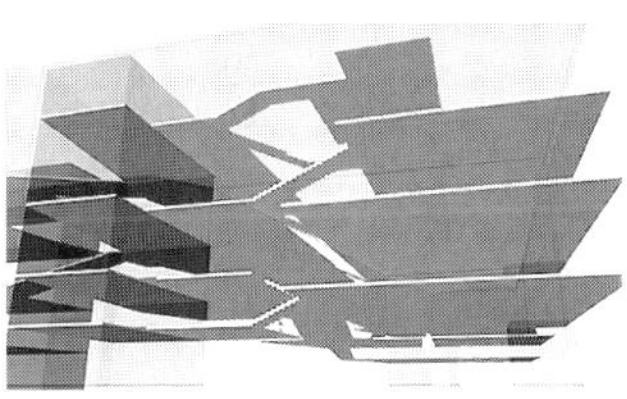

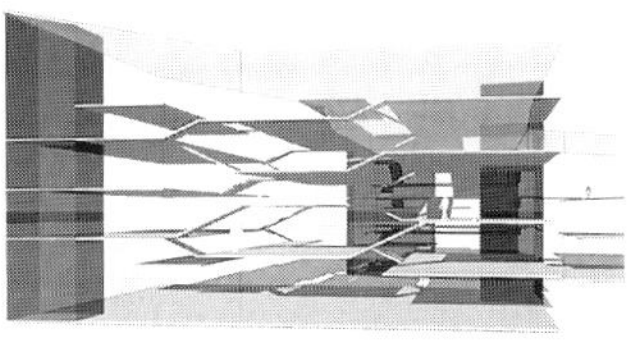

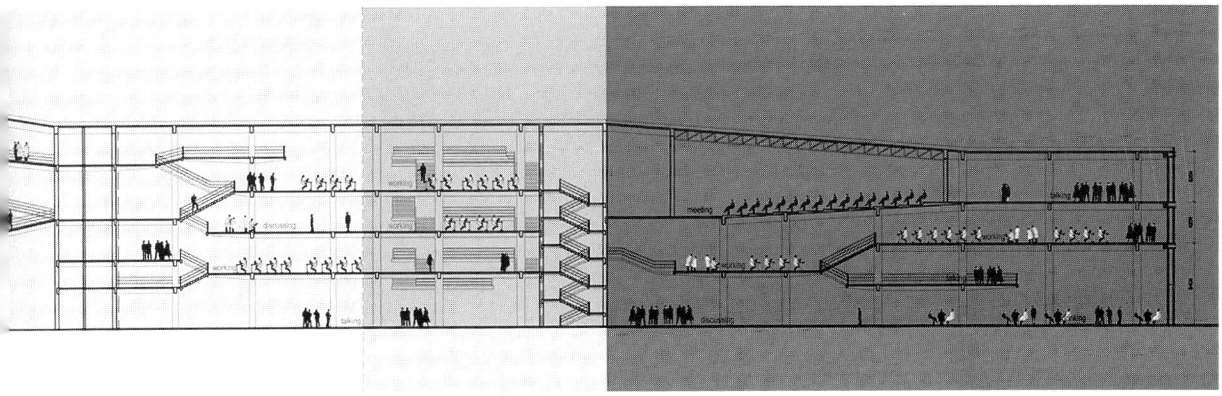

邓府巷高层住宅区设计
High-Rise Residence Design in Downtown, Nanjing

作者：柴金戈 胡晨希　指导老师：冷嘉伟

作为地处南京市城市最中心的邓府巷地段，其南北各临中山东路和长江路，近百年的法国梧桐凸显出浓重的历史韵味，而西侧的洪武北路则是一条交通繁忙的城市干道，缺乏绿化和景观。我们将一条绿带植入基地，它不仅在地面层为普通市民提供了一条连接长江路和中山东路的景观通道及商业长廊，更在地面二层为此处住宅区居民提供了独立的活动场所。结合对现今高层住宅的批判性研究，绿带的概念也随着高层住宅的结构朝垂直方向生长蔓延，在高层住宅中产生数个内凹的空中花园。为居民提供方便的活动平台。

The site is located between two historical streets, which are full of old trees, and also beside a city trunk road full of traffic and noises Landscape is rare in this district. We insert a green belt into this area, not only to connect two green streets for the city but also to provide a upper landscape for people who live here. The idea of a greenbelt also grows vertically to the high-rise upper space, creating several hanging gardens for a brand-new high-rise residence.

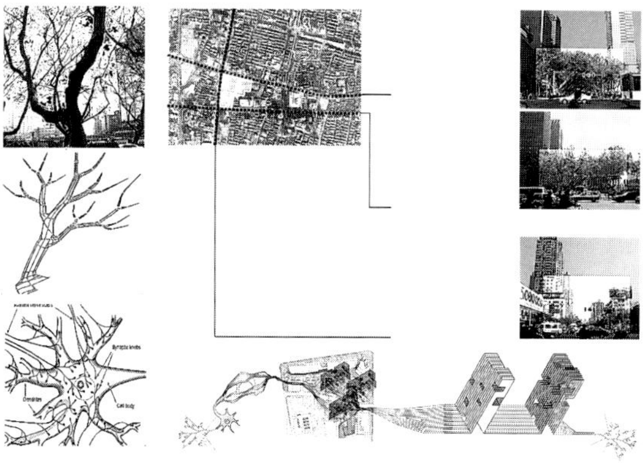

蔓延 生长 连接

一层平面

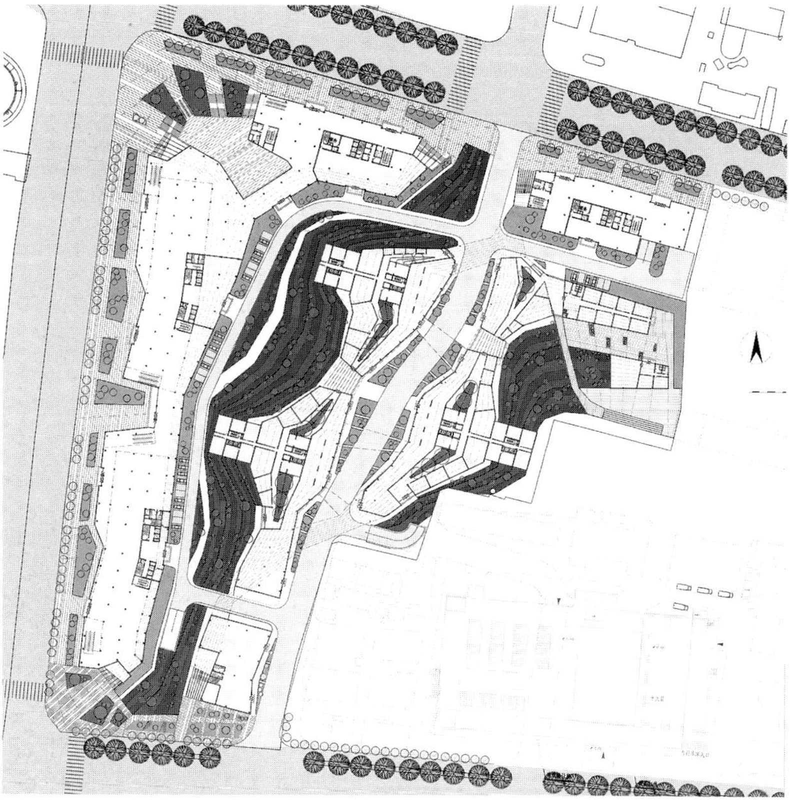

户型组合方式

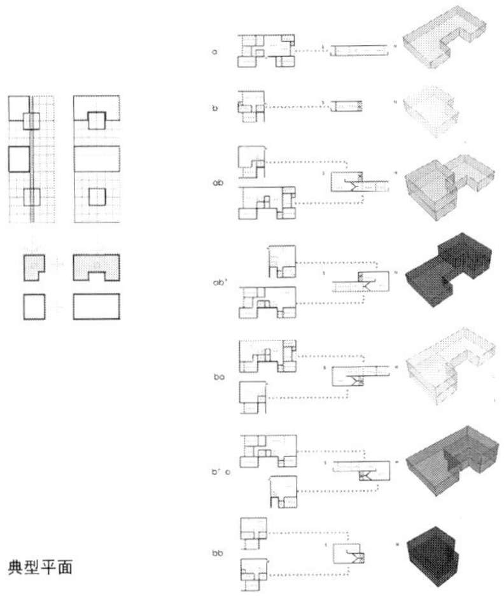

典型平面

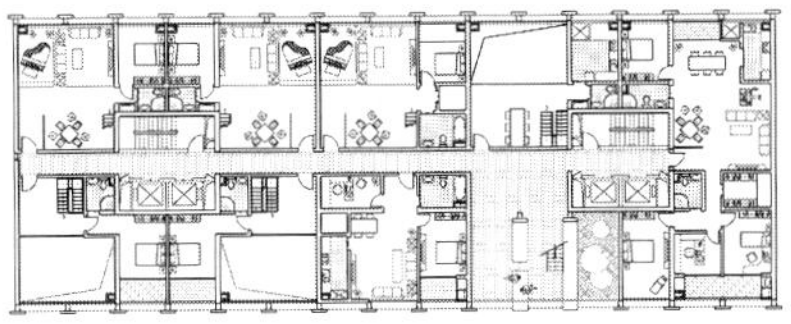

共享空中花园

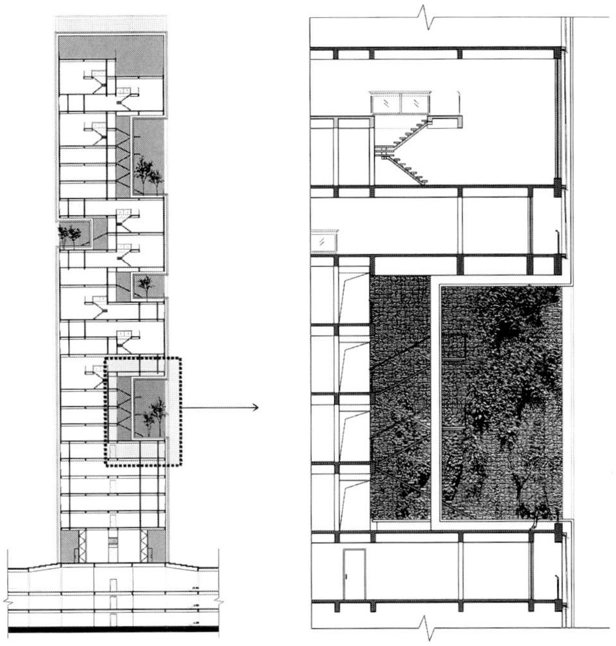

住区设计——城中村

Residence Area Design

作者：施展 曹奇琛　指导老师：张玫英

1. 大逃亡。封闭的系统必然产生异化，当内因与外因优劣而产生压力过大时，大逃亡将不可避免的产生，而所街正处在这种崩溃的边缘。
2. 无政府主义。由于大多数所街的使用者迟早都要离开，人们像使用一次性餐盒一样使用所街。
3. 脏器化。与健康的社区相比，所街缺乏的是一种可以在此安居的希望，因此将所街脏器化非不可能。
4. 生长。自发组织生长的单元具有强烈的可延续性与秩序感，一开始只是在所街与城市接壤处介入，最终通过生长使整个所街秩序化。
5. 单栋。四户为一组的单元以同样形式的交通体连接，在满足多样性的同时维护了整体感。
6. 组团。组团内部插入光体与绿化，满足整个社区高密度下的居住条件。

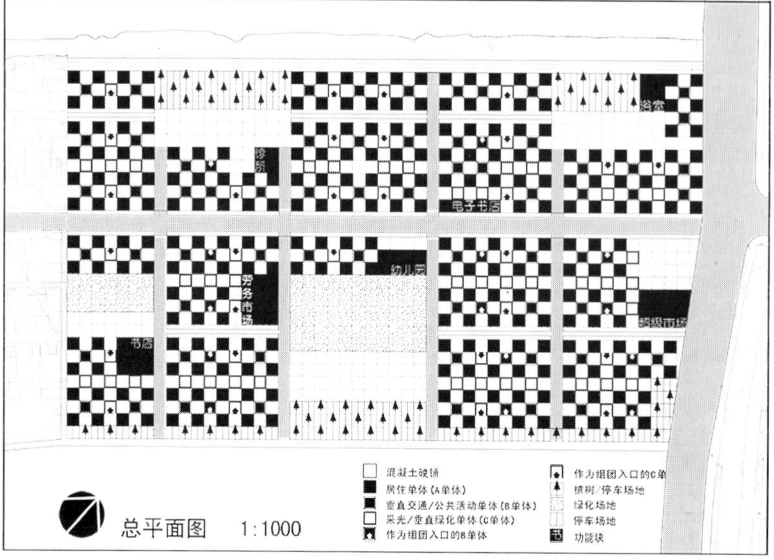

总平面图　1:1000

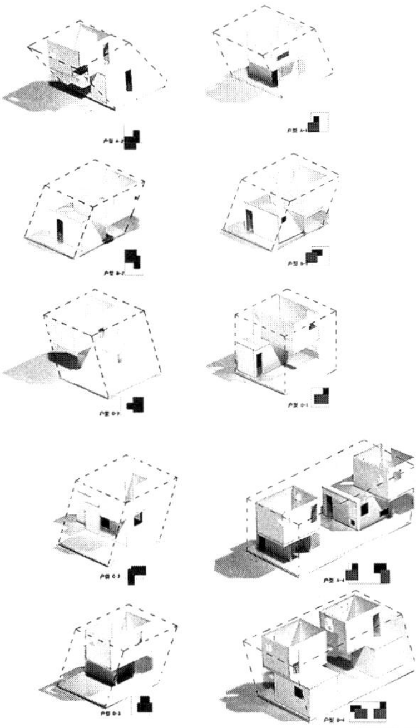

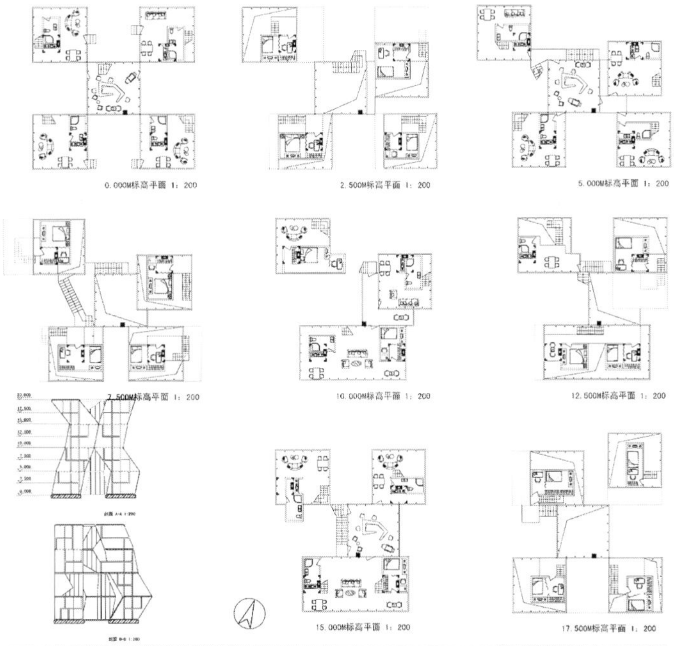
0.000M标高平面 1：200
2.500M标高平面 1：200
5.000M标高平面 1：200
7.500M标高平面 1：200
10.000M标高平面 1：200
12.500M标高平面 1：200
15.000M标高平面 1：200
17.500M标高平面 1：200

每户住宅均依空间的私密性分为两部分，卧室和卫生间分别置于上下两个盒子内，日常的起居在外部开放空间中。

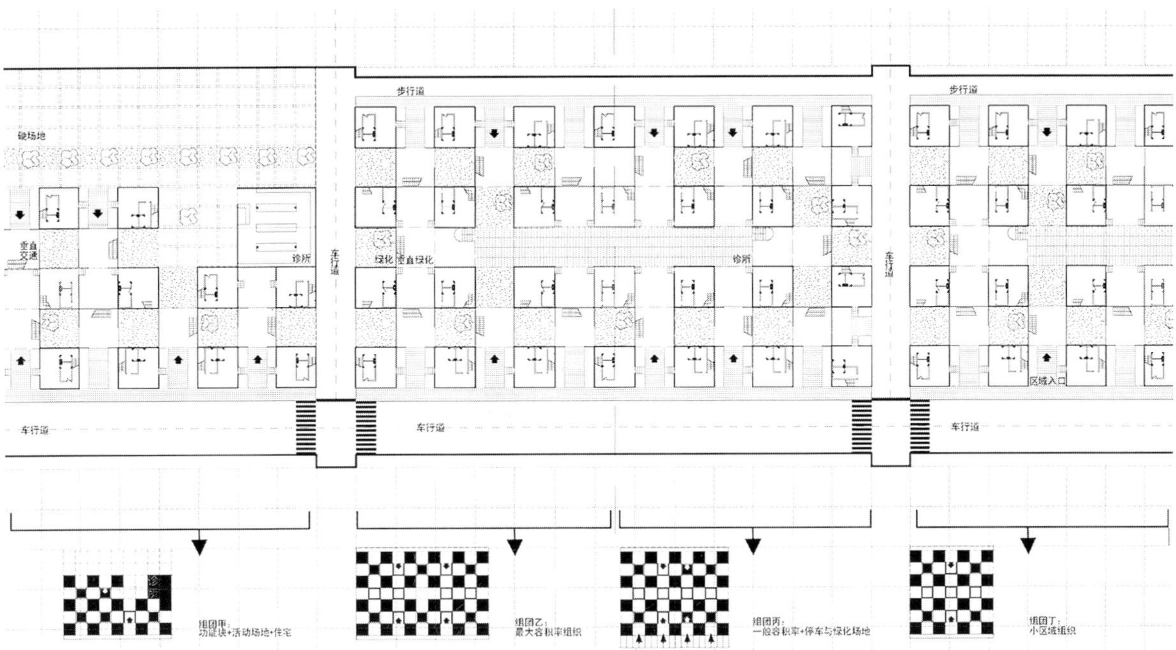
步行道
硬场地
垂直交通
诊所
车行道
绿化
垂直绿化
区域入口
组团甲：
功能块+活动场地+住宅
组团乙：
最大容积率组织
组团丙：
一般容积率+停车与绿化场地
组团丁：
小区域组织

住区设计
Residence Area Design

作者：姜汶林 何志鹏 指导老师：张玫英

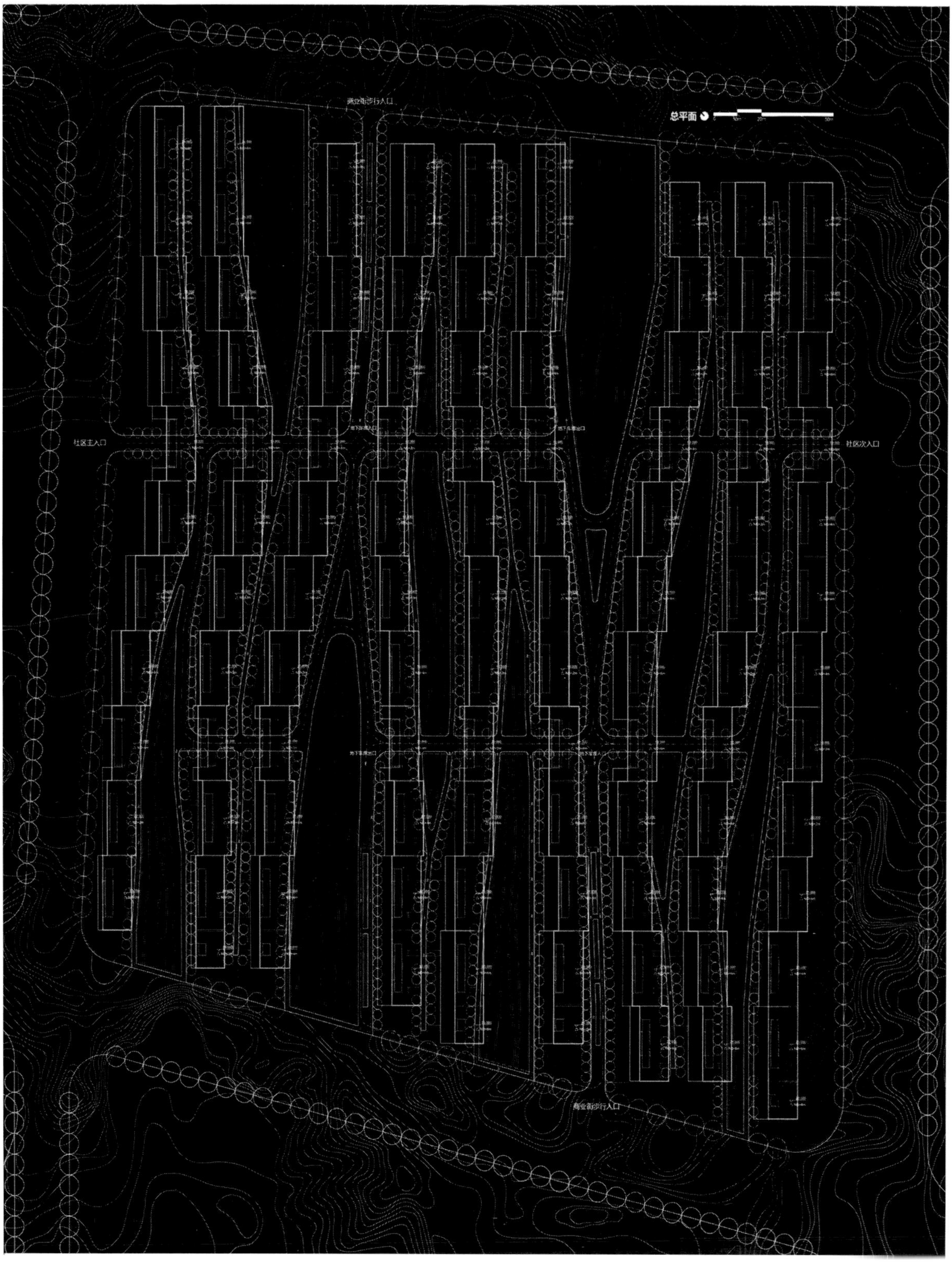

NEW DISTANCE
NEW YARD
NEW SPACE

通过研究低收入住宅的属性和特质，
创造符合低收入人群的住区空间。

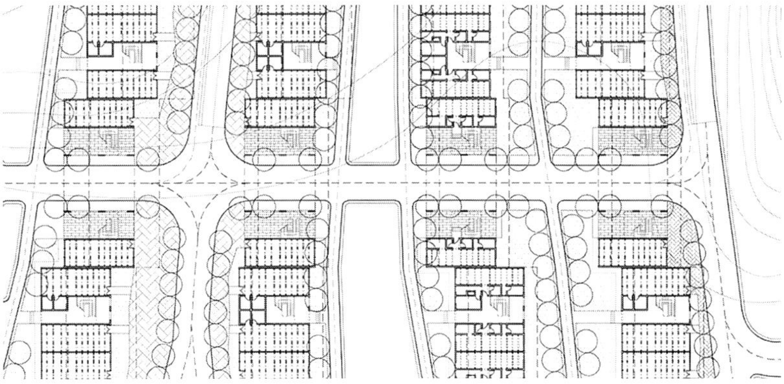

组合平面

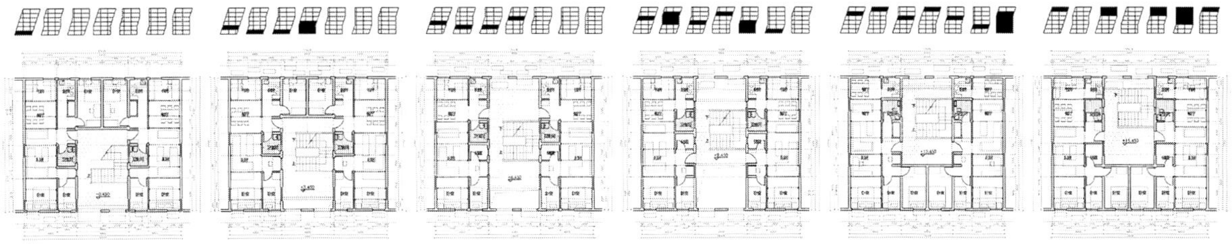

单元平面

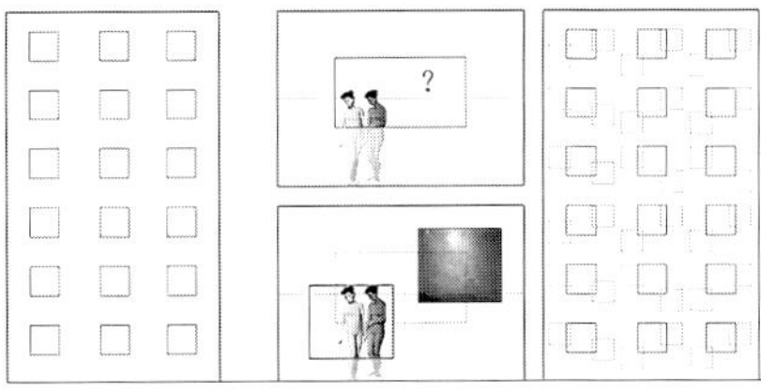

立面生成

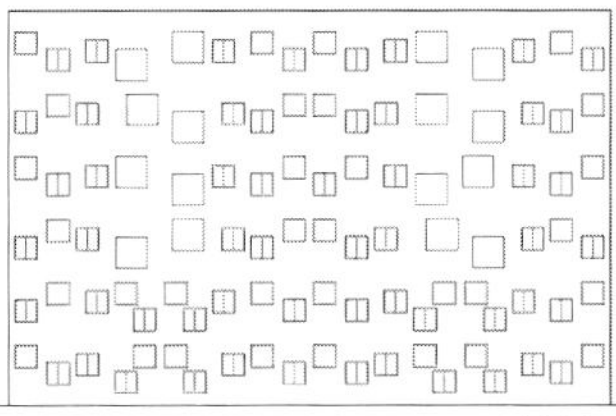

南立面

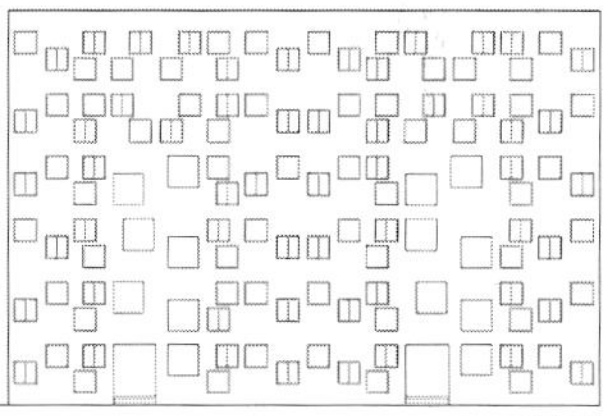

北立面

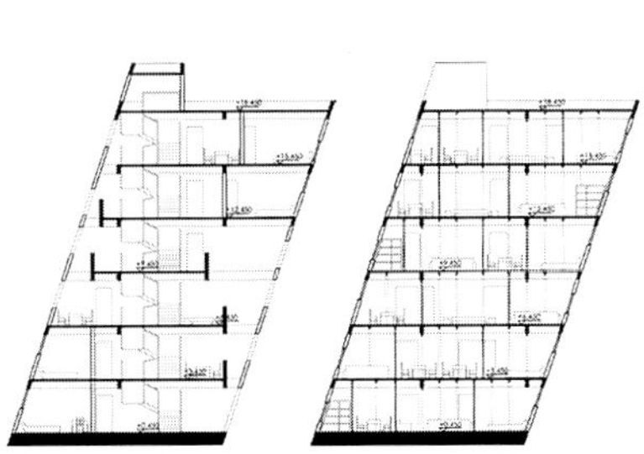

剖面

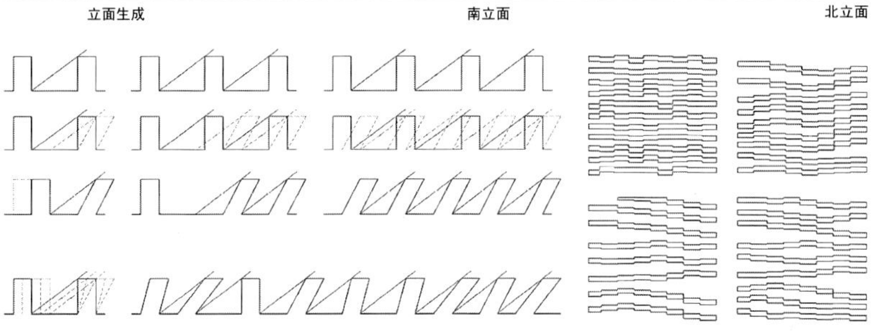

总平面生成

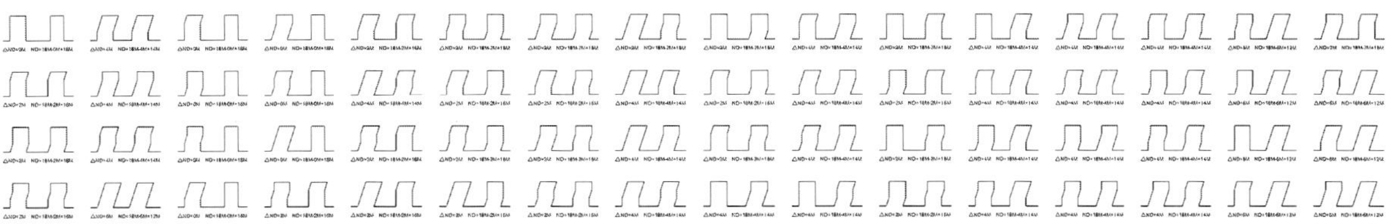

巷道空间分析

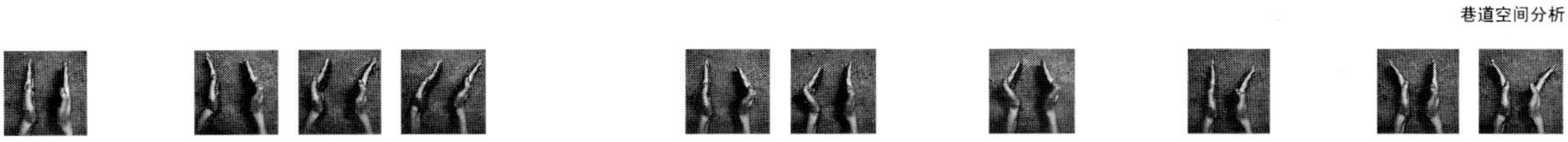

竹——材质的空间诠释
Bamboo: Spatial Interpretation of Materiality

作者：王明文　指导老师：单踊 张慧

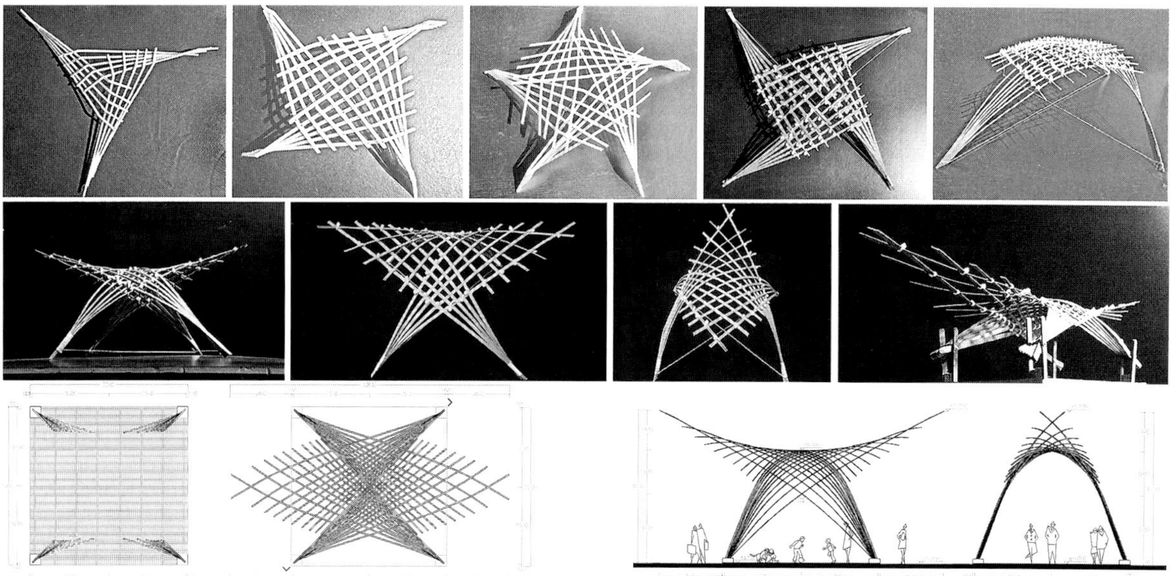

借助风车原理建造一个相互支撑体：先将杆件分成若干组，然后每组杆件下端集成一束作为结构体，上端发散开来，通过编织形成空间。将风车状的组合稍加变动，并将组数固定为四组，使所有竹子的顶端变成自由端，由于中部和底端受力且整体向上反弹使得竹子顶端会有上翘的趋势，改进后的方案不仅体现了竹子可弯曲的特点，同时也展现了其回复力所产生的反弹效果。

The foremost idea is to build a mutually-sustained body on the basis of windmill's theory: first the bars are attributed into several groups, then the ends of the bars are tied together respectively as the structural body, and the upper ends of the bars diverged into all directions. The windmill-shaped combination is modified slightly, and four-group model is chosen; the upper ends of the bars are free ends; the middle parts and the bottoms are under force and rebounding upwards, which makes the upper ends rise upwards.The revised project not only embodies the curving feature of bamboo, but also exihibits the rebounding's effect which its restoring force produces.

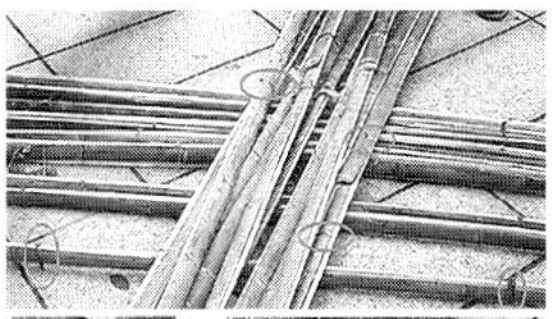

三重门
Three-Layer-Gates

作者：刘迪 唐元　指导老师：高源 阳建强 吴晓
获2006年全国高等城市规划专业指导委员会城市设计竞赛二等奖

基地位于南京总统府边的梅园新村。经常性的大量游客干扰了居民的生活。设计将社区结构分为三层即三重门。第一重门为城市共享空间，第二重门为过渡空间（社区居民共享空间），第三重门为居民私密空间。通过这种设计将基地内原住民的生活与周边地段的旅游活动剥离开来。这既维护了其生活私密性，又满足了城市旅游的需要。

The site is located in a historical area, which is near President Mansion in Nanjing. And everyday there will be a large number of visitors who bring strong disturbance to residents living around. So the objective is not only to continue the historical context, but also to reduce such disturbance. Through investigation, a structure system of three-layer-gates is found. And so based on the status quo, buildings with historical worth are preserved and some others are renewed or rebuilt by their quality and pattern.

A structure system of three-layer-gates is found: The first-layer-gate space is shared by all the people who come to the site; second-layer-gate space is shared by community; the third, the family. It's not only a type of original living there, but also a reaction to the disturbance outside.

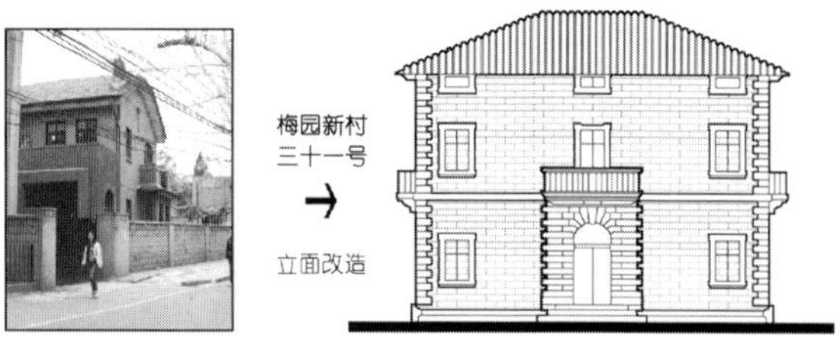

梅园新村三十一号，董必武故居立面改造方案，
去掉加建的门房部分和院墙部分，恢复董必武故居立面原貌，
作为历史旅游纪念性建筑。

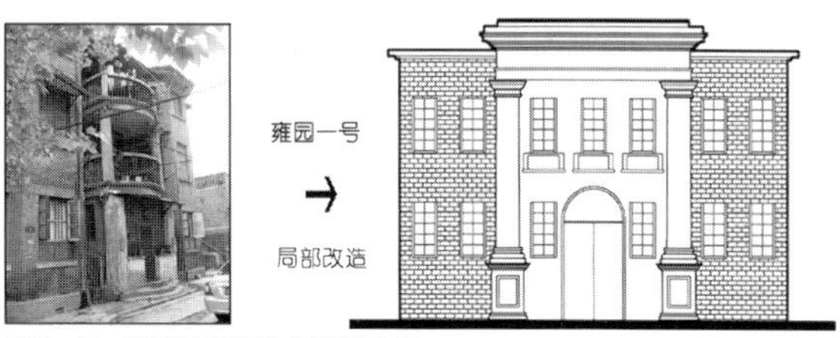

雍园一号，白崇禧故居整体结构改造方案，
去掉加建的三层部分和门前居民自建雨篷，恢复白崇禧故居原貌，
作为优秀民国小住宅建筑。

现状建筑图底分析

现状建筑质量分析

现状建筑年代及历史建筑分布

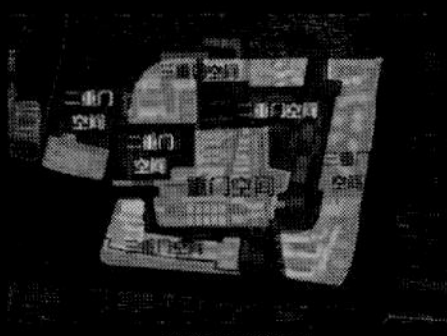

规划结构分析

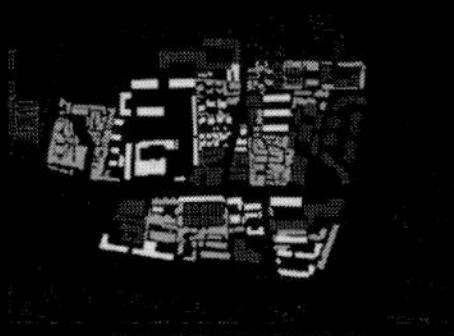

规划建筑整治方式分析

规划总平面 1:1500

规划建设图例

A 地块

- A1 特色旅馆
- A2 旅游纪念品专卖区

B 地块

- B1 原住民回迁居住区
- B2 社区停车场（30车位）
- B3 保留的原梅园饭店
- B4 社区活动广场
- B5 民间工艺研究室
- B6 社区幼儿园
- B7 社区活动中心
- B8 地下停车场
- B9 原住民回迁居住区（其中七座为保留）

C 地块

- C1 长江路旅游文化管理委员会
- C2 民俗博物馆
- C3 梅园新村纪念馆内部步行区
- C4 保留的周恩来、董必武故居
- C5 梅园新村历史纪念馆
- C6 旅游文化广场
- C7 公共厕所
- C8 艺术家工作室

D 地块

- D1 露天酒吧广场
- D2 钟岚里改造餐饮娱乐区
- D3 公共厕所
- D4 露天咖啡座

E 地块

- E1 恢复毗卢寺西花园开敞空间
- E2 毗卢寺万佛楼
- E3 毗卢寺南侧广场
- E4 社区活动广场

F 地块

- F1 保留的逸仙小学
- F2 社区活动广场
- F3 居住小区
- F4 地下停车场
- F5 保留的江苏报业大厦

G 地块

- G1 保留的工商管理大楼
- G2 地下停车场
- G3 居住小区
- G4 保留汉府雅苑高档住宅区
- G5 恢复白崇禧故居
- G6 居住小区

- P 机动车停车场
- B 自行车停车区
- S 公交车停靠站

基本用地指标平衡表

序号	代码	用地名称		面积	比例
1	R	居住用地		4.39	[illegible]
2	C	其中	商务办公用地	1.32	[illegible]
			商业金融用地	2.67	[illegible]
			文化娱乐用地	2.87	[illegible]
			文物古迹用地	[illegible]	[illegible]
3	M	工业用地		0	0
4	W	仓储用地		0	0
5	S	道路广场用地		3.82	[illegible]
6	U	市政公用设施用地		[illegible]	[illegible]
7	G	绿地		[illegible]	[illegible]
8	D	特殊用地		[illegible]	[illegible]
9	T	对外交通用地		0	0
合计		规划总用地		[illegible]	100%
其它	E	水域		[illegible]	

建筑拆改留指标统计

序号	内容	建筑面积	比例
1	[illegible]	[illegible]	[illegible]
2	[illegible]	[illegible]	[illegible]
3	[illegible]	[illegible]	[illegible]
4	[illegible]	[illegible]	[illegible]
5	[illegible]	[illegible]	[illegible]
6	[illegible]	[illegible]	[illegible]

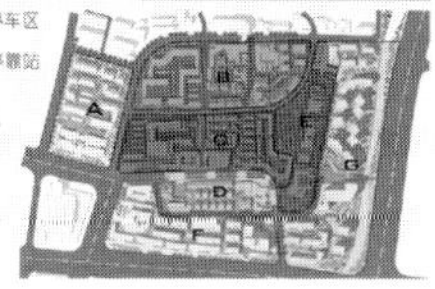

地块划分索引

收藏昨天——南京太平南路地段改造规划设计

A Renewing Design for South Taiping Street, Nanjing

作者：肖扬 计灵骏 指导老师：阳建强

太平南路作为南京市重要的商业中心，有着深厚的历史文化资源和传统商业氛围。由于复杂的社会经济变迁和城市发展，出现严重的功能性和结构性衰退。设计对太平南路的历史资源和非物质文化遗产进行了全面的梳理和深入的调查，较为准确地对太平南路的功能进行了定位，因地制宜对各类历史文化资源的保护提出了规划对策。在系统整合历史文化资源的基础上，针对不同的主题进行了精心的城市设计，较好地处理了太平南路商业中心传统特色延续和新活力注入的关系。

South Taiping Street was an important business shopping area in Nanjing. It was famous for its combination of historical cultural heritage and traditional business activities. However, under the effect of urban development and the evolution of modern socialization, South Taiping Street is no longer attractive, especially in the function of structure. In the project, it is highlight that plenty of surveys about the local historical cultural heritages and intangible cultural heritages have been done. Having analyzed lots of successful cases of urban regeneration, we take a proposal making different theme for each part of the street. Besides, we also propose the connection of South Taiping Street with the city public transport systems.

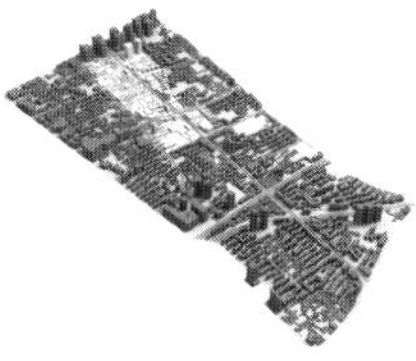

太平南路鸟瞰模型

文物保护单位分析图

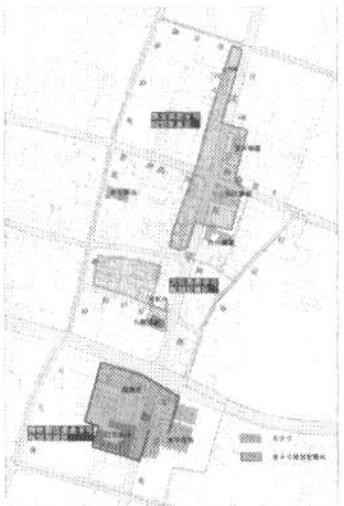

老字号分析图

建议保留建筑分析图

规划总平面图

建筑年代分析图

建筑高度分析图

建筑质量分析图

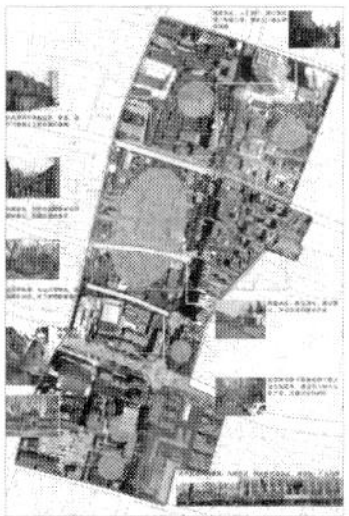

整治改造设计意向

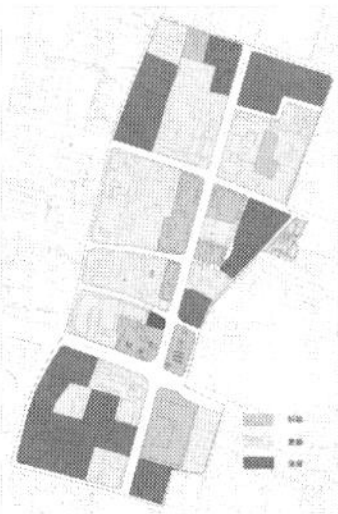

建筑更新方式规划图

特色街区规划图

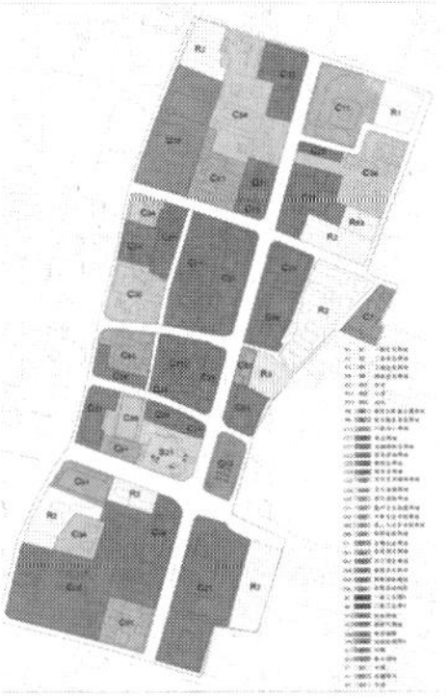

用地规划图

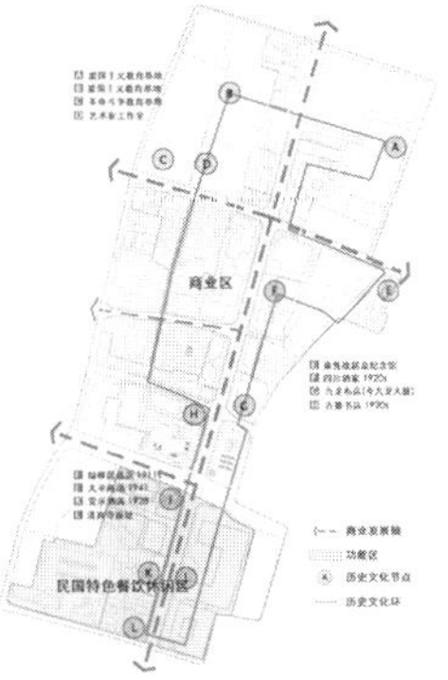

功能结构图

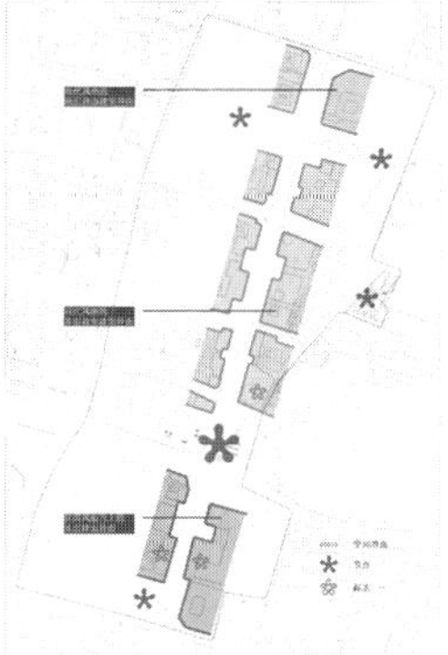

空间形态规划图

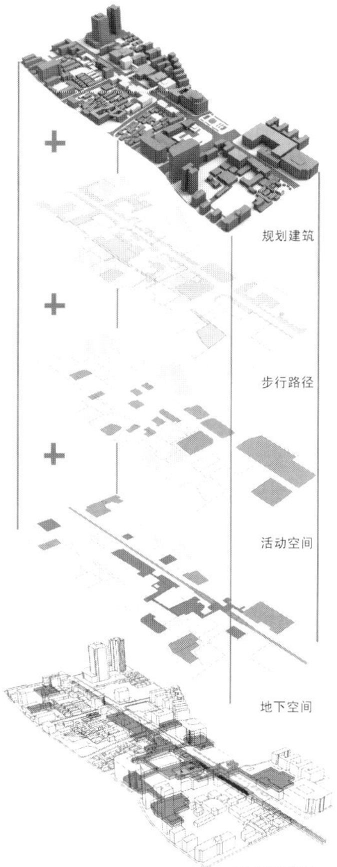

地下空间系统

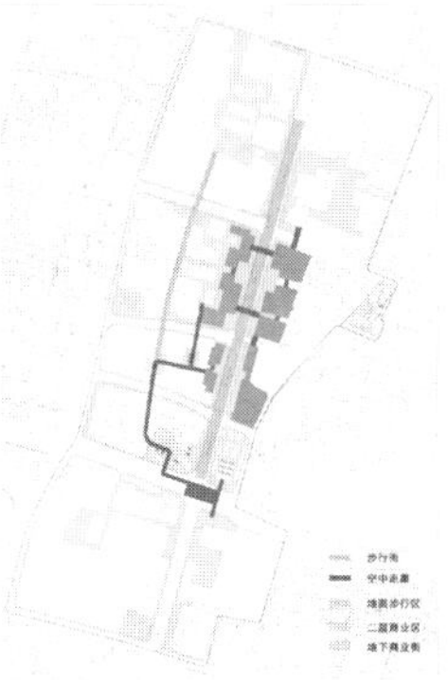

步行系统规划图

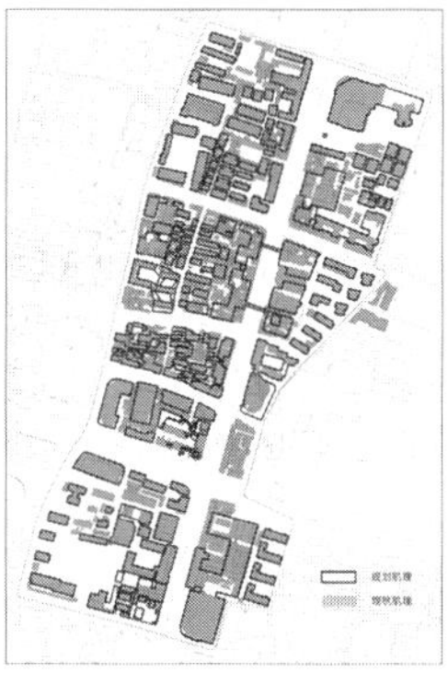

新旧建筑关系对比图

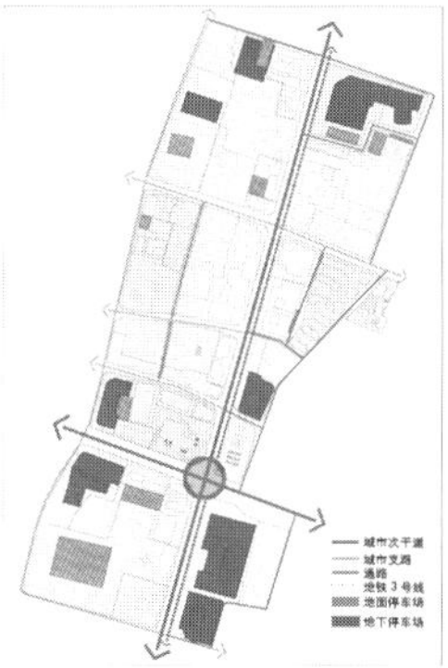

道路交通规划图

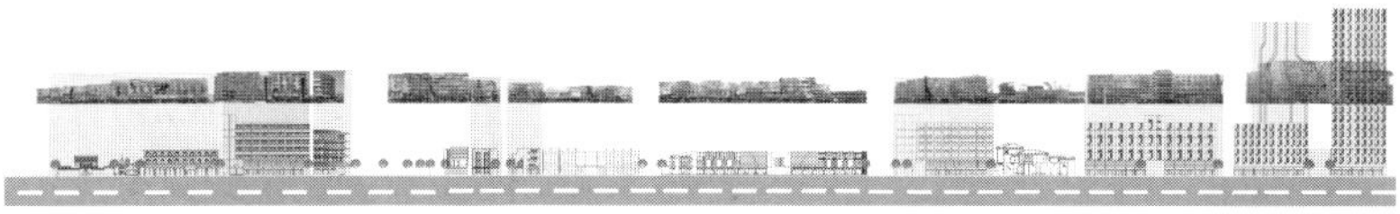

太平南路西立面改造

城市设计——场所重塑

Urban Design

作者：张殊 宫作成 指导老师：杨俊宴

获2007年全国高等学校城市规划学科本科生城市设计作业三等奖

基地位于无锡老城中心区，是现代商业包裹下的历史地段，具有典型性与代表性。历史与现代如何交融成为该步行街区设计中的主要矛盾。该方案以研究人的活动为出发点，以承载人活动的场所作为设计重点，重塑各个性格鲜明的场所。

Circulation and aggregation are the essential elements for formulating the user dynamics in a public space. Considered a public space as a perfect environment where neither masses nor particles are destroyed but to transform to other states. The dynamic of a public space can be seen as the balance between circulation and aggregation.

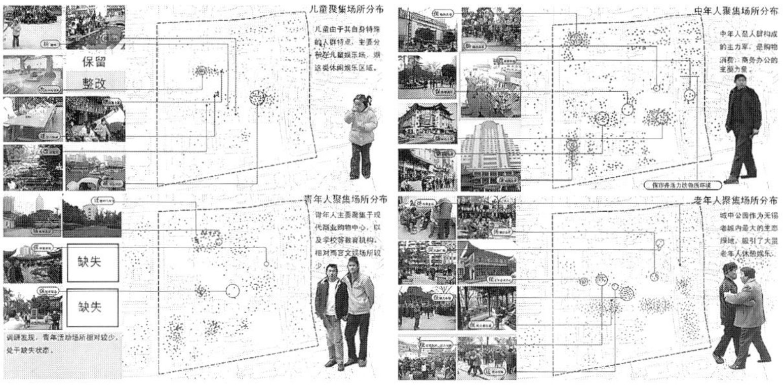

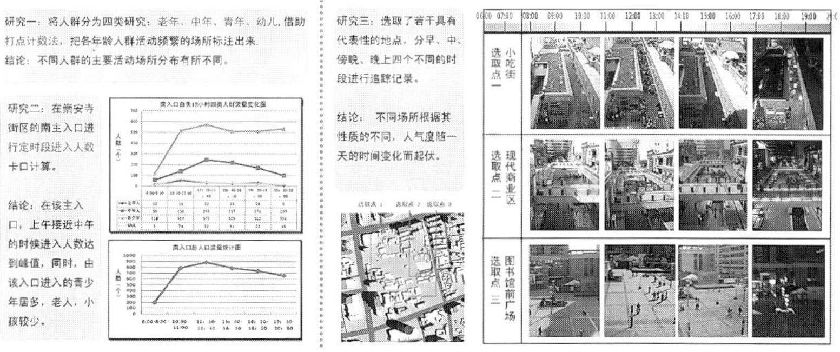

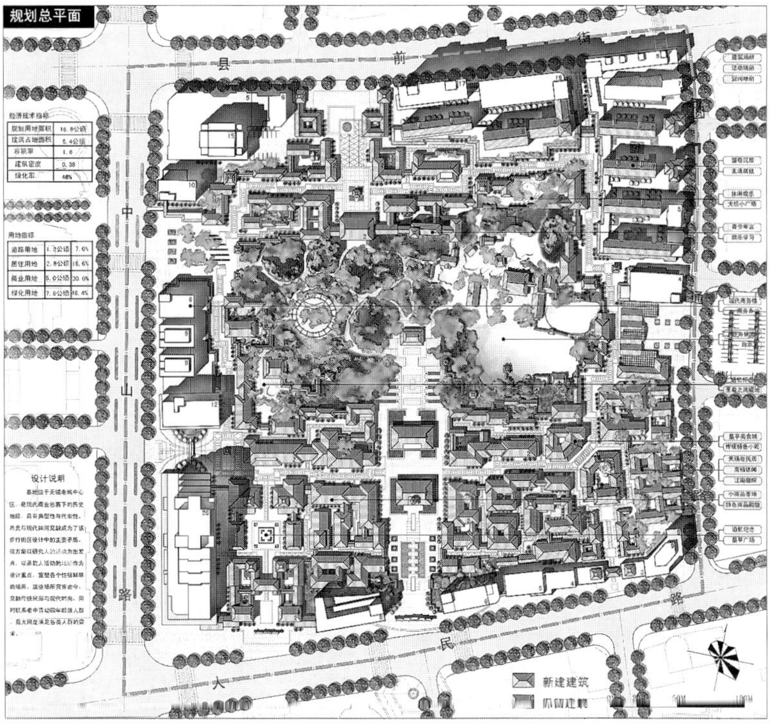

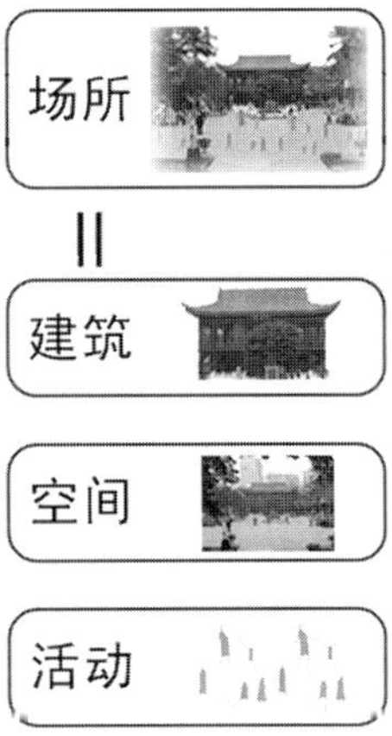

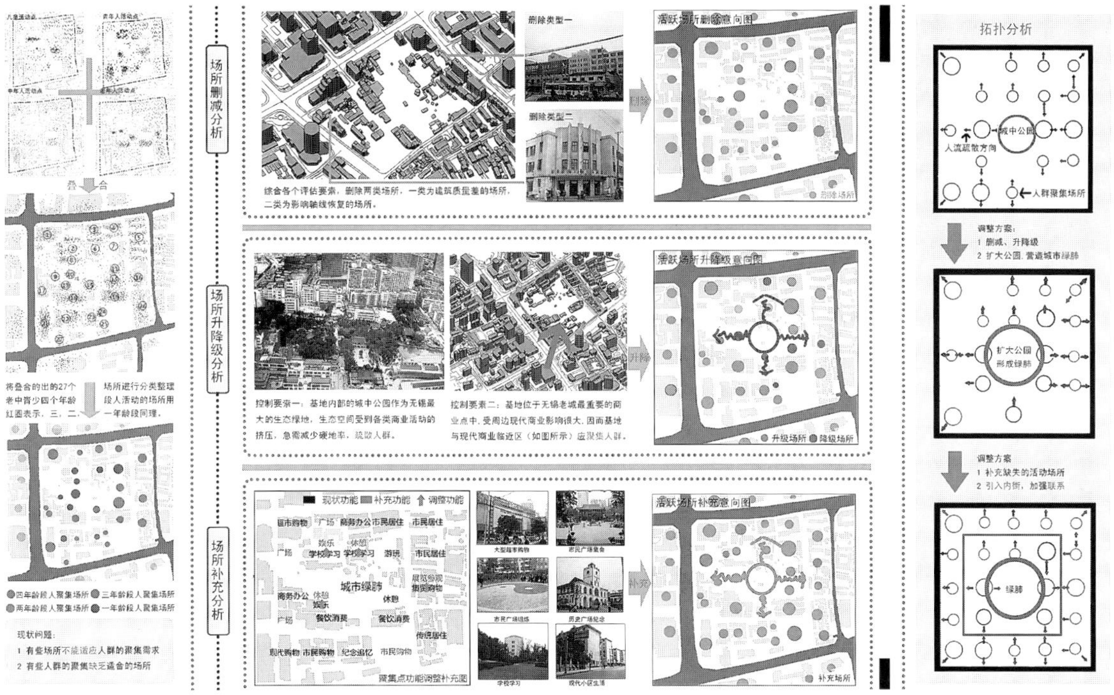
儿童活动点
青年人活动点
中年人活动点
老年人活动点
叠合
将叠合的出的27个场所进行分类整理
老中青少四个年龄段人活动的场所用红圆表示，三，二，一年龄段同理。
四年龄段人聚集场所
三年龄段人聚集场所
两年龄段人聚集场所
一年龄段人聚集场所
现状问题：
1 有些场所不能适应人群的聚集需求
2 有些人群的聚集缺乏适合的场所
场所删减分析
综合各个评估要素，删除两类场所，一类为建筑质量差的场所，二类为影响轴线恢复的场所。
删除类型一
删除类型二
删除
活跃场所删除意向图
删除场所
场所升降级分析
控制要素一：基地内部的城中公园作为无锡最大的生态绿地，生态空间受到各类商业活动的挤压，急需减少硬地率，疏散人群。
控制要素二：基地位于无锡老城最重要的商业点中，受周边现代商业影响很大，因而基地与现代商业临近区（如图所示）应聚集人群。
升降
活跃场所升降级意向图
升级场所
降级场所
场所补充分析
现状功能
补充功能
调整功能
超市购物
广场
商务办公
市民居住
娱乐
休憩
学校学习
游玩
城市绿肺
展览参观
集贸购物
餐饮消费
传统居住
现代购物
市民购物
纪念追忆
聚集点功能调整补充图
大型超市购物
市民广场聚会
市民广场锻炼
历史广场纪念
学校学习
现代小区生活
补充
活跃场所补充意向图
补充场所
拓扑分析
城中公园
人流疏散方向
人群聚集场所
调整方案：
1 删减、升降级
2 扩大公园，营造城市绿肺
扩大公园
形成绿肺
调整方案
1 补充缺失的活动场所
2 引入内街，加强联系
绿肺

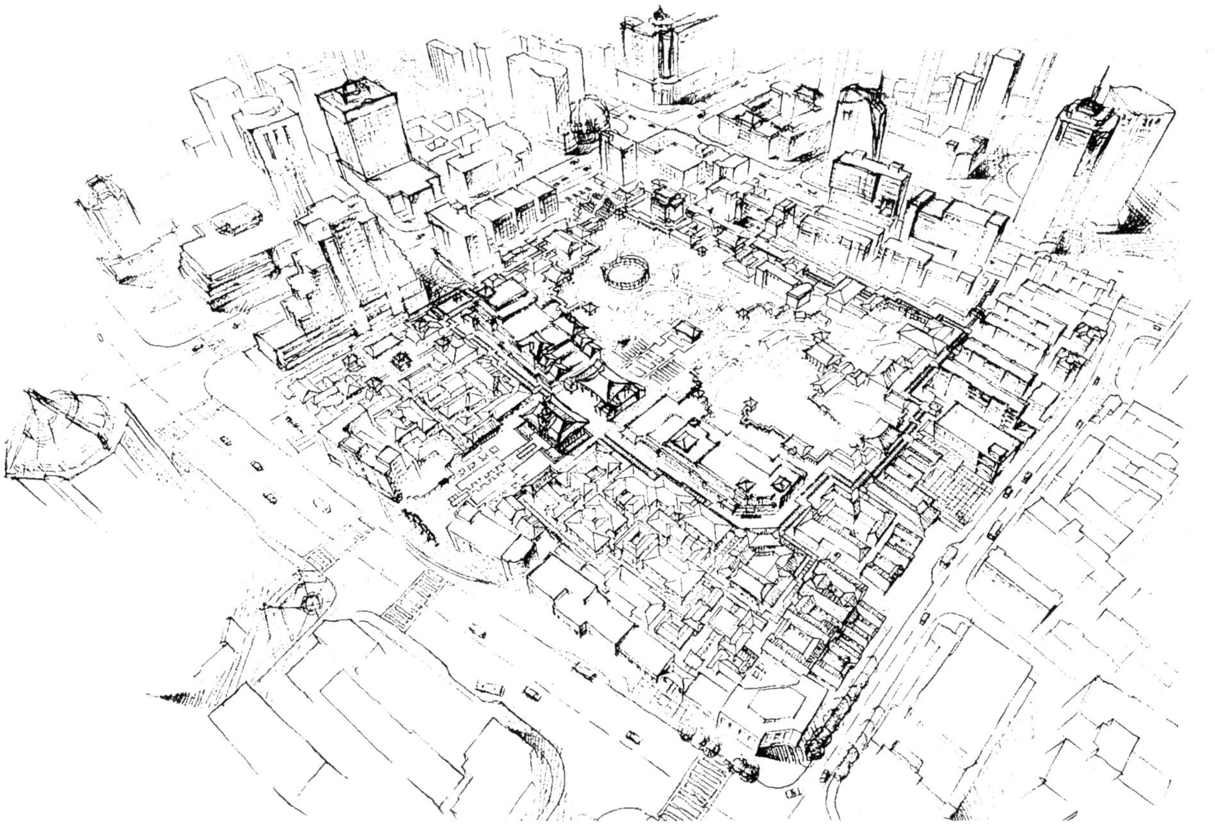

城市设计
Urban Design

作者：郑越　胥明明　指导老师：杨俊宴　雒建利　高源
获2008年全国高等学校城市规划学科本科生城市设计作业三等奖

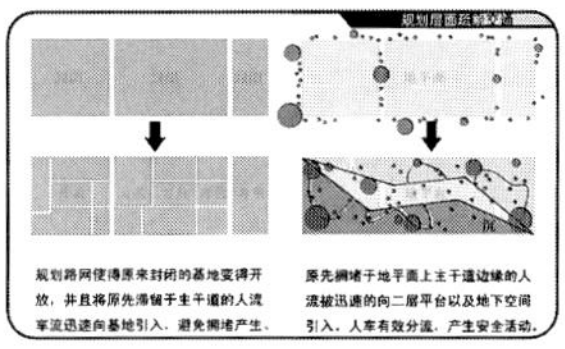

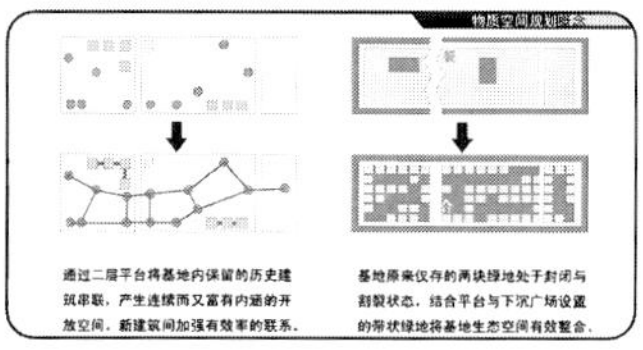

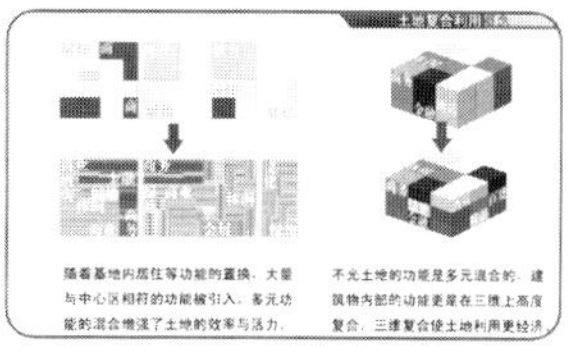

人车共面，交叉口多，产生危险！

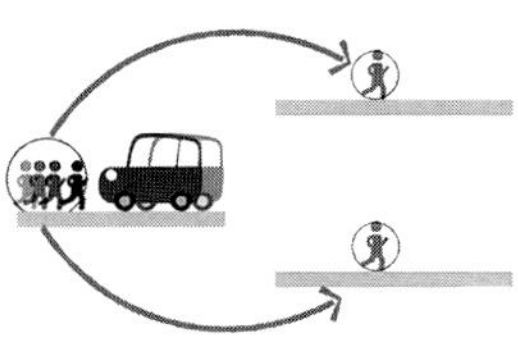

人车分流，减少危险，增加活动。

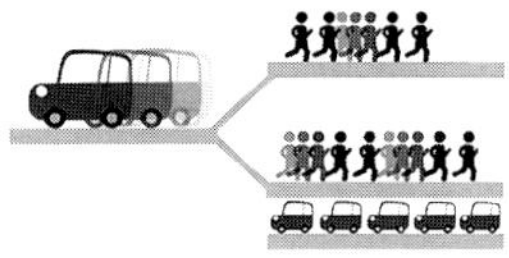

人车和谐，各得其所，高效安全。

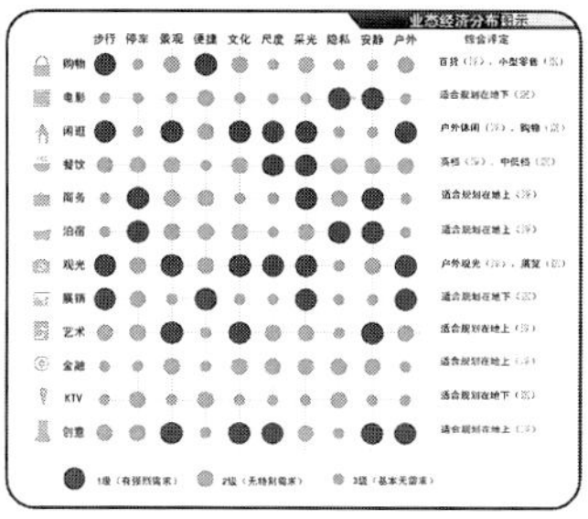

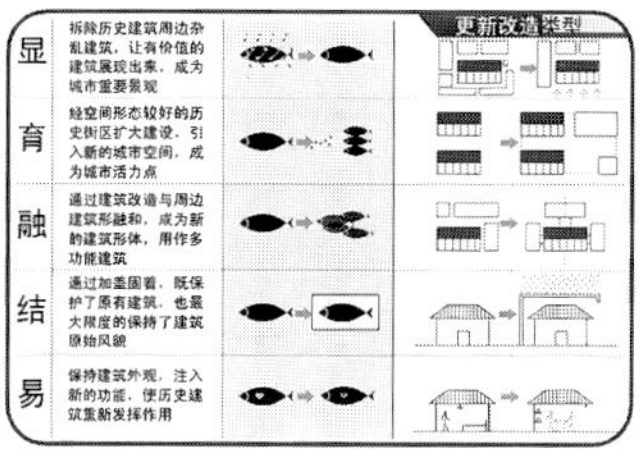

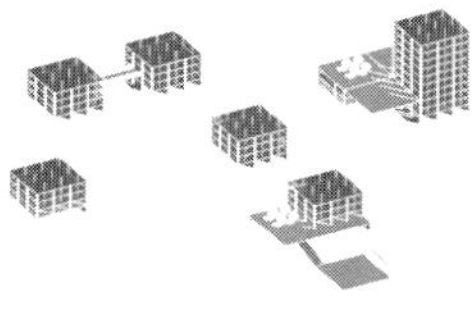

单体建筑之间通过平台系统连接

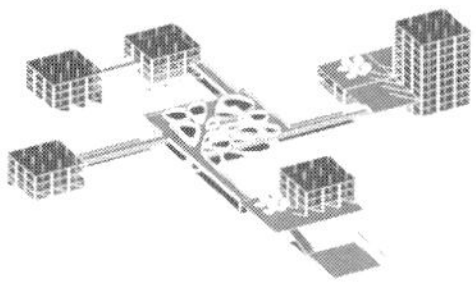

平台交汇又产生安全的交流空间

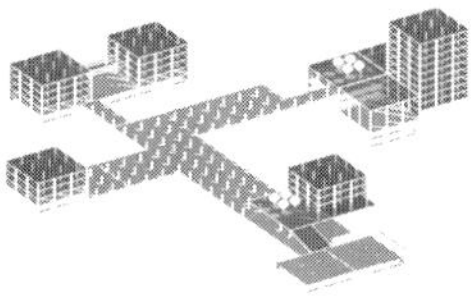

平台系统与地下交通网无缝衔接

总平面

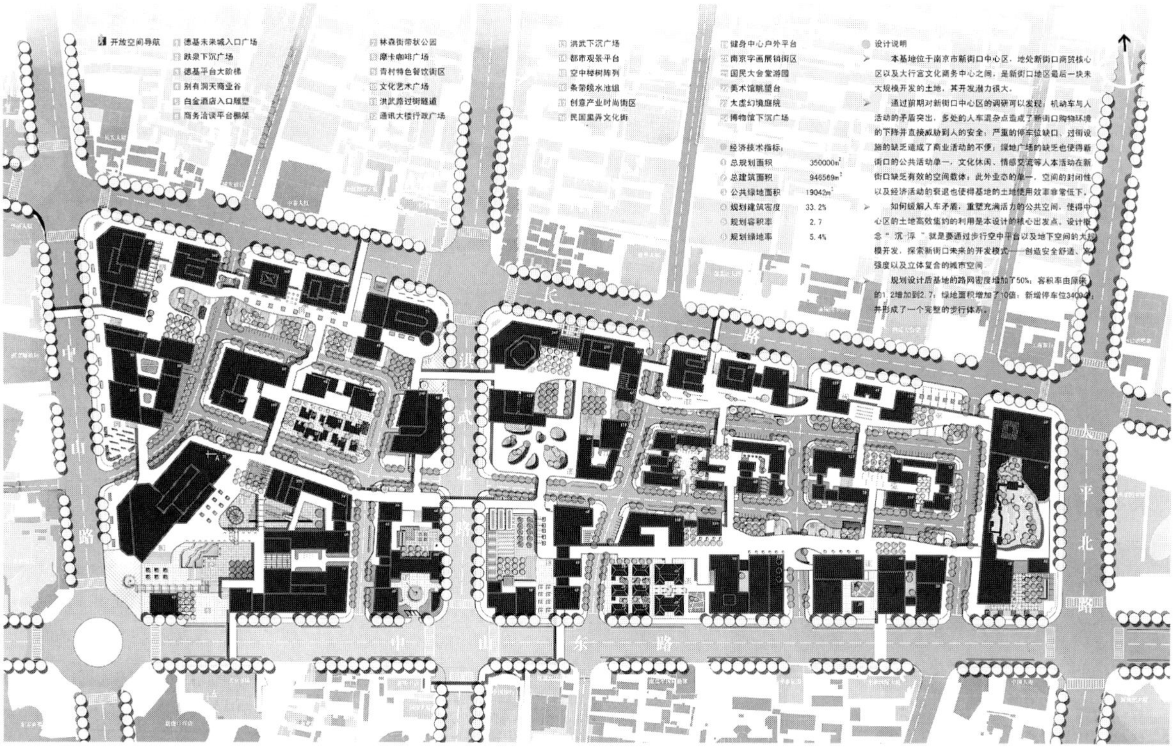

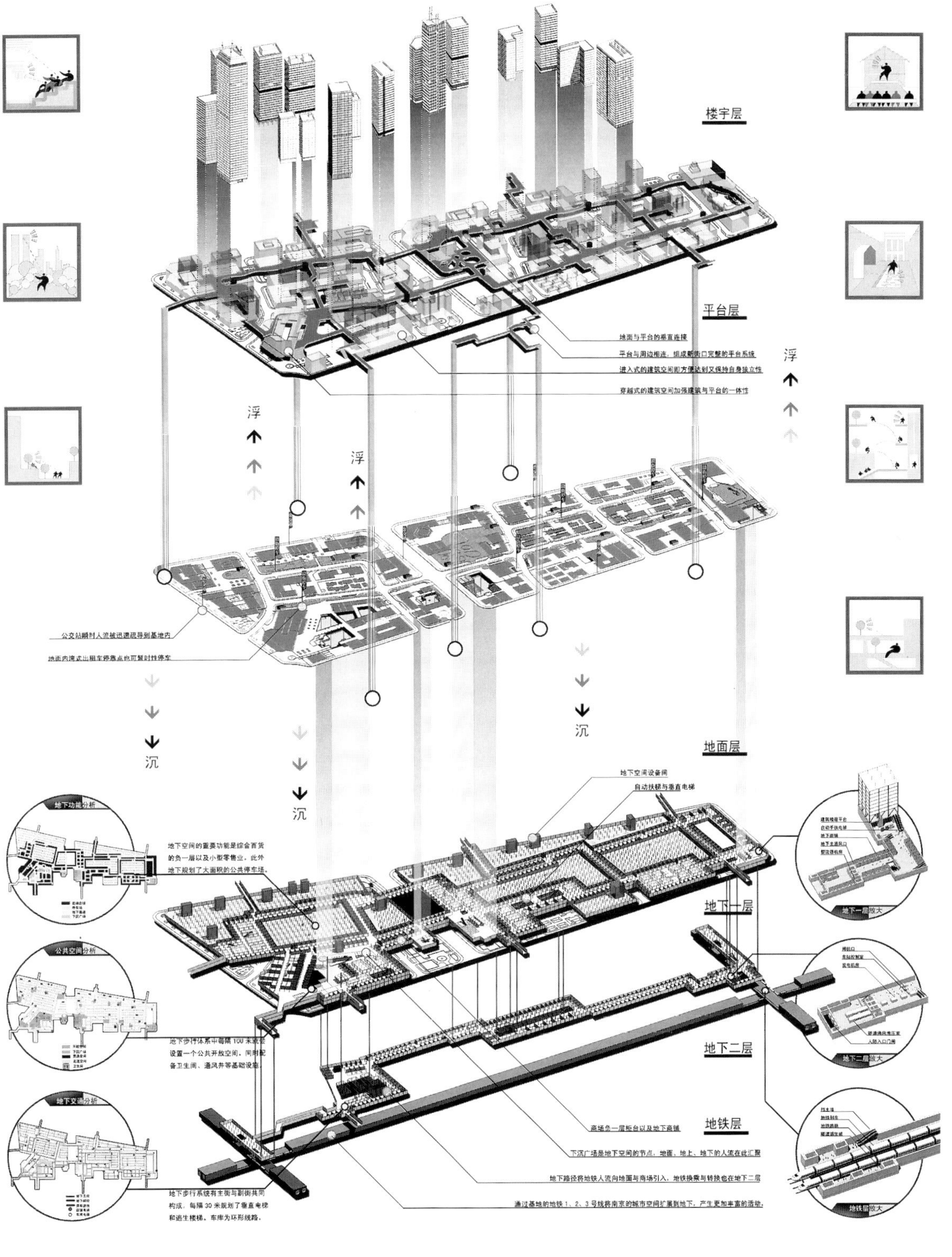
楼宇层
平台层
地面与平台的垂直连接
平台与周边相连，组成新街口完整的平台系统
进入式的建筑空间即方便达到又保持自身独立性
穿越式的建筑空间加强建筑与平台的一体性
浮
浮
公交站瞬时人流被迅速疏导到基地内
地面内湾式出租车停靠点也可暂时性停车
沉
沉
沉
地面层
地下空间设备间
自动扶梯与垂直电梯
地下功能分析
地下空间的重要功能是综合百货的负一层以及小型零售业，此外地下规划了大面积的公共停车场。
地下一层
地下一层放大
公共空间分析
地下步行体系中每隔 100 米就会设置一个公共开放空间，同时配备卫生间、通风井等基础设施。
地下二层
地下二层放大
地下交通分析
地下步行系统有主街与副街共同构成，每隔 30 米规划了垂直电梯和逃生楼梯，车库为环形线路。
商场负一层柜台以及地下商铺
地铁层
下沉广场是地下空间的节点，地面、地上、地下的人流在此汇聚
地下路径将地铁人流向地面与商场引入，地铁换乘与转换也在地下二层
通过基地的地铁 1、2、3 号线将南京的城市空间扩展到地下，产生更加丰富的活动。
地铁层放大

南立面

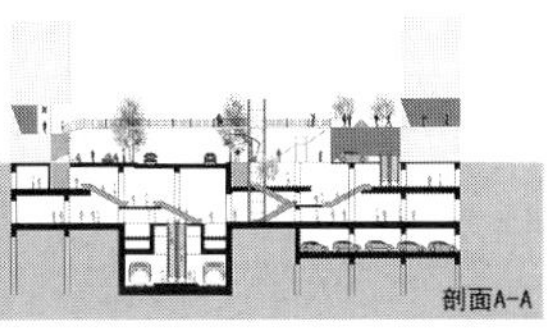
剖面A-A

扬州老城中心区城市设计
Urban Design of City Center, Yangzhou

作者：邵咪 宋亚程 指导老师：杨俊宴 雒建利 高源

昔日古城是整个扬州城的发展动力，新城发展依托老城。现今新城发展成熟反噬古城，现代元素入侵致使古城内传统元素支离破散。通过对传统公共生活元素的提取，复兴古城核心，并与现代元素共生、衍化，进而形成一个体系完整的城市中心区，辐射整个扬州城市。

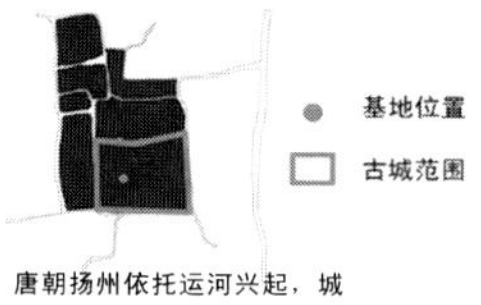

唐朝扬州依托运河兴起，城市规模较大，繁荣兴盛。

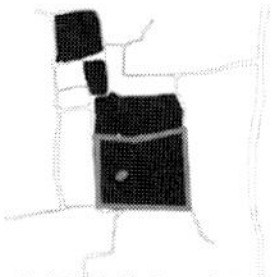

宋朝面积缩小，由于需要分三城而治。

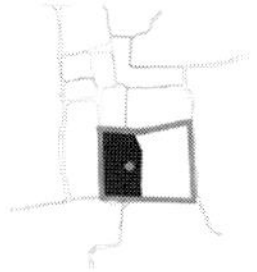

明初城市急剧减小，城市脱离运河发展。

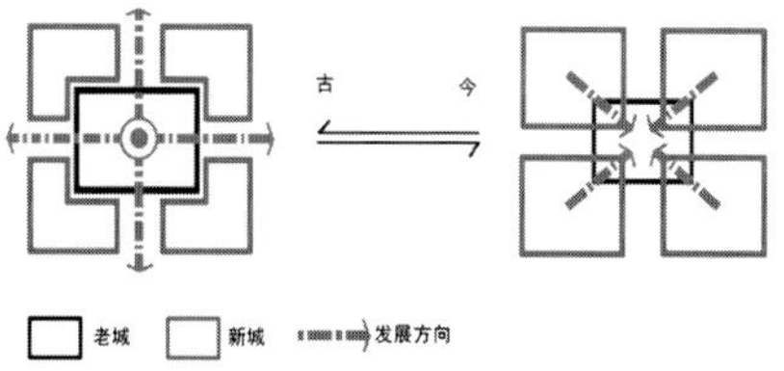

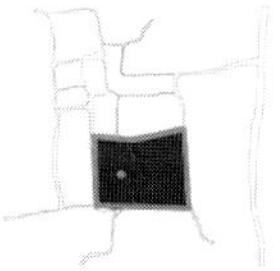

清代城市再次依托运河发展，城市规模扩大

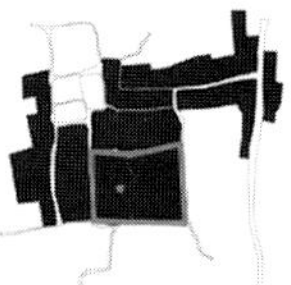

新中国初期城市面积增长速度减缓。

现今城市向西快速发展，西城面积剧增。

混搭空间=街+院

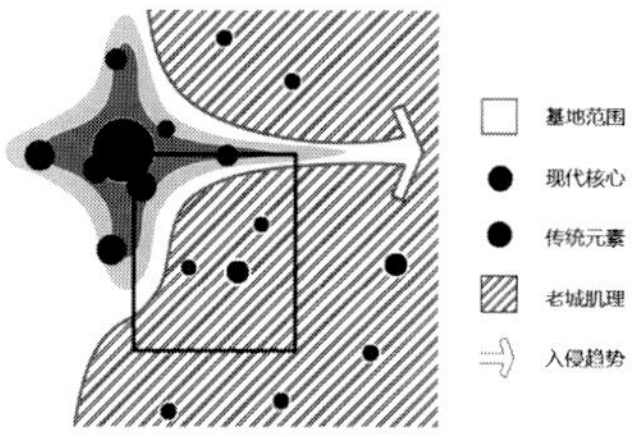

现状：
受文昌阁商业核心影响，现代商业体系较为成熟，成为整个基地甚至古城范围的重要影响元素，古城内原有传统元素，但受到现代元素入侵。

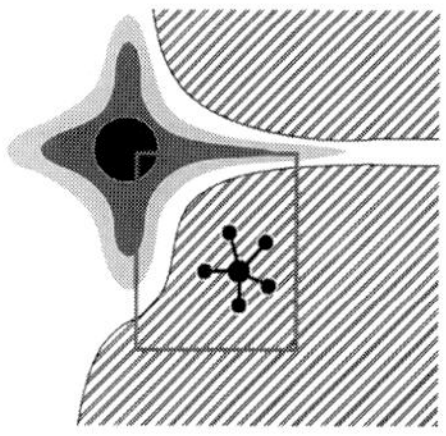

新生：
在传统居住区内建立的新生活力点，使其成为组织整个传统片区的核心，在古城范围内形成双核心格局。

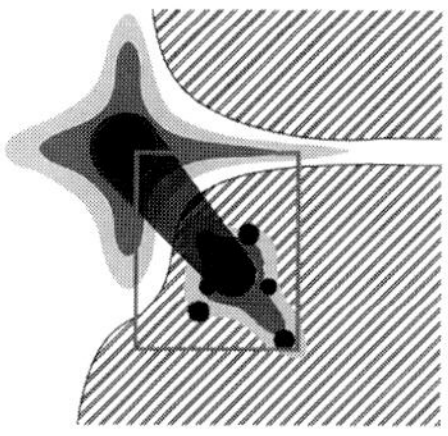

共生：
将新生的核心与原有核心串联成一个整体，形成一条连接古城和现代商业的动力带，现代和传统的力量可以共生传递。

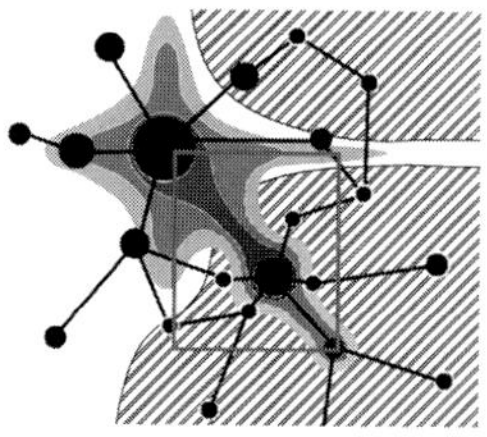

衍生：
动力带进一步发展延伸并向外辐射，带动古城和现代商业片区的潜在活力元素发展，衍生出新生力量，传统与现代和谐发展。

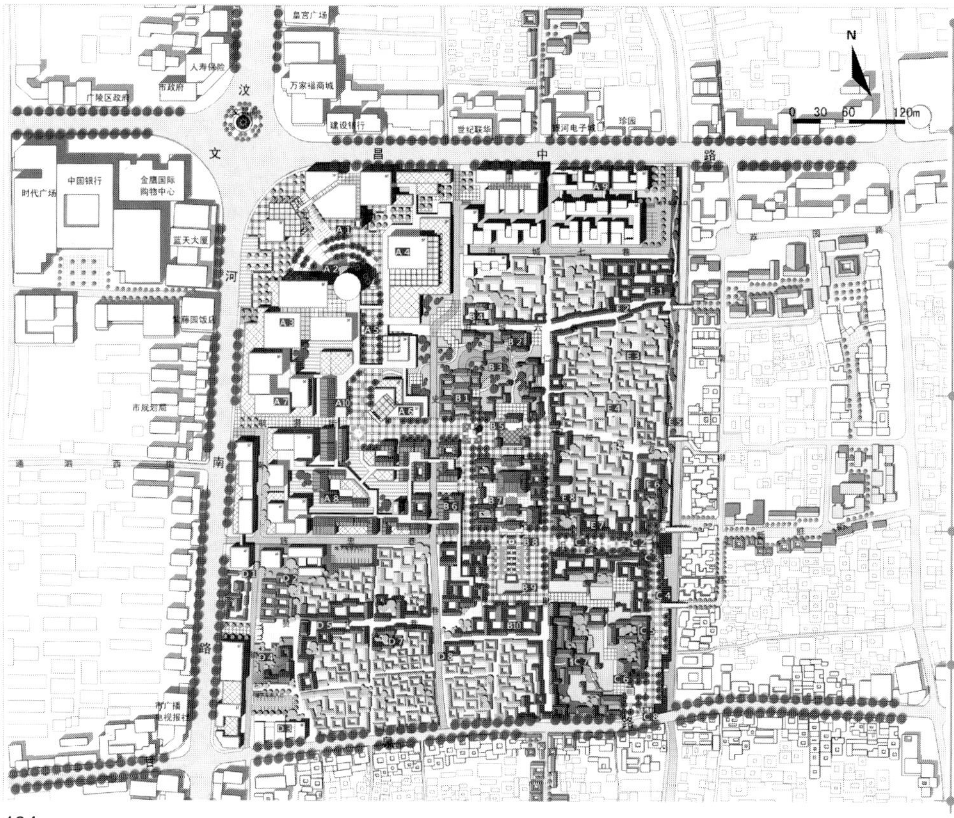

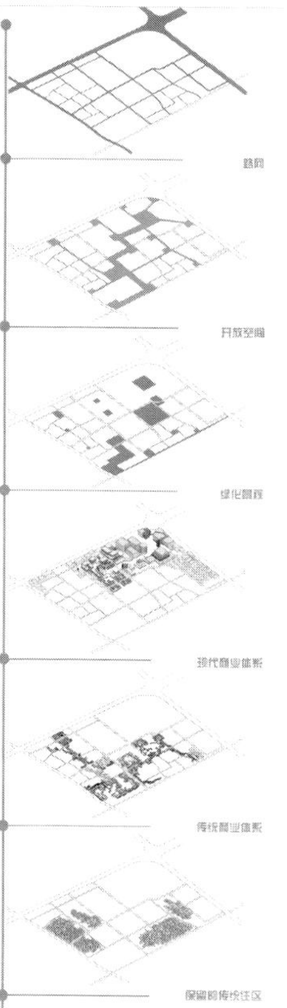

廟 庙是传统商业体系的核心元素多以庙会形式存在，空间序列沿轴线展开，仪式感较强

館 传统居住区内的文化场所文人墨客聚集于此，空间上存在轴线序列，多与园林景观结合

園 传统体系中的景观中心是休闲游走的场所，空间布局比较自由

門 城门是连接两个区域的通道，也是集市入口的标志，门内外多会形成集会场所

橋 桥连接两岸的交通流动人群较多是闹市形成的理想场所，是传统体系中的独特景观

巷 连接以上各要素的通道，基本生活设施都分布于巷道之中，建筑上采用前宅后店的形式

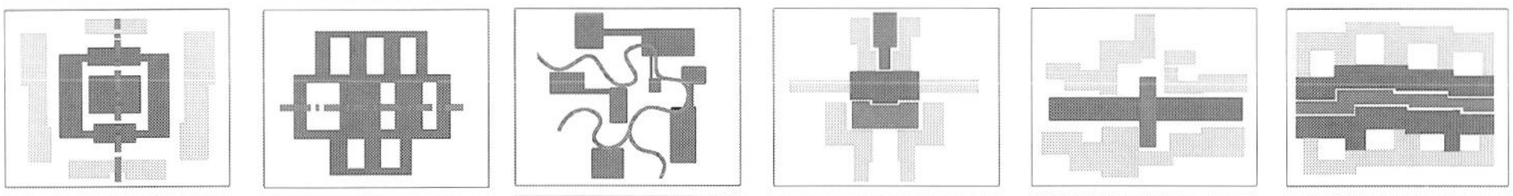

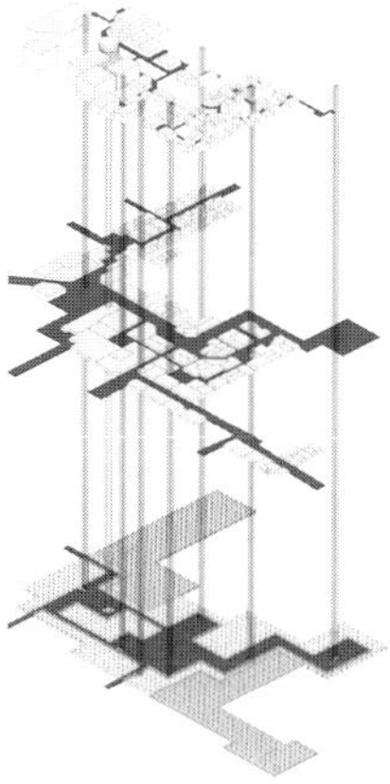

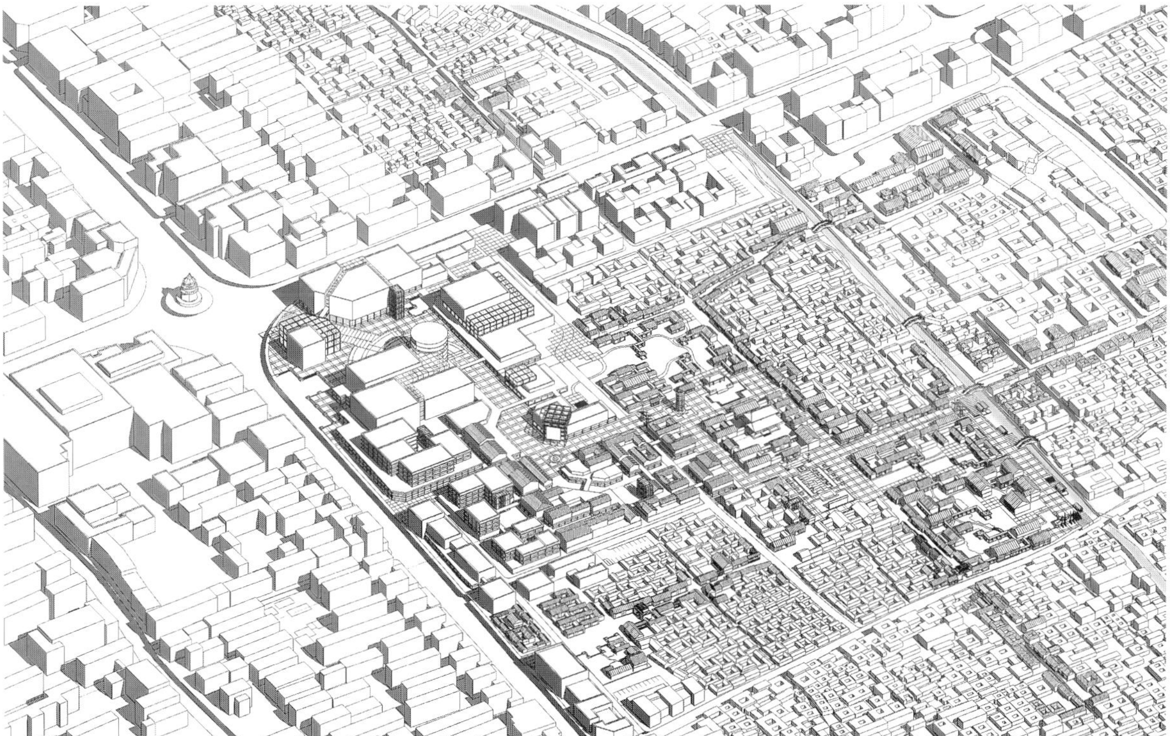

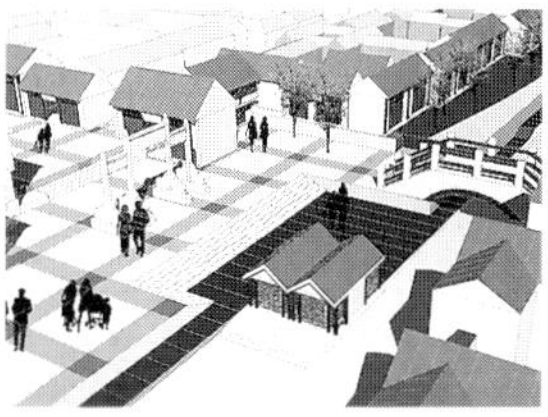

南京仙林大学城城市设计
Urban Design of University City Students' Street

作者：王洁如　指导老师：吴晓

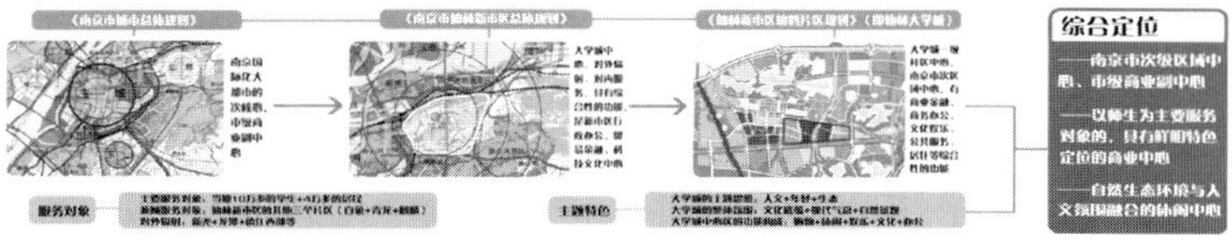

研究区域分析

在老城区的高校周围，通常都会有“学生街”的存在，那些街道曾经繁荣一时。但随着时代的进步，传统形式的学生街已不能满足大学生日益增长的物质和精神需求，“学生街”正面临转型。

本设计的基地位于快速发展中的仙林大学城，传统的街式的、“一层皮”式的学生街远远无法满足庞大的学生消费人群。因此在方案设计时，我们重新梳理了学生街的功能，融入了新时期学生的新需求。在功能“转型”的基础上，打破街式的学生街形态，引入新型的街区型商业模式，使其结合并寻找到它们之间新的平衡点，使原有孤立存在的“街”和新引入的“院”两种要素在设计上以“街＋院”的形式出现，营造出一种既亲切熟悉又蕴含着新意及活力的新型商业空间。

本方案充分考虑使用对象的特殊性，使学生街在功能和形态上“升级”，成为不同于以往的新型的学生的家园。这样的空间既非单纯的街，亦非单纯的院，而是街与院有机结合的“混搭空间”。而这“混搭空间”体现着个性和无数的可能性，打着青春与活力的印记。

Around old districts of the city, usually exist Students' Streets, which used to be flourishing. However, as the progress of the society, the traditional form of Students' Street cannot satisfy the requirement, thus facing transformation.

The project locates in fast-developing Xianlin University City. Traditional style of street as one layer cannot meet the requirement of student consumers. Therefore, we coordinate function adding new demand of students when making scheme. Upon the base of function transformation, the old form is take the place of by a new commercial style of block model, seeking balance of the two. The new form which combines the originally isolated street and newly introduced yard would construct a kind of commercial space, familiar and filled with new ideas and energy.

This project sufficiently takes into account the particularity of users, and upgrades the function and form of Students' Street to make it a new homestead. This kind of space is not simple street or yard, but mixed space combining the two. It reflects personality and possibility, full of the spirit of youth and energy.

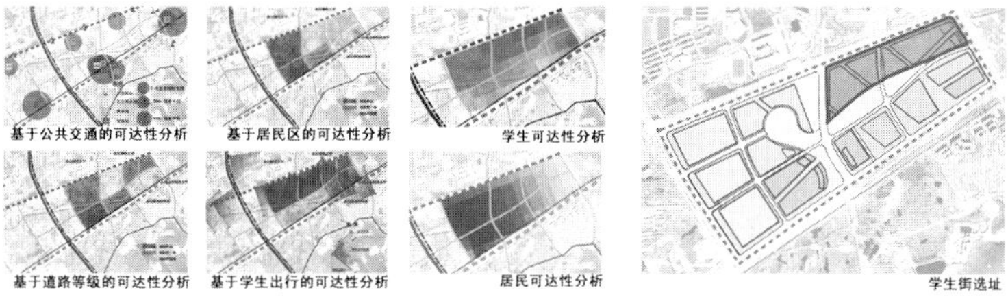

学生街选址

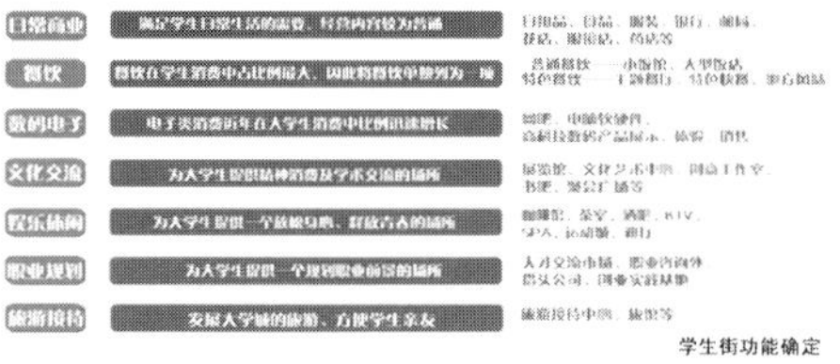

学生街功能确定

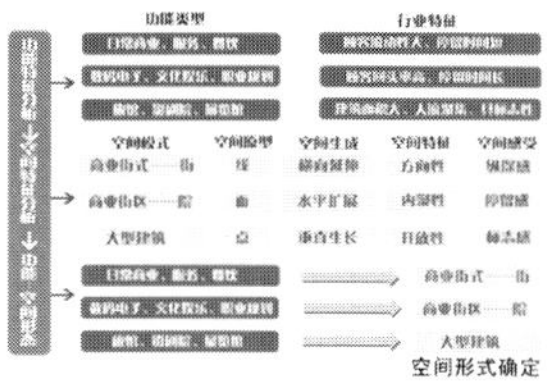

空间形式确定

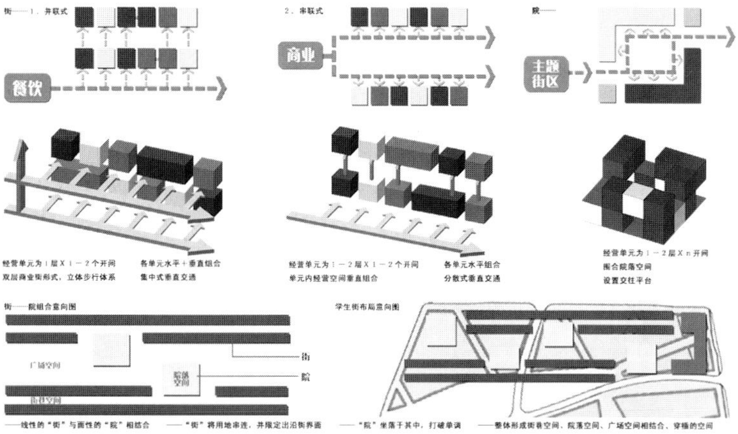

经营单元确定

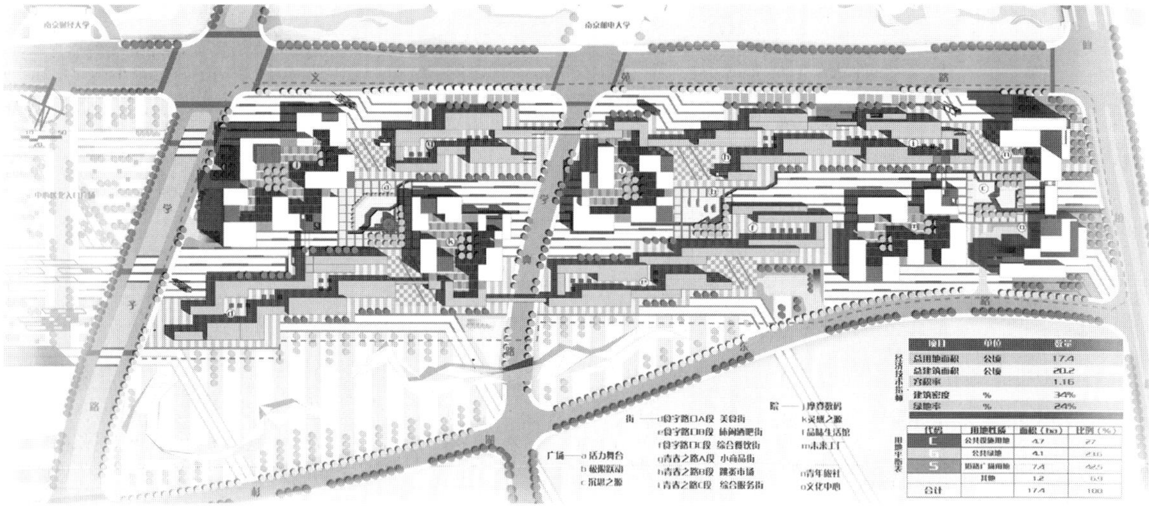

经济技术指标

项目	单位	数字
总用地面积	公顷	17.4
总建筑面积	公顷	20.2
容积率		1.16
建筑密度	%	34%
绿地率	%	24%

用地平衡表

代码	用地性质	面积（ha）	比例（%）
C	公共设施用地	4.7	27
G	公共绿地	4.1	23.6
S	道路广场用地	7.4	42.5
	其他	1.2	6.9
合计		17.4	100

入口景观透视

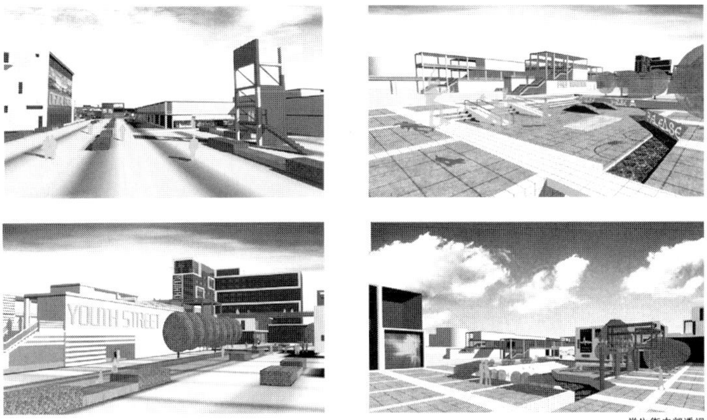

学生街内部透视

商业街

采用线型的形式进行摆放，大部分为商业街分为两层，局部三层，商业街沿街空间基本上以平面形式组织，因此商业街上下两层交通组织主要是在商业街的一端。

继承原有学生街传统，满足学生生活的基本需求。青年之路、丁字路口特色分明，在建筑空间组合及交通方式上进行了区分。

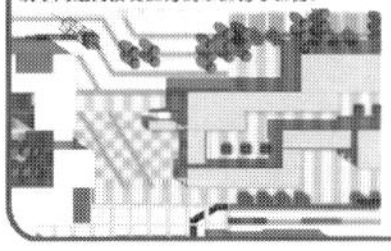

主题街区

采用曲的形式进行布局，主题街区为四层左右，主题街区的业态形式都比较鲜明，每个街区都具有各自的特色，对青年学生的一些特殊要求和满足青年的新鲜感，带动大学城中心区的活力。

街区式布局，天井式共享空间、个性化商业配套，自由空间，纵横[illegible]，个性无限度。

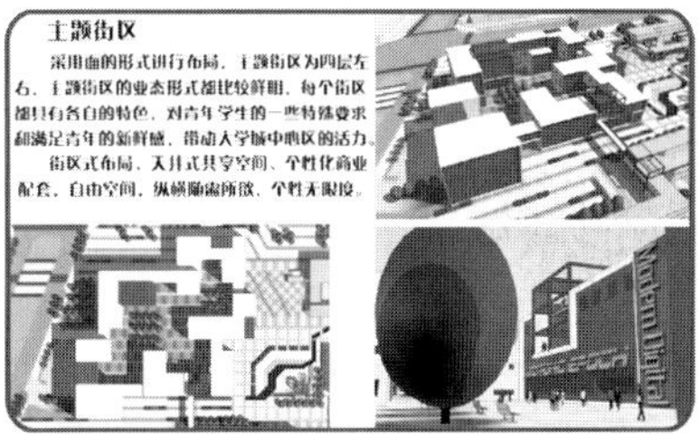

广场空间

商业街、餐饮街与主题街区之间有交通体相连，使街区及街即面和线要素不独立存在，而是有机地结合成为一体，成为新的要素，同时也限定了景观节点的开敞空间，使学生街的景观层次更加立体、活跃，满足大学生们开放的个性，及喜爱交往的性格。

院落与街道的结合之中，有节奏地形成学生街用地中的聚会交往开敞空间，新时代的大学生进行校外活动在街区与街中来回的过程中，也在有节奏感的广场中得到另一番愉悦及收获。

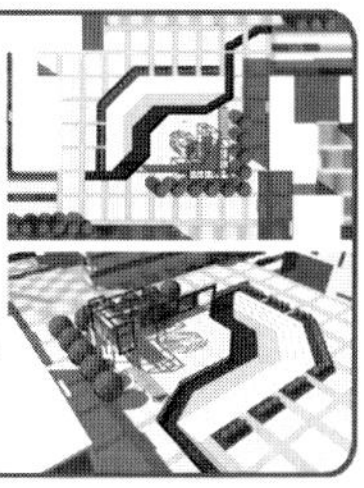

节点设计

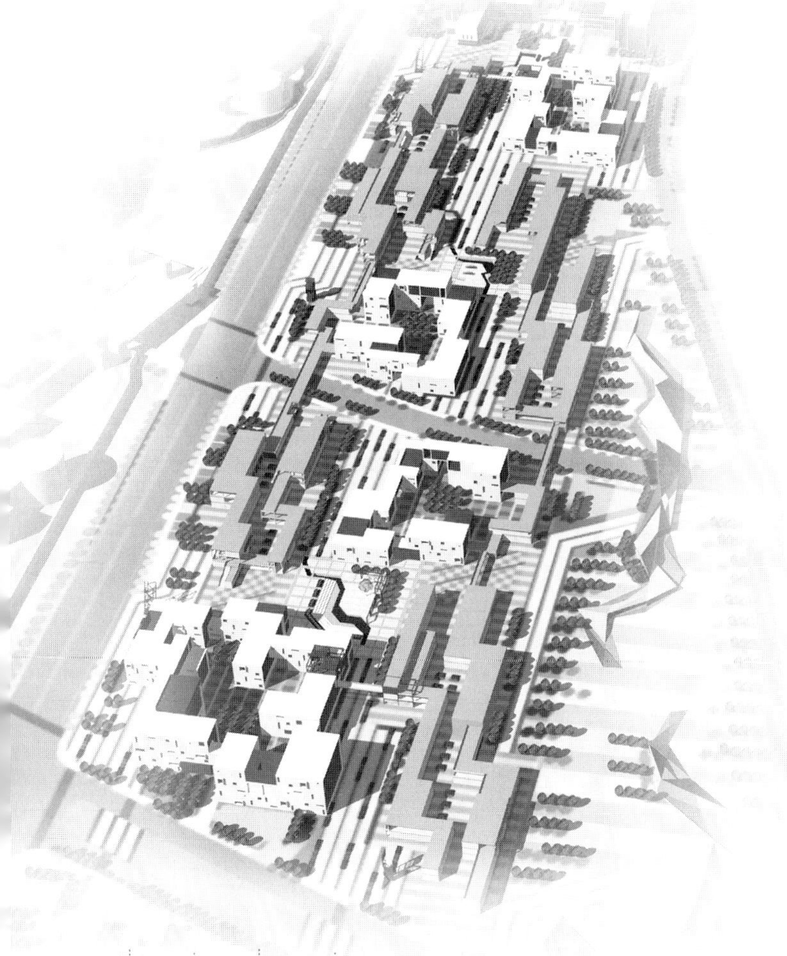

街是旧元素，街区是新趋势，街与院的组合，满足了当代大学生的传统感受的需求，同时又提供给他们接收新理念的机会。正如电影的情节和音乐演奏，街是序幕，院是高潮，二者相辅相成，有机联系，街与院不仅仅是两种城市设计基本元素的组合，也是出于满足服务对象需求的目的形成的混搭的空间形态，这正是学生这一特殊群体所需要的富有特色的步行街的形式。

Street is an old element, block is the new trend, thus combination of street and yard meets the contemporary university students' demand of traditional feeling and meanwhile opportunities for new ideas. As in movie or scenario, street is prelude while yard is climax. The mixed form is not only combination of two basic elements of urban design, but space forms to satisfy the requirement of special group, students who need characteristics.

街区活动时间分布

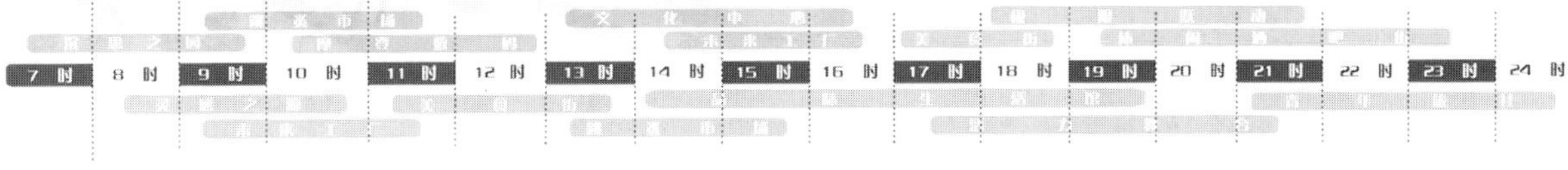

来安县汉河新区总体概念规划

Concept Plan of Chahe New Town, Lai'an

作者：赵薇 王静 陆维婷 指导老师：权亚玲

汉河新区总体概念规划的编制，主要包括基础研究以及规划方案两个部分。在基础研究中，结合汉河新区的现状以及未来发展趋势，对其进行区域功能定位研究、产业发展战略研究、空间拓展研究、空间发展模式研究。在空间拓展部分采取了GIS系统进行分析，以确定合理的发展界限。规划方案部分主要包括方案生成、规划研究范围空间布局以及新区总体规划三个部分。

Concept plan of Chahe new town, Lai'an includes basic research and planning programs. In basic research, combined with Chahe new town of the status quo and future development trend, we do research on its regional functions, industrial development strategy, extension of space and model of space development. In the research of extension of space, we use GIS analysis to determine reasonable limits of the development. The main part of the planning includes three points: the process of the plan, the scope of planning studies as well as the new town master plan.

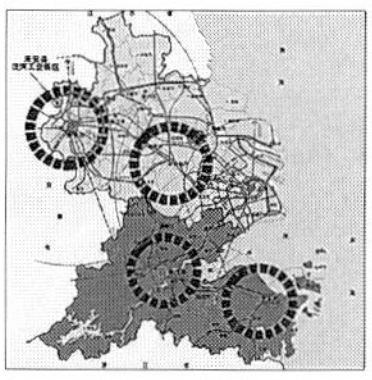
"长三角"城镇群发展的新要求

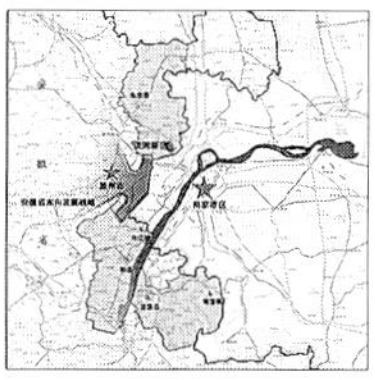
安徽省东向发展战略

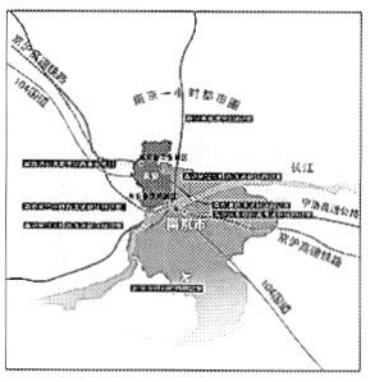
南京都市圈发展带来的新契机

规划背景

沿长江产业与城镇带层面

南京都市圈层面

南京都市区层面

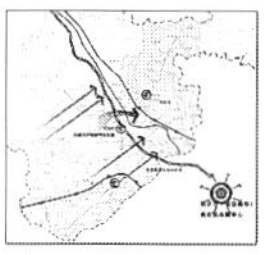
大滁州层面

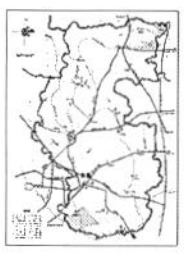
来安县层面

区域功能定位

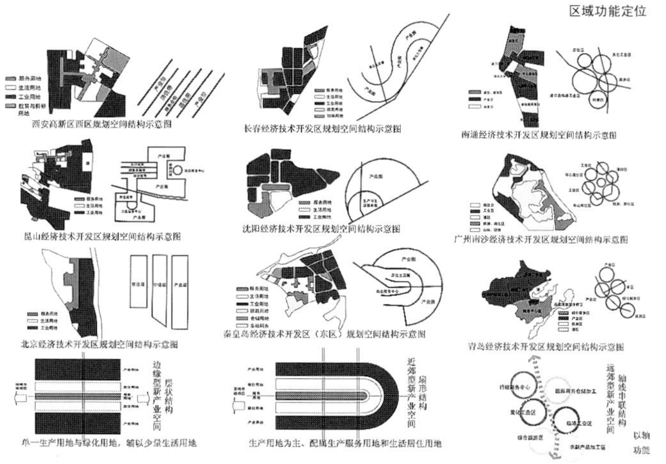
西安高新区西区规划空间结构示意图
长春经济技术开发区规划空间结构示意图
南通经济技术开发区规划空间结构示意图
昆山经济技术开发区规划空间结构示意图
沈阳经济技术开发区规划空间结构示意图
广州南沙经济技术开发区规划空间结构示意图
北京经济技术开发区规划空间结构示意图
秦皇岛经济技术开发区（东区）规划空间结构示意图
青岛经济技术开发区规划空间结构示意图
单一生产用地与绿化用地，辅以少量生活用地
生产用地为主、配属生产服务用地和生活居住用地

空间发展模式案例研究

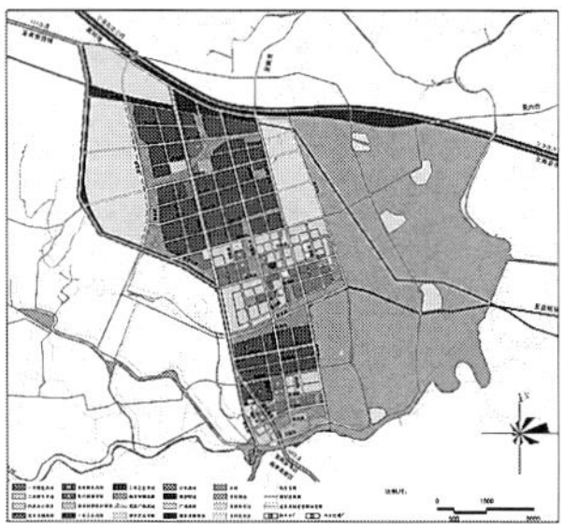
方案一

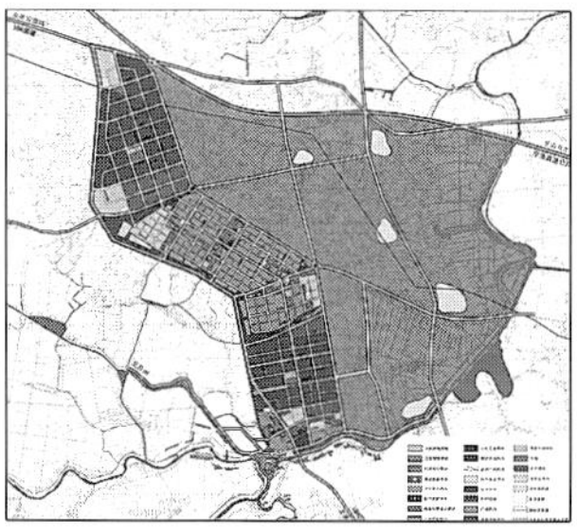
方案二

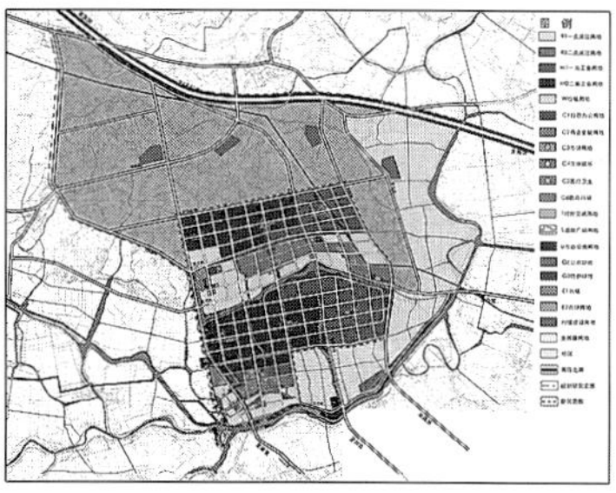
方案三

方案一

优点：
1. 充分考虑到和104国道、高速公路出入口及近期即将投入建设的长江路的联系。
2. 控制用地向圩区方向发展，维持生态系统的完善。
3. 与现状条件的结合比较好。
4. 用地布局紧凑，采用多中心的结构，对于建设时序推进比较有利。
5. 根据主导风向进行居住、工业用地的排布，对环境影响较小。
6. 在北部高速公路出入口预留发展用地，更好地应对基于出入口不可预见发展条件的考虑。

问题：
1. 建设时序形态完整性有所欠缺。

方案二

优点：
1. 与高速公路、104国道联系紧密。
2. 控制用地向圩区方向发展，维持生态系统的完善。

问题：
1. 过于依赖104国道沿线的发展。
2. 单一的功能分区造成功能布局松散。
3. 没有充分考虑到黄牌至高速公路出入口的道路设置。
4. 发展时序上有阶段性的不完整。

方案三

优点：
1. 充分考虑与南京江北新市区的呼应关系。
2. 功能布局结构性强，主次明确。
3. 强调了黄牌至文山方向上横轴的利用。

问题：
1. 用地选择对圩区的适建性考虑不足。
2. 工业包围居住的功能布局形态在合理性上有所欠缺。

多方案比较

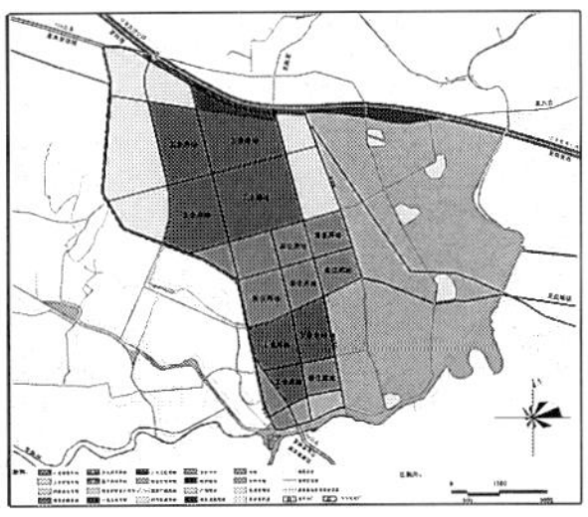
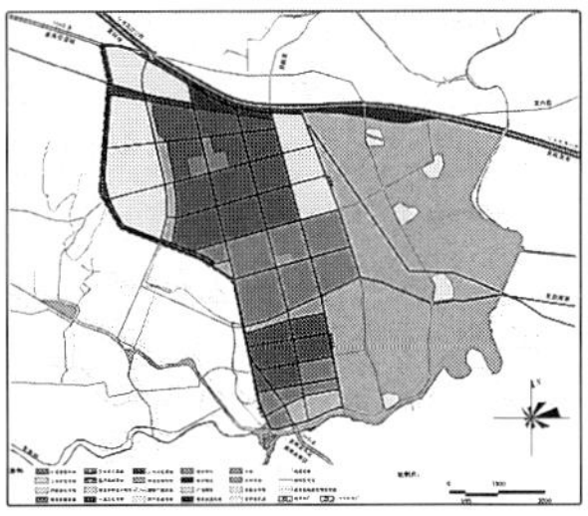
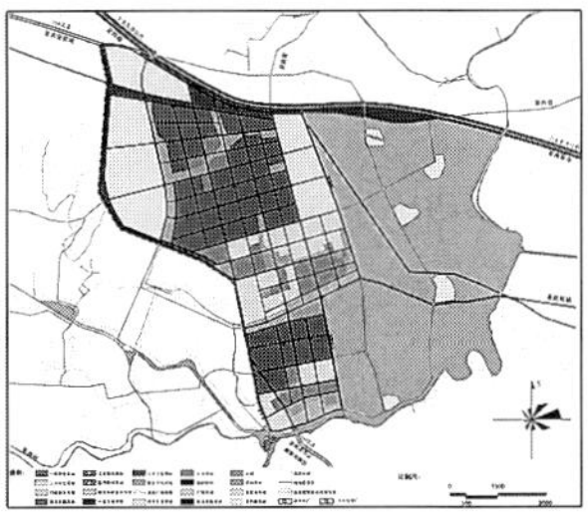
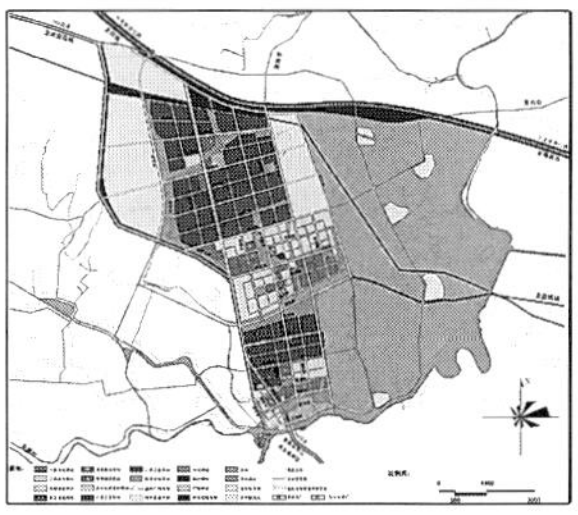

第一阶段 → **第二阶段** → **第三阶段** → **第四阶段**

第一阶段

“轴一核”结构空间布局：

以行政、办公、商业形成中心地带，辅以居住、工业用地。

基于生态格局考虑，以基地外围的水体作为新区主要的防护网络。

根据地块特点和结构布局，使每一地块建设都基于一个生长点，并最终完成新区总体建设。

规划建设长江路、新汉路形成主要的生长轴线，宁来路、瑞金路、琅琊路及黄文路等解决新区过境交通。

第二阶段

进一步强调“轴一核”结构空间布局：

突出中心用地形成生长极核，在外围居住、工业用地配以相应商业用地。

结合基地现状在工业用地范围内规划生产防护绿地，并与外围水系构成有机联系。

结合老镇区规划商业用地形成新的生长点，结合滁河规划港口。

对规划道路网调整，适当增加道路网密度。

第三阶段

“两轴三组团三核心”：

将长江路作为工业发展轴，新汉路作为居住发展轴，中心极核行政办公用地居中布置，两侧辅以商业文化用地。

保留周边大量水系和开敞空间，并与用地范围内绿地有机结合，发展渗透至各个片区。

进一步对规划道路网作调整，增加在商业、居住用地内的道路网密度。

进一步划分规划用地性质，协调各用地功能。

第四阶段

完善中部核心用地性质，各片区功能明确，密切结合交通和生态绿地。

对工业区空间发展和道路模式进行研究，确定了不同模数的工业街区结构。

充分顺应地形设置了水路结合的复合生态走廊，开敞空间具有均好性，构筑了多层次的景观体系。

路网结构清晰明确，根据不同的用地性质配设不同的道路密度。

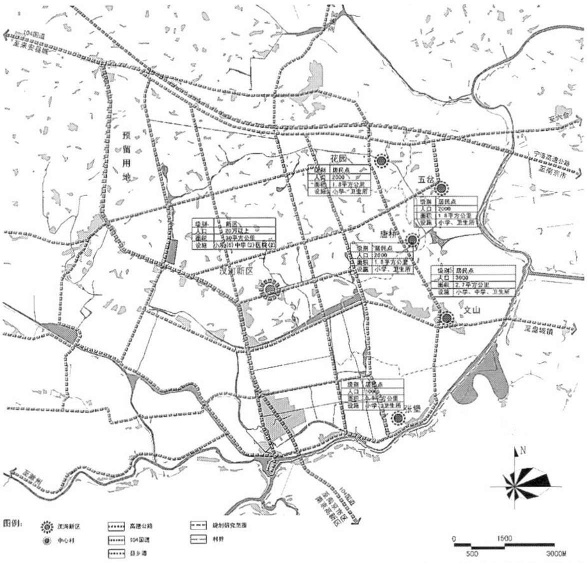

研究范围空间布局规划

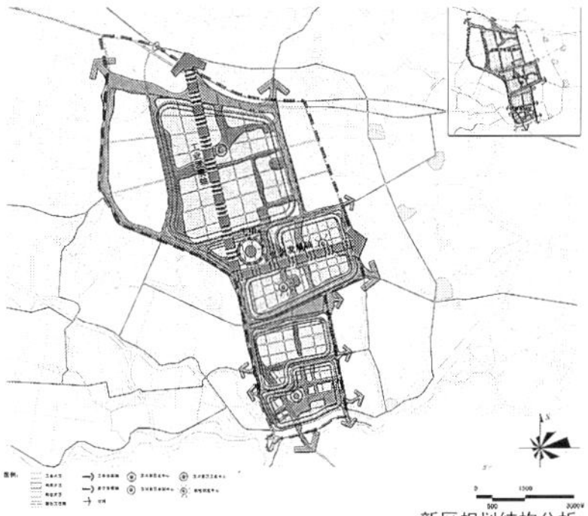

新区规划结构分析

新区道路交通规划

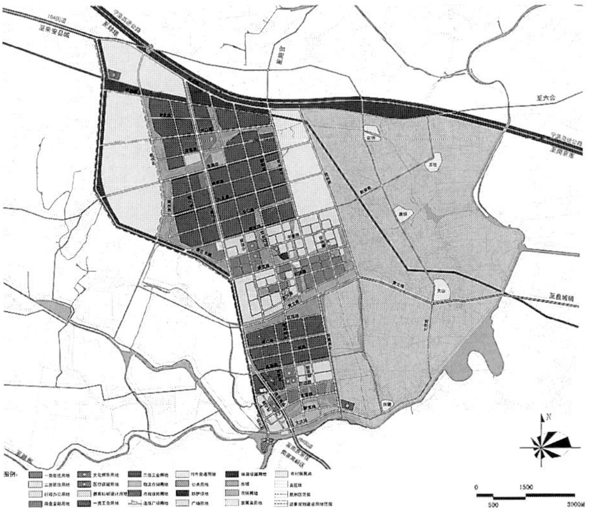

新区远景用地规划

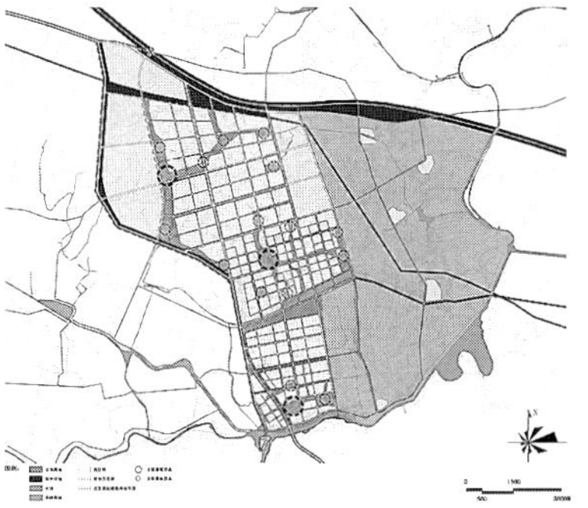

新区绿地系统规划

城镇总体规划——溧水县东屏镇总体规划［2006－2020］

Master Planning of Dongping Town of Lishui County

作者：刘坤 刘默琦 张殊 指导老师：王海卉

东屏镇地处东经119° 06’，北纬31° 34’，位于江苏省南京市溧水县东北部，是百里秦淮源头二干河发源地，距溧水县城8公里，距南京禄口国际机场18公里，距南京城60公里，是溧水县的重点中心镇。现状的常溧公路贯穿全镇，交通便利，宁杭高速位于镇界外东侧，是南京通往苏杭地区的交通要道。预计到规划期末[2020年]，镇域总人口为4.1万人，镇区人口将达到3万人，城镇化率达到70%。

As a small town in Yangtze River metropolitan area, Dongping is inevitably influenced greatly by this trend. On one hand, big cities show enormous attraction to it, while on the other hand, Dongping gets finance and technology support from big cities easily, providing it a larger stage for further development.

区位分析

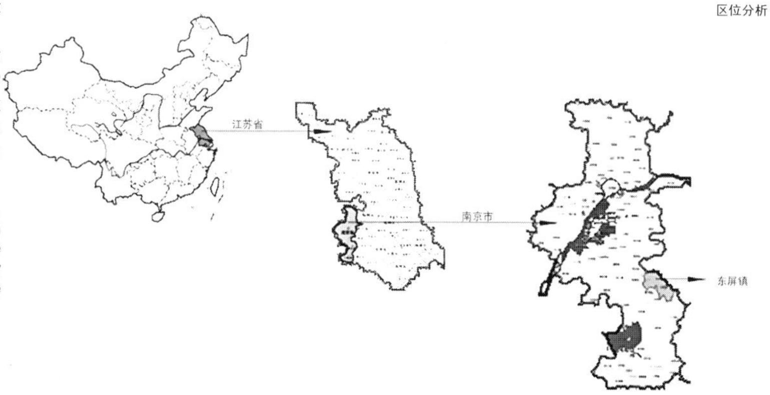

SWOT分析

STRENGTHS

[区位优势]东屏镇位于南京市南部，在南京市往南发展的重要轴线上，同时位于中心城市南京的紧密圈层内。
[交通优势]340省道、联三高速从镇域中部通过。
[优越的自然环境与资源条件]
[富有特色的苗木花卉产业]

WEAKNESS

[城市化水平滞后]
[工业现代化水平低]
[资金的制约]

OPPORTUNITIES

为了改变城乡二元结构、缩小城乡差距，南京市目前正致力于郊县城镇的发展，这对东屏来说是不可多得的发展机遇。东屏镇先后在《省域城镇体系规划》和《南京市总体规划》中被列为重点中心镇。

THREATS

[受中心城镇辐射影响较大]由于受到南京市、溧水县城集聚发展的强大吸引力，东屏镇近年来人口持续下降，产业发展出现波动。
[镇域建设用地布局分散]土地资源的利用不够经济，农业和建设用地的矛盾日益突出。

镇区旅游资源分析

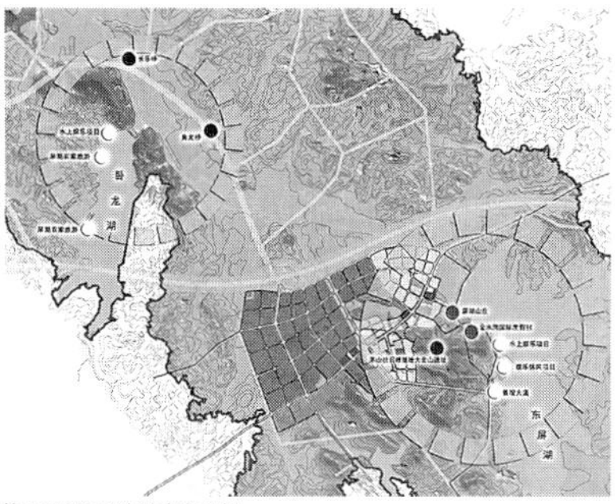

工业用地适建度等级

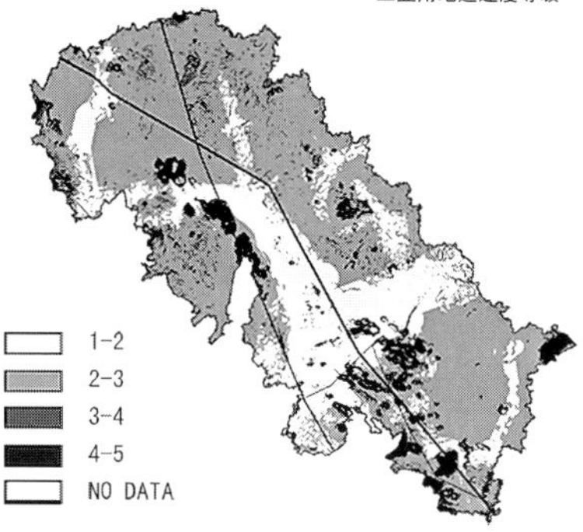

居住用地适建度等级

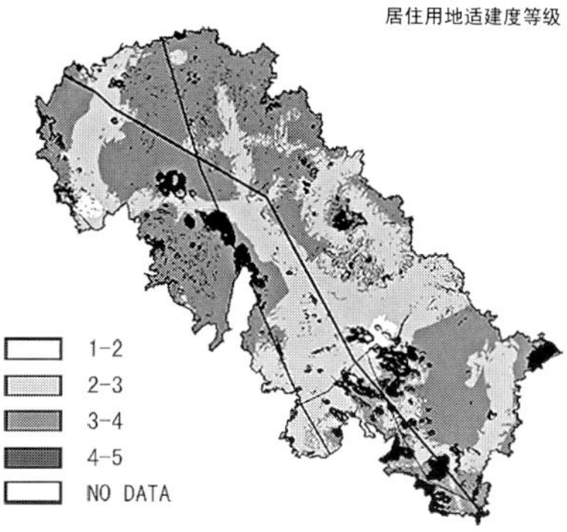

基于GIS的用地适建度分析

工业		一	二	三	四	五	权重
道路影响	一级路	<100m	100-400m	400 - 700m	700 - 900m	>1000m	0.15
	二级路	<50m	50 - 200m	200 - 350m	350 - 500m	>500m	0.1
	高速路(互通)	<1000m	1000 - 2000m	2000 - 3000m	>3000m		0.05
镇区辐射		<3000m	3000 - 6000m	6000 - 9000m	9000 - 12000m	>12000m	0.2
绿化与林地		>300	200 - 300	100 - 200	<100		0.1
水体		>2000m	1000 - 2000m	200 - 1000m	100 - 200m	<100m	0.05
坡度		<2%	2 - 5%	5 - 10%	10 - 15%	>15%	0.15
景区		>300	200 - 300	100 - 200	<100		0.1
供水管线		<50m	50 - 200m	200 - 350m	350 - 500m	>500m	0.1
高压线	500KV	>30					
	220KV	>15					
	35KV	>6					

居住		一	二	三	四	五	权重
道路	一级路	100 - 400m	0 - 100m	400 - 700m	700 - 900m	>1000m	0.1
	二级路	<50m	50 - 200m	200 - 350m	350 - 500m	>500m	0.05
	高速路(互通)	>900m	600 - 900m	300 - 600m	<300m		0.05
镇区辐射		<3000m	3000 - 6000m	6000 - 9000m	9000 - 12000m	>12000m	0.1
绿化与林地		>300	200 - 300	100 - 200	<100		0.05
水体		2000 - 4000m	1000 - 2000m	200 - 1000m	100 - 200m	<100m	0.05
坡度		<2%	2 - 5%	5 - 10%	10 - 15%	>15%	0.05
供水管线		<50m	50 - 200m	200 - 350m	350 - 500m	>500m	0.05
医疗		<300m	300 - 600m	600 - 900m	>900m		0.15
中学		<300m	300 - 600m	600 - 900m	>900m		0.1
小学		<100m	100 - 200m	200 - 300m	>300m		0.15
邮政		<300m	300 - 600m	600 - 900m	>900m		0.05
电信		<300m	300 - 600m	600 - 900m	>900m		0.05
高压线	500KV	>30					
	220KV	>15					
	35KV	>6					

反磁力之一

[农业产业化和特色农业]
构建“四位一体”经济增长点（商品生产基地、龙头企业、支柱产业、专业市场）：以城市短缺型和互补型产业、自然资源优势产业、特色手工业、自然和文化生态产业等构成吸引“反磁力”；依托中心镇，适度发展工业集中区；发展为农业产业化服务的第三产业等。

反磁力之二

[小范围人口异地城市化]
迁居至本行政区外，从事非农产业的人口城市化，称为异地城市化。小范围异地城市化战略可促使一部分农村人口向附近的“反磁力型”中心镇转移，将会对发达地带次发达地区的人口城市化起到重要的促进作用。

反磁力之三

[自然生态和文化生态]
自然生态和文化生态的魅力是“反磁力型”中心镇吸引力的来源。生态型小城镇建设原则应当包括人口集聚、生活方便、具有多样性和富于特色。其解剖结构则应具有以步行街为主的城市商业中心、便捷的对外交通、符合生物生长繁衍的生态廊道，以及镇区中心附近的农业园地。

反磁力研究

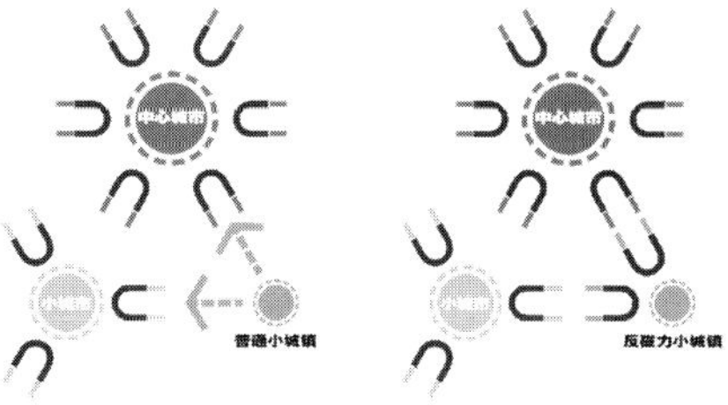

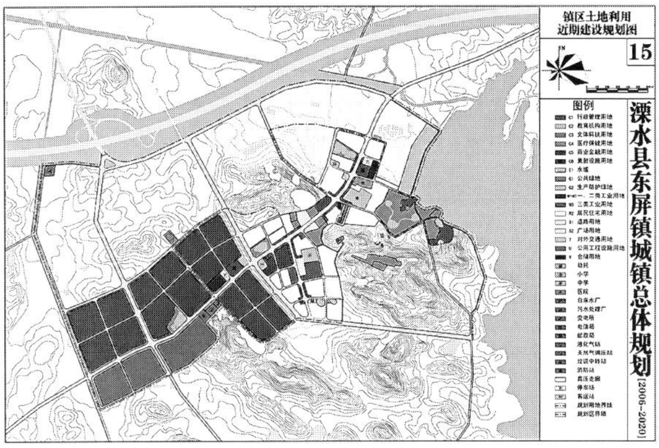

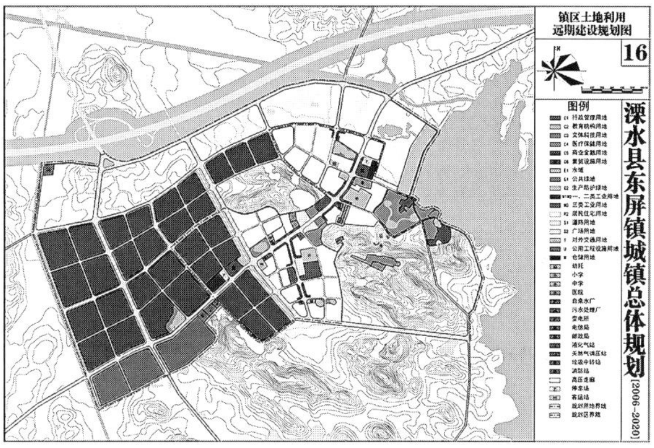

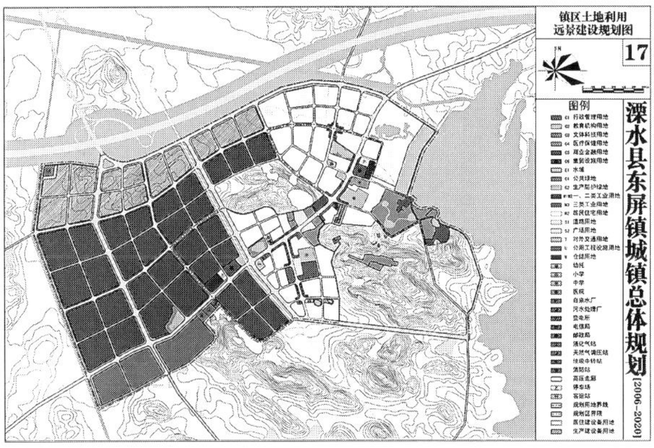

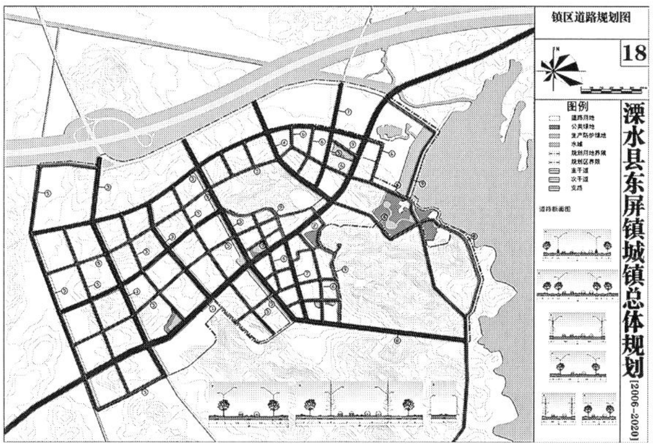

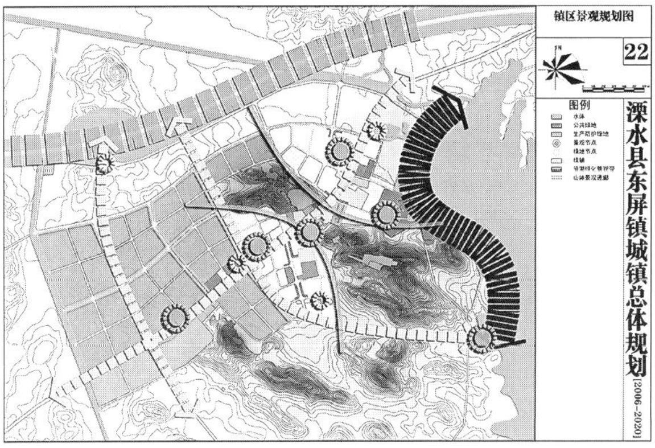

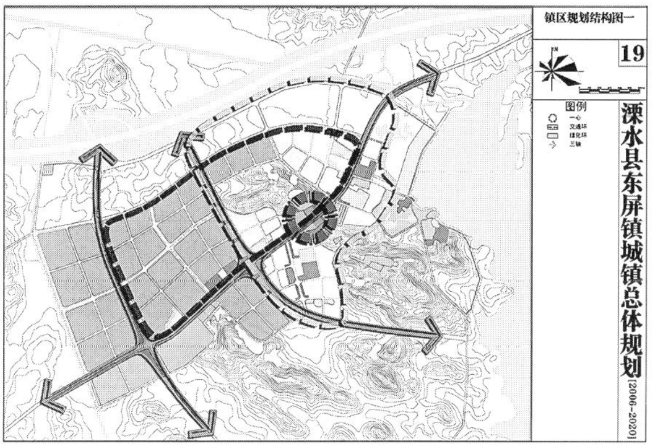

竹
Bamboo

作者：厉宏凯　指导老师：赵军 陈晓扬

每当我触摸竹子的时候，我发现自己陷于儿时的回忆之中。这种记忆来自于外婆家的竹席。当时的那张竹席油亮油亮，躺上去很清凉。小时候我经常蜷缩在竹席桶里，从编织的缝隙里看外面的世界。我所做的就是重现这些记忆。

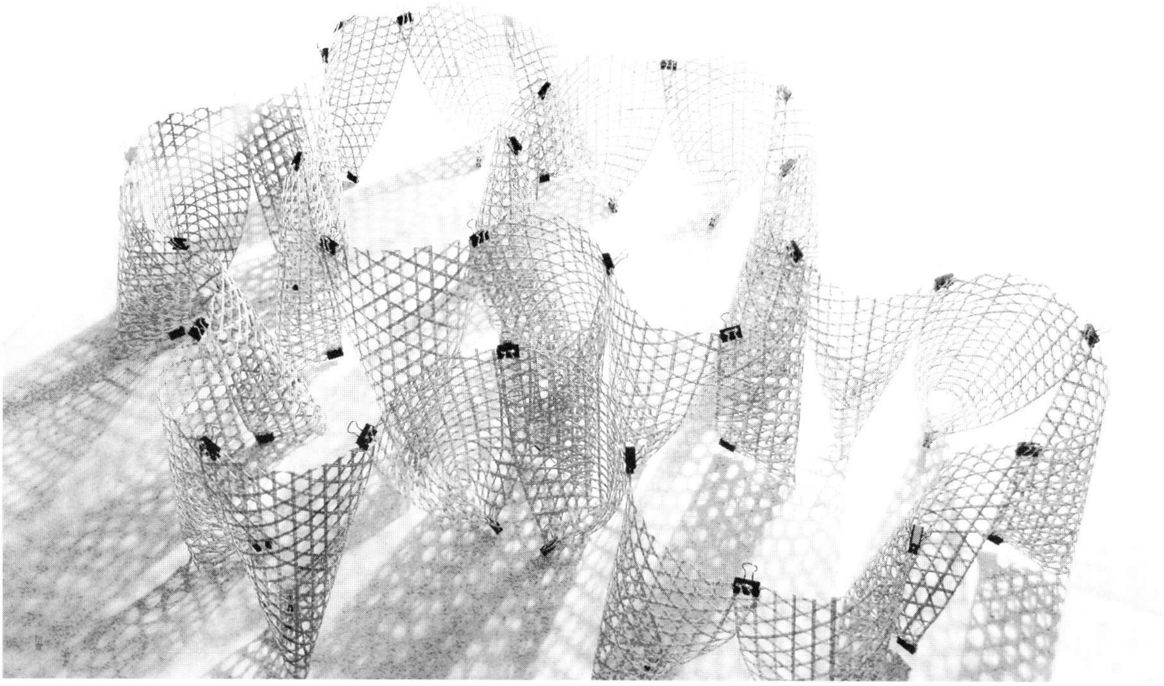

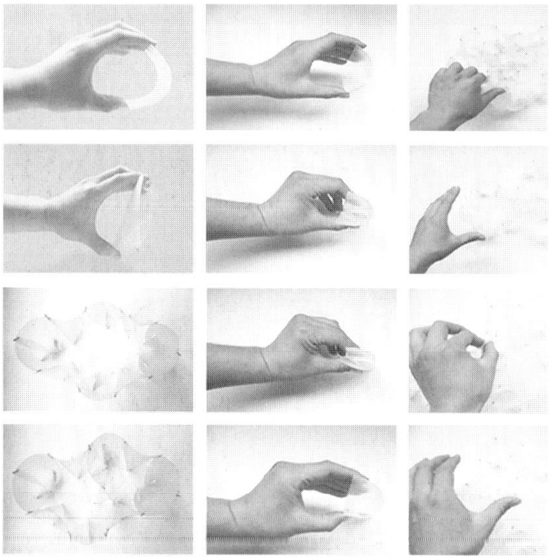

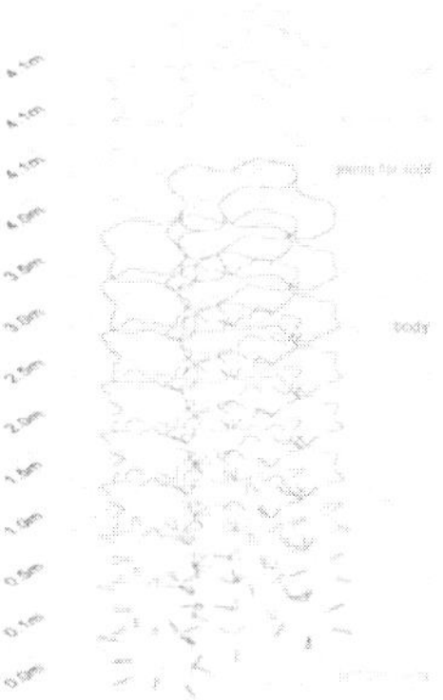

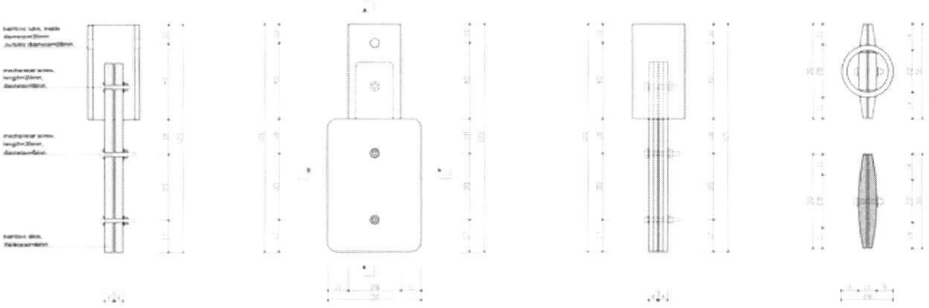

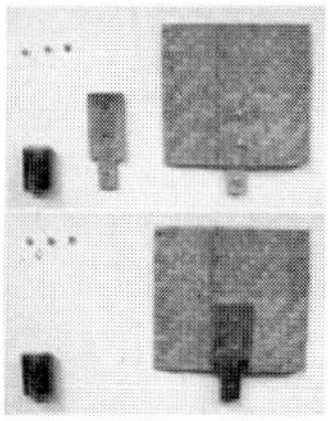

专卖店设计
Dancer's Shop Space Design

作者：李金蔓　指导老师：赵思毅

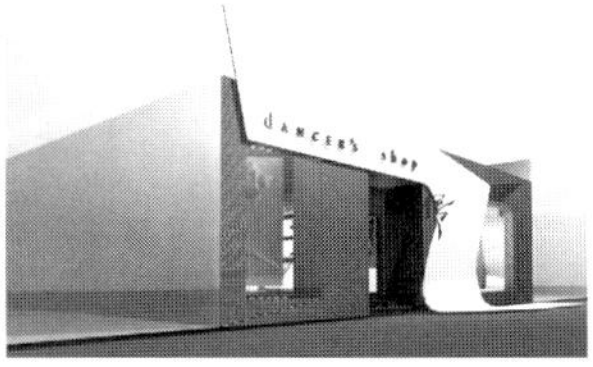

白色与黑色

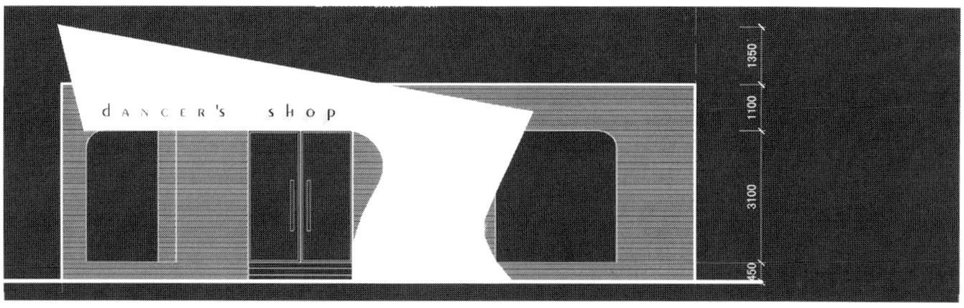

该设计源于个人对舞蹈的理解，试图通过强烈的对比来表达舞蹈的律动性。

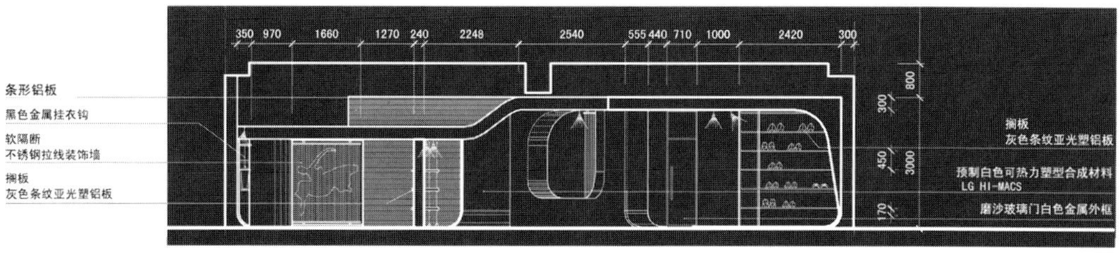

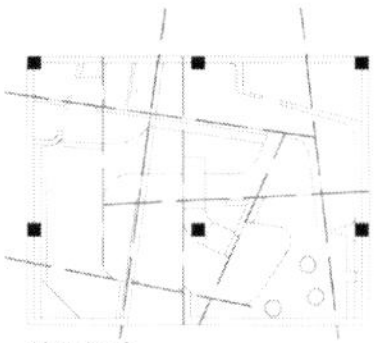

轴线关系

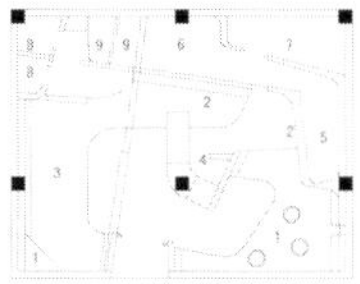

功能分区 1橱窗展示 2重点展示 3批量展示 4收银台 5仓库 6休息区 7办公区 8试衣间 9卫生间

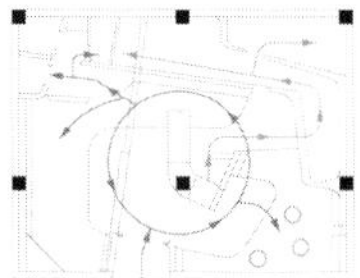

流线分析 顾客流线 员工流线

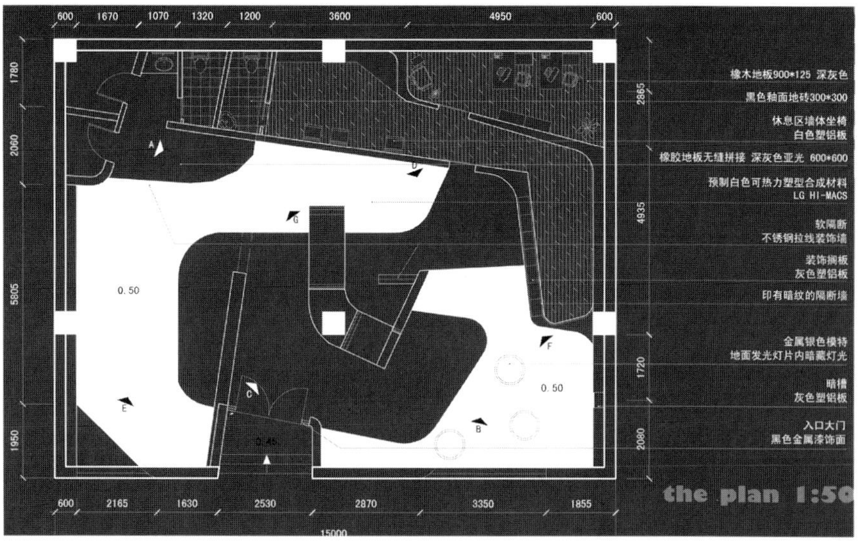

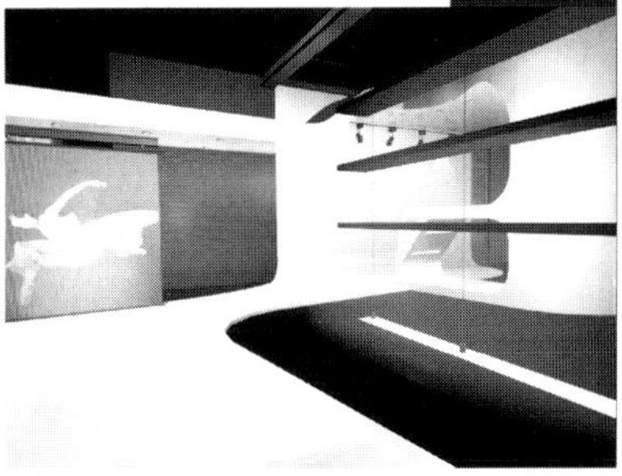

舞蹈，是一门综合的艺术，它拥有自己的表情、节奏和构图。

透入舞蹈有形的外壳，往里再往里，是人类生命灵性震颤的原动力，有动、有静，有弱、有强，有柔、有刚，有弛、有张，有涩、有畅。

——这便是律动。

*白色与黑色

*光泽的可塑性材料和亚光的铝板

*流线的大空间和直线的小细节

整体上似动非动，似静非静，亦动亦静，动静结合，动态是意识的流淌，静态是力度的凝聚，游走在动静之间。

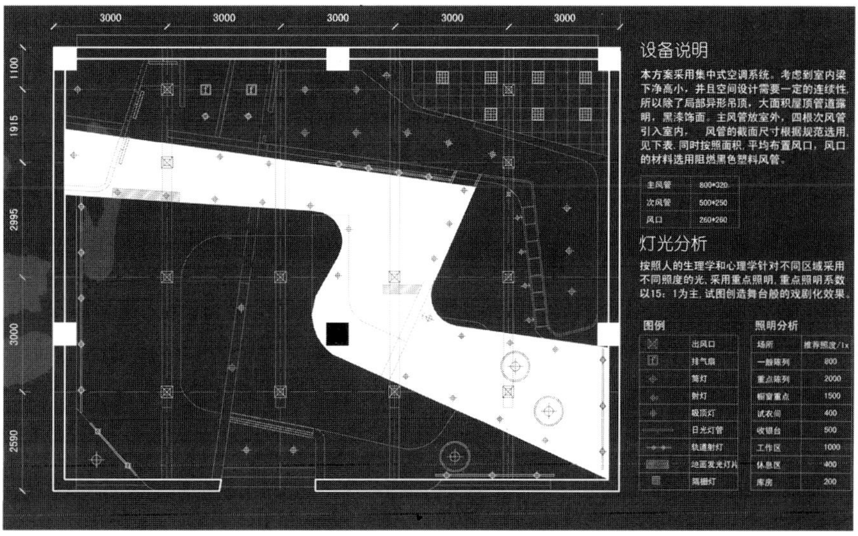

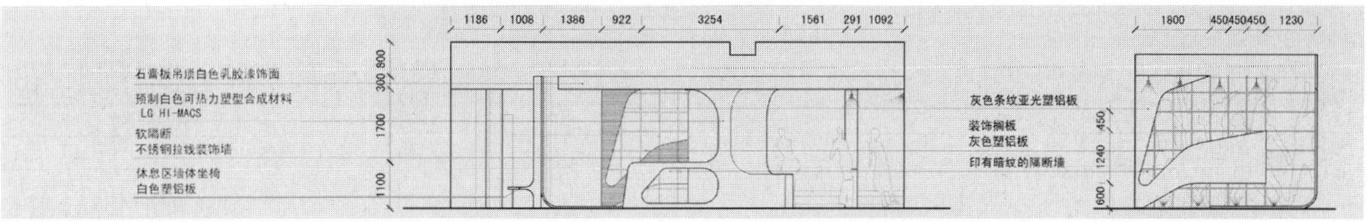

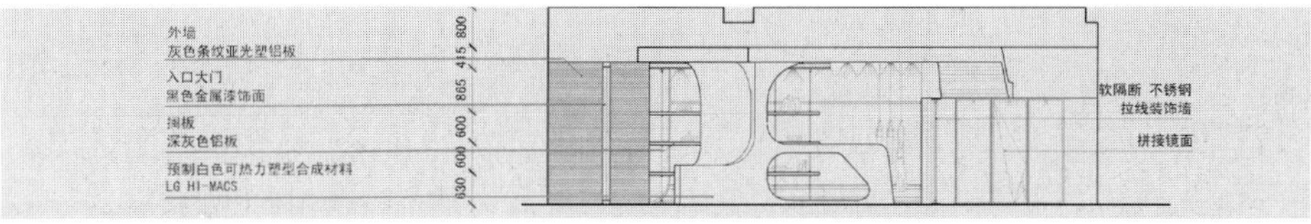

专卖店设计
Sony CD Store Design

作者：宋亦君　指导老师：赵军

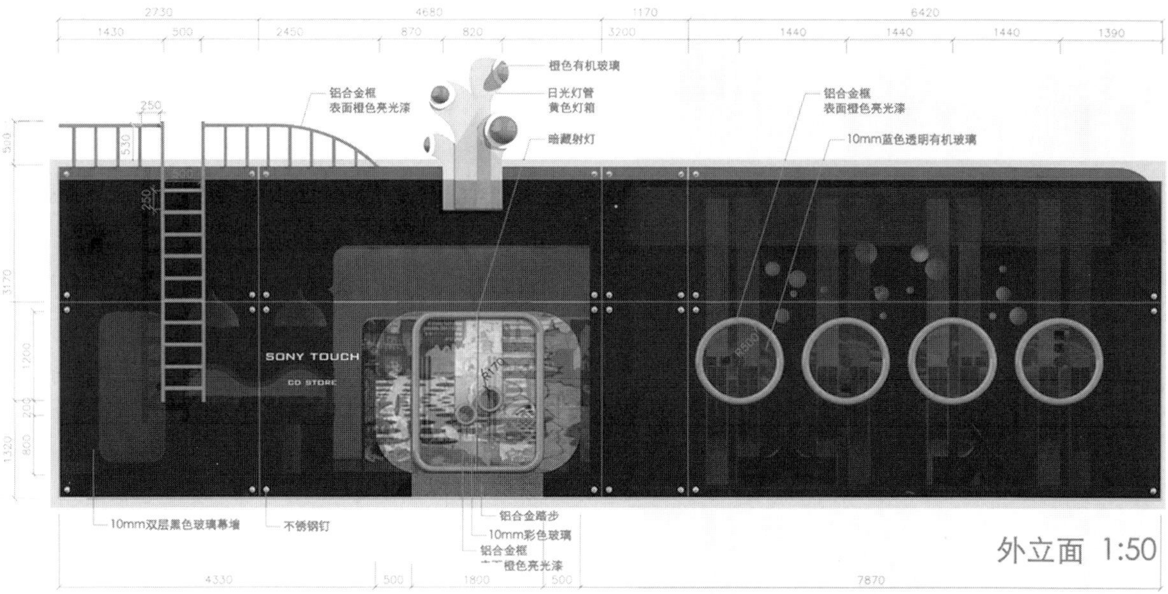

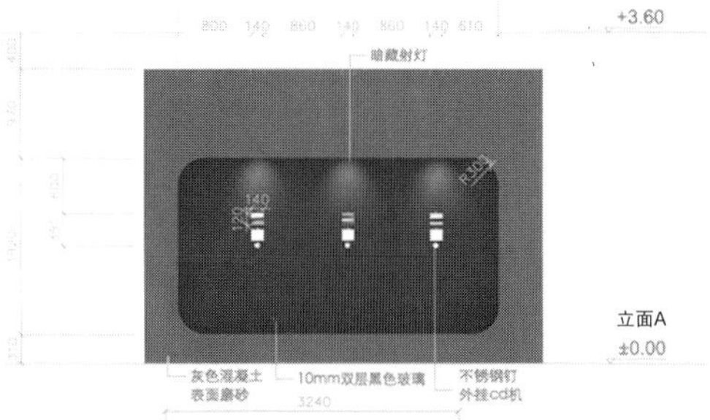

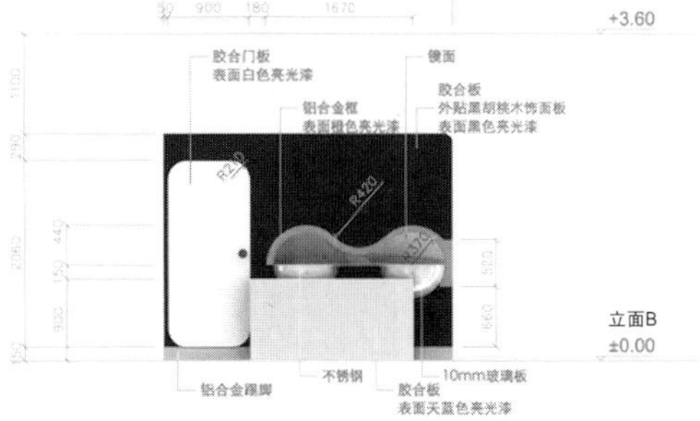

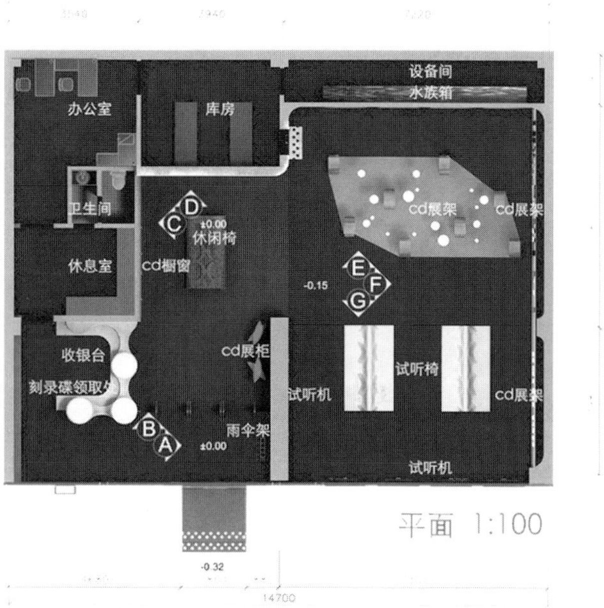

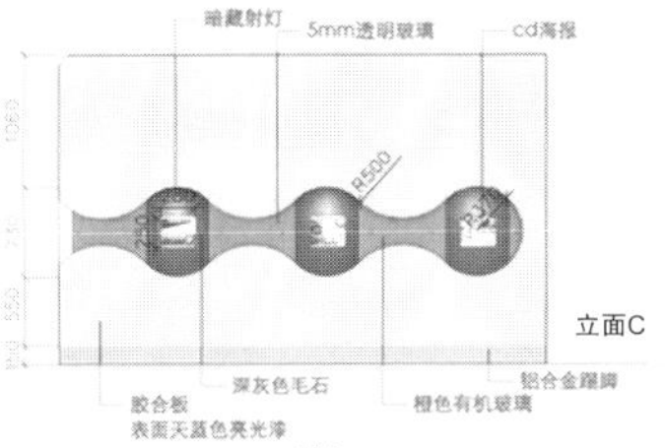

立面C

立面D

顶棚布置图例：

- φ80筒灯
- 方形筒灯
- 吸顶灯
- 天花射灯
- 垂挂式吊灯
- 镜前灯
- 埋入式日光灯管
- 嵌入式软管灯
- 1500轨道射灯
- 排气扇
- 空调主机
- 空调送风口
- 空调供气口
- 检测口
- 消防喷淋

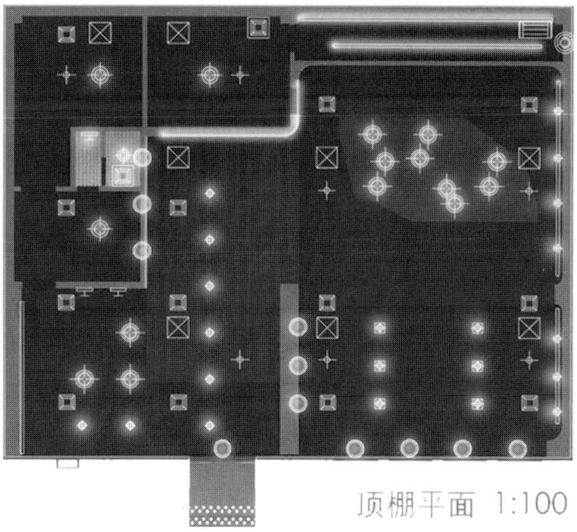

顶棚平面 1:100

空间分析

利用方案原本的室内结构，将展卖空间分割为三部分，分别为收银区、门厅和展卖区。

通过为收银区、门厅和展卖区设计不同的地面标高以及顶棚高度，形成小、中、大三个不同尺度的空间，沿着人流方向构成空间序列。

在三个空间内运用原色搭配，致力于营造轻松活泼的气氛，各个空间的色调又有所区别，冷暖交替，在对比中显现各自情调，同时缤纷的色彩又统一在深色的大背景下，有条不紊地打造时尚风格。

三区各指数说明：

功能分区	收银	门厅	展卖
地面标高	+0.00	+0.00	-0.15
顶棚高度	+2.50	+3.09	+3.60
空间形态	封闭	狭长	开放
色彩色调	冷	暖	中性

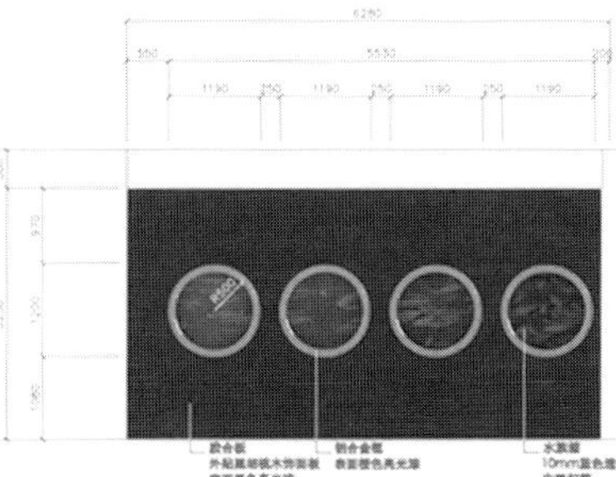

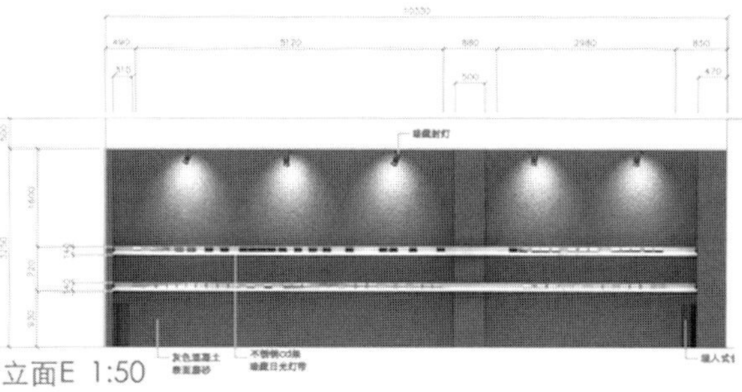

立面E 1:50

立面F 1:50

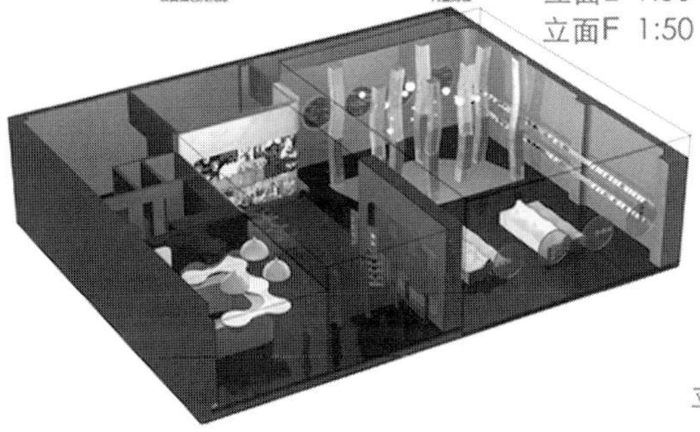

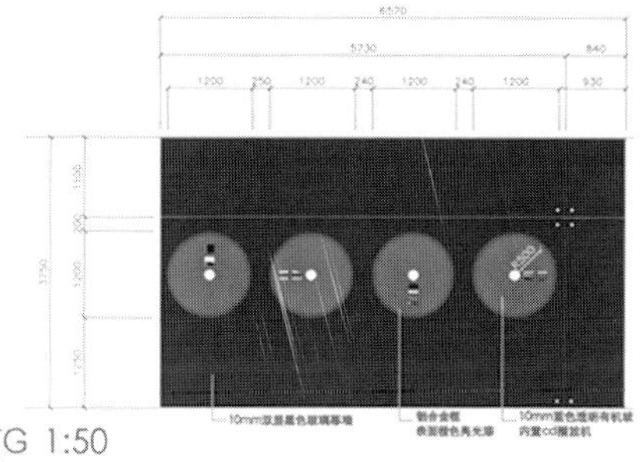

立面G 1:50

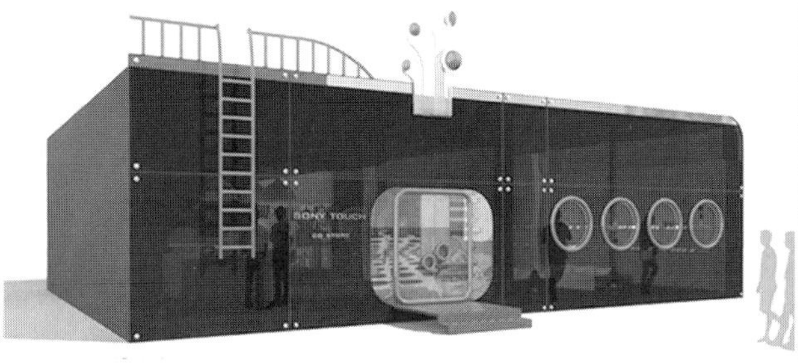

建筑设计生成法实践
Architectural Generative Design

作者：胡宏　指导老师：李飚 钱强 卫兆骥 钱敬平

2006年8月，东南大学将原作为教学楼的“前工院”北半楼划给了建筑学院。但是“前工院”在建时是按照标准的教学楼设计的，不适合建筑学院的教学的空间布局和功能要求，因此学院决定对其进行改造。在改造工程即将竣工之际，底层门厅的布置引起了大家的关注。

该方案是一项面向建造的设计项目，项目需要完成从设计到装配的全过程。因此，项目的性质就要求兼顾前工院门厅的空间状况和实际的建造要求。此外，同其他的实际工程一样，不仅要对设计本身进行探索和研究，而且要兼顾材料的特性、价格、设备的性能以及生产、运输、装配过程的各个环节。

Computer generative design employed relative algorithm implements optimization of architectural elements. Applying the tremendous ability of computing, which will emblaze architects' inspiration; it will be new architectural design implements in the architecture design aspects. The project presents the progress of choice, programming of design implements and their assist to the final construction through the exploration and practice of installation of ceiling named "ceiling Margin" of Generative Design Group (2007) of School of Architecture, SEU.

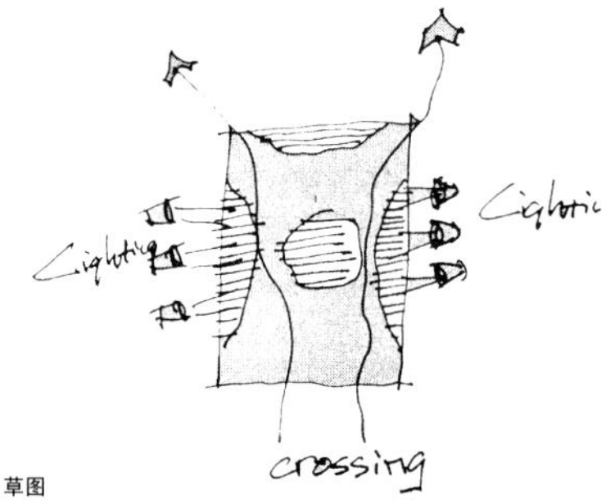

草图

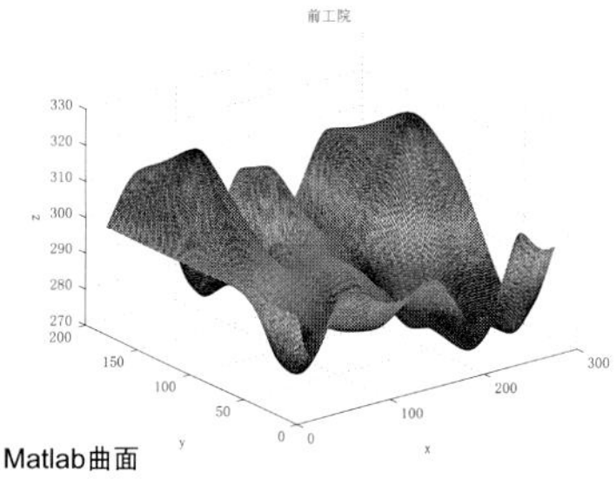

Matlab曲面

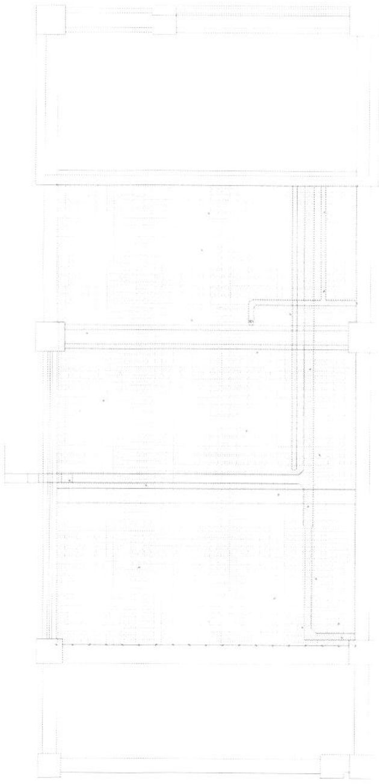
前工院平面及参数布点

模型研究及实体建造

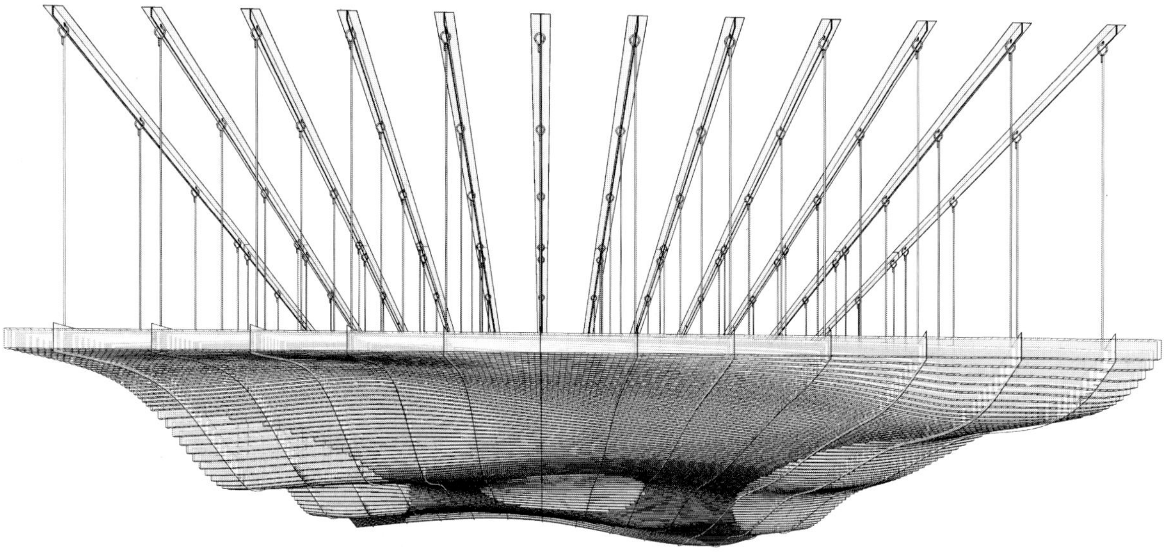

原生曲面

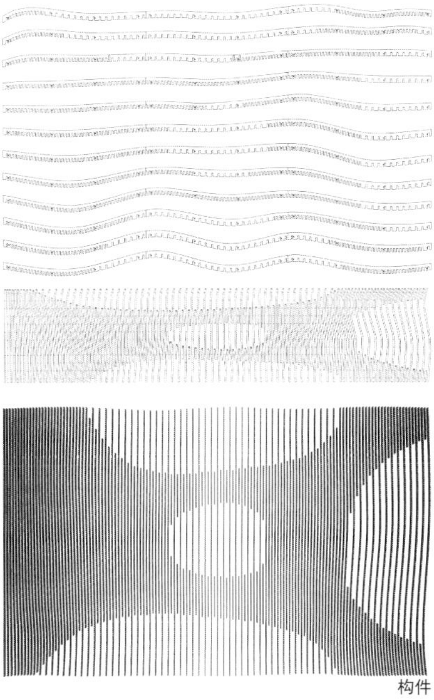

构件

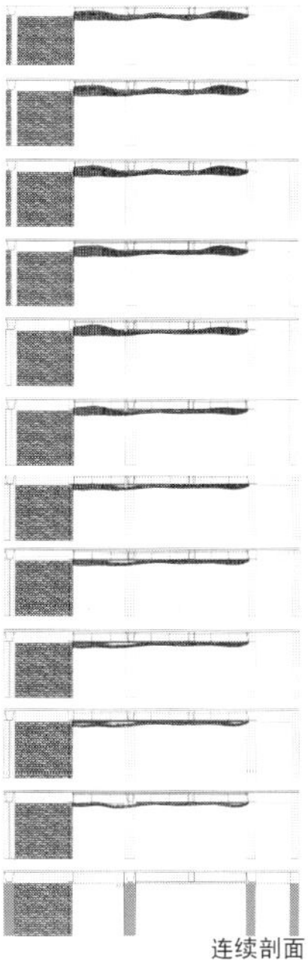

连续剖面

中外联合教学设计
International Joint Workshop

作者：许若菲　指导老师：钱强

印度加尔各答市库玛杜利地区低层高密度住宅

本次毕业设计的基地位于印度加尔各答市库玛杜利地区，基地中用地较为紧张。制作神像的供求根据当地供奉神像的节日来决定，所以在当地制作神像有高峰期，就是在每年祭祀节日附近。当地对于工人的需求也是随着高峰期的到来而有起伏。这种空间时间性的变化就对住宅提出了一个有容量伸缩变化的要求。

基地的街道，均被赋予了双重的功能，在没有行人通过的时候，通常会成为当地居民以及小孩子游乐的场所，街道空间从此功能双重化。线性的街道空间就会成为一种从公共空间到私密空间的过渡，亦成为当地的一种特色空间。室内空间因为融合了工作以及生活玩乐的功能，具有连续性，也为几种不同属性空间的转换提供了很好的先决条件，实现了高峰期与非高峰期间不同功能之间的转换。

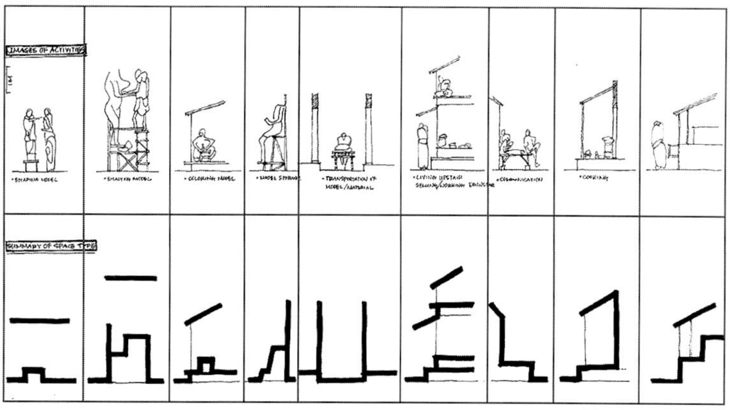

一层平面

二层平面

三层平面

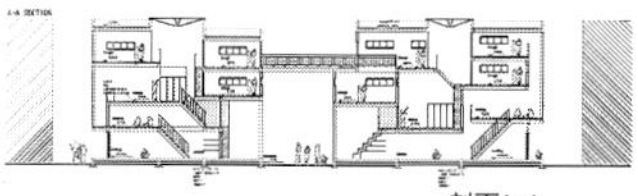
剖面A-A

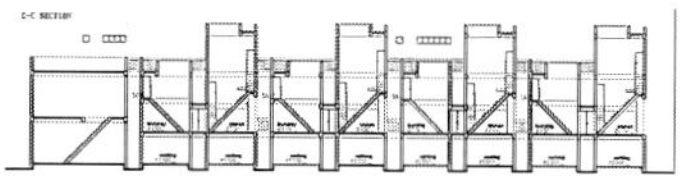
剖面C-C

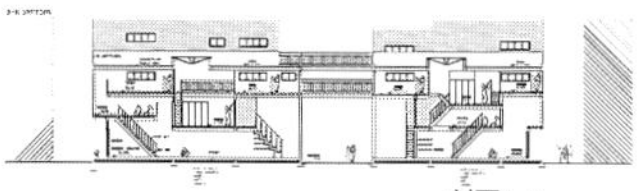
剖面B-B

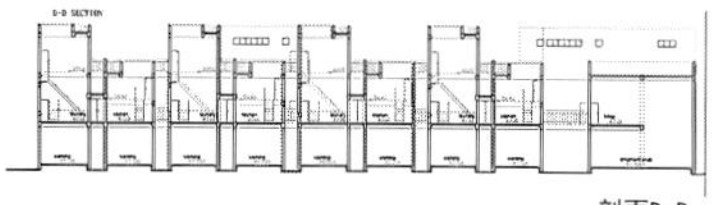
剖面D-D

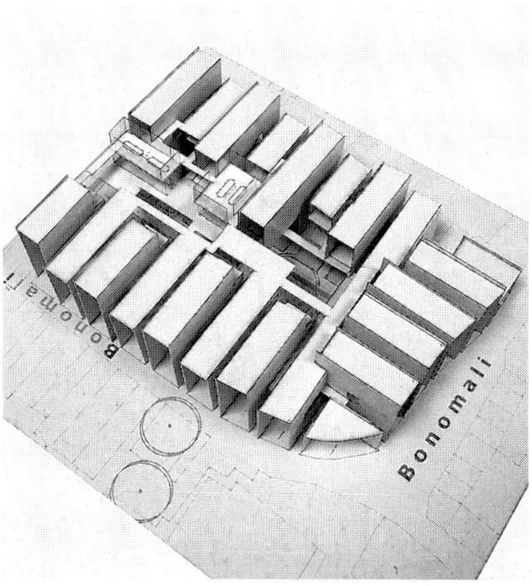

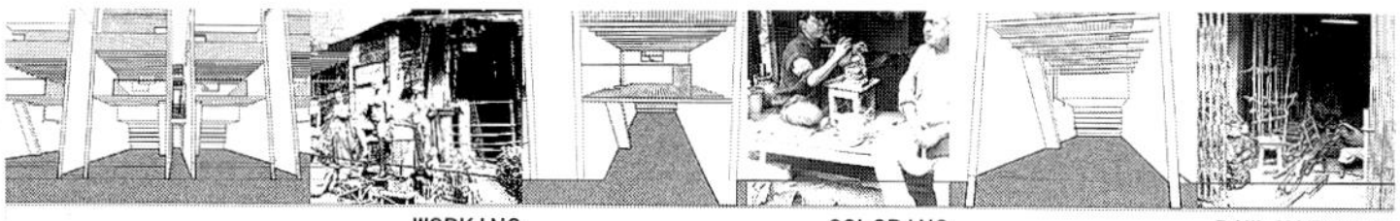
WORKING　COLORING　RAW MATERIAL

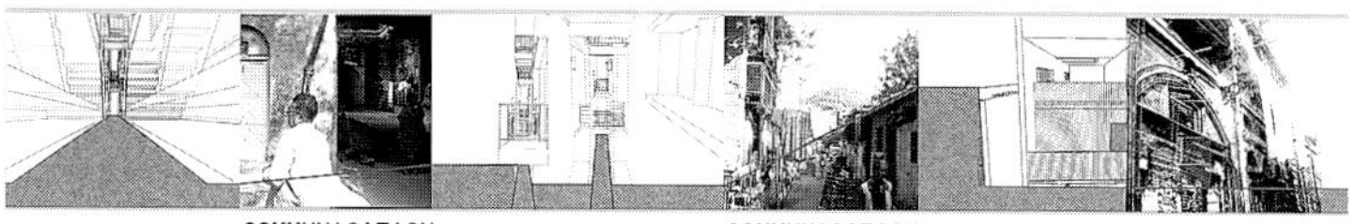
COMMUNICATION　COMMUNICATION　LIVING

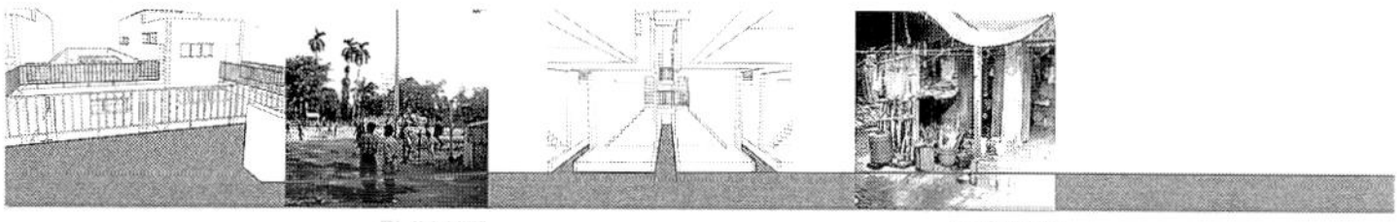
PLAYING　COOKING

西立面

东立面

In all of the Indian cities, the densest is Mumbai, followed by New Delhi, then Kolkata. The river is of great functional and religious importance to the daily routine in Kumartuli. Narrow alleys are characteristic of Bumartuli, yet small courtyards, exist for communal purposes like washing, also maximal used in the site. Even slum-dwellers survive by putting up shelter and living along pavements along the buildings.

The premise is occupied by many landlords who have inherited the building. Leftover spaces or workshops spaces on the ground floor are leased out to provide income. The premise is owned by the chief artisan who hires workers seasonally. The chief artisan possibly owns more than one studio.

Aside by the claying modeling center, residential components exist behind the wall of stores and modeling studios. The clay modeling is evidently the largest industry in Kumartuli. Working involves retrieving raw materials from the river, sculpturing of the deities, garland making, ornament crafting and storage.

Laundary and cooking are confined to the inner private realm of the courtyards deep in the heart of Kumartuli.

All of the various functions will be mixed together. There is no obvious boundary between different areas. All the activities are chained in one circulation. Life is confined like an assembly line. Different types of function own various amount of the space, large or small. All of the different types of space mixed together, reorganize to make the optimal using of space.

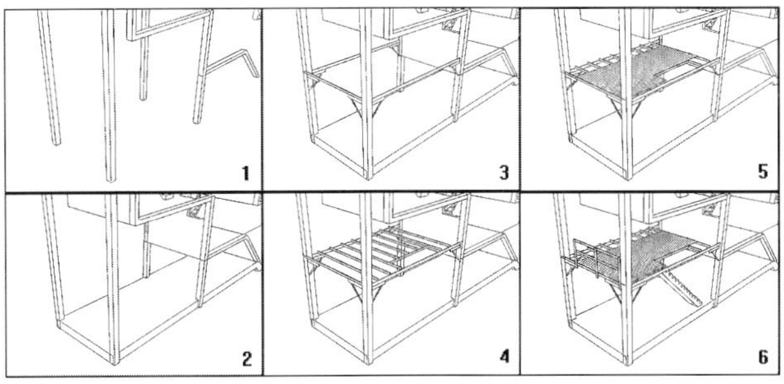

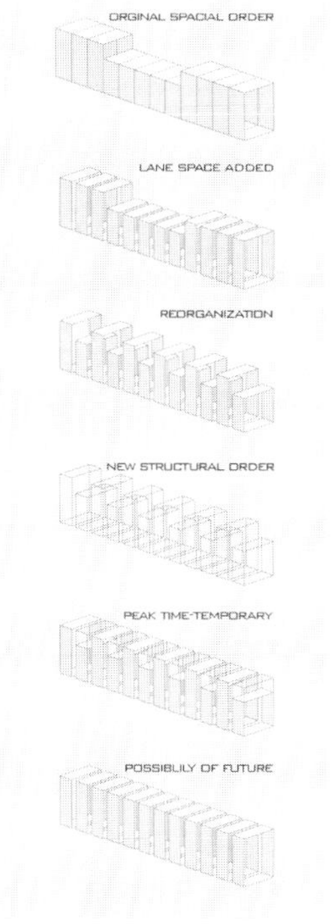

总平面

风场·水场·工场——上海世博会江南造船厂历史地段改造和更新

Regeneration and Renewal of the Historical Area of Jiangnan Shipyard, Shanghai

作者：姚昕悦 江天 何晋 袁懿 李邦健 指导老师：王建国 仲德崑 龚恺

获2008年“Revit杯”全国大学生建筑设计作业优秀奖

综述 随着上海的高速发展，生态环境的持续恶化日益受到关注。2010年世界博览会的举办为上海的城市生态改造提供了契机。基地位于黄浦江北岸，紧邻市中心，原为封闭的滨水工业区，改造后将成为城市公共空间。本方案从基地所处的风环境和水环境着手，引入“生态层”的立体绿化空间，使高速、紧张的城市得以舒缓、呼吸。

风场 生态手段上，通过建筑及植被的开敞与围合，形成一系列疏风聚风的开放空间，创造场地内适宜的风环境，通过软件计算验证逐步优化方案。

水场 充分利用水资源，通过雨水收集系统组织场地水环境，并力图达到水量平衡，在景观上活水的同时也在生态上活水，利用水体及水生植物的生态功能调节微气候。

工场 两条水廊同时打通了场地的历史文脉，在保留工业建筑物结构的同时，也使百年老厂乃至上海近代民族工业在精神上得以延续。

生态 除了种植净化水源的水生植物之外，场地内还结合不同业态的文化需要、遵循风场和水场布置原则、并考虑对既存工业污染的治理布置树种，形成错落有致、动静有别、四季交替的景观环境。

Overview As economics and society developed in Shanghai, the deterioration of urban ecological environment is more and more concerned. The hosting of 2010' EXPO provides Shanghai the opportunity to improve urban environment. The site locates to the north of Huangpu River and is closed to the city center. The aim to transform it from a closed waterfront industrial area to an open urban green space will accomplish through this design. Our scenario starts from the environment of wind and water, which are the most important elements of the local microclimate, and "eco-layer", a tri-dimensional green space, is introduced.

Wind Field A series of open spaces are created to lead or gather wind by buildings and plants. Software is used to testify and optimize the scheme.

Water Field Rainwater collecting system is applied to organize the water system in the site. Water volume achieves balance. Water is activated both scenically and ecologically. The ecological functions of waters and aquatic plants are utilized to regulate the microclimate.

Industry Field Two water-belts link the historical context, which conserves not only the industrial buildings, but the industrial spirits of Jiangnan Shipyard and even the national industry in Shanghai.

Ecology Apart from the aquatic plants for water purification, vegetation is covered in the site based on the cultural requirement, the arrangement of wind and water, as well as the treatment to the industrial pollution. The [illegible] this reconstruction

基地位置

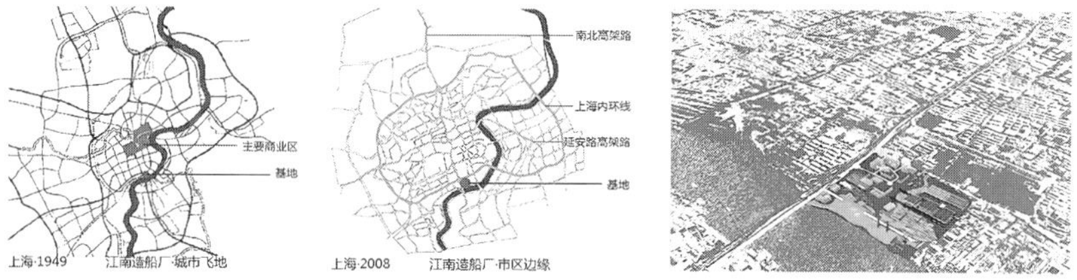

生态危机

场地特质

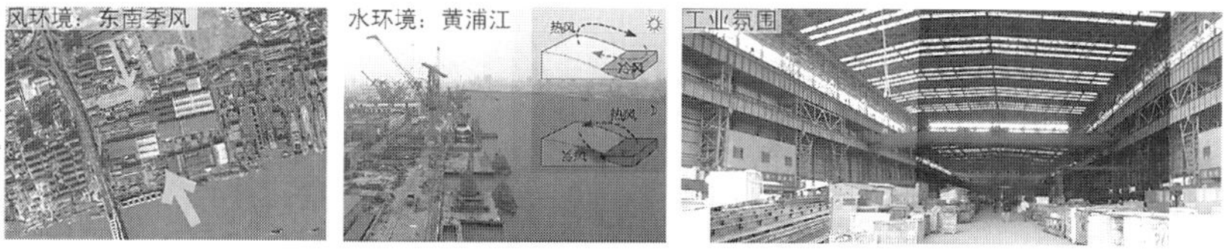

风场疏通

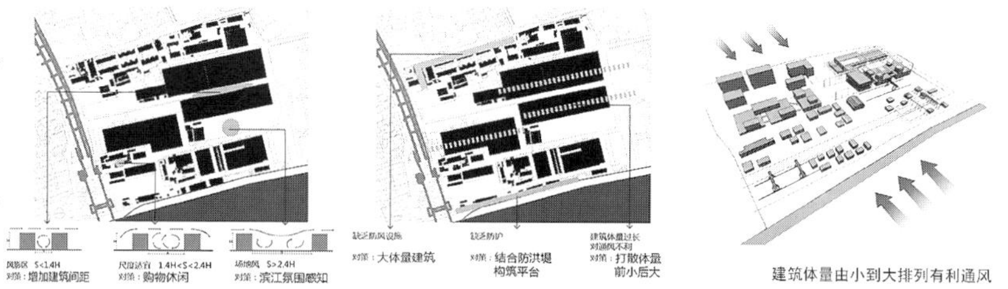

水场平衡

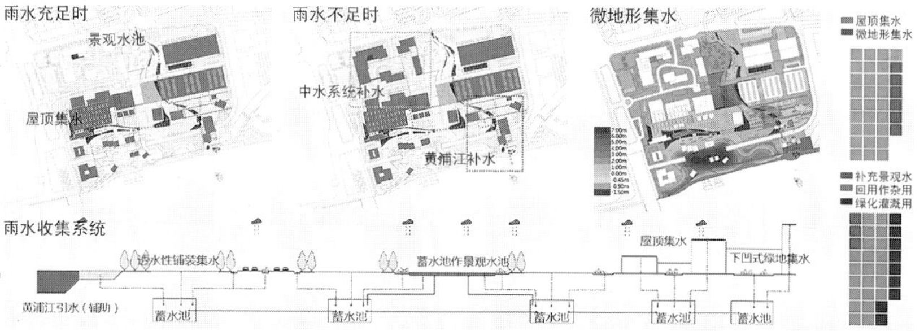

工场新生

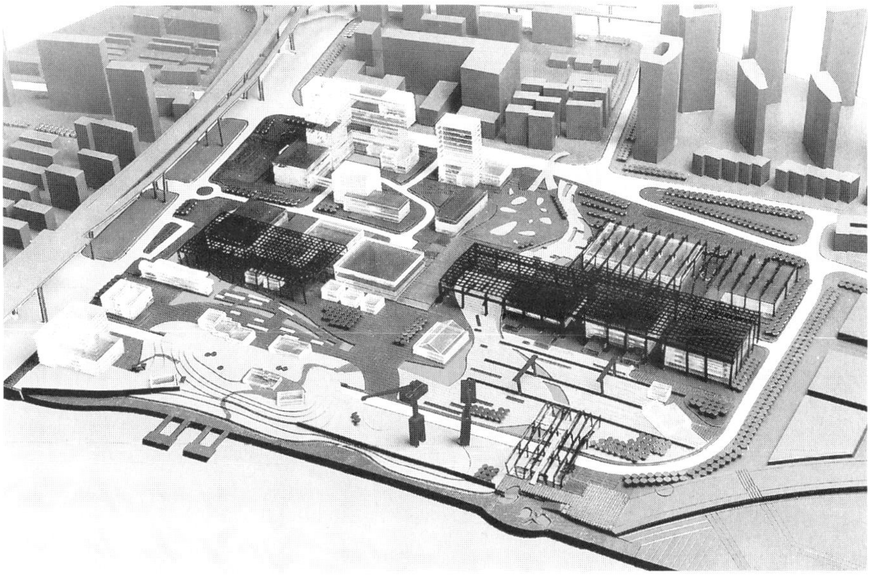

单体改造——风工厂WIND FACTORY

单体改造——水工厂WATER FACTORY

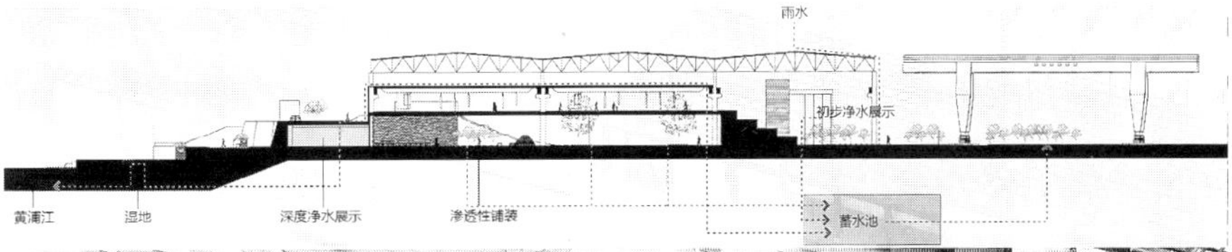

宁波市鄞州区横溪镇区控制性详细规划
The Regulatory Plan for Hengxi Town, Yinzhou, Ningbo

作者：赵薇　指导老师：段进 季松 薛松 刘红杰

通过横溪镇区控制性详细规划的编制，明确市镇的六线控制、公共配套设施、市政配套设施等强制性控制指标，对各地块的用地性质、用地面积、建筑密度、建筑控高、建筑红线后退距离、容积率、绿地率、交通出入口方位等规定性指标加以明确。同时对市镇城市设计提出指导性要求，针对不同地块的具体情况，提出建筑形式、建筑体量、风格色彩以及特殊地块的环境要求等规划指导性指标，作为城市规划管理的依据。

The regulatory planning for Hengxi town clears the town of six-lane control, public facilities, municipal facilities, such as mandatory control targets, the nature of the land around the block, the land area, building density, high-construction, construction back from the red line, the volume rate, the rate of green space, traffic directions, such as rules on import and export indicators to be clear. At the same time, the town's urban design guidance requirements for different blocks of concrete, make architectural forms, capacity of building, style and color of the special environmental requirements, such as land planning guidance indicators as the basis for urban planning and management.

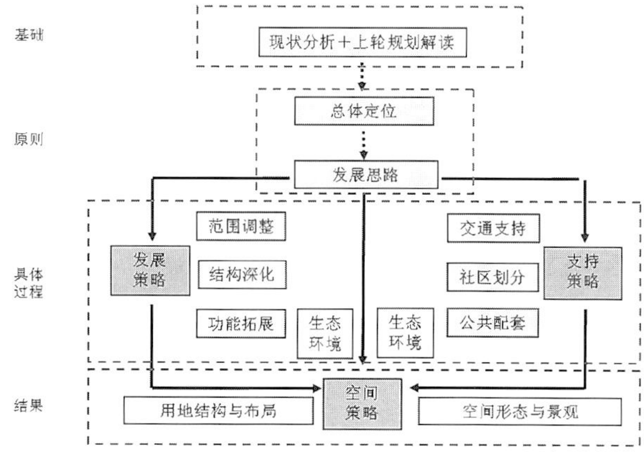

技术路线

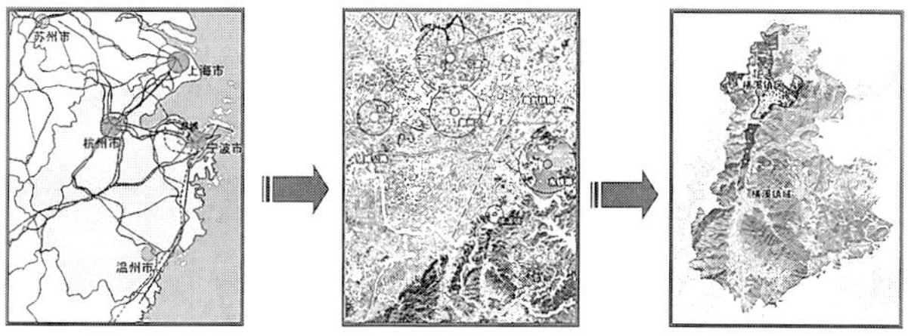

宁波市地理位置　横溪镇域地理位置　横溪镇区地理位置

背景介绍

上位规划

现状建筑质量

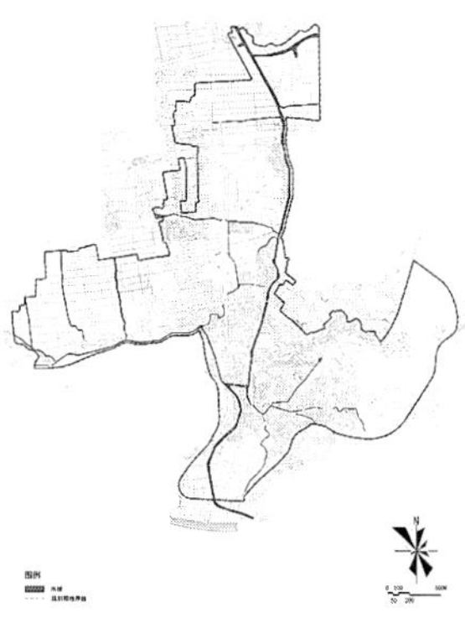

现状河流水系

现状道路交通

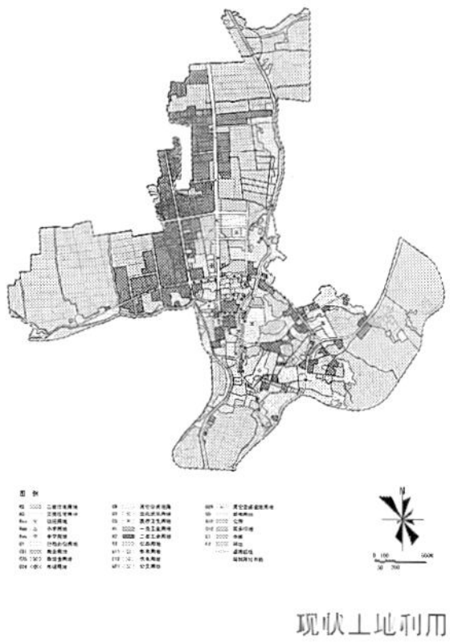

现状土地利用

道路交通系统

地块编号

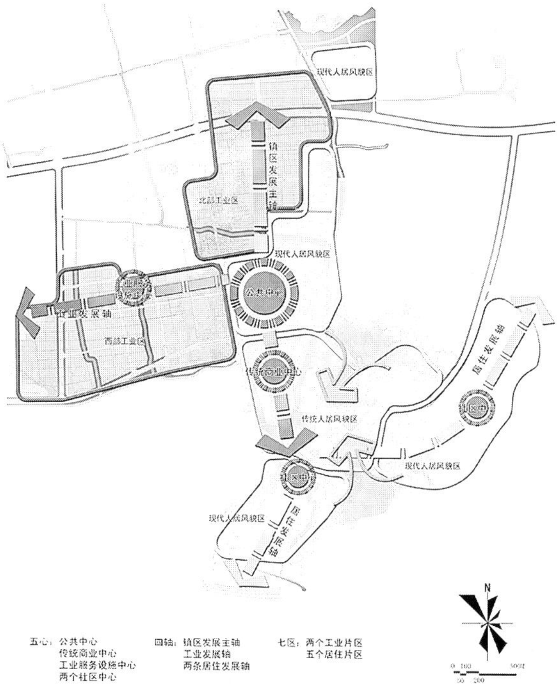

功能结构分析

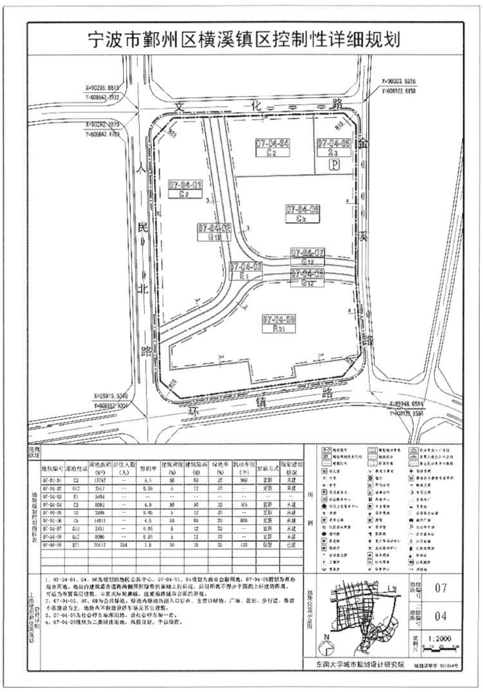

分图则

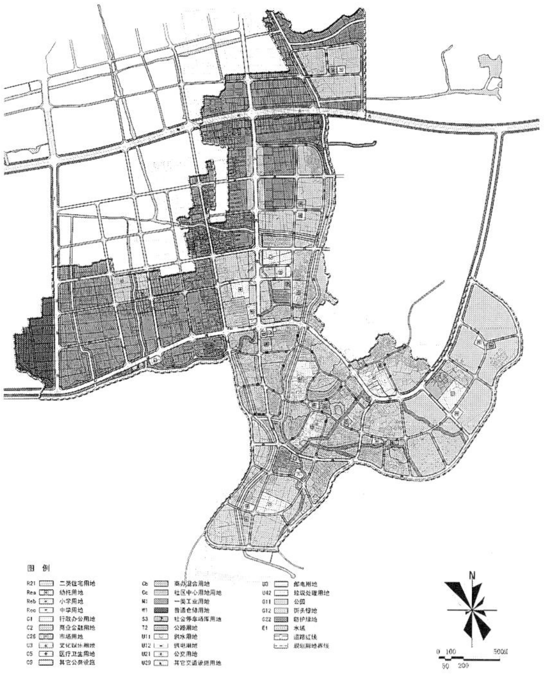

土地利用规划

设计分析与表达
Analysis and Expression in Design

主讲教师：韩冬青

作为学习、建立并展示建筑设计概念的专业技术，“分析”及其“表达”已成为现代建筑设计及研究中的关键环节之一。该课程为面向建筑设计及其理论专业硕士研究生的专业选修课，同时也向其他相关专业研究生开放。通过该课程学习，学生可以了解并掌握建筑设计中基本的分析理论和表达方法，寻找并理解设计中的主导概念、结构及过程，并能呈现设计的关键特征，从而建立起“分析—设计—交流”连续互动的设计思维方法、研究方法和操作方法，由此提升建筑设计的能力。

设计是一种创造性行为，而创造总是从模仿开始的，模仿是学习的初步形式，练习者（设计师）总是部分地依赖于自己和他人的经验，但又总是试图突破自己和他人的经验，不必讳言，几乎所有的设计者都有着纠缠于这般矛盾之中的疑惑和焦虑，更不必说是初学者了。“学习”与“创造”构成了设计练习乃至设计执业中一对最普遍的互动过程。“创造”的效率很大程度上取决于“学习”的效率。如果说案例作品(works as cases)模仿是学习的初步或直接形式，那么，到底该模仿的是什么呢？是外在的样式，还是内在的逻辑？是案例作品的终端结果，还是案例作品的形成过程？进一步问，仅有模仿是否是充分的案例学习呢？所谓“设计分析”正是用于回答这类问题的。设计分析是指以案例作品为依托，寻觅、理解并表达出一个设计的主导概念、结构逻辑和过程逻辑，进而呈现设计中最关键特征的专业工作。我们在这里讨论的设计分析，其实质是一种设计解读，是创造的逆过程，指对设计自身的一种追溯，一种从设计的结果出发倒推其过程逻辑的“反设计”。分析脱胎于模仿，又超越了模仿，甚至成为与模仿相反的学习方法。用模仿的方法接受一种知识的时候，是整体地吸收的。设计分析采取逆向的方法，它与那种整体的、感悟式的、内省式的学习方法相反，强调理性的、可以图说的、可以拆解和判断结构的方法。因此，设计分析不能完全取代模仿，但却是一种具有更高效率的学习策略。如果说设计是一种综合创造，那么，设计分析则是学习这种综合创造的必备环节和有效方法。设计分析通过专业的解析方法，使一般的对案例的感性认识转化为理性认识，有效的分析结果所具有的类型抽象特性可以使学习者获得超越于该案例作品的更具普适性的设计经验，由于这种结果取自于具体的案例，因此，它与从一般的原理说教所获得的认识相比会更生动，却又比一般的案例阅读更深刻。一个具有分析习惯的学习者由此会获得更为有效的设计策略，并有可能在其自己的设计过程中创造性地运用这些设计策略，从而弥合经验与突破、学习与创造的矛盾纠缠。

建筑设计的专业分析技术可以上溯至迪朗的古典建筑类型图解，进入现代时期以后，经过包豪斯和德州骑警的设计分析教学法，设计分析逐渐成为现代设计，包括建筑设计相关研究和教学工作中的重要环节。

2003年起，我们尝试开设“设计分析与表达”硕士生课程，从环境、空间、建构、几何与数、图解技术等方面讨论设计分析与表达的基本理论和方法。该课程共40学时。教学过程包括授课与练习两个环节，学员被要求完成某个自选设计案例或设计专题的分析工作。接下来的两项案例分析即是学员的分析习作。

As a disciplinary technique by which some concepts of design are studied and displayed, Analysis and its expression have been one of the keystones in architectural design and research. By the course, students should understand and have a good command of the basic analysis theory and the methods of expression within architectural design, looking for the main concepts, the structures and process of design, being able to display the important characters of design. Based on the reaction of analysis, design and interchange, the methods of thinking, researching and operation in the design could be found.

This course has two parts, basic theory and case study, which include following elements:

1. Meaning and significance of design analysis;
2. Contextual understanding;
3. Spatial understanding;
4. Tectonic understanding;
5. Formative ideas;
6. Diagrammatical methods in the design analysis.

1. 案例分析I
Case Study I

通过对挪威一个小型教堂的设计分析图示，从若干视角展现了设计者将设计意图向结果转化时所使用的逻辑和控制方法。同时简要论述了针对具体对象的设计分析程序，也显示了图示工具在其中的关键作用。

Through graphic analysis of a small church in Norway, the article shows the logic and control methods used by the designer to translate intent into results.The article also discusses the process of design analysis of a specific target, in which the graphic tool plays a key role.

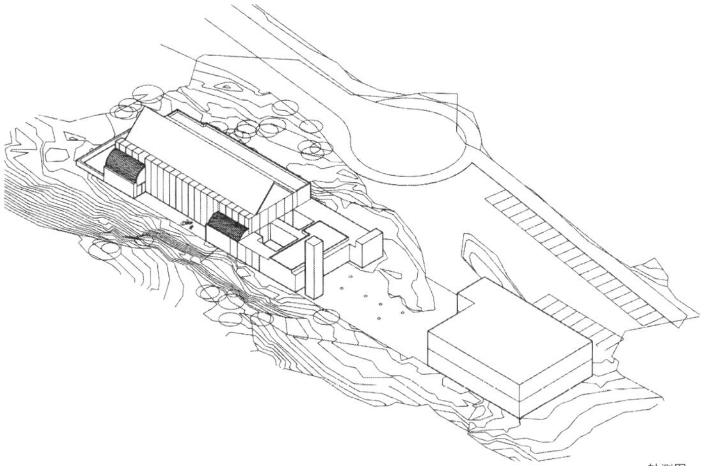

轴测图

一层平面图

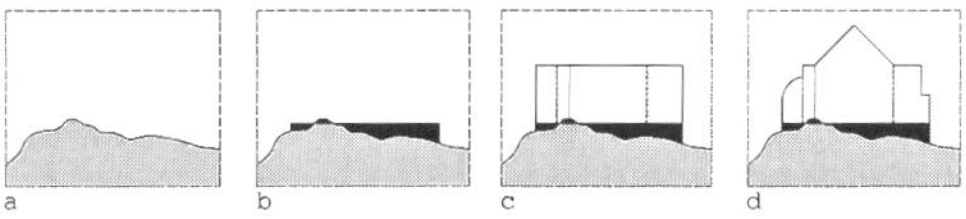

概念图解

结构的微调

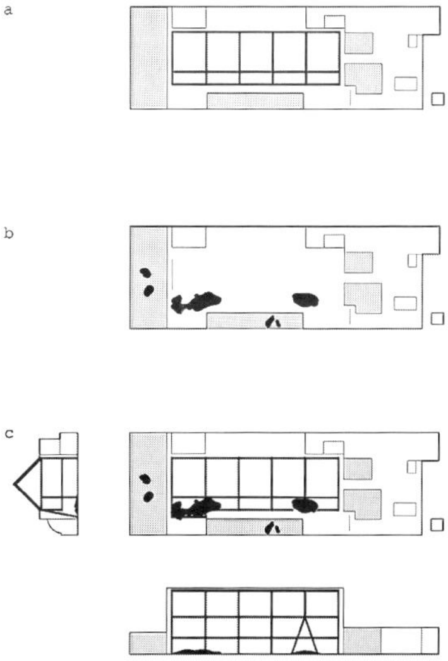

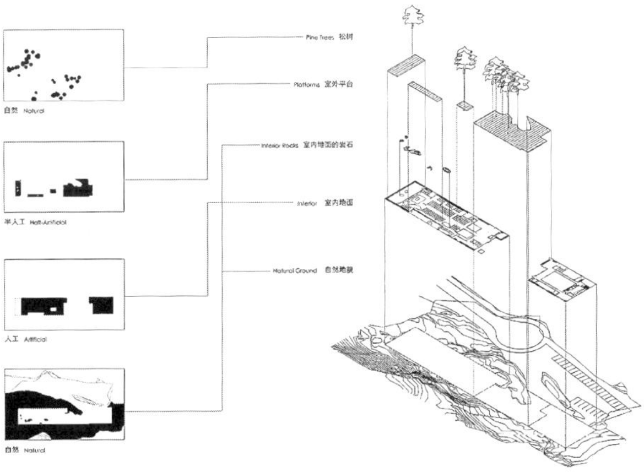

地质元素分层图

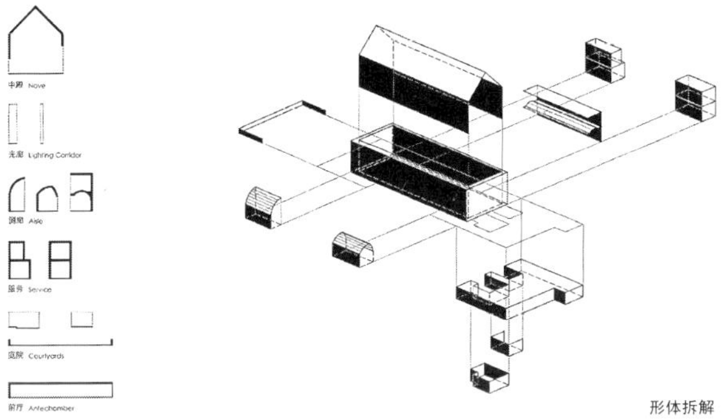

形体拆解

钢柱与地面岩石

2. 案例分析 II
Case Study II

总平面

现代主义之后，混凝土依然在当代建筑扮演着重要角色。本文从设计策划的角度解读当代设计师佩佐•范•艾利赫夏申事务所的作品坡里住宅，作者试图通过图解与模型制作去推断设计师在空间及建造设计过程中所展现的逻辑原则与方法。

After modernism, concrete is still playing an important role in contemporary architecture. The article, from the designing and planning point, is an interpretation of an project of Poli House designed by Pezo von Ellrichshausen Architects. The author tried to infer the logical principle and methods, in which the architects followed in the process of spacial design and construction period.

空间概念图示

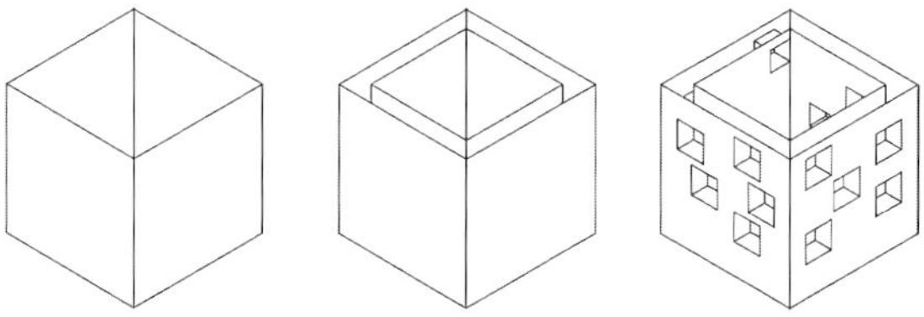

空间可达性

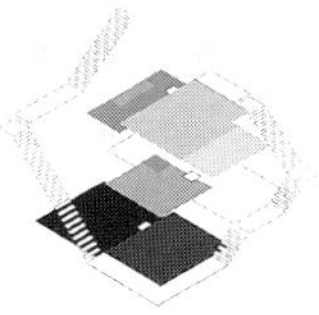

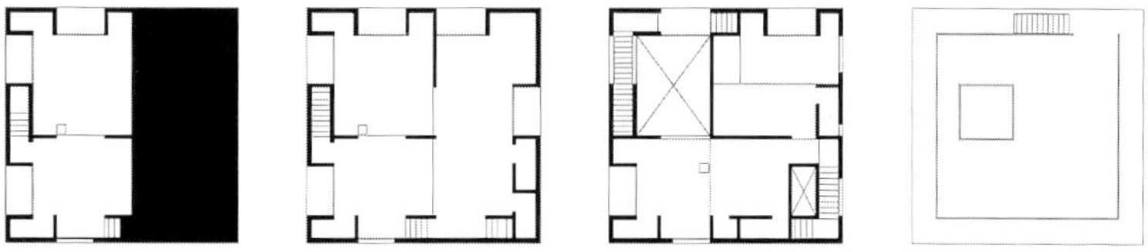
各层平面图

内部空间剖面

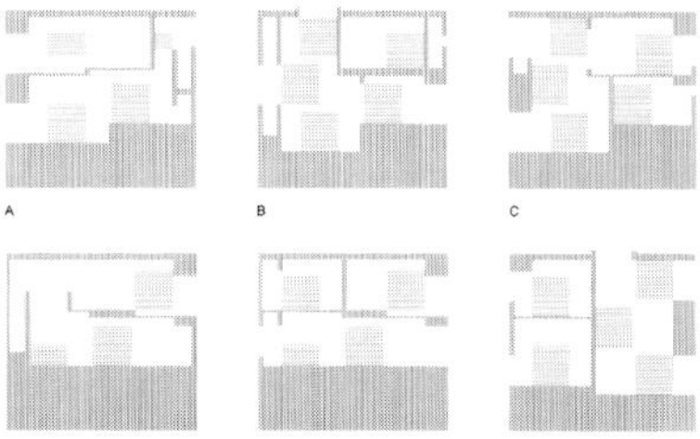

空间剖面体验

手工模型局部照片

现代城市设计方法
Modern Urban Design Methodology
主讲教师：王建国

城市设计是国内外公认的研究生阶段应该学习并在一定程度上掌握的基本能力。从含义上讲，城市设计是建筑学在城市层面上的表达和拓展，一般系指以城镇建筑环境的空间组织和优化为目的，运用跨学科的途径，对包括人、自然和社会因素在内的城市形体空间和环境对象所进行的设计工作。对现代城市设计理论和方法发展的了解、对建筑与实存环境的关系、设计场地的分析能力和综合驾驭能力是本课程对同学提出的主要要求。

一、教学目标和要求

1. 在相关先修课程基础上，一般了解城市设计的概念，熟悉其内容和历史发展。
2. 较系统地掌握现代城市设计的各种方法和操作技术，并通过案例研究检验之。
3. 完成研究报告、文献阅读或案例研究。

二、教学大纲（含章节目录）

1. 现代城市设计的基本概念及其内涵；
2. 城市设计发展的历史梗概；
3. 现代城市设计方法论演变的三个阶段；
4. 现代城市设计的理论方法；
5. 现代城市设计的操作技术；
6. 可持续发展和绿色城市设计。

三、主要参考书

1. 王建国. 现代城市设计理论和方法. 第2版. 南京：东南大学出版社，2003
2. 徐思淑，周文华. 城市设计导论. 北京：中国建筑工业出版社，1991

现代城市规划理论
Urban Planning Theory — An Advanced Study

主讲教师：董　卫

一、课程目的

本课程以专题形式讨论现代城市规划理论的发展，并以相关理论为基础开展实证性城市调查与分析，使学生了解和掌握理论的本质与特点，为今后独立开展相关研究奠定理论基础。

二、课程内容

1. 现代城市规划理论的发展过程

（1）城市规划理论的来源与发展；

（2）城市规划学科的发展阶段；

（3）城市规划理论的分类与意义。

2. 历史-空间理论研究方法

城市空间变迁理论

城市社会经济理论

3. 城市空间生成理论

城市空间规划与设计理论

后现代城市理论-政治权利框架中的城市空间

4. 城市研究

实证性研究方法——空间体验与空间阅读

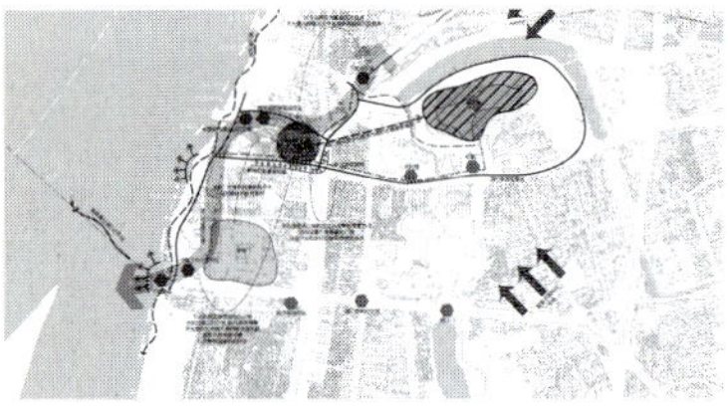
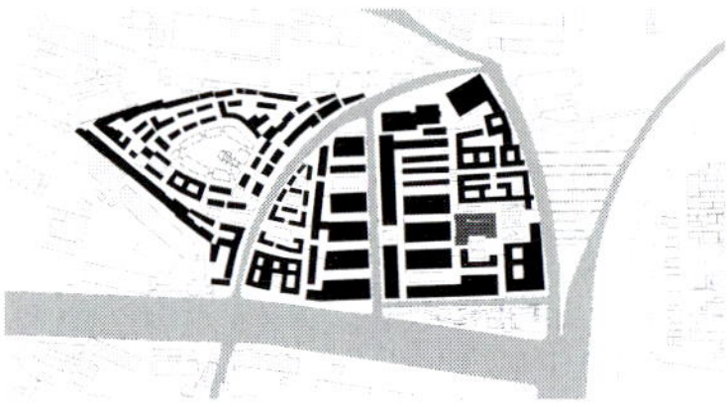
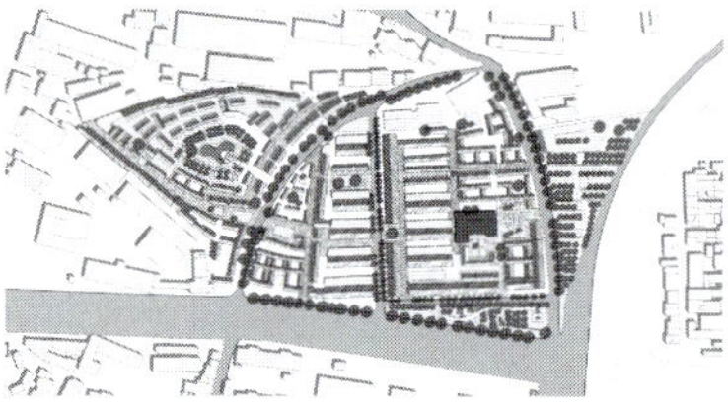

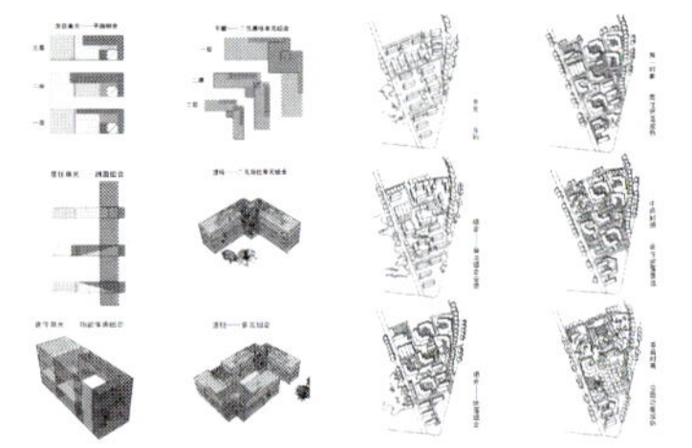
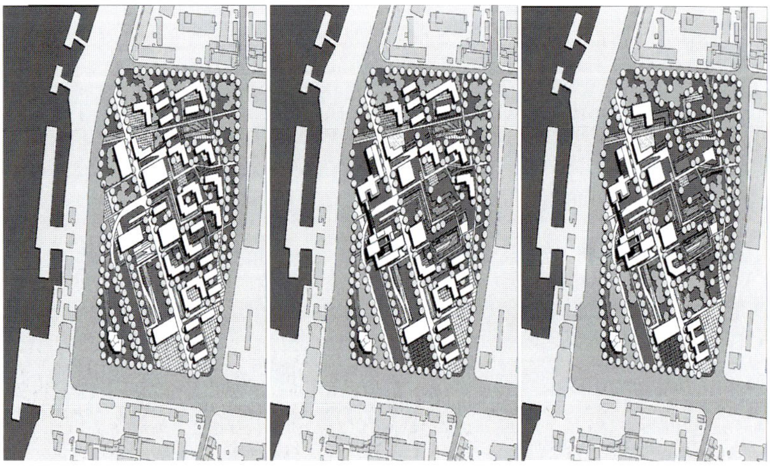
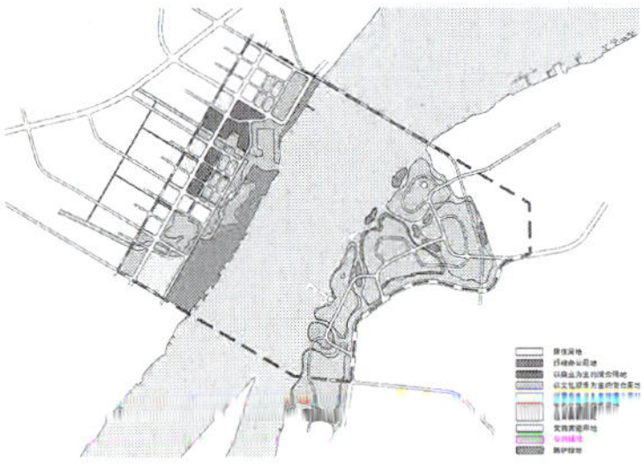
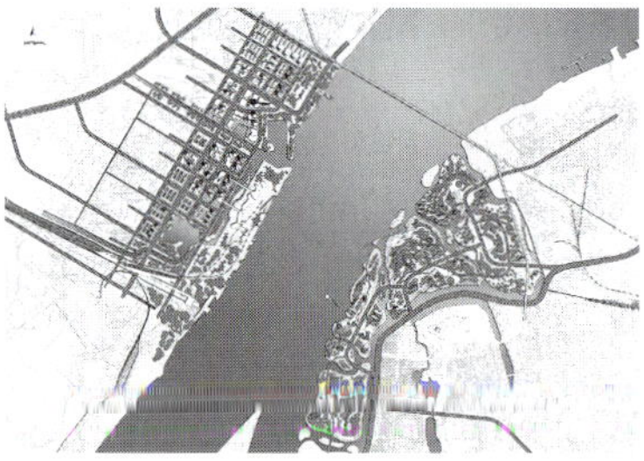
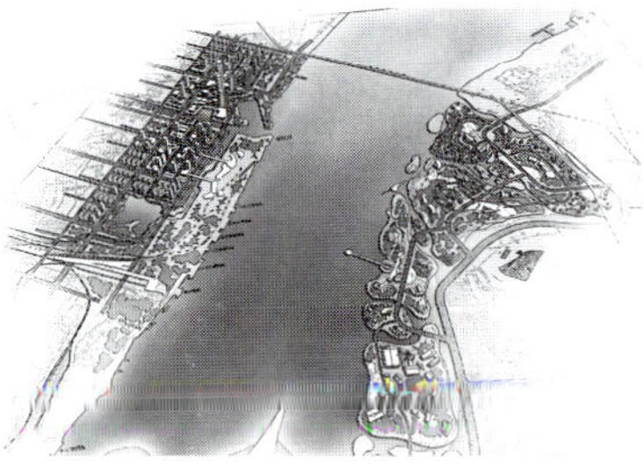

宋清营造法式

Ruler for Construction of Buildings in Song Dynasty and Qing Dynasty

主讲教师：陈　薇

教学目标和要求

通过对宋《营造法式》和清《工程做法》两部中国古代建筑法典介绍，尤其重点展开对宋《营造法式》研究性的讲课，帮助同学了解法式的方法、价值、思路和特色，掌握古建筑设计的基本原则和技巧，沟通古今在设计方法上的理念和思维，并能依法式设计古建筑。

60学时 3学分

Objects and Requirements

Through the introduction to the two ancient Chinese architectural classic books "Ruler for Construction of Buildings in Song Dynasty" and "Ruler for Construction of Buildings in Qing Dynasty", especially the research teaching of Ruler for Construction of Buildings in Song Dynasty, the students can have a better understanding of the methods, value, thoughts, and the characteristics of the rulers, master the basic principle and technique in ancient buildings design, approach the ancient ideas by modern thoughts, and then design ancient buildings in accordance with the ancient rulers.

宋清营造法式课程作业

隆兴寺摩尼殿厦两头造屋架研究

060018 刘妍
060015 于娜

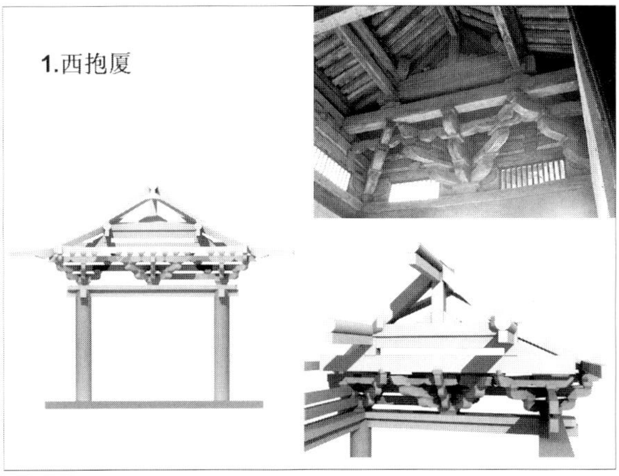

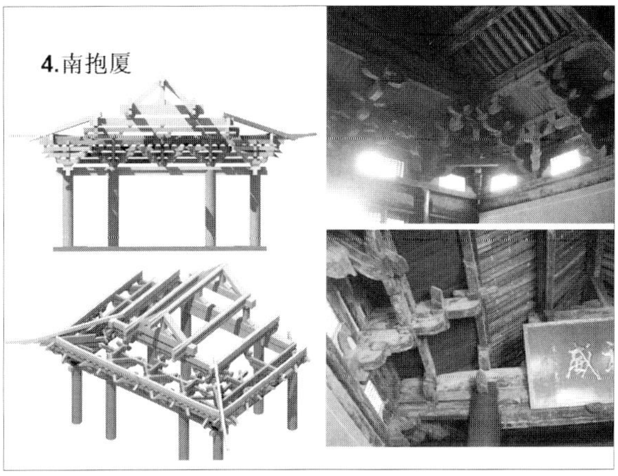

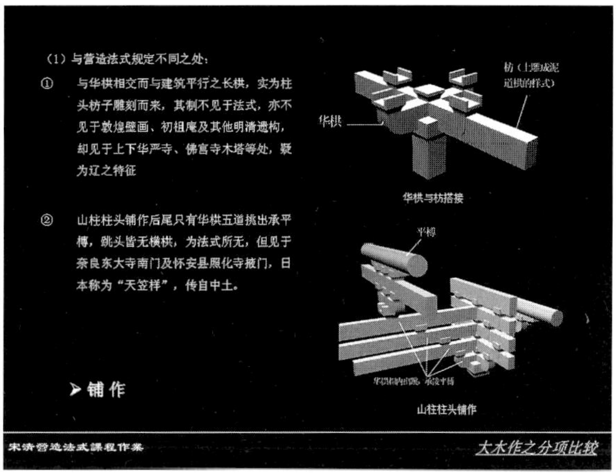

建筑遗产保护专业的一门核心课程——建筑遗产保护学课程介绍
Introduction of Architectural Heritage Conservation

主讲教师：朱光亚

建筑遗产保护专业是东南大学建筑学院从学士到博士学位都设置的新的专业，它是因新世纪建筑遗产保护工作日益受到重视，保护领域不断扩大，保护任务急剧增加的新形势而开设的。建筑遗产保护学是该专业的一门核心课程，是既为本专业也为其他专业有兴趣学习建筑遗产保护相关知识的研究生而开设的综合性课程，目前作为博士生课程开设，要求必修课程是中国建筑史和世界建筑史、营造法式和则例以及建筑学专业的本科基础课程。东南大学的这门课程的特点是，紧密结合国际学术前沿探讨的课题，紧密结合中国国情和东方历史文化的特点，以东南大学的国家重点学科——建筑历史学科的雄厚基础为依托，以东南大学建筑学院数十年来参与的中国建筑遗产保护运动的大量重大实践和理论探讨为案例，将运用与建筑遗产保护相关的各科知识围绕保护这一目标整合而成。课程的主要内容包括：问题与观念，体系与层次，基础研究，调查与评估，测绘与检测，保护规划，保护的建筑设计，保护的结构补强，修缮工艺及施工，管理与展陈，课程涉及中国学者半个世纪以来的保护实践经验和对中国国情的特点分析，也介绍了中国加入世界遗产组织以来保护运动中发生的理论、观念的变化和尚在进行的争论和思考，同时也关注了东西方文化碰撞和互动后的保护运动的新的课题。课程以理论分析为经，以案例为纬，作业以应用性为主。

Architectural heritage conservation is a new specialty in Architecture College of Southeast University. It enrolls students of bachelor, master and doctor degree. This new specialty is set up to confront the new situation such as the more attention in architectural heritage conservation, the expansion of the protection fields and the hasty increase of protection work. The course - Architectural Heritage Conservation is one of the synthetically core course for either postgraduate students from conservation or other specialities who are interested in. It is only for doctor now. The previous preparation courses are Chinese architectural history, World architectural history, Ying-zao-fa-shi, Ying-zao-ze-li and other basic architecture courses.

The course is featured with both theory and experiences. Firstly, it is combined with the latest international study topics. Secondly, it is a course concerned with Chinese conditions and Eastern Asia culture. Thirdly, it is based on the solid achievements of architectural history discipline which is National Key discipline's. Finally, it is an integration of both conservation knowledge and case studies which are from conservation practices and theory study in recent decades of Southeast University Architecture College.

The course is composed of 10 chapters, which are problems and conception, system and hierarchical structure, fundamental researches, investigation and estimation, survey drawing and examination, conservation planning, architecture conservation design, structure reinforcement in conservation, technology and construction in conservation, management and exhibition for conservation. All these chapters are linked with scholars' experiences during last half century and analysis of Chinese situation. The changes of theory, conception, argument and reflection in conservation domains since China joined in the World Heritage Organization are also introduced. Some new topics emerging during the interaction of Chinese and Western culture are also discussed. The course is organized by theory as warp and case study as weft. The assignments are mostly utilizations.

1. 浙江余姚河姆渡保护规划
Conservation Planning in Hemudu, Yuyao, Zhejiang Province

遗址概况

河姆渡遗址位于浙江省余姚市河姆渡镇，是我国长江下游一处保存情况良好的重要的新石器时代遗址。遗址的发掘为研究我国新石器时代文化增添了一新鲜资料，说明长江流域与黄河流域都是中华民族远古文化的摇篮。

河姆渡遗址发现于1973年，总面积约50，000平方米，文化堆积厚4米左右，叠压着4个文化层。遗址保存完好，内涵丰富。河姆渡遗址曾两次发掘，第一次发掘面积810平方米，其中180平方米无文化层堆积，实际发掘630平方米。第二次发掘面积2，000平方米。两次发掘出土文物主要有栽培稻谷、骨、木、石、陶等生产工具和生活用品6，193件，以及大片带榫卯结构的木构干栏式建筑遗迹和大量动植物遗骸。

河姆渡遗址揭示了7，000年前长江以南新石器时代中期最晚阶段的人类文明，在其发现之初，曾轰动了国内外学术界，此后根据河姆渡遗址的发掘成果，对河姆渡文化进行了广泛、深入的研究。它的考古发掘成果为各个学科研究，特别是对许多学科史的研究提供了极为难得的实物标本。

1982年，河姆渡遗址被国务院公布为全国重点文物保护单位。1987年划定5.4公顷保护范围与3.5平方公里建设控制地带。

Heritage Introduction

Hemudu is in Hemudu town, Yuyao, Zhejiang Province.It's one of important and well kept heritages of new stone age. It's a strong proof that Yangtze River is as important as Yellow River for culture breeding.

The heritage was discovered in 1973. Its area is about 50,000 square meters with four layers whose total height is about 4 meters. The first discovery covered 810 square meters while the second covered 2,000 square meters. Both two discoveries found out lots of tools and living stuff. Wood structure with tenors had also been found.

This heritage reveals the life and culture of people around Yangtze River about 7,000 years ago and gives real proves for further study.

Hemudu was declared as the National heritage in 1982. The protecting boundary and building control area was declared in 1987.

规划的前期分析

主要矛盾和问题

保护与城乡发展的矛盾：河姆渡遗址位于东南沿海发达地区，尽管它处于郊区，但还是与发展迅速的城乡建设产生矛盾。近年来在建控地带之内进行的建设，如杭甬高速的建设虽然经过合法程序，但是其噪音和废气污染也在一定程度上影响到遗址，对姚江南岸的景观也产生了一定的负作用。另如姚江即将升级航道，由此引起的水质的变化，噪音以及村落规模扩张，乡镇企业的发展等等都会对遗址环境产生影响。

保护与发展利用的矛盾

虽然河姆渡文化在人类考古学上有着重要的地位和价值，但是其价值并未得到较好的发掘。由于地方政府需要它带动周边经济发展，也做过这一地区的规划和设想，生态园和凤凰休闲度假村的建设正是出于这一设想，然而由于发展的定位没有更多的考虑保护的重要性，建设未加以引导和规划，保护和发展利用未能促进发展，反而成为对立面。相关规定的缺乏和管理不规范导致违法事件的产生：虽然保护范围和建设控制地带较早确定，但是缺乏合理规范的控制要求和执行力度，导致一系列的不利于保护的情况发生，比如度假村事件、开山破坏山体。

现有保护区划不能反映近20年来的考古成果。

Hemudu is in a fast developing area which leads to a lot of confliction. Waste air and water did harm to the heritage. And the expansion of Yao River and villages nearby will affect the environment.

It's hard to handle the confliction. The town government tried to build villas nearby to help tour but failed because the vision is lack of conservation. The fact means the management and the conservation needs to change to have a better control.

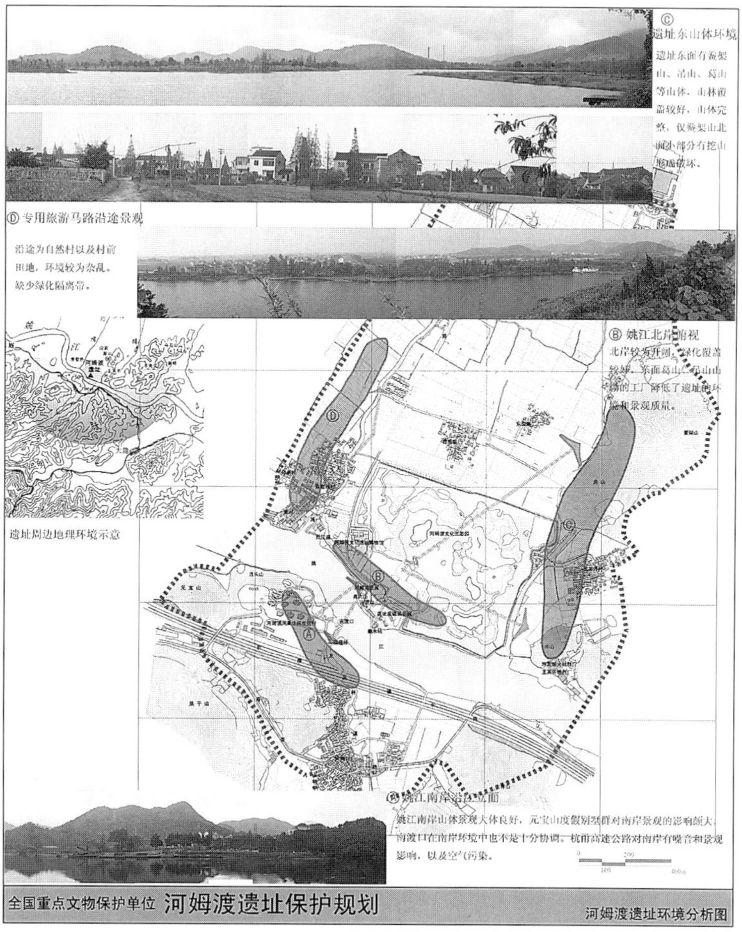

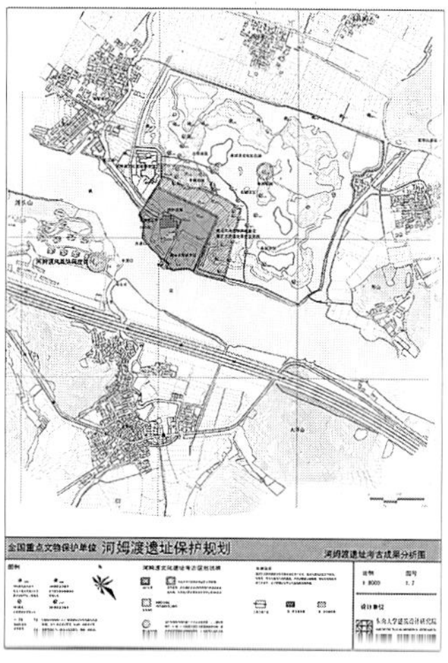

项目的难点

问题的产生

为促进河姆渡遗址的发展利用，扩大旅游接待能力，2003年，余姚市及河姆渡遗址文化旅游开发区管理委员会在尚未经过国家文物局同意的情况下，决定在河姆渡遗址南岸渡头山建设旅游项目——河姆渡凤凰休闲度假村。

度假村虽然没有破坏南岸保护主体，但对河姆渡遗址的现实环境产生了诸多的不良影响：破坏河姆渡遗址姚江南岸的地下埋藏；破坏河姆渡遗址姚江南岸部分的自然环境；扰乱河姆渡遗址景观氛围；干扰了河姆渡遗址南岸交通。

就地方上来说，这已经成为一个社会问题，开发商通过正当的途径获得建设用地，责任在政府，并且别墅的产权已经分散到几百户百姓手中，矛盾从政府和开发商之间发展成为政府和百姓之间。而保护利用的缺乏也是导致该事件的主要原因。

问题的解决

强调报批程序是首要的，在这个基础上，改善建筑群的外观使其融入河姆渡遗址的自然环境，使其功能上服务于河姆渡遗址，如果改造的效果能达到这样的预期，度假村的建设就会对遗址的发展产生有利影响和促进作用，可以较好地解决这个问题，因此最后的解决方式可以总结成以下几点：

管理权归属：　余姚市政府收回度假村管理权。

功能定位：度假村的基本功能定位为“为河姆渡遗址公园提供服务设施、兼顾相关休闲活动、弘扬河姆渡特色”的风景点，其本身应达到优秀景点的景观质量和环境质量。改造规划及设计报国家文物局批准。

In 2003, Management commission of Hemudu decided to build a villa at the south beach to Hemudu without State Administration of Cultural Heritage's permission. This leads to some serious problems such as the harm to the underground heritage and the change in landscape. All these problems then became the confliction between governments and their people. The source is the failure in handling the problem of preservation with reasonable development.

To solve these problems, it begins with the right progress and then turns to the façade design for building and function change. All steps can be concluded as follow.

The city government takes control of the management instead of the commission.The villa changes function into the service building for Hemudu.

The façade is re-designed to meet the landscape requirement.

The plan and the design are reported to Government.

规划思路

区划内的控制与整合：在建设控制地带与保护范围内的控制要求强调审批的重要性，并针对不同功能、不同保护区块实施不同控制要求。将区域资源进行整合，形成三个步骤和范围：一是核心保护区内的保护措施加强和高科技保护及展示；二是周边资源的重组和梳理，成为非单一、内容充实多样的展示群，以及各种设施的配备，以具备发展利用的条件；三是周边自然环境的生态重建，恢复山野自然环境，以达到环境的保护和可持续发展。

规划框架

内敛型保护

第一个层次将这个人文景观保护区纳入到河姆渡镇城镇总体规划中去，并将生态农业区向北延伸，与人文景观保护区相衔接，并根据宁波市的沿江生态保护计划，在姚江两岸建立50米的沿江绿化带，从生态和防洪两个方面保护姚江及周边环境。因此第一个层次是对现有区域规划思路的整合。第二个层次为保护区划的确定。保护区划的调整也是根据考古研究的新成果以及视线要求、管理情况所作出相应的调整。第三个层次为核心保护区的保护措施。

外扩型保护

外扩型保护规划是和内敛型保护相反的过程，它确立了保护发展的各个层面，体现可操作性。其主体是河姆渡遗址博物馆，从博物馆本身出发，往外扩张。它包括三个方面：一是博物馆扩张，对应博物馆管理和展示规划；二是区域影响力的扩张，这是当博物馆扩张之后，能增强对外界周边区域的影响力，带动整个镇区的建设；三是生态扩张，由生态园作为基点，向周围山脉，如四明山等等进行生态辐射，远期生态园可以东扩，形成以遗址为核心的包括周边山脉的景观生态区。

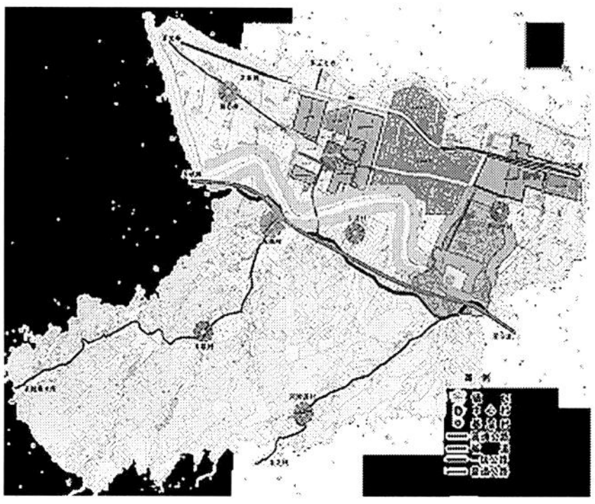

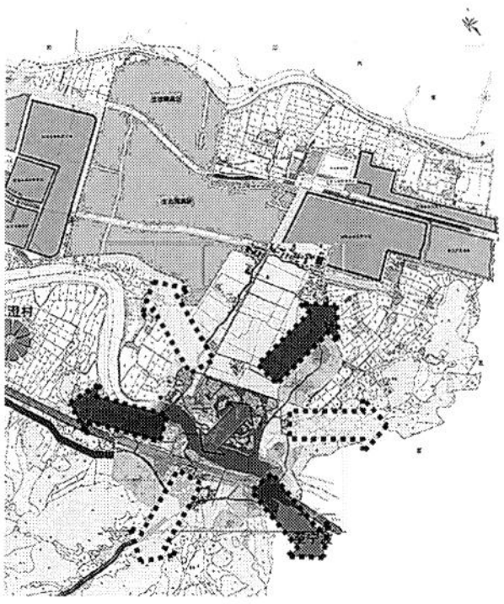

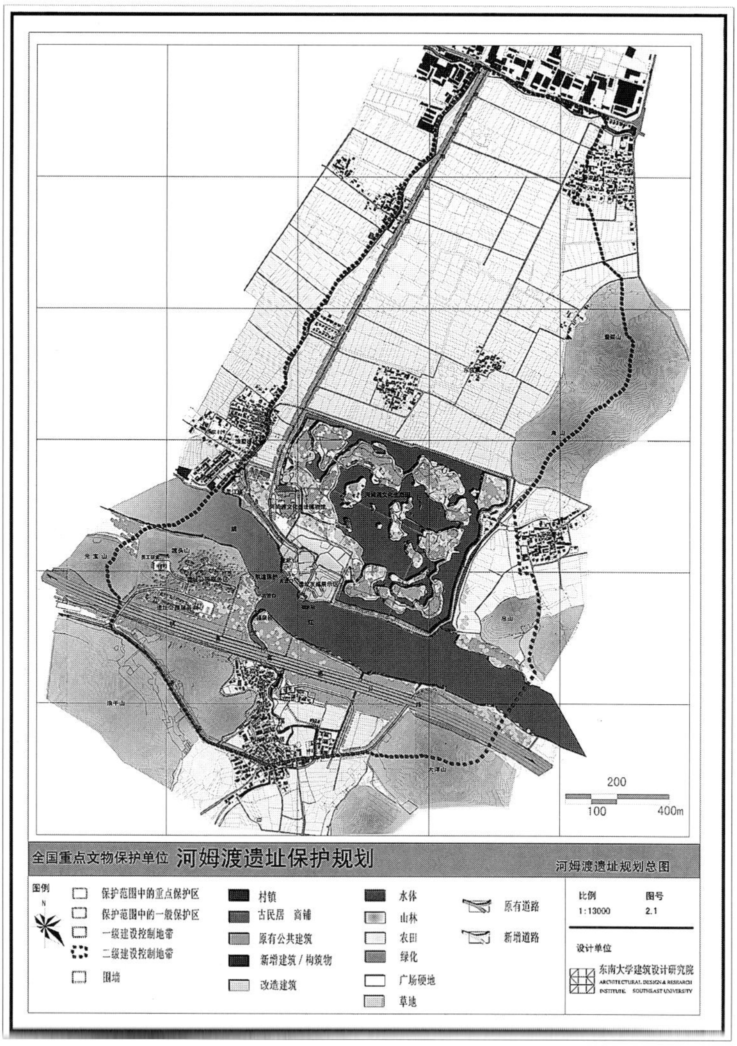

Planning Philosophy

The planning controls the area as one by 3 different levels. The core part is firmly controlled to show the heritage. The second is the contents for Hemudu and works as service area. And the third part is the landscape background.

Planning Frame

Inside Part

The first step is to enlarge the agriculture part into culture heritage. It also plans to make a greenbelt of 50 meters wide. The second step is to decide the protection area with many studies. The third step is to make conservation law.

Expansion Part

This part is to expand conservation affection. The first step is the expansion of the museum. The second step is to make the museum to affect more spaces. The third step is the eco expansion.

2. 宁波市它山堰总体保护规划
Conservation Planning of Tashanyan in Ningbo, Zhejiang Province

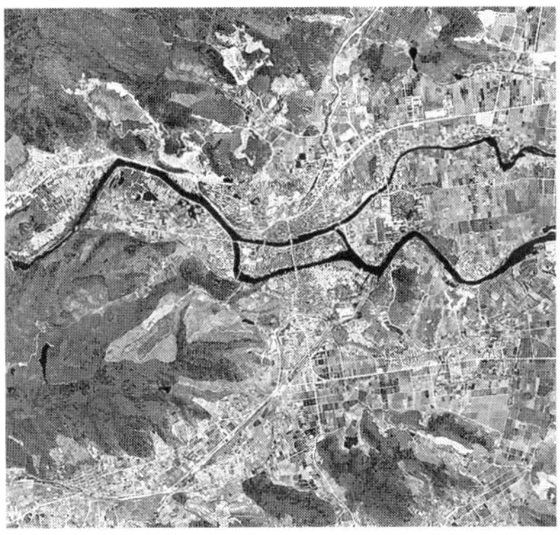

宁波市它山堰是始建于唐大和七年的重要古代水利设施，与都江堰、郑国渠齐名，是我国水利建筑史上首次出现的块石砌筑的拦河滚水坝，经历代补充完善，成为了一套完整的水利系统，于1988年被公布为国家级文物保护单位，于2000年划定保护范围和建控地带。

除本体外，它山堰还包括鄞江镇内的渠首配套设施和镇外绵延十多公里的下游配套设施，情况复杂，内容丰富。

由于水利设施不同于一般的遗址或文物建筑，长期处于使用状态而无法“冷冻”保护，因此这也就成为保护规划的重点和难点所在。

TashanYan, which is the first rock masonry dam, is one of most famous ancient water conservancy facilities. It was declared as National Heritage in 1988. The conservation area and control area were declared in 2000.

The dam and other facilities that TashanYan included are all in use today, which make it hard to do the conservation planning.

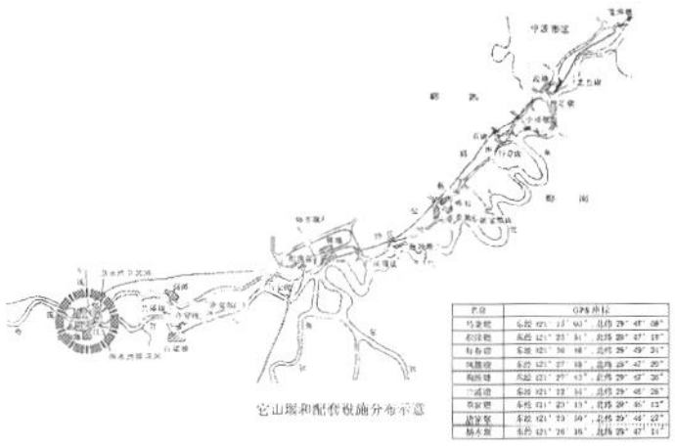

保护规划开始于对保护本体的正确再认知。它山堰之所以能成为重要的水利设施并一直得到重视，除了本身独特的建筑艺术和技术外，配套设施同样功不可没。同时，除了实际的水利作用，它山堰还对镇区的文化、历史、经济发展产生过重大影响，直至今日，仍然是“四明锁阴”的关键。

当把保护对象从堰体扩大为本体及配套设施后，周边环境与保护本体的矛盾愈发尖锐。不受控制的镇区发展已经损坏了它山堰的本体氛围，并造成文化丧失和断层。时至今日，对这些重要的保护对象，仍然没有准确的水文观测数据，使得保护工程无法展开。此外，诸如展陈、防灾、视线控制等都存在缺陷。在制定正确的保护规划政策之前，先要以图纸分析的方式一一罗列、整理上述问题。

The conservation planning begins with the recognition of Tashan Yan. In this progress, we find out that the supporting facilities are also very important. And the town nearby is also connected with Tashan Yan.

The town's nowaday development affects Tashan Yan greatly. Both the show and the conservation method are not used for today's situation. Before making planning, all these problems are listed by drawings.

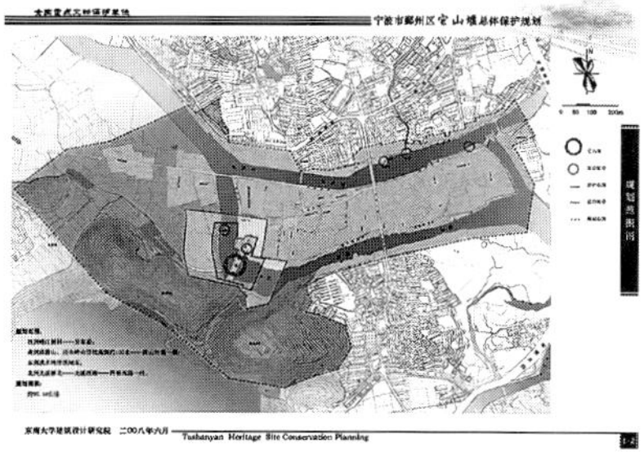

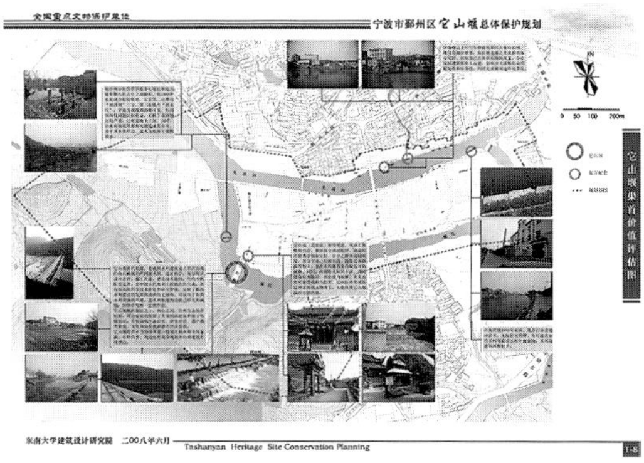

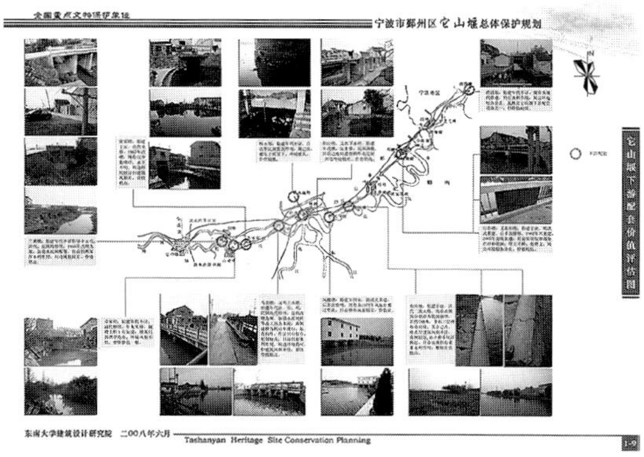

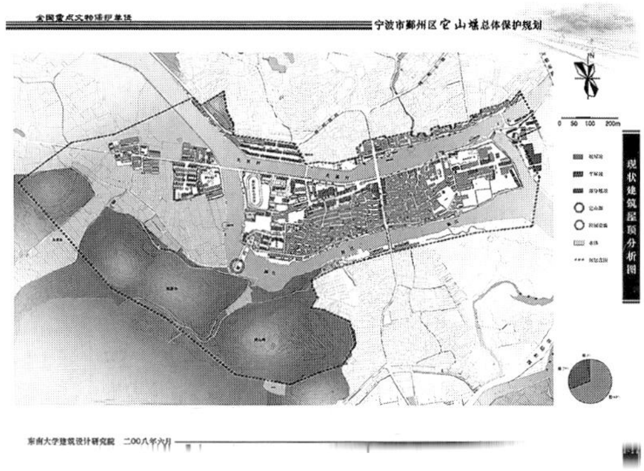

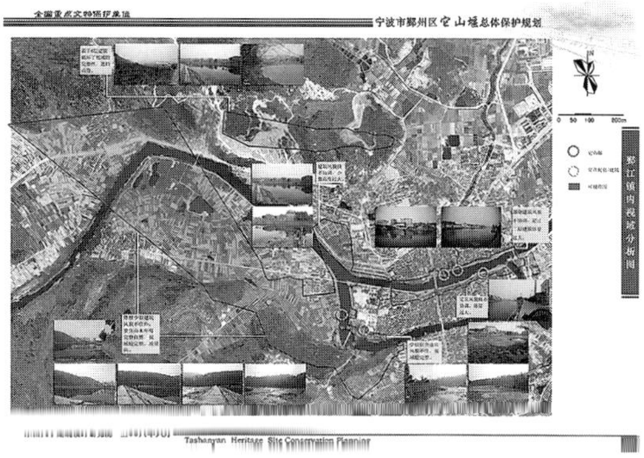

保护规划

思路

合理设置保护区划和保护措施，保证村镇和保护对象的良性互动，通过监控保证水利设施安全，将主体和配套设施完整保护和展示。

框架

三个层次：一是合理的保护范围和监控地带调整，二是设定环境协调区，三是保护本体之外的非物质遗产。

内容

包括重新制定保护范围和监控地带及措施，确定分期规划，进行展示利用引导和管理规章等。

Conservation Planning

Philosophy

To make a complete and interact Tashan Yan system conservation.

Frame

There are 3 levels.The 1st level is conservation range.The 2nd is environmental control while the 3rd is cultural heritage conservation.

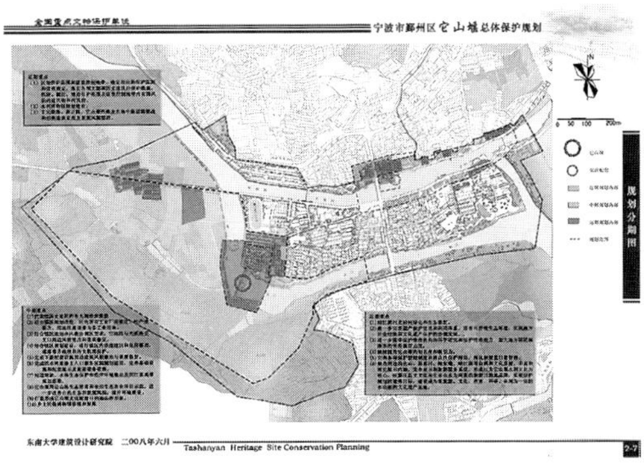

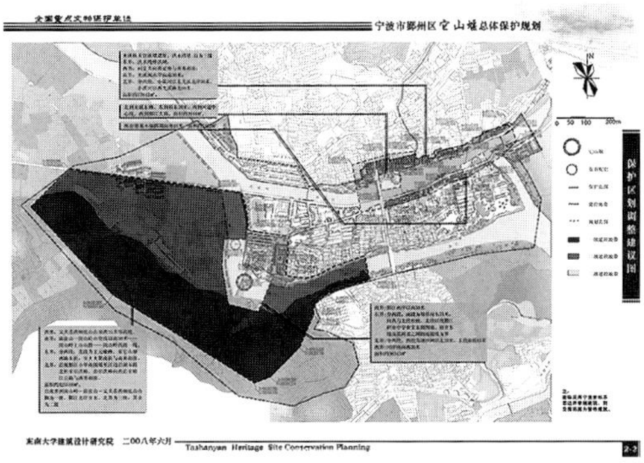

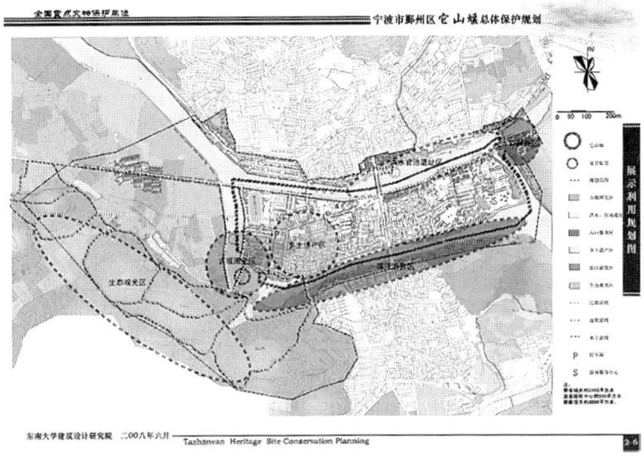

国家精品课程——建筑设计
National Level Excellent Course: Architecture Design

教学顾问

课程负责人

主讲教师

一、课程沿革

“建筑设计”是建筑学专业的主干核心课程，“建筑设计”课程教学既是专业教学的起点，也是专业教学成果的综合体现。正如国际、国内一流建筑学专业培养体系中建筑设计课程设置的共同特点，本课程贯通本科专业教学的全过程，具有多教师轮换授课、时段长、综合性和实践性强的突出特点。“建筑设计”课程教学的成效对专业建设的成败具有举足轻重的影响，该课程建设的发展和改革始终以服务和实现建筑学专业总体培养目标为宗旨，专业建设的成果也成为课程建设的重要支撑。

1927年，一批海外归国学子引进当时国际上先进的建筑教育制度和方法，最先在本校创办了中国第一个建筑学专业。80多年来，在杨廷宝、刘敦桢学部委员和童寯教授等老一辈建筑家课程创业基础上，以齐康、钟训正院士及长江学者王建国等为代表的课程教师团队又进行了不断开拓以适应社会和时代的变化，在课程整合、过程开放和创造力培养等方面不断创新，形成了以建筑设计为核心主干课，以培养 “建筑设计帅才”为目标的课程体系。东南大学建筑学院（南工建筑系）的建筑设计课程一直是中国现代建筑教育同类课程中之执牛耳者。

建系之初“建筑设计”课程采用当时国际上成熟的巴黎“布扎”设计教学模式，形成“技术与艺术相融，基本功与创造力并重”的教学理念。1950年后，随着自己培养的第二代教师的加入，中国式的建筑设计主干课程体系应运而生并逐步完善。1958年中科院学部委员杨廷宝系主任提出 “严、实、活、透、硬” （即要求要严、学风要实、思路要活、理论要吃透、基本功要硬）的理念，并一以贯之逐步形成东南大学建筑设计教学坚实的传统。20世纪，由学院从欧洲最重要的现代建筑教育基地——瑞士联邦苏黎世高等工业大学(ETHZ)留学归来的青年教师为主导，建筑设计课程率先在全国开展了“建筑设计初步”教学改革，该改革突出强调了建筑设计课程的核心内涵——对学生设计能力的有效培养，完成了“设计初步”从单一的重设计表现技能到表现与设计并重的转换，加强了系统的现代科学理性设计分析方法的运用。

20世纪，为适应现代建筑设计理论和方法发展多元目标的要求，建筑设计教学改革进一步突出了对设计关键科学问题的关注和研究，进而创建了全新的“以设计的问题类型取代功能类型”的理性教学理念。此间，课程改革也从低年级向高年级逐步推进。

2001年以来，随着突出创造性人才培养的专业建设“整合与开放”新模式的提出，“建筑设计”课程改革相应发展出“3+1”的新课程结构模式及相应的教师资源配置模式。前三年实行教学小组集体备课，年级负责人担任主讲，教师分组轮换的授课方式，注重建筑设计基本知识的传授和能力培养；四年级则实行 “教授工作室制”，由各课题方向的教师独立出题并授课、学生和教师之间实行双向选择的方式，注重基于“帅才”培养目标的设计综合和研究能力的提升。主讲教师则为各课题方向负责人及课程组织者。同时，教学理念、教材编写、教案制订与执行切合整体教学目标，交互式教学方法(Seminar)不断发展成熟，多元参与互动的设计评图制度得到确立。

近年来，“建筑设计”课程在国际化联合教学方面作出重要开拓，并已逐步形成成熟的特色方法。参与联合教学的机构包括美国加州大学伯克利分校(UC Berkeley)、瑞士联邦苏黎世高等工业大学(ETHZ)、荷兰代尔夫特理工大学等国际著名大学，并建立了实质性的学分互认的教学合作关系。

2003年，东南大学建筑学院主办了近年国内规格最高的国际建筑教育论坛，王建国院长主持大会并发表“中国建筑教育走向初探”的主旨发言，韩冬青教授发表设计课程改革最新成果。作为全国建筑学学科专业指导委员会主任挂靠单位，东南大学“建筑设计”课程建设成果多次为专指委制订全国相关建筑教学指导文件和规程提供参考。该课程在教材建设、国际、国内学生建筑设计竞赛中多次名列前茅。近年年均有10%～15%的毕业生被国际一流学校录取深造（包括MIT、哥伦比亚大学、剑桥大学、东京大学、ETHZ、TU Delft等）。

东南大学的“建筑设计”课程教学在教学理念、内容、方法、成绩考核等方面已形成独特的、连贯的课程新体系，且在国内具有重要且持续的示范作用，显著推进了中国现代建筑教育的发展，并获得广泛且积极的国际认可。教学改革成果获国家级教学成果奖两次，省部级教学成果奖三次，达到了国内领先、国际先进水平。

二、教师队伍

教学顾问

齐康院士 钟训正院士

课程负责人

王建国 教授，院长，长江学者

主讲教师

韩冬青 教授

龚　恺 教授

钱　强 教授

张　彤 教授

鲍　莉 副教授

朱　雷 副教授

俞传飞 副教授

授课教师

一年级设计　单踊 俞传飞 张嵩 张彧 郭菂 王海宁 杨靖 顾震宏 徐小东 史永高 张倩 谭瑛

二年级设计　朱雷 吴锦绣 陈秋光 陈宇 王正 张慧 王湘君 史新 虞刚 孙世界 徐春宁 雒建利

三年级设计　鲍莉 孙茹雁 夏兵 刘捷 邓浩 薛力 李海清 钱强 葛明 周颖

四年级设计　张彤 仲德崑 王建国 韩冬青 钱强 龚恺 单踊 王静 冷嘉伟 张玫英 周颖 陈薇 周琦 葛明 杨维菊 李海清

三、课程定位

建筑学专业人才的核心能力就是建筑设计的能力。“建筑设计”是建筑学专业的主干核心课程，与国际、国内一流建筑学专业培养体系相一致，该课程贯通专业教学一至四年级的全过程，具有教师多、时段长、综合性和实践性强的突出特点。“建筑设计”课程教学既是专业教学的起点，也是相关专业课程教学成果的综合运用与体现。作为专业教学的起点，学生需要从设计实践的过程中了解并明确其他相关课程的意义和作用，作为专业教学成果的综合体现，学生必须通过设计教学过程将其他课程中学习到的知识创造性地运用于建筑设计实践。该课程教学的成效对专业建设和人才培养的成败具有举足轻重的影响。

本课程教学定位一直与国际建筑教育学术渊源密切相关。从20世纪三四十年代杨廷宝教授（中科院学部委员，中国建筑教育奠基人之一）、童寯教授（著名建筑教育家，中国建筑教育奠基人之一）承袭美国宾夕法尼亚大学的学院派(Beaux-Arts)建筑设计教学理念与方法，到20世纪从瑞士联邦苏黎世高等工业大学(ETHZ)引进源自20世纪极具影响力的“德州骑警”(Texas Ranger)现代建筑教育理念，我院的建筑设计教学理念不断追踪国际建筑教育发展前沿，并结合国情进行本土化修正。

近年来开展的国际联合教学也是本课程追求国际化水平的重要手段。在不同的文化背景和知识的师生共同参与中，培养和训练学生在国际舞台上的胜任能力，在跨文化交往中的敏感性，以及在多方面地区性限制条件下的创造力。

四、课程目标

1. 以“场地与环境、空间与功能、材质与建构”为基本问题核心，学习并掌握建筑设计的基本理论知识、设计方法和表达方法。

2. 综合运用相关专业课程（如建筑历史、建筑技术等）的知识，培养创造性地提出问题、分析问题和解决问题的理论思维能力和与之互动的建筑设计实践能力。

3. 以建筑设计基本问题为核心，培养跨专业拓展的国际视野和团队合作精神和能力。

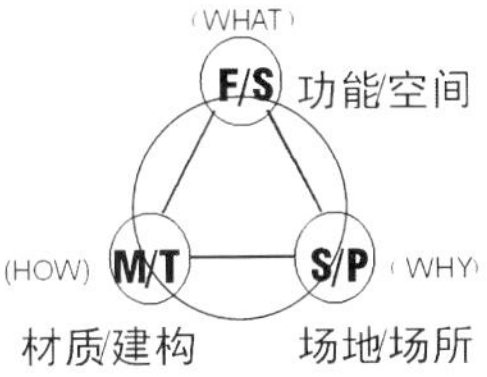

五、知识模块

“建筑设计”课程的知识模块在设计基本问题上包括“场地与环境、空间与功能、材质与建构”三个互动的组成部分；在建筑功能类型上主要包括公共建筑和居住建筑，在规模类型上包括小型建筑设计、中大型建筑设计和城市设计；在设计方法上包括基本方法和创新方法。东南大学的“建筑设计”课程的知识模块体系以设计基本问题为主线，并按照“两个阶段、三个层次”的设想（即3+1）循序渐进地串联相关的功能类型、规模类型和方法类型。达到不断巩固设计基本功，逐步发展创新能力的目标。

所谓“两个阶段”是指“建筑设计”课程一至三年的基础性教学阶段与四年级的拓展性教学阶段。所谓“三个层次”是指每一教学阶段特定的教学理念的确立、教学方案的设计和教学过程的实施。课程不同阶段的知识模块设置强调逻辑递进和连贯性，具体如下：

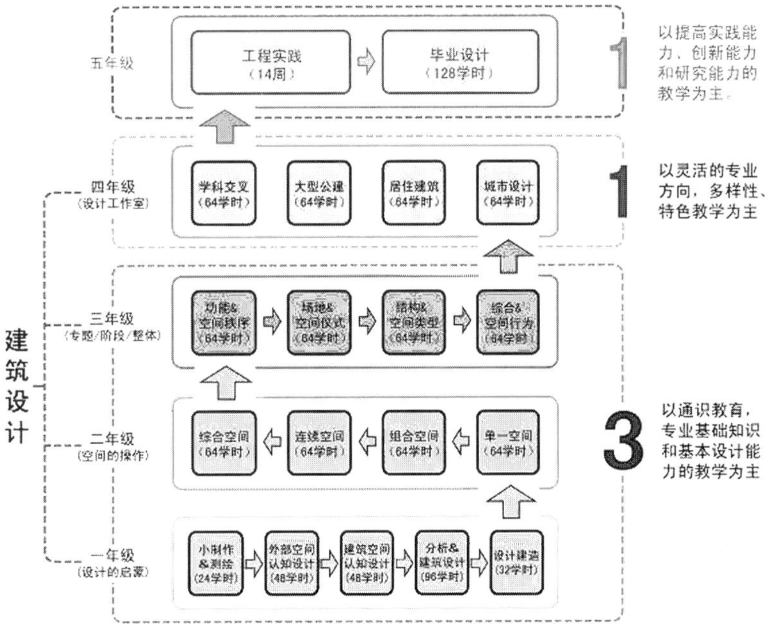

“3+1”课程结构

阶段一：即一至三年级以通识教育和基本专业知识、基本设计能力的教学为主。

一至三年级的建筑设计教学是以核心教授带头、老中青结合的教学小组为单位进行的。

一年级（建筑设计基础阶段——设计的启蒙）：256学时。学生在这个阶段要逐步培养起设计观念，理解建筑，初步掌握以设计图纸、模型作为设计研究和表达工具，熟悉基本的建筑设计的方法与过程，形成初步的建筑技术概念。同时，培养和引导学生的专业兴趣，激发学生的创作热情。

具体学时分配如下：

课 程 内 容	讲 课	实习课程设计
小制作	2	6
建筑测绘	2	14
外部空间认知	4	12
外部空间设计	4	28
建筑空间认知	4	12
建筑空间设计	4	36
先例分析	6	26
小型休闲展示建筑设计	10	54
设计建造	4	28

二年级（建筑设计初步阶段——空间的操作）：256学时。该阶段教学以空间为线索，重视设计与技术、环境的结合。通过一个学年的训练，帮助学生建立空间意识和空间思维方式。建立环境意识，理解建筑与环境的相互影响。加强对结构、材料和构造的认知，强化技术观念，认识到技术是创造空间的必要手段，了解及运用技术的影响及表现力。掌握理性的设计工作方法。

具体学时分配如下：

课 程 内 容	讲 课	实习课程设计
景区中的单一空间练习——临水小筑设计	8	48
社区中单元组合练习——青年公寓	8	64
坡地上的连续空间练习——旅游游客中心	8	56
城市中的综合空间——社区图书馆	8	56

三年级（建筑设计提高阶段——专题•阶段•整体）：256学时。该阶段教学是使学生建立整体的建筑观，以建筑的三个基本问题——功能、环境、建构为线索，由浅入深地设置若干设计练习，从单一问题发展到综合问题，强调专题性、阶段性和整体性，使学生初步掌握大中型建筑的设计方法和综合能力，培养学生掌握职业建筑师所应具备的基本知识和能力。

具体学时分配如下：

课 程 内 容	讲 课	实习课程设计
功能与空间秩序——实验中心设计	8	56
场地与空间仪式——和平纪念中心设计	8	56
结构与空间类型——博物馆设计	8	56
综合与空间行为——市民文化中心设计	8	56

阶段二：四年级（建筑设计综合阶段——设计工作室）：256学时。该阶段是具有研究性和个性化的特色教学，以“开放性、多样化、个性化”的教学模式，打破传统教研室组织机构的约束，实行“教授工作室制”，教授工作室突出研究与教学结合的个性化教学机制。学生和教师之间实行双向选择，最大限度地发挥了学生的学习热情。教学课题也因此多样化。鼓励学生在前三年设计课的基础上，学习和认识城市设计、住区设计、大型公建以及其他重要学科方向的基本理论和设计方法，重点培养综合设计能力，培育创新思维和设计研究能力的发展，形成东南大学建筑设计教学的特色。

四年级设计教学的主题是“城市与建筑”，全学年设置四大类课题为基本知识模块，即：城市设计类、住区设计类、大型公建类和学科交叉类。该四大类课题同时开设，没有前后关系。教学中鼓励进行国际合作设计和参加国际、国内竞赛，使教学更具有学科交叉和挑战性。

具体学时分配如下：

课 程 内 容	讲 课	课程设计
城市设计类课题	32	224
住区设计类课题	32	224
大型公建类课题	32	224
学科交叉类课题或以上三类任一课题	32	224

在高年级，联合教学已逐渐引入到常规的教学安排中，其基本思路是“纳入教学框架、双方互动吸收、专人全程跟踪”。

六、课程重点

1. 理论与实践的互动，强调研究型学习过程；
2. 科研与教学的互动；
3. 设计创造力的培养。

七、教学方法

1. “Seminar”讨论式教学，强调教学中的多元互动；
2. 开放性的“教授工作室制”，紧紧围绕社会发展的需求，突出研究与教学结合的个性化教学模式；
3. 国际国内联合教学(Joint studio)已逐渐成为建筑设计课程教学的常态。

八、教学手段

1. 强调师生互动，教师采用轮换制授课方式；
2. 灵活运用各种现代的教学手段，理论讲结合案例学习；
3. 充分运用徒手草图、手工模型、计算机、实体制作等多种媒质进行辅助设计。

刘迪同学获Autodesk特别奖

葛文俊等同学获北京国际学生建筑艺术双年展特等奖

九、学生获奖

近三年来，我院有二十多位本科毕业生被国际一流建筑学院录取为研究生，如美国的麻省理工学院(MIT)、哥伦比亚大学和康奈尔大学，英国的剑桥大学和诺丁汉大学，日本东京大学，瑞士联邦苏黎世高等工业大学(ETHZ)，荷兰代尔夫特理工大学，法国拉维莱特建筑学院等。这从一个侧面反映出我们的人才培养获得了国际认可。此外，2000年以来，在校学生参加国内外多个学生设计竞赛和展览共获奖30余项，奖项规格高，获奖面大，设计水准令人信服。

近年学生获得国际重要奖项情况列举如下：

1. 2004年，葛文俊等同学的“概念设计”参加北京国际学生建筑艺术双年展获得唯一的特等奖；

2. 2006年，凭借本科期间设计课程的优秀作品，骆可同学获得年度全球SOM国际学生奖学金唯一的一等奖；

3. 2007年，在英国皇家建筑师协会和美国建筑师协会共同主办的“建设可持续世界”国际建筑设计竞赛中，本科生刘迪的作品“中国湖北洪灾区生态可持续性建筑设计”项目作为亚洲地区唯一作品入围决赛，刘迪同学受邀赴美答辩并获Autodesk特别奖；

4. 2007年，张羽上、曹其琛同学在第一届世界大学生城市设计竞赛中获得创意前卫奖；

5. 2007年，朱昊昊同学获得年度全球SOM国际学生奖学金唯一的一等奖，我校学生再一次在与国际顶尖建筑院校学生的竞技中胜出。

国内奖项中最值得一提的是，自2002年起由全国高校建筑专业指导委员会主办的年度全国大学生建筑设计作业观摩与评选。这是国内最高规格的高校建筑设计作业竞赛，全国各主要建筑院系均按学生比例选送作业参选优秀作业。在历年的竞赛中我院成绩均名列前茅，2002年“选7中6”，2003年和2004年“选8中6”，2005和2006年“选7中4”，2007年又是 “选8中7”，拔得头筹。此高获奖率及其持续性在国内首屈一指。

十、课程特色

1. 基于深厚的历史积淀，传承创新传统，自成体系。课程注重教学研究，在教学理念、教学内容、教学方法、成绩考核等方面已形成连贯的新体系。这一体系在国内具有重要且持续的示范作用，并获得广泛且积极的国际认可。目前此体系仍在不断推进发展，预计三年内将“数字技术”和“生态技术”逐步融合进建筑设计主干课程，进一步优化课程体系，以适应可持续发展的时代和满足社会发展的需求。

2. 国内首创的“3+1”课程教学模式注重职业素质和创新能力的培养。三年的通识和基础教学使学生具有良好的职业素质，而其后四年级的“教授工作室制”设计教学极大地提高了学生的研究和创新能力，也调动了师生双方的积极性。

3. 跨学科、跨院校、跨国界的开放式联合教学以不同院校师生共同做一个设计为特点，以小组合作、师生互动的方式完成，不同年级采用不同的联合教学模式，目前已逐步成为教学的常态。联合教学既促进了学科交融、保证了教学与社会发展的密切联系，也培养了学生的国际化视野和合作能力。

十一、课程建设规划

1. 建筑设计教学的理念和体系的进一步探索；

2. 数字信息技术支撑平台作用下的日益开放和国际化的建筑设计教学；

3. 日益严峻的人类生存环境变迁要求建筑教育增加职业操守和环境伦理知识。

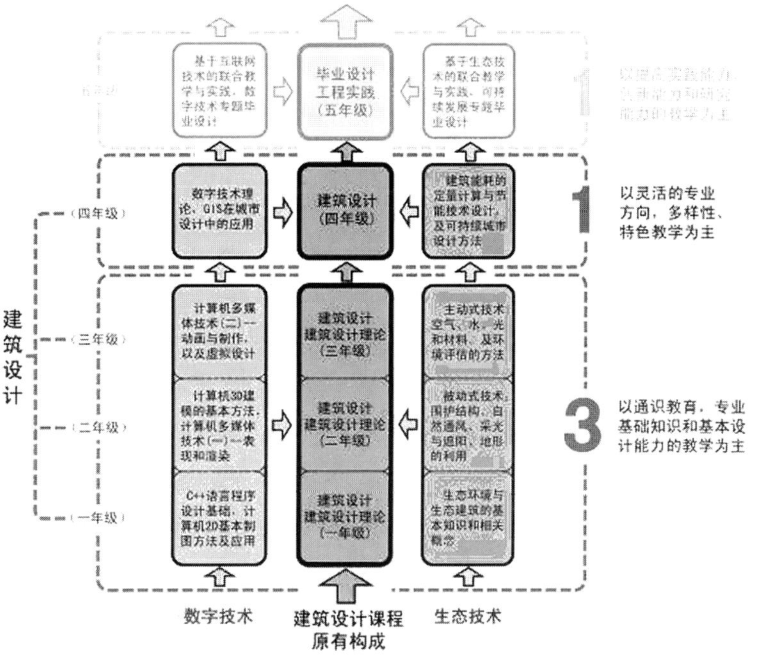

建筑设计主干课的新课程体系

国家精品课程——中国建筑史
National Level Excellent Course: Chinese Architectural History

陈　薇　Chen Wei

朱光亚　Zhu Guangya

潘谷西　Pan Guxi

胡　石　Hu Shi

诸葛净　Zhuge Jing

中国建筑史获“2005年度国家精品课程”（序号179）

一、课程简介

“中国建筑史”是建筑学基础理论教育的一部分。作为工科史学，本课程教学的主要目标是通过骨干课程和延伸课程的教学，强调建立大的建筑史观，注重理论联系实际、历史课和设计课通融思维训练，从而由宏观而微观、由系统而局部、由思维而技艺，在整体上发挥建筑史的综合作用，达到培养既具创新思维又有实际能力的建筑专业人才的目标。

本课程的内容在纵向以“中国古代建筑史”、“近现代建筑史解析”为两个主要知识模块进行教学，其目的是从整体上把握中国建筑史的发展进程、特点、思想脉络等，达到掌握中国传统建筑精华、学习判断优秀建筑思想的目的。横向由“古典亭榭与小品设计”和关于遗产保护交叉学科的课程设计组成，对进一步把握精准的古典设计手法和创造性地学习使用提供良好的平台。在实践环节中，通过“古建筑测绘”学习，巩固、加深理解中国传统建筑，由测而绘进一步了解和认识古建筑的设计手法、营造特点等。同时辅以“中国古代建筑史网络课程”，鼓励学生自行上网，在和老师的互动过程中进行讨论式学习。

课程的基本要求是：使学生通过本课程的学习，对中国建筑发展过程及其规律、理论、案例有最基本的了解，从而为建筑设计、城市规划等专业学习提供基础，也为学生进一步深造、开拓和创新提供大历史观和思维活力。

二、课程特色

教材科学，体系完整，勇于突破，追求卓越。本学科是《中国建筑史》教材的主编单位，至今已完成了五版的编写与改写工作。日前正修编第六版教材。

方法先进，多样灵活，教学相长，能力和知识共进。教学内容与教学方法、教学形式与教学手段、教学教材与教学目的多元变化、灵活运用、与时俱进，能够充分发挥学生的学习能动性。

史论结合，理论与实践通融，经典传统和开放创新并举。将实践教学与理论教学相结合，强调掌握历史中的建筑精华在手法上和技术层面的内容，并由“匠”的层面上升到“意”的层面，从而成为建筑设计和创作的必要学习过程。

主持人：陈薇
精品课程建设人：陈薇、朱光亚、潘谷西、胡石、诸葛净
课程网址：[illegible]

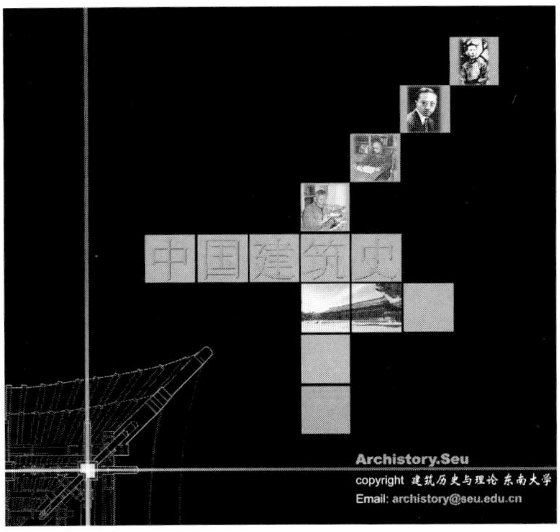

Introduction

The course of Chinese Architectural History is a part of the basic theoretical education of architecture. As a course of engineering historiography, the main aim of this course is through the key and the extension course, to construct the whole concept of architectural history of the students, emphasize linking theory with practice, and give them the thought training in history and design courses. Thus, the course of Chinese Architectural History can exert a comprehensive influence from macro to micro, from system to part, from thinking to doing to achieve the goal of cultivating the professionals integrating creative thoughts and practical ability.

Vertically, the course is divided in chronological order into two parts, which are History of Ancient Chinese Architecture and Analysis on the History of Modern Architecture. It designs to lead the students to grasp the development, the characteristics and the thought thread of Chinese architectural history as a whole, thus the students can take the finest of ancient Chinese architecture, and learn to appreciate the excellent architectural thoughts. Horizontally, the content is made up of two interdisciplinary parts, that is, Classical Pavilions and Small Structure Design and Cultural Heritage Protection, which aim to provide a good platform for students to master the precise classical design technique, and learn to use it creatively. In practice sector, the course of Survey and Draw of the Ancient Architecture helps students to learn, consolidate and further understand the ancient Chinese architecture. From surveying to drawing, students can have a more profound knowledge of the design technique, the characteristics of buildings etc. Meanwhile, the course has a part, Network Course of the History of Ancient Chinese Architecture as a supplementary sector, to encourage students to learn interactively through the communicating and discussing with teachers on the Internet.

Requirement of the course is through the course learning, students can have a basic understanding of the process, rules, theories, cases of the development of Chinese architecture, which lay a learning foundation for architectural design and city planning, and provide a great view of history and vitality of thinking for students' future learning, development and innovation.

Characteristics of the course

A scientific textbook containing a complete system and pursuing excellence: the discipline is the chief editor organization of the textbook Chinese Architectural History, which has completed the writing and editor work of five editions, and is at present revising the sixth edition.

An advanced and flexible teaching method benefits teaching and learning, promoting ability and understanding: the flexible use of the teaching content and method, teaching pattern and technology, teaching materials and objects, which advances with the times, fully inspires the students' study motive.

A course combining history and theory, integrating practice and learning, emphasizing tradition and opening: the teaching combines theory and practice, emphasizes the classics in architectural technique and technology, and upgrades appreciation level from skills to ideas, which makes a necessary learning stage in architectural design.

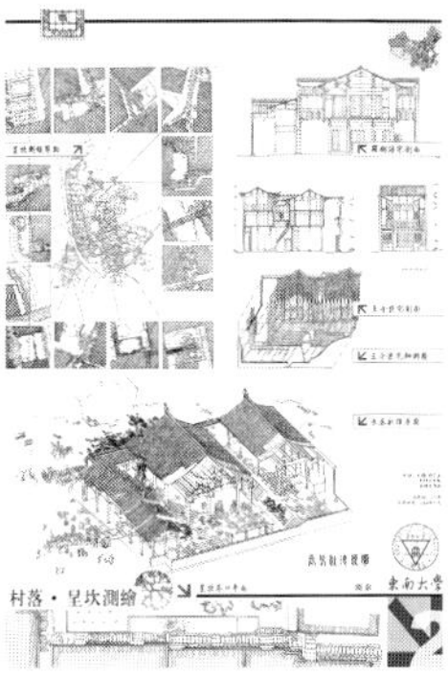

Conductor: Chen Wei
Co-builder of the Course: Chen Wei, Zhu Guangya, Pan Guxi, Hu Shi, Zhuge Jing
Website of the course: http://jwc.seu.edu.cn/jpkc

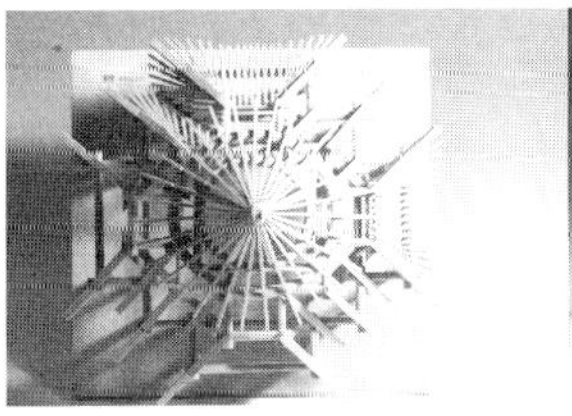

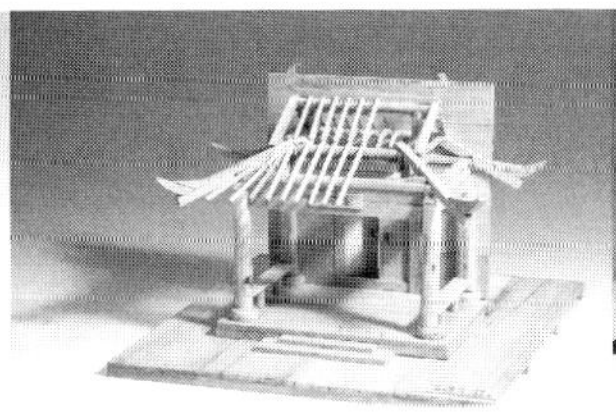

建筑构造课程教学改革简介

Introduction of Building Construction

主讲教师：李海清

建筑构造课是建筑学专业主干课，近年的教学改革目标是使之成为始于问题、基于发现、体现研究性和创造性的研究型教学，即以建筑学自主性始于营造问题的“内涵挖掘”和建筑学专业各主干课程之间的“环节联通”为导向，依靠课型设计的不断优化，在学生的学习活动和教师的研究活动之间开掘高效通道，使课内学习及时、有效地向课外研究延伸和拓展，建立学生自主、教师主导下的学习、研究和实践相结合的教学模式，对于构建与“研究型、综合性、开放式”大学建设目标相适应的研究型建筑学专业本科教学体系形成有力促进。具体而言，是从教学思想、教学内容、教学方法、教学技术、课型设计、教学组织、教学考核等方面入手，以“材料/做法”研究为阶梯，试图实现教学理念、方法和成果的创新，与建筑设计课程的教学改革形成积极互动，促成建筑技术课程教学的全面优化与整体转型——从基于工具理性的分化、孤立、单面性到富有人文精神的开放、交叉、融合。

核心问题是理论定位：建筑细部与建筑构造乃是微观层面的建筑学之主要研究对象。循此理路，建筑构造——获得、选择材料以及材料的连接，才是建筑活动的起点和首要问题。正是在这个意义上，柯布西耶关于建筑“无所不在”甚至“已经扩展到了那闻所未闻的当代制造的总体当中”的论断才具有与时俱进的深远意义——从建筑物体扩展至人居环境中的各组成要素。学生作业对于司空见惯的自行车、拉链、剃须刀、电脑、茶杯等人造物品的研究将有助于从类比、直观的角度认知建筑构造现象及其本质。

It's a common sense that teaching and learning of Building Construction is really difficult, and the reformation of courses of building technology is a global issue. Researching and discussion about autonomy of architecture seem to be helpful for problem solving or promoting, especially for the teaching and learning of building construction. In the past 10 years, some reformation strategies and projects have been executed, aimed to the new teaching system based on the idea of researching and discovering by students themselves. It's very important that we recognize the instructiveness of how to get material and different connection between materials, in a further step, the tectonic value of them is fundemental for architectural design and life. Therefore the concept of human habitation environment brought out by Le Corbusier is still an iniciation point of perfect comprehension of detail and construction design of architecture.

衣服上的机关　拉链

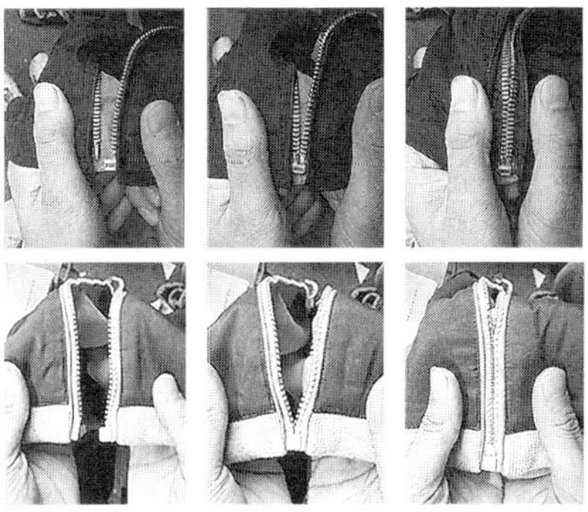

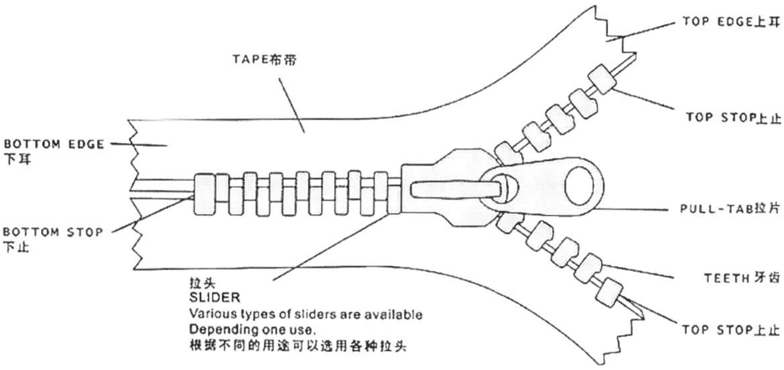

刚节点首先通过曲面限定XY方向上的移动，其次通过凹槽和突起限定Z方向上的移动。

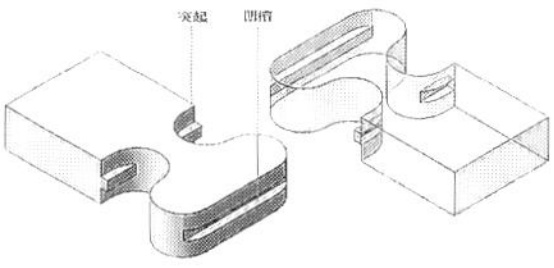

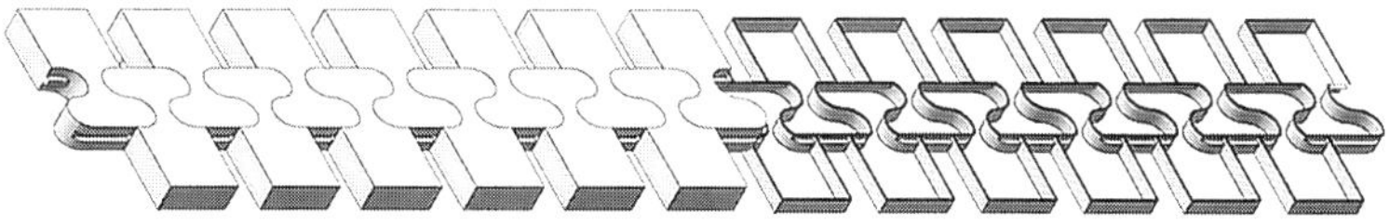

铰节点利用球面限定移动，可以转动，但不影响拉链牢固。

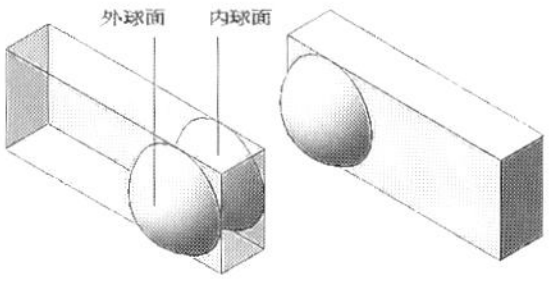

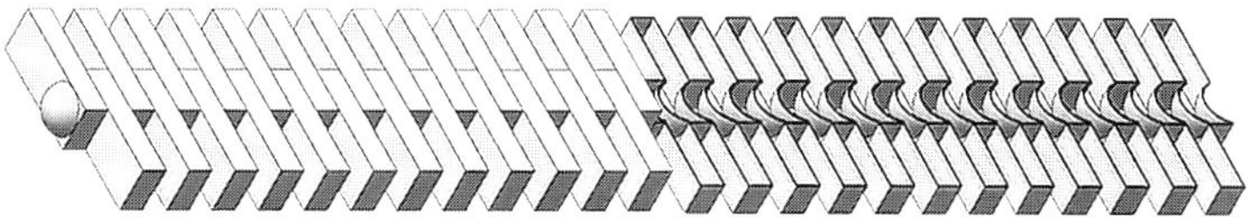

衣服上的机关　按扣

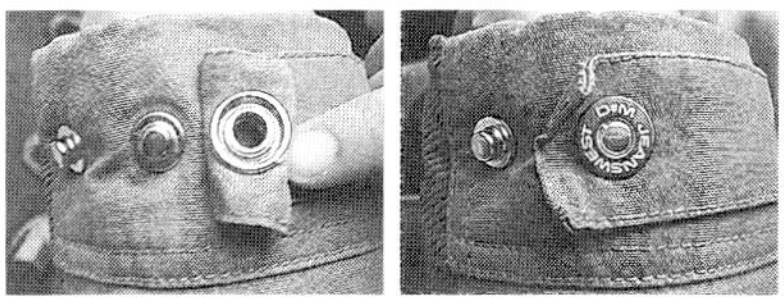

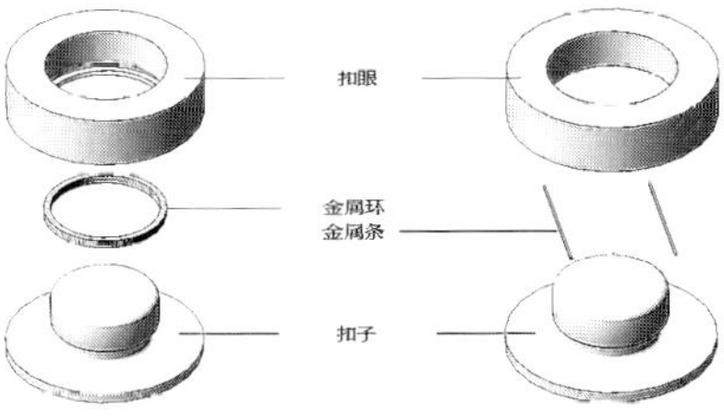

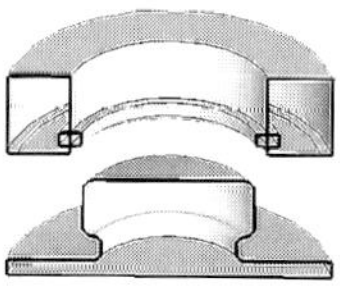

扣子插入扣眼之前，金属环处于正常状态。

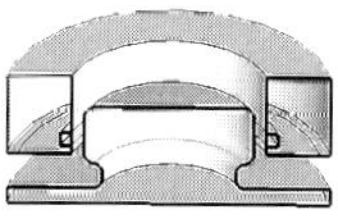

扣子插入扣眼时，扣子强迫金属环扩张。

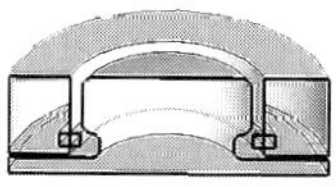

扣子插入扣眼后，金属条恢复到正常状态，使扣子不会从扣眼中轻易脱出。

三把剃须刀的比较

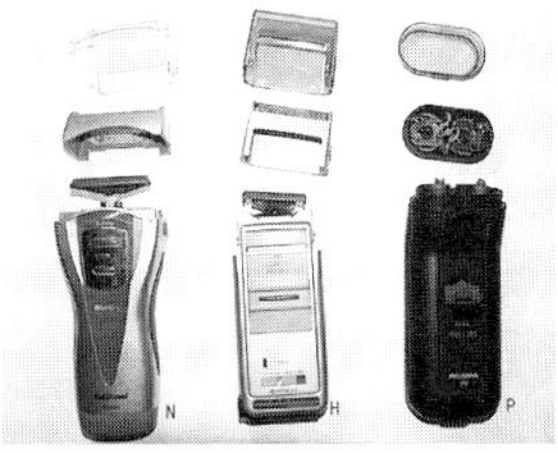

选择PHILIPS、NATIONAL和HITACHI的三款电动剃须刀作为研究对象。三款剃须刀都为一个基本功能——剃须设计，演绎出不同的形式和逻辑。主要关注内刀刃的作用原理和贴合度。

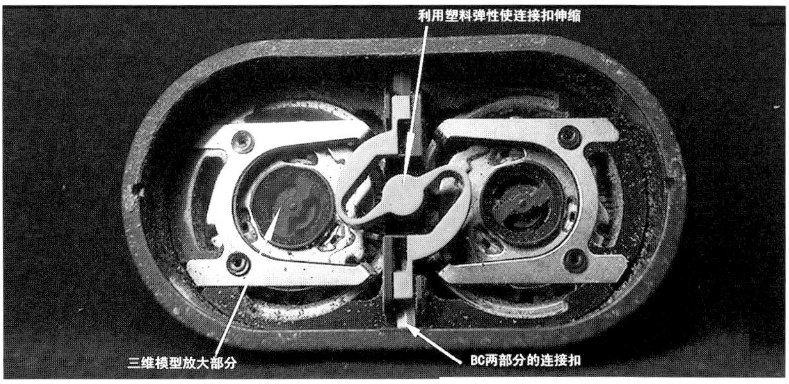

PHILIPS为旋转式，重点在于如何使机身部分的电动装置与内外刃既精确衔接又便于分离。

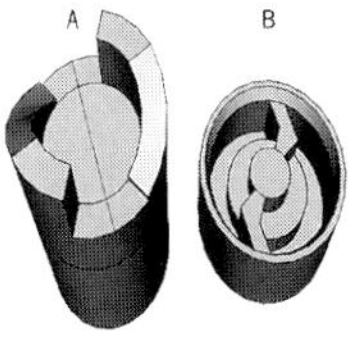

A为电动旋转头，插入B内，B带动内刃旋转。A的垂直面为逆时针旋转式的受力面，坡面则保证了AB之间准确轻松的插接。

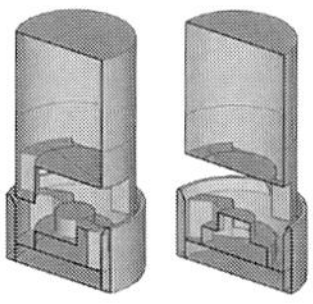

NATIONAL与HITACHI为摇摆式，重点在于外刃和机身上内刃贴合紧密。

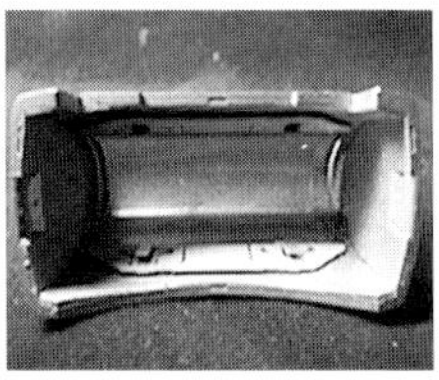

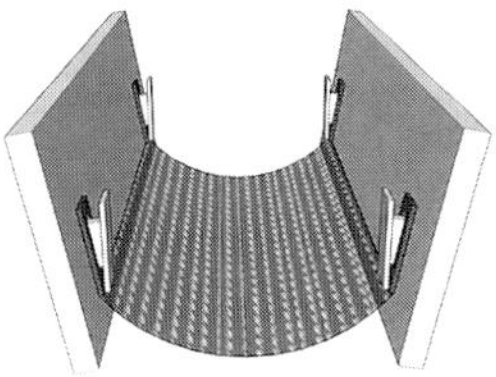

金属外刃与滑块相连，滑块扣在金属壁突出的支座上。

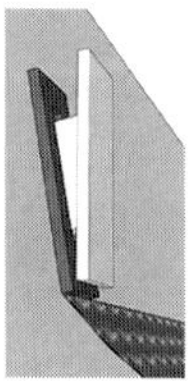

对于弹性的外刃金属片，在倾斜壁体之间如果不施外力，有恢复其自身形状的趋势。所以
情况1：刀片要挣脱变平，节点扣上b部分受力。
情况2：当机身向下顶住外刃刀片时，节点扣上a部分受力，机身上内刃很好地贴合外刃。

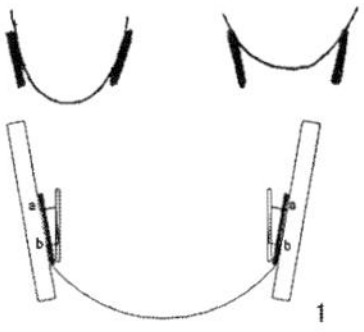

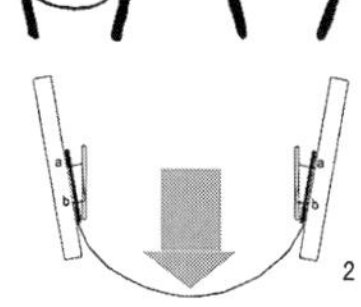

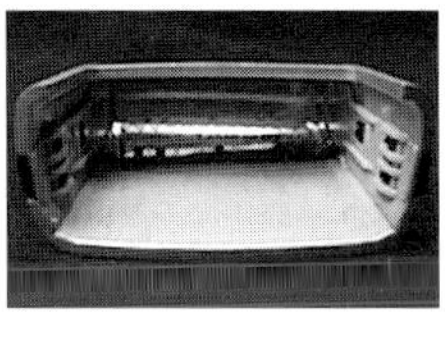

HITACHI在侧面开了小滑轨，外刃上有凸起的小头，小头在滑轨内运行，金属外刃已经自然弯曲。这种做法虽没有NATIONAL那么精彩，但也保证了内外刃的贴合和外刃刀片的固定。

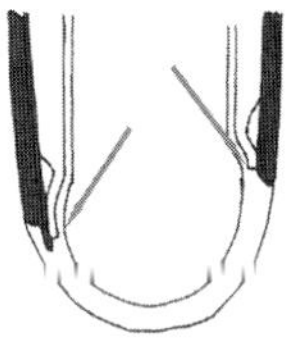

单车飞轮认知

飞轮与轴

飞轮拆解轴测

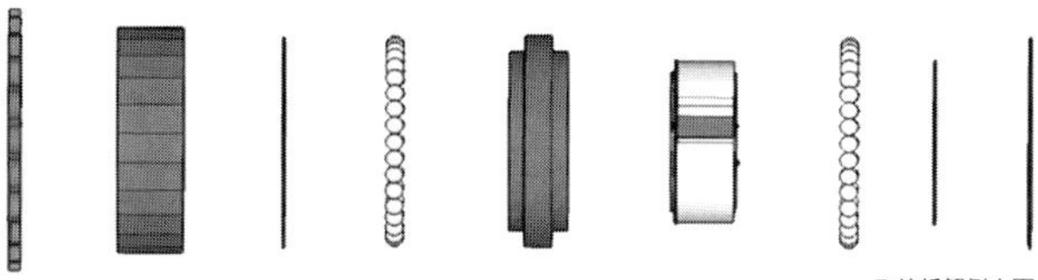

飞轮拆解侧立面

转动演示

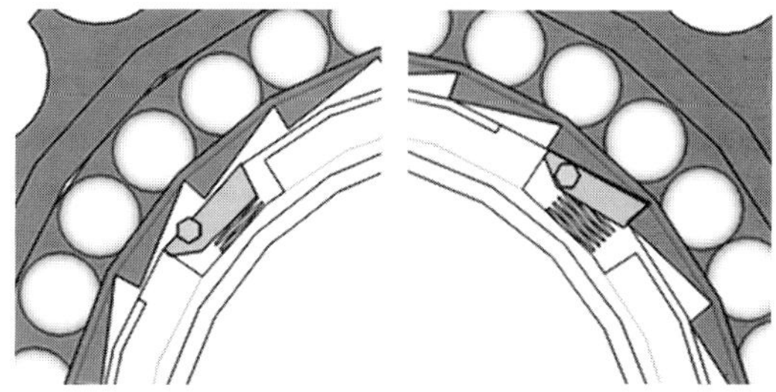

对飞轮的认知始于对单车只能单向行驶的好奇，通过对飞轮自身构造的探索，发掘其中的趣味构造。

Embarks from the curisity of how the bicycle moves unilaterally, through the research of the construction of the flywheel, find the interest of it.

纵向科研与横向实践
Research & Practice

重要科研教学项目获奖成果（省部级以上）

序号	成果名称	项目主持人	获奖时间	奖励情况，鉴定验收情况，成果转化情况
1	中国近代史博物馆文化服务区设计	齐康，杨志疆，寿刚等	2006	全国优秀工程勘察设计银奖
2	徐州师范大学教学主楼群体设计	齐康，齐昉，郑炘等	2006	江苏省优秀工程设计三等奖
3	安庆历史文化名城保护规划	吴明伟，阳建强等	2006	安徽省优秀规划设计一等奖 建设部优秀规划设计三等奖
4	钟山风景名胜区中心陵景区控制性详细规划	吴明伟等	2006	建设部优秀规划设计三等奖 江苏省优秀规划设计二等奖
5	洪泽县文化中心设计	钟训正，韩冬青等	2006	建设部行业优秀勘察设计奖 江苏省优秀工程设计一等奖
6	中国建筑史	陈薇，朱光亚，潘谷西等	2006	国家精品课程
7	城市规划教育	杜顺宝	2006	中国城市规划教育终身荣誉奖
8	南京森林公安高等专科学校主建筑群设计	韩冬青，冷嘉伟，夏兵，王正等	2006	中国建筑学会建筑创作奖优秀奖
9	长兴县图书馆档案馆设计	马晓东等	2006	江苏省优秀工程设计一等奖
10	金坛沙湖村庄整治规划	刘博敏等	2006	江苏省优秀规划设计一等奖
11	淮安市文庙慈云寺地区城市设计	孔令龙，巢耀明等	2006	江苏省优秀规划设计三等奖
12	侵华日军南京大屠杀遇难同胞纪念馆设计	张彤	2006	第五届上海国际青年建筑师作品展一等奖
13	南京市铁匠营地块商业公寓综合体设计	张彤，杨志疆，邓浩	2006	第五届上海国际青年建筑师作品展二等奖
14	基于高层建筑管控的的南京老城空间形态优化	王建国，高源，胡明星	2006	“金经昌城市规划教育基金会优秀论文”评选提名奖
15	建筑设计	张彤	2006	中国建筑学会青年建筑师奖
16	论文《设计教学呼唤技术理性——东南大学建筑学院建筑构造+建筑设计课程整合基础研究的实践探索》	李海清，方立新	2006	全国建筑技术专业委员会优秀学术论文奖
17	中国古代住居与住居文化	张宏	2007	湖北省新闻出版社 湖北省100种好书
18	西安交通大学教学主楼设计	齐康等	2007	全国优秀工程勘察设计银奖
19	河南博物院设计	齐康，李秋海，郑炘等	2007	全国优秀工程勘察设计铜奖
20	镇江人防办地面指挥中心设计	齐康，张宏，寿刚等	2007	江苏省优秀勘察设计二等奖
21	徐州汉兵马俑博物馆	张宏	2007	江苏省优秀工程设计二等奖
22	安徽大学新校区修建性详细规划	段进等	2007	江苏省优秀规划设计一等奖
23	嘉兴市沿河沿线整合城市设计	段进等	2007	江苏省优秀规划设计一等奖
24	苏州环古城风貌西段详细规划	段进等	2007	建设部优秀规划设计一等奖
25	蚌埠医学院详细规划	段进等	2007	江苏省优秀规划设计二等奖
26	大行宫市民广场景观设计	杨冬辉，唐军等	2007	江苏省城乡建设系统优秀勘察设计三等奖
27	水墨宏村	项忠孝，孙健，陈薇	2007	精瑞住宅科学技术奖：建筑文化奖，金奖（中华全国工商业联合会房地产商会）
28	复合型城市规划专业优秀人才培养	阳建强，孔令龙，吴晓，王承慧，权亚玲	2007	江苏省教学成果二等奖
29	论文《我国进城农民的居住空间探析及其对策研究——以南京市的租居型外来工为例》	吴晓	2007	第4届中国城市规划学会青年论文竞赛佳作奖（中国城市规划学会）
30	论文《中国CBD发展量化研究（1-4）》	杨俊宴，吴明伟	2007	“金经昌城市规划教育基金会优秀论文”评选三等奖
31	全国高等院校城市规划专业教师教学研究论文竞赛	吴晓，王承慧，王兴平，张倩等	2007	优秀奖4项
32	建筑教育	陈薇	2007	江苏省“333高层次人才培养工程”首批中青年科学技术带头人
33	建筑教育	陈薇	2007	宝钢教育基金会优秀教师奖
34	美国埃克森-美孚石油公司休斯总部大楼外围护结构功能提升	石邢	2007	Corner Stone Award一等奖
35	解读地景-大丰景观银杏湖公园设计随笔	成玉宁	2007	江苏省风景园林学会优秀论文2等奖

续表

序号	成果名称	项目主持人	获奖时间	奖励情况，鉴定验收情况，成果转化情况
36	江苏省沿江开发产业空间布局研究	陈雯，杨俊宴	2007	江苏省发改委优秀研究成果二等奖
37	江苏省工艺美术馆室内设计	高祥生	2007	江苏省第六届室内装饰设计大奖赛公装类奖特等奖
38	常州市万福路-常澄路城市设计与控制性详细规划	王建国、高源等	2007	江苏省城乡建设系统优秀勘察设计二等奖
39	润扬大桥综合管理楼设计	鲍莉等	2007	第6届上海国际青年建筑师作品展一等奖
40	常州市天宁区战略规划	严玲，王兴平等	2007	江苏省优秀咨询成果奖三等奖
41	刘敦桢全集	刘敦桢，刘叙杰	2008	第一届中国建筑图书奖
42	建筑教育	仲德崑	2008	中国建筑教育奖
43	建筑教育	潘谷西	2008	中国建筑学会教育特别奖
44	《建筑设计》	王建国，韩冬青，龚恺等	2008	国家精品课程
45	全国高等院校城市规划专业教师教学研究论文竞赛	高源，杨俊宴等	2008	优秀奖3项
46	威尼斯建筑双年展中国馆之——默默	葛明	2008	十一届威尼斯建筑双年展
47	新疆天山天池国家重点风景名胜区总体规划	杜顺宝，唐军	2008	江苏省城乡建设系统优秀勘察设计二等奖
48	常州城市空间景观规划设计研究	王建国，龚恺等	2008	江苏省城乡建设系统优秀勘察设计奖二等奖
49	南京溧水和凤镇张家村村庄建设规划	刘博敏	2008	江苏省城乡建设系统优秀勘察设计二等奖
50	大丰市二卯酉河景观设计	成玉宁	2007	江苏省优秀勘察设计二等奖
51	常州市特殊群体生活设施布局规划研究	严玲，王兴平等	2008	江苏省优秀规划设计奖二等奖
52	连云港经济技术开发区产业布局规划	王兴平等	2008	连云港市城乡建设系统优秀规划设计一等奖
53	汉西门风景区—小桃园片区景观设计	杨冬辉	2008	教育部优秀设计三等奖
54	南京西安门公园景观设计	丁宏伟，杨冬辉	2008	教育部优秀设计二等奖
55	宜兴团氿氿滨广场滨水地段景观设计	王建国，周小棣，徐小东等	2008	江苏省城乡建设系统优秀勘察设计奖（风景园林）三等奖
56	全国规划行业抗震救灾先进个人	徐春宁	2008	
57	Marry me project	沈颖	2008	十一届威尼斯建筑双年展
58	2008年“和成·新人杯”全国青年学生竞赛优秀组织奖	东南大学建筑学院	2008	2008年“和成·新人杯”全国青年学生竞赛优秀组织奖

专著、译著及教材

序号	专著名称	作者姓名	出版社及出版日期
1	空间研究1——世界文化遗产西递古村落空间解析	段进，龚恺等	东南大学出版社，200606
2	幼儿园建筑设计	黎志涛	中国建筑工业出版社，200607
3	城市景观的视觉评价	陈宁	东南大学出版社，200608
4	中国文人画与文人写意园林	赵思毅	中国电力出版社，200609
5	湿地概念与湿地公园设计	赵思毅	东南大学出版社，200610
6	美国现代城市设计运作研究	高源	东南大学出版社，200610
7	快速规划设计50例	黎志涛等	江苏科技出版社，2006
8	建筑师的二十岁（译著）	王静，王建国，费移山	清华大学出版社，2006
9	东南大学建筑学院建筑设计学生作品集	龚恺	中国建筑工业出版社，2006
10	中外可持续建筑实例——夏热冬冷地区可持续建筑技术（江苏篇）	杨维菊主编	中国建筑工业出版社，2006
11	绿色建筑与建筑技术	杨维菊主编	中国建筑工业出版社，2006
12	户外空间设计（译著）	俞传飞	辽宁科学技术出版社，2006
13	建筑画技法	曾琼	上海人民美术出版社，2006
14	设计先行——基于设计的社区规划（译著）	张倩译	中国建筑工业出版社，2006
15	高级室内装饰设计师	高祥生	中国机械工业出版社，2006
16	当代中国城市形态演变	熊国平	中国建筑工业出版社 2006
17	视觉设计素描	朱丹	东南大学出版社，2006
18	空间句法与城市规划	段进，比尔·希列尔等	东南大学出版社，200701
19	现代建筑与数字化设计过程（译著）	吴晓，虞刚译	中国建筑工业出版社，200701
20	信息化城市：信息技术发展与城市空间结构的互动	孙世界，刘博敏	天津大学出版社，200701
21	数字化建筑设计概论	李建成，卫兆骥等	中国建筑工业出版社，200702
22	画的记忆	齐康	东南大学出版社，200704
23	东大建筑50年学生水彩精品收集	方晓珊主编	中国建筑工业出版社，200705
24	风景入画	齐康	东南大学出版社，200706
25	山水风景与建筑	郑炘，华晓宁	东南大学出版社，200707
26	最佳人居小城镇空间发展与规划设计	阳建强，王海卉等	东南大学出版社，200707
27	中央空调系统设计	余跃进，吴雁	东南大学出版社，200707
28	夏热冬冷地区生态建筑与节能技术	杨维菊	中国建筑工业出版社，200708
29	设计结合模型——制作与使用建筑模型指导（译著）	李哲译	天津大学出版社，200708
30	居住建筑设计原理 （高校建筑学与城市规划专业教材）	胡仁禄，孔令龙， 王承慧等	中国建筑工业出版社，200708
31	学院与大学建筑（译著）	薛力，孙世界译	中国建筑工业出版社，200709
32	设计师必读	龚恺等	中国建筑工业出版社，200709
33	东南大学建筑学院建筑系一年级设计教学研究 设计的启蒙	龚恺等	中国建筑工业出版社,200711
34	东南大学建筑学院建筑系二年级设计教学研究 空间的操作	龚恺等	中国建筑工业出版社,200711
35	东南大学建筑学院建筑系三年级设计教学研究 专题·阶段·整体	龚恺等	中国建筑工业出版社,200711
36	东南大学建筑学院建筑系四年级设计教学研究 设计工作室	龚恺，韩冬青，张彤等	中国建筑工业出版社,200711
37	东南大学建筑学院联合教学成果选	龚恺等	中国建筑工业出版社,200711
38	地方性建筑与适宜技术	陈晓扬等	中国建筑工业出版社，200712

续表

序号	专著名称	作者姓名	出版社及出版日期
39	东南大学建筑学院成立80周年庆纪念专集（1927-2007）	刘先觉，安宁主编	中国建筑工业出版社，2007
40	CAADRIA2007论文集	董卫等	东南大学出版社，2007
41	城市开放空间设计(译著)	张倩译	中国建筑工业出版社,2007
42	走近798——六校联合毕业设计	许懋彦，龚恺等	中国建筑工业出版社,2007
43	亚洲城镇遗产保护与复兴实用指南	张玫英 柴洋波译	东南大学出版社，2007
44	城镇保护实例	董卫参编	东南大学出版社，2007
45	城市家园——城市住宅设计（译著）	吴锦绣，鲍莉	江苏科学技术出版社,2007
46	钢笔画技法	赵军	上海人民美术出版社，2007
47	新农村住宅建设技术问答	杨维菊主编	中国建筑工业出版社，2007
48	一级注册建筑师考试建筑设计（作图）应试指南（第三版）	黎志涛	中国建筑工业出版社，2007
49	城市与人（译著）	郑炘，周琦译	中国建筑工业出版社，200801
50	东南大学建筑学院城市规划专业学生优秀作业选	阳建强，吴晓等	东南大学出版社，200801
51	建筑物理环境与设计	柳孝图，傅秀章	中国建筑工业出版社，200803
52	梁构·建筑	戴航	科学出版社，200808
53	现代建筑理论（第二版）	刘先觉等	中国建筑工业出版社，2008
54	后工业时代产业建筑遗产保护更新	王建国	中国建筑工业出版社，2008
55	绿色城市设计---基于生物气候条件的生态策略	徐小东,王建国	东南大学出版社，2008
56	江苏城市建设的反思与重构	韩冬青，董卫，杨俊宴、王承慧参编	东南大学出版社，2008
57	园林建筑设计	成玉宁	中国农业出版社，2008
58	材料呈现——19和20世纪西方建筑中材料的建造-空间双重性研究	史永高	东南大学出版社，2008
59	中国城市CBD量化研究——形态·功能·产业	杨俊宴，吴明伟	东南大学出版社，2008
60	传统商业中心规划	杨俊宴	辽宁科学技术出版社，2008
61	数字化信息集成下的建筑、设计与建造	俞传飞	中国建筑工业出版社，2008
62	城市规划快题设计与表现	杨俊宴、谭瑛	辽宁科学技术出版社，2008
63	宽线条建筑素描	方晓珊	东南大学出版社，2008
64	建筑快图的电脑手绘快速表达	陈晓扬	江苏科学技术出版社，2008
65	东南大学建筑学院城市规划专业学生优秀作业选	阳建强，吴晓，孔令龙等	东南大学出版社，2008
66	室内建筑师辞典	高祥生	人民交通出版社，2008年
67	与城市互动的住区规划设计	杨靖，马进	东南大学出版社，2008
68	随曲合方:山东莱芜红石公园改造设计	王晓俊	中国建筑工业出版社，2008
69	风景园林设计第3版	王晓俊	江苏科学技术出版社，2008
70	第七届海峡两岸大学的校园学术研讨会论文集	阳建强，徐春宁等编	东南大学出版社，2008

重要学术论文

本学科最高级学术期刊发表论文

序号	本学科最高级学术期刊发表论文名称	作者	刊物名	卷期
1	后工业时代中国产业类历史建筑遗产保护性再利用	王建国，蒋楠	建筑学报	2006（8）
2	从建构城市生活的角度谈住宅造型设计	王承慧	建筑学报	2006（10）
3	康德论建筑艺术	郑炘	建筑学报	2006（11）
4	生态可持续发展理念下的建筑学教育思考	仲德崑，陈静	建筑学报	2007（1）
5	基于生物气候条件的城市设计生态策略研究——以湿热地区城市设计为例	徐小东，王建国	建筑学报	2007（3）
6	关于数字技术在当代建筑设计中应用的再思考	吴晓，虞刚	建筑学报	2007（5）
7	适宜技术的节约型策略	陈晓扬，仲德崑	建筑学报	2007（7）
8	当代佛教寺庙规划设计初探	李新建，朱光亚	建筑学报	2007（8）
9	与城市互动的住区规划设计实践	杨靖，马进	建筑学报	2007（11）
10	体验私家园林的变化过程——从江苏泰州乔园的扩建说起	陈薇	建筑学报	2008（1）
11	地形对城市环境的影响及其规划设计应对策略	徐小东，徐宁	建筑学报	2008（1）
12	从工厂到总部——南京泉峰国际集团总部办公楼设计	钱锋，汪晓茜	建筑学报	2008（2）
13	基于公共安全的城市设计——安全城市设计刍议	蔡凯臻，王建国	建筑学报	2008（5）
14	芬兰生态型居住区探察——以赫尔辛基的Viikki实验新区为例	吴晓，汪晓茜	建筑学报	2008（11）
15	历史性校园的价值及其保护——以东南大学、南京大学、南京师范大学老校区为例	阳建强	城市规划	2006（7）
16	美国城市设计导则探讨及对中国的启示	高源	城市规划	2007（5）
17	金陵女子大学的空间形态与设计思想评析	陆敏，阳建强	城市规划	2007（6）
18	南京高新区高新技术企业的空间扩散研究	陈家祥，王兴平	城市规划	2007（7）
19	沿海开发区一种典型深层结构：大津泰达为例	熊国平	城市规划	2007（7）
20	长江三角洲区域协调重大问题的调查研究	杨俊宴，陈雯	城市规划	2007（9）
21	建立与城市互动的住区规划设计观	杨靖，马进	城市规划	2007（9）
22	基于旅游功能策划的景区规划——以射阳岛区的总体规划为例	吴晓，吴明伟，徐伟	城市规划	2007（10）
23	南京绕城公路的生态环境影响分析及规划对策	王晓俊，王建国	城市规划	2007（11）
24	快速城市化浪潮下的文艺复兴	阳建强	城市规划	2007（12）
25	传承与演化——贵州屯堡聚落研究	王海宁	城市规划	2008（1）
26	唐山焦化厂产业地段及建筑的改造再利用	王建国，张愚，沈瑾	城市规划	2008（2）
27	美国快速城市化背景下的贫民窟整治初探	吴晓，吴明伟	城市规划	2008（2）
28	中国城市开发区群的发展与演化——以南京为例	王兴平	城市规划	2008（3）
29	郑州老工业基地更新规划的整体思考	阳建强，罗超	城市规划	2008（6）
30	住区规划中的城市设计应用初探	吴晓，阳建强	城市规划	2008（7）
31	关于城市开放空间优先的思考	王晓俊，王建国	中国园林	2007（3）
32	区划调整背景下的城市中轴线景观更新	谭瑛，杨俊宴	中国园林	2007（9）
33	可达性的悖论与问题的解决——以天山天池风景名胜区为例	唐军	中国园林	2007（12）
34	木渎景区金山采石宕口植被恢复与可持续景观设计	陈盛彬，杜顺宝	中国园林	2006（4）

本学科核心和重要学术期刊发表论文

序号	本学科核心学术期刊发表论文名称	作者	刊物名	卷期
1	新型办公建筑之构想——竹中工务店东京总部新办公大楼	钱强	建筑师	2006（6）
2	历史视野中的乡土建筑—— 一种充满质疑的建筑	吴晓	建筑师	2006（6）
3	当代中国低密度住宅设计中传统与现代的矛盾性	周琦，杨红波	建筑师	2006（6）
4	白墙的表面属性和建造内涵	史永高	建筑师	2006（6）
5	解读格雷戈·林恩	王立明，龚恺	建筑师	2006（8）
6	分析作为一种学习设计的方法	韩冬青	建筑师	2007（1）
7	从建构思维看古代建筑结构的类型与演化	张十庆	建筑师	2007（2）
8	建筑的复杂性和简单性——建筑空间与形式丰富性设计方法探讨	周琦，高钢	建筑师	2007（4）
9	“得州骑警”与“九宫格”练习的发展	朱雷	建筑师	2007（4）
10	天朝的南端——嘉靖三十二年（1553年）前后北京外城商业活动与城市格局	陈薇	建筑师	2007（6）
11	明洪武朝建筑群规模等级制度体系浅析	白颖	建筑师	2007（6）
12	“小组十”、柯布西耶与毯式建筑	陈洁萍	建筑师	2007（4）
13	物质是如何被赞美的？	史永高	建筑师	2008（1）
14	重力原则下的结构与造型	周琦，郭健	建筑师	2008（2）
15	苏州同里古镇人居环境营建的生态策略初探	鲍莉	建筑师	2008（4）
16	绿色福利：可持续发展的瑞典城市与建筑	张彤	世界建筑	2007（7）
17	卡桑-怀特建筑师事务所办公楼，斯德哥尔摩，瑞典	张彤	世界建筑	2007（7）
18	哈默比湖城的环境信息中心	张彤	世界建筑	2007（7）
19	Bo01欧洲住宅展览会，马尔摩，瑞典	吴晓，顾震弘	世界建筑	2007（7）
20	维基实验新区，赫尔辛基，芬兰	吴晓，顾震弘	世界建筑	2007（7）
21	哈默比湖城，斯德哥尔摩，瑞典	吴晓，顾震弘	世界建筑	2007（7）
22	维基实验新区生态示范住宅，赫尔辛基，芬兰	汪晓茜	世界建筑	2007（7）
23	Hedebygade街区城市生态更新，哥本哈根，丹麦	汪晓茜	世界建筑	2007（7）
24	瑞典皇家工学院汉宁南校区综合教学楼，瑞典	陈宇	世界建筑	2007（7）
25	KTHB：瑞典皇家工学院主校区图书馆，瑞典	陈宇	世界建筑	2007（7）
26	哈默比湖城“柯本”街区，瑞典	陈宇	世界建筑	2007（7）
27	两种瑞典可持续住区模式的研究	顾震弘	世界建筑	2007（7）
28	卡路斯特瑞格生态住宅，奥斯陆，挪威	顾震弘	世界建筑	2007（7）
29	绿色旅馆：桑加赛比培训与会议中心	王湘君	世界建筑	2007（7）
30	可持续性评估方法在北欧建筑设计和城市规划中的应用	王湘君	世界建筑	2007（7）
31	可持续发展的城市与建筑（翻译）	陈宇	世界建筑	2007（7）
32	当代毯式建筑研究	陈洁萍	世界建筑	2007（8）
33	多哈会展中心及塔楼（多哈，卡塔尔）	徐春宁	世界建筑	2007（12）
34	我国滨江大城市的跨江扩展	王兴平	城市规划学刊	2006（2）
35	区域分析在新城市中心区城市设计中的应用	刘伟奇，王兴平	城市规划学刊	2007（1）
36	理论·实践·思考——奖励性管制方法在城市规划管理中应用	杨俊宴，吴明伟	城市规划学刊	2007（2）
37	八十年代以来长江三角洲区域空间结构发展研究	杨俊宴，陈雯	城市规划学刊	2008（5）
38	疯狂与数字：屈米的两个公园设计竞赛方案的解读	王晓俊，王建国，苏志国	新建筑	2006（6）
39	北欧建筑师希古德·莱维伦茨述评——以圣彼得教堂设计为例	吴晓，魏羽力	新建筑	2006（6）
40	回应气候的地方建筑技术	[illegible]	新建筑	2006（12）

续表

序号	本学科核心学术期刊发表论文名称	作者	刊物名	卷期
41	文化回应技术——南京渤泥国王墓文物展览室设计有感	姚准	新建筑	2006（12）
42	从凡尔赛到拉·维莱特——试析两个园的空间构成与巴黎城市的双重脉络	朱雷	新建筑	2007（1）
43	建筑的祸福与历史铁证——兼驳黑格尔、李泽厚的建筑论	郑光复	新建筑	2007（2）
44	中观尺度的城市设计生态策略研究	徐小东	新建筑	2007（2）
45	建筑设计生成艺术的应用实验	李飚	新建筑	2007（3）
46	风格派的建筑师	桂鹏，郑炘	新建筑	2007（4）
47	从廿八都谈欠发达地区历史文化村镇的保护	薛春霖，仲德崑	新建筑	2007（4）
48	双向适宜——一种对适宜技术的文化解读	邓浩，宋峰	新建筑	2007（4）
49	地形学议题——第九届威尼斯建筑双年展回顾	陈洁萍	新建筑	2007（4）
50	问题生长突现设计——关于建筑设计及其理论专业学位论文教学的思考	韩冬青	新建筑	2007（6）
51	瑞典皇家工学院的校园演化与空间环境探析——以KTH的历史性主校区（Valhallavägen）为例	吴晓，谢泉	新建筑	2007（6）
52	问题先导突现设计——关于建筑设计及其理论专业学位论文教学的思考	韩冬青	新建筑	2007（6）
53	颐和路公馆区的历史与再生——从北京西路60号住宅的修缮改造说起	周琦，傅舒兰	新建筑	2007（6）
54	东南大学老校区的保护与更新	倪慧，阳建强	新建筑	2008（1）
55	以影像之名——电影艺术与建筑实践	仲德崑，闫苏	新建筑	2008（1）
56	图解——期待未知	韩冬青等	新建筑	2008（2）
57	开放空间应优先成为城市设计的重要准则	徐小东	新建筑	2008（2）
58	整体中的片断	陈秋光	新建筑	2008（2）
59	欧洲“移动谷”的演化与建设初探——瑞典著名的Kista科技园区考察	吴晓，孙静	新建筑	2008（3）
60	透明性的意味——透明性研究之一	史永高	新建筑	2008（3）
61	在原点上反躬自问——5.12汶川大地震引发的建筑思考	仲德崑	新建筑	2008（4）
62	震殇解惑：建筑物体的灾害性终结及其对于建筑教育的启示	李海清	新建筑	2008（4）
63	我们为什么如此建造	俞传飞	新建筑	2008（4）
64	波普风格与观念园林：玛莎·施瓦兹的园林设计评述	钱筠，王晓俊	新建筑	2008（5）
65	江南传统村镇空间要素的装饰性及其文化内涵	王海宁，季松	华中建筑	2006（8）
66	城市现代化、民主化发展中的城市景观	唐军	华中建筑	2006（9）
67	试论校园规划的整体性与延续性——以常州市戚墅堰区实验中学规划设计为例	薛力	华中建筑	2006（10）
68	有关李渔“便面窗”的分析	朱雷	华中建筑	2006（10）
69	城市精神的提炼、阐释与创造	李向锋	华中建筑	2006（12）
70	类型：行为、意象与文化内涵	刘捷	华中建筑	2007（1）
71	试论景观建筑创作中对文学修辞法的运用	金俊	华中建筑	2007（2）
72	地方建筑中的文化·技术观	陈晓扬	华中建筑	2007（2）
73	“建构”的一次尝试——从材料出发进行的“伞、门、亭”设计	薛力	华中建筑	2007（4）
74	风景建筑设计的思考——张家界国家森林公园门票站规划及单体设计	张弦，齐康	华中建筑	2007（5）
75	浅谈夏热冬冷地区办公建筑节能环保的设计策略	庞博，张宏	华中建筑	2007（5）
76	建筑的祸福是非——重建圆明园及其他	郑光复	华中建筑	2007（5）
77	浅谈现代商住楼的设计及其传统形式的引用	薛力	华中建筑	2007（5）
78	设计更为积极的“辅助空间”——对于高校建筑交通空间设计的思考	顾燕，姚准	华中建筑	2007（5）
79	城市“绿心”规划研究——以乐山市城市“绿心”规划为例	罗文军，李家军，李海清	华中建筑	2007（6）

续表

序号	本学科核心学术期刊发表论文名称	作者	刊物名	卷期
80	生长与融合——大连贝壳博物馆方案设计	刘媛，齐康	华中建筑	2007（7）
81	斯德哥尔摩的“地下艺术长廊”浅析——以地铁站点的艺术陈设设计为例	吴晓，施梁	华中建筑	2007（7）
82	福建永安青水乡土建筑测绘七则	薛力	华中建筑	2007（8）
83	回归本始——赫尔佐格和德梅隆的REHAB康复中心设计浅析	王彦辉	华中建筑	2007（8）
84	东南大学·代尔夫特大学建筑联合教学成果介绍评析	高源，杜嵘，吴晓	华中建筑	2007（9）
85	就学术讨论的效率答诸友——话语权与学术民主	郑光复	华中建筑	2007（10）
86	与城市互动的住区商业形态设计	杨靖，马进	华中建筑	2007（10）
87	瑞典高校建筑学科的教学体系探察——以皇家工学院（KTH）的建筑与环境学院为例	吴晓，阳建强	华中建筑	2007（12）
88	石屋访古	薛力	华中建筑	2007（12）
89	表皮的透明性与真实性	邓浩	华中建筑	2007（12）
90	环境对形式的作用，空间对流线的引导	薛力，顾海燕	华中建筑	2008（2）
91	传统底蕴　现代手法	刘捷，薛力	华中建筑	2008（3）
92	襄阳明代王府建筑初探	白颖	华中建筑	2008（4）
93	隆昌寺游记	薛力	华中建筑	2008（4）
94	图书馆建筑界面营造和建构策略——以青岛理工大学黄岛校区为例	仲德崑，戚立	华中建筑	2008（6）
95	古地新居——廿八都镇旅游接待中心设计	仲德崑，田志卿	华中建筑	2008（7）
98	ORDER视角下的西方建筑设计	夏娃，周琦	工业建筑	2007（1）
99	建筑职业的伦理选择——AIA伦理准则的百年历程	李向锋，仲德崑	世界建筑导报	2006（11）
100	Research on Acoustical Environment Planning of Harbour Cities	柳孝图	Journal of Southeast University	Vol.12, No.2
101	Progress of Research and Application on Noise Control Engineering	柳孝图	Chinese Journal of Acoustics	Vol.15, No.12, No.2
102	Exploration and Preservation of Petra	纳瓦福，龚恺	Journal of Southeast University	
103	古老埃及陵墓的数字建构和保护（英文版）	艾比塔，龚恺	东南大学学报（哲学社会科学版）	2007（2）
104	作为公共艺术形态的城市雕塑	施梁，吴晓	东南大学学报（哲学社会科学版）	2007（3）
105	试论我国建筑环境设计的自主创新	赵军	东南大学学报（哲学社会科学版）	2007（3）
106	立足于求租群体的住房租赁市场探察——以南京为例	吴晓	东南大学学报（哲学社会科学版）	2008（2）
107	城市规划初步教学改革实践	吴怡音，雒建利	规划师	2006（8）
108	小传统应对城市化——南京市江宁杨柳村的调查与思考	姚准	规划师	2006（8）
109	安庆倒扒狮历史文化街区的保护与更新	阳建强等	规划师	2006（10）
110	滨海开放空间的个性塑造	谭瑛	规划师	2007（5）
111	对新一轮城市总体规划编制的探索——以江阴为例	熊国平，缪敏	规划师	2007（5）
112	关于城市设计与现有规划体系衔接的思考	吴晓，魏羽力	规划师	2007（6）
113	基于效益分析的节约型城市规划方法探索——以常州天宁经济开发区规划为例	谢晖，王兴平，章建豪，严玲	规划师	2007（6）
114	竞争与竞争力导向的唐山市高新技术开发区功能定位研究	于涛方，王兴平	规划师	2007（7）
115	解读乡村景观的同质性——以福建土楼为例	姚准	规划师	2007（7）
116	苏黎世西部工业区复兴及其启示	王彦辉，顾威	规划师	2007（7）
117	城市中心区控制性详细规划编制方法探索	杨俊宴，吴明伟	规划师	2007（8）
118	土地集约利用背景下的城市地下空间开发	[illegible]	规划师	2007（10）

续表

序号	本学科核心学术期刊发表论文名称	作者	刊物名	卷期
119	世博会场馆设计的国际经验对上海世博会的启示	冷嘉伟	规划师	2008（1）
120	基于“空间准入”的开发区产业布局规划研究——以连云港经济技术开发区为例	王兴平，钱德福，齐文	规划师	2008（3）
121	香港公屋规划设计的分析与启发	杨靖，郭药，张嵩	规划师	2008（4）
122	从“小产权房”看农村土地制度的改革	王海卉	规划师	2008（4）
123	聚落形态的文化基因解析	王海宁	规划师	2008（5）
124	基于文化环境建构的校园雕塑建设研究——以东南大学、南京大学、南京师范大学老校区为例	孙静，谢泉，吴晓	规划师	2008（6）
125	基于生物气候条件的绿色城市设计生态策略	王建国，徐小东	建筑与文化	2006（8）
126	传承与创新——厦门园博园杏林阁设计	张成武，金俊	建筑与文化	2007（8）
127	苏州环古城西段风貌保护的规划与设计	段进	建筑与文化	2007（10）
128	南京河西滨江公园太阳宫景区	陈薇	建筑与文化	2007（10）
129	山高水长	朱光亚	建筑与文化	2007（10）
130	南京图书馆新馆	张宏	建筑与文化	2007（10）
131	江宁区东南大学九龙湖校园公共教学楼设计	王建国	建筑与文化	2007（10）
132	被隐藏的与被消解的：“后现代性”语境下的城市与建筑	李琦，史永高	建筑与文化	2007（12）
133	农村卫生站建筑设计研究（上）——基本原理	周颖	建筑与文化	2008（6）
134	传统的回应——记大丰市博物馆设计创作	徐小东等	建筑与文化	2008（6）
135	树城：一个超越常规的公园设计	张健健，王晓俊	国际城市规划	2007（5）
136	科技园在英国区域发展和科技创新战略框架中的作用	许景，刘伟奇，王兴平	国际城市规划	2008（1）
137	差异性的建筑教育	朱雷，藏峰	时代建筑	2007（3）
138	走向多元化与系统的中国当代建筑教育	仲德崑	时代建筑	2007（3）
139	不知晦朔 焉知春秋——2007年中建史期刊论文点评	陈薇	时代建筑	2008（2）
140	《中国近代建筑史研究》点评	李海清	时代建筑	2008（2）
141	江南古村落居民生活与水体变迁的思考	赖凌瑶，阳建强	小城镇建设	2007（1）
142	长三角村镇空间整合与规划面临的新形势与挑战	王兴平	小城镇建设	2008（4）
143	历史文化街区中居民生活延续研究	赖凌瑶，阳建强	小城镇建设	2008（6）
144	中国开发区空间配置与使用的错位现象研究	王兴平	城市发展研究	2008（2）
145	基于可持续发展准则的绿色城市设计交通策略——来自〈绿色城市主义〉的启示	王建国，徐小东	城市发展研究	2008（增刊）
146	老工业城市的转型与更新改造	阳建强	城市发展研究	2008（增刊）
147	基于城市整体发展的工业文化遗产保护	阳建强等	建筑创作	2006（9）
148	基于生物气候条件的城市设计生态策略研究——以冬冷夏热地区城市设计为例	徐小东	城市建筑	2006（7）
149	绿色着，以自己的方式——瑞士阿尔卑斯山区的三所学校	李海清	城市建筑	2006（7）
150	因地制宜 整合创新	刘捷，施梁	城市建筑	2006（9）
151	风景中的建筑	杜顺宝	城市建筑	2007（5）
152	现代竹材技术及其在建筑设计中的应用	王静等	城市建筑	2007（8）
153	寻求竖向纬度空间形态的多样性	刘捷，施梁	城市建筑	2007（10）
154	建筑形态地景化的结构形态策略	仲德崑，蒋鑫	城市建筑	2008（5）
155	传统地域文化的现代演绎——广西崇左壮族博物馆设计	仲德崑，杨宝	城市建筑	2008（9）
156	合肥文化中心	仲德崑	建筑与文化	2007（10）
157	欧洲城市规划与公共健康互动的发展演变分析	杜娟，阳建强	现代城市研究	2006（8）
158	整合中创造和谐——解读青岛大学图书馆及校前区广场改扩建设计	钱玉斋，金俊	现代城市研究	2007（1）

续表

序号	本学科核心学术期刊发表论文名称	作者	刊物名	卷期
160	历史环境中街区更新的实践与反思	冷嘉伟	现代城市研究	2007（4）
161	西欧城市更新的特征与趋势分析	倪慧，阳建强	现代城市研究	2007（6）
162	生态城市美学研究的系统建构	李哲	现代城市研究	2007（10）
163	商业化冲击下的社区变迁	史北祥，杨俊宴	现代城市研究	2008（6）
164	谈室内陈设设计中的视觉问题	高祥生	中国建筑装饰装修	2007（3）
165	室内异形空间的优化设计	高祥生	中国建筑装饰装修	2007（5）
166	谈室内柱子的装饰形态设计	高祥生	中国建筑装饰装修	2007（6）
167	室内空间中隔断的围合度	高祥生	中国建筑装饰装修	2007（7）
168	室内环境中的细部设计	高祥生	中国建筑装饰装修	2007（9）
169	室内设计中材料肌理的表现方法	高祥生	中国建筑装饰装修	2007（10）
170	国民政府外交部历史探源与修缮设计	龙潇，周琦.	中国近代建筑研究与保护国际研讨会	2006（7）
171	杨廷宝20世纪40年代小住宅设计探究	季秋，周琦	中国近代建筑研究与保护国际研讨会	2006（7）
172	关于景观学专业建设的思考	成玉宁	首届中国景观教育大会论文集，中国建筑工业出版社	2006
173	设计与建造的数字化融合及其对建筑数字技术教学的影响	俞传飞	2006年全国高等学校建筑院系建筑数字技术教学研讨会论文集	2006
174	南宋径山寺法堂复原探讨	张十庆	文物	2007（3）
175	弹性曲弯空间网壳结构的找形与承载设计	方立新	空间结构	2007（4）
176	明洪武朝分封制度下王府建筑群基址规模初探	白颖	古建园林技术	2007（4）
177	1990年以来国际新城建设趋势探讨	熊国平	地域研究与开发	2007（6）
178	谈室内设计的独立价值	高祥生	室内设计师	2007（8）
179	一个逝去时代的巨人——纪念刘敦桢先生感悟	朱光亚	中外建筑	2007（10）
180	Reading of Several Key Words in the Study of Chinese Urban History	朱光亚	建筑历史与理论研究文集（1997-2007）	2007（10）
181	中国古代木结构谱系再研究	朱光亚	建筑历史与理论研究文集（1997-2007）	2007（10）
182	水彩画《春阳和风》	方晓珊	韩中水彩画展	2007（10）
183	表面建构学的可能性	史永高	《DOMUS》（中文版）	2007（11）
184	为冷静而执著——Yksi三人组	沈颖	室内设计与装修	2007（11）
185	西方古典建筑教与学	季秋，周琦	第二届世界建筑史教学与研究国际研讨会	2007（11）
186	中国传统民居对地形顺应的生态策略	杨维菊，沙晓冬	哈尔滨工业大学学报	2007（12）
187	关于五山十刹的年代考析	张十庆	东方建筑	2007
188	基于节约理念的建筑适宜技术观	陈晓扬	建筑学会学术年会论文集	2007
189	南京站室内设计中的形式逻辑	高祥生	火车站规划、设计、管理	2007
190	场所精神的营造——谈室内专业的独立价值	高祥生	2007年中国建筑学会室内设计分会年会论文集	2007
191	From Instrument to Interface	俞传飞	2007 CAADRIA 论文集，东南大学出版社	2007
192	A New Way of Storytelling in Today's Architecture	俞传飞	2007 ISAMA 论文集，Texas A&M University, USA	2007
193	手段与方法的取舍和定位——再谈设计媒介变迁对建筑教育的影响	俞传飞	2007（北京）国际建筑教育大会论文集，中国建筑工业出版社	2007

续表

序号	本学科核心学术期刊发表论文名称	作者	刊物名	卷期
194	空间要素介入材料研究的必要性	史永高	2007（北京）国际建筑教育大会论文集，中国建筑工业出版社	2007
195	南方地区建筑节能现场检测方法讨论	彭昌海	第三届国际智能、绿色建筑与建筑节能大会	2007
196	矿区构造应力场的遥感分析	胡明星	国土资源遥感	2008（1）
197	对话：当代中国建筑发展的三个断面	赵辰，葛明，胡恒	亚洲新建筑 建筑师（台湾）特刊	2008（1）
198	作为空间表现的素材——教学空间改造中的材料运用及其表现	钱强等	室内设计师	2008（2）
199	燕王府位置新考	白颖	故宫博物院院刊	2008（2）
200	低技术条件下节能及生态建筑设计——以中国药科大学体育活动中心为例	冯志荣，周琦	建筑技术与设计	2008（5）
201	Problems of urban green space system planning in China	Wang Xiao-Jun	Journal of Forestry Research	2008
202	核心、阶段、整体——东南大学建筑学院景观学系景观规划设计课程设置	唐军	第三届全国风景园林教育学术年会论文集，中国建筑工业出版社	2008
203	求同存异——论我国风景园林教育的规范化与多元化	成玉宁	第三届全国风景园林教育学术年会论文集，中国建筑工业出版社	2008
204	Conservation and adaptive- reuse of historical industrial building in China in the post-industrial era.	Wang Jianguo, Jiang Nan.	Frontiers of Architecture and Civil Engineering in China	2007，1（4）
205	Uncertainty Analysis for Vapor Pressure Measurement	石邢	Journal of Building Physics	2007（4）
206	Implementation and demonstration of web-based consulting for architects	Qi Zhou	Information Technology Conference	2007（4）
207	Mechanics and Test Study of Three Dimensional Flexible Membrane	石邢	Building and Environment	2007（11）
208	Solving a Puzzle – A Case Study for Building Distresses Due to Foundation Movement	石邢	Structure Magazine	2007（12）
209	Ventilation Drying in Walls with Vinyl Siding	石邢	Building X International Conference	2007（12）
210	Ventilation Drying in Walls with Vinyl Cladding	Xing Shi, Eric Burnett	Proceedings of Thermal Performance of the Exterior Envelopes of Whole Buildings X	2007
211	Mechanics and test study of flexible membranes ballooning in three dimensions	Xing Shi, Eric Burnett	Building and Environment，SCI检索，EI检索	43（11）
212	The Economy-oriented Strategy of Appropriate Technology	Chen Xiaoyang,Zhong Dekun	Frontiers of Architecture and Civil Engineering in China	2008
213	既有建筑的耐久性与使用寿命预测方法	石邢	Sustainable Building Restoration and Building Physics	2008

科研项目

序号	科研项目名称	项目主持人	科研项目来源	科研到款（万元）	起、讫时间
1	基于数字技术的城市空间规划设计研究（50238010）	董卫，王建国等	国家自然科学基金“十五”重点项目	100	2003.01～2007.12
2	后工业时代中国产业类历史建筑保护性再利用研究（50578040）	王建国	国家自然科学基金	25	2006.01～2008.12
3	中国申报世界文化遗产的村镇空间生长模型研究（50378013）	段进	国家自然科学基金	24	2004.01～2006.12
4	渤海国建筑史研究（50478070）	张十庆	国家自然科学基金	24	2005.01～2007.12
5	高速城市化期城市更新规划理论与技术方法研究（50478076）	阳建强	国家自然科学基金	21	2005.01～2007.12
6	东南地区若干濒危和失传的建筑工艺研究(50678034)	朱光亚	国家自然科学基金	30	2007.01～2009.12
7	新型节能建筑维护结构热物理性能与热工设计计算研究(50678163)	杨维菊（2）	国家自然科学基金	28	2007.01～2009.12
8	开发区与城市的空间整合及规划调控研究——以长江三角洲为例(50508009)	王兴平，吴晓	国家自然科学基金	24	2006.01～2008.12
9	我国城市化背景下的流动人口聚居空间研究:演化、特征与整合(50708017)	吴晓	国家自然科学基金	20	2008.01～2010.12
10	多元化趋势下建筑师结构选型策略的调整与重建（50778037）	方立新	国家自然科学基金	30	2008.01～2010.12
11	中国当代中等收入者的社会态度研究	严翅君，高祥生	国家社会科学基金	6	2004.01～2006.12
12	村镇小康住宅关键技术研究与示范中的“徽派”传统民居型小康住宅技术集成与示范	陈薇，项忠孝等	“十一五”国家科技支撑计划重大项目	400	2007.1～2012.12
13	城市旧区土地节约利用关键技术研究（2006BAJ14B06）	赵万民，蒋一军，王建国等	“十一五”国家科技支撑计划重点项目	125	2006.11～2010.11
14	既有建筑综合改造关键技术研究与示范：既有建筑功能提升改造关键技术研究（2006BAJ03A04-01）	李爱群，李杰，金伟良，王建国等	“十一五”国家科技支撑计划重大项目	800（子项目140）	2007.01～2010.12
15	空间信息技术在大遗址保护中的应用研究——京杭大运河遗产历史文化与当代人居环境研究（2006BAK30B01）	毛锋，陈薇等	“十一五”国家科技支撑计划重大项目	130（子项目25）	2006.12～2008.12
16	村镇小康住宅关键技术研究与示范：华中发达地区示范点	周琦等（5）	“十一五”国家科技支撑计划重大项目	130	2007.03～2012.03
17	新世纪优秀人才支持计划(NCET-05-0472)	阳建强	教育部“新世纪优秀人才支持计划”	10	2006.01～2008.12
18	新世纪优秀人才支持计划	王兴平	教育部“新世纪优秀人才支持计划”	10	2008.01～2010.12
19	新世纪优秀人才支持计划	周颖	教育部“新世纪优秀人才支持计划”	10	2008.01～2010.12
20	开放、交叉、融合——走向可持续发展时代的土建类复合型人才培养和基地建设	钱强，王建国等	教育部理工类教学改革课题		2006.01～2008.12
21	21世纪土建类复合型人才培养模式创新实验区	钱强	教育部人才培养模式创新实验区		2008.01～2011.12
22	渤海国建筑史研究（20040286007）	张十庆	教育部高等学校博士学科点专项科研基金项目	6	2004.01～2006.12
23	长江三角洲区域空间演替研究（6701001028）	杨俊宴	国家发改委	20	2005.01～2007.12
24	农村居民集住区现代化人居环境构建关键技术及示范工程(BS2005005)	吕锡武，柳孝图，张宏，石邢等	江苏省科技厅重点项目，江苏省建设厅	150	2005.06～2007.12
25	柔杆编织结构分析与设计研究(BK2005066)	方立新	江苏省自然科学基金项目	8	2005.01～2007.12
26	城市住宅节能关键技术研究及工程示范（BS2005001）	谢远建，杨维菊	江苏省科技厅	10	2005.05～2007.05
27	建筑维护结构节能措施设计导则	许锦锋，杨维菊	江苏省科技厅	12	2004.07～2006.07
28	江苏省城市中心区土地集约利用的量化研究：数据评估、驱动机制与整合策略（7601000067）	杨俊宴	江苏省科技厅	8	2007.03～2008.12
29	江苏省沿江开发产业空间布局规划（7601000067）	杨俊宴	江苏省发改委	5	2005.01～2007.07
30	外墙外贴面保温系统关键技术研究（JS200626）	杨维菊	江苏省建设厅	5	2007.01～2009.12
31	[illegible]	[illegible]	[illegible]	4	[illegible]

续表

序号	科研项目名称	项目主持人	科研项目来源	科研到款（万元）	起、讫时间
32	城市规划品牌专业建设的实践和研究——立足复合型城市规划专业优秀人才的培养	阳建强，孔令龙，吴晓	江苏省教育厅重点项目	1.5	2006.01～2007.12
33	城市规划品牌专业建设	阳建强等	江苏省教育厅	10	2006～2008
34	城市新商业空间研究——以南京为例	管驰明，王兴平	江苏省教育厅高校哲学社会科学基金项目（江苏教育厅）	0.5	2005.06～2007.12
35	江苏近代建筑文化遗产研究（7601005054）	刘先觉，汪晓茜	江苏省文化厅	10	2004.01～2006.12
36	混凝土-钢组合梁结构性能研究（03y0310）	戴航等	江苏省交通厅	30	2004.07～2008.12
37	新加坡佛教建筑艺术	刘先觉	新加坡李谷建筑师事务所	20	2004.01～2006.12
38	普天信息产业上海工业园发展公司生态工业园区设计	张彤	瑞典皇家工学院产业生态系	62.5	2006～2007
39	City History and Multi-scale Spatial Masterplanning (CHaMSpaM) network	王建国（东南大学合作方）	英国工程与物理科学研究院	422240英镑	2007～2009
40	大型建筑环境舱实验系统里实现温湿、太阳辐射和风环境同步模拟的可行性研究	石邢	教育部留学回国人员科研启动基金		2008.9～2010.8
41	Sustainable Design计算机辅助设计软件在中国的现状分析及开发智能化辅助设计软件的市场需求研究	石邢	Autodesk（中国）有限公司		2008
42	Styro Stone双层隔热保温钢筋混凝土结构系统无损检测技术研究	石邢	泰锘石保温建筑科技（上海）有限公司		2008
43	中英合作老工业城市更新改造研究	王建国，王兴平	中英两国政府合作项目		2007～2009
44	旧建筑改造利用研究：南京博物院扩建设计	龚恺	澳大利亚新南威尔士大学建筑学院		2007.01～2007.02
45	江苏省新建住宅全装修质量标准	高祥生	江苏省建设厅		2007.6～2008.10
46	全装修设计施工一体化研究	高祥生，高宁	南京市建委		2008～2009
47	江苏省灯光照明标准图集	高祥生	江苏省建设厅		2007～2008
48	《江苏省建筑装饰柱子、墙体标准图集》	高祥生	江苏省建设厅		2006～2007
49	《江苏省建筑装饰装修设计文件深度规定》	高祥生	江苏省建设厅		2006～2007
50	《江苏省建筑装饰装修设计制图标准》	高祥生	江苏省建设厅		2005～2006
51	江苏省“青蓝工程”中青年学术带头人培养对象	王兴平	江苏省“青蓝工程”中青年学术带头人培养对象		2006.01～2009.12
52	国家精品课程建设：中国建筑史	陈薇等	教育部		2006.01～2010.12
53	南水北调东线江苏段建筑与环境保护发展研究（7601000069）	段进，雒建利，王兴平	南水北调东线江苏水源有限责任公司		2007.01～2008.12
54	开发区与城市的空间整合研究	王兴平	教育部聘请外籍教师重点资助项目		2007.08～2008.08
55	服务业集聚的形成机理、区域效应及调控策略研究（07JC790036）	管驰明，王兴平等	教育部人文社会科学研究青年基金		2008.01～2010.12
56	《江苏省历史街区保护规划编制导则》研究（JS2007JH13）	朱光亚（排名2）	江苏省建设厅		2007.11～2008.1
57	农村居民集聚区现代化人居环境构建关键技术及示范工程（BS2005005）	张宏（排名2）	江苏省科技厅、江苏省建设厅重点项目		2005.10～2007.10
58	江苏省大遗址保护规划研究	朱光亚	江苏省文化厅		2005.1～2006.12
59	大运河遗产保护规划编制第一阶段要求研究	侯卫东，朱光亚	国家文物局		2008
60	长城文物资源调查试点—河北省抚宁段长城敌楼测绘和文物调查	陈薇	国家文物局“十一五”重点文物普查		2006.8～2006.10
61	编制《“十一五”国家重要大遗址保护规划（第二批）》	陈薇	国家文物局		2006.8～2006.12
62	苏南城乡规划中的集约型建设用地指标体系研究（BK2008323）	王兴平	江苏省自然科学基金项目		2009.01～2011.12
63	建筑蓄能保温材料与系统的研究开发及示范	石邢（排名3）	科技部“十一五”国家科技支撑计划重大项目		2008.01～2010.12
64	华东发达地区新农村建设技术合成	周琦，杨维菊	十一五国家重点科技支撑计划	130	2008～2011

续表

序号	科研项目名称	项目主持人	科研项目来源	科研到款（万元）	起、讫时间
65	中国近代建筑保护技术研究	周琦，方立新，虞刚	江苏省文物局	4	2006～2009
66	南朝石刻被动式保护技术研究	周琦	南京市文物局	20	2005～2008
67	高淳亚溪新农村建设示范村	周琦	南京市科技局	20	2008

基于数字技术的城市空间规划设计研究

A Study on Digital Approaches for Spatial Planning and Design

国家自然科学基金“十五”重点项目(Key project of NSFC)，2003-2007　项目批准号：50238010

负责人：董卫
合作：广州市规划局 同济大学 武汉大学
项目组成员：王建国 胡明星 陈薇 傅秀章等

本课题以“城市规划设计数字化方法”研究为主线，将城市规划与设计、城市空间环境分析、城市规划管理等密切相关的方面组成一套既相互关联又相对独立的技术体系。通过对数字规划设计基础理论及相关应用技术的研究，有效整合了以GIS/VR/CAD为平台的相关计算机技术，用于从规划设计到规划管理的全过程，初步实现数字化城市规划设计与管理目标的全面整合。课题组特别以南京、上海、广州、无锡、杭州、宁波等城市为例，开展了实证性的基于数字化平台的城市空间规划设计方法研究。在大尺度城市空间设计、空间变迁分析、空间生成设计等方面取得了突破性进展。发展出基于GIS技术的城市空间规划设计支持系统(Spatial Planning and Design Support System, SPDSS)和城市规划基本数据库建设模式，这些创新性成果填补了我国在这方面的空白，具有重要的学术价值和广阔的应用前景。

课题组对我国当前城市规划设计、规划管理领域及国外相关研究的状况开展了分析和比较，为我国未来在这个领域的持续研究和发展作出了关键性的探索并奠定了良好的技术基础。

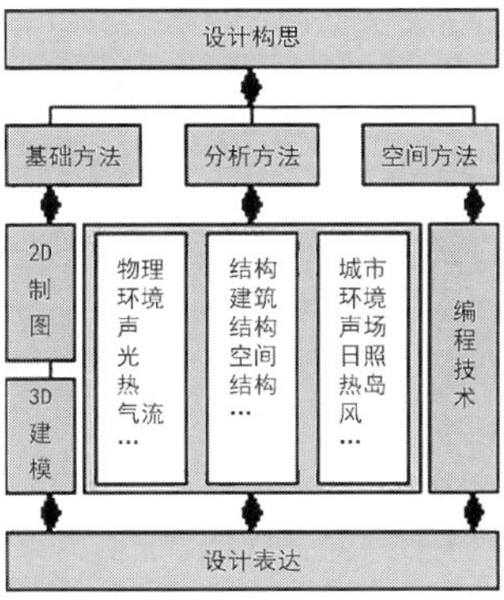

模式1：以技术分析为导向的规划设计方法

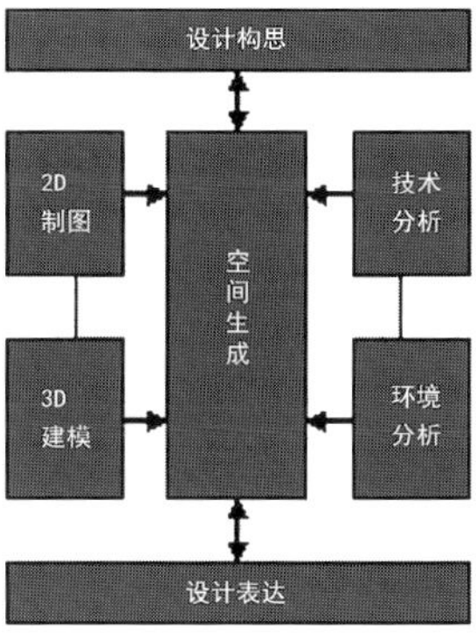

模式2：以空间形态为导向的规划设计方法

基于数字技术的规划设计方法

案例1：城市空间环境分析方法研究

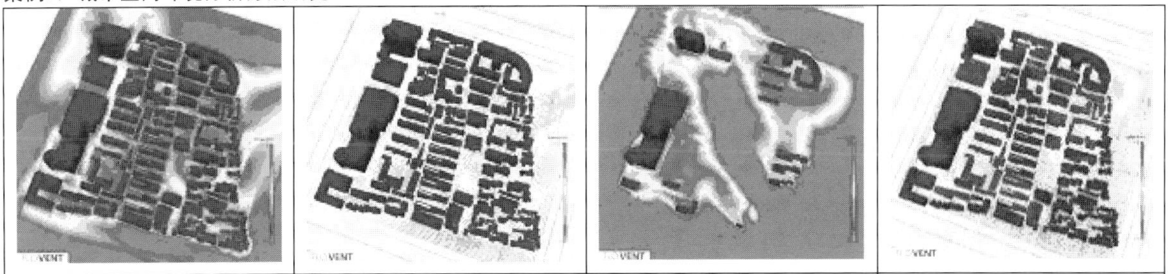

湖滨传统地块风速模拟　地块风向矢量分析　地块上空风速模拟　地块上空风向矢量分析

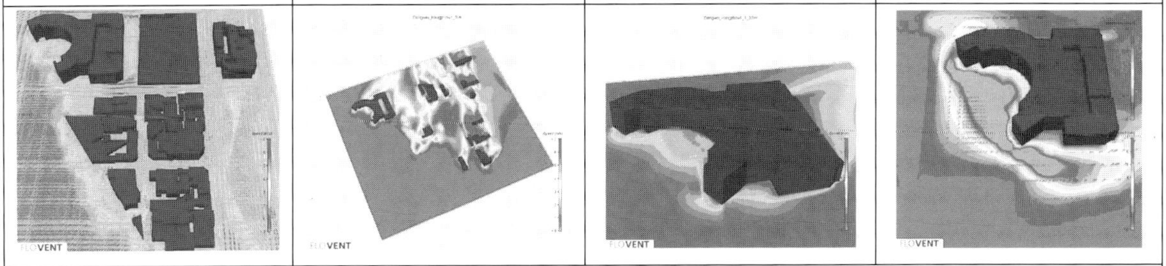

比较：湖滨现代街坊对夏季近地冷空气的阻滞作用　湖滨大体量建筑完全阻隔了夏季冷空气对城市的影响

“杭州主城区城市设计导则” 空间环境专项分析（项目主持：董卫教授，环境分析：傅秀章副教授，合作单位：杭州市规划局）

设计面积：110平方千米

解决问题：

在强化历史文化名城保护与房地产开发双重压力下如何保持湖滨地区空间形态的连续性

分析方法：

1. 建立历史空间资源数据库；
2. 利用FLOVENT软件，进行城市气流与温场分析；
3. 建立城市空间模型。

案例2：大尺度城市空间设计方法研究

生态环境分析

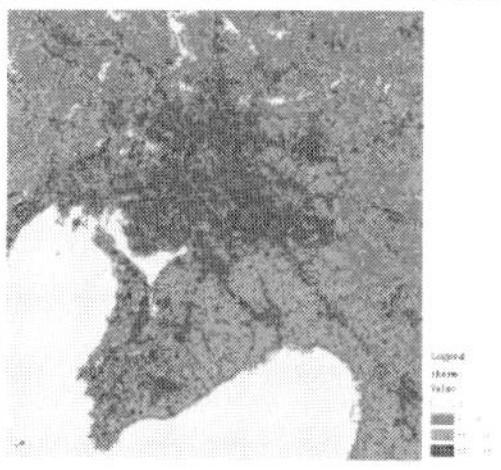

主城区热岛效应分析

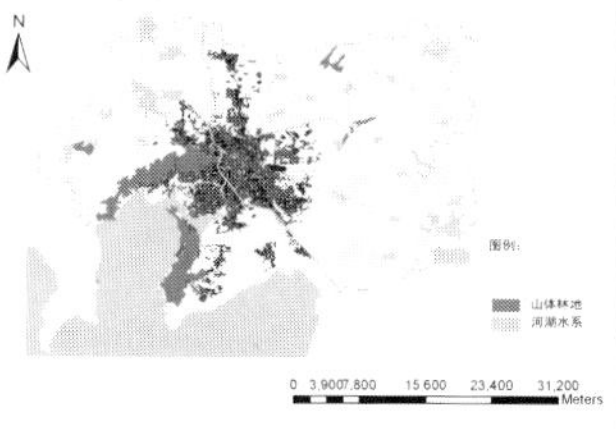

源数据图

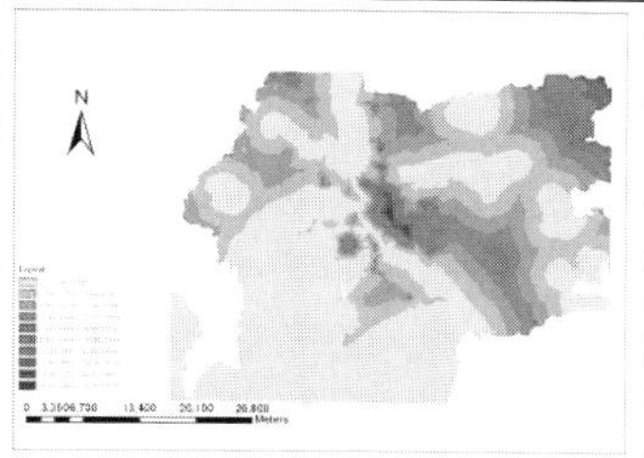

阻力面分析图

无锡市总体城市设计空间环境专项研究（项目主持：王建国教授，阳建强教授，GIS技术：胡明星副教授，合作单位：无锡市规划局）

设计面积：400平方千米

针对大规模城市扩张过程中产生的环境恶化现象提出关键性的分析方法：

1. 基于ETM遥感影像的热红外数据计算得到的无锡城区热岛效应分级图。红色部分为热岛效应明显地区；

2. 建立最小累积阻力模型，利用GIS空间分析中的成本距离法，对现状景观斑块进行生态阻力值计算，得到生态阻力面分析图，最终得到景观生态安全格局分析图。

案例3：城市空间生成设计方法研究

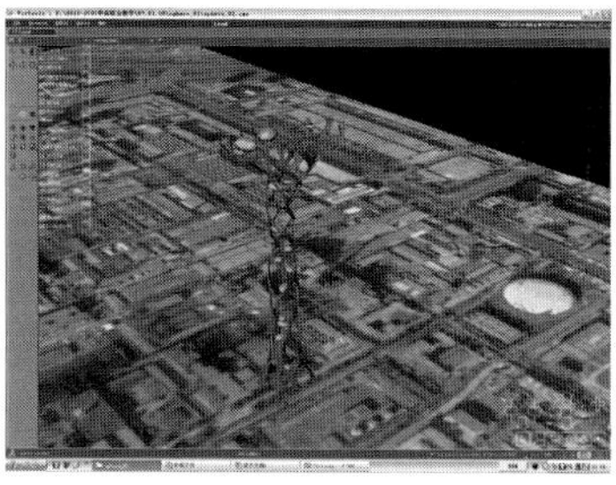

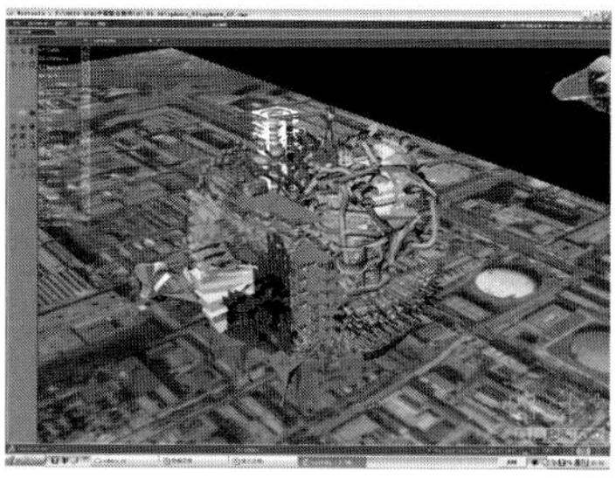

基于网络、VR和超媒体(hypermedia)方法的数字TT建模——空间生成过程(网络截图)

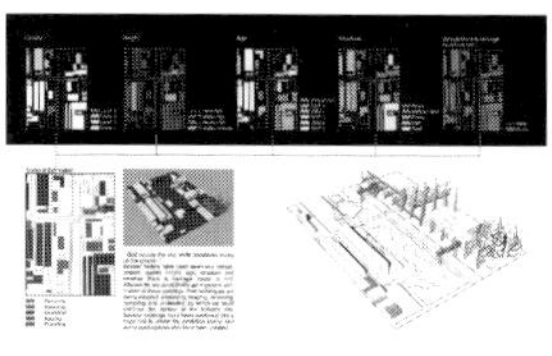

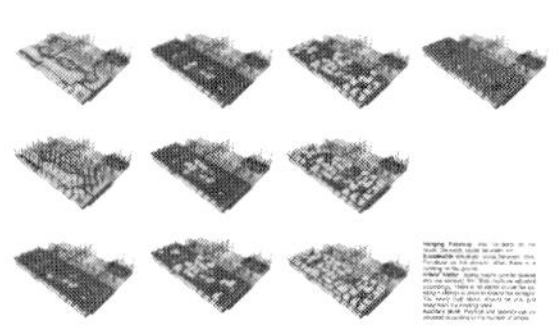

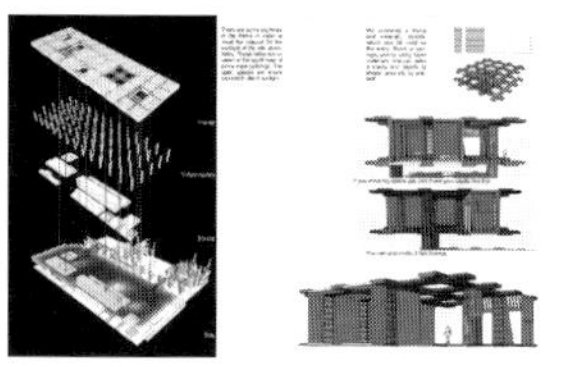

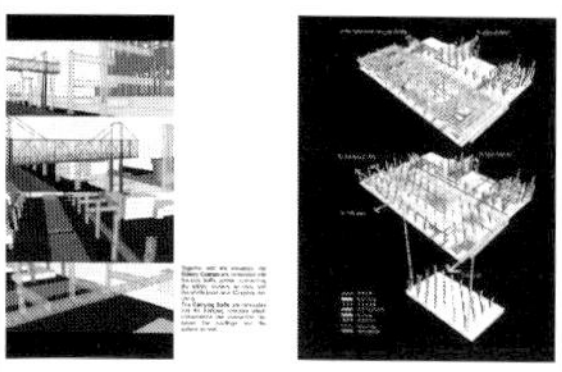

数字空间建模——空间生成与变迁分析

东南大学建筑学院·荷兰代尔夫特大学建筑系联合网络设计研究：北京751工厂改造—数字空间建模

设计主题：空间生成及数字建模研究

设计方法：多种技术联动应用，包括常规建模、语言编程、实时互动与修改

研究重点：本实验以一个直径200米的球状体为主，由24人共同完成同一建模过程，模型由24个子模型组成，共同形成一个完整的大模型，研究重点在于发展建筑层面上大尺度复杂空间建模的实用方法。空间构成采用非规则形态，以检验复杂条件下空间建模方法的可行性与可靠性

后工业时代中国产业类历史建筑保护性再利用研究

The Conservation and Adaptive-reuse of Historic Industrial Buildings and Sites in the Post-Industrial Age

国家自然科学基金资助项目(Projcct of NSFC)，2006～2008　项目批准号：50578040

负责人：王建国

产业类历史建筑及地段的保护性改造再利用是世界建筑学科发展前沿，特别是我国当今城市发展建设中一个迫切需要解决的重要科学问题。研究基于对国际间产业类历史建筑保护性改造再利用所进行的系统而有明确针对性的研究总结，旨在揭示中国城市发展更新、产业结构和布局调整、土地功能置换前提下的产业类历史建筑保护性改造再利用的合理性和可行性。澄清当今产业类历史建筑及地段保护性改造再利用的概念和学术意义；提出保护性改造再利用的对象分类和界定标准；探讨其在中国实施保护和改造再利用的基本原理，并针对中国特定的城市化历史背景构筑产业类历史建筑及地段保护性改造再利用的理论架构。经由对产业类历史建筑及地段在观念和实践层面的物质性实证研究，提出具有技术针对性的改造设计方法。

关键词：产业类历史建筑及地段；遗产保护；改造再利用；方法；中国

The conservative regeneration and adaptive reuse of the industrial historical buildings and blocks is one of the most impendent and important scientific problems to be resolved, not only in the leading edge of architectural field, but especially in the city development in contemporary China. Based on the systematic and pertinent research of the conservative regeneration and adaptive reuse of the industrial historical buildings on a worldwide scope, this research is aimed at revealing the rationality and possibility of the conservative regeneration and adaptive reuse of the industrial historical buildings under the conditions of Chinese city regeneration, modulation of the industrial structure and allocation, and substitution of land-use. The research also intends to clarify the conceptions and academic significance of the conservative regeneration and adaptive reuse of the industrial historical buildings and blocks, and bring forward the object categorization methods as well as the defining standards, probe into the principles of its implementation in China, build up a theoretical framework of the conservative regeneration and adaptive reuse of the industrial historical buildings and blocks against the background of the characteristic urbanization in China. Through the empirical study of the industrial historical buildings and blocks from both the conceptual and practical perspective, this research will finally put forward the design methods of regeneration with the technological pertinence.

Keywords: Industrial Historical Buildings and Blocks; Heritage Conservation; Regeneration and Adaptive Reuse; Method; China

本研究对世界产业类历史建筑及地段保护和再利用的案例进行了理性的分类和系统分析，较为全面地总结了国外在这一方面的经验，初步探索了在中国快速城市化进程条件下与如何保护产业类历史建筑相关的一些关键科学问题，包括：产业类建筑概念界定、分类方式、价值评定、改造措施、实施运作等；通过国内外学术会议报告、发表的论著和工程实际案例的研究，在学术和技术两个层面推进了中国在产业类建筑及地段保护和再利用方面的发展，是现阶段国内该领域研究最重要和系统的成果之一。

学术专著：

王建国. 后工业时代产业建筑遗产保护更新. 北京：中国建筑工业出版社，2008

学术论文：

1. Wang Jianguo. Conservation and Adaptive-reuse of Historic Industrial Heritage in China. Proceedings of the International Housing Symposium. Hosted by Seoul National University of Technology, Topic:Sustainable Development: Urban Habitat and Friendly Environment, Seoul Korea, 2005, pp.67-76
2. 上海世界博览会产业历史遗产保护和浦西内港码头区设计. 世界建筑导报，2005（4）：78-79
3. 产业类历史建筑保护及再利用的背景、过程和特点. 建筑趋势. 北京：中国电力出版社，2005
4. 王建国，彭韵洁，张慧，王彦. 瑞士产业历史建筑及地段的适应性再利用. 世界建筑，2006（5）：26-29
5. 王建国，蒋楠. 后工业时代中国产业类历史建筑遗产保护性再利用. 建筑学报，2006（8）：8-11
6. 王建国，蒋楠，王彦. 产业地段的创意再造，多元价值的综合平衡——以常州国棉一厂改造概念规划为例. 住区，2007（2）：62-67
7. 赵婧，王建国. 澳大利亚悉尼渥石湾码头区改造. 住区，2007（2）：80-87
8. 杨宇，王建国. 澳大利亚墨尔本港区改造和产业建筑再利用. 住区，2007（2）：88-93
9. Wang Jianguo, Jiang Nan. Conservation and adaptive-reuse of historical industrial building in China in the post-industrial era. Frontiers of Architecture and Civil Engineering in China. 2007,1(4):474-480 (Translated from Architecture Journal, 2006(8):8-11)
10. 王建国，张愚，沈瑾. 唐山焦化厂产业地段及建筑的改造再利用. 城市规划，2008（2）：88-92

学位论文：

蒋楠. 基于多重价值的产业历史建筑及地段的量化评析和改造再利用研究. 南京：东南大学，2007

王彦. 城市棕色地段更新及其城市设计对策研究. 南京：东南大学，2007

张婧. 中国产业类建筑改造的分析与研究. 南京：东南大学，2005

学术会议报告：

1. 北京市城市规划设计研究院成立二十周年学术研讨会大会特邀报告：后工业时代产业类历史地段的保护和再生，中国北京，2006年10月25日
2. 中国城市规划学会城市设计学术委员会2007年会主题报告：“产业类历史地段的保护再生”，中国株洲，2007年12月21日
3. 2007深圳香港城市/建筑双城双年展特邀报告：“后工业时代产业类历史建筑的保护再生”，中国深圳，2007年12月22日

工程研究案例：

结合研究课题，研究团队先后开展了杭州创新创业新天地（原杭州重型机械厂）规划设计竞赛、唐山焦化厂地区更新改造（政府委托）、南京7316厂地段城市改造再利用（政府委托）和常州国棉一厂更新改造方案咨询等案例的研究，其中杭州创新创业新天地规划设计是竞赛评选出的两个优秀方案之一，南京7316厂项目已经实施并于2008年11月建成。

高速城市化期城市更新规划理论与技术方法研究

Theory and Technical Method Study on Urban Renewal Planning in Rapid Development Period

国家自然科学基金资助项目(Project of NSF)，2005-2007　项目批准号：50478076
负责人：阳建强
项目组成员：冷嘉伟 孙世界 成斌 罗超 费跃 尹超 祁艳 杜娟 张帆 黄治 倪慧 曹新民 陆敏 赖凌瑶 等

中国正处在高速城市化的重要阶段，城市正面临和正在进行着物质空间和人文空间的重新建构，旧城改建正以空前的规模与速度展开，日益成为我国城市建设的关键问题，亟须拓展城市更新基础理论、规划方法及技术手段。课题针对高速城市化期城市发展呈现的复杂性、不确定性和动态性等显著特征，树立可持续发展思想，在分析现代城市更新运动的思想渊源和政策演变的基础上，选择南京、广州、杭州、安庆、无锡等城市中不同类型的典型案例，研究了高速城市化下旧城空间结构演变的内在机制及相关规律。在把握现阶段城市更新实质的基础上，从城市整体发展角度重点研究了旧城功能结构调整、新旧区发展互动、土地利用结构优化和历史文化环境保护等关键问题，总结了实现旧城空间结构转型的规划措施与有效途径。并基于GIS、VR等数字技术，完成包括规划信息提取、资源分析、评估、建档及旧城空间结构动态模拟、旧城空间变迁分析、城市空间综合评价和形态控制以及旧城市用地开发潜力研究在内的初步技术应用。研究将改变现有的城市更新规划设计思路和技术路线，形成可以应对高速城市化的城市更新规划理论和技术方法，提高城市更新规划的科学性和技术性，促进城市更新的健康与可持续发展。

关键词：城市更新；城市化；高速发展；数字技术；规划理论

Being in an important rapid development period, the old city is meeting a readjustment of physical and humane space, urban renewal increasingly becomes one of main problems of current city construction. Therefore, it is very necessary for us to expand some new theories, approaches and technologies on urban renewal. This project, in view of the complexity, indeterminate and dynamic characteristic on urban renewal, researched the internal mechanism and objective law on old city spatial structure evolution, and also studied some key problems such as mutual reaction between new city and the old city, land-use structure optimization, old city's environmental control, historic protection and so on. Meanwhile, on the basis of GIS and VR, it also attempts to explore some preliminary new-tech applications of old city information drawing, resources evaluation and spatial structure dynamic analogue.

Key words: urban renewal, urbanization, rapid development, digital technology, planning theory

主要研究成果：

1. 发表的主要论文

[1]阳建强，罗超．郑州西部老工业基地更新规划的整体思考．城市规划，2008（6）

[2]阳建强．历史性校园的价值及其保护．城市规划，2006（7）

[3]阳建强．高速城市化期的城市更新研究．城市住宅，2008（7）

[4]阳建强．老工业城市的转型与更新改造．城市发展研究，2008（增刊）

[5]阳建强等．安庆倒扒狮历史文化街区的保护与更新．规划师，2006（10）

[6]阳建强，尹超．基于生态优先的绿色规划设计．城市规划，2005（3）

[7]阳建强．南京古城格局的独特魅力与保护延续．城市规划，2004（12）

[8]阳建强，罗超，曹新民．基于城市整体发展的工业文化遗产保护．建筑创作，2006（9）

[9]阳建强．影响南京古城格局形成的深层文化因素．北京规划建设，2006（4）

[10]阳建强，罗超．广州珠江后航道洋行码头仓库区的保护与再发展，生态文明视野下的城乡规划：2008年中国城市规划学会学术年会论文集，大连：大连出版社，2008（9）

[11]阳建强.江南水乡李市的保护与发展．城市文化国际研讨会暨第二届城市规划国际论坛论文集，中国城市出版社，2007年10月

[12]阳建强．郑州老工业基地的更新与改造.中国城市发展与规划论文集：首届中国城市发展与规划国际年会，中国城市出版社，2006年6月

2. 研究成果获奖

[1]郑州市西部老工业基地调整改造规划国际咨询 国际性规划设计竞赛第一名（18平方千米，2006年5月，郑州市政府），项目负责人：阳建强　主要成员：罗超、成斌、周倜、曹新民、蔡志昶、殷祥瑞、尹莹等

[2]杭州市重型机械厂更新改造规划，全国性规划设计竞赛优胜奖，2007年，项目负责人：阳建强 王建国　成员：罗超、蒋楠、殷祥瑞、王军、王柯、陈海浪等

[3]安庆历史文化名城保护规划，2005年度安徽省优秀城市规划设计一等奖和建设部优秀城市规划设计三等奖，项目负责人：吴明伟 阳建强

渤海国建筑史研究
Research on the History of Bohai Kingdom Architecture

国家自然科学基金资助项目(Project of NSF)，2005～2007　项目批准号：50478070
负责人:张十庆

本项目为建筑研究所张十庆教授负责的国家自然科学基金资助项目，研究的对象是以渤海国建筑为中心的东北亚建筑史。

渤海国是唐朝时在我国东北及朝鲜北部地区建立的隶属于唐朝的地方民族政权，其建筑是以中国为核心的东亚建筑文化圈的重要组成部分。本研究是以东亚建筑整体为视野，对渤海国建筑历史进行的相关研究，并在东亚建筑文化圈的背景下将其与唐朝、日本、新罗以及高句丽、辽的建筑加以比较与分析，以探讨其相互间的文化传播关系。研究的重点是律令制度传播影响下的都城、宫室制度以及佛教文化传播影响下的佛教建筑。此外，本项目研究还拓展至东亚背景下的高句丽、唐宋相关建筑史问题的专题研究。本研究对于推进东方建筑研究、弥补中国建筑史的薄弱环节，以及深化和探讨中国建筑史的整体研究，都具有重要意义。本研究是东方建筑研究领域上的新成果，是目前学界关于东亚视野下渤海国建筑史及其相关史研究的最主要的研究成果。

目前主要的研究成果有：发表相关论文10篇，已完成及正在进行的相关博士学位论文4篇，完成相关建筑遗产保护研究1项，以及若干后续成果。

已完成及正在进行中的博士论文：

乔迅翔. 宋代建筑营造技术基础研究[D]. 南京：东南大学博士学位论文，2005. 10

陈涛. 渤海国上京龙泉府建筑研究[D]. 南京：东南大学博士学位论文（进行中）

张明皓. 高句丽中后期宫殿建筑研究[D]. 南京：东南大学博士学位论文（进行中）

谢鸿权. 东亚视野下的宋元建筑研究[D]. 南京：东南大学博士学位论文（进行中）

已发表的相关论文：

张十庆. 建筑与家具——家具结构与风格的建筑化发展[J]. 室内，2005(4)

张十庆. 部分与整体——中国古代建筑模数制发展的两大阶段[J]. 建筑史(21)，2005(7)

张十庆. 是比例关系还是模数关系——关于法隆寺建筑尺度规律的再探讨[J]. 建筑师(117)，2005(10)

张十庆. 甪直保圣寺大殿复原探讨[J]. 文物，2005(11)

张十庆. 关于胡床、绳床与曲录[J]. 室内，2006(6)

张十庆. 北构南相——初祖庵大殿现象分析[J]. 建筑史(22)，2006(8)

张十庆. 南宋径山寺法堂复原探讨[J]. 文物，2007(3)

张十庆. 从建构思维看古代建筑结构的类型与演化[J]. 建筑师(126)，2007(4)

张明皓. 论安岳三号墓的建筑渊源[J]. 北方文物，2007(4)

相关建筑遗产保护研究：

国家重点文保单位高句丽罗通山城保护规划研究。国家文物局专家评审、通过。

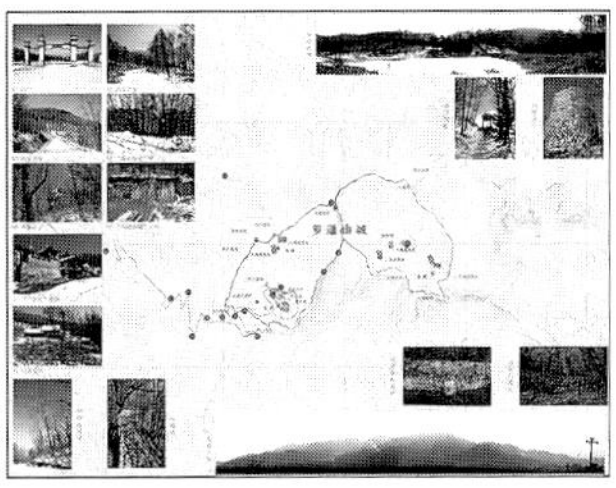

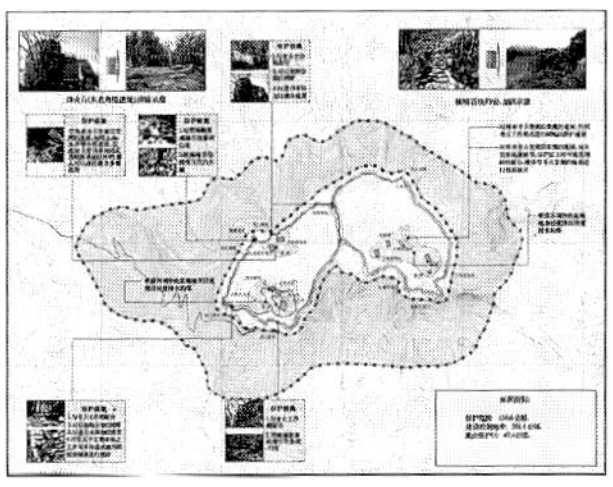

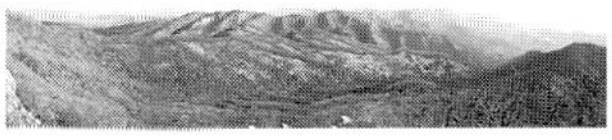

This program,supported by National Natural Science Foundation of China,is in the charge of Prof. Zhang Shiqing RIA.This is a part of oriental architecture research which belongs to basic theory research. The Bohai kingdom (AD698-926) was a local power submitted to the Tang Dynasty, in northeast China and the northern part of D.P.R. Korea, the architecture of which was an important part of the East Asia Architectural Culture Sphere with China as its core.

In the view of the whole East Asia, this program carried out the research on the history of the Bohai kingdom architecture, and analyzed the culture communication in the East Asia Architectural Culture Sphere by comparing the architecture of Bohai kingdom with the Tang dynasty, Japan, Xinluo, Gaogouli and the Liao dynasty. The research focused on the regulation of the capital cities and the royal palaces controlled by the Statutes System of Tang dynasty, and buddhist monasteries in the spreading of Buddhism. Furthermore, some special research topics about the Gaogouli architecture and the Tang-Song architecture were outspread in the background of East Asia. The effort of this program made contributions to improving the oriental architecture, to making up the weak part of Chinese architectural history, and to deepening it as a whole. The program was a new achievement on oriental architecture, and up to now it was the most important achievement from the point of view of the whole East Asia in the research of architectural history of Bohai kingdom and others related.

For this program, 10 papers have been published, and 4 dissertations for the PHD degree have been fulfilled or now being carried out, and one project about the heritage conservation of the Bohai architecture related had been finished. Some further research can be expected in recent years.

Published Papers:

Qiao Xunxiang.Basic Research on Techniques of Building House in Song Dynasty[D].PhD,2005(10)

Zhang Shiqing.Architecture and Furniture[J].Interior Design Construction,2005(4)

Zhang Shiqing.Parts and a Whole[J].Treatises on History of Architecture.Vol.21,2005(7)

Zhang Shiqing.Be proportion relationship or modulus relationship -the study on the scale regulation of FaLong Temple buildings again[J].Architect,2005(10)

Zhang Shiqing.A Trial Study on the Restoration of Main Hall of Baosheng Temple[J].Cultural Relics, 2005(11)

Zhang Shiqing.About Huchair Shengchair and Qulu[J].Interior Design Construction,2006(6)

Zhang Shiqing.The analysis of Main Hall of Chuzu'an Temple[J].Treatises on History of Architecture. Vol.22,2006(8)

Zhang Shiqing.The Discussion of the Restoration of the Schoolroom in Jingshan Temple of Nan-song Dynasty[J].Cultural Relics,2007(3)

Zhang Shiqing.The style and evolvement of the structure of ancient building from the aspect of tectonic thinking[J].Architect,2007(4)

Zhang Minghao.Marks on the Origin of No.3 Tomb of Anyue with Architectural View[J].Northern Cultural Relics,2007(4)

Chen Tao.Research on the Zushi Tower in Foguang Temple[J].Cultural Relics.

2006年至2008年主要的横向项目获奖成果
Awards of Works & Practice

序号	成果名称	项目主持人	获奖时间	获奖等级
1	武汉杨春湖地区副中心城市设计	段进，邵润青等	2006	国际竞赛第一名
2	淮安市火车北站周边地区城市设计	段进等	2006	国际竞赛第一名
3	福州市中轴线八一七路段城市设计	刘博敏等	2006	国际竞赛第一名
4	福州市中轴线茶亭街段城市设计	刘博敏等	2006	国际竞赛第一名
5	郑州市西部老工业基地调整改造规划	阳建强等	2006	国际竞赛第一名
6	盐城城南新区市中心城市设计	王建国等	2006	国内竞赛二等奖
7	镇江市新行政中心规划与建筑设计	刘博敏等	2006	国内投标第一名
8	南通市火车站广场城市设计	刘博敏等	2006	国内投标第一名
9	镇江清华山水高档居住区规划	吴明伟，王承慧等	2006	国内投标第一名
10	天目湖新镇百花广场规划设计	孔令龙	2006	国内投标第一名
11	淮安市楚州新中心城市设计	孔令龙	2006	国内投标第一名
12	江宁职业教育中心规划设计	单踊等	2006	国内投标第一名
13	南京宝华山低密度住宅区设计竞赛	周琦，章泉峰，陈思	2006	第一名
14	中国药科大学体育馆设计竞赛	周琦，冯志荣	2006	第一名
15	镇江市南徐新区行政中心设计	俞传飞	2007	国内投标第一名
16	南京尚风尚水低层高密度住宅区规划设计竞赛	周琦，陈思，章泉峰	2007	第一名
17	人民日报社南京国际传媒中心设计竞赛	周琦，杨红波，张力	2007	第一名
18	人民日报社北戴河疗养院改扩建设计竞赛	周琦，张力，朱晓洲	2008	第一名
19	南通钟秀大桥设计竞赛	周琦，东南大学建筑设计院交通分院	2008	第一名

中国近代史博物馆文化服务区设计
Cultural Service Area of Museum for Modern Chinese History

设计：齐康 杨志疆 寿刚等

获2007年全国优秀工程设计银质奖、2005年度建设部优秀勘察设计一等奖

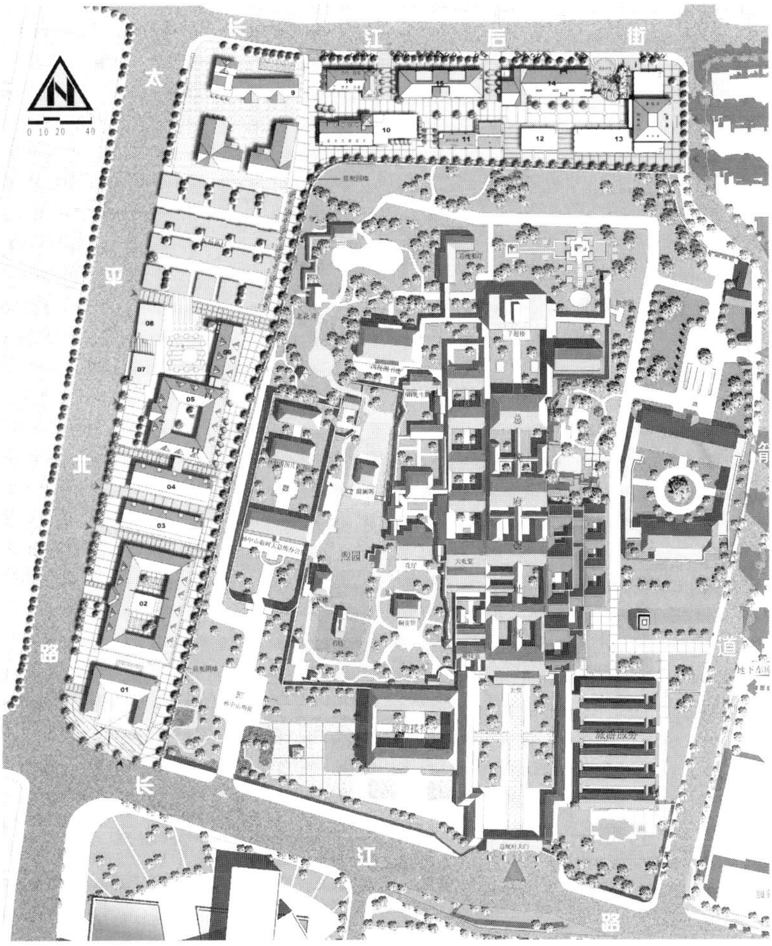

南京森林公安高等专科学校主体建筑群设计
New Campus for Nanjing Institute of Public Forest Security

设计：韩冬青 冷嘉伟 王正 夏兵
获2006年第四届中国建筑学会建筑创作优秀奖

南京森林公安高等专科学校主体建筑群包括图书馆、公共教学楼、实验楼等三幢主体建筑，三者分布在校园主轴线的两侧，其中图书馆、公共教学楼和实验楼围合成校园主广场，成为整个校园的核心。该主体建筑群的布局综合考虑了与校园整体功能、空间环境、交通组织及自然要素的相互协调关系。设计结合自然地形地貌的基本特征形成场地空间的有机变化。三幢主体建筑的造型设计与内在功能的性质相一致，并力求反映该学校的特殊气质。立面处理强调不同材质的理性表达和光影效果。空间、形体和材质上的一体化设计处理为整个校园建立了基本的格调。公共教学楼东北角高耸的塔楼对中心广场乃至整个校区结构起到必要的控制及标识作用。

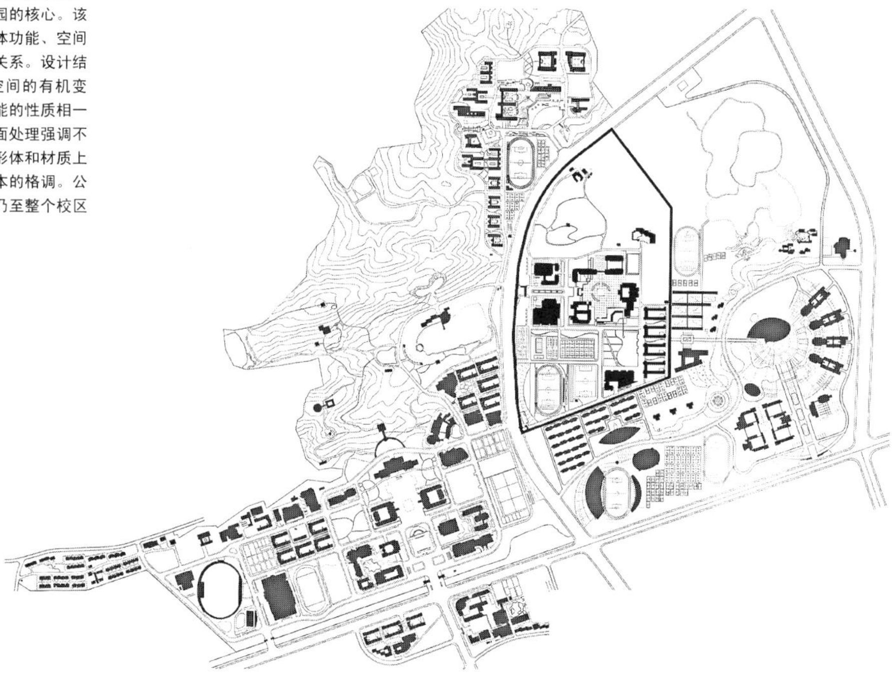

南京森林公安高等专科学校警体馆

New Campus for Nanjing Institute of Public Forest Security

设计：冷嘉伟 韩冬青 刘珏

获2006年建设部优秀勘察设计二等奖

南京森林公安高等专科学校新校区坐落在仙林大学城内。警体馆位于校园主入口空间轴线的南侧，内容包括门厅、一个1100座的比赛馆，六个教学训练馆，一个平战结合、全国最大的室内地下靶场以及体育教研室、器械室等。建筑地上二层，地下局部一层，总建筑面积14450平方米，高度19米。该馆的建设主旨是为在校学员提供一个警务技能训练、体育活动及比赛的场所。警体馆设计根据学校培养模式和教学要求合理组织功能，既反映其自身的建筑特色，又注重融入校园文化的整体氛围。以“简洁、理性、合理”为原则，强调功能和形式的结合与统一，内部和外部空间的和谐与呼应。该馆设计有别于社会公共体育馆，未贪大求全、追求形式，而是切合学校教学育人的实际需要“量体裁衣”，凸显校园体育设施应以教学、锻炼为主的本色。

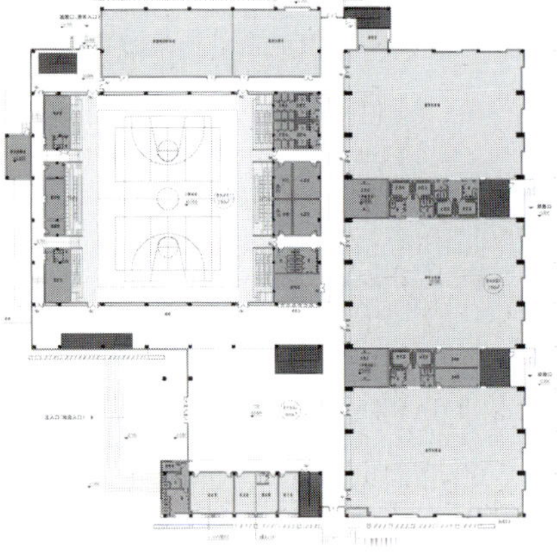

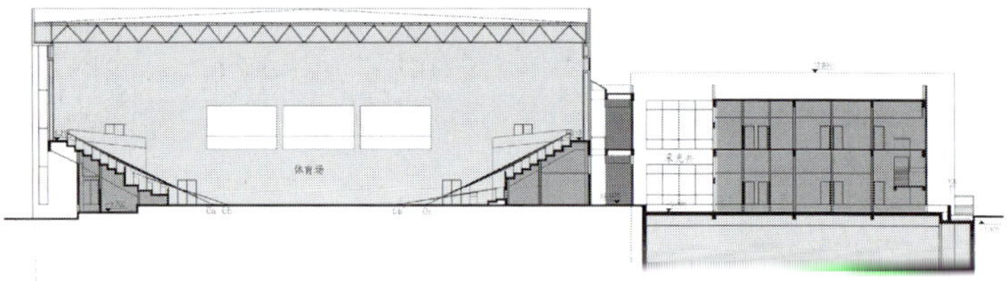

浙江新昌大佛寺景区般若谷景点设计
Da Fo Si Scenic Area, Boruo Vale Landscape Design, ZheJiang Province

设计：杜顺宝 张哲 张麒 杨冬辉等
获2006年建设部优秀勘察设计二等奖、2006年度江苏省优秀工程设计一等奖、2005年度江苏省城乡建设系统优秀勘察设计一等奖

浙江新昌大佛寺景区以大佛寺为核心。新昌大佛寺以南朝石刻大佛著称。这里原是大佛寺景区内几个路边废弃的采石宕口，成为自然景观中人为的疤痕。这种废弃地在我国风景区中很常见，如何利用改造，变废为宝，是景观设计中一个重要的课题。本设计巧妙利用宕口的高差，营造七级瀑布水景。宕口石壁上雕刻南朝三代僧人开凿大佛的历史故事，与景区的文化主题取得呼应。空间上道路两侧的宕口通过地下隧洞连结为一个完整的游览序列。

本景点设计的社会意义在于利用废弃地段改造为景点，可以节约土地资源，减少材料与资金的投入，有利于环境保护。景点于2001年建成开放，获得社会各界和国内外游客的广泛好评。

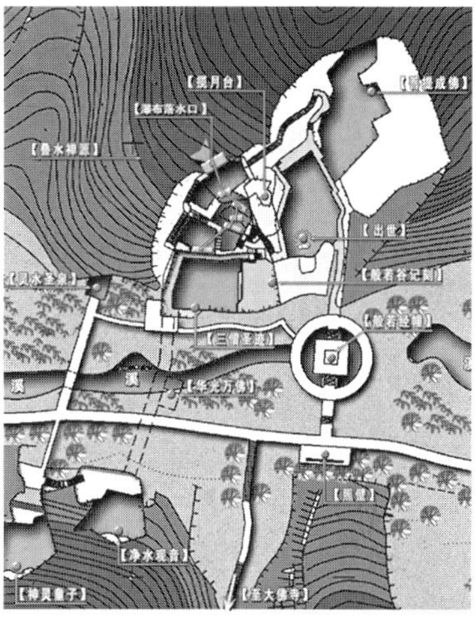

苏州环古城风貌保护工程西段详细规划设计

Detailed Planning of West District of Old-City-Ring Landscape Conservations, Suzhou

规划设计：段进 徐春宁 张麒

获2006年建设部优秀勘察设计一等奖、2006年度江苏省优秀工程设计一等奖、2005年度江苏省城乡建设系统优秀勘察设计一等奖

本次规划是城市规划设计研究院苏州环古城风貌保护规划全国竞标中选方案的延续和深化，其中西段强调“金阊十里、盘门水城”的地域主题、解决古城保护与新城发展交接处的各种矛盾、创造苏州古城保护协调区的特色是本次规划的主要构思。

按规划实施后的环古城地区，社会反应良好，先后受到包括贝聿铭、多位院士以及世界遗产中心在内的国内外专家、机构的好评，还被苏州民众评为“美丽新苏州”十大工程之首。

钟山风景名胜区中山陵园风景区详细规划
Planning of the National Park of DR. Sun Yatsen's Mausoleum

规划设计：吴明伟、杨红伟、罗仁朝、邵润青、鞠德东、张帆、朱生树、胡虹
获2006年建设部优秀勘察设计三等奖、2006 年度江苏省优秀工程设计二等奖、2005年度江苏省城乡建设系统优秀勘察设计二等奖

中山陵园风景区是国家重点风景名胜区——钟山风景名胜区的主体部分，陵园山水雄秀兼得，文化历史悠久，拥有世界文化遗产——明孝陵，著名人文景观——中山陵等众多名胜古迹。鉴于中山陵园是一个发展比较成熟的风景区，其主要矛盾在于大量驻区单位、农民住区的无序发展对景观环境的负面影响，因而加强风景名胜资源的系统性保护与风景区环境整治成为本规划的重点。

规划项目组创造性运用控制性规划方法，对六大景区开展系统研究，明确保护、利用的方式与措施，架构了风景区控规指标体系，推动风景区的可持续发展。

部分已实施项目位置示意

中山陵景区规划总图

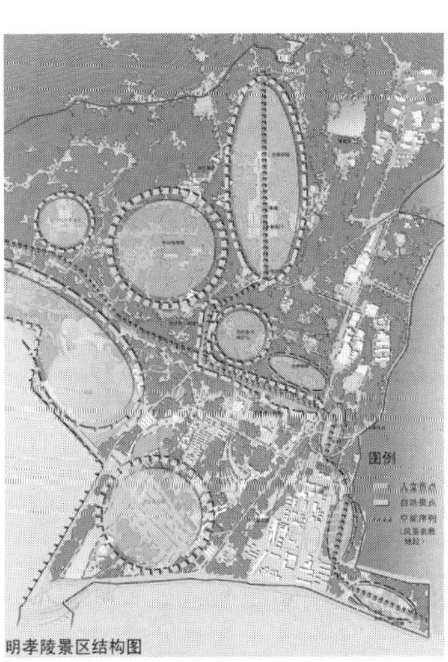

明孝陵景区结构图

风景区规划总平面图

嘉兴市环城河沿线景观城市设计

Urban Design of Ring Water System Around Jiaxing City

设计：段进 季松 张麒等

获2008年度江苏省优秀工程设计一等奖、2007年度江苏省城乡建设系统优秀勘察设计一等奖

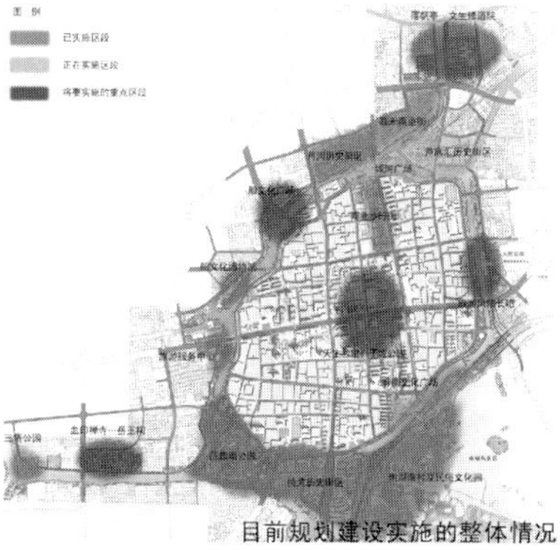

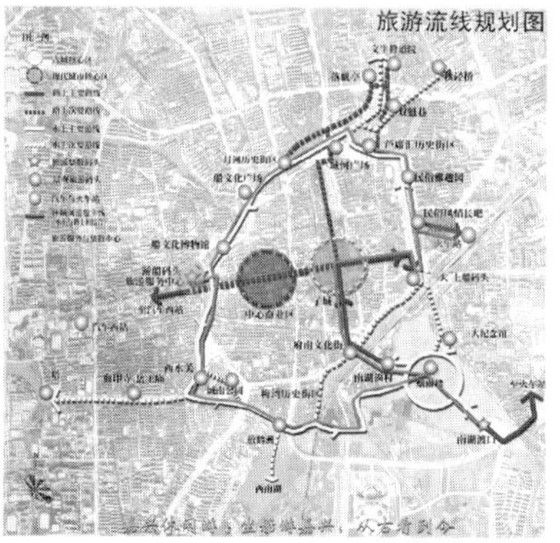

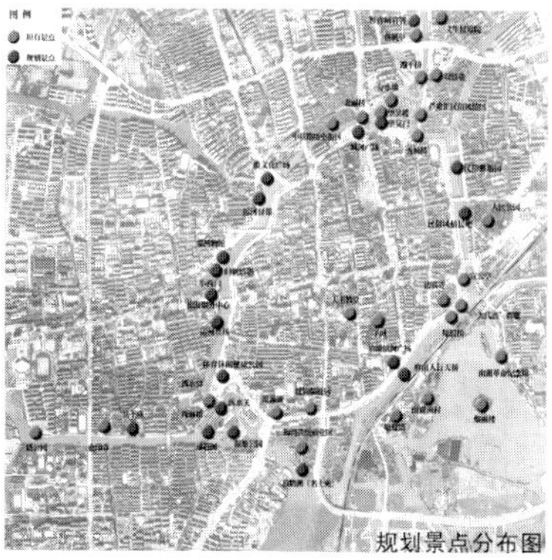

嘉兴是我国著名历史文化名城，形成于东汉，因京杭大运河而兴盛，成为南北交通要冲，水运必经之地。“一河八塘三湖”的水系资源奠定了城市“环形加放射”这一独特的江南水乡古城格局。然而，在当今快速城市化的时期，环城河地区逐渐衰败，2000年，嘉兴市政府对环城河沿线进行大力整治，形成了基本贯通全线的绿地空间，环境与景观得到了极大的改善。但是，由于活动安排欠缺、流线组织不畅、设施配套不足、文化氛围较弱等原因，环城河沿线景观带 “好看不好用”，空间使用效率低。针对现存问题，发挥现有资源优势，本次规划设计主要进行了以下几方面的创新与探索。

1. 综合物质与非物质文化遗产进行情景设计，构筑地方特色水城空间；
2. 整合公共空间与主题活动，提升空间使用效率；
3. 重视各类历史遗存的保护与有机更新，形成多元化的景观风貌；
4. 强化旅游系统的水乡特色和休闲功能，打造品牌旅游；
5. 强制控制与弹性引导相结合，确保规划的实效性。

整治后的月河历史街区沿河景观

整治后的月河历史街区鸟瞰

建成后的“船文化带”鸟瞰

改造后的范蠡湖公园鸟瞰

安徽大学新校区修建性详细规划

Site Plan of the New Campus of An Hui University

设计：段进 陈晓东等

获2008年度江苏省优秀工程设计一等奖、2007年度江苏省城乡建设系统优秀勘察设计一等奖

规划以“保护生态、构筑系统、发展人文”的理念为指导，结合现状特殊的景观与地形条件，采用轴线空间、分组团、生态化的空间布局手法，创造富有特色的大学校园，并进行了以下的创新探索：

1. 人与自然共生的结构：

因地制宜的尊重现状条件，延续“指状”地形特点，创造人工与自然两大系统共生的结构，确立校园空间形态，化不利为特色。

2. 生态景观的设计手法：

利用地段生态优势，空间组景利用各种原生态自然要素并借景丽人湖，创造生态湖景校园。

3. 有机生长的发展模式：

依特殊的用地形态，结合功能和用地特点，建构有机联系的组团化结构，创造可持续发展校园。

4. 大学精神的公共场所：

突出人文传统和人际交流，设置师生交往活动带和室外交流场所，创造大学校园精神。

5. 全过程的城市设计：

强调规划成果与实施过程的衔接，通过全过程的服务与介入，保证规划思想的落实。

江苏省洪泽县文化中心设计
Hongze County Cultural Center, Jiang Su Province

设计：钟训正 韩冬青 徐静等

获2006年度江苏省江苏省城乡建设系统优秀勘察设计一等奖、2006年度优秀工程设计二等奖

洪泽县文化中心坐落在江苏省洪泽县城新城的中心区，西侧与新建绿化广场隔路相望，北临快速干道东九道，东侧与南侧均为新区待开发地块。该项目规划用地面积58600平方米，总建筑面积15610平方米。

该项目综合了展览中心、会议、表演、文化娱乐、县图书馆、博物馆、青少年活动中心及文化局办公等众多功能。对于苏北发展中的县城来说，这种集大成的综合建设策略，十分吻合其文化生活需求与经济实力状况。因此，这种综合类型成为具有类似经济文化背景的苏北县级城市文化设施建设的新模式。这项设计面临的最大挑战就在于如何使上述各项功能既能各就各位、各得其所，又能够相互补充，彼此间构成场所资源的共享。为此，总平面布局集合了集中式布局与分散式布局两种类型的优势，将展览与会议及表演区相对独立，其余各项功能围绕一个内庭院形成围合式布局，既有利于各功能群组独立出入，各自形成自我完整的区域，并与相应的室外场地形成自然的功能渗透，同时又能够集约利用服务性设施。该布局也有利于各种功能空间实现最大限度的自然通风和采光，分体式空调仅作为一种补充性设施，这一点对于经济欠发达的小城市来说，是一种尽量降低建筑能耗及维护费用的重要策略。

建筑造型吻合于其内部功能的组织方式，并直率且恰当地表达了结构技术的基本特征，灰色面砖加白色线条及细部的处理意在表现苏北水乡城镇的文化气质，垂直向的钟楼与水平向的形体构成一种富有力度的对比，配合场地空间的组织，较好地实现了文化中心的标识性，并有利于引导公共人流自然地进入其活动场所。

The Hongze County cultural center is located in the central area of Hongze County Metro. The project integrated the exhibition center, conferences, performances, cultural entertainment, county libraries, museums, youth centers and Culture office, and many other features.To the North Jiangsu in the development of the county, such a master of building a comprehensive strategy, very inosculates its cultural life and economic strength of demand conditions. The shape of building inosculates its internal functions of the organization, the expression of the basic features of the structure is clear. The performance in details is intended to deal with urban culture in North Jiangsu quality.

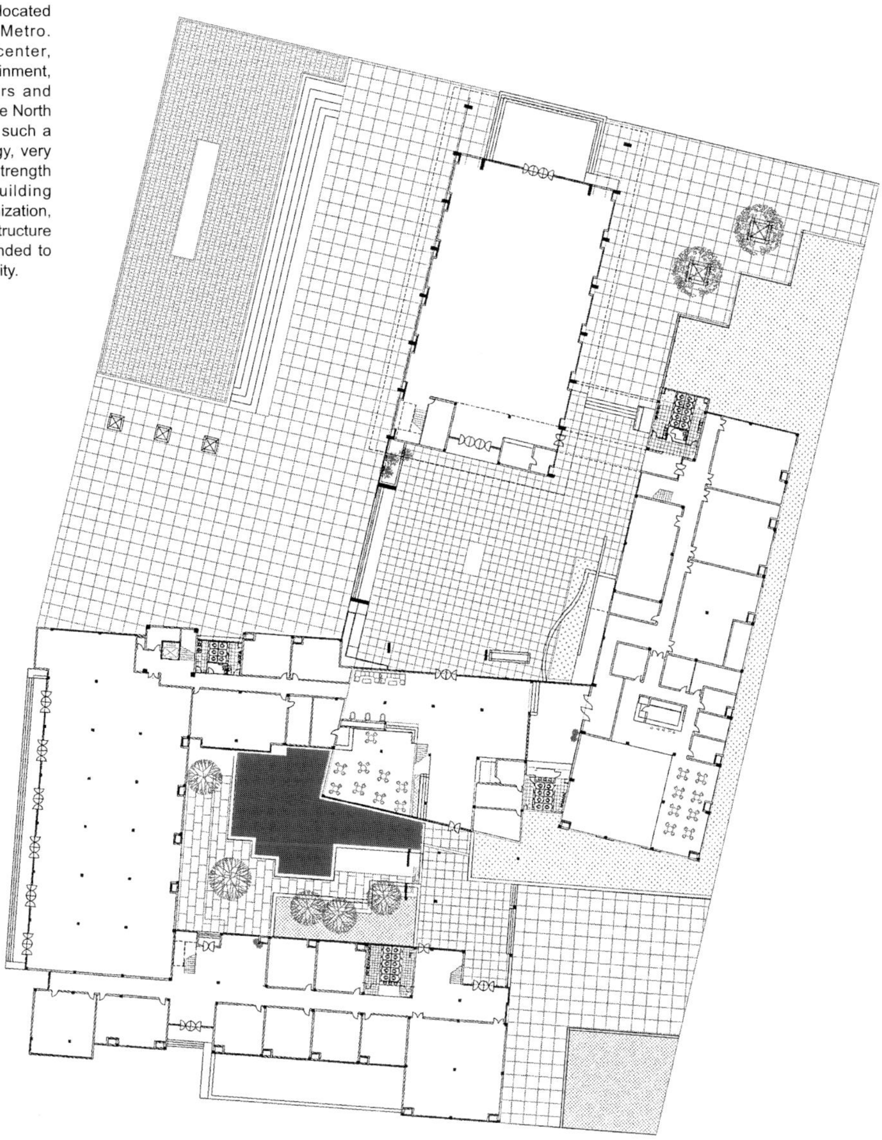

金坛市沙湖村村庄建设规划

Planning for New Village Development in Jintan, Jiangsu

规划设计：刘博敏 姚迪 徐冰华 晋劲 李凯 倪冶

获2006年度江苏省优秀工程设计一等奖、2006年度江苏省城乡建设系统优秀勘察设计一等奖

沙湖村位于金坛西港镇北部，距镇2.6千米，现有330人，150户，规划总人口830人，332户，总建设用地面积10.6公顷。现状建设分散、质量差，缺少环境卫生设施、硬质路面、公共活动设施与场所，原有地域的水乡特色正在消失。规划恢复水系活力，保持水网村落的环境特色，保持村庄发展的生命力。

在发展形态上，立足于老村整治与新村发展协同，引导农民向新村集聚，整体提高村庄环境质量与村民生活水平。规划立足于现实整治建设的经济可能性，按村庄发展中需求项目的重要性进行分类，建立菜单式、可选择的实施项目，以求在不同的初始投入条件下，都能保证建设规划实施与工作推进。农民住宅按照村民的生活生产方式，设计为联排式与公寓式住宅模式，其中联排式住宅以现状农民住宅功能空间结构为基础，形成宅、院、辅助空间组成的独立单元，具有较强的灵活性。在住宅单元组合的基础上，以空间变化丰富的街巷为基础，构成住宅群落，街巷连接节点处形成广场，提供村民户外公共活动场所，形成富有变化、反映地方特色的村庄环境形象。

Shahu village is located in the north of the Xigang town in Jintan, 2.6 km from the town. The existing population is 330, 150 families, and the planning population is about 830, 332 families, with a total area of 10.6 hectares of land for construction purposes.

The planning for Shahu village development tries to set up a new style village settlement which can inherit the local cultural and environmental characteristics, and adapt for the sustainable developmental demand. The housing design is based on the traditional local house space, including building, courtyard and auxiliary space, which is suitable for different living and farming activities.

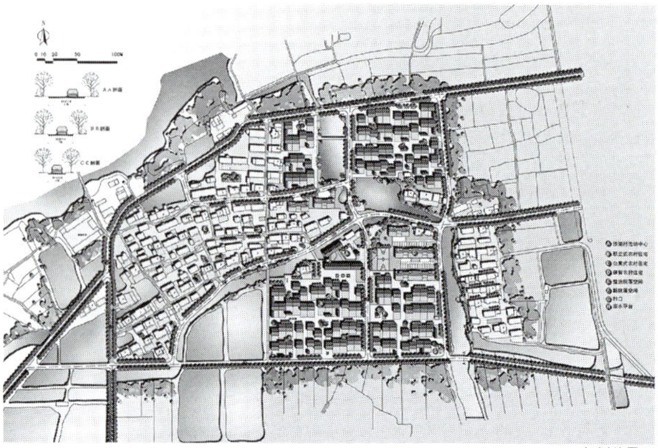

规划总平面

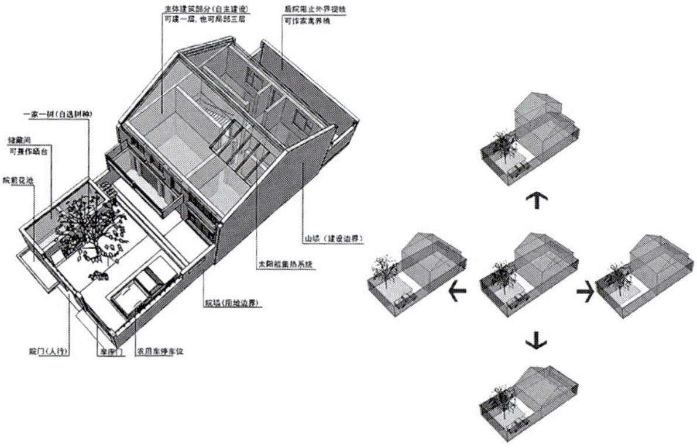

建筑单元空间示意图

村庄建设整治规划意向图

蚌埠医学院新校区修建性详细规划

Site plan on the new campus of Bengbu Medical College

规划设计：段进　邵润青等

获2006年度江苏省优秀工程设计二等奖、2006年度江苏省城乡建设系统优秀勘察设计二等奖

蚌埠医学院新校区面积45公顷，规划学生8000人。规划提出了“集约校园、活力空间”的设计理念。方案通过加强校园与城市、校园与自然、校园与师生以及校园各部分之间的互动，形成一个面向城市整体，融入绿色生机、体现人文精神、空间组织有机、富有独特魅力的活力校园。

按规划实施后的蚌埠医学院新校区，受到蚌埠医学院师生员工、兄弟院校和蚌埠市领导的普遍赞扬。

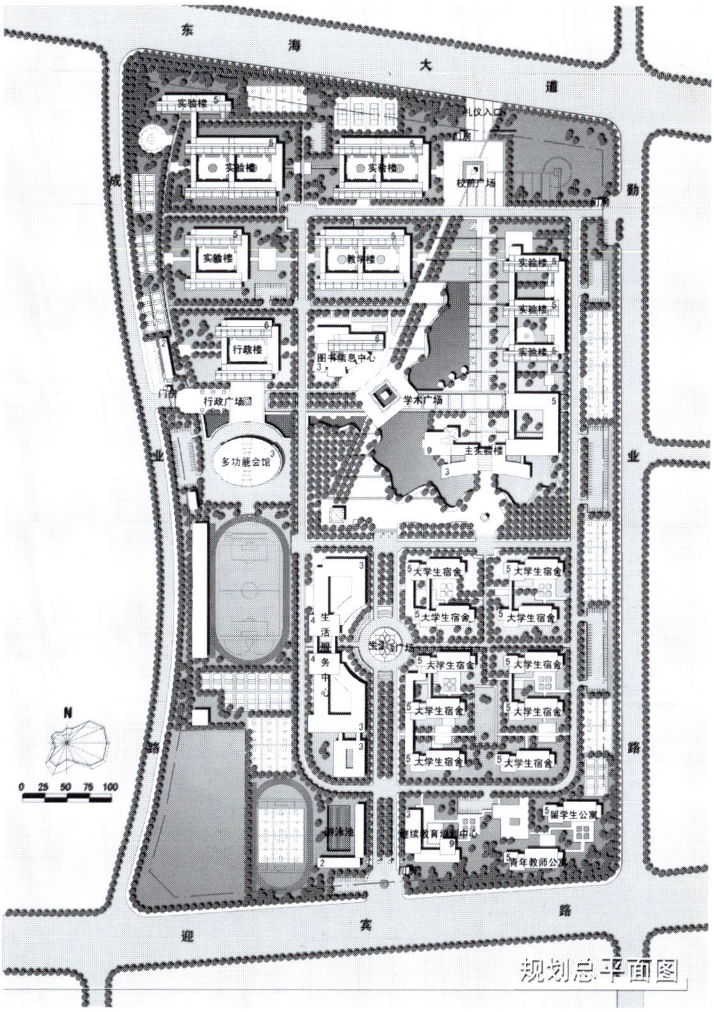

规划总平面图

徐州市汉兵马俑博物馆设计

Museum of the Terra-cotta Warriors and Horses of Han Dynasty, Xuzhou

设计：齐康 张宏 周曦

获2008年度江苏省优秀工程设计二等奖、2007年度江苏省城乡建设系统优秀勘察设计二等奖

徐州市汉兵马俑博物馆（以下简称博物馆）为中国遗址性博物馆，位于江苏省徐州市东郊狮子山西麓。建筑用地面积19380平方米，主体建筑两层，总建筑面积6706平方米，是集保护、陈列、研究、文化休闲为一体的博物馆建筑。

汉兵马俑兵阵，是全国文物保护单位。建筑基地三面环水，地势较低。原老展馆为临时性展馆，将其拆除后建新博物馆。为了保持兵马俑兵阵的真实环境，文物在原地不动的情况下，进行博物馆的施工建设，使工程难度大大提高。也正因如此，设计考虑保护性施工的特殊要求，采用相应设计措施，设计与施工密切配合，使该项目顺利完成并形成了特色。

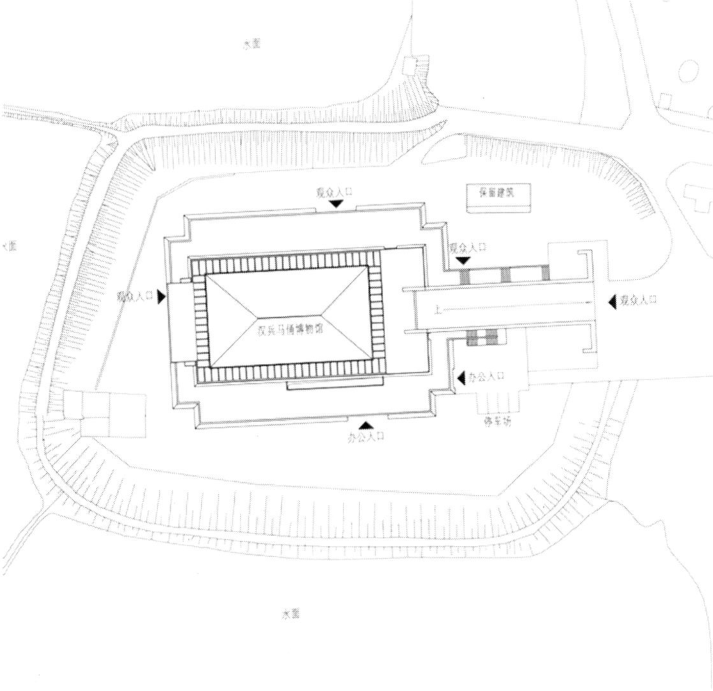

镇江市人防办地面指挥中心

Conduction Center of Civil Air Defense in Zhenjiang

设计：齐康 张宏 张振辉

获2008年度江苏省优秀工程设计二等奖、2007年度江苏省城乡建设系统优秀勘察设计二等奖

该建筑离市区较远，位于山林之间，周围绿化环境良好。基地坐落于向阳的山坡上且无建筑物遮挡，利于冬季获得更多太阳辐射热，且为利用自然光照创造了条件。基地西面为坡地且遍植绿化，起到了很好的遮阳作用，夏季利于降低建筑小环境的温度。

设计整体采用半圆形的平面围合和园林式的内院组合形式，为原本单调的办公空间增加了情趣，且为营造舒适的建筑小环境创造了可能性。利用建筑朝向，平面、剖面布置，局部处理等方面的设计策略，以达到对自然资源的充分利用。

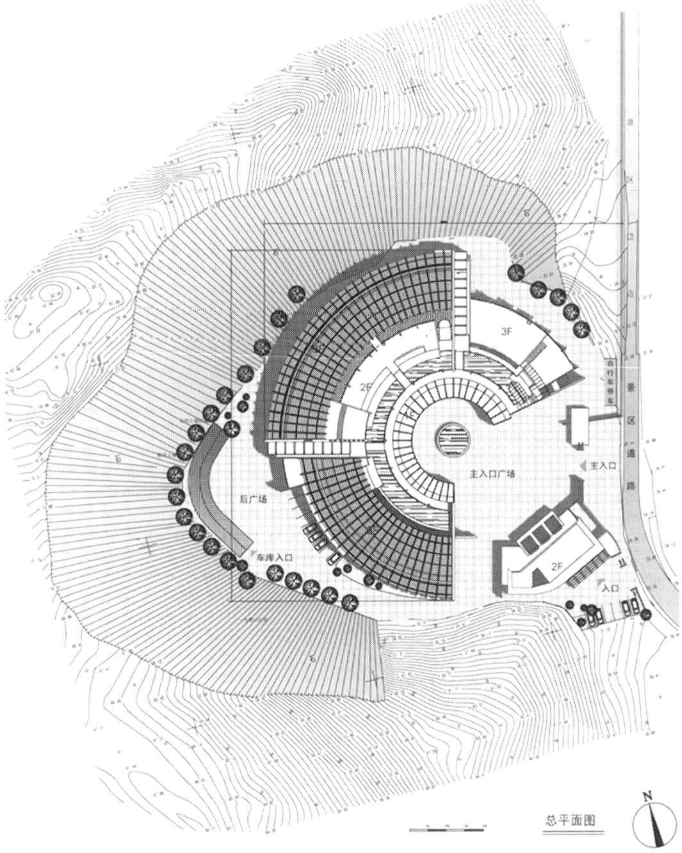

总平面图

江苏省大丰市二卯酉河景观设计
Landscape Design of the Ermaoyou River, Dafeng, Jiangsu

设计：成玉宁

获2008年度江苏省优秀工程设计二等奖、2007年度江苏省城乡建设系统优秀勘察设计二等奖

二卯酉河作为一条人工开挖形成的河道，其历史不过百余年，但对于仅有50年建城历史的大丰而言却又是城市发展历史的见证，二卯酉河及其他人工河道不仅仅在历史上发挥过重要作用，也影响着今天乃至未来大丰的城市发展，业已成为该城市景观特征的重要组成部分。保护好城市既有的纵横正交水网景观特色，使之融入新城市空间，并且成为城市景观体系的基本框架，对于大丰城市景观形态构成具有重要意义。本项目深刻发掘地缘文化，充分解读地景形态，运用全新的方式将具有农田沟渠格局的地景特征加以提炼保留并融入城市新景观体系中，使观者能够体会到地景的变迁历程。延续与强化固有的场地肌理，为行将消失的地景记谱，藉此以强化城市滨水地段景观特征的可识别性。景观带渗透南北相邻地块与河道，与新城区有机结合，成为联系相邻城市空间的重要纽带。风光带中景观节点的设置充分考虑道路、河道、视线的对位，将南北的视轴线引入二卯酉河及两岸绿地，充分利用线性景观空间的优秀，建构“简洁、明快、充满生机、富于动感”的新区城市景观新秩序。

Ermaoyou River,which was excavated by manual work,is just about a hundred years.But it is very important to the Dafeng City,which was built only half a hundred years ago,because the river not only played an important role in the history,but also affects the future of Dafeng City development. At the same time,the river has already become an important part of the city landscape characteristics.Protecting the orthogonal city water network landscape features and fit it into the new city space and urban landscape system become the basic framework for the landscape patterns of Dafeng City. This project explores the profound geo-culture, fully interpretates landscape patterns,and uses new methods to make farmland ditches landscape characteristics of the pattern of reservations to be refined and integrated into the new city landscape system.

山东省平邑县城市总体规划（2004～2020）
Master Plan of Pingyi County, Shandong Province

规划设计：孔令龙 王兴平 权亚玲 王海卉 靳涛
获2006年度江苏省优秀工程设计三等奖、2006年度江苏省城乡建设系统优秀勘察设计三等奖

《山东省平邑县城市总体规划（2004-2020）》，规划2020年县域总人口105万人、城市化水平55%、城市人口规模36万、城市用地规模38平方千米。

规划依据科学发展要求，立足当地实际，遵循科学规划、城乡和谐、有序发展、开放整合的原则，对平邑县从区域、县域和城市三个层次进行系统分析与规划，科学制定了“建设具有特色的新平邑”和城市转型发展的战略、日标与空间布局。

本规划于2005年8月编制完成，2006年3月按法定程序经临沂市政府批准实施。自批准以来，不断推进着平邑县城乡规划与建设工作向科学化、制度化、规范化发展，对其产业经济发展战略，蒙山旅游的保护和开发，区域保护和发展的强制性措施，县城的城市功能完善、优美的人居环境创建、旧城改造和新区建设等方面均起到了积极的指导作用，同时对县的经济发展及和谐社会的创建形成了巨大的推动力。

用地规划

近期规划

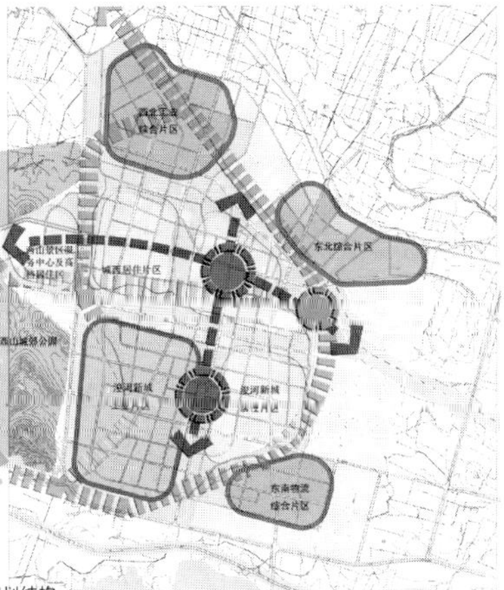

规划结构

淮安市文庙—慈云寺历史文化风貌区详细规划
Detailed Planning of the Historic Conservation Area of Wenmiao and Ciyunsi, Huai'an City

规划设计：孔令龙 巢耀明等

获2006年度江苏省优秀工程设计三等奖、2006年度江苏省城乡建设系统优秀勘察设计三等奖

规划在全面和充分调查与评价规划区历史文化资源、建筑质量与风貌、街巷网络与空间肌理以及存在问题的基础上，从城市总体发展战略高度对其进行科学的功能定位，确定发展目标——将其规划建设成为淮安市运河文化长廊中集历史文化资源展示、宗教活动、商业及休闲旅游等功能于一体的历史文化风貌区和文化旅游区。

规划坚持“科学保护、适度发展与合理利用”的设计宗旨，将历史文化资源的保护、利用与展示相结合。以历史文化资源的有效保护带动和促进文化旅游与商业的发展，以文化旅游和商业的发展进一步带动和促进文化资源的挖掘与延续。

规划确立“生态优先”、“以人为本”、“多元文化共生”的设计理念；恢复里运河生态长廊，融入里运河和楚秀园生态绿化开放空间。以人为本，建构多元文化共生的物质空间载体，使传统文化与当代文化共存。

Based on the adequate investigation and appreciation of the reconstruction zone(historical and cultural resources, architectural quality and feature, streets and lanes systems, space texture and other problems), based on the city's development strategy, this planning determines the goals of development -- to be an area of historic conservation and cultural tourism, in that area people appreciate the magic of the historical and cultural resources, religious activity, business and leisure.

This planning insists on the design tenet of "scientific protection, moderate development and rational utilization", combines the protection with utilization and display of historical and cultural resources. We advocate effective protection of historical and cultural resources in order to drive the development of cultural tourism and commerce, and the development will further promote the excavation and continuation of cultural resources.

This planning establishes the design concept of "ecology first ", "people-oriented", "multi-cultural symbiosis" in order to restore the ecological corridor of the canal. In this process, the reconstruction zone merges into the ecological open space of the canal and Chuxiu Park. We construct material space carrier of multi-cultural symbiosis, in which the traditional culture can coexist with contemporary culture.

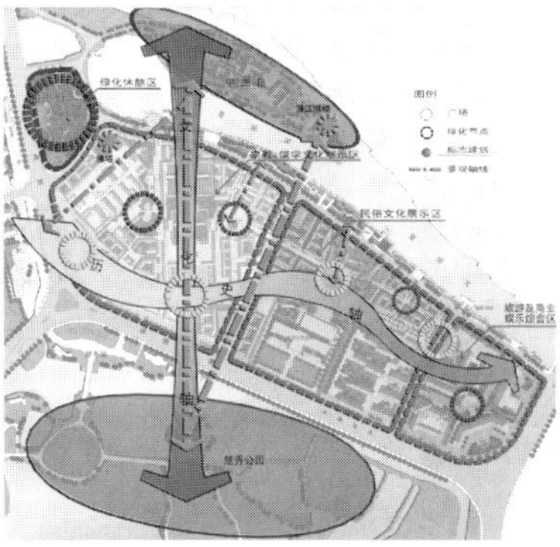

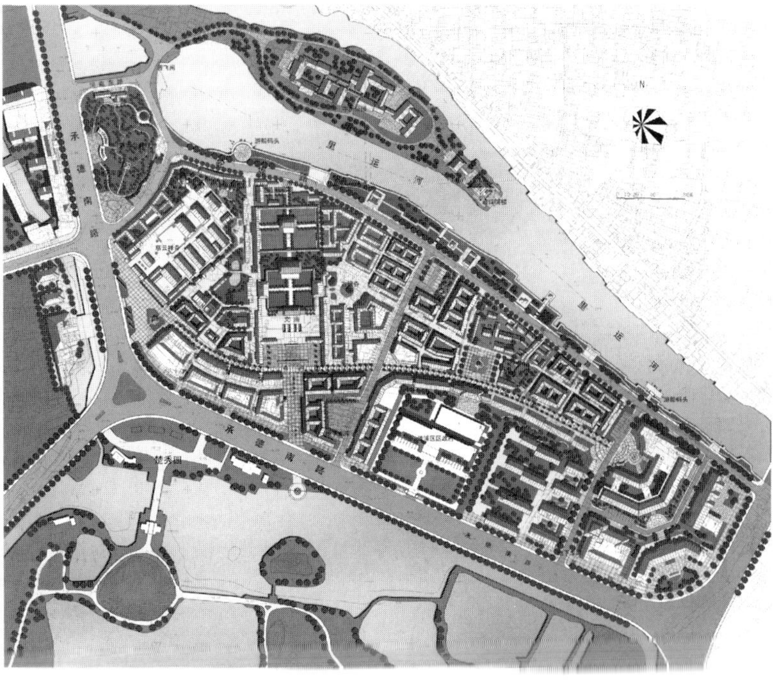

南京大行宫市民广场景观设计
Daxinggong Plaza Landscape Design, Nanjing

设计：杨东辉
获2008年度江苏省优秀工程设计三等奖、2007年度江苏省城乡建设系统优秀勘察设计三等奖

大行宫市民广场位于南京市总统府的正南面，2005年建设完成。它既是为市民、游客使用的广场，同时也具有展现民国历史文化的作用。

广场围绕两条主要轴线展开，一条是历史文化轴线，位于总统府南门，主要展现总统府从清、太平天国、民国等不同的历史文化；另一条是当代文化轴线，位于图书馆一侧，主要展现与图书馆文化氛围相适应的现代文化。

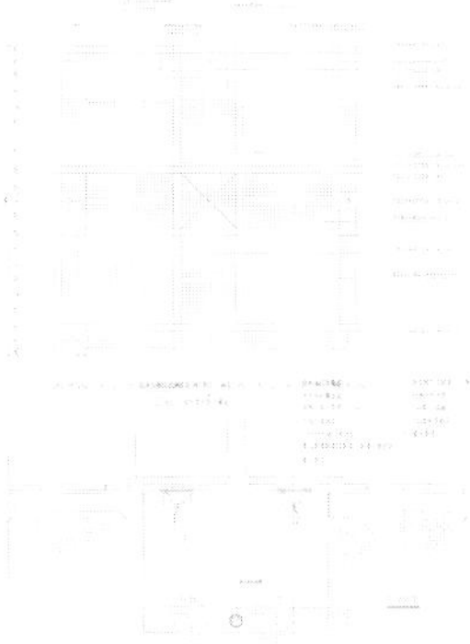

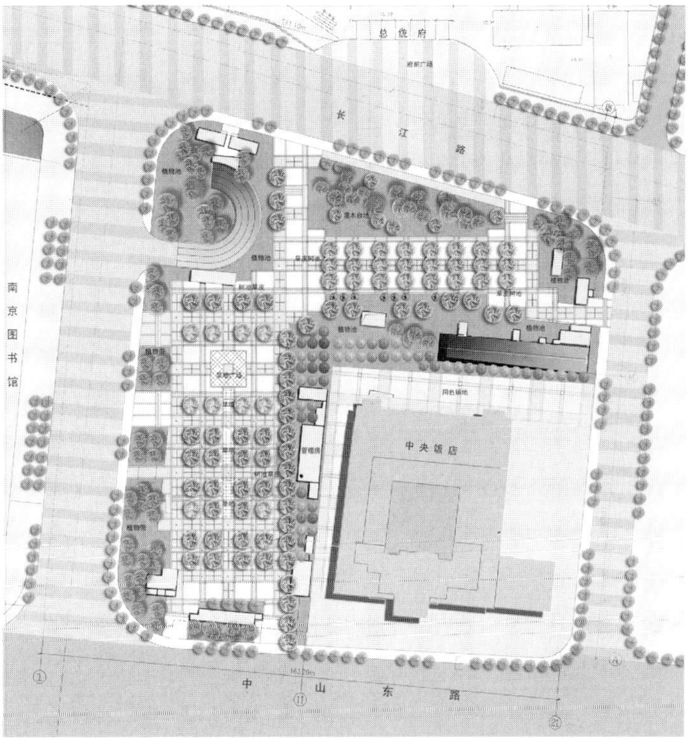

南京大石湖生态旅游度假区规划设计

Plan of Nanjing Dashihu Eco-tourism Resort

规划设计：成玉宁

获2006年南京市优秀旅游规划设计二等奖

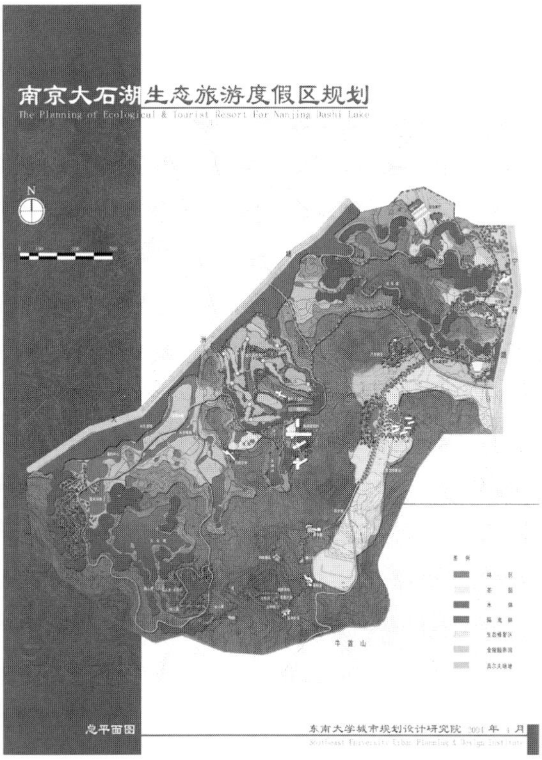

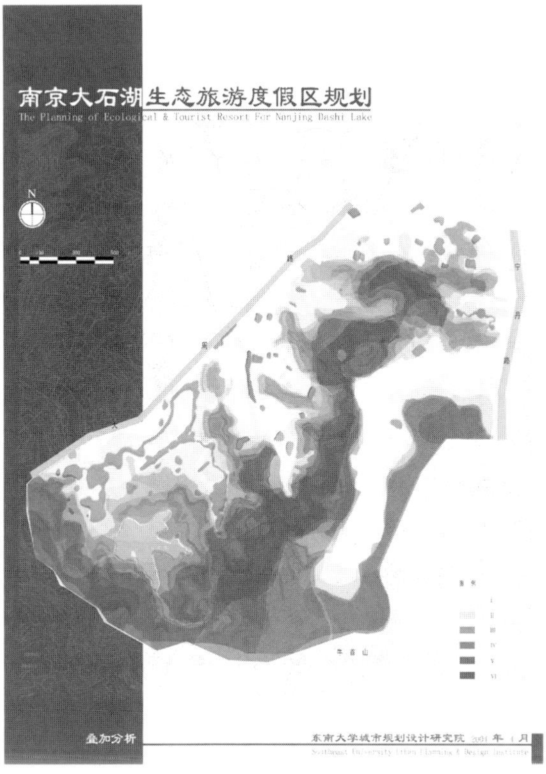

南京大石湖生态旅游度假区位于南京市郊牛首-祖堂风景区内，基地地处牛首山北麓，东侧与将军山风景区隔宁丹路相望，北侧毗邻外秦淮河风光带。本区域规划以维护并丰富生态自然景观为主，以突出自然山林、湖溪为景观特色。该区域的建成，将以独具特色的自然景观及休闲游憩项目丰富南京旅游度假文化内涵。

Nanjing Dashihu eco-tourism resort is located on the outskirts of Nanjing, in the Niushou-Zutang in scenic areas, the base is located in the northern foot of Niushou mountain.To the eastern side of the resort is the Jiangjun Mountain, and on the north side of it is the Qinhuai belt. The regional plan protects and enriches the natural landscape ecology in order to to highlight the landscape features of the natural forests and Lake Creek. The project has been a unique one with natural landscape and abundant leisure activities in Nanjing.

杭州市重型机械厂更新改造规划
Renewal and Renovation of Hangzhou Heavy Machinery Works

规划设计：阳建强 王建国等
获全国性规划设计竞赛优胜奖

杭州重型机械厂建于1958年，是大型国有重型机械加工企业，在杭州的工业结构中占有突出的重要地位，在建国初期至20世纪末一直都是杭州加工行业中的支柱企业，在几十年的发展历程中为国家作出了突出贡献。目前，城市建设的空间需求与企业的升级转型成为城市功能调整的契机。更新改造规划结合区域发展、产业选择和城市文化，拟在原杭州重型机械厂搬迁后的土地上规划建设一个环境优美、交通便利、设施先进、产业现代、服务完善，并且集文化娱乐、商业休闲、总部商务、科研孵化、都市工业为一体的多功能城市副中心。地段浓缩了杭州近现代工业化的历史进程，具有一定的历史价值。设计在客观翔实评价的基础上，确定了老工业建筑的存留，同时结合原有的厂区空间，通过精心组织，融合新的城市中心功能，形成特色鲜明的城市公共活动空间。针对城市副中心的功能特征，在保护和再利用历史遗产的前提下，很好地解决了与地块开发容积率之间的矛盾。

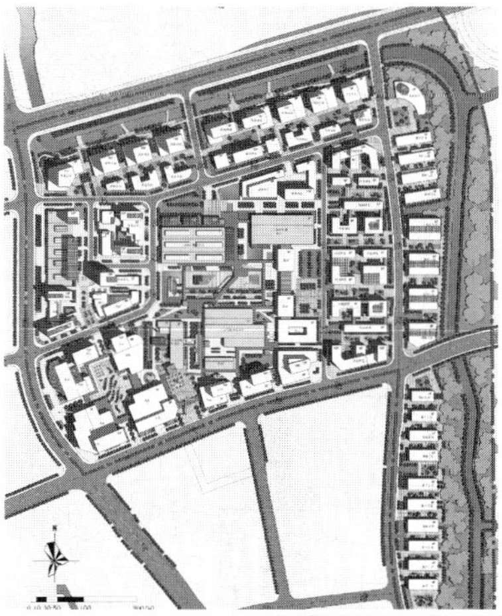
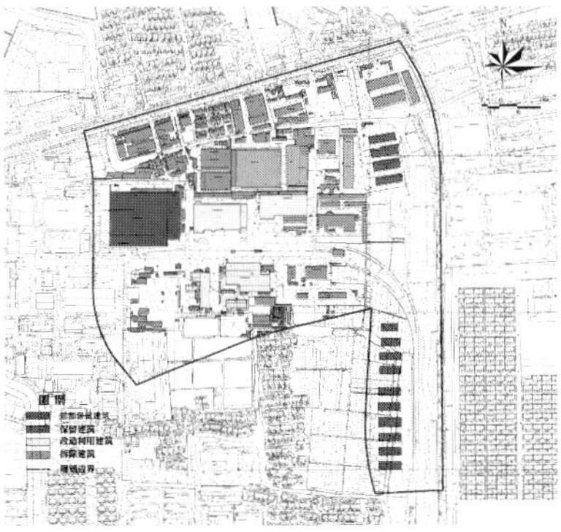

广州珠江后航道近代洋行码头仓库历史遗迹保护和利用规划研究
Research and Planning for the Modern Warehouse along the Post-Sea-Route of the Pearl River in Guangzhou

负责人：阳建强
项目组成员：罗超 魏晨 刘迪 雷禹 王颖楠 潘之潇
周静 曾志向 刘宁 章飙等

广州珠江后航道洋行码头仓库区形成于20世纪初，作为沙面地区各国洋行、公司的功能延伸，至今仍保存许多洋行码头、仓库和重要历史建筑，是特定历史时期广州乃至中国畸形对外经济关系和港口贸易发展的重要实物见证和历史遗存，具有很高的历史、文化、艺术和使用价值。近年来，随着城市的迅速发展与急剧转型，后航道滨水工业及交通运输业出现严重的结构性衰退，珠江后航道洋行码头仓库区保护工作面临巨大压力与挑战，同时也孕育着再发展的契机。规划通过对珠江后航道洋行码头仓库区的发展历史、综合价值、面临的问题及未来发展的研究，基于全面综合的历史文化保护和城市更新可持续发展思想，采取融入城市、延续历史、调整用地、优化交通等手段，选择适宜的保护和发展模式，以达到工业遗产保护和地区活力复兴的整体最优目标。规划在梳理近代洋行码头仓库的历史发展的基础上，对历史遗迹、建筑状况、土地利用状况及相关规划控制要求进行了全面调查，确定了历史遗迹的保护目标和保护原则，划定了近现代历史文化遗产的保护范围和建控地带，提出了相应的保护措施和控制要求，并在充分尊重历史文化环境的前提下，选取重要的历史地段和节点，进行城市设计。

该项目与广州市城市规划设计所合作完成。

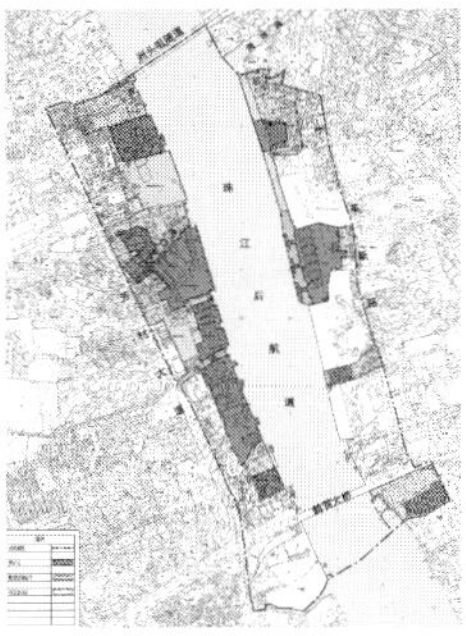
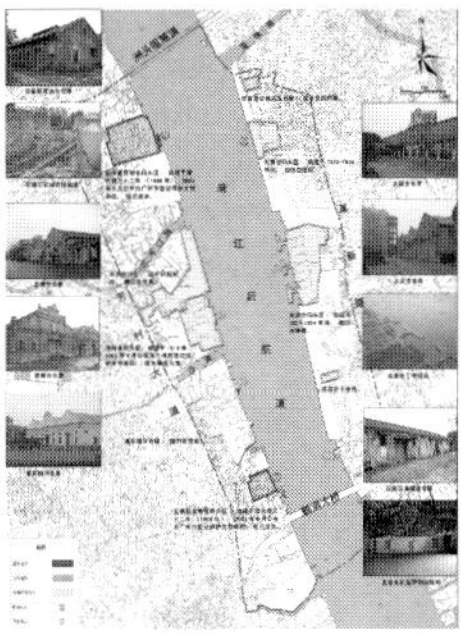
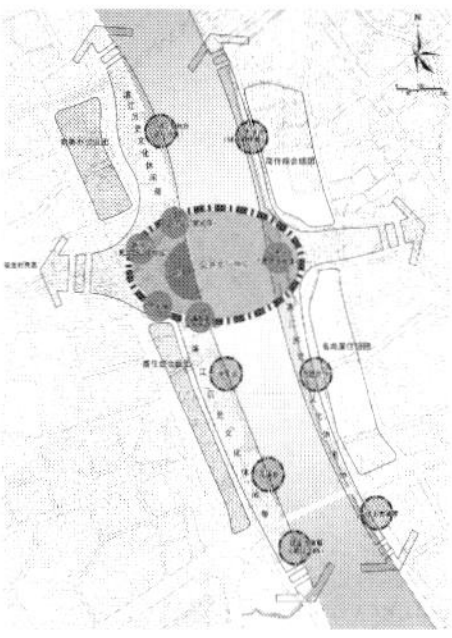
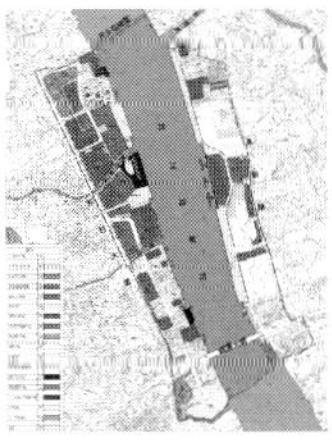
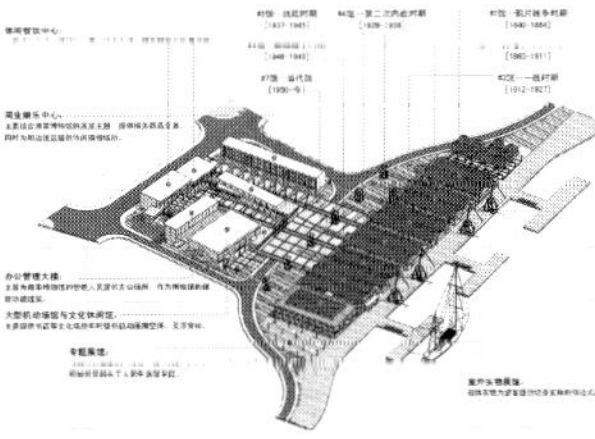
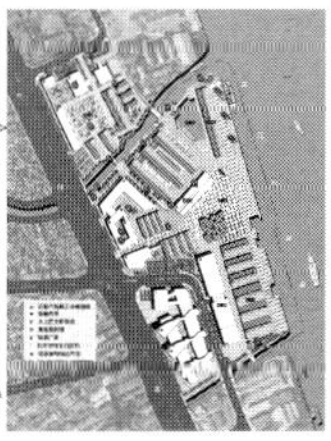
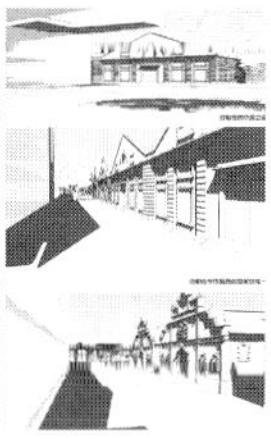

中国普天信息产业上海工业园智能生态科研楼建筑设计

ECO-POTEVIO: Sustainable Approaches to the Architectural Design of Office Building, China Potevio Shanghai Industrial Park Development CO.

设计：张彤等

国家建设部、科技部首批“十一五”绿色建筑示范工程

中国普天信息产业上海工业园智能生态科研楼位于上海市奉贤区，由中国普天信息产业上海工业园发展公司投资建设，东南大学建筑学院、东南大学建筑设计研究院与瑞典皇家工学院产业生态系联合研究设计。项目的建设旨在全面研究并在可能的条件下集成与优化采用体现可持续性原则的建筑设计策略与技术设备，开展建筑能耗与环境控制智能化系统的研发与产业化实验，创建我国冬冷夏热地区生态节能建筑的“示范工程”。

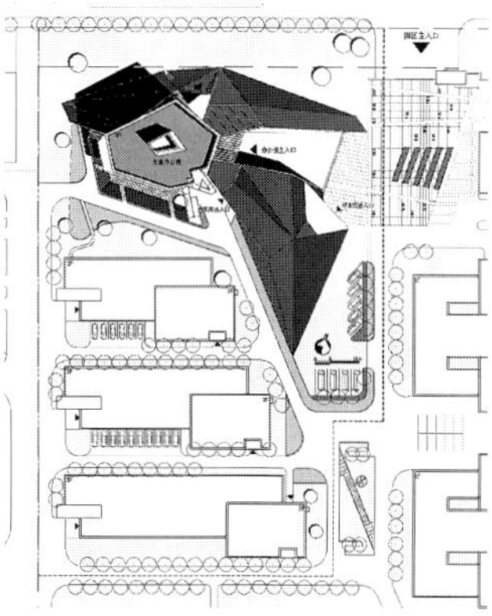

项目名称：中国普天信息产业上海工业园发展公司A1（含A2）地块一期工程生态工业园区

项目地点：上海市奉贤区沪杭公路西侧、环城北路南侧区域

项目规模：一期工程规划总用地面积：19416.4平方米，其中，科研楼总建筑面积4370.4平方米，厂房总建筑面积10069.19平方米

设计组成员：

项目负责人：张彤、毛烨

设计：张彤、毛烨、苏玲、朱君、赵玥

结构设计：王剑飞

暖通设计：许东晟

给排水设计：赵元

电气设计：罗振宁

智能设计：臧胜、张程

技术咨询：Ronald Wennersten（瑞典皇家工学院）顾震弘、彭昌海

项目协调：何颖方

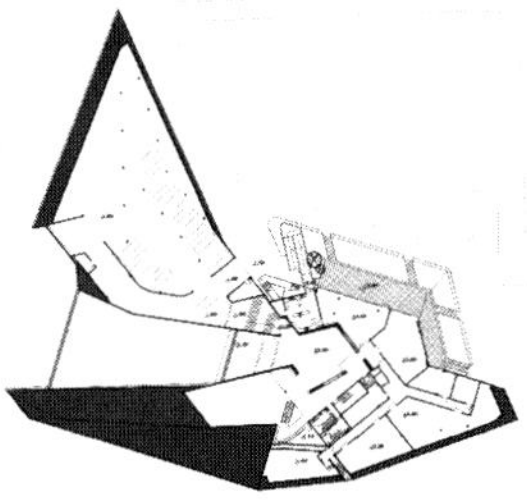

一层平面

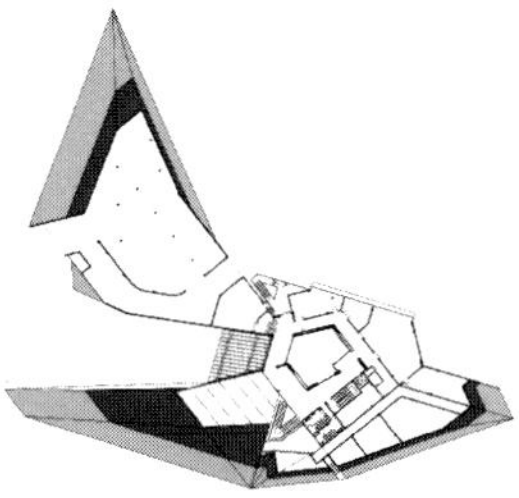

二层平面

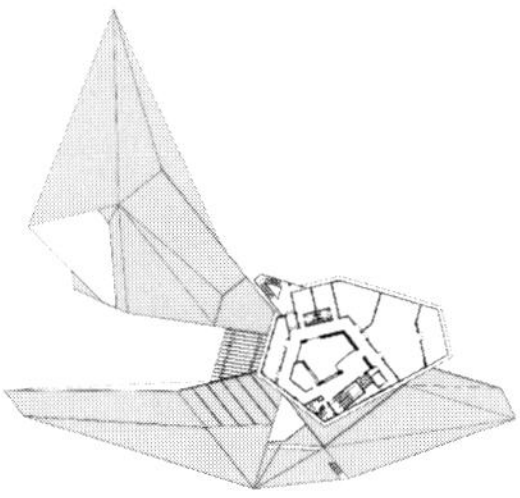

三层平面

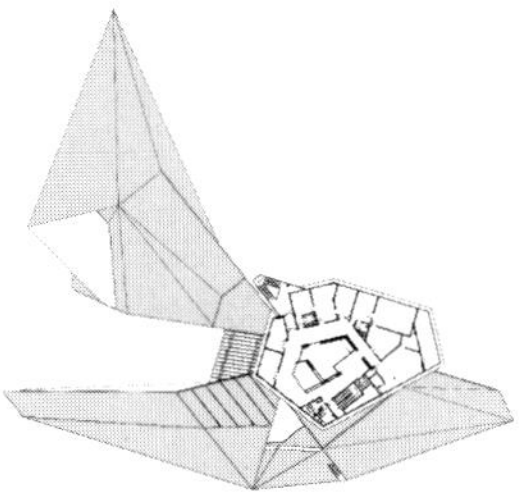

四层平面

自然通风

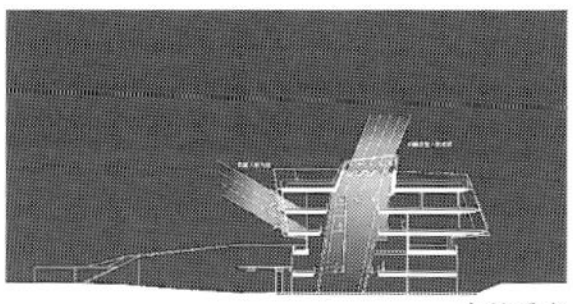
自然采光

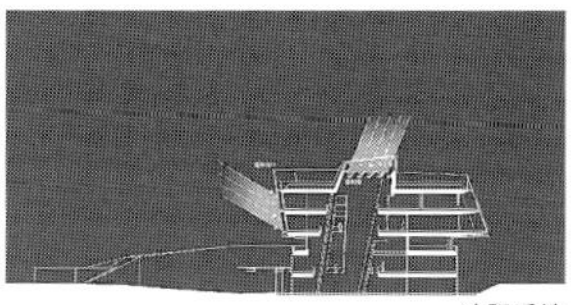
遮阳系统

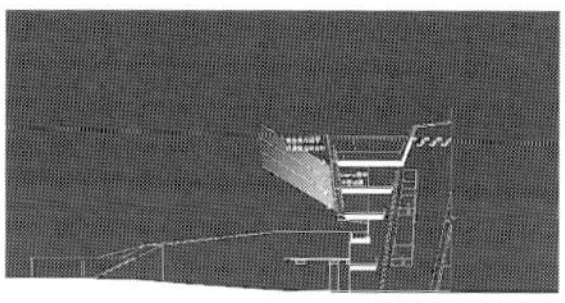
智能型双层表皮

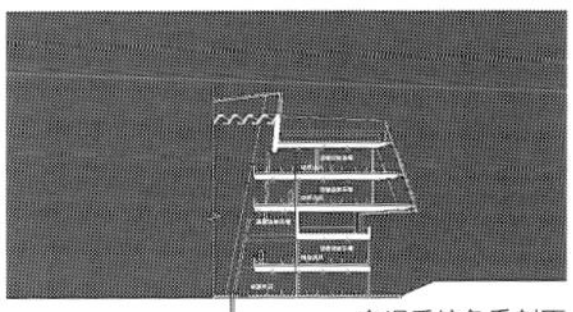
空调系统冬季剖面

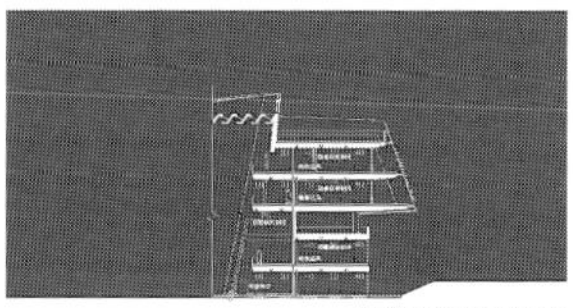
空调系统夏季剖面

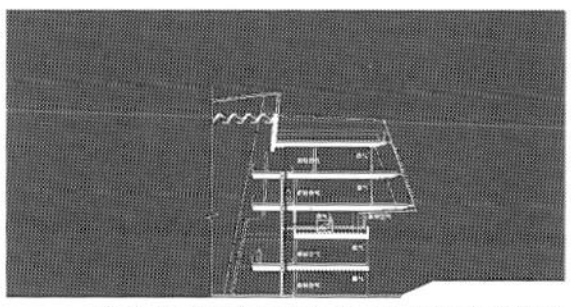
置换式新风及全热交换回收系统冬季剖面

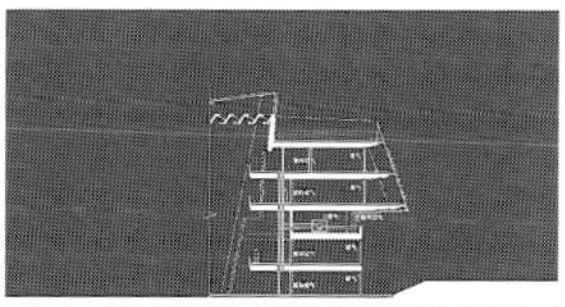
置换式新风及全热交换回收系统夏季剖面

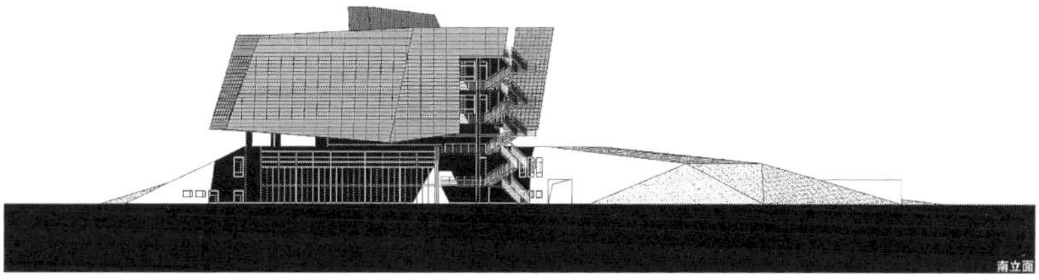
南立面

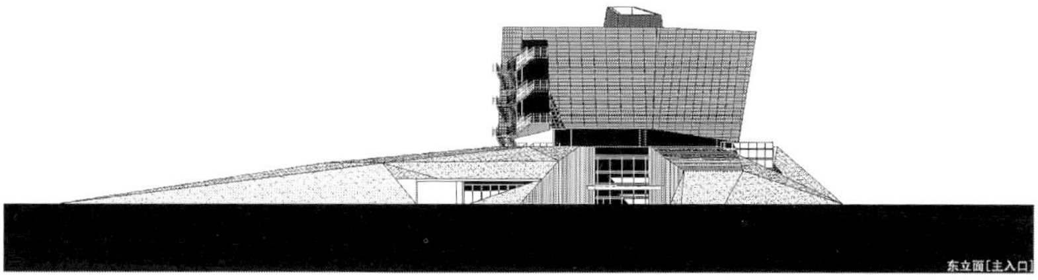
东立面[主入口]

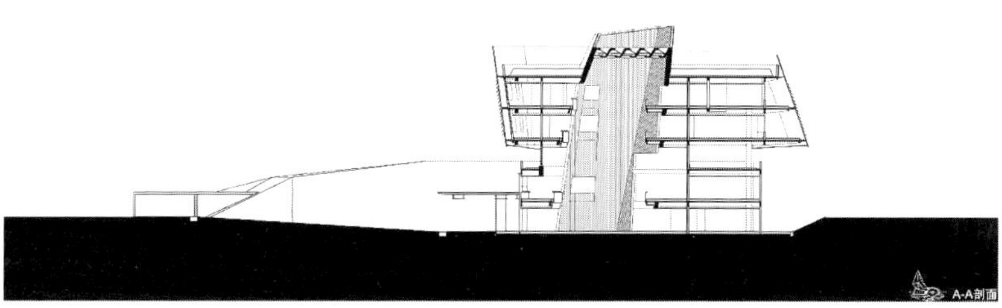
A-A剖面

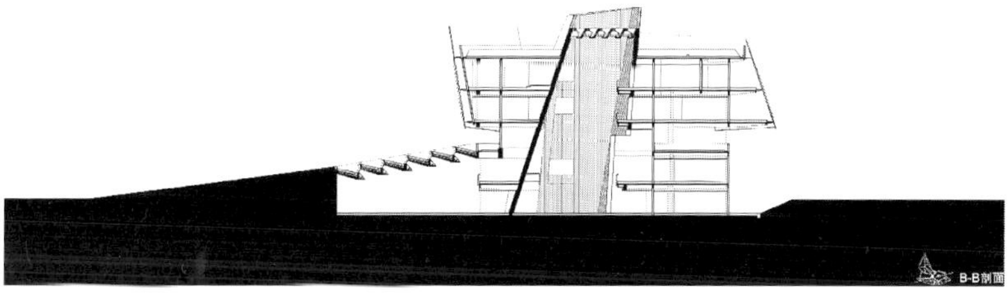
B-B剖面

江苏省工艺美术馆室内设计

Jiangsu Arts and Crafts Museum Interior Design

室内设计：高祥生

获江苏省第六届室内装饰设计大奖赛公装类特等奖

在江苏省工艺美术馆室内设计中既对原建筑设计的意向作了延续，同时又对原建筑空间作了完善和补充。设计中始终贯彻节省、环保的理念，坚持人性化设计的原则，取得了展示流线简明、功能合理、空间形态美观的效果。

外事交流与学术活动
Foreign Exchange & Academic Activities

2006年至2008年开展的国际合作项目
International and Cooperation

序号	国际交流合作项目名称	起始时间	合作对象
1	新加坡佛教建筑艺术	2004.01～2006.12	新加坡李谷建筑师事务所
2	建筑初步设计教学方法研究（本科）	2004～2007	香港中文大学
3	高舒适度／低能耗建筑设计	2006.08	苏黎世高等工业学校
4	中国制造（2）	2006.09	奥地利维也纳理工大学、新加坡国立大学
5	中国制造（3）	2006.09	奥地利维也纳理工大学、深圳大学
6	北京751创意街区合作设计（本科五年级）	2006.09～2007.01	荷兰代尔夫特大学建筑学院
7	城市发展下的景观设计（建筑系研究生）	2006.10	瑞士联邦苏黎世高等工业大学（ETHZ）
8	“破碎与透明性”联合教学（建筑系研究生）	2006.12	香港中文大学
9	普天信息产业上海工业园发展公司生态工业园区设计	2006～2007	瑞典皇家工学院产业生态系
10	南京南捕厅改造设计（研究生）	2007.01	韩国成均馆大学建筑系
11	南京博物院扩建设计（建筑系研究生）	2007.01～2007.02	澳大利亚新南威尔士大学建筑学院
12	历史地段的城市设计（建筑系研究生）	2007.05	美国Woodbury大学建筑系
13	城市专题研究（城市规划系研究生）	2007.05	美国加州大学伯克利分校（G.Cranz教授）
14	亚洲建筑史教育方式—奥地利、美国、中国教育的对照 The Way of Teaching Chinese Architecture: A Cross - cultural Comparison	2007.09	美国宾夕法尼亚大学
15	南京明城墙和罗马Aurelian城墙的比较研究	2007～2008	意大利罗马大学建筑系
16	City History and Multi-scale Spatial Masterplanning (CHaMSpaM) Network	2007～2009	伦敦大学学院等
17	变化中的互换：从南京西站到博物馆	2008.01	澳大利亚新南威尔士大学建筑学院
18	南京下关/浦口地区保护与改造概念设计	2008.02	德国
19	中国园林和韩国园林的关联性研究	2008.02	韩国汉城大学
20	中国普天信息产业上海工业园智能生态科研楼设计	2008	瑞典皇家工学院产业生态系
21	日本现代建筑与建造（建筑系研究生）	2008.05	日本
22	下关：图解、叙事与触动干预（建筑系研究生）	2008.05～06	美国Woodbury大学建筑系

2006年至2008年举办的国际国内学术会议

序号	国际会议名称	举办时间
1	“交叉文化与交叉学科下的联合设计教学”国际研讨会	2007.01
2	CAADRIA 2007——亚洲计算机辅助建筑设计研究协会2007年年会	2007.04
3	中国城市规划学会历史文化名城学术委员会年会暨城市更新国际研讨会（40人，外宾4人）	2008.10
4	联合国人居署/教科文组织高级培训班（50人，外宾30人）	2008.11
5	合作院校圆桌会议（40人，外宾20人）	2008.11
6	中瑞城市与建筑可持续发展合作研讨会（40人，外宾10人）	2008.11
7	世界人居会议（60人，外宾40人）	2008.11

序号	国内会议名称	举办时间
1	长三角研究生学会年会	2007.05
2	全国低能耗建筑研讨会	2007.06
3	东南大学建筑学院80周年庆系列研讨会	2007.09
4	海峡两岸大学的校园研讨会	2007.09

学术活动及讲座
Academic Activities and Lectures

2006-09-27，讲座：城市化建设过程中的历史文化名城保护，建设部副部长 仇保兴
2006-09-27，讲座：了解设计理论，把握城市文化，新加坡著名规划大师 刘太格
2006-09-27，讲座：现代城乡规划的理想风貌，台湾著名作家 司马中源
2006-11-01，讲座：建筑学的命题之一——自治，南京大学教授 丁沃沃
2006-11-22，讲座：与建筑同行 与大师同行，2006中国国际建筑艺术双年展艺术总监 梅可
2007-03-21，讲座：1970大阪/2005爱知 世博KEYWORD，东南大学建筑学院教授 钱强
2007-04-19，讲座：Complex Systems in Architecture beyond CAAD，
瑞士联邦苏黎世高等工业大学建筑系 Prof. Udger Hovestadt (ETHZ)
2007-05-15，讲座：导演/演员的理想剧场与空间视角，国家一级导演 陈韵强
2007-05-25，讲座：国家大剧院的风雨历程，剧场建筑专家 金志舜
2007-05，讲座：城市保护规划的未来，
同济大学建筑与城规学院副院长、同济大学城市规划设计研究院院长、教授 周俭
南京大学建筑学院副院长、教授 赵辰
清华大学建筑学院教授 边兰春
中国城市规划研究院历史文化名城研究所所长、高级规划师 张兵
中国城市规划学会秘书长、高级规划师 石楠
南京市规划局局长、高级规划师 周岚
2007-06-17，讲座：历史文化名城的编制，中国城市规划研究院历史文化名城研究所高级规划师 张广汉
2007-06-19，讲座：全球都会区域的虚拟与真实，台湾大学建筑与城乡研究所教授 夏铸九
2007-06-27，讲座：积累经验——大舍事务所的建筑实践，著名建筑师 柳亦春
2007-09-18，讲座：Protection and Management of the Urban Heritage in France,
Former Chairman of Society of State Architect and Town Planner, Bruno Chauffert-Yvart
2007-09-18，讲座：文物本体与环境的保护，
建设部历史文化名城专家委员会委员、中国古迹遗址保护协会执委、教授、博士 赵中枢
2007-09-20，讲座：Landscape Urbanism，Design Director, Colors: Urban Design Limited, Peter Owens
2007-10-20，讲座：可持续城市发展，德国著名规划师、建筑师 Albert Speer
2007-10-21，讲座：实验空间，德国艺术设计师、装置艺术家 Markus Heinsdorff
2007-10-21，讲座：近日建筑要点，斯图加特建筑与城市规划学院人居研究所所长、教授 T. Jocher
2007-10-22，讲座：重返城市，法国拉维莱特建筑学院教授 Michel Verne
2007-10-23，讲座：模块架构，德国建筑师 Stefan Meyer-Miethker
2007-10-25，讲座：综合规划：区域可持续发展的前提条件，
德国Nürtingen-Geislingen大学城市规划学院 Alfred Ruther-Merhlis
2007-10-30，讲座：Built upon Love: Architectural Longing after Ethics and Aesthetics，
著名建筑历史和理论家、加拿大McGill大学S. R. Bronfman教席教授 A. Pérez-Gómez
2007-11-16，讲座：Recent Projects，
2007 Mies Van der Rohe建筑奖青年建筑师奖得主、Office Bevk & Vasa, Slovenia主要建筑师 Vasa J. Perovic
2007-12-05，讲座：从文化啤酒厂到梦清园——中德啤酒厂改造实例比较，
同济大学建筑城规学院副教授、博士 左琰
2007-12-06，讲座：近作漫话，京都工芸纤维大学造型工学科教授、建筑家 岸和郎
2008-01-17，讲座：现代城市规划的三个重要支柱，中国工程院院士 邹德慈
2008-03-19，讲座：国外城市考察与中国城市化问题，中科院南京地理所研究员 姚士谋
2008-03-21，讲座：Urban Revitalization -- The Genesis of a Shopping Center，
奥地利著名建筑师、规划师 Peter Lorenz
2008-04-24，讲座：Planning Australian Metropolis: Issues and Governance
澳大利亚新南威尔士大学教授、Faculty Built Environment系主任 Peter Murphy
2008-04-23，讲座：通过目标寻找过程——我的建筑创作之路，
九城都市建筑设计有限公司总建筑师 张应鹏
2008-04-24，讲座：可持续性城市发展Sustainable Urbanism，
瑞典皇家工学院教授、产业生态系主任、欧洲可持续发展建筑网络会员、欧洲海岸管理网络会员 Ronald Wennersten
2008-05-01，讲座：关于日本寺庙建筑史的概论——从装饰要素的角度叙述历史性的演变，
日本奈良国立文化财研究所文化遗产部建造物研究室室长、日本建筑史学会常任委员 窪寺茂
2008-05，系列讲座：城市历史观察，法国拉维莱特建筑学院教授 Michel Verne
2008-05-21，讲座：状态，中国建筑设计研究院执行总建筑师 汪恒
2008-05-23，讲座：非到达场所，建筑家、永山佑子建筑设计代表 永山佑子
2008-05-28，讲座：平衡体系，中国科学院建筑设计研究院总建筑师 崔彤
2008-06-06，讲座：三个关于中国建筑异质性的研究，
美国密歇根大学建筑系讲师、美国北卡罗来纳州立大学建筑学院访问助理教授 王飞
2008-06-10，讲座：绘画和建筑在何处相逢，建筑评论家 方振宁
2008-06-11，讲座：学习，同济大学建筑与城规学院副教授 童明

民国科技博物馆设计
The Museum of Science and Technology in the Republic of China 1912—1949, Nanjing

澳大利亚新南威尔士大学，中国清华大学，中国东南大学
UNSW/Tsinghua University, China/Southeast University, China 2005.12—2006.05

指导教师：许亦农，James Weirick，Graham Bell，许懋彦，龚　恺，陈　薇

参加学生：
Group 1：毕若臻(UNSW)，张大为(UNSW)，相　南(SEU)，赵　婧(SEU)，刘　鹏(Tsinghua)
Group 2：李良能(UNSW)，郑宗炜(UNSW)，丁　顺(SEU)，周晓文(SEU)，黄建志(Tsinghua)
Group 3：骆彦君(UNSW)，杨清仪(UNSW)，冷天翔(SEU)，杨　宇(SEU)，刘晓霞(Tsinghua)
Group 4：张逸航(UNSW)，李慧文(UNSW)，翟　值(SEU)，苏　玲(SEU)，李久太(Tsinghua)
Group 5：陈杰君(UNSW)，艾　玛(UNSW)，张剑葳(SEU)，蒋　楠(SEU)，邬南薰(Tsinghua)
Group 6：周仁和(UNSW)，王绍豪(UNSW)，郭　健(SEU)，陈科舟(SEU)，梁晓方(Tsinghua)

Group 1
Cutting
切开

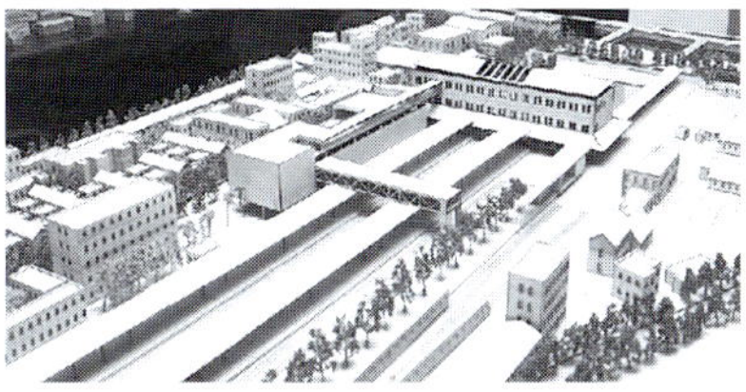

Group 2
The Gate Way of City
城市之门

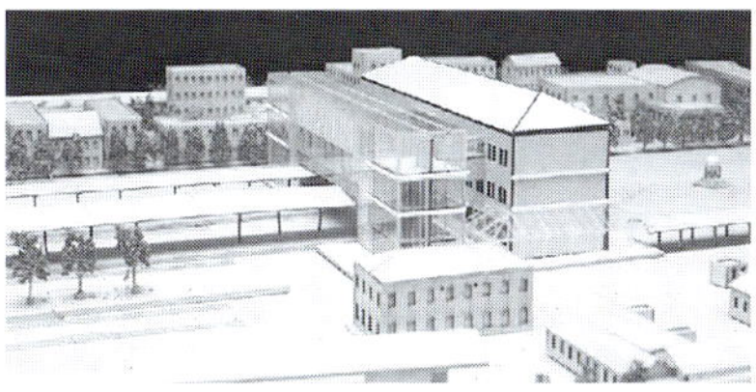

Group 3
On Track
轨迹

Group 4
Civic Space
市民空间

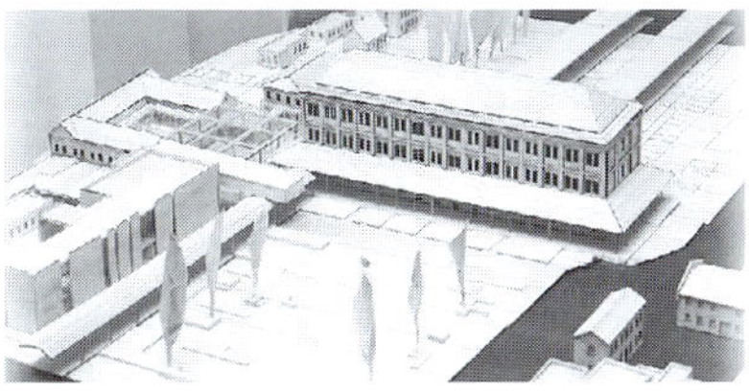

Group 5
Courtyard
庭院

Group 6
Inner Skin
内皮

高舒适度低能耗建筑设计研究——宝应行政中心建筑设计

High Comfort Low Energy: Architectural Design for Baoying Administrative Center

瑞士联邦苏黎世高等工业大学，中国东南大学
ETHZ/Southeast University, China 2006.04.17—2006.06.11

指导教师：Stephan Rutz(ETHZ)，李海清，周　颖
顾　　问：Bruno Keller(ETHZ)

参加学生：
Group 1：张　璐
Group 2：陈　佳
Group 3：史庆超，刘　杰，高庶三
Group 4：郁　倩，杨　程
Group 5：甘　昊，李　燕

Group 1

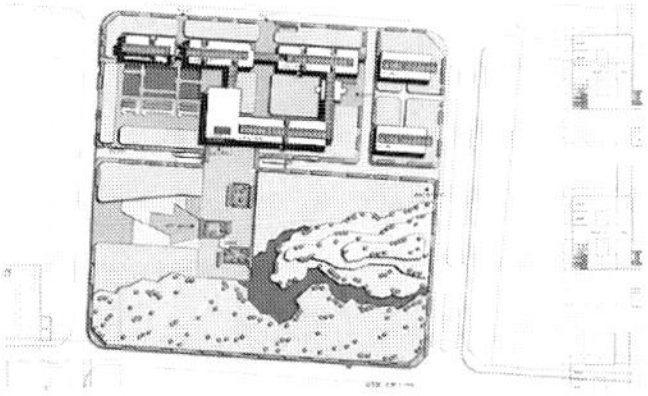

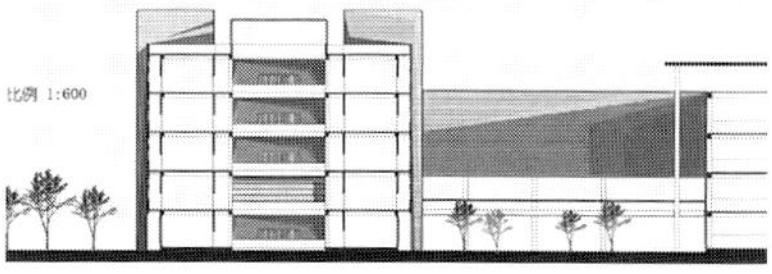

Group 2

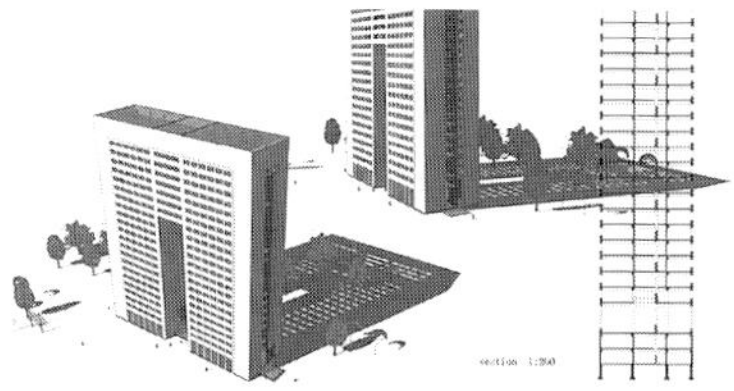

Group 3

Group 4

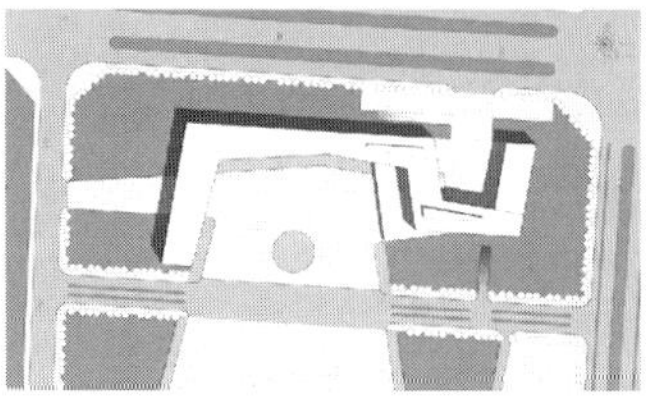

Group 5

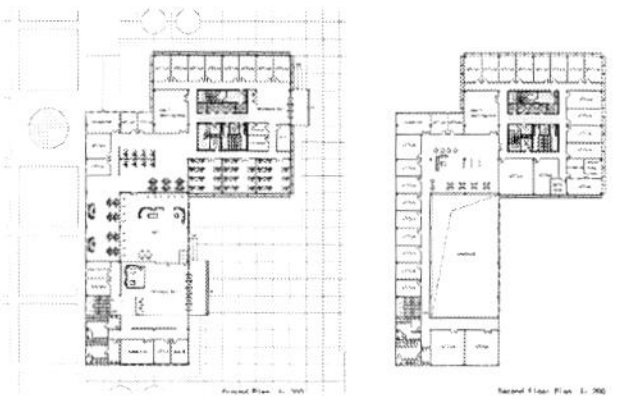

Group 6

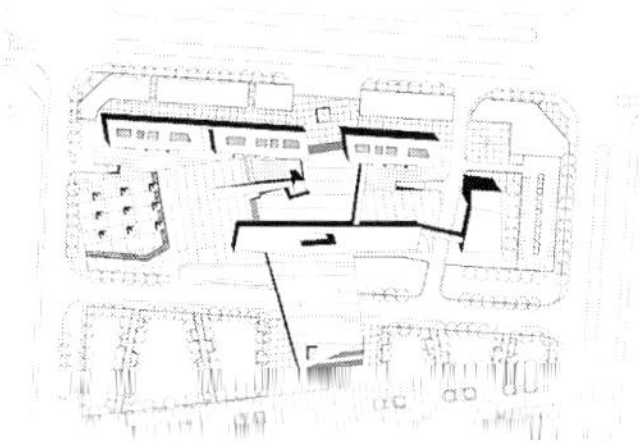

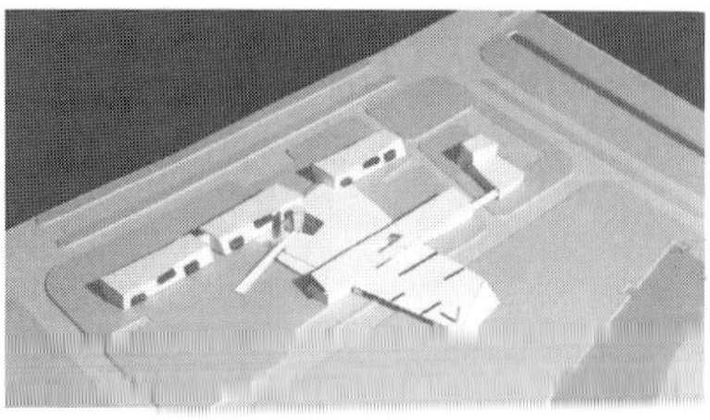

中国制造——深圳蛇口三洋厂房改造设计
Made in China: Renovation of Sanyo Factory Buildings in Shekou, Shenzhen

奥地利维也纳理工大学，中国东南大学，中国深圳大学
University of Technology Vienna, Austria/Southeast University, China /Shenzhen University, China 2006.09.02—2006.09.12

指导教师：刘尔明，Klaus Semsroth，龚　恺，Mladen Jadric，葛　明，单　皓，黄大田

参加学生：
Group 1：吉英雷（东南大学），凌鹏志（深圳大学），曹圳波（深圳大学），Maciej Boltryk(TU Vienna)
Group 2：吴海龙（东南大学），吴　昊（东南大学），胡倩文（深圳大学），Lukasz Pituch(TU Vienna)
Group 3：肖　凡（东南大学），刘凌雪（深圳大学），覃伙记（深圳大学），姜智勇（深圳大学），Margot Deerenberg(TU Vienna)
Group 4：王　柯（东南大学），常　莹（深圳大学），李云霞（深圳大学），Claudia Rohrweck(TU Vienna)
Group 5：胡　宏（东南大学），刘进红（东南大学），林晓丽（深圳大学），欧阳祎（深圳大学），Thomas Stini(TU Vienna)
Group 6：庄　悦（东南大学），刘立早（深圳大学），张　博（深圳大学），牟　裕（深圳大学），Oliver Krieger(TU Vienna)

Group 1
Fun Factory
快乐工厂

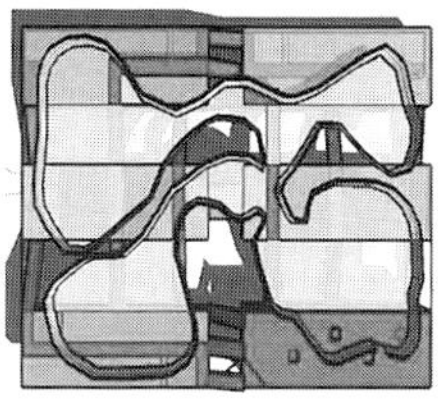

Group 2
2 Expression of Factory
工厂的两种表达

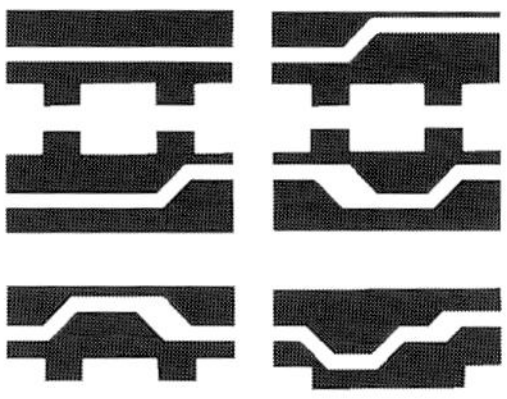

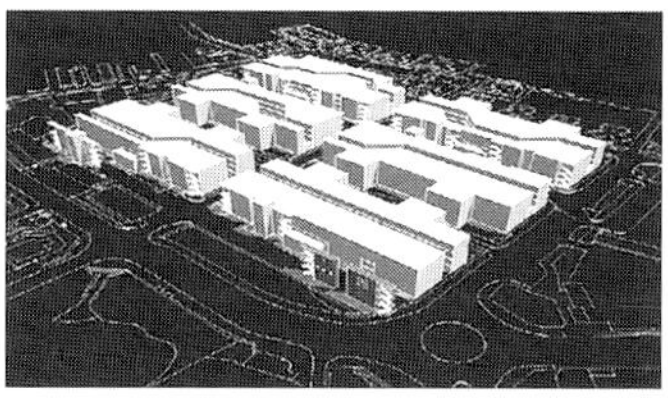

Group 3
Let Ourself Be Bebbled in the Industry
工厂幻想

Group 4
Architecture in Urban, Urban in Architecture
建筑中的城市，城市中的建筑

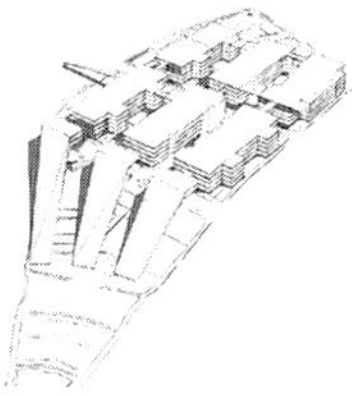

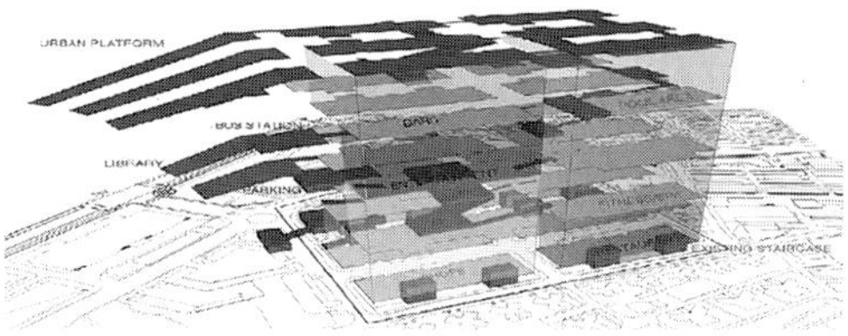

Group 5
Tree
树

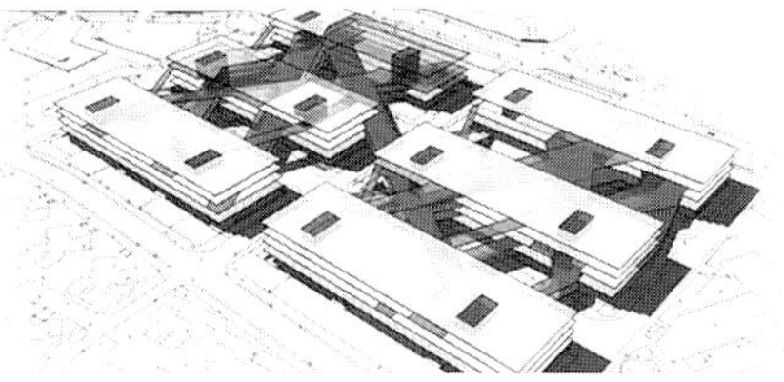

Group 6
Gathering People
会聚人群

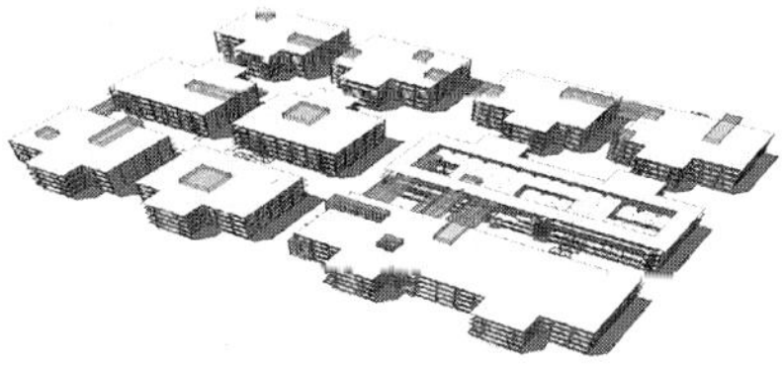

城市转化地带的景观设计——南京中华门外护城河地区

Designing Urban Landscapes in Trans-Formation: The Region of the Outer Zhonghua Gate,Nanjing

瑞士联邦苏黎世高等工业大学，中国东南大学
ETHZ/Southeast University, China 2006.10.16—2006.10.27

指导教师：Jacqueline Parish，李　雱，龚　恺

参加学生：
Group 1：李　娟，闵　铭，刘　园，董　凌
Group 2：徐　斌，崔陇鹏
Group 3：顾海燕，戴　韵，陈海宁
Group 4：骆　可，方　榕，赵　谦
Group 5：叶财华，曾　飞，张　颖，刘苏文
Group 6：严　希，曾　瑞，崔佳琪
Group 7：孙颖智，陈　染，曹　婷
Group 8：周少聪，戴国雯，许　皞

Group 1

Dynamic Belt

运动的带

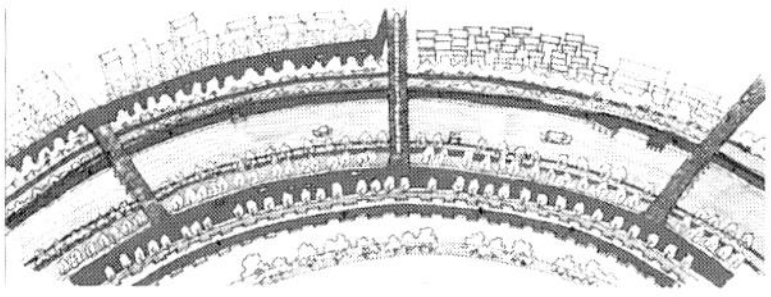

Group 2

Mapping the Path to Feel Nature & Culture

感受文化与自然

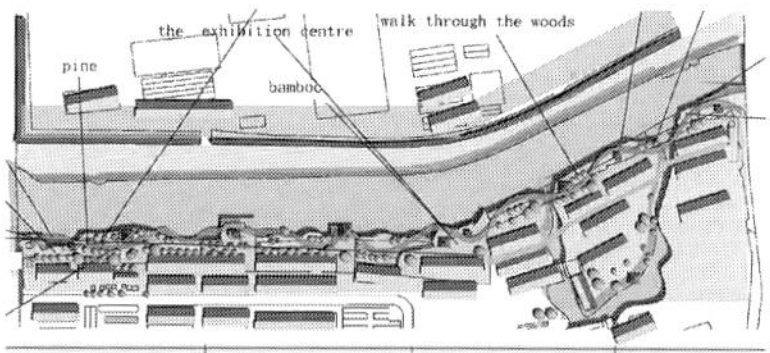

Group 3

Musical Rhythm in Landscape Design

音乐节奏与景观设计

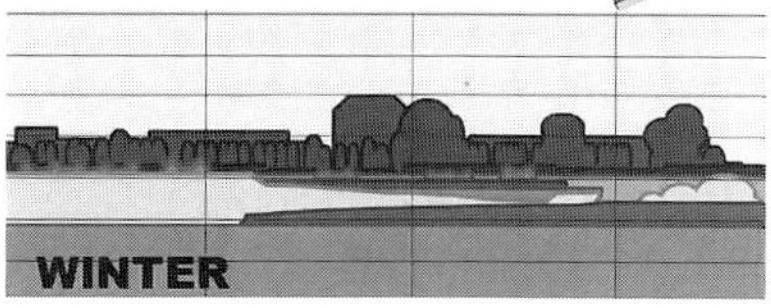

Group 4

The Mask Party at the Foot of the City Wall

城墙下的假面舞会

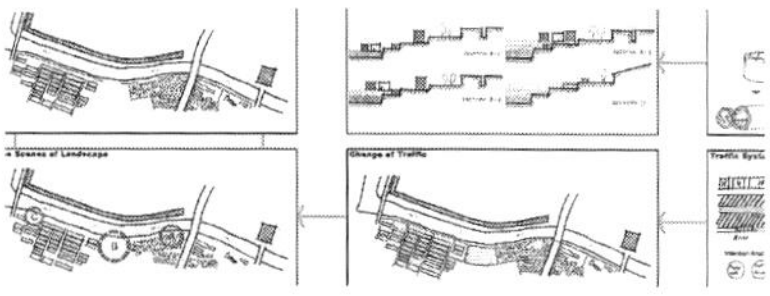

Group 5

The New & the Old -- Constrast & Merge

新与旧——对比与融合

Group 6

Communication with and within Seasonal Change

交流应四时之景而变

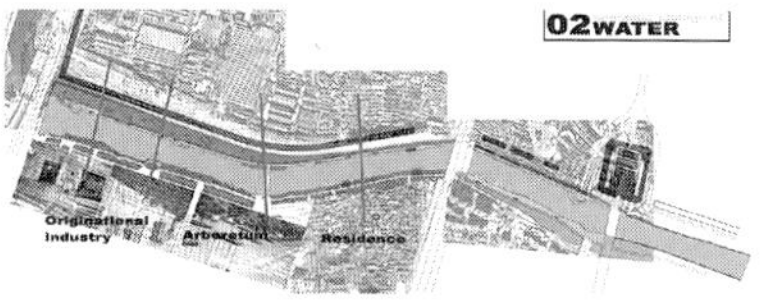

Group 7

From Loneliness to Meditation

从寂寞空间到静思空间

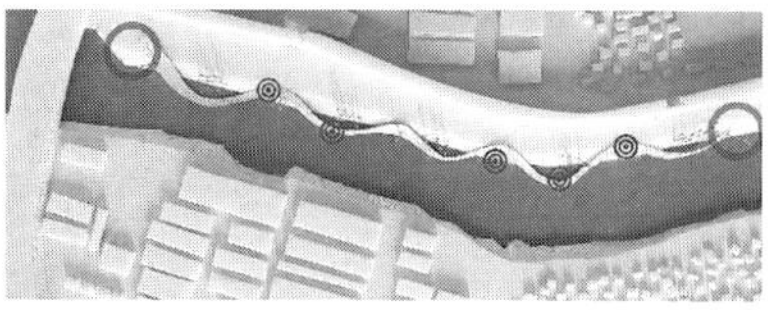

Group 8

Relating Speed in Urban Landscape

城市景观中的速度

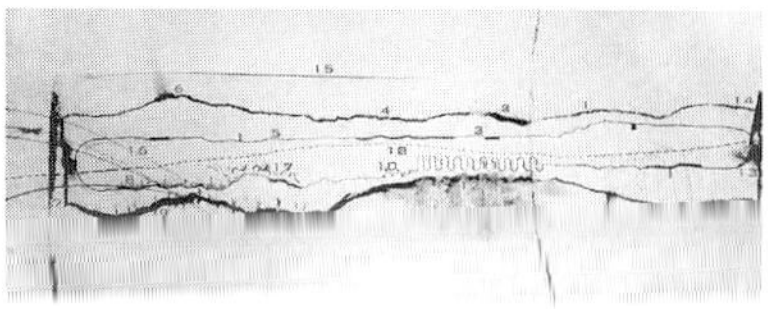

“破碎”与“透明性”——关于建筑空间组织方法的研究
Poché Versus Transparency: The Strategies of Space Organization

香港中文大学，中国东南大学
The Chinese University of Hong Kong/Southeast University, China 2006.12

指导教师：顾大庆，龚　恺

参加学生：
Group 1：蒋梦麟，韩　曼，章泉丰，李　静，钱瑜皎，王巧莉
Group 2：杨　宝，蔡　弋，彭　溪，朱　君，胡晔旻，田志卿
Group 3：邓　艳，陈　思，孙晓燕，高　阳，刘小盼

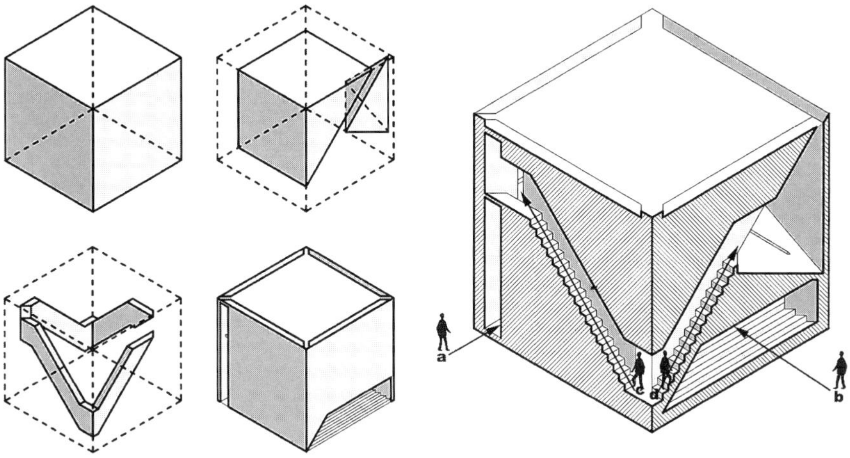

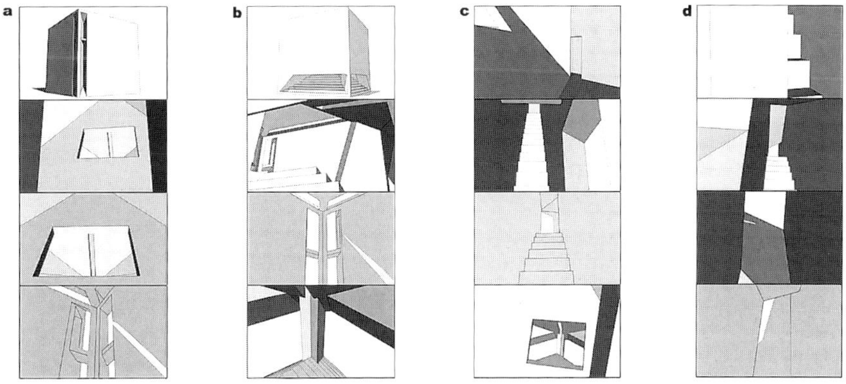

section B-B

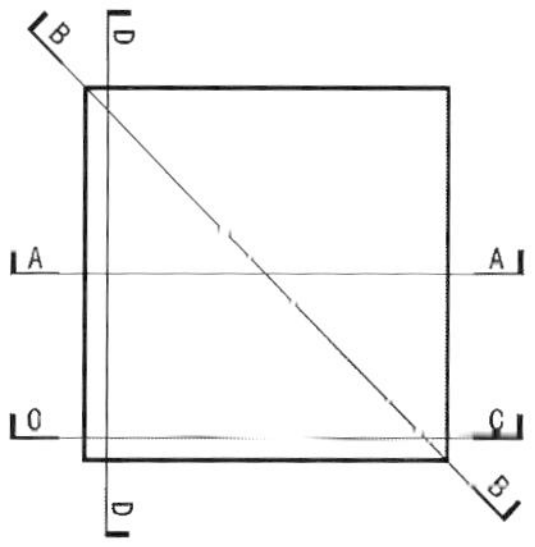

南京南捕厅传统街区改造城市设计（1）
Nanbuting Housing District Development in Nanjing(1)

韩国成均馆大学，中国东南大学
Sungkyunkwan University, Korea/Southeast University, China 2007.01.08—2007.01.26

指导教师：Yim Chang Bok，龚　恺，李　哲，刘　捷

参加学生：
Group 1：张竹容，杨　杰，黄　欢，KIM Young Joon，SONG Seungmin
Group 2：尹　莹，朱穗敏，LEE Jin Hyuk，CHUN Jaeoh
Group 3：王　烨，柏灵芝，HUH Hyo Sung，LEE EungKeum
Group 4：申世明，戴国雯，周少聪，HAN Dong O，SONG SungHyum
Group 5：蔡芝明，蔡　晶，YEO Min Gu，CHO JungWon

Group 1
Buffer Zone
缓冲空间

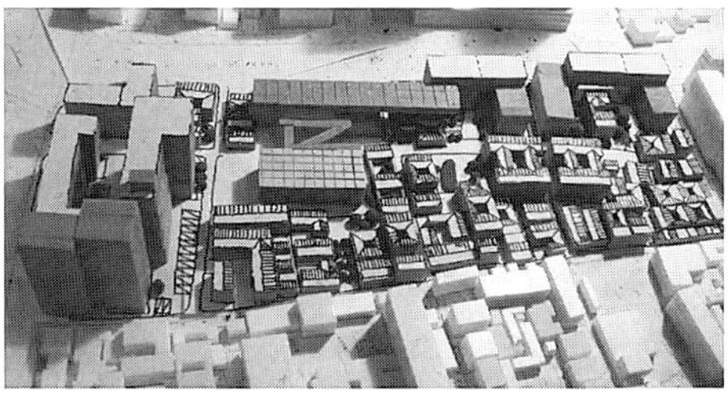
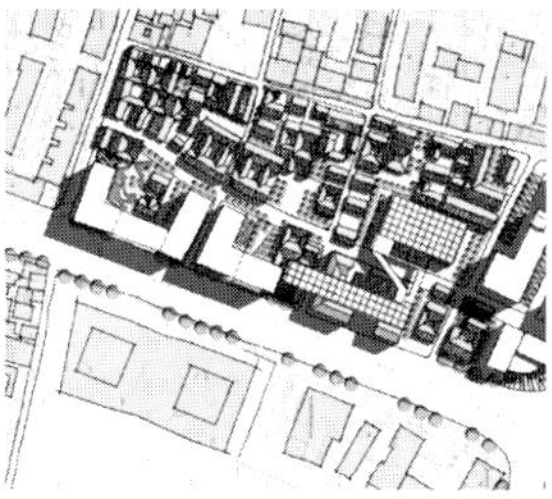

Group 2
Diversity Activity
多样活动

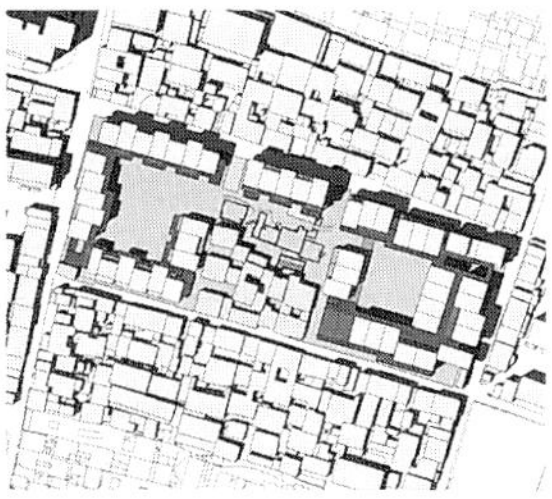

Group 3
Linkage
联结

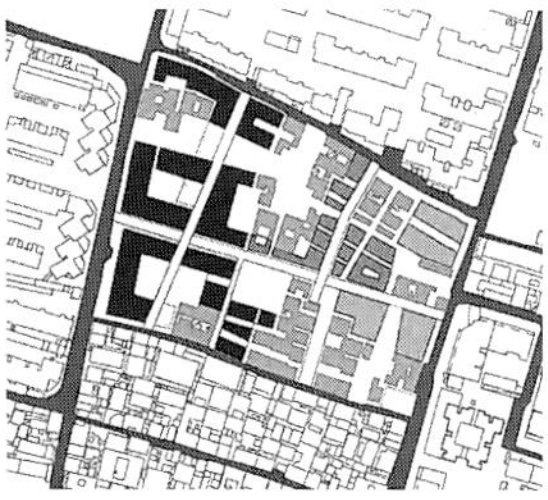

Group 4
The Carnival
嘉年华

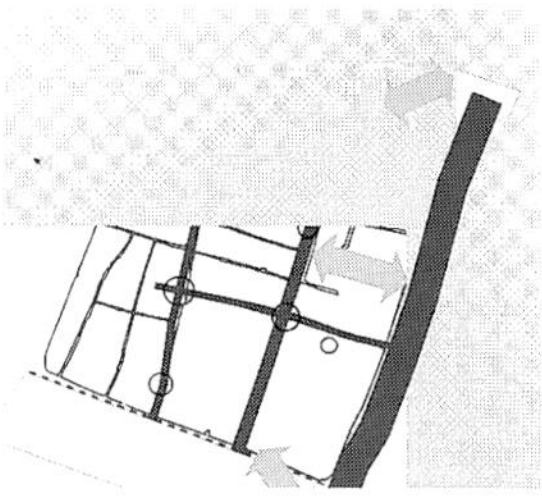

Group 5
Permeation
渗透

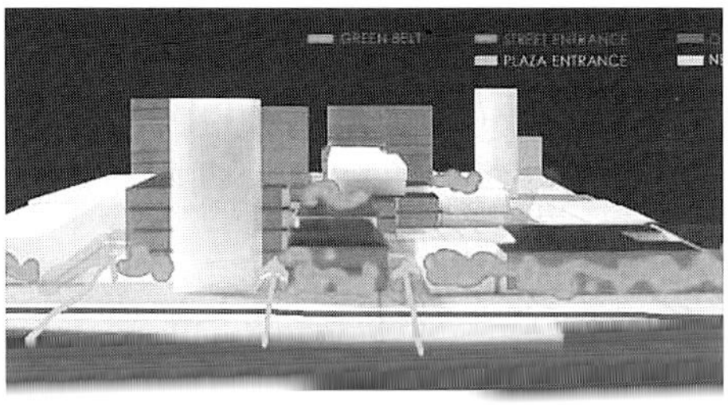

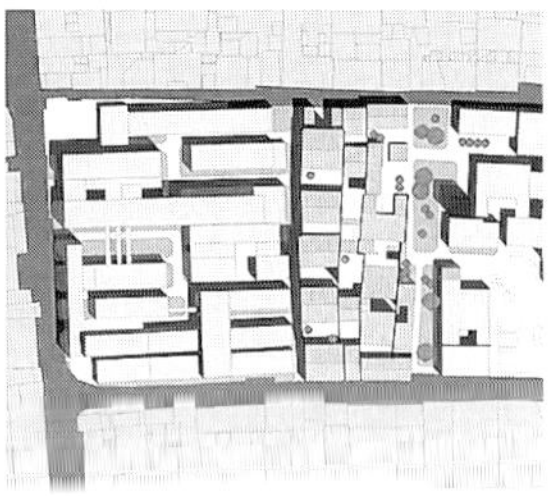

南京博物院改造扩建设计
Replanning and Redesign of Nanjing Museum

澳大利亚新南威尔士大学 中国东南大学
University of New South Wales, Australia/Southeast University, China 2007.01—2007.05

指导教师：许亦农，Linda Corkery，龚 恺，王湘君

参加学生：
Group 1：萧克良，黄旭升，Ross Laura Jade
Group 2：陈 健，张建波，陆 宇
Group 3：陈 宁，Oh Alvin Szu Chuang
Group 4：陈长易，秦 笛，张灿辉
Group 5：朱 睿，Bolton Victoria，Sungkram Krisada
Group 6：潘贞子，傅舒兰

Group 1

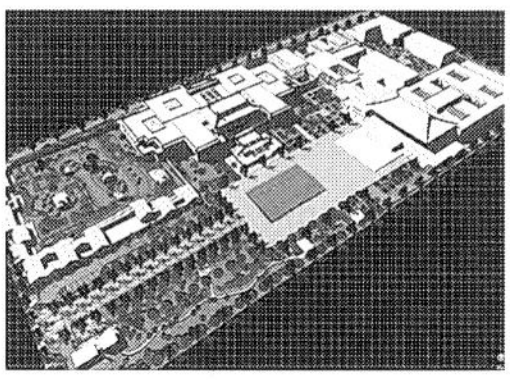

Group 2

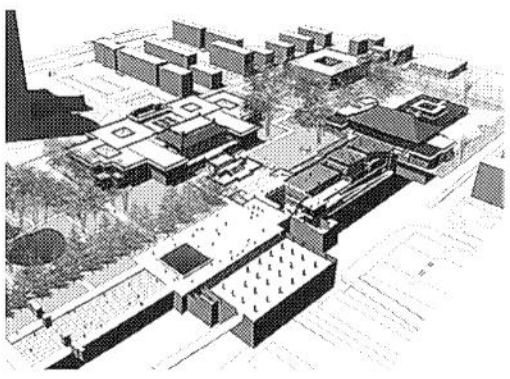

Group 3

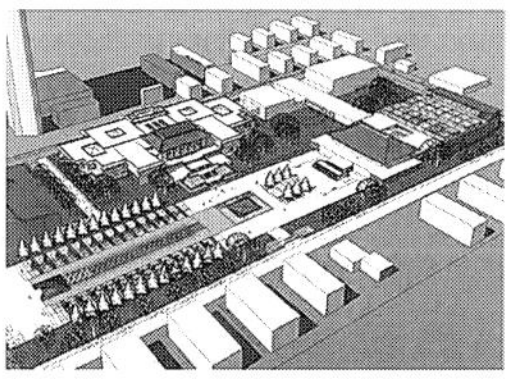

Group 4

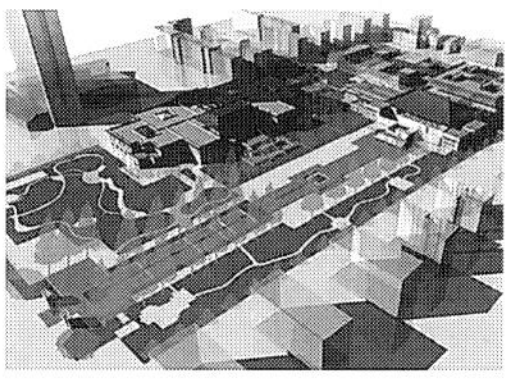

Group 5

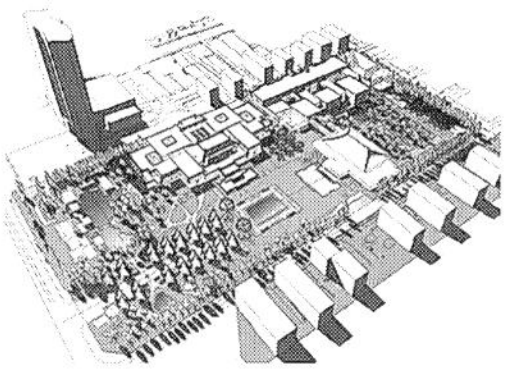

Group 6

南京南捕厅传统街区改造城市设计（2）
Nanbuting Housing District Development in Nanjing(2)

美国Woodbury大学，中国东南大学
Woodbury University, U.S.A/Southeast University, China 2007.05.11—2007.06.02

指导教师：Nick Roberts，Ingalill Wahlroos-Ritter，张 彤，龚 恺

参加学生：
Group 1：秦 笛，陈 宁，Luca Marino-Baker，Ricky Torres
Group 2：方 榕，张灿辉，Jason King，Sipan Nazartan
Group 3：李 静，朱道焓，Brtan Oknyansky，Sean Nazarran
Group 4：周艳华，闫振宇，Jonathan Hecuert，Nate White
Group 5：陆 宇，丁 瑜，韩晓峰，Danny Mascari，Coun Wysock
Group 6：陈 君，朱 君，Jennimer Baurt，Jvan Lav
Group 7：杨晓琳，张竹容，蒋博雅，Looris Nazaryans，Brice Linawe
Group 8：谢丽娜，朱 睿，Joel Cota，Biayna Boghosian

Group 1
Stratification/Stratum
分层/社会阶层

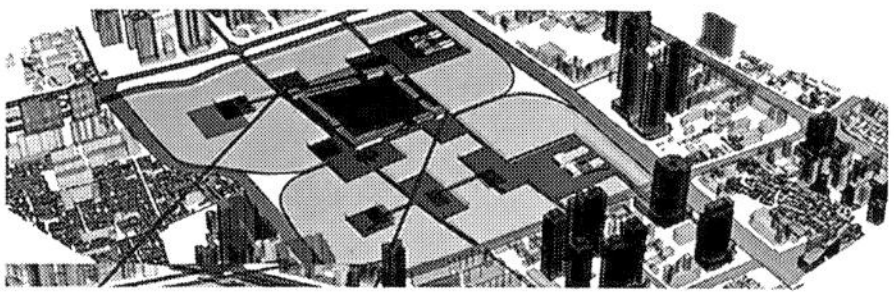

Group 2
Wall City
墙围界

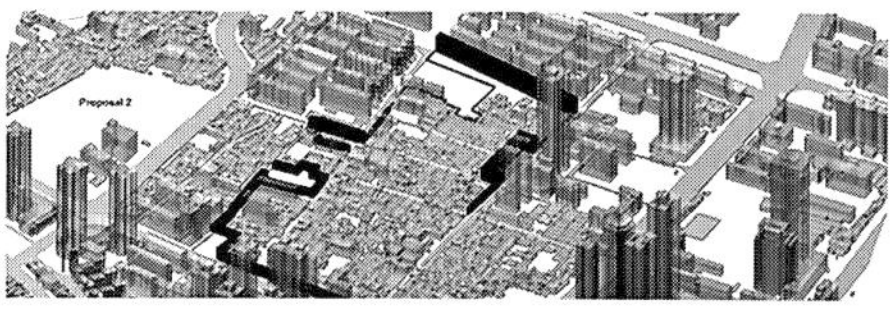

Group 3
Troubled Waters -- private Green Space
杂乱无章的水——私人绿色空间

Group 4
Acupuncture
针灸疗法

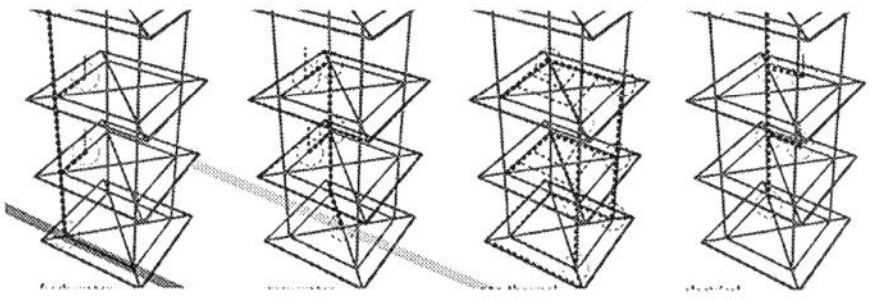

Group 5
Text(ure) City:Extracting UrbanTexture
提取城市肌理

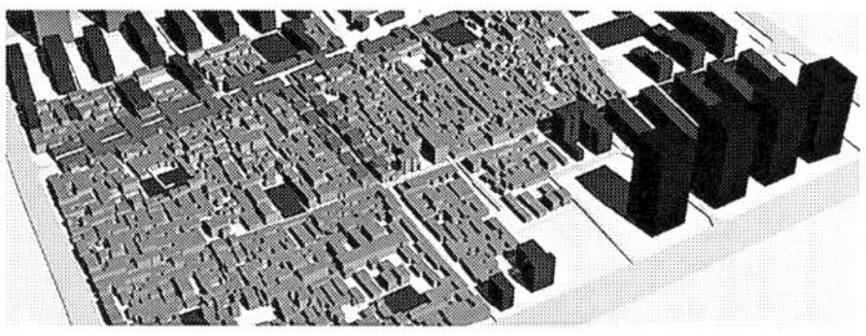

Group 6
Informal City:Adapting Complex Systems
可适应性系统

Group 7
Velo City: The City of Constant Change
不断变化的城市

Group 8
Verdigris
铜绿

交互式合作设计——北京751工厂更新与改造设计
Interactive Architecture: Renovation of Beijing 751 Factory

荷兰代尔夫特理工大学建筑学院，中国东南大学
TUD, Netherland/Southeast University, China 2007.05.11—2007.06.02

指导教师：Kas Oosterhuis，Hans Hubers，Tomasz Jaskiewicz，董　卫，张　倩，杜　嵘

参加学生：
24名（选修BK6A030 Hyperbody课程的学生，研究生+本科生）
刘　迪，经　靖，张子君，王　柯，臧公秀（东南大学本科五年级）

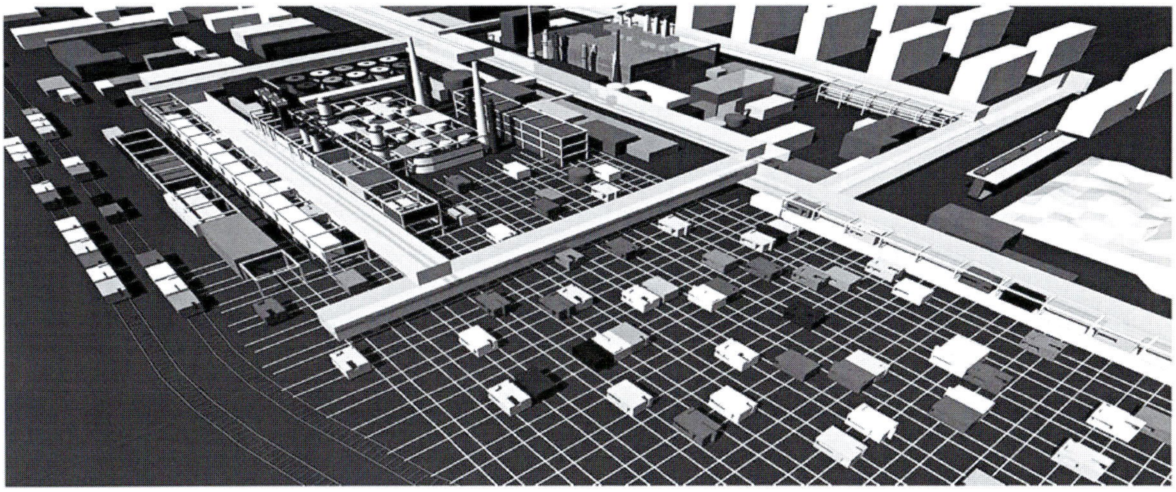

Virtools技术在本次设计中的应用

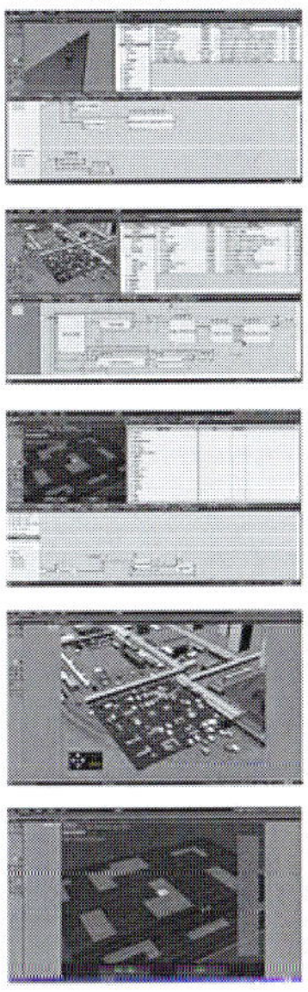

Virtools导入原始模型

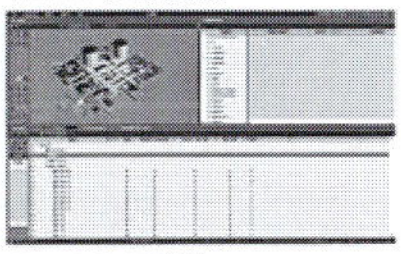

Virtools脚本编辑器

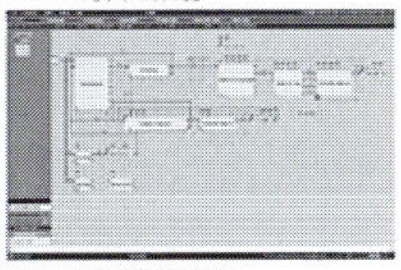

Virtools的集群操作01

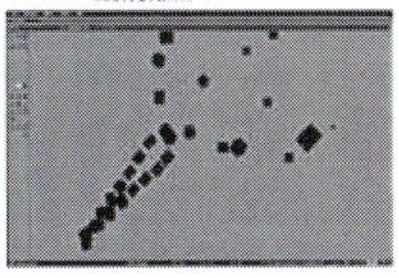

Virtools的集群操作02

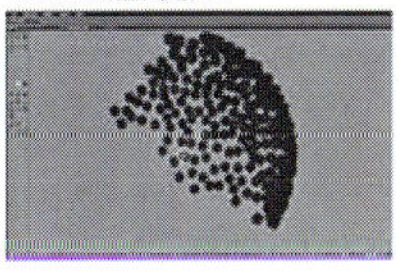

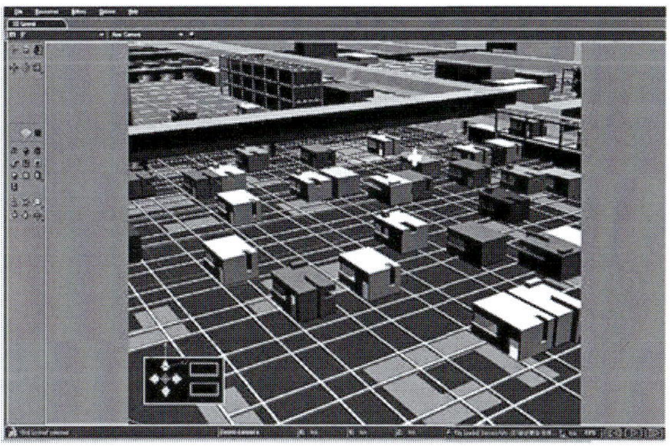

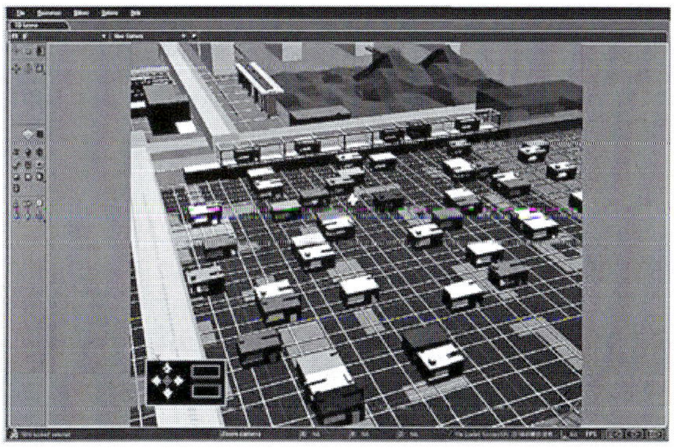

滑动单元——艺术家工作室

地块南端结合现有运输轨道，利用保留下来的厂房框架结构形成网状的水平与垂直滑动模式，新加入的滑动单元尺寸为4m×6m，两个或多个单元之间可以合并组合。为了实现单元的可动性，这里，引入一种全新的软件操作工具Virtools，用于艺术家们对自己工作室在空间上的控制。

“建设可持续世界”国际建筑师竞赛亚洲区唯一入围特别奖

中国洪灾区的可持续性设计

Shelter for Homeless when Flood

作者：刘迪　指导老师：王建国

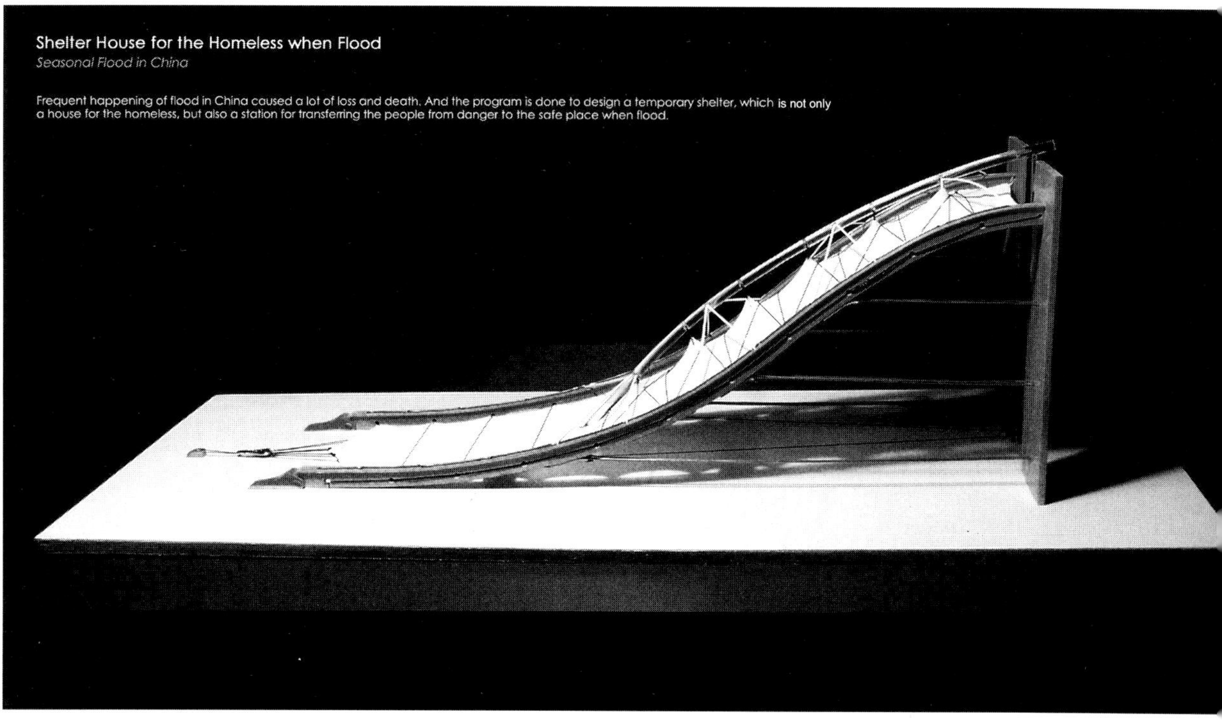

In order to find out a structure strong enough for the building against flood. Some structure modles were made for the test. Since water level continues changing when flood, horizontal steel ropes holding houses for the homeless have three different positions in a vertical direction for adapting themselves to freshet.

The concept of this bionic shape comes from a kind of aquatic worm named trilobite which holds itself in sault by its multiply feelers. Further more, the curvilinear skin of the building is more suitable to structural mechanics test, which can reduce the load of snow and hail on the surface. At the same time, the curve steel holders are also effectively designed to decompose the pression into two directions.

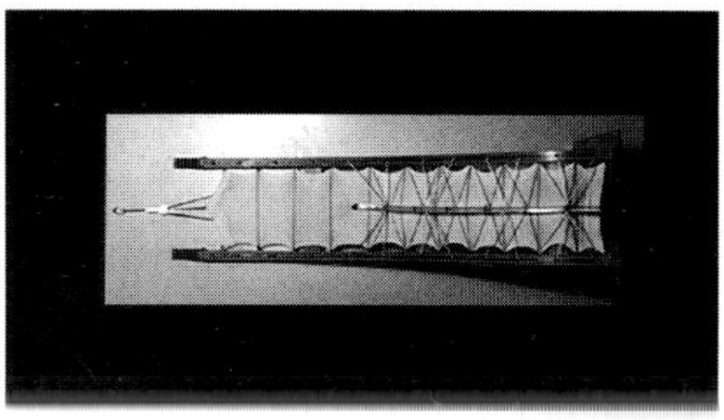

SOM奖学金中国区一等奖
SOM Scholarship

作者：朱昊昊

JIANCHUAN:
BO-AI SANITATION
September 21 2004-December 22 2004

This design is based upon the research of construction, as the essential issue of architecture. The vernacular house of Jianchuan in Yunnan is selected as the case to study, because the feature of the house is formed by earth and wood as main materials and shows clearly the construction logic on the material and structural level. In the first step, I design the wood system of construction. In the second step, the research focuses on the construction of walls with earth, which shows the reciprocity between the earth and the wood. The construction of ramming-earth wall is based on the research by Yang Baoxin.

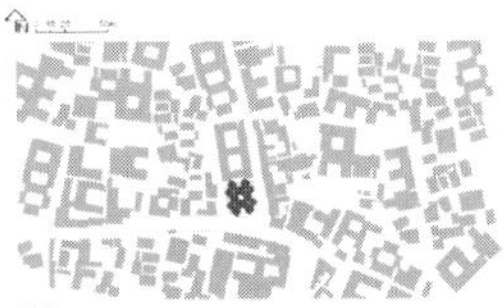
Site Plan

Wood construction

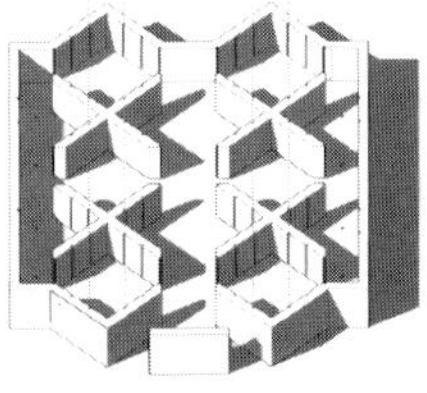
Ramming-earth wall

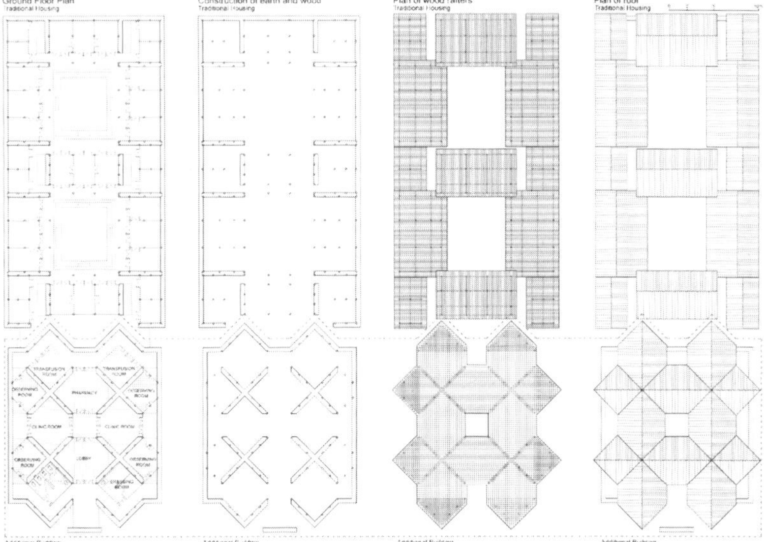

SUZHOU:
THREE HOUSES IN SECTION
March 12 2005-April 25 2005

Different from the designing method by focusing on the plan, in this section, three private houses are developed by the section. A box with 21mx15mx12m is covered by four slope roofs. Vertical walls and horizontal floors are introduced to separate and form various spaces with different characteristics, such as high, low, light or dark. Six different sections are created and two of them work together to form a house.

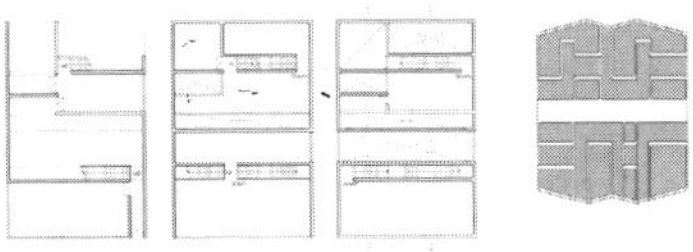
First floor plan　Second floor plan　Third floor plan

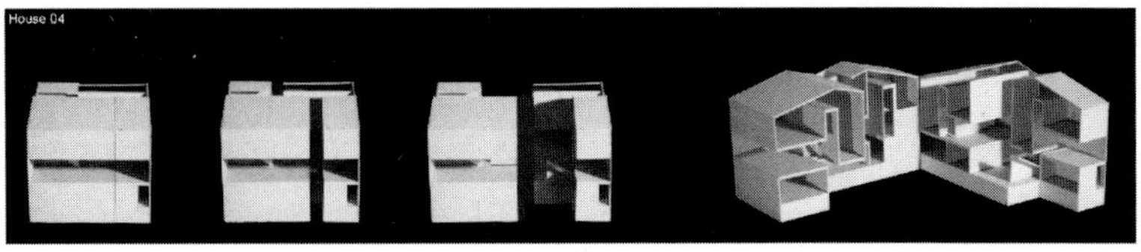

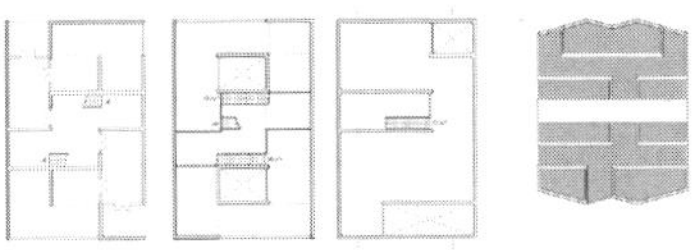
First floor plan　Second floor plan　Third floor plan

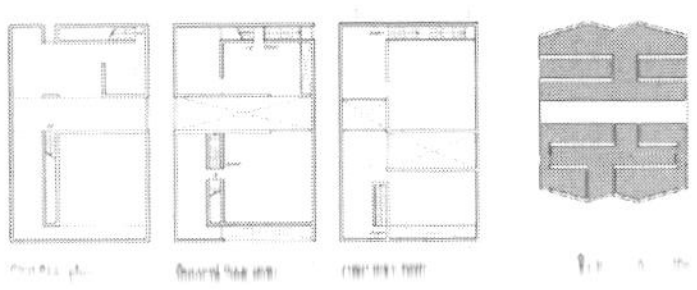

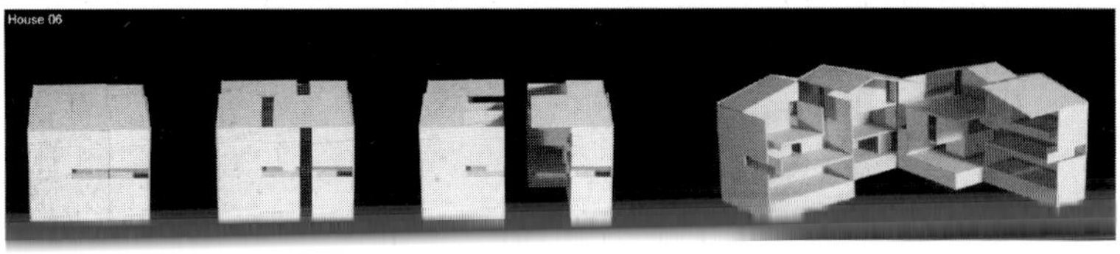

NANJING:
ADDITIONAL BUILDING WORKS
September.02 2005-September.28 2005

School of Architecture occupies a square shaped old building. It is necessary for the school to add more auditoriums and other classrooms to accommodate more students. What I am considering in the design is to find an appropriate space prototype to meet the needs of special program and to integrate the new ones with the old organically. I imagine the building to be a garden with forking paths, in which students are provided various opportunities to meet unexpectedly and to communicate with each other.

Abstraction

First floor   Second floor   Third floor   Fourth floor   Fifth floor

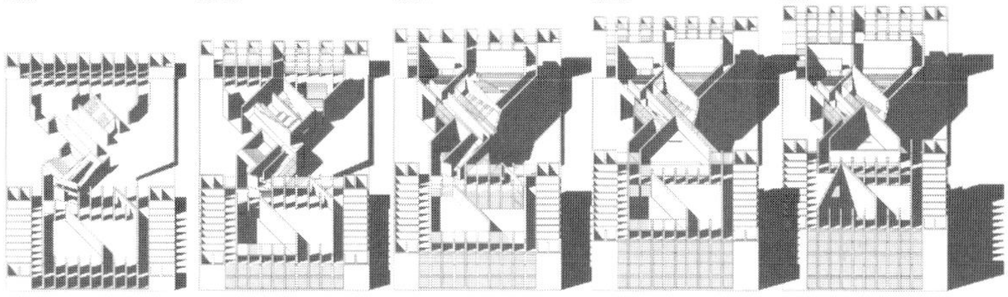

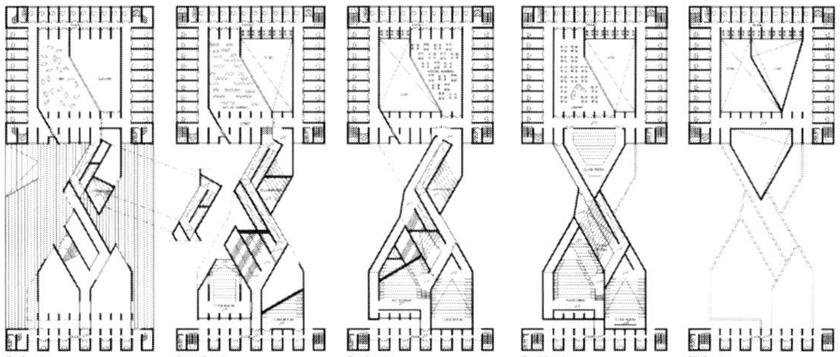

First floor plan   Second floor plan   Third floor plan   Fourth floor plan   Fifth floor plan

HUIZHOU:
CONFUCIAN SCHOOL
March 14 2004-June 09 2004

In the design, I analysis the structure of Tangyue, a typical village in Huizhou. The entrance architectures of Tangyue Village was already on a certain scale. The group of seven memorial gateways arranged in order of Loyalty, Obedience, Chastity and Righteousness. Together with square in front of the ancestral hall, these afforded the entrance views of the village with special characteristics. Two parallel streets were laid down from east to west in the development of Tangyue. Between the front and back streets, there were numerous alleys from south to north, which form a street network.

SOM奖学金中国区一等奖
SOM Scholarship

作者：骆可

"MACABRE TOWER"　　The design starts with the analysis of the surrealistic artist Zdzislaw Beksinski who always describes the world of death. The first step is to collect all his paintings and sculptures, then try to find out the artist's favourite subjects and skills. Select special art works which could particularly be the bridge between Beksinski's art and the architectural design. It is necessary to not only pick up the useful elements, but also capture the "action" which is the key point of his art. For example, the action "entangle" inspired me to create a totally new "space-structure" which ties the iron tower and the brick tower together. The only way to make this building meaningful is absorbing the soul of his art into the design.

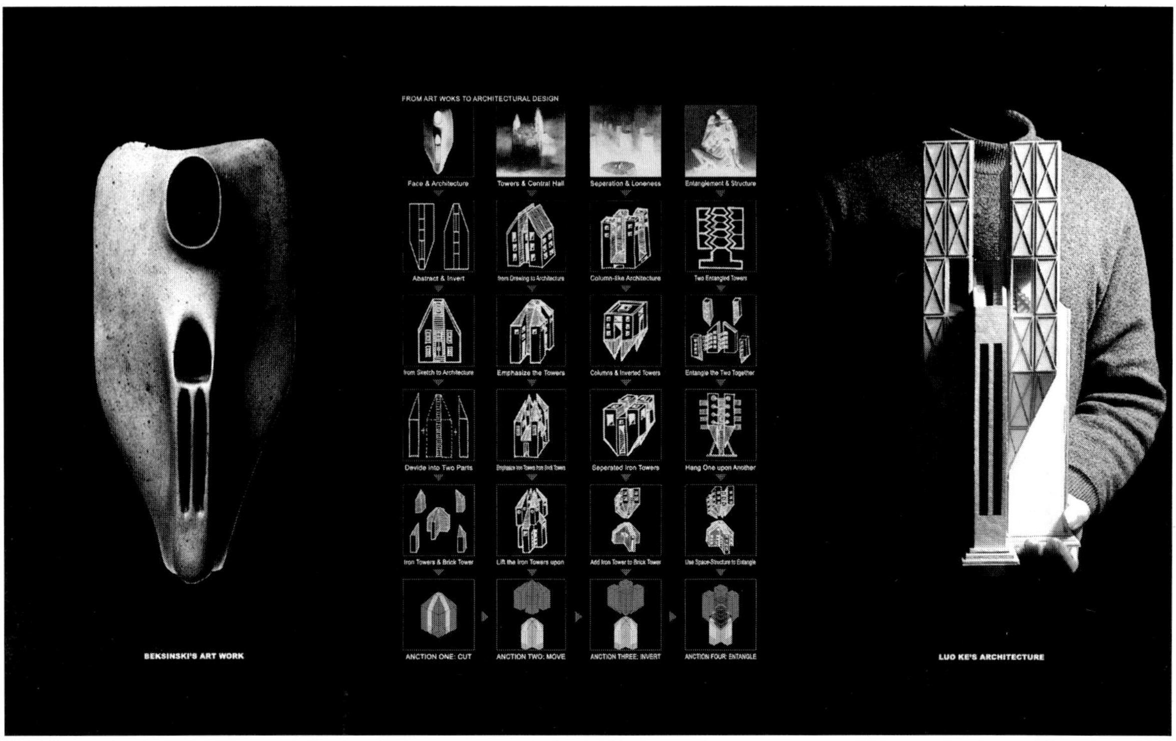

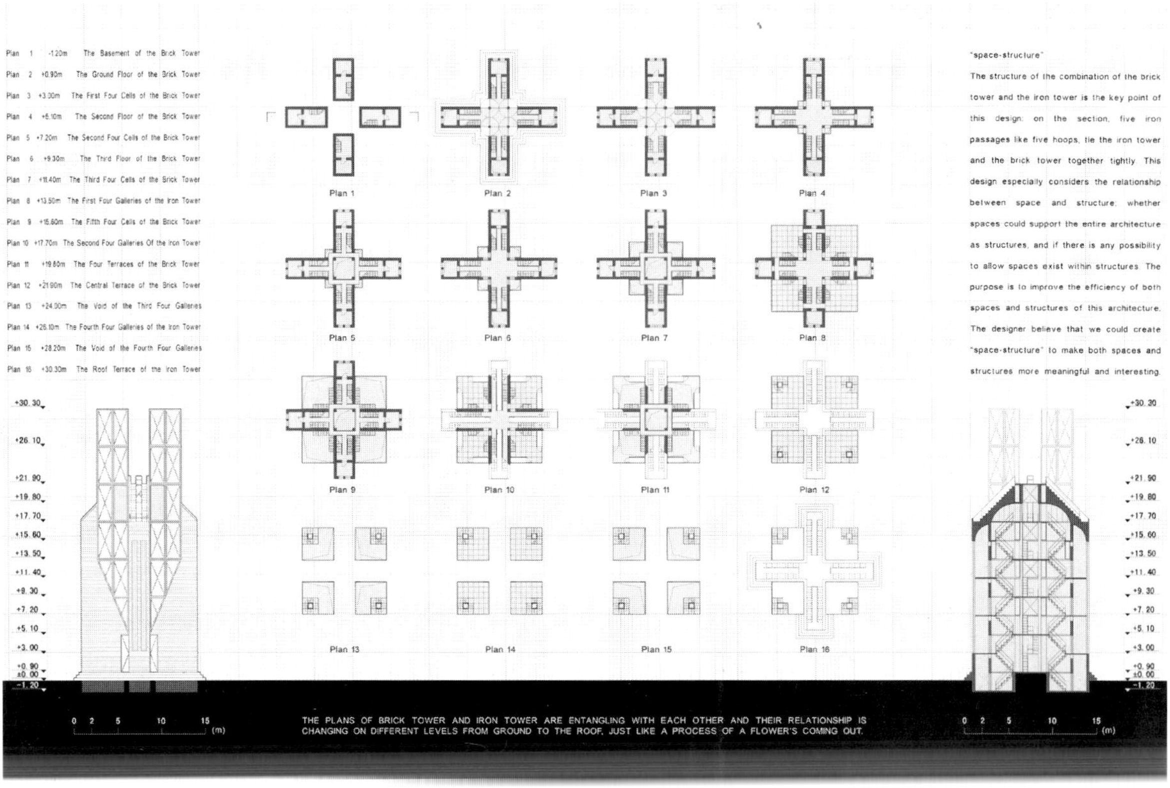

"Courtyard House" In this series, ten courtyards whose dimensions are all 24m x 24m are located along both sides of a river. Each courtyard should be designed for three or two independent families. This design tries to research on the relationships among the spaces within courtyard housing and the relationships among people living in them.

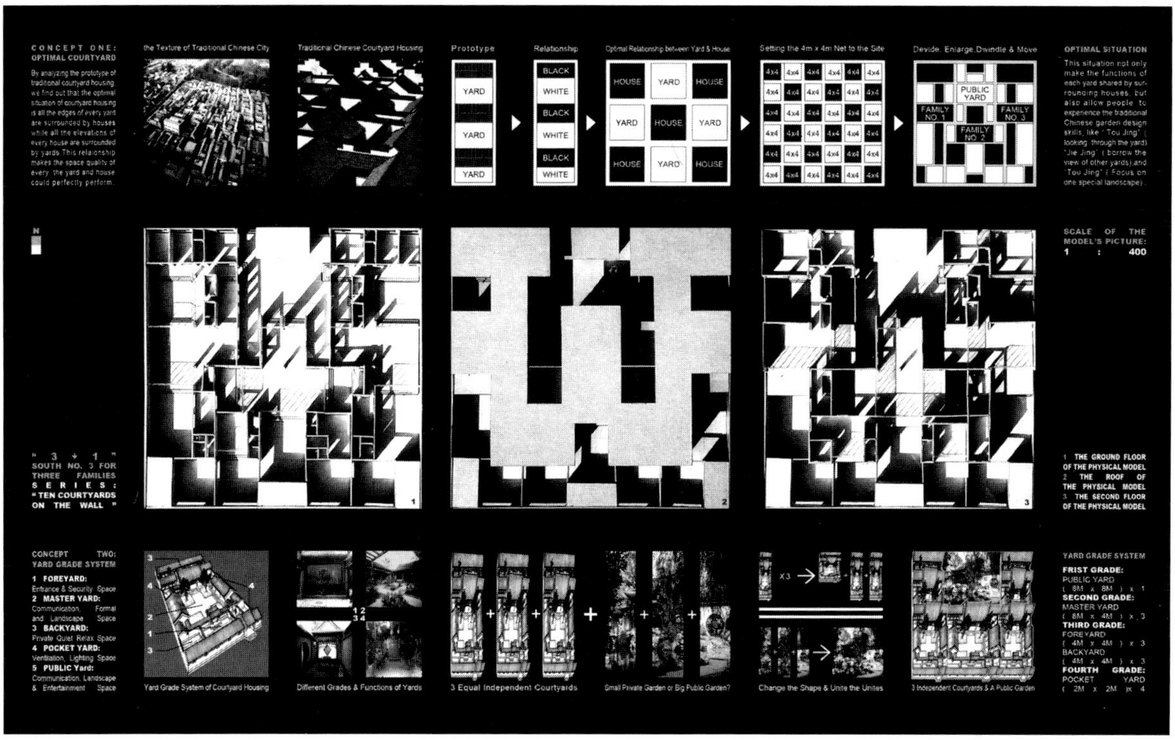

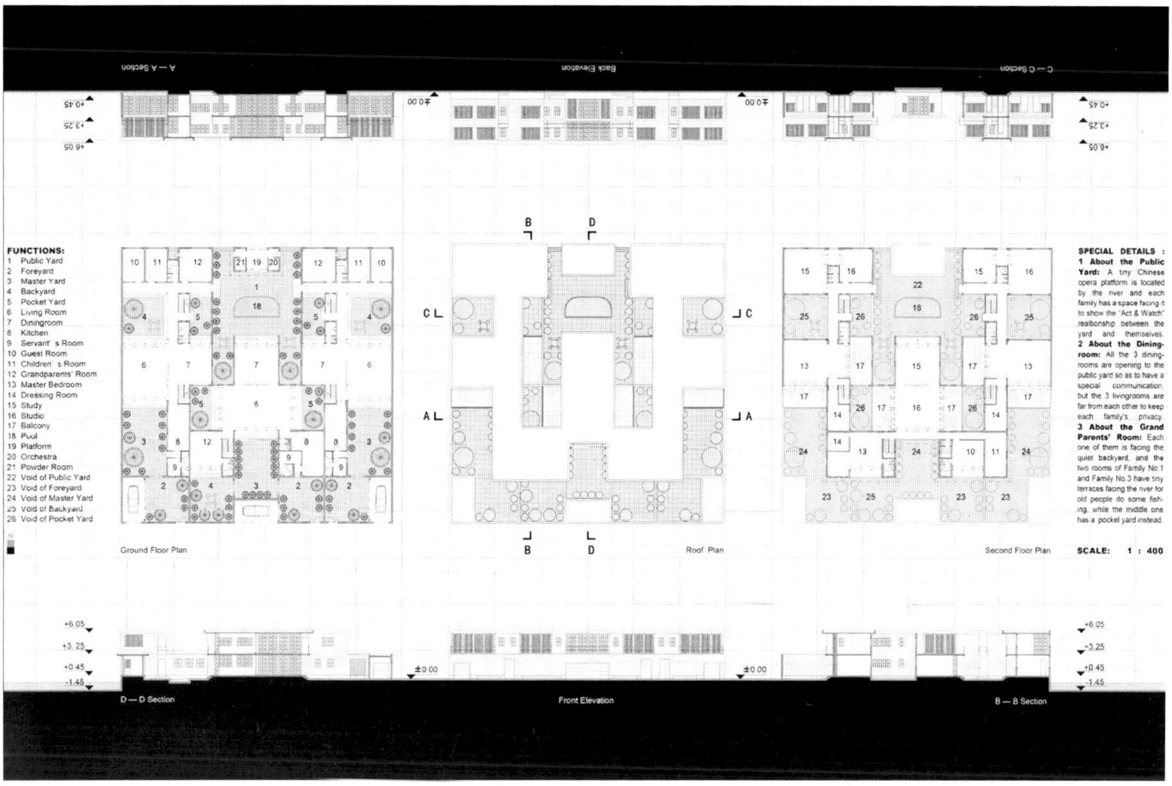

学生工作与社团活动
Students' Affairs & Activities

学生奖励
Students' Awards

前言

“绿草正含芳，梧桐映礼堂，春华豆蔻共寒窗，秋实岁月叙短长。”2007年，我们迎来了建筑学院的80华诞，在这承前启后的一年里，建筑学院的广大同学们自强不息，奋斗不止，用自己的实际行动证明了东大学子的风采。我们筹办了80周年院庆系列活动，从征召志愿者到组织行为艺术，从文化衫设计到院庆征文大赛，从纪念册的编排到院庆晚会的举办，每一个活动的背后都有我们的笑脸和汗水……

系列表彰

2006—2007年获奖集体、个人名单

1. 三好学生：李晨星　李　力　姚欣悦　栗　茜　龚　桓　胡晨希　周文婷　周　邹　朱琳君　吴梦茜　张李瑞　马晓君　张一楠　徐　文　盛　吉　张荩予　王　欣　郑克卿　顾超溢　冒蕴蓓　何舒炜　施骁夏　吴冰璐　钟晓晖　刘一歌　仇　星　孔德钟　葛　欣　樊思嘉　林明路　宫汝勃　张　佳　牛元莎　李　悠　章　恒　邢　成　陈梦婕　刘　坤　赵　薇　吴　烨　单　琳　孙贝妮　丁子玥　王　媛　汪　蕾　吴国栋　于艳成　曹　丽

   优秀学生干部：李小溪　郭晓斌　毛志伟　张一凡　戎卿文　崔毅雄

   优秀团干部：古振强　仇　星

   优秀团员：景文娟　钱逸文　何志鹏　赵晓玲　王　欣　曹　丽　孙　颖　胡佳佳　何舒炜　邵　咪　牛元莎　钟晓晖　桂　琦

   甲级团支部：011061团支部

   国家奖学金：李金蔓　顾超溢　孔德钟　蔡倩倩　申瑞雪　宫汝勃　陈梦婕　郑　浩　蔡　陶　邢　成

2. 党团建设

   东南大学2006年度 “最佳党日活动” 获奖名单

   走进北小　（一等奖）　建筑学院本科生党支部

   和谐与共融，真实记录的南京名城的昨天、今天与明天　（一等奖）　建筑学院博士生党支部

2007—2008年获奖集体、个人名单

1. 三好学生：汤梦捷　钱逸文　盛　吉　马晓君　查曼舒　游　忻　王　欣　陈梦姣　顾超溢　施骁夏　唐　薇　穆小贺　梅雪群　张李瑞　金显书　丁子玥　乔　琦　习　超　徐莉莉　曹奇琛　黄　立　夏慕蓉　王　敏　秦　静　袁　闻　仲早立　柴文远　宋一鸣　刘一歌　赵　韡　仇　星　樊思嘉　吴程辉　林明路　葛　欣　张　佳　张一凡　陶诗琦　邢　成　章　恒　张平星　刘扬慧

   优秀团干部：戴亚斐　刘一歌　贾　若

   优秀团员：罗海娇　周舒颖　顾超溢　唐　薇　孙晓倩　王　冲　毛　凯　盛　楠　邢　成　吉星帅　夏慕蓉　张倩楠　朱天睿　臧　亭

   甲级团支部：011061团支部　011071团支部

   国家奖学金：付轶飞　胥明明　王　欣　施骁夏　凌　洁　赵　韡　葛　欣　郑辰暐　韩雨晨　左　为　刘嘉阳

2. 党团建设

   东南大学2007年度 “最佳党日活动” 获奖名单

   牵手农民工子弟小学——莲花小学　（一等奖）　建筑学院本科生党支部

3. 2007年暑期优秀社会实践获奖

   2007年江苏省暑期社会实践活动优秀调研报告二等奖

   “历史文化名城的历史文化信息链接与再生——以淮安为例” 汤顶华（指导教师） 沈　旸 张　硕 金晓燕

   2007年校级社会实践优秀调查报告

   《南京市轨道交通与传统交通方式间的换乘调研》　鲍宇廷　何舒炜　黄灵卉　施骁夏

   《南京中山—浦口轮渡综合社会实践调查报告》　魏祥莉　席　震　史　谊　高　尚

   《社区管理：从“政府本位”到“公众本位”——由基层居委会向社区管理网络的转变》　邓达荣　顾超溢　陈继鹏　翟玉章

   《在现代化浪潮中飘零的“盘根草”——南京市七家湾回族社区的变迁调研》　王　慧　吴　珏　夏茂华　陈海明

4. 积极响应国家号召，支持西部地区教育发展

   2007年东南大学西部支教人员选拔，我院王均同学入选

   2007年10月我院011041、011062、012041、012061、011061五个团支部共计资助3360元帮助内蒙古准格尔旗希望之星小学四名学生（王强、郝正亨、白煦铂、韩旭）

思想教育
Social Activities

青年节无偿献血活动

2007年4月，我院组织了一次献血活动，共计有200名师生献血50100mL。“颂青春 献爱心 续希望 展真情”的主题在活动中得到彰显，提高了大家奉献爱心、挽救生命的社会意识。

看望老教师

2007年9月，学院团学联在教师节组织了看望老教师、代表同学们表达祝福的活动。同学们真切感受到他们朴实平淡而让人感动的生活，向他们送出了大家的祝福。

参观南京大屠杀纪念馆

2007年12月，东南大学建筑学院组织学生参观南京大屠杀纪念馆。通过这次活动，同学们更真实地认识了历史，激发了同学们的爱国热情。

研究生大合唱

2007年12月，我院研究生组织大合唱，表达对祖国的热爱之情。

“迎评促建” 演讲暨知识竞赛

2008年4月，响应学校团委的号召，为促进学校本科教学评估的顺利通过，开展以“迎评促建”为主题的演讲及知识竞赛，激发了同学们“知校，爱校，荣校”的热情。

烛光点亮祝福——建筑学院烛祭活动

2008年5月19日，东南大学建筑学院由本科毕业班同学发起，由院团委、院学生会牵头组织，自发地在大礼堂前举行烛祭活动，表达对“5·12”汶川大地震中死难同胞的追思和哀悼。

牵手莲花小学

2007年4月，本科生党支部邀请南京农民工子弟小学莲花小学的部分学生参观东南大学四牌楼校园，并进行一对一的交流。

走进北京东路小学

2006年11月，本科生党支部党员发挥专长，运用专业知识，帮助小学生设计布置新教室，丰富校园文化，美化校园环境。

同伴教育

2007年12月15日晚，16日全天在中大院209与校红十字会联合举办青年同伴教育活动。

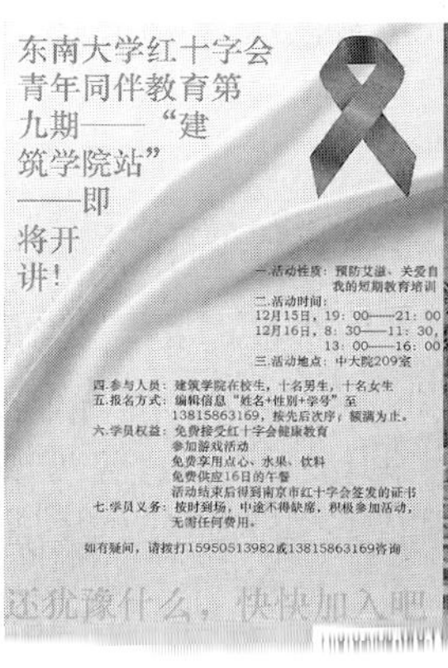

校际交流
Communications

竞赛

“现代杯设计大赛”、“金宸希望小学设计大赛”、“五合国际奖学金”、“筑森奖学金”、“南玻奖学金”等举行颁奖典礼。

交流活动

2007年5月，与浙江大学、同济大学共同筹划举办了长三角地区的学生建筑联谊。三所高校同学聚集在浙江杭州，参观了当地著名建筑，并在浙江大学进行一系列的学习交流活动。

2007年5月，我院012061班同学与南京大学二年级规划班同学进行热烈友好的学术交流，共同学习进步。

2007年9月，南京林业大学外联部同学到我校参观交流，两所大学交换了相关联系资料。

2007年10月，同济大学规划与建筑学院同学来到我校参观学习，学生会外联部予以接待并安排了相关学习交流活动。

2008年5月，与我校土木学院通过学生讲座、优秀成果展示的方式进行了相关专业的交流。

2008年5月，丹阳中学200名学生来我校进行参观交流。

建筑学院优秀学生作业展

学院学生会多次筹划举办了建筑学院优秀学生作业展。优秀作业展包括大一到大五各年级学生优秀作业展板展示、优秀模型展示、幻灯投影展示。作业展向本校及外校师生展示了我院近几年教学成果，并与相关专业师生进行了交流。

院庆系列活动
80th Anniversary Ceremony

2007年10月20日，建筑学院举行80周年院庆活动，学院围绕院庆开展了多项学生活动。在同学们的积极参与下，文艺晚会、院庆征文、优秀作业展、志愿者服务等活动都取得了圆满成功。

院庆行为艺术

2007年10月20日上午，建筑学院100多名同学在大礼堂前进行行为艺术表演，祝福建筑学院八十周年庆。

院庆系列活动之文化衫设计

院庆前期的文化衫设计，弘扬了东大建筑积淀的科学人文传统，展现了东大建筑学人的精神风貌。设计出的文化衫图案款式大方得体、富有含义，便于在院庆系列活动中使用，为院庆添彩。

院庆征文竞赛活动

学生会学习部负责组织此次活动。活动中的优秀来稿分别被汇编在院庆学生活动及征文专辑中和工作室宣传栏张贴的报纸中，并且在院庆征文竞赛后对获奖同学给予鼓励。

“建瓴东南，筑梦中大”文艺晚会

本台晚会共分为序曲——龙盘虎踞，梧桐嘉树，缘聚中大，岁月如歌，锦绣华章，尾声——金秋明月，共六个章节。历经前后共七个月的准备期。很多同学利用暑假以及开学后的课余时间，积极排练。通过老师、第32届团学联全体成员、近两百名演员的共同努力，成功地举办了建筑学院80周年庆典晚会，并获得了校友们的一致好评。

学生社团活动
Students' Activities

由于2006年学校主体搬迁至九龙湖校区，校级学生社团随之全部搬迁，而建筑学院留在四牌楼老校区，同学们课余没有机会参加生动活泼的社团活动。

2007年9月，为丰富建筑学院同学们的课余文化生活，院团委及时向校团委汇报，取得校团委和校社团联合会的支持，根据自愿、自主、自管的原则，在我院广泛倡议成立各类社团。

球社

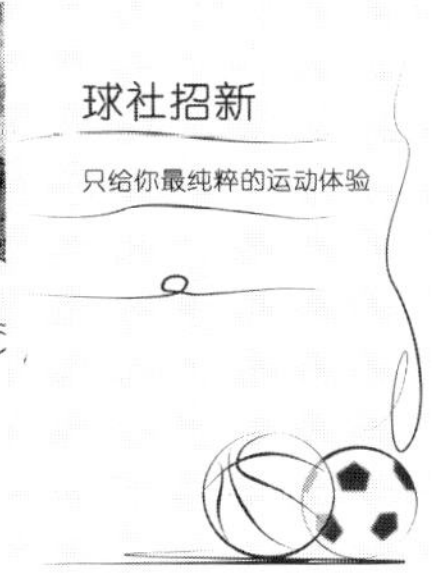

轮滑社

同学自发成立发展了十几个学生社团，如“东日计划”爱心社、摄影社、省钱协会、拉丁舞社、网球社、演讲与辩论社、文学社、瑜伽社等，覆盖文体学等多个方面。同学们热情筹备，踊跃参加感兴趣的社团，使大学业余文化生活更加丰富充实。

省钱社

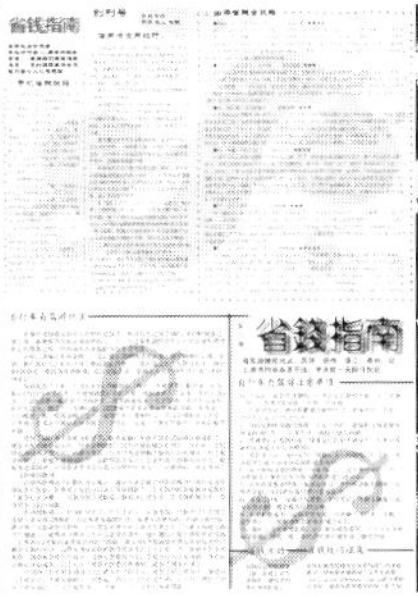

动漫社

2007年11月，学院在四牌楼和九龙湖校区联合举办关注山区失学儿童的“麦田计划”图片展，取得良好的反响。

“麦田计划”活动

“东日计划”爱心社

2008年5月12日，四牌楼校区中大院门前“东日计划”爱心社举行了隆重的募捐爱心物资运输活动，学校、学院以及天地华宇物流公司的领导出席了本次活动。“东日计划”致力于在大学生及贫困地区人们之间建立起沟通桥梁，将大学生闲置的衣物、学习用品等募集起来，运送到贫困地区。四牌楼校区同学对爱心募集活动献出了极大的热情，短短两次活动，用时两天，就募集到了近2000件衣物，最终通过物流公司免费运送到贫困地区。

文体活动
Amusements

2007年、2008年建筑之春文艺晚会

在欢乐祥和的氛围中，全院师生欢聚一堂，老师和各年级研究生、本科生，以歌舞、舞台剧等形式，迎来新的一年。晚会中涌现出一大批文艺人才，同时增进了师生之间、同学之间的友谊。

经典电影模仿秀

2007年12月15日、16日承办了校团委发起的“经典电影对白模仿秀”。

电影协会电影放映

电影协会每隔一个星期放映精彩的电影。

建筑学院超音速歌手大赛

2006年11月、2007年11月，学生会文艺部成功地举办第二、三届超音速歌手大赛。超音速歌手大赛为全院同学展现自己的风采提供了一个很好的平台。不仅可以让同学们以一种更加自信、乐观的态度去生活，也为学院各种活动的人才储备打下了坚实基础。

建筑学院2006、2007年学生田径运动会召开

所有同学或参加到争夺激烈的比赛中去，或加入到呐喊助威的队伍里来。运动会对促进建筑学院同学们的体育锻炼，增强学院的凝聚力起到了积极的作用。

万人长跑

2007年12月9日下午全院五十余名师生参加了全校“12·9”万人长跑活动。

拔河比赛

2007年5月与2008年5月，气氛热烈的拔河比赛将同学们的活动积极性和凝聚力提高了。

“中大杯”系列球赛

学院为丰富同学们的课余生活，增强体魄，培养班级的凝聚力，举办了各种球赛。包括篮球、足球、羽毛球、乒乓球等多个项目。每位同学都可以根据自己的特长及兴趣爱好报名参赛。大力开展学生体育运动，取得了良好的效果。

附录
Annex

2007届本科毕业生名单

011021班

仇鹏飞	嵇丽萍	张 璐	赵 玥	高 勤	李建红	郑 娟	宋燕燕	胡琦琦	许若菲
沈小利	周 舟	王 琦	曲敏佳	贾如君	李永强	许昱歆	邱 健	魏鹏程	方 琦
杜德章	吉英雷	束旻力	陈 嘉	赵立锋	王雁安	薛 垲	盛蓓蓓	姜 沙	史庆超
胡洪波	曾庆惠	刘 畅	阎 凯	张 芳					

011022班

朱倩如	徐 珂	郁 倩	焦 键	庄 悦	肖 凡	卿 州	王 柯	沈素兰	是 霏
吴念儒	刁芸婷	张 璐	杨 程	刘 杰	吴海龙	陈 笛	陈 锐	孟祥跃	羊 烨
龚健健	章慕懿	洪先进	孔祥恒	成 晨	胡 宏	赵 振	朱 萌	王恩琪	尚 川
袁振华	甘 昊	杨永智	卞俊卿	张 尧	郭 昀				

012021班

王颖楠	石慧敏	汤群群	洪桂萍	唐 元	徐笑亮	高一雄	周 静	曹 祯	叶玉曲
刘 宁	王惠敏	龚雪岚	潘之潇	汤雪璇	黄亦凡	刘英姿	臧公秀	陈黎娟	莫昭莹
刘春华	刘 元	张子君	郏廷炎	雷 禹	刘 迪	曾志向	杨奕人	计灵骏	柳 宁
潘钧鹏	章 飙	杨 悦	辛 生	肖 扬	葛天阳	倪 冶	经 靖	魏 晨	郑亚兰

013021班

包正怡	杨 乐	滕云飞	许文炜	郑渊丹	陈家元	王吟燕	黄筱娴	陈 璟	何云姝
许 皞	潘 鎏	张赟洁	欧阳芳芳	龚 俊	张亚伟	黄 炎	黄 林		

2008届本科毕业生名单

011031班

李晨星	黄 寅	唐颖立	葛 宁	田 天	王文卿	姚昕悦	丁晓春	吴 倩	李瑞鹏
刘彦珉	向 晖	陈博赓	李雨超	董霄霜	刘海天	徐苑枫	李 晶	张 琦	邱 滨
张志兵	罗国彬	张海纯	陈 超	肖 冰	黄 轩	汤晓伟	王 均	李 力	陆 昊
柴金戈	孙志坤								

011032班

叶茏茏	何 晋	江 天	杨 瑜	胡晨希	林晓云	卢犁梦	杨 扬	宋剑青	栗 茜
侯 薇	陈宗瑞	宋学俊	方 嘉	邱 珏	李邦健	崔 赟	陈 昇	顾晓晓	王怀宇
朱理一	李成刚	张 亮	龚 桓	徐 旺	吴伟刚	姚文轩	袁 懿	黄 磊	彭 彦
陈 超	郭 韬	申苏蓉	郭东海	谢 铮					

012031班

吴靖梅	王 静	张 佳	魏 皎	赵 薇	孙 晨	陆维婷	孟 婕	刘 坤	张 殊
华晶晶	吴 烨	吴一如	王洁如	王 淋	和 烨	陈 颖	孙丹妮	张园园	杨 洁
单俊俊	李 伟	刘默琦	毛 玮	靳 锦	沙 林	陈 沂	吴 弘	张 强	于晓淦
袁新国	吴增鑫	贾 晨	阚俊杰	宫作成	宋若蔚	莫昭莹			

013031班

周 朋	季 方	孙贝妮	于 灿	邢 玮	杨明兰	杨 莹	李直霖	李金蔓	杨成珠
钱 莉	洪丽华	卢玉婷	孙 姗	宋亦君	单 琳	王慧津	蔡 婧	廖心怡	保建道
程远鹏	朱梦雅								

2004级硕士研究生名单

美术学

周　贤	吴媛媛	李炳南	吴　莹	周　超	赵忠超	史爱明	李　昕	董　智	孟　涛

建筑历史与理论

张　延	高宜生	姚舒然	李练英	龙　潇	王　劲	张剑葳

建筑设计及其理论

杨　云	倪翔宇	张　盈	马奕鸣	徐　琦	蒋　楠	陈　栋	杨　柳	朱昊昊	张琪琳
王　华	温丽敏	辛　杨	高　钢	赵　明	陈　萍	白小松	刘　华	姚　旭	陈　卓
胡湘明	黄珂星	谢峻峰	沈花晨	余　爽	张维维	刘　园	孙霄奕	程佳佳	倪震宇
张　军	王　斌	高宏波	冷天翔	杨红波	张　珂	任　敏	方　伟	周　扬	

城市规划与设计

雷　巍	曲志华	杨芳龙	赖凌瑶	陶　亮	陆　敏	徐善彬	袁金波	顾媛媛	陈　仪
王轩轩	倪　慧	王　颖	顾渝群	孔孝云	姜洪友	胡　幸	孟祥婉	李大雁	周志达
孙晓恒	裴小明	吴晓刚	顾　洁	姚　迪	洪　苗	曹新民			

建筑技术科学

许慧锋	高　霖	耿志莹	林　宁	王　格

2005级硕士研究生名单

美术学

殷念平	侯伟伟	卢　漫	黄　江	吴天华	沈　宁	曹　莹	丁盛杰	李　吟	韩　颖
曾　伟	张永良	汪皆瑞	赵　迎						

建筑历史与理论

季　秋	纪立芳	黄　欢	杨　莹	高　琛	傅舒兰	朱穗敏	冯志荣

建筑设计及其理论

刘进红	蒋　鑫	冯　剑	彭　溪	许东锬	丁　庆	何博翔	段丽娟	陆　天	翟　值
庞　博	周天蕾	钱晶晶	陈　萌	乐　为	张　悦	谭　亮	吴　昊	张丽莉	周　婷
闫　苏	朱维吉	丁　顺	蓝　莉	胡暐昱	王　铮	李　燕	史春华	苏　玲	翟　彬
李宝童	胡晓明	郭　健	陈科舟	孟　媛	相　南	杨　宇	赵　婧	周晓义	徐　伟

城市规划与设计

叶冬黎	杨　志	嵇　岚	郑　国	陈　苑	徐冰华	胡旭明	肇新宇	于　芳	姚宇乾
李　建	晋　劲	马菀艺	关　十	陈海浪	宁　凯	卢　君	史北祥	刘伟奇	邹亦凡

建筑技术科学

吴　迪	蔡会衡	高海防	吴　薇	姜　妍	李　田	高　燕	孟海港

景观建筑学

张　峻	周　斌	罗艳宁	韦　斐	石　诺	叶　麟	郑　华

编后记

金秋十月，一部新的学院年鉴将呈献给全体师生和广大读者。

年鉴记录了东大建筑学人一年来的主要历程，它本身构成了一部小小的但却十分多元而丰富的历史。年鉴也承载着我们对未来的寄托，希望东大建筑学人在过去的基础上创造更加辉煌的未来。

许多老师和同学都为年鉴的诞生作出了贡献，他们是：

董卫

史永高

李向锋

陈洁萍

熊国平

白颖

李新建

唐静寅

习超